Managing the Business

THEORY AND PRACTICE

Thomas Zellweger

Professor of Management, University of St. Gallen, Switzerland

Edward Elgar
PUBLISHING

Cheltenham, UK • Northampton, MA, USA

Published by
Edward Elgar Publishing Limited
The Lypiatts
15 Lansdown Road
Cheltenham
Glos GL50 2JA
UK

Edward Elgar Publishing, Inc.
William Pratt House
9 Dewey Court
Northampton
Massachusetts 01060
USA

A catalogue record for this book
is available from the British Library

Library of Congress Control Number: 2016959910

MIX
Paper from
responsible sources
FSC® C013604

ISBN 978 1 78347 069 3 (cased)
ISBN 978 1 78347 070 9 (paperback)
ISBN 978 1 78347 071 6 (eBook)

Typeset by Servis Filmsetting Ltd, Stockport, Cheshire.
Printed and bound in Great Britain by the CPI Group (UK) Ltd

Contents in brief

Full contents

Preface

This textbook is the result of two observations from being a teacher and researcher in the field of family businesses. First, when I began looking for a comprehensive textbook to support my teaching, I could not find one that satisfied me. While there were numerous textbooks on entrepreneurship, human resource management, marketing and strategy, these books only covered selected aspects of the challenges and managerial practices observed in family firms. Meanwhile, there seemed to be a dearth of supporting materials for the sort of family business class that covers the full breadth of relevant topics. My aim in writing this book was not to replace the many important books, case studies and research papers already in existence on specific topics. Rather, I tried to provide an overview of what makes the family firm a unique type of organization, to integrate knowledge from practitioners and scholars, and to help readers navigate the large array of available materials. This book thus intends to guide students and practitioners through the rich insights that those involved in managing and studying family firms have accumulated in recent years.

In this attempt, the book will most likely leave some readers unsatisfied. Family firms are highly heterogeneous organizations, and their heterogeneity arises not only from the particular goals of family owners or family constellations but also from the varying institutional contexts in which the firms are embedded. The present compilation of topics, conceptual models and case studies is the result of an attempt to discuss the core topics that these firms share, and hence to explore what is essential about family firms *despite* their heterogeneity. It is inevitable that some aspects may have been overlooked or inadequately represented. This partial limitation, I think, must be weighed against the opportunity to offer insights on many of the central aspects of managing family businesses in a single book.

The second observation that led to this book relates to my work with family business practitioners. Over the years, the individuals and families I have worked with have entrusted me with their stories, challenges and questions, including: How should we approach the succession process? Who should become the successor? How do we achieve long-term success? Should I enter my parent's company? What competitive advantages do we have as a family firm? What is an adequate return on the capital the family has invested in the firm? How do we structure decision making in our family with regard to the business? When I was first confronted with these questions, I was unable to answer them satisfactorily. However, over time, and with the help of many excellent family business researchers and family business practitioners, I have arrived at some possible answers.

I am indebted to the many individuals who helped me compile this book. First and foremost to Miriam Bird, Urs Frey, Michael Gaska, Marlies Graemiger, Maximilian Groh, Frank Halter, Sonja Kissling Streuli and Melanie Richards from the Center for Family Business at University of St. Gallen. Many thanks go to Urs Fueglistaller, my co-director at the Swiss Research Institute of Small Business and Entrepreneurship at the University of St. Gallen, for creating a very collaborative, fun and entrepreneurial atmosphere. I am grateful to Joe Astrachan, Michael Carney, Jim Chrisman, Alfredo De Massis, Kim Eddleston, Marc van Essen, Luis Gomez-Mejia, Nadine Kammerlander, Franz Kellermanns, Tim Habbershon, Robert Nason, Mattias Nordqvist, Pankaj Patel, Peter Rosa, Bill Schulze, Pramodita Sharma, Philipp Sieger, Alex Stewart, Wim Voordeckers, Arist von Schlippe and John Ward from whom I have learned a tremendous amount about family firms and who have contributed to the book in one way or another. Thank you also to Heinrich Christen, Peter Englisch, Carrie Hall, Patrick Ohle, Santiago Perry, Johannes Rettig, Yuelin Yang, and Marnix van Rij. Your input and support has been invaluable. Finally, my deepest gratitude and love to Nathalie, Nikolaus and Leo, my closest family. This book is dedicated to the many individuals who share a common goal: to understand what makes family firms unique and successful organizations.

April 2017, St. Gallen & Singapore   Thomas Zellweger

1

Introduction

Writing a textbook about the management of family firms poses a particular challenge. On the one hand, family firms undoubtedly represent the largest fraction of all firms across the globe. On the other hand, there are relatively few family business classes being taught in business schools and universities today, suggesting that the market for such a book may be limited. If you are reading this book, then you are likely a manager, scholar or student who believes—as I do—that the mainstream management literature does not sufficiently describe family firms or address their managerial challenges. There are dozens of textbooks on topics such as entrepreneurship, human resource management, marketing, financial management or strategy, but hardly any about family firms.

Admittedly, the above topics are relevant to all types of firms, independent of their family or nonfamily status. But family businesses face challenges that may be more pronounced than they would be in nonfamily firms, or that may need to be addressed differently. For instance, while governance in nonfamily firms is mainly concerned with the effective structuring of the cooperation between a dispersed group of owners and a limited number of managers, governance in family firms also includes topics such as the effective collaboration of a group of family blockholders or the efficient oversight of family managers (such as children) by family owners (such as parents). Similarly, while a firm leader's exit is an increasingly relevant topic in entrepreneurship, succession has been and remains a central preoccupation in family firms. When we look at other broad topics such as strategy, financial management or even human resources, we again find that family and nonfamily firms face similar questions but that family firms address them in different ways. The goal of the present textbook is to look at these managerial topics through the family business lens and to come up with actionable strategies to promote family firm success.

1.1 Thematic focus

Although this book aims to provide guidance to practitioners in various domains, its content necessarily mirrors my training as a management scholar. This precondition brings with it some preferences that guide my approach to family firm challenges. In the best cases, the thematic focus I use in this book leads to greater conceptual clarity and simplicity. But the management scholarship approach also comes at a certain cost, which is the potential oversight of other rationales and theoretical backgrounds through which family firm behavior could be explained.

Thus, although I aim to embrace different points of view throughout the book, I mainly focus on the organizational processes in family firms and the way they can be managed to ultimately achieve firm-level success. In consequence, the main level of analysis—although I relax this assumption in the last two chapters of the book—is the firm, and to a lesser extent the family itself. The frameworks put forth in the book stem primarily from management theory and economics, with a secondary emphasis on family sociology.

Because this is a book that focuses on the management of family businesses, it explores managerial challenges that are decisively influenced by the family. This choice is a matter of my perspective. But it is a deliberate choice that strives to avoid a common pitfall in much of the current family business writing and thinking: the idea that any given aspect or behavior of family-controlled firms is decisively impacted by the family. I try to single out the specific managerial practices in family firms where the family aspect matters to a degree that is decisive for the effectiveness or ineffectiveness of the firm.

1.2 Intended audience

I wrote this book for family business students and practitioners. It is not the classical 'how-to' or 'do-it-yourself' book, filled with checklists of 'success factors' derived from looking at a few successful family firms. Rather, this book is written for people who seek guidance in dealing with the most pressing challenges faced by family firms. In trying to deal with these challenges, the book attempts to combine frameworks that have been proven in practice with the latest research findings.

This book will be most useful to you if you are:

- looking for an inclusive discussion of topics generally faced by family firms,

- a family business student trying to immerse yourself in the family business world,
- a family business owner/manager looking for actionable and at the same time tested advice about how to tackle managerial challenges, and/or
- an advisor looking for an overview of research findings relevant for your practice.

The book may not be a satisfactory resource if you:

- are looking for easy answers and one-size-fits-all solutions to complex problems,
- do not have the time to explore the foundations of practical questions, and/or
- are not interested in exploring research findings.

1.3 Structure and pedagogical tools

The book is structured along the following sections: defining the family firm, family firms' significance and economic contributions, and the typical strengths and weaknesses, governance, strategic management, succession, change and transgenerational value creation, financial management, and interpersonal relationships in family firms. Each chapter makes use of multiple pedagogical tools: conceptual frameworks, presentation and summary of research findings, case studies, reflection questions both for students and practitioners, and suggestions for background reading.

The use of literature is limited to the most relevant and up-to-date studies needed to support an argument. Thus, the studies cited do not encompass all the relevant literature, but they do represent some particularly foundational and intriguing studies and books. In addition, at the end of every chapter, you will find a list of bibliographical references suggested as background reading for a more in-depth view of the subject.

2

Defining the family business

One of the most serious challenges in many social sciences relates to the definition of the phenomenon under study. In the case of family businesses, this challenge is particularly important given that what distinguishes family firms from other types of organizations is the influence of the family on the firm.[1] Note that the distinction between family and nonfamily firm is *not* a matter of the size of the business, nor whether it is privately or publicly held. Rather, what qualifies a family firm as such is the degree to which—and the ways through which—a family controls its firm. Family firms deserve an approach to management that takes into consideration what makes them unique: the fact that they are influenced by a particular type of dominant coalition, a family, that has particular goals, preferences, abilities and biases.

2.1 The distinction between family and nonfamily firms

Students, practitioners and researchers alike often look for an easy answer to the question of what distinguishes family from nonfamily firms. In search of such a demarcation line, many have tried to assign some cutoff level for family involvement in a firm, for instance in the dimensions of ownership or management. The underlying assumption behind such an attempt is that a minimum level of family involvement is required above which a firm is defined as family firm and below which the firm is nonfamily.

In the case of ownership control, some argue that a majority stake is required for a family to exert a decisive influence on a firm. Others suggest that control is possible even without a majority ownership stake. For instance, in publicly listed companies, and in the many cases where ownership outside the family is diluted and widely held, a significant minority ownership may be enough to control important strategic decisions in a firm (such as, for instance, the appointment of board members and top managers, acquisitions, divestments, restructuring and the like). In consequence, and in the case of large and publicly quoted family firms, there is an increasing consensus that an ownership stake of 20 to 25% may be sufficient for a shareholder to have a decisive influence on strategic decisions (Anderson and Reeb 2003b; Villalonga and Amit 2006). As such, and for the case of large and publicly listed family firms, the 20 to 25% cutoff in ownership is often used as the criterion to distinguish family from nonfamily firms.

For instance, the European Commission suggests that a public firm is a family firm if a family controls 25% of voting rights. Most importantly, in countries where dual-class share ownership structures are allowed by law, an even smaller ownership stake may entitle a family to exercise control over a company. For example, in 2010, the Ford family collectively owned less than 2% of Ford Motor Company in terms of rights to its cash flows, but it remained firmly in control of the company with 40% of the voting power through a special class of stock. Accordingly, it seems reasonable that the minimum threshold of ownership rights should be applied to voting rights and not to the cash flow rights of owners (see the case study about the Ford family and Ford Motor Corporation in Chapter 6 on strategy in family firms).

Others would argue that a firm only qualifies as a family business if it is family managed as well as family owned. The underlying rationale here is that influence takes place not only through formal ownership, but also through leadership, and hence through the values and leadership styles that permeate a company. Family management is often understood as the family's involvement in the firm's top management, in many cases even in the CEO position. The use of family involvement in management as a criterion for family firm demarcation is especially common in the case of smaller firms. For large firms, and especially for publicly listed firms, family management is less often seen as a distinguishing factor between family and nonfamily firms.

At the same time, there is a good deal of literature suggesting that what makes a family firm unique is its transgenerational focus (e.g., Chua, Chrisman and Sharma 1999). That is, the wish to pass the firm on to future family generations separates family firms from nonfamily firms. The transgenerational outlook is indeed important, as it represents the critical feature distinguishing family firms from other types of closely held companies.

Some argue that, regardless of the ownership or management structure, a business can only qualify as a family firm if it has remained under family control *beyond* the founding generation. In fact, many empirical studies find significant differences between founder-controlled companies and those

Table 2.1 Family business definitions

Influence dimension	Cutoff criterion distinguishing family from nonfamily firms	Rationale
Ownership	*For small firms*: at least 50% of voting rights in family hands *For large and public firms*: at least 20% of voting rights in family hands	Ownership rights, and in particular voting rights, equip actors with a decisive power to alter the strategic direction of the firm
Management	*Small firms*: family involvement in top management team *Large and public firms*: involvement often not required	Management involvement is what allows a dominant coalition (the family) to imbue a firm with particular values and to directly influence decision making
Transgenerational outlook	Firm is controlled by a family with the intent of passing it on to the next family generation	It is the desire for transgenerational control that distinguishes a family from a nonfamily firm
Later-generation control	*First-generation firms*: founder-controlled firms *Later-generation firms*: family firms	Control that spans generations—and hence is not limited to a founding generation—is what constitutes a family firm

controlled by later generations. For instance, there is mounting empirical evidence that later-generation firms underperform founder-controlled firms on the stock market.

However, the argument that firms held by the founding generation are not family firms is not universally accepted. Many would argue that firms founded with the involvement of family members (e.g., those founded by siblings or a spousal team) or firms held by the founding generation with the intent of passing control on to some future family generation should qualify as family firms as well. These various arguments about the seemingly clear-cut distinction between family and nonfamily firms are summarized in Table 2.1.

The arguments summarized in Table 2.1 show that there is no such thing as a clear demarcation between family and nonfamily firms (for further reflection on this topic, see Astrachan, Klein and Smyrnios 2002). In their understandable attempts to come up with a decisive definition of the family business, practitioners and researchers alike have created an artificial dichotomy between family and nonfamily businesses, thereby falling prey to some serious simplifications about what family firms are and what they are not. Three such simplifications may be particularly problematic:

1. **Overlooking the heterogeneity of family firms**: Many studies that suggest a clear-cut distinction between family and nonfamily firms overlook the heterogeneity within the group of family firms. As we will see later on in this chapter, family firms are numerous among the smallest firms, but they are also found among the largest ones, and they exist in a wide variety of industries. At the same time, family firms do not share a single mode of governance structure. Some families exercise control solely through ownership and board involvement, while other families are also active in management. Similarly, some families control a single firm, while others control large conglomerates.

2. **Simplifying the definition of family**: One traditional line of thinking sees the family as a social unit whose operation is fundamentally distinct from the market. For example, in his famous work on the role of family in society, Bourdieu (1996, p. 20) argued that a family is 'a world in which the ordinary law of the economy is suspended, a place of trusting and giving—as opposed to the market and its exchange of equivalent values'. However, this view of the family neglects the particular situation of families in business, including the ways in which they have to deal with family and business issues in parallel. More generally, families are not social systems that are incapable of dealing with financial issues—think, for example, about the task of allocating income and wealth among family members.

   Furthermore, the definition of *what* a family is and *who* belongs in it may differ widely across cultures. For example, Arab families tend to be relatively inclusive in determining family membership. In China, despite the relevance of the family as a social actor, the one-child policy severely limits family sizes, with important consequences for decisions such as family succession and the intergenerational transfer of family wealth. Family structures also change over time because of changing social norms, as evidenced by the increasing number of divorces and non-marital births in Europe and the United States.

3. **Underestimating the value of studying family involvement along various dimensions**: Finally, the view that there is a clear-cut criterion that can distinguish family firms from nonfamily firms overlooks the value of examining different types of family influence. Resisting the temptation to lump various means of family involvement into one category can lead to valuable insights. For example, we may come to better understand the sources of heterogeneity among family firms as well as the managerial levers needed to alter a firm's circumstances.

Taken together, whether we like it or not, there is little to be gained from creating a family/nonfamily firm dichotomy. If we want to achieve a more refined understanding of what makes family firms unique organizations, we need to move beyond such simplistic divisions. Instead, we should ask ourselves: *what are the specific ways in which families influence their firms?*

2.2 Defining family business by type of family involvement

To answer the question posed above, we can start by examining the dimensions along which families may be involved in their firms.

A particularly prominent example of a model that seeks to capture the essential dimensions of family influence is the F-PEC model (Astrachan, Klein and Smyrnios 2002). This model suggests that family influence stems from three dimensions. First, the power dimension captures the degree of ownership control in family hands, the extent of management control in family hands and the degree to which a governance body (i.e., the board) is controlled by the family. Second, the experience dimension is represented mainly by the number of generations for which the firm has been under family control. Third, the cultural dimension accommodates the degree of cultural overlap between the family and business systems, that is, the degree of overlap between family and business values.

Building on the F-PEC model and drawing from more recent research on the channels through which families influence their firms, we can identify five dimensions of family involvement: (1) the amount of family control, (2) the complexity of family control, (3) the setup of the business activities, (4) the family owner's philosophy and goals, and (5) the stage of control in terms of the family's history with the firm. Figure 2.1 provides a graphical overview of these reflections on family involvement using what we call the *family business assessment tool*.

The family business assessment tool does not suggest an optimal positioning along the five dimensions. Rather, the benefit of assessing family involvement according to these dimensions should be twofold. First, the five dimensions are meant to shed light on the sources of family firm heterogeneity, and in particular the opportunities and challenges that come with various types and levels of family involvement. Second, the tool allows family business practitioners to open a discussion not only about the current state of family involvement, but also about the family's future involvement, and the opportunities and challenges the firm will likely face when altering its positioning along the various dimensions of influence.

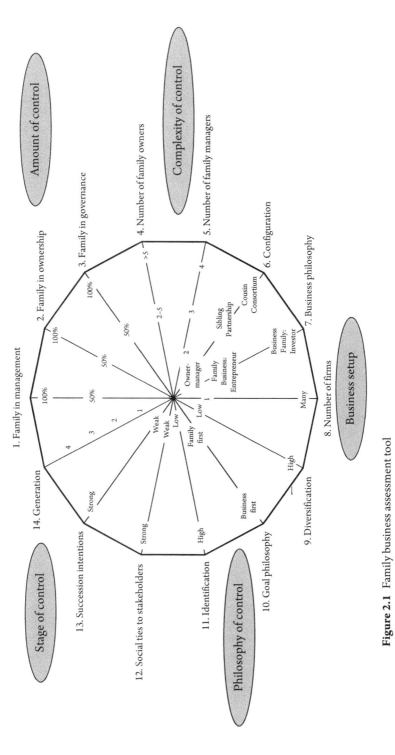

Figure 2.1 Family business assessment tool

2.2.1 Amount of family control

The control dimension captures the current degree of family involvement in ownership, management and governance functions. The current level of family control determines the degree to which the family is (potentially) able to exercise power and influence important strategic decisions. There is mounting evidence suggesting that firm performance is impacted differently by family involvement in ownership, governance and management, depending on the complexity and, in particular, size of the business. For instance, in a small firm a family-dominated ownership and management team may help performance as it represents a very efficient and lean governance form. In a larger firm, however, it may be necessary to open up ownership to outsiders to finance growth and drive performance. Moreover, given the complexity of a large firm and the expertise required to manage it, opening up management to nonfamily talent may be essential. However, in such a case, it is critical for the family to be present on the governance board to control the nonfamily managers. Depending on the type and degree of family control, family firms face different opportunities and threats, as depicted in Table 2.2.

Table 2.2 Amount of family control

	Attributes	Opportunities	Challenges
Management	100% nonfamily	Superior management expertise, given the broader population of managers to select from	Agency conflicts: control of nonfamily managers, expensive incentives, loss of family-firm-specific culture
	100% family	Efficient leadership, preservation of tacit knowledge	Lack of expertise among family managers, conflicts (e.g., altruism)
Ownership	Family with minority stake	Access to nonfamily capital and opportunities for growth	Reduction of family influence and reduced focus on family goals; short-termism
	100% family	Powerful position of family, tight control of the firm and its values	Abuse of power, limited growth opportunities
Governance/ Supervisory board	100% nonfamily	Independent advice and control	Loss of family influence
	100% family	Ensured family control	No access to external expertise and control

2.2.2   Complexity of family control

While the control dimension captures the amount of family control, the complexity dimension measures the complexity of family control. Complexity of family control rises with the number of family owners and managers. The classical owner-manager constellation represents a fairly simple governance form with one person serving as the sole owner and manager. The opportunities of this governance form are the speed and efficiency of decision making, as well as the absence of owner–manager agency problems; the challenges are the lack of access to external advice and external capital to fund growth and, most often, succession problems.

With increasing numbers of family owners and managers, the need for coordination, communication and hence family governance rises while the potential for conflict grows in parallel. With each generation the number of family members grows and owners' identification with and attachment to the firm may suffer. Table 2.3 summarizes these considerations.

Table 2.3 Complexity of family control

	Attributes	Opportunities	Challenges
No. of family owners	1	Efficient and fast decision making	Lack of external capital, undiversified owner wealth
	2–5	Committed and patient owners	Conflicts with potentially severe consequences because of deadlock
	5 or more	Committed and patient owners	Coordination among owners, lack of identification with the firm
No. of family managers	1	Efficient leadership, few control problems	Lack of expertise and dedication in later generations, succession problems
	Several	Support, commitment, trusted relationships	Relational and task conflicts
Configuration	Owner-manager	Efficient leadership and control	Role overload, responsibility
	Cousin consortium	Culture of commitment and support	Relational conflicts, coordination and communication, identification with the firm

Note: For a detailed discussion of owner-manager, sibling partnership and cousin consortium stages refer to Chapter 5 on governance.

2.2.3 Business setup

Family firms also vary in their approach to conducting business. In the first place, this variance implies that family owners have different modes of self-understanding. On the one hand, the prototypical owning family defines itself as an entrepreneurial actor that strives to nurture a firm. Most often, this means protecting and developing a single business entity, the family's legacy firm, which is active in a certain industry. When this firm is continuously successful, the family often alters its self-understanding from a 'family business' to a 'business family' mindset. In the latter case, the family as the controlling actor no longer sees itself as a nurturer, and even less so as the protector of a single business. The business family's identity is derived from an altering and parallel engagement in and development of businesses. Over time, the business family develops a significant portfolio of businesses (a family business group) that is typically controlled via a holding company or family office.

In contrast to the entrepreneurial approach, which focuses on a single business (most often, the firm in which the family has historical roots), the business family resembles an investor who seeks to deploy his/her funds in multiple businesses. Such an investment approach is unique in that the business family tries to buy, build and eventually exit businesses over long cycles. While in the family business case the controlling family derives its identity partly from its involvement in a particular firm, the business family identifies more with entrepreneurial activities in general, and thus is less dependent on a particular type of firm or industry.

The family's self-understanding and its approach to doing business are both related to the number of firms the family controls. While many family firms are 'single business operations', over time the family may opt to invest in several businesses. The differences in required competences for different numbers of owned firms are significant. For example, when a family manages a single business, industry expertise is essential. In contrast, for a family managing multiple businesses, deep industry expertise may actually be a hindrance. Managing a portfolio of companies requires the ability to develop and eventually rearrange the business portfolio, to take significant financial risks, and to invest in, develop and eventually divest from various businesses.

The third element that captures the variance in families' approaches to doing business is the degree of business diversification. Family firms often exhibit a strong preference for a core activity, product and industry. Their specialization is evidence of in-depth market, product and production know-how. While this may provide significant efficiency and reputation advantages, and

Table 2.4 Business setup

	Attributes	Opportunities	Challenges
Business philosophy	Family business: entrepreneur	Efficiency and reputation advantages	Under-diversification of family wealth
	Business family: investor	Wealth diversification, growth opportunities beyond the core firm	Complexity of portfolio management, conglomerate discount, lack of expertise
Number of firms	1	Specialization and related efficiency and reputation advantages	Nurturing of a potentially declining asset
	Many	Wealth diversification, growth opportunities beyond the core firm, career options for family members	Complexity, required corporate strategy expertise
Diversification	Low	Efficiency and reputation advantages, securing family control and ties, protection of socioemotional wealth	Heightened portfolio risk
	High	Reduced portfolio risk	Complexity, lack of focus and synergies, more difficult to identify with the firm and develop emotional attachment to it

hence protect family owners' socioemotional wealth,[2] the owners also face a significant financial risk to their undiversified wealth (Table 2.4).

2.2.4   Philosophy of family control

A prominent feature of many family firms is that their owners pursue a particular set of goals that includes noneconomic along with economic elements. This feature is often reduced to the idea that family firms try to pursue family (noneconomic) and business (economic) motives. Even though there may be synergies between economic and noneconomic goals, many family firms struggle with a (perceived) tradeoff between them. Put more bluntly, family firms struggle with the question of whether they should prioritize family-related goals over business-related goals, and hence whether they should adhere to a family first or a business first philosophy.

In the related literature, the noneconomic goals have been termed 'socioemotional wealth'. This umbrella term comprises a set of noneconomic goals that are seen as valuable by families but at the same time tend to impact the business sphere (Gomez-Mejia et al. 2011; for a further discussion of socioemotional wealth and its impact on strategic decisions, refer to Chapter 6 on the strategy). A family first approach to managing the family firm would thus emphasize socioemotional wealth, which prioritizes emotional attachment to the firm, the nurturing of the firm, the firm's public image, and benevolent social ties to stakeholders. A business first approach would prioritize innovation, change, growth and profit over such nonfinancial goals.

A prominent element of socioemotional wealth is the level of identity overlap between the family and the business, epitomized, for instance, by a shared name. Family owners with a high identity overlap with their firms are particularly concerned with the firm's public image and reputation. A bad firm reputation reflects poorly on the owners, while a positive firm reputation may cast the owners in a favorable light. Identity and ultimately reputation concerns among family owners often result in an emphasis on social actions at the firm level (e.g., pollution reduction or support for local social activity).

Benevolent social ties are another essential noneconomic goal and element of socioemotional wealth in family firms. These ties represent a preference for binding relationships that emphasize support, trust and the interdependence of firm actors (such as managers, employees, suppliers and clients) with each other and with external stakeholders. The value placed on benevolent social ties affects many aspects of firm behavior. For instance, a firm that prioritizes benevolent ties may have more internal promotions than outside hires, place a particular emphasis on organization-to-person fit for new hires (eventually at the expense of job-to-person fit) and/or exhibit a general hesitation to downsize the workforce. Because benevolent ties are particularly prominent in families and tend to grow over time, their emphasis within a firm may also denote a preference for family and senior nonfamily members over nonfamily and, in particular, junior nonfamily members in staffing and promotion decisions. Benevolent ties to external stakeholders may lead a firm to do favors for business partners (e.g., by providing referrals), to reciprocate received favors, and to nurture long-term interdependent relationships rather than focusing purely on the firm's short-term financial gain. Again, this emphasis comes with opportunities as well as challenges (see Table 2.5).

2.2.5 Stage of control

The stage dimension in our taxonomy of family control assesses the temporal aspect of the family's relationship to the firm. This dimension distinguishes family owners from other types of blockholders, such as private equity investors.

Table 2.5 Philosophy of family control

	Attributes	Opportunities	Challenges
Goal set	Family first	Continuity, long-term orientation	Unconditional preference for family members, leading to questionable capabilities, free riding and abuse of family ties
	Business first	Focus on economic prosperity	Neglect of family-firm-specific advantages
Identification	Low	Focus on economic realities	Lack of credibility as leaders, oversight of social impact of actions
	High	Concern for firm reputation, corporate social performance	Hesitation to undertake required efficiency improvements for fear of reputational damage
Benevolent ties	Weak	Ability to focus on the most economically beneficial relationships in the short term	Lack of support from stakeholders in difficult times, limited resource access from stakeholders stemming from lack of ties
	Strong	Personal, trusting atmosphere; low workforce turnover; 'good citizen' behavior	Inability to cut off underperforming employees and activities

The time horizon of the stage of control extends in two directions: it reaches back into the past (duration) and projects forward into the future (vision).

The duration of family ownership denotes the history of firm control by the family. Families with a long duration of ownership may show a heightened concern for their entrepreneurial legacy, a commitment to the historic roots of the business, and a high level of emotional attachment to the firm. In some cases, however, especially when the family is not involved in operations, the owners may experience less attachment to the firm with each passing generation. Nevertheless, for owners who are involved in operations, the passage of time only strengthens the bond with the firm. In these cases, the firm may become a veritable heirloom asset with a value that exceeds the pure financial value of the firm.

The owners' vision for the future relates to the current generation's desire to extend family control to the next family generation. If the future of the firm looks grim, the family may seek to sell or even liquidate the firm even if it has a long history of successful business activity. In such a case, the family will be

Table 2.6 Stage of family control

	Attributes	Opportunities	Challenges
Generation	First	Strong entrepreneurial spirit of founder(s)	Lack of business sustainability
	Late	Emotional attachment among owners, perseverance	Excessive legacy concern, loss of entrepreneurial spirit
Family internal succession intention	Weak	Seek most profitable exit opportunity, focus on firm prosperity without considering the family constellation	Short-termism; lifecycle of owner-manager reflected in the performance of the firm
	Strong	Long-term focus, preservation of valuable networks and knowledge, continuity of leadership	Succession planning, pressure on the next generation, forgoing financially attractive exit options

less likely to care for, develop and invest in the firm compared to a family that believes in the future of the firm and wishes to pass it on to the next generation. The stage of control, like the previous dimensions, comes with its own specific opportunities and challenges (see Table 2.6).

Taken together, the above framework seeks to capture the heterogeneity of family influence in a firm. Understanding the sources of this heterogeneity is important as the family-involvement dimensions give rise to particular opportunities and challenges for the firm and its owners. As such, the framework points to managerial tasks that are directly tied to the type and degree of family control.

The family business assessment tool and the associated framework will be most useful to family business practitioners when each dimension is considered distinctly and when discussions deal with the levels of control, interdependencies and managerial challenges that come with certain positions in the framework. As mentioned above, the family business assessment tool is not intended to point to some optimal positioning (e.g., inner versus outer circle). Rather, it should be seen as a tool that brings to light the managerial opportunities and challenges that are tied to specific dimensions of family influence.

2.3　Circle models of family influence

Practitioners and scholars alike have found it useful to define family firms as organizations characterized by the interplay of several subsystems. Figure 2.2 presents one version of the systemic view of family firms. Circle models such

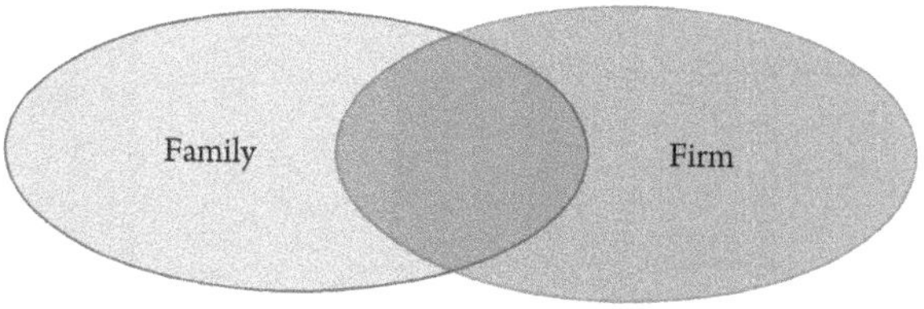

Presumed logic of
family system
- Tradition
- Emotional/irrational
- Nepotism
- Long-term perspective
- Nonfinancial values

Presumed logic of
firm system
- Renewal
- Rational
- Meritocracy
- Short-term perspective
- Financial values

Figure 2.2 Two-circle model of the family firm system

as this one are helpful because they remind us that family firms are composed of two social systems—the family and the firm—which adhere to differing, if not opposing, logics.

The depiction of the family business as a combination of largely incompatible subsystems brings to the fore the tensions inherent in this form of organization. Further, it suggests that the management of family firms can be equated with the management of tensions among the business and family systems that compete for influence. The circle model thus helps us in making sense of the underlying reasons for the tensions we observe. These tensions become apparent at various levels of strategic decision making, such as alterations at the corporate level (e.g., diversification), risk taking, investments, and research and development, but they also arise in the firm's structuring of its incentive and compensation systems. The two-circle model would suggest that the discussions around these topics are ultimately influenced by the largely competing logics of the two underlying social systems that come together in the family firm.

A much-used alternative to the two-circle model outlined above is the three-circle model of family, ownership and management (Figure 2.3). Originally introduced by Hoy and Verser (1994), this model has received wide acceptance in practice.

The three-circle model is appealing to many practitioners because it helps them to grasp the role-related complexities that individuals experience in a family firm. In total, it identifies seven types of roles that an individual can play in a family business system (see Table 2.7).

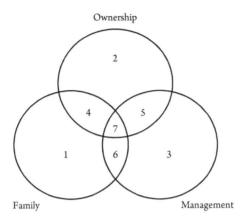

Source: Tagiuri and Davis (1996).

Figure 2.3 Three-circle model of family influence

Table 2.7 Roles and motives in the three-circle model

Number	Role	Typical motives and concerns
1	Family members who are neither shareholders nor business managers	Harmony, mutual support, long-term survival of the firm
2	Shareholders who are neither family members nor managers	Return on equity, dividends, value of the ownership stake
3	Employees or managers who are neither family members nor shareholders	Job security, salary, stimulating work environment, promotion opportunities, opportunity to become owner
4	Family members who hold shares but are not involved in management	Return on equity, dividends, information access
5	Nonfamily managers holding shares	Opportunity to benefit from firm performance and increase in value, managerial discretion
6	Family members involved in operations without shares	Get to know the firm, career path inside the firm, ways to eventually become owner
7	Family managers holding shares	Trying to be 'successful' in all three systems: family (togetherness), business (commercial and entrepreneurial success), ownership (financial success)

2.3.1 Advantages of circle models

The circle models outlined above rank among the most commonly used models to analyze family influence and governance in family firms. This is not surprising given their undisputed strengths:

1. **Disentangling the underlying logic of the subsystem**
    The key advantage of circle models is the way in which they make visible the underlying logics of family and business. They reveal the principles through which role identities, relationship modes, personal expectations and problem analysis are constructed and executed. As a result, they make us aware of the subtle contexts in which reasoning, communication and decision making take place.

2. **Enabling discussion about roles and related interests**
    The three-circle model furthers our understanding of the various roles that individuals can play in a family firm. Combined with an understanding of the expectations and motives that come with different roles, it can help us sort out and simplify the complexity inherent in the family business governance structure. Although this model provides a static assessment of the positions of individuals involved with the firm, it can also enable a discussion about how people might switch roles within the model over time.

3. **Improving our understanding of role complexity**
    The diagram makes us aware of the fact that people not only have differing interests associated with their roles, but also may wear several hats—that is, they may play different roles at the same time. This insight is important in helping us unearth the inherent complexities of family businesses as well as the sources of misunderstanding and conflict that plague many family business communications.

2.3.2 Disadvantages of circle models

Despite their clear advantages, circle models necessarily reduce real-life phenomena to conceptual models. As such, they are fraught with several important shortcomings.

1. **Flawed subsystem prototypes**
    The attributes assigned to the family and business spheres are largely overstated. For instance, it does not seem plausible that decisions and relationships are purely emotional/irrational on the family side and purely rational on the business side. Board dynamics in nonfamily firms may be very emotional, and decision making in family firms is not irrational per se. Relationships among family members may be more complex than those among nonfamily members, but they are not necessarily less rational. In the family sphere, financial considerations may be an important matter (e.g., when distributing wealth and income within a family). Circle models thus attribute certain features solely to family or business that actually occur in the other subsystem as well.

2. **Flawed functionality assumptions**

    A particularly severe disadvantage of circle models is their implicit assumption that the family inhibits the success of the business. That is, the family logic presented in these diagrams injects disturbing emotions into rational business decisions, emphasizes tradition while limiting change and innovation, and hinders rational decision making and success. Ultimately, one may conclude that because the purpose of the business is to be logical and profitable, the emotional aspect of the family is an interference that is best excluded (Whiteside and Brown 1991).

    This view, however, has two major flaws. First, family involvement is a given in family firms; by definition, a complete separation of family and business is impossible in these organizations. Second, many aspects of 'family logic' may be present and even desirable in the business sphere. For instance, support, commitment, cohesiveness and interdependence are particularly pronounced in the family context. But these features of interpersonal relationships are often much sought after in the business sphere as well. Similarly, certain attributes that are ascribed to the business sphere, such as the efficient use of resources, are a part of familial norms (e.g., think of the norm of parsimony and the family's provision of economic goods such as shelter and education). Circle models are undermined by flawed functionality assumptions about the nature of family and business systems because each is defined as the opposite of the other.

3. **Overlooked synergies between family and business**

    The polarization of family and business attributes neglects the synergies between family and business systems. The ways in which a controlling family can contribute to a business's success deserve particular attention. As mentioned above, certain social rules and norms, such as support, commitment, cohesiveness and interdependence, are particularly pronounced in the family context. However, these relationship qualities are often depicted as highly desirable in the business context as well—in particular, ironically enough, when it comes to embracing change. Stability-providing systems, which are also associated with families, have been found to be essential grounds for organizational change (see, e.g., Martha Feldman's work on routines, Feldman and Pentland 2003). Similarly, families often favor a long-term investment horizon, patient financial capital, and networks that may be highly valuable for a firm. The negative and inertial role that the diagram tends to assign to families disregards the synergies between family and business and the ways in which family attributes contribute to firm success.

4. **Simplified view of roles and communication**

    Circle models tend to obscure the challenges for actors who 'wear several hats' in the organization (in particular, see roles 4, 5, 6 and 7 in the three-circle model). For instance, a dispute between a junior (daughter) or senior (mother) family member involved in the business can be better understood and potentially solved if both sides acknowledge that the two protagonists may each speak as 'two types of people'. When the daughter criticizes a business decision by the mother, the mother may interpret the critique as inappropriate behavior by her subordinate. The daughter, however, is used to open communication with her mother in the family sphere. Moreover, she wants to position herself as a determined entrepreneur and successor who is able to successfully continue the mother's business. Similarly, a family business owner and manager whose son also owns shares and is involved in management may ask himself: when I talk to my son about the business, am I speaking to him as a father, boss or co-owner? In nonfamily business settings, we have familiar 'markers' to indicate our roles (at home as a family member, at work as a professional). These contextual markers are often missing or hidden in the family business context. In consequence, and particularly in cases where actors simultaneously occupy multiple roles, circle models tend to underestimate the complexity of communication and decision making.[3]

2.4   Family firm identity

Interestingly, not every family firm that qualifies as a family business under the criteria suggested above defines itself as such. For instance, in a study of private family firms in the United Kingdom, Westhead and Cowling (1998) found that 17% of firm leaders in the sample did not perceive themselves to be part of a family firm despite the fact that the firm was majority controlled by a family. Conversely, 15% of the firm leaders in the sample perceived their firm to be a family firm despite a low level of family control. These findings point to the relevance of the firm's self-perception. Some firms may want to conceal family influence due to legitimacy concerns for instance on the stock market, as the financial community and minority shareholders may fear nepotism and expropriation by the controlling family. However, other firms may openly portray themselves as family firms in order to project an image of tradition, relationship quality and reliability. Therefore, some argue that the classification of a family firm depends not only on objective governance criteria, but also on the degree to which the controlling family projects a family firm image to its internal and external stakeholders.

2.5   Family business definition used in this book

The discussion above is evidence of the lively debate about the essential aspects of family firms. We have seen that there is significant value in separating the dimensions of family influence to unearth the distinct opportunities and challenges tied to family control. Still, as a reader you may well ask about the common denominator this book uses for family firms and the type of family firm for which the concepts discussed in the book are particularly suitable. With these concerns in mind, we suggest the following working definition:

> **Family business definition used in the book:**
>
> A family firm is a firm dominantly controlled by a family with the vision to potentially sustain family control across generations.

This definition of family business is aligned with the prominent definition of Chua, Chrisman and Sharma (1999) and emphasizes two central features:

- **Dominant control in the hands of family**: The channels through which this control is exercised may vary significantly depending on the complexity, size and age of the firm and on the particular value system and goals of the family, as shown above.
- **Transgenerational outlook**: This aspect is critical when distinguishing between any closely held company and a family firm. It points to the particular relevance of succession and long-term value creation, aspects that are either absent or less relevant in nonfamily firms.

We will emphasize different parts of the definition above when discussing different topics in this book. For instance, in the discussion on governance, we will explore the element of 'dominant control' in more detail. When discussing succession, we will emphasize and explore the 'transgenerational outlook'. And when exploring the strategic management of family firms, we will explore how both elements in conjunction impact the strategic choices of family firms.

Of course, how one chooses to define a family firm has implications for the prevalence of the family business phenomenon around the world. This will be the topic of the next chapter.

? REFLECTION QUESTIONS

1. What are the particular advantages and disadvantages of using the two-circle model to describe family firms?

2. What modes of family influence may be overlooked when one determines family control only in terms of ownership, board and management involvement?
3. What are the potential sources of conflict between family owners involved in management and those not involved in management?
4. Why are there so many communication problems among family members who work together in the family business?
5. For a family firm you know: what is its position in the family business assessment tool? And what are related challenges and opportunities?
6. For a family firm you know: position the family members, shareholders, board members and managers in the three-circle model. What are their goals and concerns?

NOTES

1 The terms 'family firm' and 'family business' are used interchangeably throughout this book.
2 Socioemotional wealth is defined as the total stock of affect tied to the firm by the family, such as benevolent ties, familial control, identity and reputation, just as emotional benefits. For further details refer to the related literature by Luis Gomez-Mejia and colleagues, which is further explored in Chapter 6 on strategy.
3 To remedy this confusion in family business communications it can be helpful to clarify the boundaries between roles and indicate the role from which one is speaking at a particular moment.

BACKGROUND READING

Anderson, R. C., and D. M. Reeb (2003b). Founding-family ownership and firm performance: Evidence from the S&P 500. *Journal of Finance*, 58 (3): 1301–1328.

Astrachan, J. H., S. B. Klein and K. X. Smyrnios (2002). The F-PEC scale of family influence: A proposal for solving the family business definition problem. *Family Business Review*, 15 (1): 45–58.

Bourdieu, P. (1996). On the family as a realized category. *Theory, Culture and Society*, 13 (3): 19–26.

Chua, J. H., J. J. Chrisman and P. Sharma (1999). Defining the family business by behavior. *Entrepreneurship Theory and Practice*, 23 (4): 19–39.

Gomez-Mejia, L. R., C. Cruz, P. Berrone and J. De Castro (2011). The bind that ties: Socioemotional wealth preservation in family firms. *Academy of Management Annals*, 5 (1): 653–707.

Hoy, F., and T. G. Verser (1994). Emerging business, emerging field: Entrepreneurship and the family firm. *Entrepreneurship Theory and Practice*, 19 (1): 9–23.

Tagiuri, R., and J. Davis (1996). Bivalent attributes of the family firm. *Family Business Review*, 9 (2): 199–208

Villalonga, B., and R. Amit (2006). How do family ownership, control and management affect firm value? *Journal of Financial Economics*, 80 (2): 385–417.

Westhead, P., and M. Cowling (1998). Family firm research: The need for a methodological rethink. *Entrepreneurship Theory and Practice*, 23 (1): 31–56.

Whiteside, M. F., and F. H. Brown (1991). Drawbacks of a dual systems approach to family firms: Can we expand our thinking? *Family Business Review*, 4 (4): 383–395.

Zellweger, T., K. Eddleston and F. W. Kellermanns (2010). Exploring the concept of familiness: Introducing family firm identity. *Journal of Family Business Strategy*, 1 (1): 54–63.

3

Prevalence and economic contribution of family firms

In a famous article, Aldrich and Cliff (2003, p. 575) wrote that 'one hundred years ago, "business" meant "family business", and thus the adjective "family" was redundant'. Business *was* family business. And to a certain degree, this remains true today. The following sections explore this issue by addressing the prevalence and economic contributions of family firms around the globe (for further discussion, please refer to Bertrand and Schoar 2006).

3.1 Prevalence of family firms worldwide

Depending on the definition one uses, roughly 70% to 90% of all firms across the globe are family firms. However, given the lack of a shared definition among the studies on this topic, the exact estimates and their international variation should be taken with a grain of salt.[1] For some regions we have more fine-grained data illustrating the link between the definition used and the significance of the family firm phenomenon. The following subsections explore these links in more detail.

3.1.1 United States

For the United States, Astrachan and Shanker (1996) suggested that family firms make up 74.9% of the 27.09 million total firms located in the United States[2] when family firms are defined as businesses with at least limited involvement of the family in ownership, board and management. This share drops to 45.0% of firms if we require the firm to be run by a family member, and to 15.1% of firms when we require a family firm to be under the control of the same family for more than one generation and that more than one family member is involved in management.

3.1.2 Europe

The European Commission, which uses a fairly narrow definition of family business, finds that 70% to 90% of all firms in the European Union are family firms.[3] The European Commission defines a private family firm as:

> A firm, of any size, . . . if: 1) The majority of decision-making rights is in the possession of the natural person(s) who established the firm, or in the possession of the natural person(s) who has/have acquired the share capital of the firm, or in the possession of their spouses, parents, child or children's direct heirs. 2) The majority of decision-making rights are indirect or direct. 3) At least one representative of the family or kin is formally involved in the governance of the firm.

We can assume that these criteria are cumulative (i.e., a firm must meet all three criteria to be classified as a family firm). For the case of publicly listed firms, the European Commission suggests:

> 4) Listed companies meet the definition of family enterprise if the person who established or acquired the firm (share capital) or their families or descendants possess 25 per cent of the decision-making rights mandated by their share capital.

Country-level data on the prevalence of family firms across Europe can be found in Mandl (2008). The following overview of the share of family firms in Europe (Table 3.1) was adapted and extended from Flören, Uhlaner and Berent-Braun (2010).[4]

Table 3.1 Share of family firms across various European countries

Country	Share of family firms in %
Austria	80
Belgium	70
Finland	86
France	75
Germany	95
Italy	93
Netherlands	69
Spain	75
Sweden	80
Switzerland	88
United Kingdom	69

3.1.3   Asia and Pacific Rim

Information on family firms is less comprehensive for this region. In Australia, a KPMG family business survey (2013a) suggests that 67% of all firms are family controlled. In China, we have only sparse data on the prevalence of family firms. However, an increasing number of studies is investigating publicly quoted family firms in this country, and there is some evidence suggesting that family business is the organizational form of choice of most non-government-controlled business activity. For instance, it has been suggested that Chinese family firms control a proportion of the country's economic wealth that is larger than their relative share in the population of firms (see Lee 2006). Sun Yat-sen and Zhejiang Universities estimate that 85.4% of China's private enterprises are family owned. In Singapore, 80% to 90% of industrial companies are reported to be family firms (Lee 2006).

3.1.4   Middle East/Gulf countries

The Middle East is a particularly interesting context for the study of family firms. According to *Tharawat* magazine, around 75% of the region's private economy is controlled by roughly 5000 families. Here, not only do family businesses dominate the economy, but family control is also concentrated in the hands of a few very powerful families. This observation points to an underlying social pattern that distinguishes the Middle East regional economy from most Western economies—or, at least, from common depictions of Western economies. While business-controlling families in the Western world are often described as solitary actors, in the Arab world the web of familial relationships tends to reach beyond the immediate family and encompass a larger number of people. This social form is reflected in a concentrated network of economic activity in which the ultimate owner of a business is not a single family as defined in narrow Western terms, but an extended group of family members who pool their economic activity, wealth and resources.

In the Arab world, the type as well as the execution of family influence matters to a particular degree. For instance, control structures and management styles may depend on the owner's religious affiliation, as the wide array of Islamic sectarian groups fosters different management styles, from authoritarian to consultative (Raven and Welsh 2006). These divergent styles make it difficult to impose a clear-cut definition of the family firm or degree of family influence. In an authoritarian setting, for example, the controlling family may seem to have a relatively small share of involvement in the executive board, but may actually control a large fraction of power.

3.1.5   Latin America

Looking to Latin America, we again find that family firms play a very prominent role in the regional economy. Depending on the data source, between 65% and 98% of all businesses are reported to be family firms (Flören 2002). For the overall prevalence of family firms as part of the total population of firms, only limited data is available. Nevertheless, the Latin Focus Consensus Forecast suggests that in Brazil the majority of all firms are family controlled, and that in Chile family control is the dominating governance form to the extent that 90% of all firms are under family control.

3.1.6   Africa

Rosa (2014) provides a rare glimpse into the particularities of family firms in Africa. As he reports, until the nineteenth century, most Africans lived in small tribal societies pursuing a mixture of traditional subsistence-based hunting, gathering and agriculture. The isolation of most African peoples from developments in Europe and Asia meant that until the arrival of Portuguese traders in the sixteenth century, followed by the Dutch and the English in the eighteenth century, family businesses as economic entities that manage resources to achieve a monetary profit were largely absent on the continent. Family businesses thus did not really take off in Africa until the height of the colonial period in the mid-nineteenth century.

In the nineteenth century, some colonies in Africa opened up for European settlement (such as those in modern-day South Africa, Angola, Mozambique, Kenya and Congo). Rosa (2014) reports that today there are still two South African families of European origin who appear prominently on the *Forbes* list of the world's wealthiest people—namely, the Rupert family, which controls the luxury conglomerate Richemont, and the Oppenheimers, who own the De Beers diamond empire. In other African countries, where white settlement was either banned or discouraged by the colonial governments, the gap tended to be filled by South Indian and Middle Eastern (mainly Lebanese) migrants.

Balunywa, Rosa and Nandagire-Ntamu (2013) report that the development of (family) businesses by African natives themselves was severely handicapped by European powers and local governments in the colonial and the post-colonial periods. In the colonial period, the incentives of the colonial governments favored non-Africans. From the time of national independence until the 1990s, the socialist policies of many African governments suppressed the development of indigenous capitalism. This trend against the development of local businesses was exacerbated by political instability and civil wars in many former colonies.

In his intriguing account of the evolution of family firms in Africa, Rosa (2014) distinguishes the following types of family businesses in sub-Saharan African countries today:

1. Traditional trading merchant businesses of mostly Muslim business families, many with an ancient trading tradition stretching back to medieval times and beyond. These may survive in some East African coastal areas, in Ethiopia and in areas of cross-Saharan trade.
2. Family businesses of Europeans who settled in Africa, the oldest of which in South Africa date back to the eighteenth century. These are most common in former colonies with significant white settlement.
3. Family businesses of Asians who came to Africa in colonial and more recent times and established businesses. They are particularly common in East and Southern Africa. New waves of South Asian as well as East Asian migrants are still coming over in the early 2000s, adding to the stock of family businesses of Asian origin.
4. Small-scale family businesses of indigenous Africans who are enjoying the freedom to participate in business after years of discouragement during the colonial and early post-colonial periods. These are very common in all countries, and range considerably in size and dynamism within the overall small-scale category.
5. Large-scale indigenous African family businesses that have blossomed in countries where liberalization and capitalism have been encouraged by governments. The twenty-first-century generation of entrepreneurs is particularly dynamic and forms the base of a new group of indigenous African family businesses with highly educated founders.

Africa thus presents a rich context in which to study the impact of colonial forces and migration on the evolution of family firms. Despite wide regional variance in the origin of these firms and the infancy of the research on family firms in Africa, the results so far show that family firms are emerging in Africa at a very fast rate and that they represent the largest share of all firms on the continent. As elsewhere, the micro family firms are an especially large group. These small family firms, whether created out of necessity or opportunity, significantly contribute to the economic growth of African countries.

3.1.7 Summary

All in all, we find an emerging picture of the family business phenomenon with two central facets. First, family firms are the dominant form of organization across the globe, in emerging as well as in more established economies. In all countries in which studies on the topic were conducted, family firms represent the majority of firms, even when the definition of family firm is rather narrow. Given the evidence, it seems reasonable to assume that families control between 70% and 90% of all firms worldwide. Second, an international comparison of the prevalence of family firms is challenging given that the studies exploring the phenomenon use very different family firm definitions. On the one hand, this lack of comparability is frustrating. On the other hand, it is questionable whether a 'one-size-fits-all' definition can realistically render the family firm phenomenon across such different national and cultural contexts. Given the variations among corporate governance regulations and preferences, as well as among definitions of family, a globally standardized definition of family business will likely over- or underestimate the phenomenon in local circumstances.

3.2 Economic contribution of family firms

If, as we estimate, 70% to 90% of all firms are controlled by families, one may wonder what their contribution to the economy is (e.g., in terms of employment or GDP). The economic contribution of family firms will likely depend on these firms' average size. If, on average, family firms are smaller than their nonfamily counterparts (e.g., in terms of employment, total assets and sales volume), the share of their contribution to the economy will likely be smaller than the share these firms represent of the total number of firms.

3.2.1 Size of family firms

Family firms are particularly prominent among small to mid-sized enterprises (SMEs), a pattern that tends to be consistent around the globe. For instance, in her study on family firms in the European Union, Mandl (2008) finds that the family business sector is dominated by SMEs, and particularly by micro enterprises with fewer than ten employees. For Germany, among companies with an annual sales volume of less than €1 million, the share of family businesses is as high as 97%. The share of family firms decreases to 86% among those with €1–5 million in annual sales volume, to 74% among those with €5–10 million and to 58% among those with €10–50 million.[5]

However, this trend should not lead us to expect family firms to be absent among large firms or, in particular, among publicly listed firms. In Germany, according to the Institut für Mittelstandsforschung as many as 34% of companies with an annual turnover of more than €50 million are family businesses. Similarly, in Luxembourg, Norway and Sweden, research suggests that about 30% of the largest companies are family businesses. In Belgium, the share of family firms among large companies is even higher, at about 50%. And as the International Family Enterprise Research Academy (IFERA) pointed out in 2003, not only is Walmart, the world's largest enterprise, a family business, but 37% of Fortune 500 companies are also family firms.

Evidence of the economic power of the largest family firms in the world can be found in the Global Family Business Index (for more details about the largest family firms in the world refer to www.familybusinessindex.com).

3.2.2 Contribution to employment

As we might expect given the negative link between firm size and family firm prevalence, we find that family firms contribute to employment at lower levels than their fraction of total companies would suggest. Nevertheless, family firms employ a large portion of the workforce worldwide. Astrachan and Shanker (2003) suggest that family firms employ 62% of the workforce in the United States. In the European Union, family firms account for about 40% to 50% of employment (Mandl 2008). And in the Middle East, *Tharawat* suggests that family firms create about 70% of employment. Even taking into account the limitations of the available data and the variance across regions, these figures show that family firms are responsible for significant economic contributions around the globe.

3.2.3 Contribution to GDP

The available data on the contribution of family firms to GDP is very limited. For the United States, Astrachan and Shanker (2003) suggest that family businesses are responsible for 64% of GDP. For the European Union, we find a wide spectrum of estimates. Depending on the definition of family business—and also on the use of aggregate economic output metrics, such as GDP versus GNP—the share attributed to family firms ranges from about 40% to 70% (Mandl 2008). In the United Kingdom, there is data suggesting that family firms contribute roughly 25% of GDP (Institute for Family Business 2011). Meanwhile, in Switzerland, the share of GDP attributed to family firms is estimated at about 60% (Zellweger and Fueglistaller 2007).

And in India, KPMG (2013b) estimates that family firms account for two-thirds of GDP, 90% of gross industry output, 79% of organized private sector employment and 27% of overall employment (for additional information on the structure and challenges of Indian family firms, see Ramachandran and Bhatnagar 2012).

3.2.4 Summary

In sum, we find that family firms have a dominant influence on the economic landscape around the world. More specifically, family firms are more prevalent among small firms than among large ones. Still, some of the largest firms across the globe are family controlled. Worldwide, we estimate that family firms account for about 40% to 70% of employment and GDP.

3.3 Institutional setting and the prevalence of family firms

The findings on disparate family firm presence across the globe are not only caused by variance in the definition of the family firm. More fundamentally, family firms may be more or less prevalent in different regions because of underlying social forces that affect their success (e.g., industries or political contexts). To illustrate this proposed link between the institutional setting and the prevalence of family firms, we will examine the industry affiliation and stock market listing of family firms.

3.3.1 Industry affiliation of family firms

An often-heard argument for the superiority of family firms is that family control equips a firm with specific abilities. For instance, the long-term commitment of families and employees, the atmosphere of mutual trust and benevolent relationships, and the close ties to the local community that are characteristic of family firms should allow them to develop some competitive advantages over nonfamily firms. If this is true, family firms should be particularly successful and ultimately prevalent in industries in which stable personal relationships and trusted community ties are important. Think, for example, of the food retail and gastronomy industries, in which customers tend to favor trusted retailers, restaurants and hotels. For these services, which deal with products that are important for daily life, it may be particularly important to 'know what you're getting' and from whom you're buying. Customer loyalty is more likely to develop in this context when the supplier and the customer get to know each other over multiple interactions.

It is not surprising, then, to find that family firms are particularly present in service industries. For the United Kingdom, one finds the highest concentrations of family firms (next to agriculture) in hotels and restaurants (85%) and in wholesale and retail (77%) (Institute for Family Business 2011). Likewise, a study investigating sector distribution among publicly listed German and Swiss firms finds that 67% of all firms in the food industry are family firms (compared to roughly 35% of all publicly listed firms). In the wholesale and retail industries, family firms represent 70% and 55% of all firms respectively. Similar findings about the prevalence of family firms in service-based industries are reported for other European countries (Mandl 2008) and for India (Ramachandran and Bhatnagar 2012). Conversely, industries in which family firms tend to be underrepresented include manufacturing, high-growth industries and financial services (Willers 2011).

Along with the service industry, family firms seem to be particularly prominent in the agricultural industry (Institute for Family Business 2011). For instance, 89% of all firms in the UK agricultural industry are family firms. Comparable results are reported for other countries such as India. For Brazil, São Paulo Business School suggests that family-owned farming enterprises comprise 84% of the rural firms in the country. In Chile, family firms are concentrated in agricultural and related industries, such as farming, food and beverage services, mining, textiles, fishing and fish processing, and forestry (Latin Focus Consensus Forecast).

In addition to the service industry and the agricultural sector, several industries stand out for their tendency toward family control. The global beer industry is an impressive example of this phenomenon: ABInBev, SABMiller, Heineken, FEMSA, Carlsberg and many smaller companies are still controlled by their founding families. Some of the world's largest car manufacturers—including Volkswagen, Ford, Toyota, PSA Peugeot Citroën, Fiat, BMW and Tata—are also under family control. In the United States, six of the seven largest cable system operators, including Comcast, Cox, Cablevision and Charter Communications, are controlled and partly managed by their founders or the founders' heirs. Eleven of the twelve largest publicly traded newspaper companies in the United States are also family controlled. This finding is particularly noteworthy given the important social and political impact media companies can have in national and regional markets. Investigating family control across industries, Villalonga and Amit (2010) find that, consistent with the hypothesis that family firms have a competitive advantage in certain industries, firms and industries are more likely to remain under family control when their efficient scale and capital intensity are smaller, when the environment is more noisy (and monitoring needs are therefore greater) and when there is less stock turnover (reflecting longer investor horizons).

Summing up, we find family firms to be particularly prevalent in the retail, wholesale, agriculture, food manufacturing, gastronomy, hotel and media industries. Family firms are less prevalent in capital-intensive industries and in the financial industry.

3.3.2 Stock market listing of family firms

Another often-heard argument is that family control is an efficient response to weak formal institutions. That is, family control can help mitigate the weak protection of property rights and rule of law that firms may experience in emerging market countries (Gedajlovic et al. 2011). For instance, where the protection of property rights is underdeveloped, leaving minority owners with few possibilities to fight against expropriation by majority blockholders, the trust developed by the family may help ease investor concerns. Similarly, where legal enforcement of contracts is limited and capital markets are inefficient, family ties and the trust-based relationships, support, familial resources and networks associated with them may serve as a substitute for the lack of institutional quality. Family firms should thus be particularly prevalent in settings with weak formal investor protection, as trusted relationships with family members, the family's reputation and strong social ties should help these firms enforce contracts and access critical resources in an otherwise resource-scarce environment.

This institutional perspective on family firms is partly reflected in an analysis of the presence of family firms on the global stock markets. La Porta, Lopez-De-Silanes and Shleifer (1999) find that the prevalence of family firms on the stock market rises with the decreasing quality of minority owner protection (see also Faccio and Lang 2002). In cases where minority owners have less protection—for instance, in a dual-class share structure with voting and nonvoting shares—it may be particularly attractive for family owners to take their firms public, as family blockholders can retain control despite listing the firm on the stock market. In general, family firms seem to prevail when the institutional environment is relatively weak, supporting the argument that family firms may be better placed to navigate less regulated environments. Interestingly, even in the United States and many other Western countries, where institutions are presumed to be relatively strong, up to 30% of all firms listed on the stock market are family controlled.

1. What is the estimated contribution of family firms to GDP and employment? What is their share among the total population of firms?
2. Why are family firms more prevalent among small firms than large ones?
3. In which industries are family firms particularly prominent? And why might this be so?
4. Why are family firms more prevalent in countries with weak formal institutions?
5. What is your assessment of the predominant role of large family firms in many developing countries for the overall economic development of these countries?
6. Why are family firms more prevalent on the stock market in countries with relatively weak formal institutions?
7. What are the advantages and disadvantages of applying the same family firm definition in different national and regional contexts?

NOTES

1 For data on the significance and economic contributions of family firms in various countries, see the online repository of the Family Firm Institute, www.ffi.org, and there the section on Global Data Points.
2 Data retrieved from the US Bureau of the Census, 2007 Economic Census: Survey of Business Owners.
3 The respective report can be downloaded at: http://ec.europa.eu/enterprise/policies/sme/promoting-entrepreneurship/family-business/family_business_expert_group_report_en.pdf. It provides an interesting overview of the structure and challenges of European family firms.
4 For a detailed study of family firms in Germany, see Klein (2000).
5 Source: Institut für Mittelstandsforschung, IFM, Bonn. For the United Kingdom, refer to the Institute for Family Business (2011). For more details see also Flören (1998) and Frey et al. (2004).

 BACKGROUND READING

Aldrich, H. E., and J. E. Cliff (2003). The pervasive effects of family on entrepreneurship: Toward a family embeddedness perspective. *Journal of Business Venturing*, 18 (5): 573–596.

Astrachan, J. H., and M. C. Shanker (1996). Myths and realities: Family businesses' contribution to the US economy—A framework for assessing family business statistics. *Family Business Review*, 9 (2): 107–123.

Astrachan, J. H., and M. C. Shanker (2003). Family businesses' contribution to the US economy: A closer look. *Family Business Review*, 16 (3): 211–219.

Balunywa, W., P. Rosa and D. Nandagire-Ntamu (2013). 50 years of entrepreneurship in Uganda, ten years of the Ugandan global entrepreneurship monitor. Working paper, University of Edinburgh.

Bertrand, M., and A. Schoar (2006). The role of family in family firms. *Journal of Economic Perspectives*, 20 (2): 73–96.

Faccio, M., and L. Lang (2002). The ultimate ownership of Western European corporations. *Journal of Financial Economics*, 65 (3): 365–395.

Flören, R. (1998). The significance of family business in the Netherlands. *Family Business Review*, 11 (2): 121–134

Flören, R. (2002). Family business in the Netherlands. *Crown Princes in the Clay: An Empirical Study on the Tackling of Succession Challenges in Dutch Family Farms*. Breukelen, the Netherlands: Nyenrode University, Chapter 1.

Frey, U., F. Halter, T. Zellweger and S. Klein (2004). *Family Business in Switzerland: Significance and Structure*. IFERA, Copenhagen.

Gedajlovic, E., M. Carney, J. Chrisman and F. Kellermanns (2011). The adolescence of family firm research: Taking stock and planning for the future. *Journal of Management*, 38: 1010–1037.

Insitute for Family Business (2011). *The UK Family Business Sector*. Oxford Economics.

Klein, S. (2000). Family businesses in Germany: Significance and structure. *Family Business Review*, 13: 157–181.

La Porta, R., F. Lopez-De-Silanes and A. Shleifer (1999). Corporate ownership around the world. *Journal of Finance*, 54: 471–517.

Lee, J. (2006). Impact of family relationships on attitudes for the second generation in family businesses. *Family Business Review*, 19 (3): 175–191.

Mandl, I. (2008). *Overview of Family Business Relevant Issues: Final Report*. Conducted on behalf of the European Commission, Enterprise and Industry Directorate-General: KMU Forschung Austria.

Ramachandran, K., and N. Bhatnagar (2012). Challenges faced by family businesses in India. Indian School of Business, Hyderabad.

Raven, P., and D. H. B. Welsh (2006). Family business in the Middle East: An exploratory study of retail management in Kuwait and Lebanon. *Family Business Review*, 19 (1): 29–48.

Rosa, P. (2014). The emergence of African family businesses and their contribution to economy and society: An overview. Working paper, University of Edinburgh.

Villalonga, B., and R. Amit (2010). Family control of firms and industries. *Financial Management*, 39 (3): 863–904.

4

Strengths and weaknesses of family firms

Any chapter-length discussion of the typical strengths and weaknesses of family firms will be unable to fully account for the tremendous heterogeneity within this group of organizations. As we have already seen, family firms vary widely in terms of size, industry, regional context, and the type and level of family involvement. Still, an overview of the most common strengths and weaknesses of family firms is useful because it should point to the most critical aspects of running a family firm. From a practical standpoint, the list of typical strengths and weaknesses may serve as a self-assessment tool indicating critical issues and opportunities for improvement in a given firm. The strengths and weaknesses discussed in this chapter thus represent potential sources of competitive advantage and disadvantage which will be important for the strategic positioning of the firm.

4.1   Typical strengths of family firms

1. **Fewer conflicts of interest between owners and managers**

   One important strength of family firms is the alignment of the interests of owners and managers who are from the same family. Interest alignment may spare family firms costly control and incentive mechanisms and lead to fewer agency conflicts between owners and managers. In order for a firm to see these benefits, however, two conditions must be met: first, family members must be present at both the ownership and the management levels. Second, the family must exhibit harmonious and benevolent relationships among family members. It should be clear that not all family firms will meet these conditions—just think of the rampant media reports of conflicts in the controlling families of high-profile firms, or of the conflict you may have experienced in your own family relationships (even if your family does not control a firm). Nevertheless, the central argument here is that family relationships between owners and managers typically bring about a particular level of trust and goal alignment, which spares family firms costly monitoring and incentive alignment systems.

2. **Efficient leadership**

   Efficient leadership is an advantage that is related to the lower owner–manager agency costs described above and to the incentive that family blockholders have to ensure the efficient use of their resources. Efficient leadership relies on the lean organization of managerial work and should result, for instance, in more parsimonious, cost-conscious company administration and smaller headquarters. This quality includes the ability to take and enforce decisions more quickly because of the family's powerful position and the trusting relationships and shared goals and values among the family managers involved.

3. **Resource advantages**

   The family-influenced resource base called *familiness* (Habbershon and Williams 1999) is another proposed source of the competitive advantage of family firms. For example, consider the following resources:

   - **Human capital and knowledge**: Family firms may have advantages in developing and upholding deep, long-term knowledge about products, markets and clients.
   - **Financial capital**: Family firms tend to have very loyal (family) equity investors that provide patient capital (i.e., capital that is invested in the firm for the long run and that does not require a fast return).
   - **Social capital**: Family firms often have unique networks with clients, suppliers, industry experts, capital providers and community leaders that they can draw from for support.

   These are just a few examples of the resources that may fall under the concept of familiness; others, such as physical assets for example, may qualify as well. The important point is that resource advantages form the basis for important competitive advantages in family firms, an idea that we will return to in Chapter 6 on strategy.

4. **Long-term orientation and continuity**

   Family firms tend to pursue long-term goals. This is reflected in lower turnover in top management and in longer investment horizons. The long-term view allows family firms to pursue strategies (such as market development, innovation and internationalization) that are costly in the short run but highly profitable in the long run. These types of strategies are harder to pursue for firms that employ a shorter time horizon. Also, family firms' tendency to pursue one strategy consistently may increase their credibility among stakeholders. Family firms tend to act on chosen strategies and deliver on their promises, whereas nonfamily firms may make more erratic strategic moves due to frequent changes in top management.

5. **Culture of commitment and support**

   Family involvement in a firm and the related social norms of support, harmony and benevolence often give rise to a very particular form of corporate culture. This culture tends to be characterized by a heightened commitment among family and nonfamily employees. For example, family firm employees may be willing to contribute beyond expectations and to support the firm in difficult situations, thus increasing the firm's resilience. In return, employees may not earn the highest wages, but they often benefit from greater job security. The resulting atmosphere of trust and mutual support is absent in many nonfamily firms, which tend to promote a more impersonal corporate culture.

6. **Identity and reputation**

Family-controlled companies are also unique because family owner-managers stake their money and often even their personal names and reputations on the firm. As a result, there is a heightened awareness at the ownership and firm levels about the public perception of the firm and its offerings. The concern for reputation at the family ownership and management level translates into a firm-level goal of maintaining the firm's success and the respect and trust of its stakeholders. In turn, family firms often benefit from a trusted reputation. Given the reputation concern, family firms also prioritize the development of strong brands over time. The long-term horizon of family firms mentioned above helps firms achieve the reputation-related goal of brand building.

4.2 Typical weaknesses of family firms

1. **Dependence on family**

A critical feature of family firms relates to their dependence on the family as constituting stakeholder. The controlling family's formal and informal power allows it to determine the fate of the company, for good or ill. This power harkens back to the classical right of the owner to use (*usus*), enjoy (*usufructus*) and abuse (*abusus*) the property in question. The family's dominating influence may be used to the benefit of the company as a whole, for instance via lower owner–manager agency costs compared to nonfamily firms. However, the firm may also be exploited or mismanaged by incompetent or even unethical (family) owner-managers. The dependence on a family may be a blessing for the firm, as outlined in section 4.1, but it may also be a curse.

In addition, relational conflicts between family members or between branches of the family can be very destructive for the firm under family control. Conflicts may impair a firm's ability to take important strategic decisions and can lead to organizational paralysis. In such cases, because the exit for one party is often very costly—for both financial and emotional reasons—the firm itself may be at risk.

2. **Agency costs because of altruism**
    The classical argument is that family firms should have lower owner–manager agency conflict, as outlined above. However, family relationships between owners and managers may give rise to other types of agency problems (agency costs due to altruism). A prominent example is the case of nepotism, in which family members are appointed to positions not because they have the abilities required for a specific task, but simply because they are family members. Nepotism may lead to inappropriate staffing decisions and hence to an adverse selection problem (Schulze et al. 2001). In addition, it signals to other firm members that ability and performance are not the essential criteria for employment or promotion. This has the effect of undermining the perception of fair treatment and reducing employee motivation, especially among employees with the highest level of expertise.

    Family-related agency conflicts may also come in the form of family members (e.g., children) free riding on the goodwill of other family members (e.g., parents). Children working in the company may abuse parental loyalty and love, for instance by shirking their duties or failing to comply with governance rules. In such cases, when parents resist sanctioning their children (e.g., by reducing their salaries or even terminating their employment), children may take unilateral advantage of their family status. Alternatively, parents may free ride on the benevolence of their children and the norm of filial support. For example, parents who are still involved in the firm may oppose necessary innovations and adaptations proposed by the younger generation.

    Taken together, these cases show that many family firms do not escape owner–manager agency costs, but incur them in a different form. Unlike nonfamily firms, which may be more likely to suffer from the misalignment of owner–manager interests, family firms are more likely to suffer from the ill effects of altruism between family members.

3. **Succession challenges**
    Probably the most challenging part of managing a family firm relates to the succession problem. In his study of manufacturing companies in the United States, Ward (1987) finds that only 30% of all family firms 'survive' succession as independent family-controlled and managed companies. Over three generations, this share drops to only 3%. Although the change from family to nonfamily control does not necessarily represent a failure for the firm, many family firms consider succession to be an important concern. These firms face the following questions (among others):
    - Is there somebody in the family who wants to take over?
    - If yes, is he/she able to do the job?

- What role should the successor(s) play in the firm?
- Should the predecessor have a role in the firm after handing over control?
- How should younger family members enter the firm, and what should they be responsible for?
- How do we structure governance, management and the firm overall so that a successor can take over?

The solutions to these questions are highly individualized and require a cross-disciplinary approach that takes into account interpersonal, managerial, financial and legal aspects. Ownership transfers between parties without family ties are more or less standardized corporate transactions. But the questions above touch upon family- and firm-related aspects in parallel, which adds a significant level of complexity. A transfer of corporate control in the absence of family ties obeys the logic of the market, and hence follows the norms of opportunism, maximization of personal profit and self-interest. A transfer of ownership between family members, however, involves family norms that largely conflict with market logic, such as unconditional support and loyalty. This results in a challenging negotiation process, as evidenced by the time needed to reach consensus. Family succession often involves conflicts, power struggles and emotionally laden discussions about justice and fairness—and ultimately love and money.

4. **Resource constraints**

   Counterbalancing the resource advantages mentioned above, family firms also face some resource disadvantages. For instance, relying on family to fill management positions limits the availability of nonfamily talent and may also spark frustration among nonfamily managers about a perceived nonfamily 'glass ceiling'. If nonfamily managers believe that important decisions are always left to family managers, they may conclude that they will never actually reach the inner circle of the firm.

   Similarly, relying on the family as the main source of financial capital may impose a serious constraint on innovation and growth. Because of their heavy investment in the firm, most business-owning families have a fairly undiversified wealth position, which could limit their willingness to take risks—even ones that might ultimately benefit the firm. Given these possible constraints, one should carefully consider whether and in what ways a particular family firm faces resource advantages (positive familiness) and disadvantages (negative familiness) (Habbershon and Williams 1999).

5. **Declining entrepreneurial orientation**

   By definition, any firm has to be entrepreneurial to survive. A firm's entrepreneurial orientation includes an inclination to take risks, a proactive stance toward new strategic actions and an overall goal of autonomy. Over time, however, firms mature, and as a result of their (past) success and resource accumulation, firms and their owners may lose their entrepreneurial drive and hunger for growth and success. In mature family firms, family orientation, and hence an excessive focus on harmony and continuity, may lead to the sort of complacency that is incompatible with entrepreneurship (Lumpkin, Martin and Vaughn 2008). The decline in entrepreneurial orientation is by no means inevitable, and may be counteracted by suitable governance structures and the owners' continued support of entrepreneurship. Nevertheless, keeping up an entrepreneurial spirit across generations is a serious challenge for many family firms.

6. **Role ambiguity**
Actors in family firms often have to play multiple roles. In the most complex cases one actor may be active in management, ownership and family at the same time (refer to the three-circle diagram in Chapter 2 for more details). The multiple and sometimes conflicting perspectives inherent in these roles complicate decision making and communication. For instance, from the family's viewpoint it may make sense to continue a failing business operation. From an ownership perspective, however, closing or divesting the failing unit will increase the value of the ownership stake. And from a managerial standpoint, it may make sense to try to turn the unit around—but this will require a new capital injection from the owners. These differing points of view may coincide in family business actors (especially in family owner-managers), posing severe challenges for the people involved: What should I do? Which hat do I wear in this particular situation? Who am I today, and who am I tomorrow?

Role overlap in family firms requires a tolerance for ambiguous situations that cannot be resolved by considering only one dimension of the problem. By definition, a family firm cannot simply negate one of its constituting elements; the family and the firm are both necessary to this organizational form. Of course, governance structures can be set up to reduce role ambiguity, for example by specifying whether a context or a decision applies to family, ownership or management. Nevertheless, role ambiguity poses severe challenges for family firms and may result in confusion, frustration and conflicts among actors.

Table 4.1 summarizes the strengths and weaknesses of family firms.

Table 4.1 Typical strengths and weaknesses of family firms

Typical strengths	Typical weaknesses
Lower traditional agency costs	Dependence on family
Efficient leadership	Agency costs because of altruism
Resource advantages	Succession challenges
Continuity and long-term orientation	Resource constraints
Culture of commitment and support	Declining entrepreneurial orientation
Identity and reputation	Role ambiguity

Table 4.2 Bivalent attributes of family firms

Attribute	Positive manifestation	Negative manifestation
Overlap of management and ownership	Lower owner–manager agency conflict	Agency conflict because of altruism
Resource base influenced by family	Resource advantage: e.g., tacit knowledge, patient financial capital, networks	Resource disadvantage: e.g., limited amount of financial capital and managerial talent
Long-term orientation	Entrepreneurial investment strategy that can tolerate uncertain or longer time until positive returns	Complacency, inertia and unwillingness to act on opportunities
Family-influenced culture	Commitment, trust and mutual support	Control, distrust, fear
Shared identity	Loyalty, strong sense of mission	Sense of being constantly surveyed, limited scope for individual development
Simultaneous roles	Quick and effective decision making	Norm confusion, anxiety in decision making, lack of objectivity in business decisions

Source: Adapted from Tagiuri and Davis (1996).

4.3 Bivalent attributes of family firm characteristics

From the above list of advantages and disadvantages, it is easy to see some potential links and reinforcing effects. For instance, a long-term orientation strengthens family firms' ability to develop a strong reputation. Also, the powerful position of the controlling family should strengthen the pursuit of a unique strategic path. At the same time, it is conceivable that one source of strength may limit the deployment of another potential strength. For example, the concern for reputation and legitimacy may actually limit the pursuit and timely deployment of strategies that are novel, unique and/or not part of proven (industry) standards.

Moreover, the distinction between advantage and disadvantage may be far from clear cut. For instance, having family members in management and ownership may bring about the advantage of aligning the interests of both groups. On the other hand, because of the altruistic ties between family members, the same attribute may give rise to altruism-induced agency problems. In fact, most of the advantages/disadvantages do not have purely positive/negative valences. Rather, they are bivalent as shown in Table 4.2.

Taken together, it should now be clear that family and business are not necessarily opposing forces. Just as a business can be a valuable resource for a family (e.g., by providing income), a family can be a valuable resource for a firm. The question, then, is *how* one should organize the link between family and business, and hence the choice of appropriate governance structures. This will be the topic of our next chapter.

4.4 CASE STUDY

More than a move to Mexico

by Michael McGrann

For 50 years, brothers Ed, Mike and John Smith ran their clothing manufacturing and merchandising business in relative harmony. In 1980, John died, leaving Ed to run the manufacturing division and Mike to run the merchandising division. Ed and Mike operated with a high level of autonomy within their own divisions, and for many years were able to agree on key strategic issues impacting both divisions.

This harmony began to break down, however, as the brothers approached retirement and the successor generation's involvement grew. Mike felt that his niece, Jennifer (Ed's daughter), was somewhat disorganized and that she had poor leadership skills. Ed felt that his niece, Kimberly (Mike's daughter), was smart, but 'not as smart as she thinks', and that she would do anything to get rid of her cousin Jennifer. John's children, Dan and Martha, were not employees of the business; however, Dan served on the board of directors.

The tensions related to these issues reached a boiling point when Mike decided to retire and named Kimberly to succeed him as President of the Merchandising Division and Chair of the Board. In an effort to calm the tension, Jennifer and Kimberly called an ownership meeting to discuss the coming leadership transition. Ed's son, Robert, and John's daughter, Martha, were not invited. After a discussion of the difficulty the group was having with a local bank, the discussion turned to succession.

CASE STUDY *(continued)*

Table 4.3 Smith Inc. Ownership Group

	Branch 1	Branch 2	Branch 3
Senior generation	**Ed Smith**: President of Manufacturing Division	**Mike Smith**: Semi-retired	**John Smith**: Deceased
Successor generation	**Jennifer**: Director of HR and VP Sales **Robert**: Not involved	**Kimberly**: President of Merchandising Division	**Dan**: Board member **Martha**: Not involved

Mike: 'I know there is some concern about my decision to retire and to promote Kimberly, but she is ready—and the performance of the merchandising division proves it. In fact, we need to begin evaluating all family employees and compensating them based on that performance.'

Ed: 'We agreed years ago that the merchandising division was always going to be more profitable than the manufacturing division because of the market it operates in, and that we would compensate family members equally.'

Jennifer: 'Dad, I have no problem being evaluated and compensated based on my performance, but Kimberly and I can not agree on what is a fair compensation plan.'

Mike: 'Of course you can't. Your division is a sinking ship. You have been losing money for three years, and you don't want to be held accountable for it. For example, the amount of scrap on your shop floor is unacceptably high, and your labor costs are out of control. We need to move to Mexico, like our consultant suggested.'

Ed: 'How can you say that? You know we have made huge improvements in efficiency, and labor costs are a fact of life when you manufacture in this city. And I can't believe you are still talking about Mexico . . . I thought we decided that issue. Don't you have any loyalty to our community?'

Kimberly: 'If we are going to continue growing, we have to address losses in manufacturing— and relocating our plant or sourcing overseas is the most viable option. We can't continue with our acquisition strategy as long as the manufacturing division is a noose around our necks.'

Ed: 'You are as cold-hearted as your father. And besides, I am tired of this growth-through-acquisition stuff. Do you know what that has done to our dividends?'

Dan: 'Jennifer, how long will we continue to lose money in manufacturing? Is there any plan in place to turn things around?'

The meeting ended shortly thereafter when Ed and Mike began to physically threaten each other.

 REFLECTION QUESTIONS

1. Ed and Mike ran the business peacefully for 50 years. How is it possible that they would come to blows now? What are the contributing factors?
2. Why is the discussion about moving to Mexico so difficult?

CASE STUDY *(continued)*

3. If the manufacturing division were doing better would 'everything be ok'? Are they just fighting about manufacturing losses?
4. What are some of the issues impacting the success of the successor generation? When did they start?
5. It is hard to have difficult performance conversations with family members. What are the key criteria for having them successfully? Is it too late for this family group? Why or why not?
6. If you were advising this family, what action steps would you recommend in order to save this family business?

? REFLECTION QUESTIONS

1. What are typical strengths of family firms?
2. What are typical weaknesses of family firms?
3. Consider the following statement: 'If family is involved in ownership and management, family firms are naturally protected against agency conflicts.' Do you agree? Why or why not?
4. What are typical resource advantages and disadvantages of family firms?
5. In what way could the long-term orientation often attributed to family firms become a source of competitive advantage? In what way could it be a disadvantage?
6. What does 'role ambiguity' mean in the context of family firms? Why is it a typical weakness of family firms?
7. Some argue that, over time and generations, family orientation (concern for harmony and continuity) overtakes entrepreneurial orientation (concern for innovation and growth). Put differently: family orientation will eventually suffocate entrepreneurial orientation. Do you agree? Why or why not? How would you ensure this is not taking place?
8. In what ways are family and business logics opposed? In what ways are they complementary?
9. Name some attributes, decision-making criteria and norms usually attributed to the family that might be beneficial for the firm. In what ways are they advantageous?
10. What do we mean when we say that family firms have 'bivalent' attributes?
11. Why is a shared identity and strong family cohesion not always beneficial for business families and their firms?

BACKGROUND READING

Habbershon, T. G., and M. L. Williams (1999). A resource-based framework for assessing the strategic advantages of family firms. *Family Business Review*, 12 (1): 1–25.

Lumpkin, G. T., W. Martin and M. Vaughn (2008). Family orientation: Individual-level influences on family firm outcomes. *Family Business Review*, 21 (2): 127–138.

Schulze, W., M. Lubatkin, R. Dino and A. Buchholtz (2001). Agency relationships in family firms: Theory and evidence. *Organization Science*, 12 (2): 99–116.

Tagiuri, R., and J. Davis (1996). Bivalent attributes of the family firm. *Family Business Review*, 9 (2): 199–208.

Ward, J. (1987). *Keeping the Family Business Healthy*. San Francisco, CA: Jossey-Bass.

5

Governance in the family business

Governance refers to the system of structures, rights and obligations by which corporations are directed and controlled. A firm's governance thus specifies the distribution of rights and responsibilities among the different constituents of the corporation—in particular, among the board of directors, managers and shareholders, but also among other stakeholders such as auditors and regulators. It specifies the rules and procedures for making decisions and provides the structure through which corporations set and pursue their objectives. The particular corporate governance regulations of any given firm reflect its social, regulatory and market environments. Ultimately, governance is a mechanism for monitoring the policies and actions of corporations that aims to align the interests of stakeholders and create value for them.

Given this definition of governance, we may ask why we should bother with governance in the family firm context. After all, since the owning family often participates on the board and in management, family firms should have innate incentives to ensure interest alignment among these groups. This appears to be a reasonable argument, and it may likely hold in many small family firms where a united family is active in management, board and ownership.

It turns out, however, that this view is a rather idealistic one. In practice, there have been many prominent attempts by family firms to set up sophisticated governance structures, and many advisors offer specific services to help families set up governance structures and supporting documents such as family charters. This observation leads us to ask an important question at the outset of our chapter on the governance of family firms: why do family firms need governance structures?

5.1   Why do family firms need governance?

In this section, we will discuss three main reasons why family firms need governance structures: (1) the motivations of family owners, (2) the governance problems particular to family firms and (3) the limited functionality of traditional mechanisms used to curb governance problems for family firms.

5.1.1 Motivation of family owners

The traditional approach to corporate governance tends to make simplified assumptions about the motivations of the family owners who make up the firm's dominant coalition. This perspective sees families as blockholders, that is, as owners with controlling stakes in the shareholdings of a company. According to this orthodox view, blockholders' primary motivation should be to increase the financial value of their ownership stake. Thus, individual family owners should act as part of a united, monolithic group of actors who are fully aligned toward achieving this financial goal.

The traditional perspective also assumes that the controlling family has an undiversified wealth position due to its concentrated ownership in the family firm. A natural consequence of this wealth exposure is risk aversion. Compared to minority nonfamily owners, the family will be much more hesitant to incur significant risks at the firm level given the drastic financial consequences for the family in case of failure.

Another consequence of the family's undiversified wealth position is the incentive it provides the family to carefully select and supervise managers who are mandated to run the firm on their behalf. An implicit but important assumption here is that (family) blockholders do not need to be competent themselves to run the firm. This task is delegated to nonfamily professionals.

Families as blockholders should also have the power and financial incentive to monitor and eventually sanction inefficient managers. In particular, they should protect the firm from predatory managers who might try to expropriate the owners.

In sum, the classical agency literature tends to depict family blockholders as natural stewards who always know what is best for the firm and act as a force for good. As a result, this view of family owners assumes there is no need to monitor the family.

A brief comparison of these theoretical attributes with family firm reality shows that traditional assumptions about family blockholders are often inaccurate in practice. First, family business practitioners and researchers have long discussed the fact that family firms, and by extension their owners, do not only strive for financial goals. The goal set of family firms prominently includes a concern for reputation and transgenerational control and for benevolent ties within and among the family, the firm and community stakeholders. We will return to the relevance of these socioemotional goals in the strategy section (Chapter 6) of the book.

In addition, there are often family blockholder conflicts and hence misaligned interests within the group of family blockholders. For instance, family owners may disagree about the amount of risk the firm should take on, the time horizon of various strategies, their emotional attachment to the firm and their need for dividends. Moreover, the relationships among family members may be tarnished by personal squabbles. When each family blockholder has both the power and incentive to fight for influence over the firm and the family's assets, these squabbles can lead to intense battles within the family ownership group. In consequence, family shareholders often do not act as a unified block, but represent a group of owners with diverse interests and preferences.

What is more, blockholders can use their power to the detriment of other owners. For example, nonfamily minority owners may be expropriated by family blockholders via the extraction of private benefits of control (e.g., private family expenses that are paid for by the firm), or via a high level of family risk aversion that results in conservative investment and growth strategies (Claessens et al. 2002).

The question of the competence of family blockholders is another point of debate. Managerial or entrepreneurial abilities are only imperfectly passed down from parents to children, so that across generations these abilities revert to the mean of the total population (Bertrand et al. 2003). Thus, the desire for transgenerational family control and family leadership may result in an adverse selection problem. The specter of incompetence looms large when family members are appointed to top positions, as they may overestimate their own abilities, select incompetent managers and board members, and/ or install inappropriate monitoring and incentive schemes. As such, ensuring that competent family members monitor and eventually also manage the firm is a dominant concern among family firms in practice. In the absence of appropriate governance regulations, family members and other stakeholders are hard-pressed to limit the family's detrimental interference in the firm. The need for competent family members even in a supervisory role challenges the passive and somewhat detached role that is assigned to the family in the classical perspective.

We can draw two main conclusions from the discussion above. First, the standard agency assumptions about the role, preferences and abilities of blockholders do not necessarily hold for the case of family owners. Despite family owners' overall incentive to ensure the firm's prosperity, they can become a curse for the business through their particular preferences and their power to interfere in the firm. Second, while in nonfamily firms most of the governance work is focused on goal and incentive alignment between owners and managers, governance in family firms has to focus on the effects of the family's preferences and outsize power. Family owners often have to impose governance regulations on themselves so that their involvement remains a blessing and does not turn into a curse.

5.1.2 Functionality of traditional governance mechanisms in family firms

A further reason why governance is needed in family firms is that these firms are partly immune to the disciplining effects of traditional governance mechanisms. To illustrate this argument, consider the internal and external governance mechanisms that are conventionally used to cure firms' control problems and increase their efficiency (Table 5.1).

Looking more closely at the functionality of internal governance mechanisms in family firms, we find that boards of directors are less likely to be installed in family firms, especially in small ones. Where they do exist, they tend to be staffed with family members or friends of the family. These boards may fulfill the function of ensuring family control, but they do not help the firm access outside expertise and independent advice. In turn, concentrated ownership gives the controlling family the incentive and power to align the behavior of nonfamily managers with the family's interests and goals, thus resolving some principal–agent conflicts. However, misaligned interests among family owners, as well as the problems between family and nonfamily minority owners, remain unsolved. With regard to performance-based pay, family firms often opt against such compensation systems. What is more, given the family's strong wish to uphold family control, these firms forgo one of the most prominent incentive mechanisms, namely managerial ownership in the firm.

When we look at external governance mechanisms, we again find only limited functionality in family firms. In nonfamily firms, the product and labor markets and the threat of takeover serve as disciplining mechanisms. If a product, a manager or the firm as a whole underperforms, the markets will intervene and better products, managers or owners will take over. Family control in a firm partly removes these potentially positive effects. For example, family owners may hang on to poorly performing products due to

Table 5.1 Functionality of internal and external governance mechanisms

Internal governance mechanism	Governance role	Functionality in family firms
Board of directors	Has the ability and independence to monitor and advise managers	Less likely to be installed in family firms and, if so, is often dominated by family members or other insiders
Concentrated ownership	Blockholders have the incentive and power to ensure the efficient management of the firm	Highly relevant in family firms, with two possible consequences: (1) stronger monitoring of managers and hence lower principal–manager agency conflicts; (2) expropriation of (nonfamily) minority owners and adverse selection (i.e., appointment of incompetent family members to top positions)
Performance-based pay	Alignment of manager's and owner's interests	Less likely to be used for family managers; limited willingness to provide shares to nonfamily managers

External governance mechanism	Governance role	Functionality in family firms
Product market competition	Underperforming firms and products are outcompeted	Family firms often seek niches to protect themselves from competition, or they persist with ailing products due to legacy concerns
Managerial labor market	Underperforming managers replaced with more competent ones	Often less relevant, since top management positions are filled by family members (who are less likely to be fired)
Threat of takeover	Underperforming firms are easy takeover targets	Strong ownership control and legacy concerns limit the takeover threat

legacy concerns ('this is the product that made us big'). Alternatively, they may be unwilling to fire underperforming managers because they are family members or have strong ties to the family. Finally, family firms tend to be protected from takeover threats by tight family ownership control.

In sum, family control undermines many of the potentially positive effects of traditional internal and external governance mechanisms. To be fair, not all family firms suffer because of their immunity to traditional governance mechanisms—but many family firms do. Family firms that want to curb the governance problems particular to this form of organization need to impose governance regulations on themselves and comply with them.

5.1.3   Specific governance problems in family firms

So far we have discussed that governance in family firms is required because family owners have motivations that do not fit the traditional agency assumptions that underlie much governance thinking. Also, we have seen that many beneficial internal and external governance mechanisms are not very functional in family firms. The need for appropriate governance structures in this type of firm becomes even more apparent if we think of the various and sometimes subtle ways through which family influence can limit the efficient working of a firm. Table 5.2 provides a non-exhaustive list of family-firm-specific governance symptoms and underlying governance problems.

Table 5.2 Symptoms and underlying governance problems in family firms

Governance symptom	Description
Favoritism/adverse selection	Owners appoint family members or dependent nonfamily members to top positions, which leads to a lack of independent and competent control and advice
Harmony	Altruistic feelings and a concern for harmony blur decision making and the quality of monitoring
Glass ceiling	Top positions are restricted to family members only
Consumption of perquisites	Owners pay private expenses with company money
Insider trading	In public firms: family owners exploit their privileged information access when trading with company shares
Nonfinancial goals	Owners pursue socioemotional goals to the detriment of financial value, e.g. supporting loss-making legacy activities
Related-party transactions	Especially in family business groups: the performance of a single firm suffers because of the corporate burden, bailouts to firms in financial trouble and buying/selling at nonmarket prices among group companies
Tunneling	Especially in family business groups: transfer of funds to the firm where the family has the most cash flow rights
Heightened costs of capital	Nonfamily investors in family firms require compensation for the various risks related to family control
Unspecified involvement of family in the firm	Required qualifications and entry levels for family members who wish to work in the firm are not specified and result in conflict
Inappropriate interference of family owners in the firm	Family owners do not adhere to the governance structures and inappropriately interfere in the firm's operations
Conflict among family owners	Family owners disagree on topics such as risk, growth, dividends and time horizon, obstructing the further development of the firm
Inability of family owners to speak with one voice	Family owners are unable to structure internal communication and decision-making processes

Often, the destructive effects of many of these governance problems are barely perceptible from outside the firm in the short run. However, they may be revealed in comments regarding symptoms such as the following:[1]

- It is really sad to say, but my son should not have been appointed CEO. He is simply not up to the job. But what can you do as a father, he is my son.
- My brother is not working hard enough. Our salaries should reflect the difference in responsibilities and performance between the two of us.
- It is really annoying: we have repeatedly lost our best employees after only a short period of time they have been with the company!
- It is so difficult for us to find highly qualified employees.
- There may be nonfamily shareholders in our firm, but we as a family and controlling owners basically do what we want in the firm.
- Even if I'm not actively involved in the business, I still own shares. Why shouldn't I get the same information access as the family members who are in the business?
- What do you mean, you took a $100 000 loan from the business?
- What happens if my brother thinks that his son should be promoted, but I disagree?
- With six family members on the board, shouldn't some be getting off?
- What happens if my cousin gives his wife company stock and then they get divorced?
- Shouldn't the business buy its group health policy from me? I am family!

Many of the symptoms may seem purely family related (e.g., am I allowed to work in the firm?). However, they can raise more fundamental questions (e.g., which qualifications should family members possess when entering the firm? At what level should family members enter the firm?). These questions ultimately trickle down to the firm level (e.g., who will be the next CEO?), with important strategic consequences for the firm (e.g., should we enter this business activity or not?).

The above lists of governance symptoms, while not comprehensive, can be tied to four underlying governance problems, namely (1) *altruism-induced governance problems*, (2) *owner holdup governance problems*, (3) *majority–minority owner governance problems* and (4) *family blockholder governance problems*. These governance problems manifest in the triangle of family owners, managers and minority owners.

1. **Altruism-induced governance problems**
   This first type of governance problem unfolds when family owners supervise family managers. The related governance problems result from

Family owner

Minority owner/
other stakeholders

Conflict between family owner and family manager
- Altruism: it is difficult to sanction somebody you love
- Danger of free riding by family managers, adverse selection of managers
- Solution: control- and incentive systems even for family managers, careful selection
  of managers, independent of family status

Managers

Figure 5.1 Altruism-induced governance problems

the fact that in family firms family members interact not just on the basis of contractual agreements (e.g., labor contracts), but also on the basis of familial ties, and related social norms such as mutual support, benevolence and trust. Under this perspective, parents have the inclination to support and favor children over nonfamily members. In turn, under the norm of intergenerational altruism, children are obliged to support parents (Schulze et al. 2001). Altruism is problematic in the governance of companies as it (1) leads to adverse selection based on family status over competence, (2) makes it hard to sanction someone whom one loves (e.g., parents sanctioning children, and vice versa), and (3) creates an incentive for the parties (e.g., children) to shirk and free ride given the expected benevolence and inability to sanction by the other party (e.g., parents). The solution to this problem is that even for the case of family presence in both ownership and management, family firms have to set up control and incentive systems, assess family member performance and foresee sanctioning mechanisms for underperforming family members. These arguments are depicted in Figure 5.1.

2. **Owner holdup governance problems**

The second type of governance problem unfolds when family owners supervise nonfamily managers. This governance problem is linked to the power of the family as controlling owner to steer the firm in very particularistic and personalistic ways. The power of the family owners equips these owners with the opportunity to freely determine the fate of the company, for the good or ill of the firm. For instance, the family may come to decide not to grow the firm as this would mean opening up management to nonfamily members. Also, the owning family may appoint family members to top positions, which sends a strong signal to nonfamily managers that it is not primarily performance that accounts for promotion but family status. Thus, managers and employees will

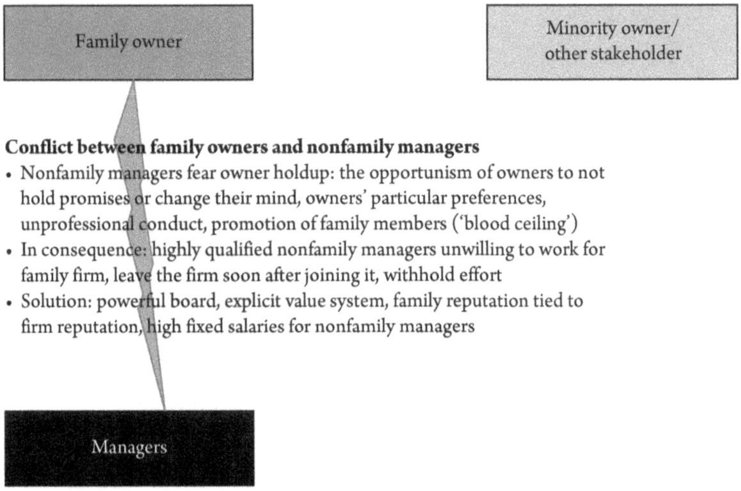

Figure 5.2 Owner holdup induced agency problems

come to feel that the unfettered power by the owner (i.e., only the owner can control the owner in the firm) exposes them to potential risks of misconduct, temperament, change of mind and opportunism by the owners. The consequence of such owner holdup (Schulze and Zellweger, 2016) is that family firms will find it difficult to attract and retain highly skilled managers and motivate their employees to go the extra mile and commit beyond what is required. Solving these threats is not easy because the family has to impose limits on its own discretion. In practice, family business owners 'tie their hands' by appointing powerful boards, tying their personal reputation to the one of the firm, openly committing to certain value systems, religious beliefs or management styles, or having to pay high fixed salaries to attract and retain top talent (Figure 5.2).

3. **Majority–minority owner governance problems**
   The third type of governance problem is linked to the relationship between family owners as controlling owners, and some minority owners, eventually along with other claimants to the firm, such as creditors (Claessens et al. 2002). The majority and minority owners may be in disagreement about goals, level of risk taking and information access. More overtly, the family owners may abuse their power and govern the firm as if it belonged to them alone. These problems are particularly severe in the presence of dual-class shares through which the family has excessive control over the firm (e.g., the family has super voting shares). Also, in business groups, such as diversified conglomerates, the family may use its power to divert funds to itself or to firms in which the family has the highest stakes in the cash flows (for further details refer to the

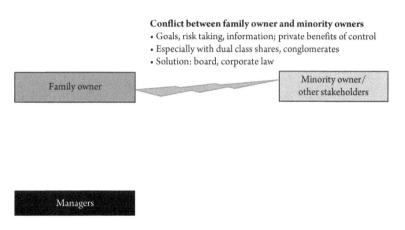

Figure 5.3 Majority–minority owner governance problems

below excursus on family business groups). Installing independent board members and the protection of minority owners by law are the usual solution to this type of problem (Figure 5.3).

4. **Family blockholder governance problems**

The fourth type of governance problem relates to unaligned interest *within* the group of family owners (Zellweger and Kammerlander 2015). The family owners may be in disagreement about the overall strategy with regard to their investments (risk taking, dividends, time horizon, emotional attachment) but also about influence of family members in the organization (board representation, transfer of shares within the family, involvement of in-laws, family employment in the firm; see Table 5.2 for more details). These problems are often tackled through shareholder agreements, board representation and family governance (Figure 5.4).

In essence, governance in family firms seeks to solve these four foundational governance problems.

Because these foundational governance problems primarily appear at the family and ownership levels, many family firms are able to keep them private for some time. But if left unsolved, they tend to result in severe problems— first at family level, and then at the ownership and managerial levels. For instance, some family members may feel that they are kept out of important conversations and decisions and only get information 'through the grapevine'. When different people get different/inconsistent messages, they may fill out incomplete information with their own assumptions and lose trust in the group. Family members who no longer trust each other will build alliances inside and outside the family with the goal of securing influence. The resulting power struggles carry over to the ownership level and may persist

Figure 5.4 Family blockholder governance problems

for long periods of time due to high exit costs. Ultimately, these conflicts end up at the management level—as, for example, when nonfamily managers have to deal with family squabbles in the boardroom.

One common strategy that firms use to avoid addressing these problems is to procrastinate. This strategy, however, prolongs conflicts rather than solving them. In the longer run, managers may become aware of the tensions among family members and their inability to communicate. In the worst cases, managers may even experience strategic inertia, which is the result of the controlling owners' inability or unwillingness to take important strategic decisions for the firm. The efficient functioning and performance of the firm may suffer as a result. For instance, the most dynamic managers may leave the company because of their frustration with the family.

Excursus: Governance problems in family business groups

In emerging countries, many large family firms are structured as business groups, that is, as conglomerates of diversified holdings controlled by a family. These family business groups—called *grupos* in Latin America, and *zaibatsu* or *keiretsu* in Southeast Asia—are most often structured as pyramids. In family business groups, the families in control sit at the apex of the pyramid and control the various vertically aligned investments over a control chain. Family business groups represent a particularly fertile ground for majority–minority governance problems. Business groups are particularly prevalent in emerging countries, but also appear in more developed countries, which is why some further remarks about their specific governance problems seems particularly warranted (for further details, see Carney et al. 2011; Morck and Yeung 2003).

CASE STUDY

Governance challenges at Citychamp Dartong Co. Ltd.

Citychamp Dartong is a Chinese publicly listed company engaged in property development and the manufacturing of enameled wires. In 2011, the company sold 63 100 tons of wire, totaling in sales of $9.2 billion. The company distributes its products in domestic and overseas markets. The ownership structure of Citychamp Dartong appears in Figure 5.5.

The family's control over Citychamp Dartong and the cash flow it generates can be determined as follows.

Han Guolong, the founder of Citychamp Dartong, owns 80% * 36.16% * 100% * 16.39% = 4.74% of Citychamp Dartong's cash flows. But his actual control over Citychamp Dartong, which is determined by the weakest link across the vertical control chain, is larger: min (80%, 36.16%, 100%, 16.39%) = 16.39%. The ownership/cash flow rights (4.74%) is equal to the product of all ownership shares across the vertical control chain, but the actual control is determined by the weakest link across the control chain. Xue Lixi, Han Guolong's daughter-in-law, owns 68.5% * 26.74% = 18.32% of Citychamp Dartong cash flows, but controls min (68.5%, 26.74%) = 26.74% of the firm.

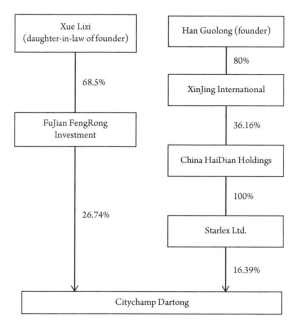

Source: Amit et al. (2015).

Figure 5.5 Vertical control chain of Citychamp Dartong[2]

CASE STUDY *(continued)*

The Han family's combined cash flow rights in Citychamp Dartong thus amount to 4.74% + 18.32% = 23.06%, but the family's actual control is 16.39% + 26.74% = 43.13%. The family holds four out of nine board seats in the company, which represents its strong influence. This case of a pyramidal family business group illustrates several control-enhancing mechanisms and mainly the majority–minority governance problems that come with them.

First, through the group's pyramidal structure, the family is able to exercise substantial control over Citychamp Dartong (43.13%). This share is significantly larger than the family's share of cash flow rights in the company (23.06%). Thus, with a limited ownership stake, the family is able to exercise disproportional control over the firm.

Second, the family has incentives to use this excessive influence (sometimes called a wedge; 43.13% − 23.06% = 20.07%) to ensure that cash flows are tunneled through the control chain and ultimately accrue at the very top of the pyramid. In practice, this means that the family compels firms inside the group to buy at higher than market prices from other group firms in which the family has a higher cash flow stake. For instance, Citychamp Dartong may be obliged to buy products from XinJing International, in which Han Guolong owns an 80% stake. Similarly, the family may use its influence to implement bailout payments or financing across the group: for instance, Starlex Ltd. may be required to lend funds to FuJian FengRong at favorable conditions.

Third, while such structures lead to a lack of transparency and eventually to inefficiencies for the management and firms involved, they are particularly problematic for the nonfamily owners that invest alongside the family in some of the group's firms. These minority owners not only have limited control, but also risk having their funds diverted by the family blockholders to the apex of the pyramid.

Finally, it is sometimes argued that under weak institutional settings, as is often the case in emerging countries, business groups can help remedy the detrimental effects of inefficient capital and labor markets. In this view, business groups should be particularly proficient at filling 'institutional voids' because the multiple firms that form the group help each other with money, talent and intermediary products. Moreover, family blockholders should have a natural interest in securing the financial stability and performance of their conglomerates, not least to secure their wealth and the reputation of their firms and families.

Of course, family blockholders may use their influence to the benefit of all shareholders. The empirical evidence over a multitude of studies on family business groups, however, supports a more negative view—namely, that families exploit their powerful position in family business groups to extract money for their own gain and to the detriment of firms and non-family minority investors at lower positions in the pyramid.

5.2   Typical governance constellations in family firms

By now it should be clear that even in family firms—where one would expect family bonds to naturally align family members, owners, the board and the management team—some form of governance is necessary. We have seen that some of the traditional assumptions about blockholders do not hold for family blockholders, that many of the traditional governance mechanisms do not work well in the family firm context, and that family firms exhibit unique governance problems.

In our attempt to shed light on the practical aspects of governance, we must start by acknowledging that the governance challenges in family firms vary significantly with the development stage and complexity of family, owner-ship and management structures. Consider the extremes of the continuum of governance complexity: at the lower end, a single owner-manager may control a firm without the presence of a board, other top managers or other owners. At the other end of the spectrum, multiple members of a family may control a large portfolio of companies.

Given the heterogeneity of family, ownership and business structures, there is no one-size-fits-all governance solution for family firms. In practice, we typically find four types of governance constellations. These constellations, along with their particular challenges and governance needs, are depicted in Table 5.3.

In the owner-manager stage, family firms are mainly concerned with corpo-rate governance. Along with general oversight of the firm, access to external and independent expertise is especially important. The critical challenges at this stage are access to and acceptance of external advice as well as succession planning.

When a firm passes into the sibling partnership and cousin consortium stages, the need for governance at the family and ownership levels increases. Shareholder agreements are put in place defining the entry, transfer and exit of family ownership (ownership governance). At the family level, families may define their shared values and vision for the firm, set up employment policies for family members, nurture emotional ties and identification with the firm, ensure the education of next-generation owners and try to instill an entrepre-neurial spirit among owners who are increasingly distant from firm operations.

In the family enterprise stage, corporate, ownership and family govern-ance become increasingly sophisticated. A particular challenge in the family enterprise constellation is the switch from a *family business* mindset (in

Table 5.3 Four typical governance constellations in family firms

	Owner-manager	Sibling partnership	Cousin consortium	Family enterprise
Definition	Ownership and management in the hands of a single family member	Ownership and management shared among siblings	Cousins as owners	Extended family controls portfolio of business activities
Typical business structure and stage	Often a smaller firm in the founding stage	Often a mid-sized firm	Often a mid-sized to large firm	Often a portfolio of companies including large, multi-divisional firms
Family constellation	Single family member (often the founder, hence first generation) actively involved in the firm	Siblings from single family branch (most often second generation) involved in the firm	Cousins of two or more family branches (often third or later generation) involved in the firm	Later generation of founding family in various roles in various family and business governance bodies
Ownership constellation	Single family owner; some non-controlling owners may be present	Siblings co-own firm; most often, two or three owners	Cousins co-own firm; most often, three to seven owners	Often more than eight family owners; eventually also nonfamily owners
Management constellation	Owner-manager	Siblings as co-managers	Designated family member(s) and/or nonfamily manager(s)	Often delegated to nonfamily managers
Key advantages	Strong control over firm, rapid decision making, cost-efficient governance	Trusted relationships between siblings, common values and goals	Dedicated and patient family owners, limited complexity of shareholder structure	Families as entrepreneurial and patient investors; buy, build and also exit firms
Key challenges	Access to and acceptance of outside expertise, abuse of power, dependency on owner-manager, succession	Rivalry, qualifications, complementary competencies, distribution of responsibilities, interlocking ownership	Old rivalries, decision making in family, roles and related qualifications, identification, family cohesion, entrepreneurial spirit	Identification with firm(s) and investor role, decision making in family, roles and qualifications, cohesion, business complexity
Typical governance activities	Board of directors, succession planning	Board of directors, shareholder agreements, employment policy, performance-based pay, fair process in decision making	Board of directors, shareholder agreements, family meetings and agreements, educate professional owners, nurture emotional ties to firm, establish common vision, nurture entrepreneurial spirit	Board of directors, shareholder agreements, family meetings and agreements, educate professional owners, family council, foundation, family office, establish common vision, nurture entrepreneurial spirit

Source: Inspired by Carlock and Ward (2010).

which a family controls a single firm that has been under family control for generations) to a *business family* mindset (the family sees itself as an entrepreneurial investor who buys and builds but also exits businesses). This constellation makes it hard for owners to identify with the firm, as it now includes various and changing business activities. Oftentimes, next to the ownership and family governance tools outlined above, family governance now also includes structures such as family councils (subgroups of family members who manage business- and ownership-related matters for the extended family), family offices (which manage family wealth) and family foundations (which engage in philanthropic activity).

Over successive generations, family firms often pass through more than one of the above four stages. However, depending on the growth of the business activity and the controlling family, a family business may also remain in one stage. For instance, a firm may remain small and be passed down from one owner-manager to the next owner-manager. But as business activity grows in size, multi-divisional firms or family business groups usually emerge. At the same time, the number of family shareholders grows, which pushes the firm toward sophisticated governance structures. This dynamic view is depicted in Figure 5.6.

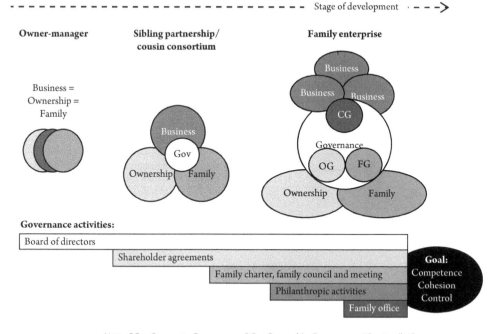

Note: CG = Corporate Governance; OG = Ownership Governance; FG = Family Governance.

Figure 5.6 Governance constellations and related governance activities

Figure 5.6 shows that there is no one-size-fits-all solution to family firm governance. Depending on the constellation, governance activities have to be more or less sophisticated. Independent of the constellation, however, governance serves three overarching goals:

1. **Competence**: Securing competence on the side of the family as the ultimate owner and decision maker for any business activity. Competence in business-related questions is crucial to take decisions that are in the best interest of relevant stakeholders, in particular the family itself.
2. **Cohesion**: The social and economic power of a group of individuals vitally depends on the cohesion and the alignment of individuals within that group. Only an aligned and cohesive group of family members is able to keep together and direct business activities in the desired strategic direction.
3. **Control**: Last but not least, governance activities help the owners to exercise control, for instance by monitoring management. Control should never be given completely out of hand of the family. Delegation of decision making may be a prerequisite for growth. But as the ultimate owner the family should never fully delegate control.

5.3 Performance implications of governance constellations

The previous section highlighted the particular challenges for family firms as they pass through the owner-manager, sibling partnership, cousin consortium and family enterprise stages. Often, family business owners have very strong

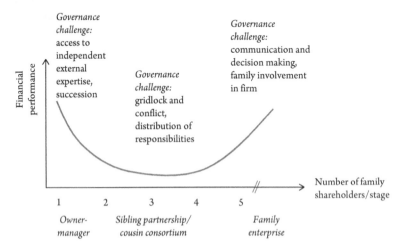

Figure 5.7 Typical governance constellations and performance implications

opinions about what the 'best' constellation is. Looking at some empirical studies, we find a U-shaped relationship (see Figure 5.7) between family governance constellation (proxied by the number of family shareholders) and financial performance. It turns out that the sibling partnership and (to a lesser degree) cousin consortium constellations are the most vulnerable to governance conflicts, which ultimately result in negative performance consequences for the firm.

Entrepreneurs often argue that the owner-manager constellation is the optimal governance form because it best aligns the interests of owners and managers. In this constellation, decisions can be taken rapidly and firm-related sibling rivalry and family conflicts are minimal or nonexistent. These advantages do lead to significant performance advantages in many cases. However, they are balanced by other potential governance challenges, such as the firm's dependence on the intellectual and physical abilities of the owner-manager him-/herself and access to (and acceptance of) independent external expertise. In addition, the firm's heavy reliance on its owner-manager makes succession a particularly critical issue. Succession challenges may come from both the owner-manager (who wants to shape the organization according to his/her preferences and may be unwilling to let go) and the successors (who hesitate to 'fill the shoes' of the previous owner-manager and assume his/her duties).

Sibling partnerships and cousin consortia appear to be particularly vulnerable governance constellations. These constellations are threatened by an unclear distribution of managerial roles among family members and ownership deadlock among powerful family owners. Sibling partnerships are often constituted by two to three family members from the same generation, all of whom fulfill managerial roles. Unfortunately, these roles are often not clearly defined or delineated, leading to misunderstandings, rivalry and ultimately conflict. Tensions also tend to take place at the ownership level, with 50/50 gridlocks or 33/33/33 block-building efforts that result in strategic inertia and declining performance.

In such constellations, family members sometimes face a loyalty challenge: should they focus primarily on the interests of their own nuclear family or family branch or, alternatively, the family as a whole and hence the overall success of the firm? All too often, controlling families operate not as a united group but as a loose congregation of family subgroups with differing goals. These families tend to be overly concerned with the *vertical* distribution of interests within the family tree, that is, the differing interests of the individual family branches. But great families in business move toward *horizontal* thinking—that is, toward the creation of a unified group of family owners, or what James Hughes called the 'horizontal social compact' (Hughes 2004).

Overcoming the differing goals of loosely related and sometimes even hostile subgroups of family owners and moving toward the family enterprise stage, in which the family works as a united entrepreneurial actor and blockholder, is probably one of the biggest challenges for family firms if they wish to create lasting value.

Most family firms perform better in the family enterprise stage than in the sibling partnership/cousin consortium stages. In the family enterprise stage, ownership deadlocks are less likely to occur because ownership is usually more diluted within the family. The governance challenge now becomes one of structuring communication and decision making among a relatively large number of family members. To deal with this task, many families set up a family council with a limited number of family members. Many firms also find that it is extremely important at this stage to establish rules about how and when family members are allowed to occupy management roles inside the firm.

While the sibling partnership/cousin consortium stages seem to be more demanding than the owner-manager or family enterprise stages, especially in light of their negative performance impact, in practice we observe a significant number of family firms that perform well even in these middle constellations. Thus, we cannot simply recommend one of these stages as optimal. Rather, a firm will do best if the individuals involved recognize the governance challenges and remedies tied to their particular constellation.

5.4 Untangling corporate, ownership, family and wealth governance

The above overview of the typical governance constellations indicates that not all family firms need sophisticated governance tools and activities. However, especially in the sibling partnership, cousin consortium and family enterprise stages, family firms have to deal with structuring four areas of governance: corporate, ownership, family and wealth governance. As Table 5.4 shows, these are distinct areas of governance with specific goals, relevant topics, governing groups and forums for discussion. Keep in mind that not all firms need to make all types of governance arrangement. In line with the idea of requisite complexity of social systems, the sophistication of governance (and hence the extent to which the family not only needs corporate governance, but also ownership, family and wealth governance) will depend on the

Table 5.4 Overview of corporate, ownership, family and wealth governance

	Corporate governance	Ownership governance	Family governance	Wealth governance
Goal	Efficient cooperation of shareholders, board and managers	Efficient cooperation among family owners	Efficient cooperation of family in matters related to the firm; commitment and identification	Efficient administration of family wealth
Topics to be addressed	Selection, supervision and advising of top management, strategic guidelines for business	Entry and exit of shareholders, execution of ownership rights	Family involvement in board, management and ownership of firm; new entrepreneurial activity; philanthropy	Organization of wealth administration, pooled versus individual wealth administration, access to and distribution of wealth, diverging family preferences
Governing group	Board of directors	Shareholder group	Family council	Family council/Investment committee
Forum for discussion	Board meeting	Shareholder assembly	Family assembly	Investment committee
Leader and role	Chair of the board: Steward of family business	Pool speaker: Steward of family ownership	Chair of the family council: Steward of family values	Family wealth manager: Steward of family wealth
Guiding tool	Board regulations and strategic guidelines	Shareholders' agreement	Family charter	Family charter, wealth governance setup

complexity on the side of business and family. In this way, the approaches discussed in this chapter should prepare you to make an informed choice about what is most relevant to you, your family firm or the clients you are advising.

What makes family firms unique with regard to governance is the addition of two governance areas—family and wealth governance—which are absent in nonfamily firms. In the following sections, we will thus put a particular emphasis on family and wealth governance. We will conclude the chapter by combining family, wealth, ownership and corporate governance in an integrated framework.

5.5 Corporate governance

Corporate governance is concerned with the efficient cooperation of the board, managers and shareholders. Given the extensive literature on this topic for firms of all types, we will limit our discussion to the most central aspects of corporate governance for family firms.

In today's corporate world, corporate governance systems broadly fall into two categories: one-tier and two-tier board systems. In a one-tier board system, the members of the board of directors (sometimes also called a governance or supervisory board) are allowed to be both executive directors (top managers of the company) and board members. In contrast, in a two-tier board there is an executive board (also called a management board, consisting solely of executive directors) and a separate governance board (which includes no executive directors). Countries such as the United States, the United Kingdom, Canada, Brazil, Japan and Australia have adopted the one-tier board system, while countries such as Germany and the Netherlands have a two-tier board system.[3]

The distribution of power and roles among shareholders, board and management is extremely important in ensuring the efficient cooperation of these groups. The shareholders appoint a board of directors whose duty is to promote shareholder interests. In turn, the board appoints, advises, monitors and eventually dismisses the top management team, in particular the CEO. This distribution of roles and responsibilities is depicted in Figure 5.8.

Although the corporate governance pyramid draws clear boundaries between roles, in family business practice, the lines are often blurred. Family members may occupy several roles at the same time—for example, a family owner may be part of the board and serve on the top management team, while a nonfamily member serves as the CEO. The presence of individuals at various

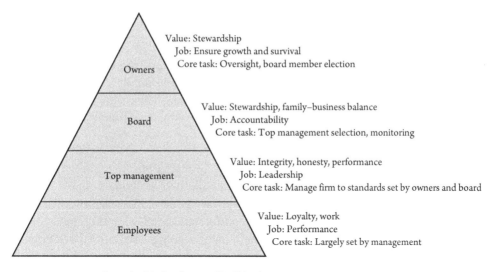

Source: Joe Astrachan, Kennesaw State University.

Figure 5.8 Corporate governance roles

levels of the corporate governance pyramid simultaneously can easily lead to confusion about who is allowed to say and do what. Thus, this structure may undermine the unambiguous distribution of power and control, which is an important component of effective corporate governance.

The problem of role ambiguity is exacerbated in family firms because family members often have the formal and informal power to give orders and speak to actors across all hierarchical levels. While the family's hands-on involvement is a positive sign of care for, control of and identification with the firm, transgressing a predefined governance role can easily spark frustration. Think, for example, of a nonfamily CEO whose orders to his/her employees are constantly undercut by a family owner (such as a former family CEO or a powerful family owner) who gives contradictory orders to employees. The family also needs to realize that the CEO, not the owners, will (should) be the main point of contact for employees.

If the family involved in ownership is a large one, not all family members should be in close contact with the CEO. The family should comply with the corporate governance functions described above and may eventually form committees such as a family council to speak to the appropriate people across multiple levels.

5.5.1 Picking the right people for the board of directors

In larger family firms, the family usually does not place family members in management positions. In these cases, the family exercises control mainly through representation on the board of directors. Family members bring the family's point of view to the board and ensure alignment between family, ownership and corporate interests, while nonfamily board members may contribute critical business acumen and industry expertise.

For many family owners, it may be tempting to hire the family's accountant or lawyer as a board member. After all, these individuals know the family's personal and business circumstances in detail. However, they may have underlying interests that are not perfectly aligned with the family or the firm—for example, securing their own ongoing commercial relationship with the owners or with a subgroup of owners. In some cases, they may not be independent enough and/or may not be willing to take a critical stance vis-à-vis family members. The following criteria can help a family firm decide if a candidate is appropriate for board membership:

● Does the individual have the skills, knowledge and time to do the board job?
● Can the individual communicate with managers on equal footing?
● Does the individual have the necessary managerial skillset?
● Is the individual knowledgeable about the family's dynamics *and* the challenges of the business?
● Why might the individual be willing to become a board member? Ideally, he or she should not be motivated primarily by money or status.

5.5.2 The role and involvement of the board of directors

In most countries, the board of directors is responsible for the following tasks:

● Set strategic guidelines for management based on guidelines by owners in terms of:
  – behavioral principles for board and top management,
  – growth goals,
  – financing (leverage/rating), stock market listing,
  – compensation system.
● Appoint, monitor and dismiss top management team members, including the CEO.
● Invoke the general assembly.

- Set dividend policy (in terms of level and stability of dividends).
- Review the business strategy with the top management.

The example below may provide some guidance on the definition of the roles and responsibilities of the board of directors in a family firm. These corporate

---

Example: Governance regulations and the role of the board of directors

Board of directors

A. Mission of the board of directors

1. The board of directors is defined as a body that deliberates issues with the goal of reaching consensus.
2. The principles articulated in this document will form the guidelines to be replicated for all boards of directors at the individual company level.

B. Formation and composition

1. The board of directors shall comprise XX persons in line with the articles of incorporation and the bylaws of the Group's companies.
2. At the time of signing of this charter, the board of directors shall comprise all lead-generation family members and the founder's spouse.
3. Each of the Family Branches shall always be represented on the board of directors of the Group. At the time of signing of this Charter, the Family Branch of the late XX is represented in the board of directors by the founder's spouse. Should there be a vacancy on the board of directors such that a Family Branch is not duly represented therein, a representative of the affected Family Branch shall be elected to the board of directors. In nominating family members to the board of directors, consideration should be given to the individual's commitment to family and ability to add value to the family as a whole.
4. Members of the board of directors serve for a 5-year term, at the end of which they will be eligible for re-election.
5. Mandatory retirement is required at the age of 65.
6. The board of directors shall elect a chair from among their number. The chair is appointed for a term of 3 years.
7. The board of directors may elect or appoint a secretary, preferably from the Junior Committee.
8. Should it be felt that the board of directors is not fulfilling its mission and responsibility to the family, the shareholders may vote to dissolve the board of directors and re-elect a new board by a written resolution of a XX% majority of the shareholdings.

C. Meetings of the board of directors

1. The board of directors shall meet quarterly under the overall responsibility of the chair to:
   a. Discuss and take major decisions regarding investments, divestments and new ventures.
   b. Discuss and agree on the strategic plan and revisions for the businesses.
2. In order to properly conduct board of director meetings:
   a. An agenda shall be prepared by the chair of the board and shared with the board members 2 weeks before the meeting. Directors may submit topics they want to have included in the agenda to the chair. These should be received by the chair 18 days before the date set for the meeting so they can be incorporated into the agenda.
   b. Financial highlights shall be prepared and circulated by the chair to all board members together with the notice of meeting and the agenda before the meeting.
3. Minutes shall be kept of all meetings of the board of directors. The chair and secretary shall be responsible for the minutes. All major points of agreement will be minuted together with agreed action points, due date and name of the person responsible for the follow-up. These should be signed by all directors for avoidance of misunderstandings regarding agreements arrived at.

D. Authority of the board of directors

1. The board of directors shall have all powers to operate the companies in the Group as it sees fit.
2. The board of directors shall make decisions and reach agreements through voting by simple majority, except where otherwise specified in the bylaws.

E. Role of the chair of the board
The chair of the board shall be responsible for:

1. The organization of and invitation to board meetings.
2. The preparation of the meeting agenda.
3. The preparation and distribution of meeting minutes to all members of the board of directors.
4. The safekeeping of a copy of the minutes of the board of directors' meetings, signed by all members of the board of directors.
5. The management of board meetings.
6. The communication with the shareholders.

The secretary of the board will support the chair in administrative and procedural functions with respect to board meetings.

regulations are written down in the bylaws of the company and need to be aligned with the local jurisdiction. Please note: commercial law foresees corporate governance regulations, such as, for instance, the inalienable duties of the board and the top management. Hence, the family is most often not completely free to adapt bylaws but needs to respect the legal specifications.

Collaboration with top management is essential to the effective functioning of the board of directors. The board has to control the management team, not the other way around. Thus, the relationship between the board and top management should not be too close. At the same time, however, this relationship should not be characterized by mistrust or fear, which might incentivize management to hide critical information from the board instead of seeking its advice. Effective boards are as close as necessary to management but no closer.

5.5.3 The board's involvement in strategy formulation

A moment of truth for the quality of cooperation between board and management comes with the formulation of the firm's strategy. In some firms, the board sets the strategy, which is then executed by the management. Alternatively, the management may define the strategy without consulting the board. Neither approach is ideal. In the first case, the board may be missing information from operations that would help define the strategy, and management may not be fully committed to the strategy's implementation. Most importantly, a board that is overly involved in strategy formulation may lose its ability to correct the failures in that strategy—and thus, it may be less effective in monitoring management and protecting shareholder interests. In the second case, the board is left out of the decision-making process and is unable to play its advisory role. One potential 'middle way' between these two approaches is the sequential approach depicted in Figure 5.9.

Effective boards do not have a static role, but dynamically adapt their involvement in operations depending on the circumstances. On one end of

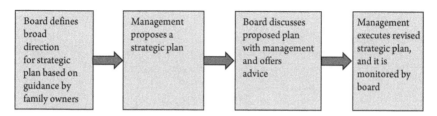

Figure 5.9 Cooperation between board and management in strategy formulation

the continuum there is the passive board with limited activities, participation and accountability. This board mainly ratifies management's preferences, placing the CEO in a particularly powerful position. On the opposite end of the continuum, the board makes decisions that management implements and fills gaps in management expertise.

5.6   Ownership governance

Ownership governance legally defines firm-related ownership aspects. The general principles of family involvement in ownership—such as the overall ownership strategy (e.g., tight or loose control over the firm, whether or not to launch a public offering of shares, IPO) and the age at which family members can become owners—may be covered by family governance, which we will investigate in the next section. However, many families come to the point where they require a legally binding shareholders' agreement (Ward and Aronoff 2010). Shareholders' agreements thus transform the general ownership principles (as defined by the owners, such as defined in family governance) into a legally binding document. Such shareholders' agreements often cover the following topics (for a more detailed overview of the usual content of shareholder agreements, see Chemla, Habib and Ljungqvist 2007).

1. **Execution of voting rights**
    Voting agreements are often the centerpiece of the shareholders' agreement. Family members may pool their voting power in order to control voting outcomes at shareholders' meetings (e.g., when electing members of the board of directors). For example, the family shareholder group may include representatives of different branches. Each branch, sometimes independent of its share quota, may be allowed to delegate a representative to the board of directors. Alternatively, the family shareholder pool may see itself as a single group of owners out of which the most suitable representatives are appointed to the board, irrespective of branch representation.
2. **Transfer of shares**
    The shareholders' agreement should address the following questions regarding transfers of shares:
    *   When do family members have the right or the obligation to sell stock? 'Tag along' provisions ensure that if an offer is made to the majority shareholder for its shares, the minority shareholders can decide to sell their shares to the same purchaser on the same terms. 'Drag along' provisions ensure that if a majority share-

holder wishes to sell his/her shares, he/she can force the minority shareholders to sell their shares to the same purchaser on the same terms.

- When one family owner wants to sell, who has the right of first refusal to acquire these shares? The owner's nuclear family, followed by his/her family branch, and then by the other branches in proportion to their current shareholdings?
- Under what circumstances does the company have the right to buy back stock (e.g., death of an owner)?
- What if the business/the beneficiaries of the right of first refusal cannot afford to redeem the shares of an owner willing to sell?
- If an owner wants to sell, how quickly does he/she have to notify the other owners and what is the deadline by which they have to use their right of first refusal?
- What is the valuation formula for the shares? Is there a family discount, defined as the rebate compared to an estimated market value when shares are passed on inside the family?

3. **Stalemates**

Shareholders' agreements may also include buyout agreements in case of conflict. Conflicts among shareholders may be resolved through a third-party valuation or other clauses. For instance, a shotgun clause allows a shareholder to offer a specific price per share for the shares of the other shareholder(s). The other shareholder(s) must then either accept the offer or buy the offering shareholder's shares at that price.[4]

4. **Dissolution of shareholder agreements**

Under which conditions (e.g., percentage of agreement among family owners, expiry date) can the shareholders' agreement be dissolved? What happens to the shareholders' agreement when a family shareholder dies?

As mentioned above, shareholders' agreements are legally binding documents. Given the heterogeneity of national regulations and ownership constellations, the above overview should be seen as a general guideline that should be adapted and formalized in cooperation with a legal expert.

5.7 Family governance

Before delving into the details of family governance, we should remember that sophisticated family governance regulations are not equally relevant across the owner-manager, sibling partnership, cousin consortium and family enterprise constellations, as shown in section 5.2. The following discussion of family governance is particularly relevant for families who are in or wish to transfer into the sibling partnership, cousin consortium or family enterprise stage. In it, we will explore various family governance tools that come with increasing complexity on the family side (as a further source of inspiration you may also refer to Koeberle-Schmid, Kenyon-Rouvinez and Poza 2014).

5.7.1 Goal and topics of family governance

The overarching goal of family governance is to secure the efficient operation of the family in matters related to the firm. As with any other type of governance regulation, family governance defines a preferred means of collaboration inside an organization or a social group. However, family governance also addresses a more fundamental question, namely the values and core beliefs of the family. Defining a values-based foundation for the subsequently defined family governance regulations (which address, e.g., family involvement in the business) is important for two main reasons: (1) it gives family members a strong reason to stick together, and (2) it provides a common ground from which the family can hammer out the details of family governance.

Broadly, family governance addresses the following topics: the fundamental values and goals of the family; family involvement on the board, in management and in ownership; the family's stance toward new entrepreneurial activity; and eventually also philanthropy. Not all of these aspects are relevant

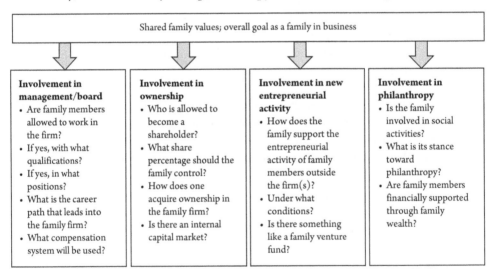

Figure 5.10 Topics of family governance

to all firms and families. Typically, family values and family involvement in management/board and ownership are the dominant topics. Other topics will be more or less relevant depending on the size/complexity of the family and the firm.

These topics of family governance are depicted in Figure 5.10 and are further specified in the next sections.

5.7.2 Family values and goals

Before setting up sophisticated governance structures, families in business should reflect on their fundamental values and beliefs. Establishing a set of norms is important as it can help guide the definition of governance rules and regulations at a later stage. For instance, a family could consider the following topics:

- **Overarching values**: What are the core values that we believe characterize us as a family? What values do we honor, and what values do we reject?
- **Mission**: What is our overarching goal as a family? Here, families could clarify their stance toward acting jointly versus individually, or how important it is for the family to control a company or, more generally, to be in business.
- **Who we are**: Families as social groups are often very concerned about delineating the boundaries of the family group. Who is part of the family, and who is not? In which aspects of our lives do we wish to work together jointly, and in which aspects do we act as individual actors?
- **Values about being in business**: In broad terms, what is the family's goal with regard to business growth, risk taking and entrepreneurship? Even at this early stage of discussion, the family may work on clarifying its stance toward the business.

As mentioned above, the values established through this discussion can act as rough guidelines for all subsequent family governance discussions. Just as important, value statements represent important reasons for family members to commit to a common cause and hence create cohesion.

5.7.3 Family involvement in management

Family governance should clarify family involvement in firm management. For example, the family may address the following questions:

- **Are family members allowed to work in the family firm(s)?**
  Some families allow or even encourage family involvement in operations, while others may try to avoid confusion by forbidding family employment in the firm.
- **If yes, in what positions and with what qualifications?**
  The family may wish to make a statement about hierarchical levels/positions and the related qualifications necessary for family employment. Some families adhere to the philosophy that family members should be allowed to work in the firm as long as they apply for the position using the same process that nonfamily members do. The ultimate criterion then should be whether the respective family member has the qualifications needed for the open position. Other families may restrict family employment to senior management positions to secure family control of operations and to avoid conflicts that result from employing family members as employees while having a nonfamily manager who is farther up in the hierarchy.
- **If yes, what career path leads into the family firm?**
  Some may argue that to learn the business in detail, family members should enter the firm at the factory floor (or equivalent level). However, once a family member enters the firm, he/she will inevitably be seen as part of the owning family, and will most likely not be treated as a regular employee. Family members in entry-level positions may not receive independent feedback and may be promoted (or not promoted) purely because they are part of the family. Family members entering the firm at lower hierarchical levels may also be drawn into internal power struggles in which nonfamily managers try to lobby for their interests via family members under their control.

  Alternatively, when entering the firm at the senior management level, family members can have significant influence as they represent the owning family's point of view in the firm. While entering into management can make it easier for next-generation family members to leave their mark on the firm, they may have to work harder to be accepted by long-time nonfamily managers. Family members may quickly advance to senior management jobs that are more difficult to reach for nonfamily members, causing resentment and feelings of injustice. Moreover, nonfamily managers may be hesitant to confer legitimacy on family members who have limited experience inside (and possibly outside) the firm.

A middle way in this dilemma is lateral entry for next-generation family members. In this model, a family member first has to gain significant senior management experience in a job outside the family firm. Then, once a senior management position opens up in the family business, the family member enters the firm via a series of trainee positions that expose him/her to the firm's various departments/activities. This phase may last from several months up to a few years. Finally, the family member is fully promoted to the senior management position. We will return to these ideas in Chapter 7 on succession.

● **How should family members be compensated?**

A family governance code should include a statement about compensation levels. This statement should probably refer to the market-rate compensation that is commensurate with the position's responsibility

---

Example family employment policy

The following policy is excerpted from a family charter:

Family employment policy:
Family harmony is our top priority. It is well recognized and documented in research on family businesses that an area of frequent family conflict is that of employment in family businesses. In order to ensure that we have good quality opportunities available wherever possible while reducing potential flashpoints to a minimum, the following rules of engagement apply to family employment in the Group.

1. Our philosophy is that all family members are encouraged to contribute to the growth of the family legacy in whatever way they are able. Their involvement in the family business should be a positive experience and contribute to growth in the individual, the business and family relationships.
2. Direct descendants of XXBB are encouraged to work in the family businesses provided they meet the entry criteria and there are suitable job vacancies available. In-laws will not be offered employment in XX Group of Companies and all other businesses controlled by our family (the Group). The business environment is fertile ground in which the weeds of misunderstanding can take root. As we treasure close family ties with our in-laws, we have chosen to exclude in-laws from employment in the Group in favor of maintaining good family relationships. This rule is not applicable to in-laws currently employed in the Group at the date of signing of this Family charter.
3. To be eligible for employment in the Group, the respective family member shall meet the following conditions:
   a. Work experience of 2–3 years outside the family businesses.
   b. Join at entry level or commensurate with training and education.
   c. Hold a university degree.

---

     d. Enter into a full-time job governed by a legally binding employment contract. Exceptions can be made under special circumstances subject to the approval by the board of directors.

     e. Receive market-rate compensation.

4. The performance of family members employed in the Group shall be evaluated in accordance with the job role and requirements of the respective employment contract.

5. Wherever possible, family employees should not have a direct reporting line to their parents.

6. All direct descendants of the founder are welcome and encouraged to take internships with the family-controlled businesses during school/university holidays.

Source: UBS Family Advisory.

(for more details on family firm compensation, see Aronoff, McClure and Ward 1993).

- **How should the employment of family members be terminated for non-performance?**

  Family governance regulations should also consider what to do when a family employee fails to meet performance standards. For top management positions, classical corporate governance routines may dictate that the decision falls to the board of directors (comprising family and nonfamily members). For other positions, family owners should leave the decision to the direct superior of the family member in question.

5.7.4 Family involvement in ownership

Family governance should also make a statement about the family's ownership strategy. Note however: ownership related statements as part of family governance need to be aligned with the legally binding regulations laid out in an eventual shareholders' agreement. Family involvement in ownership as part of family governance could, for instance, specify the share percentage the family intends to hold in the company (currently and over time), the family's stance toward stock market listing, how next-generation family members get shares and how shares are broadly passed on within the family.

The primary wish of many business families is to perpetuate family ownership. Still, family owners are well advised to review their ownership strategy from time to time. For instance, as a result of succession within the family, the next-generation family owner-manager may wish to consolidate his/her ownership position and buy out dispersed family owners over time (such activity has been labeled 'pruning the family tree'). Alternatively, a family may seize an attractive opportunity to sell out, or the family may wish to pay out part of the family or fuel new growth through an IPO.

In order to transfer shares within the family, family firms often use a branch structure. This means that shares must first be offered for sale within the same family branch, and then to the other branches prorated according to current ownership.

Family governance regulations such as a family charter define the general principles of family involvement in ownership. Although a family charter attempts to create commitment and accountability among family members, it is only emotionally binding due to its small degree of detail.[5] A shareholder agreement transforms the principles of ownership governance outlined in the family charter into precise and legally binding obligations and defines how family shareholders exercise their shareholder rights at shareholders' meetings. For further details on family shareholders' agreements refer to section 5.6.

Taken together, family governance should address the following ownership topics:

- Current and future ownership strategy.
- When and how do family members become owners?
- Must family members meet certain requirements to be owners?
- Can in-laws be owners?
- Can nonfamily managers own stock?
- What is the base percentage that the CEO should own?
- What is the base percentage that the family as a whole should own?
- What happens with children from first and second marriages regarding ownership?
- Can a trust hold stock for the benefit of the family or others?
- Is there something like a family internal capital market and, if yes, how is it organized?

Example of family involvement in ownership

The following guidelines are excerpted from a family charter:

A. General principles

1. The following provisions cover the family's ownership in the family-controlled companies. Other assets such as financial assets are excluded from these provisions.
2. The provisions included in the articles of incorporation of the companies, their bylaws as well as the family's shareholders' agreement shall apply.
3. The shareholders' agreement is drafted in such a way that each family branch has the same shareholding and that such shareholding remains in such branch, if possible. Within the branch, decisions are made by simple majority vote.
4. We encourage family member ownership in the family-controlled businesses (the Group). Direct descendants shall be welcomed into the shareholder community through a gift of shares in the Group granted by the respective family branch. As we recognize spouses as full family members, spouses will be similarly welcomed into the shareholder community.
5. All shareholders will sign a shareholders' agreement, the purpose of which is to secure the family's continued control of the businesses.

B. Share transfer and disposal

The transfer and disposal of shares in the Group by the shareholders are governed by the provisions in the family's shareholders' agreement, the articles of incorporation and the bylaws of the Group's companies. In the event of any discrepancy, the provisions in the shareholders' agreement shall apply.

1. Each shareholder is bound by the shareholders' agreement, which is to be signed at the time of the acquisition or gifting of shares in the Group. All current shareholders will sign the shareholders' agreement at the official ceremony to formally launch this Family charter.
2. The shareholders' agreement is set up to the effect that the shares of each family branch remain in such branch.

5.7.5 Family involvement in new entrepreneurial activity

Family governance can determine the ways through which the family supports the entrepreneurial activity of next-generation family members. It is not uncommon for senior-generation family members to find that the succeeding generation lags behind expectations in continuing the legacy of the family firm. Meanwhile, next-generation family members who aspire to grow new businesses under the family umbrella may also find it difficult to roll out their plans (Au and Cheng 2011).

CASE STUDY

Family venture fund by the Mok family, Hong Kong[6]

A sophisticated form of family venture fund has been set up by the Mok family from Hong Kong. For the family's next generation, Dr. John Mok has set up a family nurtured spin-off scheme as a way for family members to keep some ties to the family business while at the same time starting their own entrepreneurial venture. The scheme is not a one-off tool to lure next-generation members to new ventures. Instead, it should be seen as a system supported by a culture of learning, a transgenerational leadership development program, a family angel scheme, and professional management. The system should be sustainable in itself instead of requiring continuous family input (see Figure 5.11).

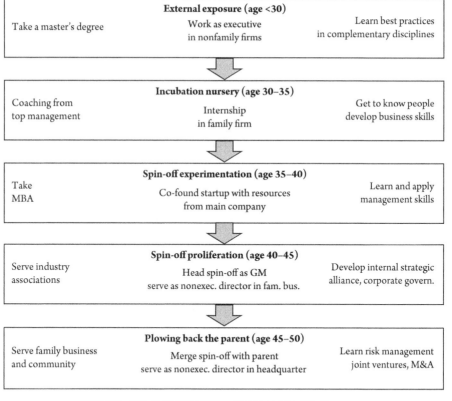

Note: GM = General Manager; M&A = mergers and acquisitions.

Source: Adapted from Au and Cheng (2011).

Figure 5.11 Family venture scheme by the Mok family, Hong Kong

A sophisticated scheme to support new entrepreneurial activity by next-generation family members makes particular sense in cases where junior family members have difficulty finding capital, networks and knowledge outside the family firm (e.g., in less developed countries). The necessity of a family venture scheme may be less pressing—and the opportunities tied to it less attractive—when next-generation members can find these resources outside the family firm (as is often the case in more developed countries).

Some families solve this dilemma and support the entrepreneurial activities of the next generation through a family venture fund. To be funded, family members must present a business plan of their intended venture (e.g., to the nonfamily members of the board) that is scrutinized for its commercial viability and its eventual synergies with the family's main business interests. The family charter could help structure the venture fund by defining the assessment process and criteria for the proposed venture, the conditions placed on funding, and the maximum amount of funding. Well-structured family venture funds are valuable because they provide family members with an opportunity to experiment as entrepreneurs without risking a larger investment or the family firm.

5.7.6 Family involvement in philanthropy

Family governance can help define the family's (joint) engagement in philanthropy. To this end, the family may specify the general purpose of its philanthropic activities. It may also wish to make a statement about the eventual support of family members in need. Relatedly, the family can support the education of its members through an education scheme.

Family business owners tend to be highly concerned with the social impact of the firm and the family, as discussed in Chapter 6 on strategy in family firms. Thus, it should not be surprising that many family firms are engaged in some sort of philanthropic activity. Along with its direct positive social impact, philanthropic activity is often tax exempt and has an identity-forging effect for the owning family that should not be underestimated. For family owners who are not engaged in firm operations, philanthropic activity may be an additional reason to commit to the firm and its objectives. In this way, philanthropic activity can also fulfill a governance role.

5.8 Wealth governance

The fourth pillar of governance in the family firm context, wealth governance, has not received due attention in the governance debates thus far. At first glance, the administration of family wealth seems to be a topic of wealth management, and thus belongs to the realm of financial advisors, estate planners and banks. However, upon closer scrutiny we will see that family wealth governance has a direct impact on families' ability to build and preserve wealth over time. Family wealth governance thus deals with the question of how families efficiently organize and monitor the management of their wealth so as to preserve and grow it in the long term (Zellweger and Kammerlander 2015).

We open our reflection on family wealth governance with an important observation: much of the governance thinking in family business implicitly follows the assumption that one united family controls a single firm. This may hold true in the case of younger, smaller family firms. But in later, more developed stages of families and businesses, this view is an inappropriate simplification.

Treating the family as a unified, monolithic actor dismisses the possibility of heterogeneous interests, goals and preferences among individual family members. But behind the façade of a seemingly united family, individual family member interests may diverge, for instance in terms of time horizon, liquidity needs, risk aversion, emotional attachment to the firm and, in general, what to do with the family's wealth.

Just as important, the assumption that families control only a single asset, that is, 'the family firm', deserves closer scrutiny. Indeed, successful and, in particular, 'old money' families often possess assets that significantly exceed the boundaries of a single firm. This diversity of business activity is reflected in studies on family business groups (e.g., Carney and Child 2013) and transgenerational entrepreneurship (e.g., Zellweger, Nason and Nordqvist 2012), as well as family wealth management and estate planning that prioritize the extended and often complex asset base of entrepreneurial families (e.g., Amit et al. 2008; Rosplock 2013). The multiple asset perspective is, however, not only a wealthy family phenomenon and challenge. Even families controlling smaller firms often hold more than corporate assets (i.e., their stake in the family firm), in many instances also owning real estate, and having some liquid wealth.

Acknowledging heterogeneous interests among family firm owners who often control more wealth than the stake in the family firm creates some challenge about how to administer the wealth. A first way for business families is to set up a shareholder agreement that regulates the access and transfer of shares of the family firm. However, such contractual agreements are unable to deal with the wealth not held under the roof of the firm. To coordinate heterogeneous family member interest over a more or less complex asset base, an important and growing number of business families defer to an organizational solution to administer their wealth (Carney, Gedajlovic and Strike 2014), such as by setting up a family office or a family trust (Rosplock 2013).

The wealth administration structures chosen by families vary in the degree to which they separate family members from their wealth. As we will see in more detail below, the stronger the separation of the family members from their wealth, the more limited is the family's access to the wealth and hence the smaller are the opportunities for disruptive infighting among unaligned family members about it. From this perspective, wealth administration vehicles that restrain access to wealth, such as, for instance, via family trusts, are attractive to many wealth creators (such as founders) as they limit the outbreak of conflicts among family members (such as children) with differing interests.

Families who separate family from wealth need to defer to some expert advisor who manages their wealth. A complex and large asset base creates a more urgent need to formalize control structures via the delegation of monitoring and asset-consolidation functions to expert and dedicated managers (i.e., some sort of fiduciary) who are entrusted with the custody of the family's wealth. There are direct costs associated with having experts manage the family's assets (such as salaries for the hired experts), as well as classic agency costs due to the separation of ownership and management of family wealth. These costs may be partly mitigated if a competent family member is the fiduciary. In most cases, however, where the fiduciary is nonfamily, this manager has a particularly powerful position as an intermediary between the asset owners (the family) and the asset managers (e.g., the managers of the various assets, such as the family firm). When owners place assets in the hands of intermediary agents such as trusted advisors or dedicated governance entities (e.g., family offices and trusts), they further separate ownership and control by inserting a first-tier agent between themselves and the second-tier managers of the various assets.

The promised advantage of establishing a trust and entrusting family wealth administration to professional managers (first-tier agents) is based on the idea that these incentivized experts will oversee and monitor the actions of the various managers (second-tier agents). But the particular problem that arises when owners install a first-tier agent who watches a set of second-tier agents is that the first-tier agent may start to act as the owner. Blind trust, an atmosphere of strict confidentiality, lack of competence at the level of the family owners, and a legal setup that confines the owners' discretion over the assets (e.g., trusts in common law countries, or foundations in most civil law countries) create significant opportunities for self-interested activity by the fiduciary. Often, the fiduciary need only establish a trusted relationship with a few family members and secure his/her delegation of authority in order to start acting as the principal (Zellweger and Kammerlander 2015).[7]

The fiduciary may use the authority conferred on him to put his/her actions in a favorable light, and to align his/her interests with those of second-tier service providers to take advantage of the owners rather than protecting their interests. Admittedly, a fiduciary can use his/her influence in a non-partisan, personally disinterested way and act in pure dedication to the maintenance of the family social system (Strike 2013). But because fiduciaries often operate under relatively light regulations[8] and are securely positioned in the center of a network of contractual relationships with various types of managers and advisors, they have many opportunities to acquiesce to second-tier agents, pocket kickbacks for the services they contract or impose preferences that run counter to the owners' interests. Mitigating these double-agency conflicts is especially costly for owners, as they must deal with agents in multiple tiers who have multiple, idiosyncratic opportunities to be in misalignment with the owners' interests (Zellweger and Kammerlander 2015).

In sum, family wealth governance is concerned with keeping together family wealth. Family wealth is under threat of being pulled apart by family members, in particular in later generations, who have differing views about what they would like to do with it. An often-chosen strategy to keep wealth together and hence align family member interest is to separate family from assets. But doing so is costly. Not only will the family have to bear direct costs from installing an intermediary who takes care of family assets, but the family also runs into double-agency costs because it requires oversight of second-tier agents by an expert monitor as the first-tier agent. In their wealth governance, families thus face a tradeoff: either the family solves the problem of misaligned interests among family members or the family separates themselves from the assets. But establishing such a cushion between the family and the assets and installing a first-tier agent (e.g., an intermediary or fiduciary) leads to double-agency costs.

In practice, families typically choose between four wealth governance constellations. These constellations separate family from wealth to

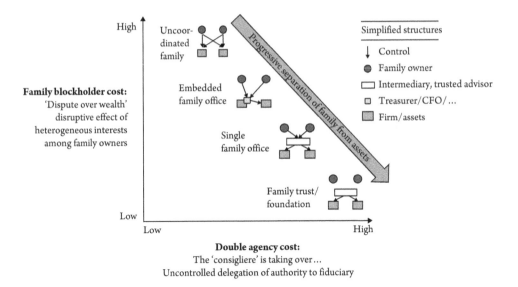

Source: Zellweger and Kammerlander (2015).

Figure 5.12 The four wealth governance constellations

different degrees and hence eliminate the disruptive effect of heterogeneous family interests to different degrees. The stronger the separation of family from assets the more prevalent should be double-agency costs (Figure 5.12). In the following we will take a closer look at the four governance constellations.[9]

5.8.1 The uncoordinated family

The uncoordinated family pertains to a governance form wherein control over the management of family wealth is kept in the hands of the family, without any coordination of family member interests. As such, there is no separation of family and assets. Without the coordination of heterogeneous familial interests, each family owner has unmediated and potentially uncontrolled access to the family's assets within legal confines (e.g., marital, heritance and testamentary law; contracts of inheritance). This constellation is likely prevalent among families with a powerful patriarch or matriarch or among families with a history of limited family and asset complexity, which has rendered the alignment of family owner interests unnecessary. As such, it is particularly prominent among founding and second generations. Yet families of later generations with more complex ownership structures might also be unable or unwilling to separate the family and its assets, for instance to minimize the related expenses of setting up and running a wealth management system and to ensure privacy (Zellweger and Kammerlander 2015).

The lack of coordination, however, may result in significant disadvantages for the family. Most importantly, the absence of coordinating mechanisms represents a fertile ground for family conflicts to play out. Heterogeneous interests of family members and access to wealth provides them with incentives to tunnel resources to themselves before relatives are able to do so. These dynamics can take the form of overt infighting for the family's wealth, or more subtly, incentives for thriftless, extravagant and wasteful lifestyles. A divergence of interests thus induces a race to the bottom over the family's assets; it will appear rational for many family members to engage in an unseemly internal struggle for power and money.

Consequently, despite advantages in terms of minimized expenses, increased privacy and, particularly, the lack of double-agency costs (due to the absence of an intermediary), the uncoordinated family constellation is highly susceptible to family conflicts. Moreover, in this constellation, welfare losses for the family emanate from forgone economies of scale and knowledge advantages that would accrue to all owners from deference to professionals and coordinated action, especially in terms of the management of wealth and the joint exercise of monitoring and control as a united group.

Taken together, the uncoordinated family therefore constitutes a very fragile governance form and, over the longer run, represents a recipe for the dissolution of family wealth and the decline of the family as the collective owner of wealth (Colli 2003; Franks et al. 2012). The fragility of the uncoordinated family may be temporarily mitigated by the involvement of a powerful family representative, such as the founder of the family's fortune or a senior patriarch/matriarch who holds uncontested authority over other family members. Alternatively, a will can block family members' transgressions and unrestrained access to the family's wealth. But as soon as these restraints are lifted (e.g., owing to the death of the founder or patriarch/matriarch), the disruptive forces that fuel the downward-spiraling lemmings race for the family's money will begin. Similarly, poor asset performance will place the uncoordinated family under increased pressure. Family members have incentives to maintain the status quo and to subordinate their individual interests to the interests of the family as long as performance is satisfactory. Declining performance, however, is likely to bring diverging interests to the fore and to create an incentive for individual family members to run for the exit. These arguments are further illustrated with the case study of U-Haul.

CASE STUDY

Family feud weighs down U-Haul

In the early hours of August 6, 1990, Eva Berg Shoen, 44, was shot to death as she slept in her deluxe log home in Telluride, Colorado. Why would anyone kill this pleasant, blonde, Norwegian-born woman who had moved with her family to the area for its small-town atmosphere? Her father-in-law, Leonard Samuel (L. S.) Shoen, who founded the U-Haul truck and trailer leasing empire in 1945, called it an 'assassination'. He suggested to authorities that the killing might be related to a long-running family feud over control of the company, which has close to $1 billion in annual sales.

Eva's husband, Dr. Sam Shoen, happened to be away the night of the murder. Sam Shoen is embroiled in the family dispute and had resigned as U-Haul president three years ago. Some people in town wondered if the killer might have meant to murder Sam instead of Eva. The wild family feud has pitted sibling against sibling—of which there are a dozen, by three different mothers—and some of these offspring against the eccentric patriarch. In recent years, the two sides have duked it out in the boardroom and the courtroom—and literally at last year's annual meeting, where some of the brothers came to blows.

The murder, in fact, occurred as the factions were fighting over a lawsuit, filed by U-Haul International and its parent company, Amerco, contending that L. S. Shoen, his son Sam, daughter Mary Anna and son Michael revealed confidential financial information about the company to outsiders. The suit also claims the group secretly plotted a takeover, possibly with the intention of selling the company to outsiders, and slandered the company, with the result that its credit rating was reduced. It seeks $30 million in damages. Eva Shoen herself was not an Amerco shareholder and wasn't actively involved in the dispute.

The seeds were sown years ago for this bitter battle of money, power and ego. After his first wife died, leaving him with six children, Shoen married the 23-year-old daughter of a neighbor, who bore five children. They divorced, and he married again and had another child. Thinking that his children would eventually run the company together, he began turning over chunks of Amerco stock to his seven sons and five daughters. They ultimately held 95%, leaving him with just 2%. He had set the stage for a mutiny.

In the mid-1970s, troubles began brewing among the four oldest sons—Sam, Mike, Edward J. (known as 'Joe') and Mark—who had moved into top management. The orange and white U-Haul vehicles, once synonymous with do-it-yourself moving, has recently begun losing ground to rivals such as Ryder System, based in Miami. U-Haul's revenue rose, but profit sank. In 1979, Joe and Mark Shoen resigned in a dispute over the company's direction.

Mark recalls that he and some of his siblings also resented the fact that they never received dividends on their Amerco stock holdings. '(We) were millionaires in name only', said Mark Shoen, now U-Haul president. 'We were told we were wealthy, but we didn't have enough money to buy a car.' When Mark got into some financial difficulty in 1980, he said, he asked his father and brother Sam to buy some of his stock, but they refused. L. S. has said

CASE STUDY *(continued)*

Mark and Joe set about drumming up support among their other siblings to wrest control from him because they disagreed with his management style.

Four years ago, they succeeded in booting their father out of the chair's post. But he didn't give up, insisting that the rival groups of children attempt to work together at the company. The arrangement failed miserably. In 1988, L. S. and Sam attempted a comeback coup with the support of some wavering relatives. But Joe foiled this by selling 8099 shares to five nonfamily company executives, and cemented his control. L. S. then filed suit in an Arizona state court, contending that the stock sale was illegal. The case was dismissed, but L. S. has appealed.

Then, in early 1989, son Joe, chair of Amerco, cut off his father's retirement compensation. 'I'm basically bankrupt', L. S. Shoen said recently. 'Well, maybe not bankrupt', he added, but he was forced to sell his big house in Las Vegas. Once firmly in control, Joe and Mark Shoen instituted a 'back-to-basics' approach, unloading the diversified businesses, scaling back the workforce and investing $1.2 billion to upgrade the fleet of 66 000 trucks and 1 00 000 trailers.

Always plenty nasty, the Shoen family feud has taken its most vicious turn with the death of Eva Shoen. The mere implication that family members had something to do with plotting the murder has outraged those on the inside at U-Haul. They have lashed back in a response reminiscent of the cat fighting between J. R. and Bobby Ewing in the television series *Dallas*.

By most accounts, Eva Shoen was an attractive, friendly woman who took an interest in her children's schooling, did volunteer work and enjoyed skiing and raising dogs. After the murder, Sam Shoen, a medical doctor who no longer practices, offered a $250 000 reward for information leading to an arrest and conviction. He also planned a memorial service and asked that his sibling rivals, the U-Haul 'insiders', not attend.

 REFLECTION QUESTIONS

1. What is the underlying reason for the family conflict about the control of the firm?
2. How does the family conflict impact the firm?
3. What type of agency problems do you recognize in this case?
4. What could have been done to avoid the conflict?
5. What elements of this extreme case can be observed in other business families?
6. Looking at U-Haul today: how does the family control the firm today?

Source: Inspired by an article by Martha Groves, *Los Angeles Times*, September 4, 1990.

5.8.2 Embedded family office

In the case of an embedded family office, the family appoints a fiduciary from within the existing asset structure to manage its wealth. For instance, and as often observed in practice, the family may ask the accountant, treasurer or chief financial officer of the family firm to also manage the family's wealth. In so doing, the family delegates the management of part of the family's affairs to a nonfamily member but does so within the original structure. In addition to their job in the firm's operations, embedded family officers are, for instance, entrusted with the management of the family's liquid wealth and real estate and are responsible for fulfilling related services such as personal bookkeeping and tax filings. As such, there is a low level of separation between the family and its assets (Zellweger and Kammerlander 2015).

This governance structure is particularly attractive to families with a trusted manager embedded within the family firm seeking a convenient and cost-efficient solution to the family's wealth governance challenges. Such a structure may evolve from the progressive success of the focal family firm and the accumulation of wealth on the side of the family over time and generations.

While embedded family offices bundle the individual family members' wealth management activities, they provide only limited guidance on how to handle the diverging interests of family members. Moreover, embedded family offices often create an incentive for family owners, and eventually even non-owning family members, to escalate their personal demand for subsidized services from the embedded family office, particularly when the embedded family office offers its services to the family for free or below-market costs.

At the same time, however, the embedded family officer will gain preferred access to owners and their most private financial circumstances and will thus emerge as an influential information and power broker. Such an embedded family officer may be tempted to steer decisions in a direction that mainly serves his/her own interests, that extends his/her sphere of influence, and that undercuts the position of the CEO to whom he/she reports. Such double-agency costs will likely be particularly pronounced if large fractions of the total family wealth are managed through the embedded family office (Zellweger and Kammerlander 2015).

Regarding further costs, it is also important to consider that an embedded fiduciary serves two masters, the family and the firm, which sometimes have diverging interests. The ensuing dilemma about which master to serve comes in many forms, such as a risky private investment for which a family member seeks financial backing from the firm, family members' preference for tax structures that protect their private interests to the detriment of the firm, or pressure to pay dividends when the firm needs additional equity injections. Given the family's influence, it can be difficult for the embedded fiduciary to oppose the family's wishes. Such governance inefficiencies are costly for a firm's minority owners, creditors and other family owners. Additionally, because the embedded fiduciary takes orders directly from both the CEO and family owners, the CEO is placed in the difficult sandwich position of having a subordinate who is simultaneously the trusted advisor of the party to whom the CEO reports. Such a hybrid hierarchical structure stands in sharp contrast to unambiguous and efficient control structures. The CEO thus lives with a costly substructure that does not actually serve the company and operates outside his/her immediate control, but under the direct protection of the family owners. As a consequence, resources may be allocated according to family-political criteria instead of firm-level efficiency-based criteria, which highlight further important inefficiencies for a firm's minority owners, creditors and any family owners who do not have access to the services of the internal advisor (Zellweger and Kammerlander 2015).

Additional costs of the embedded family office constellation arise not only from the opportunistic behavior of the embedded fiduciary, but also his/her potential incompetence in fulfilling certain tasks (such as asset-management decisions regarding the family's wealth) for which the fiduciary is often untrained. In sum, embedded family offices align differing family member interests to only a limited degree but give rise to some level of double-agency costs. Embedded family offices engender majority–minority-owner/creditor agency costs from the fulfillment of various services for the family and from governance inefficiencies due to the hybrid hierarchical position of the embedded fiduciary.

CASE STUDY

The embedded family office

The relevance of embedded family offices is underlined by Rosplock's guide for affluent families (2013). She suggests that, in the United States, there are 9000 single-family offices and 12 000 to 18 000 embedded family offices. Embedded family offices play a role in managing family wealth in other countries as well. For example, a study by Credit Suisse and the University of St. Gallen found that the CFOs of mid-sized German family firms manage on average 60% of the family's private wealth.

In a prominent call to separate private wealth from the family business, Flanagan and colleagues (2011) from Family Office Exchange (FOX) note that managing private wealth from within the company comes with tax-related and legal risks. According to US law, an individual or family cannot take a tax deduction for the management of their personal affairs

CASE STUDY *(continued)*

inside the business. Moreover, the embedded family office may be considered a shareholder relations department and fall under the definition of a registered investment advisor, causing a regulatory burden for the firm. Most importantly, liability from owning or insuring personal property through the company exposes the business to intra-family disputes and external lawsuits based on family member actions.

5.8.3 Single-family office

Wealthy families often pool their private assets and delegate private wealth management to a family office. While single-family offices manage the affairs (i.e., family and wealth-related governance) for one family alone, multi-family offices provide services for several families. The single-family office is set up as a distinct organizational entity and acts as an organizational intermediary between individual family members' interests and the family's assets. The motivations for setting up a single-family office are manifold:

● Independence from third parties, especially banks.
● Privacy.
● Greater control over assets and better investment controlling.
● Cost advantages, for large fortunes.
● Minimized tax obligations.
● Professionalized management of family and wealth complexity.
● Parents fear that the next generation lacks competency to manage family wealth.
● Parents wish to restrict individual family members' access to family wealth, believing that such access will damage their initiative, self-esteem and social relationships.

Overall, single-family offices tend to cover the following services: asset management, investment planning, controlling, reporting, tax planning, real estate management, succession planning, asset allocation, family governance, private equity, corporate finance and philanthropy.[10] The service level of a single-family office mainly depends on the amount and complexity of the family's wealth and on the service needs of the owning family.

In the end, a family office has to be assessed in terms of the benefits and costs it generates for the family. Given the partly noneconomic nature of some of the benefits, such as the prevention of extravagant lifestyles among junior family members or the coordination of access to wealth inside the family and hence the opportunity to limit family disputes, this is a challenging task. Whether a single-family office is the right type of wealth governance vehicle will depend on several factors, such as (1) the amount of family wealth, (2) the complexity of family wealth, (3) the family's need for confidentiality, (4) the range and (5) exclusivity of services, (6) the need for customization and (7) the ability to exercise special projects. The more pronounced these needs are, the more justified a single-family office appears. Otherwise, an outsourced solution with a financial institution and other service providers is more justified.

One of the central benefits of family offices is that they serve as a unifying force for the family: they thwart the centrifugal forces within the family, generational drift and the related dilution of wealth, so that the family preserves its cohesion and power across time. The single-family office should also be less susceptible to costs that harm minority owners and creditors. In contrast to the embedded family office, where the costs are at least partly passed along to minority owners and creditors, in the single-family office the family itself pays the bills.

But these advantages come at significant costs. For instance, direct costs arise from implementing and running the family office outside the current asset structure. Even though single-family offices tend to be small (in the United States, the average number of employees in a single-family office is about five to eight employees), the personnel costs, as well as costs for office and technology infrastructure, are often significant when considered in proportion to the wealth to be managed. For example, the Boston Consulting Group (2013) estimates that the total operating costs for a single-family office are about $1–2 million per year. Other authors estimate the total annual operating costs to be about 0.70 to 1.50% of assets under management.[11] Thus, in the US and European contexts, a single-family office setup is warranted only when there are several hundreds of million US dollars liquid wealth under management.[12] These figures explain why many single-family offices over time transform into multi-family offices.

The overall efficiency of the family office is a significant concern for the family. Thus, family owners are incentivized to carefully monitor the cost-conscious behavior of family officers. The agency costs in the relationship between the family principal and the family officer are relatively easy to keep in check because of the strong incentive among principals to monitor the cost efficiency of the family office and to hold the family officer accountable.

At the same time, however, single-family offices should be prone to double-agency costs. The relationships between the family officer and the various service providers (e.g., asset managers who are hired by the family officer) are much harder for the family principal to monitor and sanction. Because the family principal has limited insight into the family officer's dealings with the service providers, the family officer has significant opportunities for self-interested behavior. For instance, service providers and asset managers may flatter the family officer and offer various rewards in exchange for purchasing their services, and ultimately obtain access to the family's wealth. Capitalizing on the principal's limited insight, and equipped with a significant information advantage, second-tier agents may try to collude with the first-tier agent so that they can pursue their own interests at the expense of the principal.

Admittedly, these double-agency costs are of lesser concern in the presence of a trusted advisor who rises to a state of pure rationality, disinterest and stewardship. Nevertheless, the single-family office is prone to direct costs from running the family office as well as double-agency costs from delegating the management of family affairs to hired experts.

CASE STUDY

The Jacobs family

The Jacobs family's original business, coffee trading, went through several acquisitions and divestments over the generations. By 2013, the family's portfolio of businesses and wealth was governed by the following structure (Figure 5.13).

Jacobs Holding serves as the family's investment holding, which administers the family's main corporate assets (the main investment currently is Barry Callebaut, the world's largest chocolate producer). The family owns another organization (Niantic Holding) that manages large parts of the family's liquid wealth and smaller private family investments.

Ninety percent of the votes in Jacobs Holding are held by the family directly, the remaining 10% of the votes are in the hands of Jacobs Foundation. Jacobs Foundation holds 100% of the capital of Jacobs Holding and is thus the main financial beneficiary of the income generated by the Holding. Jacobs Foundation is a charitable organization established by the family to facilitate innovations for children and youth. Through this foundation, the family is also the main sponsor of Jacobs University in Bremen, Germany, the family's hometown. The family sends multiple members to the board of trustees of the foundation, including its president, but represents a minority of all board members.

As the organizational chart shows, the family has tight control over Barry Callebaut via a stake of 50.01% held through Jacobs Holding and a 15% stake held directly by the family members themselves. In the core investment, Andreas Jacobs, the head of the family, serves as the chair of the board. Agri business holds several smaller assets, including Newsells, a horse breeding service.

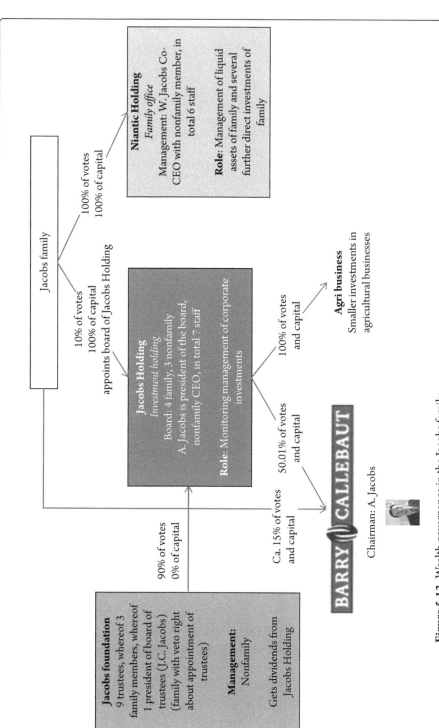

Figure 5.13 Wealth governance in the Jacobs family

 REFLECTION QUESTIONS

1. How does the Jacobs family keep control over its assets? What are the respective roles of the various boards/organizational entities in the organizational chart?
2. How does the governance structure mitigate the potential for diverging interests within the family?
3. How does the Jacobs family try to counter owner-manager and double-agency costs that might arise from this complex asset and family structure?

5.8.4 Family trust/foundation

Families may also opt for a form of wealth governance with a very strong delegation of control to an intermediary. Typically, in common law countries, such as the United States, the United Kingdom, Japan, Scotland, Israel and some Latin American countries, this takes the form of a trust. In civil law countries, including most continental European countries, there are provisions for trust-like relationships such as foundations. What is common to these arrangements is that a transferor (in the trust: the settlor) allocates wealth in a trust or a foundation to the benefit of a recipient (the beneficiary). To this end, the transferor installs a manager (the trustee) who promises to manage the wealth for the benefit of the recipient and consistent with the ex ante instructions of the transferor (Sitkoff 2004).

In all international variations of trust law, the beneficiary forgoes all property rights in the wealth placed inside the trust and has very limited ability to monitor the trustee. The trustee, not the beneficiary, wields ownership rights over the trust. The beneficiary's dependence on the trustee, along with his/her low visibility into the details of the trust, facilitates the trustee's rise to the role of powerful gatekeeper. While the trustee holds the power over the trust, the beneficiaries bear the full risk.

In the family firm context, family trusts are common vehicles for structuring family affairs as they come with several attractive features (Zellweger and Kammerlander 2015). In part, families may opt for trusts for tax reasons: in the United States, for example, trusts spare the family federal estate and generation-skipping taxes. Most often, parents set up trusts for the benefit of their children. They do so to limit their children's access to wealth due to fear that the children will ruin the assets (e.g., the family firm), or conversely, that the wealth will ruin the children (e.g., by tempting them to indulge in extravagant lifestyles or undermining their sense of initiative). Trusts are often envisioned as a means of avoiding family blockholder conflicts which are detrimental to both the assets and the family. To a large degree, trusts also allow settlors to preserve the status quo and enshrine their lifetime achievements and thus satisfy some sort of longing for immortality. Taken together, trusts provide the following advantages:

- Protect firm from family squabbles and unqualified family members.
- Protect family from wealth and extravagant lifestyles.
- Secure control: limit exit opportunities and fragmentation of wealth.
- Alignment of family owner interests.
- Tax benefits.
- Privacy.
- Economies of scale from cash pooling.
- Coordination of dynastic ambitions, such as family member education, amenity investments or philanthropy.

Despite strict legal standards, in many cases the law is an insufficient substitute for monitoring of the trustee. The beneficiary has virtually no control over the trustee's actions and limited ability to exit the relationship by removing the assets from the trustee's control. In US law, for instance, there is no monitoring mechanism in place to protect the beneficiary (e.g., court supervision or the stock price of a publicly held corporation). In other words, trusts cannot make use of the important internal and external governance mechanisms to monitor and sanction managers that are available in the corporate world.

Three types of control costs should therefore accrue in trusts. First, appointing a trustee or multiple trustees to manage family wealth leads to direct costs from the bureaucratization of wealth in trust form. To administer a diversified portfolio of assets, trustees need to be professionals with asset-management expertise and require an associated level of compensation for their services.

Second, and as noted above, trusts create significant principal–agent agency costs; more precisely, they create settlor–trustee and beneficiary–trustee agency costs. The former refers to the trustee's potential lack of loyalty to the ex ante instructions of the settlor who established the trust. The latter conflict refers to the trustee's potential lack of loyalty to the beneficiary and to his/her opportunity for self-interested behavior. These two subtypes of principal–agent agency costs are impossible to solve in the classic way by monitoring and incentive contracting. Indeed, managerial ownership— a particularly effective incentive mechanism—is unavailable for trusts. In addition, there is no efficient market for stakes in private trusts, which would provide a price signal and thus a metric for trustee performance. To some degree at least, the trustee thus becomes a manager without an owner.

Finally, trusts may also lead to severe double-agency problems. When delegating a task to a manager with wide discretion but without close monitoring, it is extremely difficult to ensure the alignment of second-tier agents with the interests of the beneficiary. It may be tempting for the trustee to allocate generous fees from second-tier agents to the trust corpus and to engage in collusive dealings with asset managers. Put differently, because the first-tier agent already has significant opportunities for self-interested behavior, the second-tier agent is even less likely to be aligned with the interests of the beneficiary, and may collude with the trustee to the detriment of the beneficiary. This double-agency problem has a further facet that is important to keep in mind when establishing a trust: the trustees are required to manage the trust corpus, that is, the assets that are held in the trust, in a careful manner. According to US trust law, for instance, this duty of care translates into a duty to conservatively allocate the assets held by the trust. This duty runs counter to the interest of dedicated investments in a single or a few private firms whose shares cannot be easily traded. Entrepreneurial investments are by definition risky. As such, trusts, which direct the trustee to avoid risks and diversify wealth, are at odds with inherently risky entrepreneurial investments. Trusts thus indeed allow family owners to secure family control over assets. And trusts may represent a suitable legal form for the administration of liquid wealth, for instance to fund some charitable activity. But from a macroeconomic point of view it is at least debatable whether trusts lead to a suboptimal entombment instead of reinvestment of capital for value-creating, entrepreneurial uses (for further details refer to Zellweger and Kammerlander 2015 and Sitkoff 2004). In sum, family trusts/foundations to control firms come with some important disadvantages:

- Administrative costs.
- Lack of loyalty of trustee to instructions by settlor and to trustee.
- Opportunistic behavior by trustee who starts acting as if he/she were the owner of the trust assets.
- Lack of efficiency in administration of trust assets in consequence to lack of oversight and disciplining outside pressure.
- Inertia and unwillingness to take entrepreneurial risks by trustee by fear of liability claims.

5.8.5 Which wealth governance constellation is best?

Business families who control some assets and consist of multiple members with interwoven financial interests will have to carefully weigh the pros and cons of any chosen wealth governance constellation. On the one hand, a wealth governance constellation may suffer from the diverging interests of family owners and hence from family blockholder conflicts (uncoordinated family, partly also the embedded family office). These conflicts weaken the family's joint exercise of power and undermine the preservation of family wealth, leading to its more or less rapid dissolution over time. On the other hand, a wealth governance constellation may incur double-agency costs, whereby family officers or trustees start to behave like the owners (single-family office, family trust). In these cases, family wealth is kept together but at significant governance costs for the family.

If family business owners wish to preserve wealth across generations, the uncoordinated family is a particularly problematic governance constellation given its inability to motivate coordinated action among family members. This is especially true for families with numerous members and significant assets.

Given that many business-owning families wish to preserve wealth across generations, we should also consider the stability of the four wealth governance constellations and their varying tendency to dissolve family wealth over time. In the uncoordinated family constellation, where individual family members have the incentive to capture a large share of family wealth before their relatives can do so, family wealth is likely to be dissolved and distributed to individual family members fairly rapidly. In embedded family offices, family wealth is kept intact, but is at risk of being managed by family-political rather than efficiency-based criteria. Single-family offices should also be able to preserve family wealth, but at significant administrative and governance costs. Finally, trusts maintain family wealth and encourage risk-averse management at significant agency costs, which are likely to gradually deplete family wealth over time.

The four governance constellations discussed here are not the sole means of administering family wealth, nor are they mutually exclusive. For instance, some families may wish to outsource part of their wealth and governance complexities to a multi-family office while performing some parts of the task themselves. Alternatively, families may use governance constellations in parallel. For instance, they may establish a single-family office to manage liquid wealth and a trust/foundation for their philanthropic activities.

In practice, many families who have created substantial wealth over generations through their firms have done so by moving from the uncoordinated family to an embedded family office to a single-family office constellation. At any given stage, the family needs to carefully assess the pros and cons of the constellation and counter the expected governance problems by defining rules of conduct for family members and eventual officers and establishing appropriate monitoring mechanisms. For the cases of embedded and, in particular, single-family offices, the families will also have to supervise the family officer's dealings with second-tier agents. As can be seen in the case of the Jacobs family (see the case study above), long-term successful families establish a finely balanced governance structure to keep owner-manager, family blockholder and double-agency costs in check.

5.9 Governance documents: code of conduct and family charter

Having laid out the four governance areas of family, ownership, corporate and wealth governance, we turn now to their integration. One way for the family to consolidate these pieces and to document its chosen governance structure is to develop a family charter.

5.9.1 Family charter

The family charter is one of the most frequently used governance tools for families in business (Montemerlo and Ward 2010).[13] As mentioned above, the family charter is not a legally binding document, but it emotionally binds family members to a joint and concerted governance of business, ownership, family and wealth. Depending on the complexity of the family and its business operations, family charters will differ in their level of detail and sophistication. Building on the previous discussion of the four governance areas, a family charter could thus comprise the following elements.

Possible structure and content of a family charter

1. Objectives of the family charter
2. Family values
3. Corporate governance (refer section 5.5)
   a. Role of the board of directors
   b. Appointment of board of directors
   c. Appointment of top management

---

4. Ownership governance (refer to section 5.6)
   a. Execution of voting rights
   b. Transfer of shares
   c. Stalemates
   d. Dissolution of shareholders' agreement
5. Family governance (refer to section 5.7)
   a. Family involvement in management/board
   b. Family involvement in ownership
   c. Family involvement in new entrepreneurial ventures
   d. Family involvement in philanthropy
   e. Family assembly/family council
6. Wealth governance (refer to section 5.8)
   a. Family's desire for the joint administration of family wealth
   b. Preferred wealth governance constellation
   c. Eligibility of family members for family wealth management
7. Social activities of the family
   a. To be adapted to family needs
8. Governance documents
   a. Family charter: setup and eventual changes to document
   b. Further documents: setup and eventual changes to document
9. Signatures
10. Appendices:
    a. Family tree
    b. Legal background information: rules for marriage settlement, inheritance/gift contracts

Many families in business, and especially those who are under threat of drifting apart, are well advised to clarify the values important to the family members. A discussion about and the formulation of family values is an important stepping stone for family business governance. Value statements often serve as a noncontroversial step toward more formal arrangements. Value statements also create cohesion and a point of reference and identification for family members. Also, they can serve as guiding principles for various further questions, such as succession, and strategic questions in the firm. In a values statement, families may wish to clarify family and business values and the alignment between family members. Think, for example, of statements about the importance of the family as a social group versus the role of the individual family member, the vision for the family and the business, ethical standards, growth, risk taking, entrepreneurship and the like.

Some families go as far as defining a code of conduct. In contrast to a family charter, the code of conduct not only defines the values important to the family, but tries to ensure their manifestation. To really 'live' their family values, families may wish to uphold certain traditions, such as family gatherings, which symbolize and transmit family values within the family, and in particular from older to younger generations. These values are made tangible through family gatherings, or further specified activities such as family philanthropy. Some families even go as far as reviewing adherence to code of conduct. Without policing family members, a code of conduct may be helpful for reviewing family members' adherence to family norms and values. For instance, a code of conduct may help specify how family members should communicate with the press and how they should approach public appearances on behalf of the firm. It is important to review the code of conduct and a statement of values from time to time. Values and behavioral norms that seem reasonable at one point in time may become outdated. On a regular basis (every few years), codes of conduct should be reviewed for their functionality in light of the current challenges and beliefs in the firm and the family.

Example 1: Code of conduct

- Treat one another with respect.
- Keep negative statements about the family out of the public realm.
- Commit to one joint event per year.
- Meeting/communication principles: be prepared, listen to understand not to respond, one person speaks at a time, no personal attacks, maintain confidentiality, commit to improvement.

Example 2: Code of conduct—The Mogi Family Creed

- **Item 1**: Family members should recognize that harmony is of utmost importance . . . fosters mutual respect . . . permits family members to focus on prosperity in business and on the longevity of the fortunes of the families.
- **Item 7**: Each employee should be treated without personal prejudice and be placed in the most appropriate position according to his capability and achievements . . .
- **Item 14**: When beginning a new business consult with family members.
- **Item 16**: Give as much money from your personal earnings to society as possible. Source: Yates (1998).

This example of a family charter should be treated as a general guideline of the topics that the charter may address. As mentioned above, the topics covered in a family charter and its level of detail will vary from case to case. When seen in conjunction, any such activity and document has the goal to ensure a cohesive, competent and controlling family.

5.10 Governance bodies: family assembly and family council

In bringing corporate, ownership, family and wealth governance together, larger families sometimes work with specific governance bodies such as the family assembly and the family council.

The family assembly comprises all family members above a certain age (e.g., above 18). In many business families, the members of the family assembly are at the same time the family shareholders. Sometimes, however, non-shareholding family members are also part of the family assembly.

Depending on the number of family shareholders/members, the family assembly may elect a family council from its members. The family council serves as the family assembly's governing group and manages the family's business and financial affairs. More specifically, the roles of the family council are to:

- serve as an executive committee of the family assembly,
- develop and change the family charter on behalf of the family assembly,
- ensure adherence to governance guidelines, as defined in the family charter,
- manage family activities that ensure cohesion, competence and control (e.g., family meetings, next-generation gatherings), and
- provide guidance to the family owners and business directors regarding the family's values and goals.

Oftentimes, members of the family council are eligible to be members of the governance board(s) of the firm(s) controlled by the family. Various combinations are conceivable, as depicted in Figure 5.14. The preferred combination will largely reflect the complexity of the family (the more complex the family, the higher the need for coordination within the family and hence the installation of a family council) and the complexity of the business (the more complex the business, the higher the need for expert involvement on the board(s)).

Figure 5.15 shows an example governance structure of a US-based family controlling a publicly listed company. In its third generation, the family shareholders today comprise roughly thirty members, four of which are part of the family council, with two serving on the board of directors (one of them is part of the family council, the other is not). Because the firm is publicly listed, next to the two family representatives on the board there are also three

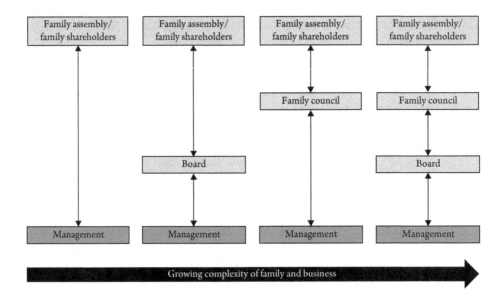

Source: Adapted from Kormann (2008).

Figure 5.14 Use of governance bodies

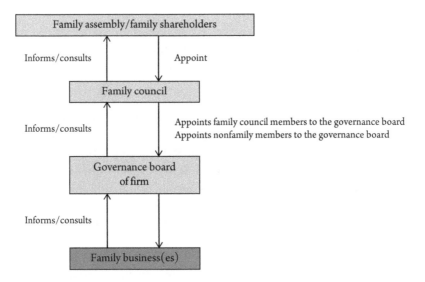

Figure 5.15 Example governance structure of US-based family

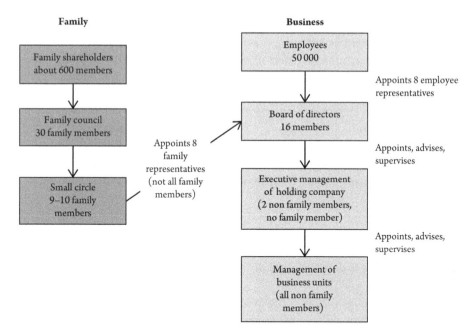

Figure 5.16 Integrated governance at Haniel

further board members who represent the large group of minority, nonfamily owners.

Haniel, a large, privately held German conglomerate owned by roughly 600 family shareholders, provides an extreme example. As can been seen in Figure 5.16, the family has adopted a sophisticated governance structure that defines the ways in which it controls the firm. The assembly of family shareholders appoints 30 members to a family council, and a small circle of the family council appoints family and nonfamily members to the board of directors of the company. In their family governance, the Haniel family specified that no family member should be allowed to work inside the firm(s). Following German law, the board of directors of Haniel must be composed of an equal number of owner and employee representatives.

5.11 Integrated governance in family firms

Thus far, we have treated the four governance domains (corporate, ownership, family and wealth) separately. Effective governance, however, ensures that the four governance areas are aligned and form an integrated governance system.

We will take family governance—which encompasses the values and over-arching goals of the family—as a starting point. In this governance domain, the family defines the rules of engagement for its members in the management and ownership of the firm. These statements set guidelines for ownership governance, for instance by forming the foundation of the shareholders' agreement. Family governance also serves as the basis for corporate governance, for example by setting standards for staffing decisions for the board and the top management team, or for the dividend policy. Finally, family governance impacts wealth governance to the extent that the family coordinates wealth management among its members and the governance thereof.

The family charter, which is the guiding document of family governance, brings these elements together and delineates the core principles of family, corporate, ownership and wealth governance. This integrative perspective of governance is depicted in Figure 5.17.

In developing such an integrated governance system, it is important to start with the overarching values and beliefs of the family as discussed in our section on the code of conduct. These values guide the more detailed formulation of corporate, ownership, family and wealth governance regulations, as discussed above.

When formulating the governance regulations across these four domains, it is important to make sure that they are consistent and complementary. For instance, if the family charter delineates some rules about the internal transfer of shares as part of family governance, these regulations should be reflected in the shareholders' agreement. Remember that a shareholders' agreement is a legally binding document; as such, any other governance regulation, such as a family charter, must be aligned with its rules.

After a family defines its elementary family and ownership principles, it will have to formulate the appropriate guidelines for corporate and wealth governance. Within these guidelines, the rules of engagement for family members in corporate and wealth governance deserve particular attention. With regard to corporate governance, the rules for the formation, composition, decision making and authority of the board of directors are especially important. Larger and public companies often include these rules in the board regulations. Of course, the family is not completely free in the way it shapes corporate governance regulations and has to respect the legal constraints in this process.

With regard to wealth governance, family members will have to specify whether they want to coordinate their wealth management and, if so, through

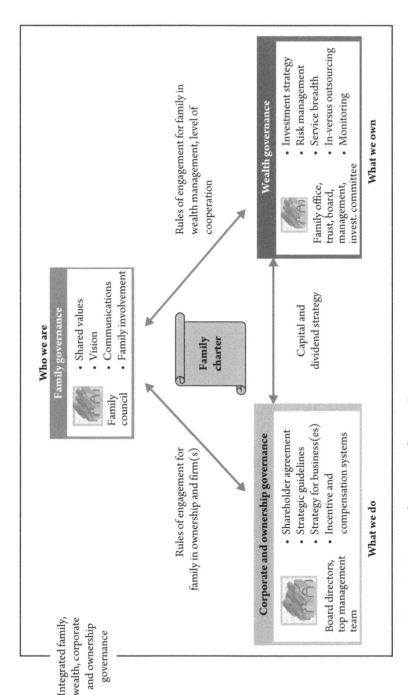

Figure 5.17 Integrated governance framework

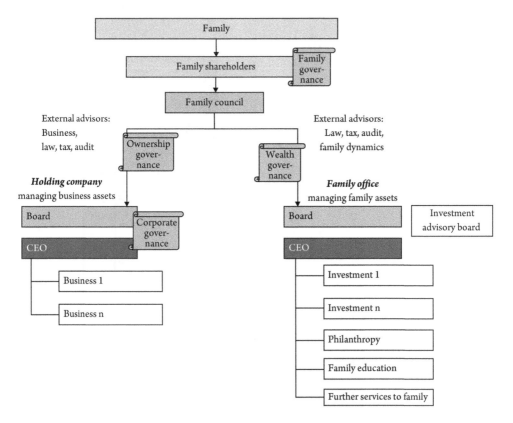

Figure 5.18 Integrated governance: an illustration

which governance constellation (e.g., embedded family office, single-family office, trust or some other combination) they will do so.

Taken together, this procedural approach should enable the development of a consistent and integrated governance structure that is aligned with the overarching values, beliefs and goals of the controlling family. In the ultimate development stage, and for the case of a large family controlling significant corporate and non-corporate assets, families often develop a dual structure composed of a holding company, controlling the corporate assets, and a family office, controlling the non-corporate assets. This structure is held together by family, corporate, ownership and wealth governance regulations (see Figure 5.18 for more details).

5.12 CASE STUDIES

Beretti Holdings—More than a retirement decision

Beretti Holdings AG is a publicly listed company controlled by the Beretti family. The firm was originally founded by Peter Beretti in 1920. Over the years, the firm has grown significantly and has become a diversified holding company with an annual turnover of approximately $900 million. The firm's activities include the production of roof tiles, coating liquids and industrial cooling equipment and the lease of production equipment. The family currently controls 60% of the firm's equity, with the rest of the shares held by various public investors.

Beretti Holdings owes much of its success over the past 20 years to the managerial talent of Marcus Mandell, the firm's long-term CEO, and to the business acumen of the president of the supervisory board, Robert Beretti. While Marcus Mandell is a nonfamily employee, Robert Beretti is a third-generation family member. Both men are in their early 60s. Another Beretti family member, Thomas Brennan (45 years old), oversees the industrial cooling division, with an annual sales volume of about $150 million. The supervisory board consists of Robert Beretti (president), Thomas Brennan and three non-family members. The current governance structure of Beretti Holdings AG is as follows (Figure 5.19).

The family shareholders are bound by a shareholders' agreement that foresees preemption rights and, in particular, valuation principles for share transfers. The preemption rights stipulate that shares should be kept among family shareholders. In case of a share transfer, the members of the owner's nuclear family should have the right of first refusal, after which the shares are offered to other families within the same branch of the family tree and finally to the other family branches. The structure of the Beretti family is as follows (Figure 5.20).

In a meeting of the supervisory board last year, Robert Beretti announced that he would be retiring next year. Marcus Mandell, the current CEO, also announced his retirement for the end of next year. Subsequently, disagreements arose in the Beretti family about how these positions should be filled. Until this point, the family shareholders traditionally followed the lead of Robert Beretti.

In recent years, the complexity of the firm's shareholding structure changed dramatically. Where before there were three second-generation family shareholders with equal 33% ownership stakes, there are now 18 third-, fourth- and fifth-generation family shareholders. In total, the family consists of roughly 40 members, including non-shareholding spouses and children. This complexity has not facilitated the decision-making process at all; in fact, the family shareholders seem to be paralyzed and unable to take a decision.

Regarding the selection of the president of the supervisory board, there were two camps among the family shareholders: the first camp, mainly represented by the family branches of Mia and Nathalie Beretti, favored a solution in which each family branch would send a

CASE STUDY *(continued)*

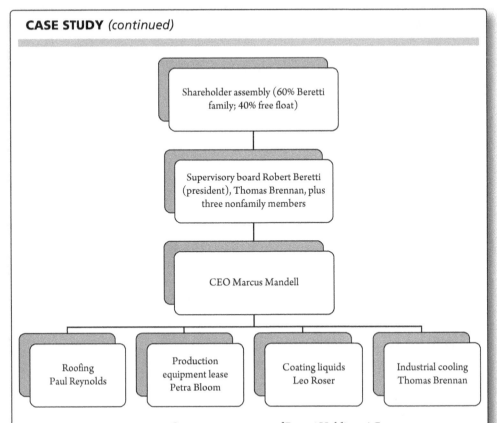

Figure 5.19 Governance structure of Beretti Holdings AG

family representative to the supervisory board; the second camp, consisting mainly of Peter Beretti's family branch, suggested forming a single pool of family shareholders that would select a number of representatives for the supervisory board independent of their affiliation with a family branch.

Discussions about CEO succession were equally contentious. One group of family members was pushing for Thomas Brennan to become the CEO. They argued: 'Thomas knows the firm very well. He already serves on the supervisory board, so why not make him CEO as well. He is one of the family.' And behind closed doors, they added: 'Thomas will do his best as CEO, because if he does not perform, he knows that he will most likely lose his family as well as his job.' Other family representatives proposed a different plan: 'We should hire a professional CEO who is able run the company without any family biases or burden. Thomas is doing a fine job as head of the industrial cooling division, but we do not see him being the CEO.'

Communication among the family shareholders was far from optimal. On the one hand, long, unstructured emails were sent to 23 family shareholders asking for their opinions. On the other hand, some family shareholders met at a private event and came up with a solution

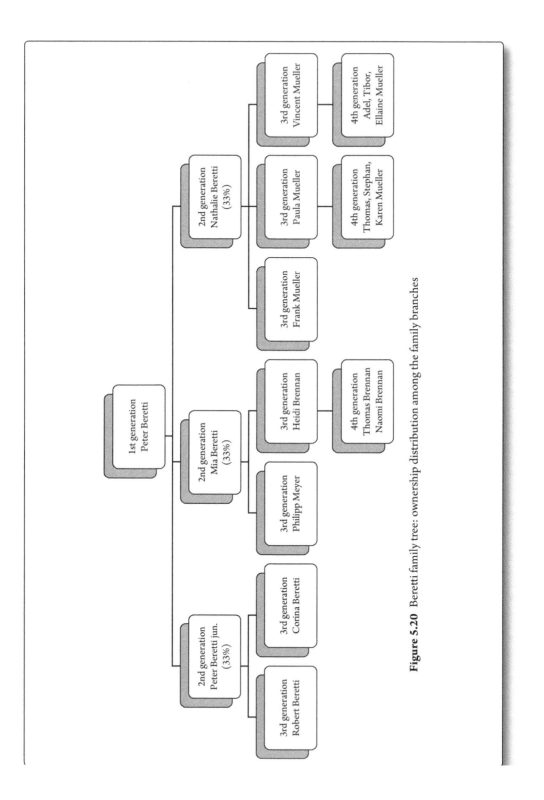

Figure 5.20 Beretti family tree: ownership distribution among the family branches

CASE STUDY *(continued)*

which they saw as final and binding for all shareholders. Frustrated by these developments, other family members suggested establishing governance bodies so that the discussion and ultimately the decision-making processes could be structured in a meaningful way. The question was, what type of governance bodies?

The family's challenges were brought to the fore when the Berettis finally decided that one family representative should replace Robert Beretti on the supervisory board. There were two candidates from the family. The first was Robert Beretti's wife Julia, a 50-year-old human resources consultant. Robert and Julia Beretti have no children. The second candidate was Tibor Mueller, a private equity consultant from the fourth family generation. The family hired an executive search firm to determine which of the candidates was best suited for the supervisory board job, and the search firm suggested that Julia was the most competent. Unfortunately, however, the Mia and Nathalie Beretti family branches were unwilling to support Julia. They argued: 'It's time for the other two family branches to have some involvement too.' Finally, Tibor Mueller was elected to the supervisory board.

 REFLECTION QUESTIONS

You are called by Robert Beretti to help the family navigate the challenges related to these family governance issues. After a long conversation with Robert and a nonfamily supervisory board member, you decide that you need to answer the following questions:

1. What should the election process of the supervisory board look like? More specifically, what do you think of the two camps' suggestions?
2. What is your advice concerning the election of the CEO? Who should become CEO, and what are the advantages and disadvantages of the proposed solutions?
3. What governance bodies are needed, and what should their respective responsibilities be?
4. How should the family organize the process of building a better governance structure to ensure that the outcome is supported by the family shareholders involved?

CASE STUDY

Family venture fund in a Colombian business family

The owning family of a large multi-divisional family firm in Colombia decided to set up what it called the 'Seed Fund'. This fund was established for two reasons: (1) to fuel new entrepreneurial ideas for the current business operations, and (2) to help next-generation family members start their own entrepreneurial careers. In establishing the seed fund, the family defined the following objectives:

CASE STUDY *(continued)*

- Promote the development of new, independent companies by family members.
- Establish next-generation family members' entrepreneurial credibility with family, employees, customers, suppliers and other parties.
- Build entrepreneurs' self-esteem.
- Develop skills and allow experiences.

The fund is structured in the form of an irrevocable and sustainable revolving trust. The management of the trust is given to a group of three investment bankers, all nonfamily members, who have no other role in the family's or the firm's governance. Family members are entitled to propose a business plan to this committee and may receive a loan of up to $70 000 per business idea. The three trustees decide on the approval of the loans, which are to be paid back with an interest rate that is roughly 50% below the market rate. The seed fund supports business ideas exclusively; it does not support family members' education or any other nonbusiness-related activity.

The performance of the loans is monitored by a bank and by the three trustees. Once a year, the family council meets with the trustees; at this meeting, the council receives an overall report on the trust, but no details about the individual loans or companies.

Over the years, the seed fund has helped to start up multiple new businesses in the retail, restaurant, agriculture, industrial production and auto repair industries, all of which are controlled by family members.

 REFLECTION QUESTIONS

1. What are the pros and cons of setting up such a seed fund?
2. Why is the seed fund not directly monitored by the family council?
3. Under which legal and cultural conditions might such a family seed fund be particularly successful?

? **REFLECTION QUESTIONS**

1. What are the four typical agency problems in family firms?
2. What are the central domains of family, ownership, corporate and wealth governance?
3. Explain the dynamic evolution of governance regulations in a family firm that moves successively through the following stages of corporate governance: owner-manager, sibling partnership, cousin consortium and, finally, family enterprise.
4. Provide an example of how family governance problems may trickle down to the ownership level and finally impact the managerial level.
5. Some family firms apply a branch structure to their decision making. For instance, when selecting family members for the board of directors, they give each branch of the family tree the opportunity to appoint one person to the board. What are the potential advantages and disadvantages of this structure?

6. What are the advantages and disadvantages for next-generation family members when entering the family business at the shop floor, and what are the advantages and disadvantages of entering in a top management position?

7. Should in-laws be included in ownership, or should they be excluded? Why?

8. What are the pros and cons of placing family wealth in a trust or foundation?

9. Over the last few years, Miller Ltd., a private manufacturing company, has grown significantly. The nonfamily CEO and CFO approach the family owners regarding the possibility of setting up a share compensation scheme for the nonfamily top managers. As a family owner, what advantages and disadvantages do you see in this proposal?

10. What is the overarching goal of setting up a family charter?

11. Please describe the typical content of a family charter.

12. A business-owning family with multiple members owning a small portfolio of companies and assets approaches you because of your expertise in family governance. You are asked to advise the family in developing a family charter. How would you approach the task? Please lay out a process model about how you would work with the family toward completing the charter. And what are the issues to be addressed in the charter?

NOTES

1 I am indebted to David Bentall, University of British Columbia, for some of these examples.

2 The percentage indications refer to the cash flow rights, which in this case are equal to the voting rights. For further information refer to Amit et al. (2015).

3 Germany's two-tier board system requires equal representation of owners and employees on the board of directors. See, for example, the discussion of Haniel in section 5.10.

4 For a helpful discussion of the disadvantages of shotgun clauses, see the Wikipedia entry on 'Shotgun clause' (accessed December 19, 2014).

5 Even though family charters and therein family ownership regulations may appear not to be legally binding, it seems interesting to see how a court would decide about this question.

6 This example is taken from Au and Cheng (2011).

7 Think, for instance, of the illustrious '*Consigliere*' in Mafia movies.

8 For example, in the United States, under the Dodd–Frank Wall Street Reform and Consumer Protection Act family offices are exempt from various reporting and regulatory obligations that apply to banks and other asset managers (the so-called Private Adviser Exemption of the US Investment Advisers Act of 1940).

9 The following descriptions of the four governance constellations are taken from Zellweger and Kammerlander (2015).

10 The services are ordered in declining relevance for European single-family offices. In the United States, philanthropy tends to have a more prominent role, while in many Asian family offices philanthropy plays a minor role.

11 Note, however, that these estimates exclude asset management fees and other costs charged directly to family members' investment portfolios.

12 On the cost structure of family offices, see Rosplock (2013) and the study by the Boston Consulting Group (2013).

13 Family constitution and family charter can be used synonymously.

 BACKGROUND READING

Amit, R., Y. Ding, B. Villalonga and H. Zhang (2015). The role of institutional development in the prevalence and performance of entrepreneur and family-controlled firms. *Journal of Corporate Finance*, 31: 284–305.

Amit, R., H. Liechtenstein, M. J. Prats, T. Millay and L. P. Pendleton (2008). *Single Family Offices: Private Wealth Management in the Family Context*. Research report. Philadelphia, PA: Wharton School.

Au, K., and C. Y. J. Cheng (2011). Creating 'the new' through portfolio entrepreneurship. In P. Sieger, R. Nason, P. Sharma and T. Zellweger (Eds.), *The Global STEP Booklet, Volume I: Evidence-based, Practical Insights for Enterprising Families*. Babson College, 17–21.

Bertrand, M., S. Johnson, K. Samphantharak and A. Schoar (2003). Mixing family with business: A study of Thai business groups and the families behind them. *Journal of Financial Economics*, 88 (3): 466–498.

Carlock, R. S., and J. L. Ward (2010). *When Family Businesses Are Best: The Parallel Planning Process for Family Harmony and Business Success*. Basingstoke, UK: Palgrave Macmillan.

Carney, M., E. R. Gedajlovic, P. Heugens, M. Van Essen and J. Van Oosterhout (2011). Business group affiliation, performance, context, and strategy: A meta-analysis. *Academy of Management Journal*, 54 (3): 437–460.

Carney, M., E. Gedajlovic and V. Strike (2014). Dead money: Inheritance law and the longevity of family firms. *Entrepreneurship Theory and Practice*, 38 (6): 1261–1283.

Carney, R.W., and T.B. Child (2013). Changes to the ownership and control of East Asian corporations between 1996 and 2008: The primacy of politics. *Journal of Financial Economics*, 107: 494–513.

Claessens, S., S. Djankov, J. P. H. Fan and L. H. P. Lang (2002). Disentangling the incentive and entrenchment effects of large shareholdings. *Journal of Finance*, LVII (6): 2741–2771.

Colli, A. (2003). *The History of Family Business, 1850–2000*. Cambridge: Cambridge University Press.

Flanagan, J., S. Hamilton, D. Lincoln, A. Nichols, L. Ottum and J. Weber (2011). *Taking Care of Business: Case Examples of Separating Personal Wealth Management from the Family Business*. London: Family Office Exchange (FOX).

Franks, J., C. Mayer, P. Volpin and H. F. Wagner (2012). The life cycle of family ownership: International evidence. *Review of Financial Studies*, 25 (6): 1675–1712.

Hughes, J. E. (2004). *Family Wealth—Keeping It in the Family*. New York: Bloomberg Press.

Koeberle-Schmid, A., D. Kenyon-Rouvinez and E. J. Poza (2014). *Governance in Family Enterprises*. New York: Palgrave Macmillan.

Montemerlo, D., and J. Ward (2010). *The Family Constitution: Agreements to Secure and Perpetuate Your Family and Your Business*. New York: Palgrave Macmillan.

Morck, R., and B. Yeung (2003). Agency problems in large family business groups. *Entrepreneurship Theory and Practice*, 27 (4): 367–382.

Rosplock, K. (2013). *The Complete Family Office Handbook: A Guide for Affluent Families and the Advisors Who Serve Them*. New York: Bloomberg Financial.

Schulze, W. S., M. H. Lubatkin, R. N. Dino and A. K. Buchholtz (2001). Agency relationships in family firms: Theory and evidence. *Organization Science*, 12 (2): 99–116.

Schulze, W., and T. Zellweger (2016). On the agency costs of owner-management: The problem of holdup. Working paper, University of Utah and University of St. Gallen.

Sitkoff, R. H. (2004). An agency costs theory of trust law. *Cornell Law Review*, 69: 621–684.

Strike, V. M. (2013). The most trusted advisor and the subtle advice process in family firms. *Family Business Review*, 26 (3): 293–313.

Ward, J., and C. Aronoff (2010). *Family Business Governance: Maximizing Family and Business Potential*. New York: Palgrave Macmillan.

Zellweger, T., and N. Kammerlander (2015). Family, wealth, and governance: An agency account. *Entrepreneurship Theory and Practice*, 39 (6): 1281–1303.

6

Strategic management in the family business

How much does the issue of strategic management in family firms really matter? That is to say, is it something that researchers and practitioners need to address? To find out, we can ask if the following two conditions apply: first, if strategic decision making in family firms differs from that of non-family firms, and second, if family firms differ from nonfamily firms in the origins and ultimately also levels of their competitive advantage. The present chapter is dedicated to these two questions.

We will start out with some observations about strategic decision making in family firms. More specifically, in the first part of this chapter, we will explore how the particular goals of controlling families impact the strategic decision making of family firms. In the second part of the chapter we will examine several concepts to explain sources of competitive advantage and disadvantage for family firms.

6.1 Strategic decision making in family firms

It is a central observation of many family business practitioners and researchers that family firms pursue nonfinancial goals alongside financial ones. In fact, this particular feature has even been considered to be a defining element of family firms (Chua, Chrisman and Sharma 1999). However, the question of what firms' nonfinancial goals actually *are* remains contested. Also, while many argue that these goals matter for strategic decision making and ultimately for a family firm's success, more insight is needed into *how* these nonfinancial goals alter strategic decision making.

6.1.1 Socioemotional wealth (SEW)

Over the years, many researchers have tried to unravel the nature of family firms' nonfinancial goals. In today's scholarship, 'socioemotional wealth' (SEW) is widely used as an umbrella term to describe the phenomenon of

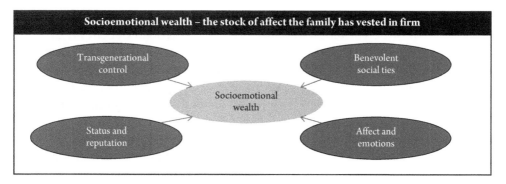

Figure 6.1 Dimensions of SEW

nonfinancial goals in family firms. SEW is defined as the total stock of affect that the family has vested in the firm (Gomez-Mejia et al. 2007). Ultimately, this boils down to the idea of the family's emotional attachment to the firm, which is similar to the concept of 'emotional value' (Zellweger and Astrachan 2008).

SEW is said to consist of four distinct dimensions, each of which captures a specific aspect of the nonfinancial value that family business owners derive from being in control of the company (Figure 6.1).

1. **Transgenerational control**
    Transgenerational control captures the utility a family has by controlling the firm with the intent to pass it on to future family generations. First and foremost this implies that the current family owners value the opportunity to pass the firm on to their descendants. For multi-generation family firms, however, emotional attachment may also derive from the family's entrepreneurial tradition of controlling the company. Transgenerational control allows family business owners to keep a cherished asset in family hands across generations and hence to establish a family legacy. Note that this form of control is distinct from long-term control per se. Although transgenerational control implicitly emphasizes a long-term perspective, it is the long-term control *in the hands of the family across generations* that makes this a unique feature and a source of perceived value.
2. **Benevolent social ties**
    Benevolent social ties capture the degree to which members of controlling families value relationships with individuals characterized by goodwill, mutual support, benevolence and loyalty. Benevolent social ties represent a humane way of interaction that stands in contrast to the

cold, contractual logic in which relationships are maintained only if they provide a material return over a short period of time (Berrone, Cruz and Gomez-Mejia 2012). They emphasize the importance of the long term, the practice of referrals, and mutual support. Actors who nurture benevolent social ties are not necessarily selfless people or pure altruists. But they do tend to think that results are best in the long run for all parties involved, including themselves, when actors are mutually supportive— even if one party incurs some disadvantages in the short run, such as when a favor is not returned immediately. Benevolent social ties are often associated with healthy relationships observed within families. But these ties may also reach beyond the family sphere, for example to long-term employees, customers, suppliers or other business partners.

3. **Identity and reputation**

    Identity and reputation, the third dimension of SEW, captures the degree to which the controlling family extracts value from identifying or being identified with the firm. For instance, in a local context, a person's social standing may be elevated by his or her affiliation with the family that controls a certain firm. This may be particularly true if the firm supports social or philanthropic activities or if the firm is a significant employer in the region. Over time, the controlling family may benefit from the reputation of the firm as an important and respected actor in the community. Of course, the intertwined nature of family and firm identity is a double-edged sword. For instance, if the firm is publicly accused of financial or ethical misbehavior, the family's reputation suffers. When the firm is well regarded, however, the family benefits. This effect should be particularly strong in cases where the family and firm share one name.

    We should note here that the positive and negative effects on reputation may serve not only as a source of perceived SEW for the family, but also as a sanctioning mechanism that pushes the family firm to comply with certain ethical standards. We will explore this issue in more detail in our discussion of the sources of competitive advantage for family firms.

4. **Emotions and affect**

    Family business owners may derive nonfinancial value from the pleasant emotions or affect they experience because of their association with the firm. For instance, family business owners may feel deeply satisfied by their connection to the firm and by their efforts to help it grow. This connection may also induce moments of pride and happiness. The family business owner's association with the firm and with the family's entrepreneurial activities in general leads to a level of affect that is absent among nonfamily owners. In this light, the firm is a cherished possession to which the owners affectively commit.

It is unlikely that the four dimensions of SEW are completely independent from each other. For instance, a positive reputation likely coincides with positive feelings. At the same time, however, it is conceivable that a family could value transgenerational control but experience few benevolent social ties (e.g., if the firm had to downsize its local workforce). This possibility shows that it is not unproblematic to lump all four dimensions of SEW together into a single score. Despite some important recent critique (see, for instance, Schulze and Kellermanns 2015; Chua, Chrisman and De Massis 2015; Miller and Le Breton-Miller 2014[1]), at this stage, SEW is a useful umbrella concept that can help us understand the strategic preferences of family firms and their root causes.

The *preservation* (and less so the increase) of SEW is an essential concern of family firms. This fact is important for our understanding of family firms' strategic decision making. In economic terms, SEW is one of the main reference points for family owners, next to financial wealth concerns, and, by extension, for their firms' strategic decisions. The attractiveness of a decision thus partly depends on its impact on SEW: all other things being equal, the more negative the impact of a decision for SEW, the less attractive the decision will appear. Family firms are only willing to accept losses in SEW and engage in actions that detract from it if (1) the firm and/or its owners are compensated in a way that is commensurate with the perceived loss in SEW, such as when a decision is highly attractive from a financial standpoint, or (2) the course of action is required to save the firm, which is itself the source of all SEW and financial wealth. It is typically understood that the pursuit of nonfinancial goals in the form of SEW normally detracts from financial goals: hence, there is an assumed *tradeoff* between the pursuit of financial wealth and the preservation of SEW.[2]

6.1.2 Distinctiveness of financial and socioemotional viewpoints

Prominent family business research suggests that family firms care for both financial goals (maximization of financial wealth) and socioemotional goals (preservation of SEW). When family firms must prioritize one goal over the other, however, socioemotional considerations often trump financial ones (e.g., Gomez-Mejia et al. 2007). To understand the peculiarity of strategic decision making in family firms, we must clearly distinguish between the financial and socioemotional points of view.

From a purely financial viewpoint, firms should try to improve their status by maximizing the financial wealth of the owners. Managers who assess whether they should undertake a certain action should evaluate the impact of their decision on the shareholders' future financial wealth. In this assessment, actors should be completely rational, as they have access to all relevant information; that is, they should focus on the maximum expected return given the associated risks. From this point of view, taking risks is considered desirable as risks are compensated at adequate returns.

The socioemotional viewpoint differs from this perspective in fundamental ways. The actor who takes the socioemotional point of view strives to preserve the family's current endowment of SEW. Instead of maximizing financial performance, he or she 'satisfices': that is, the actor aims to achieve a level of financial performance that is sufficient in light of the actor's particular aspiration level for the performance of the firm (Cyert and March 1963). That aspiration level is likely to be determined by the minimum financial performance the firm needs to achieve in order to secure the continued pursuit of SEW. Thus, family firm owners and managers may ask: to preserve our family's current SEW—for instance, to ensure that the firm remains under family control in the future—what performance level do we need to achieve? These actors will be guided not by their expectations of some (uncertain) future financial return, but by their experience with the effort needed to preserve the status quo.

Note that financial performance matters from both points of view. An actor who prioritizes SEW understands that this wealth is dependent upon the long-term survival of the firm, which in turn depends upon financial performance. But while for the financially motivated actor financial performance is the relevant output measure, for the socioemotionally motivated actor it is an input measure. He/she will see financial performance as an indicator of whether the firm's activities are meeting the level needed to secure his or her nonfinancial goals. The actor's perspective on financial performance is related to his or her appetite for risk taking, which is high under the financial regime (risks lead to higher expected financial returns) and low under the SEW regime. Under the SEW regime, actors are risk averse because, all other things being equal, risk threatens the status quo and hence detracts from SEW. The two opposing views are represented in Table 6.1.

While the above considerations shed some light on decision making at the individual or family level, the implications for strategic preferences at the firm level are significant. For example, take human resource practices: the financial viewpoint would emphasize selection based purely on the technical qualifications of the candidate, without regard to whether that candidate is internal or external. The SEW viewpoint, which emphasizes seniority and experience with the firm and relational ties, would value the internal candi-

Table 6.1 Guiding principles of the financial and socioemotional viewpoints

	Financial viewpoint	Socioemotional viewpoint
Mode of action	Status improving	Status preserving
Wealth focus	Prospective financial wealth	Current SEW
Informational role of financial performance	Output	Input
Theme of choice	Maximizing	Satisficing
Rationality of actors	Rational	Boundedly rational
Dimensions relevant for choice	Achievable performance given associated risk	Performance needed to preserve status quo
Basis for choice	Expectations about future opportunities	Experience with past achievements
Incentive to take risks	High	Low

date more. From this point of view, an internal candidate is more valuable because he or she presumably knows the firm well, fits into its culture, and has earned some amount of trust from other people in the firm. Over time, he or she gains more trust, experience and merit and moves up in the firm's hierarchy. Compensation at a firm with an SEW viewpoint is more likely to be fixed and equal among managers, as individual performance is balanced against collective performance and salary levels. The decision-making style may also be different under the SEW regime. For example, actors who emphasize SEW will prefer to compromise, save face and maintain harmony rather than initiate confrontation.

The SEW viewpoint has significant implications for strategy at the corporate level. Diversification is seen as detrimental for SEW as it waters down a firm's image and reputation, limits identification opportunities for the family, dilutes the attention a manager can give to previously close relationships, requires more diverse expertise and reduces the value of a single historic activity and related knowledge base inside the family and firm. A similar logic applies to internationalization, which tends to be viewed critically because it detracts from the firm's local roots and requires an engagement with cultures and people that the firm is less familiar with. In general, under an SEW point of view, people will generally try to 'stick to their knitting'.

6.1.3 How SEW impacts strategic decision making: a framework

In sum, we can conclude that nonfinancial goals as reflected in SEW have a profound impact on strategic decision making in family firms. Taking into

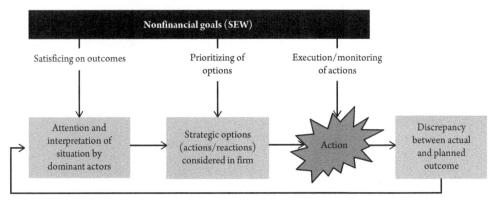

Source: Adapted from Kammerlander and Ganter (2015) and Ocasio (1997).

Figure 6.2 How SEW impacts the strategic decision-making process

consideration a typical decision-making process, we expect SEW to bias the prioritization of strategic options, the execution and monitoring of the resulting actions and, finally, the interpretation of outcomes from these actions (see Figure 6.2).

The SEW regime thus alters priorities in relation to the strategic options to be considered in at least three important ways. First, it favors options that preserve SEW even if this means that financial wealth will not be maximized. Second, SEW is likely to change the ways in which actions are executed and monitored. SEW should lead to a preference for incremental and subtle change and a close monitoring of the consequences of the actions undertaken. Third, once the outcomes of the actions become clear, actors will examine the discrepancy between the aspirational and the actual outcomes. For this part of the decision-making process, SEW should induce actors to satisfice; that is, they will try to achieve a financial outcome that is sufficient for the continued pursuit of SEW. If actual performance does not meet aspirations, family firms will engage in change; however, if actual performance exceeds aspirations, the firm may see no need to take action.

6.1.4 Some evidence of SEW in family firm behavior

Do family firms really behave according to the predictions of the SEW framework? Evidence from various studies of both private and public family firms suggests that, all else being equal, SEW is indeed a critical reference point for family firms. For instance, we find that:

1. Family firms are less diversified than nonfamily firms, even though their owners with concentrated wealth positions would benefit from diversification to reduce portfolio risk (Anderson and Reeb 2003a).
2. Family ownership is negatively related to investments in research and development (R&D), even though family firms would normally benefit from such investment (Chrisman and Patel 2012).
3. Family firms are less likely to engage in divestments, even though they would benefit from the expected positive performance effects of doing so (Feldman, Amit and Villalonga 2016).
4. Family firms prefer to stay independent, even though choosing another organizational form (such as joining a cooperative) would reduce business risk (Gomez-Mejia et al. 2007).
5. Family firm owners tend to overestimate the financial value of their firms in case they wish to pass on the firm to future family generations (Zellweger et al. 2012).

These represent just a few of the many studies that lend support to the idea that family firms consider SEW as their main point of reference, with significant impact on the strategic management of the organization.

6.1.5 Preference reversal under vulnerability

Despite the overall prevalence of the SEW viewpoint, family firms may be willing to give priority to the financial viewpoint and accept SEW losses under certain conditions. For instance, in the above-mentioned studies researchers have found that when family firms and their owners become vulnerable they may be inclined to diversify, invest in R&D, engage in divestment and alter their organizational form. Vulnerability leads family firms to reverse their usual preferences and pursue more standard economic strategies. The nature of family firm vulnerability may take various forms, such as when

- firm performance declines, threatening the survival of the firm as a whole;
- the firm possesses low levels of slack (unused) resources that would help buffer against business risks; or
- there is public pressure (such as media pressure) to apply more standard economic decision-making criteria.

Under these circumstances, family firms may be brought to engage in change, face economic facts and take significant risks to alter and improve their situation. The idea of preference reversal under one type of vulnerability cue,

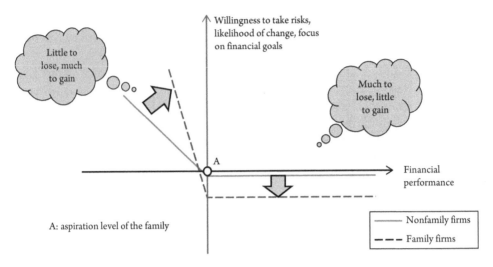

Figure 6.3 Preference reversal under threat

decreasing performance, is depicted in Figure 6.3. We find that if things go well and performance exceeds the aspiration level (often conceptualized as the difference in the firm's current performance in comparison to its past performance, or in comparison to the current performance of competitors), there is very little willingness to change. Actual performance at aspiration level signals to the family owners that SEW is secure. When performance deteriorates, however, family owners experience a growing sense of urgency, as SEW as well as money may be at stake. Family firms under threat exhibit a heightened propensity for change and risk taking. Fearing the loss of the complete 'family silver', family firms are willing to take significant risk to reverse the undesired situation.

Given the behavior of family firms facing vulnerability, it would be an oversimplification to conclude that family firms are risk averse in general. It is true that family firms are less inclined to take risks under low vulnerability, such as when performance exceeds the aspiration level, because taking risks endangers SEW. When performance exceeds the aspiration level (to the right of point A in Figure 6.3), there is little to gain but much to lose from taking risks. But when the firm is under threat (to the left of point A in Figure 6.3), this preference reverses and the financial viewpoint is given priority; now, there is little to lose and much to gain. Family firms under threat switch to an emergency mode of action and take significant risks.

CASE STUDY

Henkel's Genthin plant

Henkel is a publicly listed German family firm with roots that go back to 1876. The company operates worldwide with leading brands and technologies in three business areas: laundry and home care, beauty care and adhesive technologies. Henkel holds globally leading market positions in both consumer and industrial businesses with well-known brands such as Persil, Schwarzkopf and Loctite. Headquartered in Düsseldorf, the firm employs around 47 000 people worldwide.

In the firm's history, the production site of Genthin has a special place. The company's founder, Fritz Henkel, built the site in 1921–22. In 1923, the first Persil detergent, today one of the firm's top consumer brands, rolled off the production belts. In 1944, the site had a production capacity of 160 000 tons per year. In 1945, however, the Genthin site was expropriated from Henkel by the Soviet military, and in 1949 it became a state-owned production facility under the control of the German Democratic Republic (East Germany). Following the reunification of East and West Germany in 1989, Henkel reacquired the Genthin site in 1990. At the time of this reacquisition, the family owners were well aware of the historic significance of the Genthin plant. Family members had even heard that there was still furniture on the site engraved with Fritz Henkel's name. In subsequent years, Henkel invested a significant amount of capital in the site to renew the production facilities and make them profitable. However, the plan failed despite ongoing attempts to bring the site up to speed. After years of significant losses, the site was closed in 2009 and some remaining assets were sold.

 REFLECTION QUESTIONS

- Where do you see evidence of SEW considerations in the story of Henkel's Genthin plant?

Summing up, we have seen that SEW serves as an umbrella term for a controlling family's nonfinancial goals. SEW serves as a reference point for family business owners and is composed of four distinct drivers: transgenerational control, benevolent social ties, identity and reputation, and emotions and affect. In general, family firms seek to preserve their current SEW endowments, even if this may partly detract from financial performance. At a strategic level, the preservation of SEW leads family firms to avoid actions that threaten SEW, such as diversification, divestments and downsizing. The pursuit of SEW generally leads to risk aversion at the firm level. However, when a family firm is under threat, its owners become willing to take massive risks to save the firm, since the firm is of course the source of all financial wealth and SEW.

6.2 Conceptualizing the competitive advantage of family firms

The SEW perspective is undoubtedly useful in explaining family firms' strategic preferences, especially when it comes to their seemingly irrational behavior. The same perspective, thus far at least, has not been very helpful in explaining the variance in the competitive advantage and disadvantage and ultimately the performance of family firms. Large-scale empirical studies find important variance in performance among family firms (Carney et al. 2015; Gedajlovic et al. 2011). For instance, Anderson and Reeb (2003b) found that family firms outperform nonfamily firms quoted on the US stock market. Later studies found that public family firms outperform nonfamily firms only in cases when the founder is still the CEO or when the founder is chairman and works with a hired CEO (Villalonga and Amit 2006). Still other studies suggest that what really matters for family firm performance is whether the founder has to deal with his/her relatives or not, and that in many cases lone founder firms are the ones that outperform (Miller et al. 2007).

Many of the family business performance studies that have been conducted around the world find that family firms not only perform well but also frequently outperform nonfamily firms (for a review of family business performance studies, see Amit and Villalonga 2013). However, the positive view of the family form of governance is not universal; some argue that family managers and owners who are securely entrenched in their positions may withhold effort, or that they tend to expropriate organizational stakeholders (e.g., minority owners) via the consumption of private benefits of control. Still others suggest that family firms exhibit resource constraints, for instance when it comes to access to financial capital, which hampers growth.

Overall, the link between family influence and firm performance is a highly contested one. In light of the confusion around this issue, it may be helpful to take a step back from the approach that directly compares family and nonfamily firm performance and ask the following questions instead:

1. To what degree is family influence good for firm performance? (*degree perspective*).
2. Under what conditions is family influence good for firm performance? (*contingency perspective*).
3. What organizational processes drive family firm performance? (*process perspective*).

The *degree perspective* assumes that family influence is not good or bad per se. Rather, this perspective assumes that family influence unfolds as a force for good up to a certain level of family influence. Beyond that threshold level negative effects materialize that hamper performance. Proponents of this view argue that at low levels of family influence performance suffers, as the family may be either unable to monitor selfish managers or unwilling to provide valuable resources to the firm. Above a certain inflection point, however, performance suffers, as the family limits access to external capital and expertise and views the firm not necessarily as an engine for wealth creation but as a vehicle for familial self-enhancement, in both financial and nonfinancial terms.

In contrast, the *contingency view* asks: under what conditions do family firms outperform? This point of view looks for contextual and organizational factors that either strengthen or weaken the link between family influence and performance. For instance, we might examine the institutional variables at the societal level, such as the protection of minority owners, the availability of financial and human capital in public markets, law enforcement and overall economic development. The contingency perspective assumes that family firms are particularly successful under certain institutional regimes (e.g., under weak institutional settings where they are able to fill institutional 'voids') (Khanna and Palepu 2000). Next to these societal-level contingency variables, at the organizational level we might consider the presence or absence of control-enhancing mechanisms (such as dual-class shares or pyramid structures), the independence of the board of directors from the family, or the presence or absence of the founder.

Finally, the *process view* tries to open the black box between family influence and firm performance and asks what particular organizational processes family firms put in place to compete. A prominent view here is the resource-based view, which argues that family firms possess a unique set of resources and capabilities given the interaction with the family (e.g., Habbershon and Williams 1999; Sirmon and Hitt 2003). Another conduit through which family influence drives performance is the ability to enact nonconforming strategies, as family control provides firms with wide latitude to pursue, for example, long-term as opposed to short-term goals (e.g., Carney 2005; Zellweger 2007). Still other scholars argue that the competitiveness of family firms can be linked to their ability to accommodate and harness synergies between seemingly competing forces, such as those between family and business, tradition and innovation, or exploitation and exploration (e.g., Schuman, Stutz and Ward 2010; Stewart and Hitt 2010). In addition, the view of identification and brand building as a further source of competitive advantage falls within the process perspective. Family firms reap performance advantages via high levels of identification among family as well as nonfamily members, such as long-term employees, the wider stakeholder community in general, and customers in particular (e.g., Dyer and Whetten 2006; Miller and Le Breton-Miller 2005; Zellweger, Eddleston and Kellermanns 2010). The process view also encompasses the idea that family firms may have certain advantages when it comes to innovation. Family firms may have strong explicit and, in particular, implicit knowledge about specific organizational or production processes. These firms embrace innovation later than their nonfamily counterparts. Once the innovation is agreed upon, however, they adopt it more quickly and with more stamina (Koenig, Kammerlander and Enders 2013).

In the following section, we will zoom in on the most prominent arguments to shed further light on the elusive link between family influence and competitive advantage, thereby putting particular emphasis on the process and contingency perspectives addressed above. We will look specifically at the agency, resource-based, organizational identity, institutional and paradox-management arguments.

6.3 The agency perspective

The agency perspective is one of the approaches most often used to explain the competitiveness of family firms. In fact, the family business literature has both actively used the agency view and contributed to its advancement. Agency theory is primarily concerned with the efficient governance of the firm, and therein in particular with the collaboration between owners and managers. What is called 'principal–agent agency costs' are the costs that arise for owners if they wish to ensure that managers act in the owners' interests. Agency theory has been progressively expanded to explore other types of governance relationships, notably the one between majority and minority owners but also between the owners and the lenders of debt capital. Today, this theory would make the following predictions about the efficient governance of family firms.

6.3.1 Aligned interests of family owners and family managers

Traditionally, family firms are said to have low principal–agent agency costs. This argument is rooted in two assumptions about the governance of family firms: first, in many family firms owners are also managers (i.e., owner-managed family firms), whereby the interests of owners and managers are naturally aligned. Those who own the company also manage it, which makes expensive monitoring and incentive schemes unnecessary. Second, even when owners and managers are not the same people but belong to the same family (e.g., when parents are owners and children are managers), the trust, benevolence and information exchange that is unique to family relationships should align their interests and again make control and incentive systems unnecessary.

Given these two mechanisms, family firms that have family members in both ownership and management positions should have a natural competitive advantage. Family firms should outperform nonfamily firms because they can spare themselves expensive monitoring of and incentive compensation for the managers. Consequently, practitioners seeking levers to improve performance in such firms should ask:

- Is there a trusting atmosphere that ensures that the interests of family members in ownership and management will be aligned?

6.3.2 Misaligned interests of family owners and family managers

The positive view discussed above is contested by scholars who take a closer look at the nature of family relationships. Qualifying the standard agency assumption, Schulze and colleagues contend that when owners and managers are family members, family firms suffer from distinct agency problems that are rooted in altruism (Schulze et al. 2001). It is argued that altruism may undermine the efficient cooperation of family members involved in ownership and management. In the first place, altruism compels parents to care for their children. But even though altruism fosters trust and mutual support, children (or other family members) who benefit from (parental) altruism may have an incentive to free ride and shirk their duties. Such free riding and shirking occurs because parents are hesitant to monitor and sanction their children (or other close relatives) for their misconduct, for example by reducing their salary or firing them for underperformance ('I cannot fire my kid'). Doing so would harm the parents' family relationships.

Because altruism also biases parental perceptions ('My kids are such hard workers!' or 'My kids are so smart!'), family members are likely to appoint managers because of family ties and not performance-based criteria, a phenomenon which has been labeled adverse selection.

This view challenges the standard agency view, which assumes that family owned and managed firms should benefit from increased performance.

Rather, the performance of family firms may suffer as a consequence of altruism-induced agency costs. Therefore, even in family firms it should become necessary to install a monitoring and incentive alignment mechanism between family owners and family agents, which depresses the performance of the firm.

Thus, when the family is involved in both ownership and management, practitioners seeking levers to improve firm performance should ask:

- While altruism is an important aspect of familial relationships, does it undermine the professional working relationship between family members engaged in the firm?
- Are children free riding on the goodwill of parents?
- Are parents free riding on the goodwill of children?
- Do we appoint managers really based on their capabilities or based on family ties?
- Do we have to put in place some sort of monitoring and incentive scheme (e.g., performance-based pay, stock ownership plan) for family members working in the firm?

6.3.3 Family owners harming nonfamily managers

As already alluded to in Chapter 5 on governance, family firms experience efficiency losses that are linked to problems with regard to the hiring, retention and motivation of skilled nonfamily managers. This is because the nonfamily managers sooner or later will understand that this firm is ultimately a family affair, whereby the family who is in firm control of ownership retains full discretion about how it runs the firm. Indeed, since only the owners can control the owners in a firm, the controlling family is completely free to run the firm according to its own preferences, in very particularistic, even unprofessional ways. The nonfamily managers, either before or after signing an employment contract with the family firm, will come to understand that—to some degree at least—the family firm remains a two-class organization. As a nonfamily manager you will always be at the mercy of the family owners, who can change their minds, not hold promises or unilaterally exploit the managers once they have made investments in the employer, such as when the employee has developed skills that are less valuable outside the firm, or once he has bought a house in the neighborhood of the employer for instance. Such owner holdup (Schulze and Zellweger 2016) does not always happen out of opportunism by the owner to exploit the dependent employees/managers but may also take place because of honest disagreement about the interpretation of ambiguous information.

The consequence of owner holdup is that family firms will find it difficult to *attract* and *retain* highly skilled managers, and *motivate* their employees to go the extra mile and commit beyond what is required. Solving these threats is not easy because the family owners have to impose limits on their own discretion. In practice, family business owners 'tie their hands' by appointing powerful boards, tying their personal reputation to the one of the firm, by openly committing to certain value systems, religious beliefs or management styles, or by having to pay high fixed salaries to attract and retain top talent.

Thus, when considering the threat of owner holdup which hampers the hiring, retention and motivation of skilled nonfamily managers, practitioners seeking levers to improve firm performance should ask:

- Do we run our firm applying professional management practices?
- Do we keep our promises vis-à-vis our employees?
- How do we make sure that managers can have a career in our firm?
- How do we make sure that our firm is seen as a great place to work?

6.3.4 Family owners monitoring nonfamily managers

Families tend to own controlling stakes in their firms and to control those firms rather tightly. In many cases, the family holds a majority if not 100% ownership stake. In publicly listed firms, a significant but lower than 50% ownership stake can be enough to determine the fate of the firm. In addition, in most cases the family's ownership in the firm represents the lion's share of that family's wealth. Family owners are thus block owners with an undiversified wealth position that is tied to the firm(s) they operate. In consequence, they have the power as well as the financial incentive to curb self-serving behavior by managers—what has been called the 'monitor in place' argument. Thus, in cases when the family holds a controlling ownership stake but is not involved in management, practitioners seeking levers to improve firm performance should ask:

- How tight is the control of the family over the firm?
- Do we have access to all information about the firm?
- As owners, are we in the position to challenge the views of the management and to dismiss unsatisfactory managers?
- As owners, do we have the necessary skills to assess strategic decisions in the firm?
- How do we incentivize our managers?
- How do we avoid excessive risk taking by managers?

6.3.5 Family owners expropriating nonfamily minority owners

Family blockholders may not always behave in a way that maximizes the wealth of all shareholders. In fact, they may expropriate nonfamily minority owners in various ways. Family blockholders may extract private benefits from the firm, such as when the firm pays for private expenses of its family owners. They may force the firm to engage in activities that serve the financial interests of the family, such as making transactions with other firms controlled by the family at unfavorable prices for the firm in which the family is not sole owner. The family may enforce a dual-class share scheme, which limits the influence of nonfamily owners. Similarly, the firm may be forced to engage in the family's pet projects, which contribute to the family's social status but reduce financial performance. What these measures all have in common is that they are valuable to family owners but costly to nonfamily owners. Given their high degree of control, family block owners thus take other owners 'hostage'. These agency conflicts are called principal–principal conflicts or agency conflicts between majority and minority owners, and have been found to significantly depress firm value (Claessens et al. 2002). The conditions of such agency conflict suggest that concentrated family ownership—that is, family block ownership—should be bad for firm performance.

Certainly, private benefits of control will be bad for the nonfamily owners, and eventually other stakeholders, such as creditors of the firm. These nonfamily stakeholders may, however, be willing to accept some level of private benefits of control extracted by the family, in exchange for the proper monitoring of (nonfamily) managers.

Thus, practitioners seeking levers to improve firm performance should ask:

- Does the family use its power for the benefit of all shareholders and other stakeholders, or just to enrich itself?
- What is the type and level of private benefits of control we extract from the firm?
- Are they acceptable in light of the success of the firm, the size of the firm and in comparison to competitors?
- What are the eventual pros and short-term and long-term cons of extracting private benefits of control?

6.3.6 Family owners in conflict with each other

Family blockholders do not always act in a united fashion. Family blockholder conflicts represent misaligned interests *among* blockholders, that is, among family owners. In the majority–minority-owner agency conflicts discussed above, individual minority owners face a collective action problem, as the minority owners carry all the costs from their efforts (e.g., monitoring) but given their small stake in the firm benefit from the outcome of such activities only to a very limited degree. Minority owners thus have little incentive to fight their expropriation by the majority (family) owners.

In contrast, because conflicting blockholders tend to control significant shares of the asset(s) and have significant personal wealth invested in the firm, they have the power and incentive to influence key strategic decisions so as to enforce their individual preferences. For instance, even though the family owners may be aligned in their overall wish to increase the value of their ownership stake, they may still exhibit heterogeneous preferences on important strategic questions, such as those about risk taking, dividends, diversification, hiring of family members and the like (Zellweger and Kammerlander 2015).

Family blockholders may thus use their prominence against other family blockholders to enforce controlling access to the firm's money. For example, they may unseat undesired directors and board members, adapt bylaws in their favor, and enforce change in the direction of their individual interests. Because of the high stakes involved, the blockholders have an incentive to escalate the conflict, which makes it particularly costly to mitigate.

Family blockholder conflicts have a negative impact on firm performance, as the blockholder in power has substantial opportunities to extract private benefits of control at the expense of the other blockholders. Battles among family blockholders are also likely to create loyalty conflicts among board members and nonfamily management over which blockholder to follow. What is more, family blockholder conflicts create an atmosphere of mistrust and uncertainty about a firm's future that can cause inertia around strategic choices and hamper the firm's agility and ultimately its competitiveness. In addition, conflicts within the family blockholder group are costly for the family itself as they weaken the family's unified exercise of power and thus undermine the powerful monitoring of nonfamily managers. Fissures inside the family ownership group may also make the firm an easier takeover target, as some family members may conclude that it is best to sell out, and if possible to a nonfamily buyer. Finally, these centrifugal forces within the family poison family cohesiveness and undermine the continued control of the firm.

Thus, in the presence of multiple family blockholders, practitioners seeking levers to improve firm performance should ask:

- How aligned are the interests and views of different family blockholders?
- What are the obstacles against concerted action and what are the viewpoints of family blockholders?
- What family and ownership governance mechanisms should we put in place to align the interests of all family owners?

6.3.7 Summary and case study: family firm competitiveness from an agency perspective

In sum, the agency perspective suggests that the competitive advantage of family firms is contingent upon the firm's governance form. That is, it depends upon the more or less efficient cooperation of owners and managers as well as the cooperation inside the shareholder group. See Figure 6.4 for an overview.

Combining the above arguments, one might conclude that family control *up to a certain level* results in performance advantages, as it reduces the classical agency conflicts and allows powerful blockholders to monitor managers. However, the above outlined negative effects kick in, as depicted in Figure 6.5.

Various studies have investigated the impact of ownership concentration on firms' financial performance. Overall, and for the case of publicly listed companies, these studies reveal that the optimum range of voting control is between 30% and 50%.

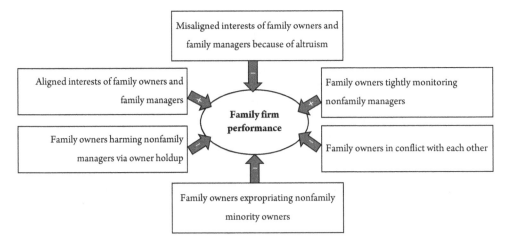

Figure 6.4 Overview of agency costs in family firms

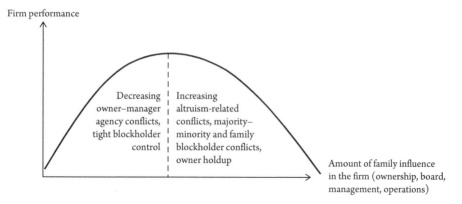

Figure 6.5 Combined agency perspectives

How the Ford family controls Ford Motor Company

By early December 2010, Henry Ford's heirs had never held a smaller stake in Ford Motor Company. Today the Fords collectively own less than 2% of the automaker, but—as in 1956, when the company went public—they remain firmly in control with 40% of the voting power through a special class of stock.

This stake was worth ten times more than it was in 2008, during the financial crisis, and the family's influence over the company remains as strong as ever. The relative size of the founding family's stake has shrunk, particularly during the past few years, as Ford has issued new common shares to raise capital and preserve its liquidity through the worst industry crisis in decades.

Is that such a bad thing? The family's desire to preserve its corporate legacy no doubt helped keep Ford out of bankruptcy in 2009, as both General Motors (GM) and Chrysler succumbed to the crisis. While its rivals were dealing with government bailouts, Ford grabbed more than two points of market share, returned to profitability and began repairing its heavily leveraged balance sheet. Now all shareholders are reaping the benefits, with Ford stock climbing from $1.58 in February 2009, at the depths of the industry crisis, to about $16.50 a share in 2010. Ford Motor by early December 2010 was worth $57 billion, up from $4.8 billion less than two years ago. The value of the family's stake has grown, too, from a mere $133 million in early 2009 to $1.2 billion in 2010.

But corporate watchdogs worry any time there are two unequal classes of stock, and they're particularly concerned when a founding family like the Fords wields so much clout despite owning such a tiny piece of the company. 'At 2% why should they be calling the shots?' said Prof. Charles M. Elson, head of the University of Delaware's Center for Corporate Governance. 'Given their economic interest at this point, why should they be standing in front of the other 98%?' 'It's like having a monarchy instead of a democracy',

CASE STUDY *(continued)*

added Nell Minow, co-founder of The Corporate Library, which specializes in corporate governance issues. Lately, she admits, things seem to be going well for Ford, whose chairman, William C. Ford Jr., fired himself as chief executive in 2006 to hire an outsider, Alan Mulally. 'But I would argue the (dual-class) system has not always worked well at this company.'

Ford declined to comment, but referred to a previously issued statement in response to a shareholder proposal to eliminate the dual-class structure. 'The Ford family's involvement with the Company has greatly benefited all shareholders, and the long history of Ford family involvement in and with the Ford Motor Company has been one of its greatest strengths.'

How did they wind up with just 2% today? The dilution happened gradually at first, but accelerated over the last decade. In 2000, shortly after Bill Ford became chairman, the company underwent a complex recapitalization that included a $10 billion special dividend and the issuance of some 600 million new common shares. The move diluted the family's holdings from 5.9% to 3.9% at the time, but cemented their grip on the company by protecting their Class B stock from dilution.

Then, in 2006, as it tried to mount a turnaround, Ford began a series of efforts to raise capital, including convertible debt offers and the issuance of new stock and warrants. Ford began printing stock certificates faster than the US government prints money: 286 million new shares in 2007, 217 million shares the following year and 925 million shares in 2009. In 2010, Ford issued another 274 million common shares as part of a $1.9 billion debt conversion. As the number of outstanding shares increased, the family's relative stake declined.

In 2010, 86 extended family members hold all 71 million Class B shares, plus a negligible amount of common stock. Ford's total common shares outstanding, including the Class B shares, is approximately 3.8 billion. Dilution aside, all those extra shares helped save the company. With the extra liquidity, Ford was able to reduce its debt by $12.8 billion this year, lowering its annualized interest costs by nearly $1 billion. A healthier balance sheet in turn helped drive up Ford's stock price.

Given what happened to GM's previous shareholders in bankruptcy, investors are likely to overlook any distaste for the fact that their shares are being diluted while the family remains firmly entrenched, said Patrick McGurn, special counsel for Institutional Shareholder Services. 'It's one thing to see your ownership diluted over time', he said. 'It's another thing to see it wiped out altogether.'

 REFLECTION QUESTIONS

1. How does the Ford family control and influence the firm?
2. What agency problems do you recognize?
3. How should the various agency problems impact Ford's performance?
4. What are the advantages and disadvantages of the Ford family's control?
5. Overall, is the Ford family's control a curse or a blessing for the firm?
6. Would you buy Ford stock?

Source: Adapted from an article by Joann Muller, forbes.com, December 2, 2010.

6.4   The resource-based perspective

The resource-based view assumes that resources are the foundation of firms' sustained competitive advantage and performance (Barney 1991). Resources are understood to encompass both the tangible and intangible assets of the firm. To generate a sustainable competitive advantage, firms must possess and combine resources that are at once valuable, rare, inimitable and non-substitutable (often referred to as the VRIN criteria of resources). It is the cumulative combination of these attributes that is essential for a firm's success.

In their attempts to use resources to build a sustainable competitive advantage, firms have to take a dynamic approach. Resources can be built, acquired, recon-figured, traded and disposed. No company can be completely self-sufficient when it comes to resources: at least to some degree, every firm is dependent on outside resources ('resource dependence'). Over time, the efficient use of resources results in capabilities and finally in core competencies.

6.4.1   Familiness

Applying the resource-based view to family firms has resulted in new insights into their competitive advantage. For example, some scholars have argued that family firms possess unique types of resources as a result of the interaction between the family and the firm. This idea has been termed 'familiness' (Habbershon and Williams 1999).

Definition of familiness:

The unique bundle of resources a firm has because of the interaction between the family and the business.

More recent accounts suggest that it is not only the family's contribution of resources that matters for performance, but also the family's configuration of resources (Sirmon and Hitt 2003). While the resource endowments of a firm may be important, these resources must also be configured effectively through an appropriate strategy to achieve a competitive advantage.

Family thus interferes in the resource management process at two levels. First, the family contributes certain resources to the firm, such as financial capital, networks or knowledge. Second, the family interferes in the resource management process through the configuration of resources, that is, through resource selection, deployment, bundling, leveraging and also

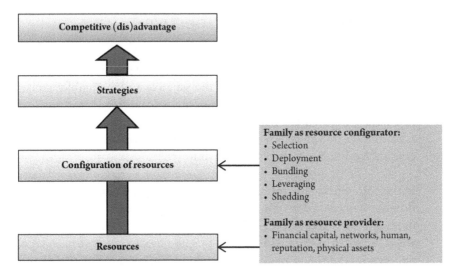

Figure 6.6 Family involvement in the resource management process

shedding (Sirmon and Hitt 2003). The family's involvement in the resource contribution and configuration process is depicted in Figure 6.6.

The familiness concept foresees that family-provided resources are potential sources of both competitive advantages and competitive disadvantages. For instance, while deep tacit knowledge (human capital) may be a source of strength because it is hard to imitate, it may turn into a disadvantage because it is also hard to multiply, which hampers growth. Similarly, strong networks may be valuable in a fairly stable and local market, but the same networks may become obsolete and even hinder the evolution of the firm when it comes to entering new markets (e.g., international markets) for which new relationships have to be secured. Hence, family-provided resources can turn into positive or negative familiness. Moreover, family influence might hamper the acquisition or development of certain crucial resources such as quick access to capital on the stock market or the hiring of 'top talents'.

6.4.2 Family as resource provider

Families typically provide their firms with a distinct set of resources. The most prominent of these include financial capital, human capital, social capital, physical capital and reputation.

6.4.2.1 *Financial capital*

The provision of financial capital by the family is essential to family firms, which are distinguished from nonfamily firms precisely by the more or less tight control of family ownership with a transgenerational outlook. The nature of the money provided by the family may have various facets beyond the sheer nominal amount. For example, financial capital can come in forms and 'qualities' varying along dimensions such as type (equity/debt), amount, availability, cost and investment horizon.

But beyond these obvious features, the money provided by family has some unique contractual features that are important to recognize as they can be directly linked to sources of competitive advantage and disadvantage. These features are displayed in Table 6.2.

Table 6.2 shows that financial capital in family firms has unique features. The amount of capital that can be provided by the family tends to be limited, as the family serves as the firm's principal capital market unless the firm is publicly listed. This resource restriction is normally seen as a disadvantage for this type of firm. At the same time, limited availability encourages owners to use the resources efficiently and parsimoniously.

Family members may be willing to provide capital at lower than market rates of returns in exchange for socioemotional advantages, in particular the continuation of the firm in family hands. In sum, financial capital in many family firms, in particular private ones, tends to have distinct features that may turn into competitive advantages (positive familiness) but also disadvantages (negative familiness).

Because family-provided capital tends to have a longer investment horizon—that is, family investors are willing to wait for longer periods of time than nonfamily investors to be paid back—it is often referred to as 'patient capital'. Family-provided capital can thus serve as a competitive advantage, as it enables long-term strategies that are difficult to imitate. These strategies are valuable when it comes to investing in projects with uncertain payback periods such as innovation or more general entrepreneurial projects.

The provision of financial capital from a family to a business it controls is particularly unique due to some contractual features that the standard arm's-length relationship between borrower and lender lacks. For instance, the specification of contracts may not include all possible details and eventualities (such as interest rates and payback periods), and (re)payments may lack

Table 6.2 Familiness in financial capital

Aspect of resource provision	Typical feature in family firms	Source of competitive advantage	Source of competitive disadvantage
Amount of capital	Often limited	Parsimony and efficiency	Limited resources hampering growth
Cost	Lower	Lenders compromise on financial returns in return for socioemotional returns, such as due to familial altruism	Lower profit discipline by borrower, perceived pressure on borrower to perform
Time horizon	Extended	Patient capital enables entrepreneurial activities with uncertain and longer payback	Inactivity/inertia, lack of profit discipline
Specification of contracts	Incomplete (e.g., when raising money from parents to start company)	Allows stepwise flexible adaptation to context	Free riding by borrower
Strictness of (re) payments	Repayment may be temporarily postponed	Flexibility through temporary freezing of payments	Free riding by borrower
Power rules	Family internal (not capital market or law)	Quick and efficient agreements despite insufficiently specified contracts	Escalation and lock-in of family conflicts, reciprocity expectations of parents
Transferability	Non-transferable to family outsiders	Valuable, non-substitutable and inimitable financing advantage	Mutual dependence, free riding on trust of lender by borrower
Renegotiation possibility	Available	Flexibility advantages through redefinition of conditions depending on progress of investment	Free riding by borrower

strict definitions so that they may be temporarily postponed. Power rules follow a family logic in which agreements are not usually legally enforced but are handled within the family, which may provide cost and speed advantages in settling disputes. Preferred access to the family capital market is restricted to family members, which makes this type of resource non-transferable and hence difficult to imitate. Financing conditions may be renegotiated, which provides the family borrower with flexibility advantages.

6.4.2.2 Human capital

Human capital represents the acquired knowledge, skills and capabilities of a person that allows for unique and novel actions. Family firms create a distinct context for human capital (both positive and negative). Some argue that the quantity and quality of human capital in family firms are limited. For example, when family owners appoint ill-qualified family members to top management positions because of their family ties, they deplete the quality of the firm's workforce. Moreover, qualified managers may avoid family firms due to their exclusive succession, limited potential for professional growth, lack of perceived professionalism and limitations on equity participation (Sirmon and Hitt 2003).

While family firms may have a less qualified workforce when quality is measured by higher education, the quality of their human capital benefits from long-term employees, particularly those who are highly experienced (although not necessarily highly trained). For example, family firm employees may have deep firm-specific knowledge about production processes and client demands, which often makes up for a lack of external training. At these firms, job experience and tacit knowledge, paired with a trusted atmosphere, supports knowledge transfer and mutual learning, which in turn drives the creation of competitive advantages.

In addition to the employees, family members themselves can also be regarded as an important and unique source of human capital. This is particularly the case when a long-tenured and committed family CEO—who has learned the business from scratch and who knows the firm, its products and its customers by heart—is at the helm of the company. Moreover, in many cases, family members are willing to show extraordinary commitment due to their personal identification with the firm (for instance, by working significantly more hours than agreed upon if needed).

6.4.2.3 Social capital

Social capital involves relationships between individuals or between organizations and is defined as the sum of the actual and potential resources embedded within, available through and derived from the network. Social capital can affect a number of important firm activities such as resource exchange, the creation of intellectual capital, learning, supplier interactions, product innovation, access to markets and resources as well as entrepreneurship (for an overview, see Hitt et al. 2001).

Social capital is composed of three dimensions: the structural, the cognitive and the relational. The structural dimension is based on network ties and the configuration of the network (whom one knows), the cognitive dimension on a shared language and narrative, and the relational dimension on trust, identification and obligations. Each of these dimensions is embedded within the family and in the family firm's ties with stakeholders (Sirmon and Hitt 2003). For instance, over the years families establish strong network ties within and across industries (e.g., with other entrepreneurial families). Family members tend to understand each other particularly well given their shared language, life experiences and history. Further, because of the trust and shared values within families, family social capital tends to be strong. The extended physical presence of family members and their long-term relationships with network partners supports the creation of even more social capital in family firms.

Families are thus particularly good at creating social capital and can use this resource advantage to the benefit of their firms. For instance, the family firm can build more effective relationships with customers, suppliers and support organizations (e.g., banks). In doing so, the firm garners resources from its network. Thus, family firms may be particularly effective in reaping the rewards of networks (Sirmon and Hitt 2003).

These considerations suggest that the availability of social capital may be a strong source of positive familiness. Again, however, we find that a source of competitive advantage may turn into a source of disadvantage under certain conditions. For instance, social capital may 'age', losing its influence, energy and value over time. Moreover, a network is most valuable when the context is stable. In changing environments, and in particular in the context of rapid change, long-term relationships tend to become less valuable or even detrimental to the firm, which needs to establish new contacts and ties. In essence, ties that bind may turn into ties that blind. The closed and trusted network which once was the basis for the firm's success now threatens to promote the status quo and lead to inertia, thus turning into negative familiness.

6.4.2.4 *Physical capital*

Physical capital includes tangible resources such as property, plant and equipment and can come in the form of the particular location or setup of a plant, store or building. Location-based physical assets may be valuable as they are inherently difficult to imitate. For instance, a retail store location in a downtown shopping area may provide an enduring competitive advantage via the preferred customer access. Similarly, the location of a plant may ensure access to production materials that are unavailable elsewhere (e.g., raw materials such as minerals, food or chemical products). Physical assets can also lead to a competitive advantage by providing lower purchasing or production costs.

Given their historical roots, many established family firms have unique physical assets. These assets may come in the form of real estate in valuable locations (e.g., vintage hotels at unique historical locations, or logistics facilities along international transport routes). Over the years, family firms may have also set up production machinery and capacity that are hard to copy. However, depending on the industry and region, the value of such physical assets might deplete over time. What was once an attractive location might become less valuable due to economic, political or environmental developments. If firm owners do not recognize and react to such evolutions in a timely manner, a former asset might turn into a liability.

6.4.2.5 Reputation

Family firms are often said to possess unique reputations and brands (Miller and Le Breton-Miller 2005), such as being trustworthy and quality-driven. The credibility and trustworthiness of family firms in the marketplace as well as in the wider stakeholder community (e.g., local opinion leaders, suppliers and competitors) is often tied to the personal engagement and visibility of family members within their firms. This seems to be particularly true in the case of eponymous firms, that is, firms that bear the name of the family or family founder.

A firm will not necessarily benefit from a price premium simply because it is known to be a family firm. However, customers will value a family's long-term personal engagement with the firm—as evidenced, for example, in higher customer retention and referrals—which is a resource that is hard to imitate (Binz et al. 2013). Here again it is important to consider the opposite side of the coin: although family firms may have a reputation for reliability and quality, they may also stand for resistance to change, stagnation and outdated business processes. Hence, the relevant question is not whether a firm has a family business reputation, but whether that image is a source of positive or negative familiness.

Some argue that there is a further noteworthy type of capital, termed *survivability capital*, defined as the pooled personal resources that family members are willing to loan, contribute, or share for the benefit of the family business (Sirmon and Hitt 2003). Survivability capital can take the form of free labor, loaned labor, additional equity investments or monetary loans. Emphasizing the continued success and in particular the transgenerational survival of the business, survivability capital can help sustain the firm during poor economic times. Given the family's loyalty to the business, survivability capital serves as a safety net or insurance mechanism upon which the firm can draw in times of financial peril.

The above list of resources makes no claim to completeness. Further resources, such as the firm's corporate culture or organizational processes and routines, may matter too. But for the sake of parsimony, the above discussion of financial, human, social, physical and reputational capital should be helpful.

Of course, not all family firms exhibit all the familiness features outlined above. For larger and in particular public firms, familiness related to human capital should be less relevant. But even for large family firms, the control of equity by the family, and hence the provision of financial capital, can be a source of competitive advantage. Keep in mind, too, that familiness features do not always manifest as a competitive advantage. Familiness can be absent in certain resources and may even be a source of competitive disadvantage, as summarized in Table 6.3.

Table 6.3 Familiness in various resource pools

Type of resource	Definition	Positive familiness	Negative familiness
Financial capital	Patient capital without threat of short-term liquidation	Long-term loyal investment, efficiency pressure, free from short-term profit pressure enabling entrepreneurial strategies	Limited availability of family capital, no equity participation for employees
Human capital	Acquired knowledge, skills and experience of employees	Deep and hard to copy firm-specific knowledge and long-term experience	Lack of access to formally trained and educated personnel
Social capital	Resources embedded in networks, accessed through relationships	Access to knowledge, innovation and new business	Outdated and closed networks
Physical capital	Property, plant and equipment	Preferred location, physical resource access, cost advantages in sourcing	Outdated buildings and machinery
Reputational capital	Image as reliable and trustworthy company	Close customer ties, information access, customer loyalty and referral	Reputation for unwillingness to change, stagnation and outdated processes

Source: Adapted from Sirmon and Hitt (2003).

6.4.3 Family as resource manager

As outlined above, the family not only serves as a resource provider, but also as a resource configurator. Resource configuration takes into account that firm performance not only depends on the amount of resources available (e.g., money), but also on the organization's ability to put these resources to efficient use. Building on Sirmon and Hitt's (2003) classification, we consider the following elements of resource configuration.

Selecting resources
Family firms tend to take care to select resources that fit into the organizational culture and its routines (e.g., they look for a person–organization fit by selecting employees that fit into the firm's culture and its production processes). Given the limited funds for acquiring resources, family firms have an incentive to make sure they select the right ones, that is, the resources that can be put to efficient use. Family firms should thus have an advantage in the accuracy with which they select and add resources. However, this may come at a cost in the form of limited resource heterogeneity, which could hamper creativity and innovation in the firm.

Deploying resources
Resource deployment refers to the adoption, rollout and implementation of new resources in the organization. Family firms face challenges in resource deployment as their long-term established processes and decision-making patterns impede the adoption of new resources and capabilities. Actors may perceive new ways of doing things as an intrusion and as a sign that decision makers no longer trust their capabilities. Moreover, path dependences lead actors to uphold traditional ways of doing things that are proven but eventually also outdated.

Bundling resources
The bundling of resources refers to the creative (re)combination of resources, in particular of resources that are available inside the firm. The family firm's intimate and trusted relationships, the strong commitment of its organizational members and the sense of community among its employees foster knowledge and idea transfers across hierarchies. This creates a deep and shared understanding of how things are done inside the firm. That is, actors in family firms have a knowledge advantage about who possesses what skills and expertise inside the organization. Employees and managers in family firms are known to possess high levels of firm-specific tacit knowledge, which accumulates during their typically long tenures within the organization. Tacit knowledge in turn is important for resource

configuration and bundling, and has been found to increase the innovativeness of family firms (Koenig, Kammerlander and Enders 2013).

Leveraging resources

Family firms should be well qualified to leverage resources, that is, to put resources to efficient use. Building on established core competencies, family firms should be able to assess the value of a resource and to leverage it competently, in a way that positively contributes to the firm's competitive advantage. Resource deployment in family firms is generally guided by parsimony, which allows for higher efficiency. The constraints on resources and the family's simultaneous desire to maintain ultimate control over the firm motivate family firms to strive for prudent resource deployment. Lower governance costs in family firms—which stem from family owners' ability to closely monitor top managers, as well as high levels of flexibility and a lack of bureaucracy—further enable the efficient leveraging of resources (e.g., for innovation) (Duran et al. 2016).

Shedding resources

Inhibited by emotional ties, nostalgia and the escalation of commitment among actors who originally provided a given resource, family firms should be particularly hesitant to shed resources. This hesitation can become costly if these resources do not generate income. Moreover, an actor's unwillingness to give a valuable resource to somebody who can put it to even more efficient use may lead to forgone opportunities for value creation for the firm.

Taken together, family firms seem to have advantages in resource selection, bundling and leveraging. However, these firms should normally be at a disadvantage in the deployment of new resources and the shedding of existing resources.

6.4.4 Turning familiness into business strategies

The resource-based perspective has been widely adopted in family business theory and in practice. Ultimately, this perspective should help us understand the ways in which business strategies can link family-influenced resources on the one hand and competitive advantages on the other. Three examples of business strategies based on positive familiness are provided in Figure 6.7.

The first example refers to Hilti, a producer of drilling machines and other building equipment with about $4 billion in sales. The firm is located in Liechtenstein and is controlled by the Hilti family via the Martin Hilti family

Family-influenced resource	Strategy	Competitive advantage
Deep market knowledge	Strategic market extension	Growth in a stagnating market
Local network	Unique contacts with authorities and customers	Development of real estate projects in a very short time
Patient financial capital	Early entry in new markets	First mover advantage

Figure 6.7 Linking positive familiness to competitive advantage

trust. Hilti and its controlling family have always emphasized client proximity, which is evident in the firm's direct sales activities, its wholly owned stores and its sophisticated customer relationship system. The firm's ability to advise clients with complex construction needs, along with its recent fleet management solution for drills and other machinery, contributes to Hilti's customer focus. While the overall construction and construction supply industries have stagnated in many of its markets, Hilti has been able to grow and attract market share thanks to its unique market knowledge.

Ventresca and Sons is another company that builds its competitive advantage on positive familiness. As a small construction company with around 25 employees located in rural Greece, it has unique insights into the local real estate market. Supported by close ties to local authorities and real estate agents, the company has been highly successful in developing turnkey real estate projects at a pace and at locations that its competitors cannot match.

Finally, the private and family-controlled German company Remondis has grown significantly since its foundation in the 1950s. The firm is active in the waste disposal and renewable energy business, reaching sales of about €6.8 billion in 2012. This fabulous growth as a private company is due to the family's willingness to invest patient financial capital in the firm, reinvest their money in it over time and, over the last 20 years, to acquire over 1000 firms. The family's use of resources has allowed the company to expand rapidly and be the first to enter new markets, in particular in Eastern Europe (see Figure 6.7).

While the family may be the source of unique strengths as outlined in the examples above, it can also become a source of grave weaknesses. In the first example depicted in Figure 6.8, the firm's competitive disadvantage stems from enduring stagnation at the firm level, which is induced by the family owner-

Family-influenced resource	Strategy	Competitive disadvantage
Decision-making style	No company development	Dynamic employees leave the company
Owner-centric culture	Founder: 'In this company no other companies are bought!'	Missed chances for development
Human capital: management team	Family membership comes first	Company lacks innovation as a result of under-qualified management

Figure 6.8 Linking negative familiness to competitive disadvantage

manager's unwillingness to delegate. All major decisions in this company have to cross the entrepreneur's desk, which over time has become a threat to the firm. The company's competitive disadvantage became apparent when some of the most dynamic and entrepreneurial managers decided to leave.

The second example bears witness to a family firm with a very autocratic business culture. The controlling family and its views about proper management are represented, for example, in stark statements such as the following: 'In our firm we will never acquire another company.' This may not sound at first like a source of disadvantage. However, it became apparent over time that competitors were happy to exploit the family's unwillingness to exit its declining business and seize new business opportunities, for instance through acquisition. Over time, this firm was outcompeted.

The last example tells the story of a family firm that was unwilling to appoint non-family members to the top management team. The firm did have a management board, which on paper included nonfamily members. However, this board never had an active role in the firm's management. While family management should surely not be generally equated with unprofessional management, in this particular case the firm clearly suffered from a lack of qualified top management.

A useful way for practitioners to assess the familiness profile of a firm is to review the firm's resource base while searching for sources of positive and negative familiness. Of course, the family may not have an impact on all the resources the firm needs to compete. This is especially true for larger companies.

Below we describe the familiness profile of a family-controlled food producing company. We found that this firm had positive familiness in terms of

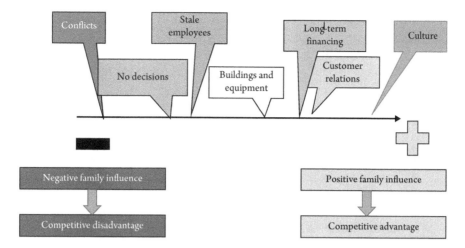

Figure 6.9 Example familiness profile

long-term financing, loyal customers and a very strong corporate culture. At the same time, we also found negative familiness in tensions between the two brothers who owned the firm, a stale workforce, and outdated buildings and equipment that slowed down production processes. Figure 6.9 shows these various aspects of familiness on a continuum from negative to positive.

This assessment helped the firm and its owners start a dialogue on the levers for its future success. At the level of positive familiness, the discussion centered on the question of how to further solidify positive qualities such as the firm's strong corporate culture. At the level of negative familiness, the owners discussed concrete issues that hampered the evolution of the firm. They also discussed how negative familiness could be eliminated and what the obstacles were in this process.

6.4.5   Summary and case study: family firm competitiveness from a resource-based perspective

Summing up, the resource-based perspective explains performance variation among family firms by suggesting that to different degrees family firms possess valuable, rare, inimitable and non-substitutable resources (VRIN resources). Positive familiness, defined as the family's positive influence on the firm's resource base, often comes in the form of patient financial capital, deep tacit knowledge, experienced employees, strong networks, unique physical assets and reputational capital. What matters for success, however, is not only resource endowment, but also resource configuration abilities, such as resource selection, bundling and leveraging. Family firms often have the advantage in these areas. However, family firms are normally at a disadvantage in the deployment of new resources and the shedding of existing resources. Familiness is tied to the competitive advantage of companies through the pursuit of business strategies in which resources are configured.

Practitioners who seek to explain or build a performance advantage based on the resource-based perspective should ask themselves:

● What are the critical resources in our firm now and in the future?
● How does the family impact these resources? Where do we have positive, neutral and negative familiness?
● How can we exploit positive familiness? What strategies can we use to turn positive familiness into a competitive advantage? What are the obstacles along the way?
● How can we overcome negative familiness? What obstacles do we face? Can we partner with or acquire new resources?

CASE STUDY

Familiness analysis of a family firm

Take the example of a family firm—maybe even your own family firm—and explore its familiness profile. In doing so, consider the following questions, which should allow you to tie your firm's familiness profile to its strategic goals:

1. What is the central strategic goal of the firm?
2. What are the resources needed to achieve this goal?
3. How does the family impact these resources: positively, neutrally or negatively? Develop a familiness profile for your firm (for an example, see Figure 6.9).
4. How can you secure or strengthen positive familiness?
5. How can you overcome negative familiness? What are the potential obstacles?

6.5 The organizational identity perspective

The resource-based perspective asked how firms achieve a competitive advantage through particular resources and their configuration. In contrast, the organizational identity perspective focuses on what an organization stands for and on how it is perceived. Organizational identity captures the most central, distinctive and enduring aspects of an organization (Albert and Whetten 1985). It describes the collective behavior and identity of the firm and provides a sense of continuity and of distinctiveness. Organizational identity is said to reside in the organization's history and values, and is continuously expressed through interactions within the firm and with actors outside the firm. It shapes and is shaped by the firm's strategy.

In addition to identifying 'who we are' as an organization (as opposed to those outside the organization), organizational identity also determines how members of the firm should behave and how outsiders should relate to them. When employees identify with the firm, they feel a sense of belonging to the organization as a whole; put differently, the organization becomes a symbolic extension of the employee's self (for the conceptual foundations of organizational identity see, for instance, Albert and Whetten 1985; Ashforth and Mael 1996; and Ravasi and Schulz 2006). In order to link organizational identity to a firm's competitiveness, we must ask how the firm's identity—and by extension, its image and reputation—drive performance.

6.5.1 Intertwined identities of family and firm

Many small firms, and even some large ones, actively advertise the fact that they are family businesses. Think, for instance, of the many vineyards and restaurants around the world that proudly present themselves as a 'family estate winery' or 'family-managed restaurant'. But why do large multinationals such as SC Johnson or Mars actively communicate that they are family-controlled firms? Is there a positive link between family firm identity (i.e., being known as a family business and projecting the image of a family firm to stakeholders) and firm success? Answering these questions requires that we take a step back and first ask why organizational identity is particularly relevant in the family firm context. Then, we can link our observations to the behaviors of family firms.

6.5.1.1 *The particular relevance of identity and identification in family firms*

Controlling families tend to identify strongly with their firms and thereby link their family identity with that of the firm. Below, we outline several possible reasons for such an identity link.

The family's history is often tightly interwoven with the firm's history, with the result that the family and firm's images and reputations are tightly connected as well. This may be particularly true if the firm bears the same name as the owning family. In such cases, the identities of the family and the firm become mutually dependent, and observers such as clients, suppliers and the wider public directly associate the controlling family with the firm and vice versa.

The intertwinement of identities is further fostered by the strong local roots and links to the social community in which the firm is embedded that many business families have developed. For example, in contrast to a distant and impersonally structured pension fund, family owners can be easily identified and are readily available as symbols of what the firm stands for. The family can thus be held accountable for the actions of the firm.

Family members may also strongly identify with the firm because of how difficult and undesirable it is to leave either the family or the firm. Even family members who are not actively involved in the firm will be linked to the firm's identity by virtue of their family ties. When family members are directly engaged with the firm, leaving often involves severe personal losses, including unfavorable sale conditions for owned shares, less attractive working conditions outside the family firm, or even damaged family relations.

When family members link their identity to that of the firm, they may benefit from the firm's reputation. Being seen as part of the family firm's success will inflate family members' self-esteem. Family firm identity then becomes a source of nonfinancial, that is, SEW. Of course, this effect works both ways: a favorable family firm identity reflects positively on the family, while a negative family firm identity tarnishes the family's identity and public reputation.

While the overall identification of family owners with their firms tends to be stronger than the identification of nonfamily actors with their firms, not all family firms decide to communicate a family firm image. Some family firms do not emphasize their family business status, and some even hide it. Other family firms—including SC Johnson, and the many small firms that advertise with slogans such as 'our family serving your family for generations'—place great stress on their family firm identity.

Below we list some examples of family firms that strongly emphasize their family firm identity and status on their corporate websites (taken from Binz and Schmid 2012).

SC Johnson: 'We understand family because we are family. Not a squabbling-in-the-back-seat kind of family. (Well, not usually.) But a glad-we're-in-this-together kind of family. So we understand the joys and strains you feel every day.'

Bechtel: 'Building on a family heritage that spans more than 100 years, we will continue to be privately owned by active management and guided by firmly held values.'

Mars: 'As a family-owned company for nearly a century, we are guided by our Five Principles: Quality, Responsibility, Mutuality, Efficiency and Freedom.'

Walmart: 'At the heart of Walmart's growth is the unique culture that Mr. Sam Walton built. His business philosophy was based on the simple idea of making the customer No. 1. He believed that by serving the customer's needs first, his business would also serve its associates, shareholders, communities and other stakeholders.'

Koch Industries: 'Koch Industries, Inc. is named for Fred C. Koch, who developed an improved method of converting heavy oil into gasoline in 1927. His entrepreneurial drive formed the foundation of what would eventually become the largest private company in the United States.'

6.5.1.2 *Linking family firm identity to corporate reputation*

Family members who identify with their firms will as a corollary be concerned about their firm's reputation. The historical links between the family and the firm, the family's local roots, its increased exit costs, and the fear that the firm might damage the family's reputation all contribute to the family's concern about how the firm, its products and its strategic decisions are perceived by the public. Because a broad set of stakeholders—including clients, employees, suppliers and also the press—shape the firm's and thereby the family's reputation, the family has an incentive to generate a favorable corporate reputation that allows them to 'feel good about who they are and what they do' (Deephouse and Jaskiewicz 2013). Such family-induced corporate reputation concern has two notable consequences at the firm level. First, family firms should be inclined to engage in corporate social responsibility (CSR) actions to satisfy reputation-forming stakeholders (Zellweger et al. 2013). Second, the family should take an interest in the branding of the firm's products. We will explore these two implications in the following.

6.5.2 Corporate social responsibility in family firms

One consequence of a family's heightened identification with the firm and their resulting concern for family and business reputation is that family firms will strive to be seen as 'good corporate citizens'. Family firms thus have incentives to invest in CSR. Indeed, Dyer and Whetten (2006) find that family firms in comparison to nonfamily firms are more socially responsible organizations, and perform better than nonfamily firms along several CSR dimensions. Similarly, Berrone et al. (2010) suggest that family firms invest more than nonfamily firms in anti-pollution activities, even if this comes at significant costs. Driven by the desire to preserve a favorable reputation in their local communities, family firms thus have a particular incentive to embrace socially responsible behavior.

More recent accounts of CSR activity in family firms move beyond investigating the *levels* of CSR activity to explore the *ways through which* family firms enact socially responsible behaviors and thereby achieve legitimacy. For instance, in the chocolate, coffee and tea industries, producers face significant social and environmental concerns, such as irresponsible labor practices (e.g., child labor) and ecologically non-sustainable production methods (e.g., overexploitation of natural resources, deforestation and the like). In this context, labels that certify compliance with international CSR standards have become the preferred way for most producers to signal to customers and to the wider community their socially responsible behavior.

A closer look at the family firms in the chocolate, coffee and tea industries, however, revealed that a significant number did not choose to adopt compliance labels (Richards, Zellweger and Gond 2016). In fact, some of these family firms took an active stance against product labels by drawing from other legitimization strategies related to their family status. For instance, Laederach, a Swiss mid-sized chocolate producer, markets its products with the slogan 'Laederach—the chocolate family'. Asked about the background of this slogan, the family owners suggested that the production chain from the farmer to the consumer was part of a family-like network based on values such as trust, responsibility and mutual respect. The company's website declares: 'we know our partners at home and abroad and value their work. Closeness, expertise and responsibility are the basis for genuine partnerships that are socially, ecologically and economically oriented.' Laederach thus adopted an alternative way to signal credibility that is not (or at last not mainly) based on the traditional labeling strategy. The firm tries to achieve legitimacy via its family business status, which translates into values and behaviors that appear to be at least as credible as the labeling strategies embraced by competitors such as Lindt and Nestlé—and, unlike the compliance label, this status is impossible to copy.

6.5.3 Branding in family firms

A family's identification with its firm is reflected not only in socially responsible firm behavior, but also in the firm's branding efforts. High levels of identification with the firm, a long-term and stable governance structure that spans family generations, and the resulting concern for a sustainable, consistent and trusted image create the perfect grounds for brands to develop (Miller and Le Breton-Miller 2005). While each family and hence family firm identity is unique to a certain degree, it is useful to ask on a general level what the family business cue evokes (e.g., with customers). What do customers expect when they buy from a family firm?

6.5.3.1 *Family firm image: the particular role of relational qualities*

Studies exploring the above question suggest that being seen as a family firm brings with it particular *relational qualities* (Binz et al. 2013). For instance, some have argued that the desire to protect corporate reputation in family firms drives family firms to provide excellent customer service. The continued interaction between clients and the firm's long-term employees creates a trusted atmosphere and promotes personal relationships. Family firms are generally said to be trustworthy, good employers that support good causes and care about the environment (Craig, Dibbrell and Davis 2008). These 'soft' attributes positively influence costumer preferences.

Relational qualities of family firms that positively impact customer preferences:

In comparison to nonfamily firms, family firms are seen as particularly:

- sympathetic
- personal
- trustworthy

- credible
- authentic

Interestingly, family firms fare worse in comparison to nonfamily firms when assessed along the dimensions of innovativeness and overall performance. Binz et al. (2013) suggest that relational qualities (such as being sympathetic, trustworthy, credible and customer-centric) drive family firm reputation among clients far more than business-related qualities (such as being innovative or attracting above-average performers). Building on these relational qualities seems to allow family firms to differentiate themselves from their nonfamily competitors in the marketplace.

6.5.3.2 *Family firms as brand builders*

In exploiting their relational qualities, family firms should be able to build unique brands that draw on the following four brand 'ingredients':

Tradition
For instance, Underberg, the producer of an herbal digestive drink, has established a unique brand based on the tradition of its product. Since

1846, the so-called semper idem claim has signaled to customers an unchanged, proven and traditional production process despite the fact that the production processes have in fact been significantly overhauled and modernized since the firm's establishment. Still, the firm's products benefit from Underberg's traditional aura.

Honesty, trust and reliability

L.L. Bean, the US-based clothing and hardware retailer, has a lifetime, 100% customer satisfaction guarantee that contributes to the firm's image of honesty, trust and reliability. Family firms are uniquely placed to project this type of image. At L.L. Bean, its trusted image and related branding campaign goes back to the company's founder, Leon Bean, who claimed: 'I do not consider the sale complete until the goods are worn out and the customers still satisfied.'

Quality

HiPP, the producer of baby food, serves a market that highly values trust and quality. After all, what parents would not want the best food for their children? HiPP's quality promise is simple but convincing. Claus Hipp, one of the company's family owners, appears on every product and states '100% organic—I guarantee this personally'. The family's very personal quality commitment helps HiPP products stand out from competitors such as Nestlé.

Personal relationships

Not many things matter more to people than the security of their material wealth. Private banks service this delicate need, and some of the most successful among them are family controlled. For instance, J. Safra Bank is a family-controlled private bank with Lebanese origins that aims to establish very long-term and personal relationships with their clients. Being a family's banker is a matter of trust and only pays off once a personal relationship is established between the firm and the client. The long-term tenure of family and nonfamily employees supports these personal relationships.

Brand consistency

Given their concern with maintaining a consistent reputation at both family and firm levels, family businesses are motivated to ensure a consistent branding strategy that avoids dilution of the brand's promise. For instance, Estée Lauder, the family-controlled cosmetics company, has a 150-page manual explaining how its products are to be sold in a consistent way across the globe.

Brand protection

Similarly, the firm's concern with maintaining a consistent image and reputation should ensure that the brand remains genuine. New products should only appear under the family's brand name if they have been extensively tested. Family brands are often tied to a narrow product or market niche in which they tend to have an iconic status. Brand extensions to new markets and products may appear attractive at first sight. But family owners may prefer to protect the core brand, a choice which may limit growth but which guarantees further core market penetration.

Secrecy

Close personal ties, particularly in small and private family firms, make it easier to keep market and marketing knowledge, sales figures and production recipes a secret. Family products and brands are often impossible to copy and thus benefit from an aura of uniqueness and exclusivity. For instance, Sefar, a global family-controlled-and-managed producer of technical filtration textiles, is hesitant to file a patent for its production knowledge. The family CEO explains:

> If we file a patent with our latest technology, it is certain that my competitors will start copying me. We prefer to keep the most critical production knowhow secret. And as a private, locally embedded family firm we have certain advantages in this. Clearly, our products and our brand benefit from this halo of exclusivity and unrivaled perfection.

Indoctrination of values

Preserving a brand requires that the brand's promises and values are reinforced on an ongoing and consistent basis. The personal presence and engagement of the family ensures that the brand's promises and values are

---

Excursus: Family firms in the luxury goods industry

In the 2013 list of the most valuable luxury brands compiled by Millward and Brown we find that seven of the ten most valuable brands are family controlled. Brands like Louis Vuitton, Hermes, Gucci, Prada, Rolex or Chanel are under family control. Most of them are not in the hands of the founding families anymore, but are owned by large family-controlled multinationals such as LVMH or Richemont.

Establishing a strong brand in the luxury goods industry takes particular abilities. In order to charge a significant price premium for luxury goods—in comparison to less exclusively positioned competing products,—a firm must establish an image of mastery and craftsmanship that is reflected in the superior quality of the product. This pedigree ideally comes from a unique lineage and heritage.

> However, luxury products must also be accessible only in select locations. Luxury goods need to have a certain degree of scarcity to reach an exclusive status. Moreover, in order to be successful, they must convey a particular kind of personality and be linked to a certain social status.
>
> Family firms are well positioned to tap into the luxury goods markets. Their abilities to build brands (through attention to tradition, honesty, quality and personal engagement) and preserve them (through personal engagement, consistency, protection, secrecy and indoctrination of values) perfectly fit this special industrial context.

not empty words. Ideally, family members are role models for the behavior and values of the firm and its products. The firm may also carefully select employees who fit the firm's culture and value system. As a result, family firms should have advantages in motivating employees to uphold their unique value systems and to deliver on the promises of their brands.

6.5.4 How a family firm image drives financial performance

Our reflections on the incentives among family firms to be concerned with reputation raises the question of whether this concern also pays off in financial terms, that is, performance. Indeed, there are various external and internal processes through which the family's identity and reputation concerns drive firm performance (for more details, see Zellweger, Eddleston and Kellermanns 2010).

Customer focus
Through their advantages in sympathy, trust and authenticity family firms can create an image and reputation that is impossible to copy. Because each family is unique to a certain degree, even other family firms will be unable to copy a particular family firm image. This image may be a highly valuable resource as it positively impacts customer satisfaction, loyalty and purchasing volume. The relational benefits of ongoing and trusted ties to customers allow family firms to introduce new products and services at lower cost. Family-based brand identity enhances the firm's ability to persuade customers to make purchasing decisions based on the perceived attributes of the seller (Craig, Dribbell and Davis 2008). Despite these benefits, however, the lower credibility of family firms in the areas of innovation, growth and internationalization limit family firms' ability to charge a price premium for their family-controlled status. The financial benefits of projecting a family firm image materialize instead through the relationship-based benefits discussed above, and hence through family firms' customer (as opposed to product) focus (Figure 6.10).

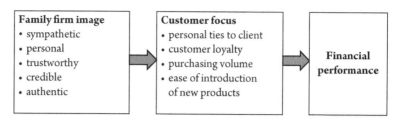

Figure 6.10 Family firm image, customer focus and financial performance

Extended family of stakeholders and embeddedness advantages

The family's identification with the business and the family and firm's desire for sustainable business practices establishes an 'extended family' of stakeholders (e.g., suppliers and customers) who support the firm's principles (such as loyalty, fairness and respect). This may provide a firm with important embeddedness advantages which accrue, for instance, in the form of customer referrals and new business opportunities. However, given family firms' local ties and entrepreneurial reputations, they may also be offered as-yet unexplored and unrelated business opportunities (e.g., entering a joint venture with another business family or taking over another firm). The embeddedness advantage may manifest through support for the family and the firm in difficult times. This support stems from the reciprocal exchanges the family and the firm have established with the local community.

Preferred resource access

The family's dedication to a business activity that is sustainable over long periods of time, eventually across generations; its concern for reputation; and its encouragement of benevolent relationships inside the firm should enable it to attract unique resources.

For instance, the features listed above lead family firms to carefully manage their financial resources and to honor their financial commitments to banks. Banks may understand that family firms value having a secure opportunity to raise money in the future, a fact which lowers family firms' likelihood of default and hence may justify lending money to them at favorable rates. Indeed, in their study of S&P 500 firms (US public firms), Anderson, Mansi and Reeb (2003) find that the cost of debt for family firms is about 0.40% lower than for nonfamily firms.

An underexplored advantage of family firms relates to their image as employers. For employees who value loyalty, continuity and trust, working for a family firm may seem especially attractive. The family firm brand signals a personal work environment in which individual performance is valued alongside personal relationships, group performance and the long-term sustainability of operations and relationships. For employees looking for a long-term employment relationship, family firms may thus appear to be humane employers whose causes are worth championing.

Incentive to perform for family managers and owners

The intertwined nature of personal, family and firm reputations creates a common nonmonetary incentive among family members involved in the firm to perform individually and as a group and to ensure the performance of the firm. This willingness to perform is particularly evident in difficult times, when family members have a heightened incentive to persevere and thereby make their firms more resilient.

Shared point of view among family managers and owners

Family managers and owners who identify with the firm and participate in it develop a shared point of view. This, in turn, leads to higher cohesion, a shared strategic consensus and the ability to make decisions quickly.

Stewardship behavior and goal alignment of nonfamily managers

If the wider organization and in particular the workforce embraces the values and goals of the family, the firm may realize unique advantages through stewardship and entrepreneurial behavior. In addition, the adoption of the family firm identity by employees ensures the combination and alignment of the ideas, goals and capabilities of family and nonfamily managers.

6.5.5 The dark side of family firm identity

The positive depiction of the family firm image cannot be left unqualified, unfortunately. When family and firm identities are integrated, both firm and family may face severe challenges.

Low perceived ability to innovate, change, grow and internationalize

A family firm image not only has positive aspects. Surely, in the utmost number of cases, family firms are seen as trustworthy, credible and authentic, as depicted above. At the same time, however, family firms are seen as less credible in comparison to nonfamily firms when it comes to the ability to innovate, change and grow. Family firms also tend to be perceived as fairly small and local organizations. These assigned attributes are disadvantageous for product markets in which size, innovation and growth matter. Thus, it is shortsighted to assign only positive attributes to the family firm image.

Conformity pressure for the firm

Given their high visibility, family business owners are targets for public conformity pressures. As employers, important taxpayers and/or local opinion leaders, family businesses and their owners may be pressured by the press or by politicians to comply with their demands. In good times, the press may legitimize the family form of governance. In more difficult times, however, the press and the wider public may renounce the family and the family members involved in the firm and call into question their legitimacy or the appropriateness of their firm-related decisions (Berrone et al. 2010). Such conformity pressures may make the firm hesitant to embrace bold strategies and lead instead to conservative strategies designed to uphold a desired image in the public realm.

Conformity pressures for the family

Research has suggested that family control and strong family identification with the firm can cause heirs to feel locked into and dependent upon the firm. If heirs feel intense pressure to join the family business despite their reservations or personal preferences, they may come to resent their dependency upon the firm and lack of autonomy from the family. In particular, next-generation members of a prominent family may feel smothered by their involvement in the family and the firm. They may feel that the firm is a 'family handcuff' that hinders their independent development.

Groupthink among managers

A heightened level of identification with the firm and the family may cause managers to engage in groupthink, in which the desire for harmony or conformity in the group (i.e., the family and firm) results in suboptimal decision-making outcomes. In such cases, group members isolate themselves from outside influences and try to minimize conflict and reach a consensus decision without critical evaluation of alternative ideas or viewpoints. Groupthink also entails the loss of individual creativity and independent thinking. The dysfunctional group dynamics of the 'in-group' produce an 'illusion of invulnerability', or an inflated certainty that the right decision has been made. Thus, members of the 'in-group' (i.e., the family and its long-term nonfamily managers) significantly overrate their own abilities in decision making and significantly underrate the abilities and viewpoints of outsiders (the 'out-group'). Groupthink thus creates an illusion of control in which actors confuse the stability of their emotionally rigid, rule-based assumptions with stability in the external world.

Expropriation of nonfamily stakeholders

The press may present positive examples of family firms, but it also frequently presents family firms that partake in harmful stakeholder behavior. Research suggests that strong family identification with the firm can create an 'us-vs.-them' mentality that causes the family to place their needs above those of nonfamily stakeholders. Strong family firm identity can encourage family members to ignore or eliminate controls that prevent fraud or even to rationalize fraud. Although social bonds generally tend to reduce negative behaviors, high levels of group cohesion can actually spur deviant behavior. Specifically, strong bonds can sometimes produce organizational norms that conflict with universal (societal) standards of behavior. As a result, family members can feel pressure to follow organizational norms even when they violate universal standards. Norms in family firms tend to be very strong and can become the dominant reference point for family members that follow a 'family first' philosophy. Indeed, deviant norms have been argued to be a root cause of fraudulent activity and scandal by family firms (Kellermanns, Eddleston and Zellweger 2012). Not all families that strongly identify with their firms seek a positive impact for their stakeholders; in fact, some may selfishly exploit their environment.

Role blurring for family managers

Along with the firm-level disadvantages described above, strong family firm identity may also lead to disadvantages at the level of the family. Sundaramurthy and Kreiner (2008) show that the question of whether the family exists for the business or vice versa is a particularly salient dilemma for integrated family firms. This question can cause considerable ambiguity and conflict, while tensions arising from role blurring can evoke defenses such as splitting, repression or denial. Splitting entails polarizing behavior and the formation of subgroups, whereas denial involves ignoring the tension and pretending that it does not exist.

Security concerns for family

Family members who control larger firms are often perceived as wealthy individuals in their communities. Under extreme circumstances, and in particular under insecure institutional conditions, controlling families can be threatened by blackmailing, robbery or even kidnapping. For instance, an Indian controlling family that sold its shares to a firm listed on the New York stock exchange (NYSE) found the names of its family members and the amount of money that each received from the sale on the NYSE website. For security reasons, the family decided to register its children under false names in their kindergarten.

6.5.6 Some empirical findings on the family firm image–performance link

Some research findings may help to consolidate our thinking about the pros and cons of family firm image. Clearly, family firms have competitive advantages stemming from an identity that positively contribute to performance, as discussed above. However, it would be inappropriate to disregard the disadvantages that stem from family firm identity. Investigating the link between family firm image and performance for a group of Swiss private family firms, we found that firm performance (measured in terms of firm growth) was highest when the firms emphasized not only their family firm image, but at the same time also their willingness to take entrepreneurial risks. Accordingly, there was a dual performance process: one built on the past, and hence the family firm image; and one built on the firm's future, represented by entrepreneurial risk taking. The family firm image path had a weaker link to firm growth than the entrepreneurial path. This dual growth path was found to be fueled by the controlling family's expectation about the successful management of the firm.

6.5.7 Summary and case study: family firm competitiveness from an identity perspective

The identity perspective explains performance variation among family firms by suggesting that the inextricable identity link between family and firm forms the basis for family firm success. It is assumed that the heightened identification of the family with the firm creates a heightened reputation concern at both the family and firm levels. This not only results in branding and CSR efforts, but also in tangible performance benefits.

Through a strong customer focus, an extended family of stakeholders, preferred resource access, an incentive to perform for family managers, stewardship behavior, goal alignment among nonfamily managers and participative decision making, family firms benefit from their identity as a family firm.

But all that glitters is not gold: a family firm image (being known as a family firm) has disadvantages as well. For the firm, the disadvantages come in the form of conformity pressures; a lower perceived ability to innovate, change and grow; groupthink; and the expropriation of nonfamily stakeholders. Overall, we have seen that a family firm image contributes best to performance if it is paired with a heightened willingness by the firm to take entrepreneurial risks. This combined view is depicted in Figure 6.11.

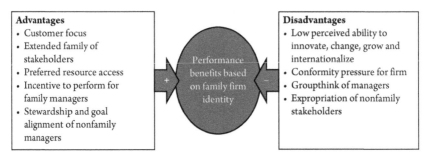

Figure 6.11 Identity advantages and disadvantages of family firms

Practitioners who seek to explain and build a competitive advantage from the perspective of family firm identity should ask themselves:

- Are we known as a family firm?
- What are the advantages and disadvantages of our family firm image?
- How can we best turn qualities attributed to us—that is, that our firm is sympathetic, personal, trustworthy, credible and authentic—into a competitive advantage?
- To what degree do we exploit the family firm identity advantages?
  - Who are our most important stakeholders and have we secured their goodwill?
  - How can we exploit the fact that we are a family firm on the job market?
  - Have we developed a shared point of view inside the family and the firm about what the firm stands for and what we would like to achieve?
  - Do we motivate stewardship behavior?
  - Do we benefit from improved decision making by allowing everybody to share his/her views and to be creative?
- How can we avoid the negative effects of a family firm image, such as:
  - Low perceived ability to innovate, change, grow and internationalize.
  - Groupthink: the false assumption that our own view of the environment is always the correct one.
  - Expropriation of nonfamily stakeholders.
- How can we combine a concern for our identity and historical roots with a strong emphasis on innovation, change and risk taking?

CASE STUDY

Branding and CSR at HiPP

Below you find a screenshot of the corporate website www.hipp.com. HiPP is 100% owned by the Hipp family and mainly produces baby food and children's products (Figure 6.12). Originally founded in Germany, the company today has a global reach with products that are 100% organic.

Figure 6.12 Screenshot from HiPP website

On the company's website, Claus Hipp, a fourth-generation family member, states

> Here at HiPP, we've pioneered the natural benefits of organic ingredients for 60 years. HiPP Organic began in 1956 when Georg Hipp converted the family farm into one of the first organic farms in Europe. While others were moving into intensive farming, Georg stuck to his beliefs. He wanted to create the very best food for babies, made carefully from only the finest, organic ingredients. Good, tasty food that would help them grow and develop healthily and happily.

Regarding organic food and CSR, the HiPP website states:

> Stricter than EU organic: The HiPP Organic Guarantee stands for purest quality. Babies and toddlers are highly sensitive, so organic food is the ideal choice for their diet. However, statutory

CASE STUDY *(continued)*

organic quality marks alone offer no guarantee that raw materials are genuinely free from pollutants. For this reason, we subject our products to extremely rigorous testing, applying standards that extend beyond the legal norm for organic foods. Raw materials receive their first inspection from our staff straight after delivery. If our inspectors have any complaints the goods are not even accepted. The objective is to use only the purest ingredients, so we analyze them for traces of over 1000 different substances. Only the products that pass our comprehensive inspection system earn the HiPP Organic Seal of Quality and end up in our jars.

On the website, Claus Hipp himself promises:

Now in our fourth generation, we have a special responsibility for the future. We want our children and grandchildren to inherit a world worth living in, and worth loving—a goal that has inspired us for over five decades.

It's one thing to talk about sustainability—but quite another to embrace it every day as the responsibility at the core of entrepreneurial action. Whenever we make decisions and develop new products, the first thing we do is to ask: What effect will they have on the world of tomorrow? The philosophy of our company focuses on conservation of nature, respectful treatment of nature's precious resources and protection of biodiversity, and with good reason. Our products are primarily designed for parents who want to feed their children as healthily as possible and give them a future worth living. For the past six decades we have done our utmost to give them the best support in this important task. But our responsibility also extends to our suppliers, our staff and their families. Because we know from experience that long-term success needs a strong foundation of ethical values—including responsibility for all creation.

Sincerely

Prof. Dr. Claus Hipp

? REFLECTION QUESTIONS

1. What image does HiPP try to project to the market?
2. Do you find this image to be credible? Why or why not?
3. Would you be willing to pay a price premium for HiPP products? If yes, for what reason?
4. Do you find it problematic that HiPP has not or has only partially adopted international safe food labels?
5. From the point of view of customers, what is the benefit of having the family strongly involved in the branding efforts of the firm?
6. What are the benefits for other stakeholders, such as employees, of seeing the family so personally engaged in the firm?
7. What opportunities and threats might the family face because of their open involvement in the firm (e.g., their personal guarantee of product quality)?

6.6   The institutional perspective

In their famous book *The Modern Corporation and Private Property*, Berle and Means (1932) hypothesized that as firms grew, concentrated (family) ownership would be replaced by the separation of ownership and control. The idea of an inevitable trend toward atomistic shareholder structures and the delegation of management to professionals was shared by Fama and Jensen (1983), who predicted that an organization would be penalized by its failure to separate ownership and control. Put differently, the concentration of ownership and control in family hands should be bad for performance and ultimately lead to the decline and disappearance of this type of organization (Morck, Wolfenzon and Yeung 2005).

Peng and Jiang (2010) have pointed out, however, that this evolution has not materialized, or at least not to the expected extent. Indeed, even in the United States about 20% of all publicly listed firms are family controlled. Family firms represent 30% of the total in their sample of publicly listed firms located in North America, Europe, Asia and Latin America (Peng and Jiang 2010). As La Porta, Lopez-De-Silanes and Shleifer (1999) note, on a worldwide basis, the separation of ownership and control is actually an exception rather than the norm; in fact, corporations are very often controlled by families. At the same time, these authors find significant international variance in the presence and ultimately success of family-controlled companies. For example, while all firms quoted on the stock market in Mexico are family controlled, this share drops to 0% in the United Kingdom. (For further comparisons in East Asia and Europe, refer to Claessens, Djankov and Lang 2000 and Faccio and Lang 2002.)

The institutional perspective has become a further prominent view to explain the variance in the presence and ultimately the success of family firms under various institutional regimes. The advocates of the institutional perspective suggest that institutions, defined by the formal and informal 'rules of the game' (North 1990; Scott 1995), can both enable and constrain organizational actions. For economic institutionalists (e.g., North 1990; Williamson 1985), institutions matter because they reduce transaction costs and uncertainty. For neo-institutionalists in sociology (e.g., DiMaggio and Powell 1983; Meyer and Rowan 1977), conformity with institutions confers legitimacy, and a lack of legitimacy can lead stakeholders to withdraw their support. Thus, the illegitimate firm may have reduced resource access and may ultimately have poorer organizational performance.

The institutional perspective is based on the idea that firms perform best when they are able to adapt to the institutional environment in which they are embedded. For example, institutional thinking holds that family firms should perform best if they adhere to the socially accepted norms of 'how business is done' and 'how firms should be run' in their specific societal context. Put differently, firms excel if they comply with the accepted 'rules of the game'.

This argument has been further developed at the micro level (the strategic choices of individual firms vs. the generally accepted strategic choices within a field) and at the macro level (the prevalence/absence of certain types of organizations in economic systems such as countries). We address both of these views below.

6.6.1 The micro view: strategic conformity of family firms

The micro view of institutional theory contends that firms' governance structures will determine whether strategic or institutional rationales prevail in their strategic decisions. Applied to the case of family firms, a strategic rationale implies nonconformity in firms' decision making. For example, family firms, free from the short-term preoccupations of public shareholders, can afford to pursue unique strategies based on the distinctive and powerful influence of the controlling family (Carney 2005). Much of the familiness literature that emphasizes the unique resources of family firms reflects such strategic thinking (Arregle et al. 2007).

In contrast, the institutional view maintains that family businesses should be associated with greater quests for legitimacy and therefore conformity (Miller, Le Breton-Miller and Lester 2013). The degree to which a family firm adopts conformist strategies—strategies that reflect the prevailing norms about how firms should operate in a certain context such as an industry—will likely depend on whether the firm is private or public. Private firms may have an easier time pursuing nonconformist strategies because they face less public scrutiny, in particular by the media, outside investors and analysts, compared to firms listed on the stock market. Publicly listed firms, in contrast, find their behavior constantly scrutinized with regard to the generally accepted norms of doing business (the appointment of outside board members, the adoption of international reporting standards, transparency rules, executive compensation plans, portfolio optimization via acquisitions or divestments etc.). Outside stakeholders, such as the press and in particular financial analysts and commentators, tend to view family firms with suspicion because they often do not adhere to the classical agency standards about how publicly listed firms should be operated. Family firms' preferences for maintaining family control, appointing family executives and pursuing SEW raise legitimacy concerns among nonfamily stakeholders.

When a family firm is public, its stakeholder base may be discomfited by the intermingling of family and business logics.

Ultimately, family firms may fear that they will have difficulty finding external support (e.g., access to capital, high-quality job applicants or favorable coverage by the press and analysts). According to the institutional argument, family firms should have strong incentives to compensate for their unorthodox governance structures by trying to appear legitimate and adopting strategies that signal conformity (Miller, Le Breton-Miller and Lester 2013).

The pursuit of conformist strategies by family firms is, however, not only motivated by the attempt to compensate for the legitimacy deficit that stems from the firms' somewhat unusual governance structures. In addition, compliance with generally accepted norms such as ecological regulations may directly benefit the owning family itself through its effects on reputation and SEW more broadly.

In the end, the institutional view maintains that conformity has positive outcomes in the form of better resource access, more support from stakeholders and better performance. In a study testing these predictions, Miller, Le Breton-Miller and Lester (2013) indeed find that family firms are more likely to conform to industry norms and by extension to the larger firm environment. With increasing family influence, the firm's capital intensity, ratios of R&D to sales and advertising to sales, financial leverage, and dividend policy will be closer to their respective industry medians. These conforming strategies ultimately lead to a higher return on assets (ROA). Interestingly, however, these strategies do not affect the firm's stock market performance.

More broadly, the institutional argument at the micro level maintains that family firms have incentives to adopt conformist strategies because of public scrutiny and suspicion as well as the family owner's intrinsic motivation to appear legitimate. These strategies in turn drive performance through improved resource access and stakeholder support (Figure 6.13).

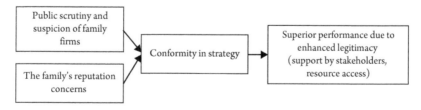

Source: Adapted from Miller, Le Breton-Miller and Lester (2013).

Figure 6.13 Conformity pressure and the performance of family firms

6.6.2 The macro view: family firms under various institutional regimes

Next to the micro perspective outlined above, the institutional perspective has also been applied to explain macro-level differences, and in particular the prevalence but also the prosperity of family firms in certain regions around the globe. The macro view has been especially popular in analyses of family firms and family business groups from emerging countries, in particular from Asia and Latin America. These countries are often characterized by weak institutions, as evidenced by low protection of property rights (e.g., the protection of minority owners), arbitrary or insufficient law enforcement, and underdeveloped financial and labor markets (see also the related discussion of agency problems at the beginning of this chapter).

The agency view portrays such environments as ideal breeding grounds for the abuse of power by local elites, who may expropriate the firm's stakeholders and in particular minority owners. This view emphasizes the opportunities that family blockholders may have for graft, abuse of power and the exploitation of their position for personal financial benefit at the expense of other stakeholders. From the agency perspective, emerging market family firms are depicted as parasites (Morck, Wolfenzon and Yeung 2005).

The institutional perspective is more optimistic about the behavior of family firms in weak institutional environments. This perspective sees family firms as paragons (Khanna and Yafeh 2007), and suggests that family firms should be well suited to fill the institutional 'voids' that arise in the absence of strong institutions. The core of the institutional argument at the macro level is that family firms can provide compensational practices that offset the disadvantages that firms face when trying to do business in weak institutional environments. These compensational practices come in several forms:

Social networks
Social networks and in particular informal ties are critical in environments where formal institutions (e.g., courts, security exchanges, banking systems and labor markets) are absent or unreliable. Knowing the right people and being able to count on their support is critical in the absence of functioning factor markets. Research on family versus nonfamily firms in transitioning economies indicates that family firms possess stronger social capital and are better able to exploit personal and informal connections (Miller et al. 2009).

Trust-based relationships

Family firms tend to be skilled at developing the kinds of trusted, long-term relationships that are especially valuable when contracts are difficult to enforce (Gedajlovic and Carney 2010). In fact, when formal legal and regulatory institutions are dysfunctional, founding families would be well advised to run their firms directly. Under low-trust circumstances, bestowing management rights to nonfamily, professional managers may invite abuse and theft. Family ties provide informal norms such as unconditional trust, mutual support, deference to family authority and altruism that are particularly useful in reducing transaction costs when the formal market-supporting institutions are lacking (Banalieva, Eddleston and Zellweger 2015).

Self-help through intermediary resources

In weak institutional environments, firms must rely on 'self-help' to replace the function of missing institutions. Family influence can be a key resource in such environments because families may be more willing to support their firms with needed resources (Gedajlovic et al. 2011). Family influence can minimize the problems associated with institutional voids and resource scarcity by providing firms with internal and external financing, intermediate products, human capital and knowledge. In such situations, minority shareholders recognize the role the family plays in ensuring the survival of the firm.

Reputation

Without regulatory protection, prospective shareholders may only be willing to entrust their funds to businesses with owners they know, respect and trust. As a firm seeks to acquire resources and develop trading partners, its reputation in the community becomes key. The reputation of the controlling family ensures cooperative behavior that is needed to honor reciprocity and promote continued exchange between trading partners over time. Greater family influence and associated family reputation thus serve as reliable contract initiating and enforcement mechanisms in environments where formal institutions (such as commercial law) are weak or absent (Aguilera and Crespi-Cladera 2012).

Tight and stable control

Long tenures allow family leaders to develop enduring relationships with external stakeholders and to commit their firms' resources on a 'handshake'. External partners tend to see family members in management and board positions as stable representatives of their firms, with the influence to make commitments and the ability to honor them (Verbeke and Kano 2010).

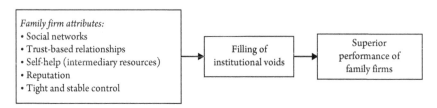

Figure 6.14 Family firm attributes, filling of institutional voids and performance

In sum, in an environment where institutions are weak and where external mechanisms are of little help in governing corporations, family ownership is a critical and positive driver of firm value.

Please note that both the agency and institutional perspectives predict a prevalence of family firms in underdeveloped institutional settings. The agency view suggests that this prevalence is due to the opportunity for family blockholders to expropriate nonfamily stakeholders, in particular nonfamily investors, which should lead to lower firm performance. In contrast, the institutional perspective attributes the prevalence of family firms to the inherent advantages such firms have in weak institutional environments; in this view, family involvement is advantageous to all stakeholders and results in better firm performance (Figure 6.14). Both views have found some empirical support. Overall, however, there is mounting evidence that family firms perform particularly well in weak institutional environments.

6.6.3 Family business groups: an institutional perspective

The prevalence of family business groups in many countries is the direct result of an institutional context that favors certain organizational forms. Business groups are defined as firms that, although legally independent, are bound together by a constellation of formal and informal ties and are accustomed to taking coordinated action (Khanna and Rivkin 2001). This type of firm is ubiquitous in many countries; think, for example, of Japan's *keiretsus* and *zaibatsu*, South Korea's *chaebols*, Latin America's *grupos*, Hong Kong's *hongs*, India's *business houses*, Taiwan's *guanxiqiye*, Russia's *oligarchs* and China's *qiye jituan* (Carney et al. 2011). While conglomerates and multi-divisional firms are also complex interconnected organizations, business groups are different in that they exhibit a more complex web of coordination mechanisms, such as multiple and reciprocated equity, debt, and commercial ties between top managers.

Many attribute the predominance of business groups in certain countries to market failures and poor-quality legal and regulatory institutions. According to this view, business groups emerge to internalize transactions in the absence of reliable trading partners or legal safeguards guaranteeing transactions between unaffiliated firms. Business groups in general have been said to be advantageous under weak institutional contexts as their scale and scope compensate for market insufficiencies through internal intermediation; for example, they can provide credit checks, internal transactions and pooled resources for their member firms. In their important study about business group performance, Carney et al. (2011) suggest that affiliates perform relatively well in contexts characterized by 'soft' voids in labor and financial market institutions, but also that business groups add no value in contexts lacking 'hard' infrastructure (e.g., telecommunication and transportation) and in fact damage affiliate performance in settings with underdeveloped legal institutions.

Family relationships in the inner leadership circle of a business group may enhance the group's intermediary role and contribute to the group's performance. Indeed, the inner circle of family business groups is often dominated by people with family ties or other kinship ties, such as a shared region or hometown, which creates an atmosphere of mutual exchange and support (Luo and Chung 2005). Kinship ties among group leaders make it easier to pool financial and human resources and exchange know-how and information. Family business groups are thus particularly well placed to internalize activities that are otherwise absent due to limitations in a society's financial, legal and labor market institutions that may jeopardize the exchange of products and services between arm's-length trading partners. In such contexts, family business group ties mitigate the problems created by institutional voids, function as an insurance policy in case of financial problems and offer access to resources that are unavailable to unaffiliated firms (Carney et al. 2011). From an institutional point of view, belonging to a family business group thus comes with significant advantages for the affiliated firm. These advantages tend to be higher in large business groups.

Still, it is important to also acknowledge the disadvantages for firms affiliated with business groups. Affiliate firms may carry a heavy *corporate burden*. Such bureaucratic and control costs tend to be particularly high in very diversified business groups. Costs for the affiliate firm also come in the form of *pyramiding*—that is, the control of many businesses with limited capital investments through a set of cascading parent–affiliate relationships (for details, see the discussion of control problems in family business groups in Chapter 5 on governance). As outlined by Masulis, Kien Pham and Zein (2011), smaller firms at the bottom of the business group pyramid benefit most from the internal capital market and the group's reputation. In contrast, firms in the middle level of the pyramid suffer most from group affiliation as they serve as bailout and intermediate institutions that are often called upon to support other group affiliates. Costs also materialize through *tunneling*, a process in which dominant shareholders transfer assets or profits from peripheral to core firms in which they hold relatively greater equity ownership. Affiliate firms are often *more leveraged, diversified and locally oriented* than their standalone counterparts, which explains part of the performance discount that many affiliate firms incur.

6.6.4 Some international comparisons

Given the above discussion of the prevalence of family firms under various institutional regimes, it is interesting to explore how that prevalence changes over time. Carney and Child's (2013) study of family firms' presence on public markets in East Asia in 1996 and 2008 suggests that family control has decreased slightly but remains the most dominant ownership form (Figure 6.15), with the total share of family firms in the region dropping from 51.6% in 1996 to 46.1% in 2008 (Carney and Child 2013). Their findings further suggest that the state has become a much more prominent owner of public corporations.

Despite this overall trend, there is significant variance among countries, as depicted in Figure 6.16. The sharpest decline of family firms happened in Taiwan and Thailand, while in the Philippines family firms became more prevalent. Interestingly, even in Japan, a country with strong institutions, the presence of family firms increased.

6.6.5 Summary and case study: family firm competitiveness from an institutional perspective

In sum, the institutional perspective suggests that family firm performance hinges on the firms' ability to comply with and adapt to the institutional context in which they are embedded. In other words, performance depends upon the firms' ability to efficiently deal with the 'rules of the game' that prevail in the societal context in which the firm is embedded.

The micro view within the institutional perspective suggests that family firms have incentives to seek legitimacy from their stakeholders, which they achieve by conforming to industry standards and hence generally accepted ways of doing business (such as industry norms, benchmarking, compliance with quality certification, and reporting standards). Family firms seek conformity because of the public scrutiny and suspicion that they face as publicly listed firms and because of their reputation concerns (i.e., the desire to appear as

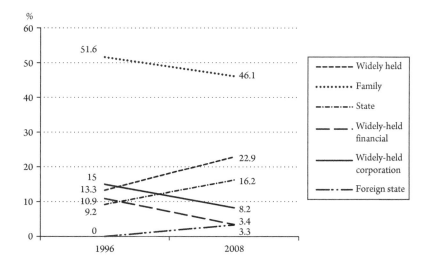

Source: Carney and Child (2013).

Figure 6.15 Share of types of organizations from 1996 to 2008 in East Asia[3]

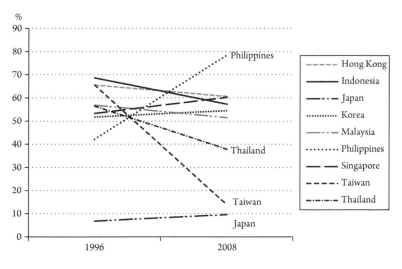

Source: Carney and Child (2013).

Figure 6.16 Change in prevalence of family firms in East Asian countries 1996–2008[4]

legitimate and reputed players). The pursuit of conformity ultimately contributes to performance via improved resource access and community support.

The macro view within the institutional perspective emphasizes that family firms are particularly good at filling institutional voids, for instance when property rights are insufficiently protected or labor and capital markets are dysfunctional. Drawing from their social networks, trust-based relationships, self-help, willingness to provide intermediary resources, reputation, and tight and stable control, these firms are able to compensate for the lack of institutional quality. In weak institutional settings, family firms are often organized as family business groups. Family business groups are particularly suited to internalize activities that are otherwise absent owing to limitations in a society's institutions that jeopardize transactions between arm's-length trading partners.

Practitioners who seek to explain and build a competitive advantage from an institutional point of view should ask themselves:

From a micro-institutional point of view:
- To what degree do we conform to industry standards and to generally accepted ways of doing business? How do we benefit from such a strategy?
- How can we improve our public legitimacy as a family firm?
- Which resources do we have access to given our conforming behavior?
- What other resources do we need to secure that we are currently lacking?
- What threats and missed opportunities do we risk if we comply with generally accepted ways of doing business instead of pursuing our own unique strategic path?

From a macro-institutional point of view:
- How developed is our institutional context in terms of: property rights protection, minority owner protection, law enforcement, development of equity and debt capital markets, labor markets, transportation and telecommunication?
- How can we compensate for institutional voids by drawing from our:
  - social networks,
  - trust-based relationships,
  - self-help and willingness to provide intermediary resources,
  - reputation,
  - tight and stable control?
- Is our governance structure adapted to our institutional environment? What are the pros and cons of being organized as a business group?

6.7 The paradox perspective

Despite numerous attempts to establish a link between family involvement and firm performance, the results are alarmingly inconsistent. Admittedly, inconsistent empirical findings are not uncommon in the social sciences. These findings can be attributed in part to definitional issues, measurement challenges, sample composition and, more broadly, contextual factors. What

CASE STUDY

Samsung Group

Below you find an overview of the Samsung Group shareholdings in the year 2010, which was simplified in 2014 to a more traditional holding structure (Figure 6.17).

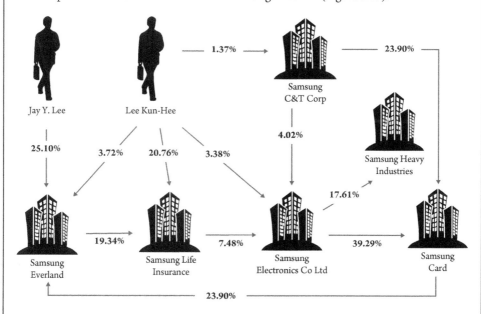

Figure 6.17 Samsung Group shareholdings in the year 2010

? **REFLECTION QUESTIONS**

1. What problems and opportunities do you see for the family owners of such a structure?
2. What are the advantages and disadvantages for the individual firms affiliated with the Samsung family business group?
3. Assume that you are small nonfamily shareholder in Samsung Electronics. What are your concerns and hopes about investing in this company?

is particularly disturbing in family business research and practice, however, is the inconsistency in the conceptual and theoretical arguments about how a controlling family contributes to firm performance.

Interestingly, all of the conceptual attempts to explain a link between family influence and performance that we have discussed so far contain arguments for both positive and negative effects. For instance, in agency theory the alignment of family owners and managers should lead to higher performance. But problems stemming from altruism can undermine these advantages. Similarly, family firms may benefit from positive familiness. But remember also that the resource base of the firm may suffer from negative family influence (negative familiness). Likewise, the organizational identity approach lends itself to positive but also more pessimistic accounts of family influence. Think, for instance, of corollaries of heightened family identification with the firm such as resistance to change and groupthink.

Whether one adheres to a positive or negative view of family influence, one must acknowledge that the link between the two is not as straightforward as expected. Both the positive and negative views receive solid support, reflected in succinct theoretical reasoning and wide empirical evidence. Given this complexity, it may be useful to take a step back and refer to our initial thoughts about the possible links between family influence and the competitive advantage of family firms.

In Chapter 2 of this book, where we reviewed various definitions of family firms, we discussed that family and business are partly incompatible social systems. In this orthodox view, introducing the family system, with its emphasis on tradition, unconditioned loyalty and support, into the business system undermines the efficient functioning of the firm. In consequence, a family orientation should lead to performance shortfalls in the firm.

The paradox perspective, which we introduce here, tries to overcome the tensions inherent in the tradeoff and contingency perspectives of family firms. The paradox perspective argues that the tradeoff and contingency views of family firms are biased toward linear consistency. Seeing family and business as juxtaposed and mutually exclusive forces may overlook the inherent synergies between these two worlds and the benefits that may arise from combining them in terms of managing tensions, paradoxes and inconsistencies (for some background reading on paradoxes and tensions in management refer to Smith and Lewis 2011 and Sundaramurthy and Lewis 2003).

6.7.1 What are paradoxes?

The paradox perspective assumes that tensions persist within evolving systems such as firms, and that these tensions can be used in ways that increase the efficiency of the organization. While contingency theory focuses on identifying the conditions under which organizations are more driven by certain factors (e.g., family vs. business interests), the paradox perspective asks *how* firms engage with these competing factors simultaneously.

The paradox view thus moves away from the idea of the simultaneous existence of incompatible dimensions in which managers are urged to overcome disjunctions. Rather, the paradox perspective suggests that actors should seek synergies between these seemingly incompatible dimensions and strive to harness efficiency advantages from complexity (Zellweger 2013). Smith and Lewis (2011, p. 382) define paradox as

> contradictory yet interrelated elements that exist simultaneously and persist over time. This definition highlights two components of paradox: (1) underlying tensions—that is, elements that seem logical individually but inconsistent and even absurd when juxtaposed—and (2) reactions by managers and firms that try to reach synergies from the seemingly competing forces.

This perspective of paradox alludes to the idea that we often face management challenges that are contradictory and complementary at the same time, in which one force enables and helps constitute the other (think, for example, of Yin and Yang as discussed in classical Chinese philosophy).

6.7.2 Tensions and paradoxes in the family firm context

Dealing with tensions is a central challenge for managers in both family and nonfamily firms. For example, there may be tensions between short-term and long-term focus, centralization and decentralization, internal and external sourcing, regional and international focus, exploration and exploitation to name a few. But the paradox perspective seems to impose itself on the study of family firms to a particular degree given the constitutive and inextricable link between family and firm in this type of organization. Demands for unconditional love, long-term focus and stability are often attributed to the family sphere, while demands for meritocracy, short-term focus and adaptation are often attributed to the business sphere (Stewart and Hitt 2010). As shown in Figure 6.18, family firms thus face the particular challenge of dealing with how to best link family and business in order to realize the synergies between the two systems.

Note that the list in Figure 6.18 is not a complete one, and that neither side of the tensions listed can be attributed to the family or the business system alone.

In dealing with tensions in family firms, we may be tempted to seek simple, linear and unidirectional solutions, driven by the belief that such solutions are best able to cut through the complexity of life. This may be partly due to the convenience of such rules: they give us simple and actionable advice about what to do in a particular situation. They also appear to result from empiricist approaches to management, with methods that originate from a natural science rather than a social science tradition. Think, for example, of mechanical and quantitative methods such as cost–benefit analyses, net present value assessments, target–performance comparisons and benchmarking. These methods suggest unidirectional cause-and-effect relationships between input and output, stipulate the existence of a single correct solution to a problem, maintain that this solution can be (best) found with quantitative methods, and hold that all the information needed to derive the solution is quantifiable in monetary terms. We are educated to reason along these lines: that is, we are trained to be logical,

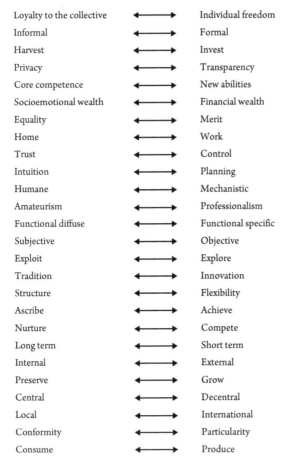

Loyalty to the collective	⟷	Individual freedom
Informal	⟷	Formal
Harvest	⟷	Invest
Privacy	⟷	Transparency
Core competence	⟷	New abilities
Socioemotional wealth	⟷	Financial wealth
Equality	⟷	Merit
Home	⟷	Work
Trust	⟷	Control
Intuition	⟷	Planning
Humane	⟷	Mechanistic
Amateurism	⟷	Professionalism
Functional diffuse	⟷	Functional specific
Subjective	⟷	Objective
Exploit	⟷	Explore
Tradition	⟷	Innovation
Structure	⟷	Flexibility
Ascribe	⟷	Achieve
Nurture	⟷	Compete
Long term	⟷	Short term
Internal	⟷	External
Preserve	⟷	Grow
Central	⟷	Decentral
Local	⟷	International
Conformity	⟷	Particularity
Consume	⟷	Produce

Figure 6.18 Paradoxical tensions stemming from the combination of family and business

consistent, precise and unambiguous, and to think in terms of wrong and false answers.

Unfortunately, however, many of the tensions described in Figure 6.18, and hence many challenges that are inherent in everyday management, do not lend themselves to such simplistic reasoning.

6.7.3 The promise of a paradox perspective for family firm management

One approach to solving the tensions listed in Figure 6.18 would be to say: let's forget about the left side and focus solely on the right side. It would be tempting to assign the attributes on the left side to the domains of family, irrationality and dysfunctionality, and to dismiss them as features that cloud the rational decision making needed for doing business. If we do so, however, then we ignore the opposing force and simply choose the other extreme as the dominant paradigm. This either/or approach is aligned with the opinion that you have to choose between family and firm, and that you have to decide whether you are a 'family first' or 'business first' family firm.

The either/or approach would likely lead to suboptimal and dysfunctional solutions. A paradox approach, which tries to harness the synergies between family and business, seems much more useful for managing family firms, for the reasons detailed below (Zellweger 2013).

First, there seems to be a largely overlooked common ground between family and business systems. While certain social rules and norms, such as support, commitment, cohesiveness and interdependence, are particularly pronounced in the family context, they are neither absent nor incompatible with the efficient functioning of the business sphere. Indeed, relationships characterized by these norms are often depicted as highly desirable in the business context. Just as important, certain attributes that are ascribed to the business sphere, such as the efficient use of resources, are found in familial norms such as parsimony and the provision of economic goods such as shelter and education.

Many family firm studies are undermined by flawed ontological assumptions about the nature of family and business social systems because they begin by defining each system as the opposite of the other. This line of research often assigns a negative and inertial role to family. However, even stability-providing systems, which are often associated with families, are essential grounds for organizational change (see, e.g., Feldman and Pentland 2003). In particular, the family may have a role in enabling as well as absorbing change. Family and business systems are not orthogonal, and the incompatibility of their respective social norms is largely overstated.

Second, the overwhelming prevalence of family firms in economies around the world challenges the tradeoff perspective between family and business goals. If most family firms pursue socioemotional goals that accrue at the family level, such as dynastic control, benevolent ties, positive affect and reputation, these nonfinancial goals cannot only detract from financial performance. If they did, the family firm as an organizational form would have disappeared long ago.

Similarly, it is unlikely that families uniformly deprive their firms of necessary resources. As depicted in the familiness literature, families often provide unique resources to their firms, such as patient capital, survivability capital and tacit knowledge, which serve as the basis for competitive advantage. In addition, because family firm owners are concerned not only about money, but also about resources such as reputation and social capital, the family and the firm do not systematically compete for the same resources. Thus, families should be seen as critical resource providers rather than systematic resource 'extractors'.

Fourth, and on a more general basis, a reductionist approach to family firm management neglects opportunities related to the combination of family and business that can help avoid the dysfunction that undermines organizational effectiveness. In fact, organizational theorists (e.g., Bateson 1972; Cameron 1986) suggest that without the tension that exists between simultaneous opposites in organizations, entropy occurs. That is, there is a process of self-reinforcement whereby one attribute in the organization perpetuates itself until it becomes extreme and ultimately dysfunctional. Effectiveness is achieved not by the mere presence of mutually exclusive opposites, but by the creative leaps, flexibility and unity that these opposites make possible. Thus, resolving the simultaneous contradictions in an organization and pursuing logical consistency may actually inhibit firm performance by eliminating the creative tension that paradoxes produce.

Taking all this into consideration, we suggest that 'professional' management in family firms should shift from a tradeoff or consistency perspective of family control to a paradox perspective (Figure 6.19).

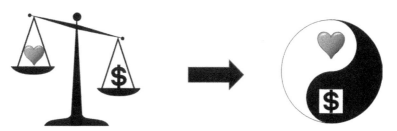

Figure 6.19 From a tradeoff to a paradox perspective

6.7.4   Management approaches to dealing with tensions

Building on the perspectives above, we arrive at four fundamental ways to approach the challenge of combining conflicting views of family and business systems (see Table 6.4).

One way forward is to *avoid* the other logic entirely (hence, to conceal and ignore). Firms that state they are a 'family first family firm' or a 'business first family firm' would fall into this category. Such a radically selective strategy is appealing to many executives as it suggests that the leadership of the family firm is simple and mono-rational. This may be a temporary solution, but the demands of the alternative view will emerge sooner or later, and they will be more challenging to accommodate the longer they are put off.

A second way forward is to *adopt* the alternative view. For instance, familial relationships may be reduced to contractual relationships that follow a cold economic rationale without the warmth and compassion that normally prevail between family members. Alternatively, the business may imitate family norms, for example by avoiding accountability and rejecting a performance orientation. However, this strategy lacks the critical and creative discourse that would harness the synergies between the two views. In the adoption scenario, one view still becomes extreme and ultimately dysfunctional.

Decision makers may also seek to *compromise* by minimizing the problems on both sides and settling for partial compliance. Family business owners who pursue compromise realize that some family influence on the firm is unavoidable and focus on limiting the family's negative impact while maximizing its benefits. In a similar vein, family business owners may seek to segment family influence temporarily (e.g., putting off increased family involvement until a later date) or organizationally (e.g., relegating family members to a part of the business where they can do no harm) (Schuman, Stutz and Ward 2010). Defining a policy for the firm's employment of family members is an example of such a strategy.

Table 6.4 Strategies for dealing with differing views of family and business systems: from selection to integration

	Strategy	Definition	Tactics	Opportunities	Threats	Examples
Selection ↓ Integration	Avoid	Avoid confrontation with the other view	Conceal, ignore	(Temporary) upholding of simplified view	Re-emergence of other view in inconvenient ways and times	Family firms that claim the family has no say in the firm
	Adopt	Adopt the other view	Imitate, give in	Conflict avoidance	Absence of critical and creative discourse; entropy (dominant view becomes extreme and dysfunctional)	Family firms that conceal the family aspect; 'we are a family first family firm'; 'we are a business first family firm'
	Compromise	Partial adoption of the other view whenever convenient, partial conformity	Negotiate, ponder, appease, segment	Involvement of multiple views	Conflict between multiple views, costly and time-consuming process needed to achieve compromise	Family employment policy
	Synthesize	Attempt to combine both views in the creation of a new view	Allow seemingly opposing opinions, seek common grounds and goals	Understand differing views, create integrated view that combines best of both perspectives	Challenge to create legitimacy for the new integrated view	Performance-based pay for family members; stock market listing of family firms

Source: Adapted from Thornton, Ocasio and Lounsbury (2012).

Finally, some may wish to *integrate* family and business views to form a new, combined strategy. Firms following this strategy would emphasize the common ground and shared goals of family and business (e.g., the long-term success of both systems), nurture a common understanding of their differing views, and emphasize the opportunity to create an integrated perspective that combines the best of both. For example, actors following an integration strategy may try to harness the focus on performance and accountability attributed to business systems along with the concern for mutual support and focus on the long term inherent to the family system. The integration strategy is hard to implement as it requires actors to acknowledge and value two worldviews that, when taken alone, are only partly compatible. But firms that are successful in these attempts will end up with a corporate culture and an approach to doing business that is very hard to copy. For instance, publicly listed family firms combine the demands of the financial markets with the stability of the family blockholders. In the end, family firms that achieve an integration of family and business will avoid 'family first' or 'business first' slogans, choosing instead to depict themselves as family *and* business first firms.

Avoiding and adopting are more selective approaches to dealing with tensions between family and business perspectives, while compromising and synthesizing are more integrative approaches. The guiding assumptions of an integrative and hence paradoxical approach to the strategic management of family firms are:

1. Family firms are inherently paradoxical organizations. Given the intertwined nature of family and business, family firms have to deal with two seemingly competing forces.
2. Family and business, however, are not *necessarily* competing forces. In fact, synergies may be achieved by linking these two perspectives.
3. Given that family and business are intertwined and that there are opportunities for creating synergies between them, family firms should ask themselves how they can exploit the family aspect in their firm.
4. Linking family and business in a synergistic way will ultimately increase the competitive advantage of the firm.

6.7.5 How the management of paradoxes drives firm performance

One of the best-researched paradoxes in the business sphere is the one between exploration and exploitation. Research on this subject examines the challenge of managing innovation, radical change and the search for distant solutions on the one hand and efficiency increases, marginal improvements

---

Dealing with paradoxes: the example of family employment policy

Family firms face the peculiar dilemma of whether to appoint family or nonfamily members to management positions. Decision makers dealing with this challenge have the following options:

1. **Avoid/choose**: Decision makers pick one side (family or business). For example, the firm might decide not to allow family members to work in operations.
2. **Adopt**: Family members are allowed to choose their own jobs in the firm.
3. **Compromise**: For example: family members are allowed to work inside the firm after two years of experience outside the company. Or: two members of every family branch (and only two) are allowed to work in the firm.
4. **Integrate**: Instead of choosing between fixed rules and no rules, owners agree to seek synergies between family and business in employment policy. Family members are not explicitly excluded from the firm, but their inclusion is expected to be synergistic (i.e., it should increase the overall effectiveness of the firm). For example, family members are allowed to work in the firm but must apply for a job opening. When applying for top management functions, family members have to self-assess their strengths and weaknesses and come up with a career plan. Any family member who wants to work in the firm must understand the advantages and disadvantages of doing so as well as the associated expectations (e.g., be a role model).

Source: Adapted from Schuman, Stutz and Ward (2010).

---

and the search for more proximal solutions on the other hand (March 1991). Focusing on exploration alone can be dangerous, as a firm may enter a downward spiral of trial and error without generating the necessary funds in the short run to finance this experimentation. Similarly, focusing on exploitation alone can be dangerous, as it may lead a firm to cling to current ways of doing business and miss the technologies and business models that will be relevant in the future (in other words, this strategy may be the equivalent of rearranging the deck chairs on the *Titanic*). The ability to simultaneously perform exploration and exploitation has been labeled 'ambidexterity', and has been said to lead to superior performance in firms.

While the ambidexterity argument applies to all types of firms, family firms should be particularly proficient in managing the exploration/exploitation paradox. Indeed, in a recent study among roughly 100 small to mid-sized private family firms in Switzerland we were able to confirm this hypothesis. We found that leaders in family firms are more aware than their nonfamily

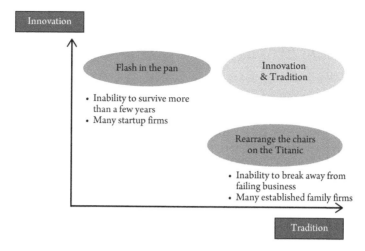

Figure 6.20 Tradition and innovation in family firms

counterparts of the inherent tensions that exist in the management of their firms and more optimistic that these tensions can be resolved in a productive manner. This attitude has a positive effect on a firm's ambidexterity and hence on the simultaneous pursuit of exploration and exploitation. Because family firms are more inclined to embrace these inherent tensions than non-family firms, they also see superior profits.

A similar tension exists between the focus on tradition and the focus on innovation. Many family firms seem to exploit this tension by suggesting that they can draw from a long tradition while at the same time keeping up with the times and embracing the future. Like the ambidexterity idea, the tradition/innovation paradox assumes that tradition and innovation are to a certain extent opposing forces. The best family firms realize that the 'problem' with this tension cannot be resolved, but it can be managed; thus, they engage in activities that are at the same time innovative *and* traditional. This paradoxical strategy allows family firms to draw from their inherent strength and to position themselves in a way that is both successful and difficult to imitate. The tradition/innovation tradeoff is depicted in Figure 6.20.

6.7.6 Paradoxes at play: innovation in family firms

A particularly intriguing context in which to study the paradoxical nature of family influence is innovation in family firms. On the one hand, family firms tend to be risk averse and may thus avoid risky investments in R&D and

In the feet of the ancestors—Research reveals the power of innovation through tradition

What helps family businesses to achieve breakthrough innovations? Trying to answer this important question researchers Alfredo De Massis and Josip Kotlar found innovation patterns that challenge conventional thinking on how innovation is best achieved. More specifically, the two researchers suggest that conventional approaches toward innovation are strongly orientated toward the future and that innovation managers are typically encouraged to downplay the past—'to discard it in order to make way for the new', as the two researchers say in a press release by the University of Lancaster in early 2014. In their research they found, however, that the past and the historic tradition of a firm can be a source of innovation. In their study of highly innovative family firms such as Beretta (an Italian firearms manufacturer founded in 1526) and Vibram (a producer of rubber soles and compounds, founded in 1937) the researchers found four distinct practices these firms deploy to leverage their past for current innovations.

1. **Historical narratives**
   The history of the firm and its traditions is actively communicated both to outsiders and, critically, to those within it. Websites, books, historical archives, multimedia and other techniques are used to continuously recall the past, so that the memories evoked become as strong for employees and managers as for the family. Beretta, for example, has a corporate museum housed in the oldest part of the company. 'There is a very clear intention behind this: namely, that in order for the innovators within the company to understand the past and to translate and use it, they have to be culturally close to those past elements', says Kotlar.

2. **Retaining the ancestors**
   Notable past members of the family are also given a very visible presence within the company. 'These firms tend to celebrate their ancestors and use symbols to put tradition into the minds of their innovators', explains De Massis. 'They tell stories about their ancestors, and hang portraits of them in the factory. So a whole new generation, all the family members, really share that kind of vision. They are very good at building the ancestor into a mythological figure.'

3. **Eliciting emotions**
   Events and shared experiences are used to instill the sense of tradition, ensuring it becomes part of the way of life for new generations and something to which they develop a strong emotional attachment. In Vibram, the family have a tradition of hiking together on a mountain first conquered by their ancestor, and it was the desire of some members to do these hikes barefoot that proved the inspiration for the FiveFingers shoe—a product that has been a breakthrough for the company in terms of market revenues. Likewise, at Beretta there is an annual summer retreat to the family villa. The family uses this place to convey the values of the past. Each new generation is also taken hunting with relatives at the age of around 15 or 16, almost as a ceremonial rite of

passage. De Massis and Kotlar suggest that these habits are meant to elicit emotions which seem to be important to create a particular attachment to those habits and a continued engagement for the future success of the firm.

4. **Corporate governance**

   Next to corporate governance, family governance seems to be a further critical contributor to family firm innovativeness. Put differently, practices that serve to maintain family values and identity and preserve the links with the past. The families that De Massis and Kotlar studied seem to have established more or less institutionalized processes of thinking strategically about who they are, what they are about and what they are doing. That happens both in the family and in the business.

   Can other firms learn from these examples? The beauty of tradition as a source of sustainable competitive advantage is that it is not easily imitated—the tradition is particular to the company. Yet innovation managers from other companies can still learn from the principles behind this approach, says De Massis. 'As long as a firm has some kind of tradition, whether in the firm itself or in the local region, innovation managers can imitate these practices.'

innovation. On the other hand, however, this conservative stance does not seem to hurt performance—overall, (private) family firms seem to outperform nonfamily firms (Carney et al. 2015). The question is: how do family firms manage the tension between their conservative attitude toward investing in innovation and the undisputed need to be innovative to survive in the market?

These insights point to the ability to manage the tension between tradition and innovation. Beretta is a particularly intriguing company in this regard because its motto—'prudence and audacity'—actually incorporates this fundamental tension. While 'prudence' suggests a careful, cautious mindset, 'audacity' emphasizes fearlessness and risk taking. With a sales volume of about €500 million in 2013, Beretta also carefully manages other tensions, such as the one between craftsmanship and automation in its production processes, or its local roots in Italy and the global reach of its products. At Beretta, the question is not whether to emphasize innovation or tradition. Rather, innovation *is* tradition.

The examples of Beretta and Vibram show that family firms seem to have unique ways of achieving innovation that challenge the standard assumptions about how innovation is best achieved. Standard practice suggests that the ideal way to achieve innovation is to increase investment in R&D. But maximizing investments in R&D does not seem to be the preferred path of family firms, despite the fact that some of them are highly innovative. To untangle this puzzle, we distinguish between innovation *input* on the one hand and innovation *output* on the other, as we did in our study of the innovativeness of family firms (Duran et al. 2016).

Risk aversion among family owners leading to lower innovation input . . .

Much of the research on the innovation behavior of organizations focuses on innovation input, which is defined as resources—such as money and workforce—that are dedicated to the exploration and exploitation of new opportunities. The relative size of the innovation input (for instance, investment in R&D as a proportion of revenues) is mainly dependent on the risk propensity of the key decision makers in an organization. Although innovation input is necessary for long-term firm sustainability, it is frequently seen as a risky investment.

Decision makers in family firms are generally risk averse because family members often invest large portions of their wealth in the firm and thus lack asset diversification. Consequently, family firms tend to prefer less risky investments in capital expenditures (CAPEX) such as production machinery and buildings (Anderson, Duru and Reeb 2012). Furthermore, because R&D projects frequently require capital from outside investors (e.g., raising bank debt and/or appointing outside managers and consultants), family members may see such efforts as leading to a loss of control and, thus, as a threat to their SEW. While non-investment in R&D might put the firm's long-term sustainability at risk, investment in R&D has an immediate negative effect on the family's SEW. Thus, we were not surprised to find that innovation *input* was lower in family firms than in non-family firms.

. . . while parsimonious resource orchestration leads to higher innovation output

While innovation input should normally enhance innovation output (e.g., the number of patents or new products), the ability to convert innovation input into innovation output varies across firms. Some firms may be particularly efficient at allocating and utilizing R&D investments, a process that is referred to as resource orchestration (Sirmon et al. 2011). In our study, we found that family firms are particularly efficient at turning innovation input into innovation output for two main reasons (Duran et al. 2016).

First, the firm-specific human capital and knowledge in family firms support an efficient utilization of resources. Employees and managers in family firms are known to have high levels of firm-specific tacit knowledge, which accumulates during their typically long tenures. Furthermore, the typical characteristics of a family firm, such as the firm's trust-based culture, the strong commitment of its organizational members, and its sense of community, also foster knowledge and idea transfers across hierarchies and thus promote innovative behavior. Although long employee tenure and strong commitment may hinder radical innovation, they have a positive effect on incremental innovation.

Second, the external networks of family firms make them particularly suited for innovative activity. Family firms' nonfinancial goals, including the preservation of strong ties to external stakeholders such as suppliers and customers, help them to build strong social capital. In turn, social capital helps these firms translate R&D resources into innovation output. For instance, knowledgeable network partners can help identify promising trends and inventions and provide valuable, timely feedback throughout the development process. This support can help reduce complexity and development costs and accelerate the development cycle (e.g., through preferred access to lead customers, tests of early stage innovations and referrals to new suppliers and customers).

Third, resource investment and deployment in family firms generally follow the parsimony principle (Carney 2005), which allows for higher efficiency. Decision makers in family firms strive for prudent and efficient resource use due in part to resource constraints and the desire to maintain control over the firm's deployment of resources. Lower governance costs—which stem from family owners' ability to closely monitor top managers as well as greater flexibility and less bureaucracy—further enable the efficient use of resources dedicated to innovation. In sum, family firms' human capital in the form of tacit knowledge, their social capital and the guiding principle of parsimony allow these firms to achieve higher innovation output than nonfamily firms (Duran et al. 2016).

The fact that family firms can turn lower innovation input into higher innovation output points to an intriguing paradox. Apparently, family firms face a constraint in the form of lower innovation input. But instead of suffering from this apparent disadvantage, this circumstance is transformed into an advantage, in this case through advanced resource management skills (Figure 6.21). This is a particularly intriguing case in which the seemingly opposing forces of family and business can be synthesized into a competitive advantage.

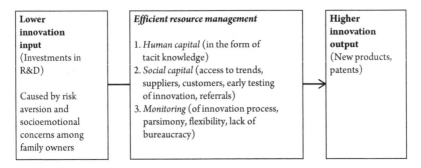

Figure 6.21 Turning lower innovation input into higher innovation output in family firms

6.7.7 What it takes to manage paradoxes: collective mindfulness

From early childhood on, we are trained that problems are here to be solved, and we are meant to make them disappear. The challenge with paradoxical situations such as those depicted in Figure 6.18, however, is that they cannot be solved—only managed. Finding a 'solution' to these paradoxes would require us to pick one side of the apparent conflict, thereby forgoing the benefits of the other side as well as the synergies between the two. The ability to manage such paradoxes efficiently requires what we call a family's 'collective mindfulness', or the controlling family's ability to make use of paradoxical thinking to seek synergies between the family and the firm (see Zellweger 2013). The following behaviors and attitudes indicate mindfulness in controlling families:

- Consciousness of bivalent attributes of family involvement.
- Hesitation to pick a family- or business-first perspective.
- Acceptance of and even appreciation for paradoxical situations.
- Tolerance for ambiguity: paradoxes cannot be solved rapidly.
- Willingness to engage in constructive debates.
- Reluctance to simplify.
- Wariness about biased perspectives.
- Avoidance of rule-based assumptions about the environment, as often seen in checklists.
- Prioritization of resilience, reliability and affordable loss.
- Sense of responsibility among firm owners.

6.7.8 Summary and case study: family firm competitiveness from a paradox perspective

In sum, the proposed paradox perspective does not negate the idea that family and business systems are social systems with partly contradictory logics. Rather, the paradox perspective considers the underlying tensions between family and business, but also between other contradictory aspects within companies, as avenues for achieving synergies from the seemingly competing forces.

Practitioners who seek to explain and build a competitive advantage from a paradox perspective in family firms should thus ask themselves:

- Where do we find synergies between aspects of the family and of the firm?
- Do we favor a 'family-first', a 'business-first' or a 'family-business first' philosophy?
- How can we best combine tradition and innovation?
- Are we simultaneously concerned with long-term firm survival and short-term change?
- Do we take risks while considering the maximum affordable loss?
- Do we accept and even appreciate paradoxical situations?
- To what degree do we tolerate ambiguity without seeking quick fixes?
- Is there a willingness to engage in constructive debates in our family and firm?
- Are we reluctant to simplify?
- Do we avoid rule-based assumptions about the environment, as often seen in checklists?

CASE STUDY

Managing paradoxes

According to Simon et al. (2005), family firms are confronted with the following seven paradoxes:

1. Family influence as a resource *and* a threat for the firm.
2. Be loyal toward the nuclear family *and* the extended family.
3. Combine short-term investor interests *and* the long-term survival of the firm.
4. Fulfill the expectation of the family for equal treatment *and* comply with the inequality paradigm in the business context due to differing personal achievements.
5. Ensure growth *and* independence.
6. Ensure adaptability in the business context *and* the continuity of family traditions.

CASE STUDY *(continued)*

7. Provide protection within the family context *and* ask for performance and personal exposure in the business context.

 REFLECTION QUESTIONS

Put yourself in the shoes of a family business owner-manager who has to deal with these paradoxes.

1. For each paradox, what are the threats involved in 'solving' the contradiction by opting for one side of the conflict and neglecting the other?
2. How would you go about managing each paradox?

6.8 Generic strategies for family firms

Given the heterogeneity of family firms and the various ways to explain their competitive advantages, attempts to identify generic strategies that family firms use to compete may seem futile. Still, the various conceptual approaches introduced above point to some common underlying themes. For instance, our discussions about SEW and the family firm's associated concern with reputation, branding and CSR point to the fundamental relevance of identity and image in family firms, a feature which may be leveraged in a competitive strategy.

Similarly, our examination of family firms' unique resources (e.g., tacit knowledge, social capital, human capital, patient financial capital), the unique ways in which these firms manage their resources, and family firms' ability to leverage their tradition to come up with new products suggest that family firms may have an edge in innovation.

Finally, family business owners' concern with keeping and perpetuating family control, their unwillingness to accept outside investors, and the related limitations on their access to outside resources suggest that family firms should be strongly concerned with efficiency.

Based on these considerations, we propose three generic competitive strategies that are shared by successful family firms (Table 6.5).

6.9 Tools for strategic management in family firms

The above sections have provided a rich foundation for the possible content of a successful family firm strategy. The previous sections have discussed in

Table 6.5 Three generic strategies of family firms

	Family aspect	Examples
Trusted brand	• Intertwined identities of family and firm • Concern for family and corporate reputations • Desire for transgenerational family control • Personal involvement of family members • Undiversified investment of family in firm	Fashion and luxury houses, hotels/ restaurants, wineries
Innovation champion	• Tacit knowledge about and experience with production processes • Networks with clients, suppliers, opinion leaders • Patient financial capital, allowing long-term innovation investment • Ability to leverage tradition in an innovative way • Resource constraints, parsimony and risk aversion lead to focus on efficient use of investments in innovation	German Mittelstand companies
Efficiency perfectionist	• Limited access to financial capital • Strong control by powerful families who work with their own money • Reinvestment of dividends • Parsimony of owners • Limited costs of equity capital as firms are often inherited from one owner to the next	Supermarket chains (Aldi, IKEA, Lidl, Walmart)

substantial detail the 'what' of strategy making in family firms. But we have not yet addressed the question of 'how' to develop a strategy—that is, the process through which a family develops a strategy for its business. This 'how' question, and hence the process of developing a strategy in a family business, will be the focus of the next few lines.

A critical question in this context is when the family should be involved in the strategy process. Given that the family is in most cases the controlling owner and therefore carries the ultimate risks and responsibilities associated with the firm, the family's role in defining the firm's strategy is a critical one. Family involvement thus should not be postponed until the moment of strategy implementation, but should be introduced early on, so that the family itself proposes the critical guidelines for strategy development. Ideally, the family provides the impetus for the strategy-making process. The strategy is then developed in a parallel and mutually inspiring collaboration between the family and the business.

From family values to the mission of the business

At the most basic level, the family defines its values. Then, the family comes up with a mission statement that may be encoded in a family charter. This is a critical input for the firm's mission. For instance, if the family fails to set down guidelines, the business side may envision a future for the firm that is not compatible with the owners' values.

From the family's guidelines for family control to the vision and strategy for the business

Once these normative guidelines are set, the family may progressively translate these values into strategic guidelines for the family, its wealth and its business(es). At the level of the family, family owners may have to make a statement about the current and future governance constellation (e.g., controlling owner, sibling partnership, cousin consortium or family enterprise; see Chapter 5 on governance for more details). At the level of family wealth, the family should determine whether wealth derived from the firm will be administered jointly or separately. Finally, at the level of the business(es), the family may set broad strategic guidelines about growth, risk taking, internationalization and third-party capital. These guidelines at the family, wealth and business levels are important in formulating a vision and strategy for the business (e.g., with regard to growth, investments and businesses to enter or exit).

From family, wealth and ownership governance to professional corporate governance

The family will also have to determine its stance and influence level in various firm governing bodies and eventually even in the firm's operations (see Chapter 5 about family governance). At this point, it is important for all family members who either hold a significant fraction of ownership or who work, have worked or wish to work in the firm to determine what their current and future role vis-à-vis the firm should be. It is not only the family's combined stance toward the firm that matters, but also the individual family members' visions of their personal involvement in the firm and the discussions they hold around this topic.

Depending on the family's goals for family wealth management, wealth management expertise may need to be secured and structures (i.e., embedded, family office or family trust) may have to be built (see the discussion about wealth governance in Chapter 5). Ownership governance in turn determines the relationships among family shareholders, voting rights and access to and transfer of shares. It also defines the family's involvement in the governing bodies of the firm, particularly its relationship with the board (see the discussion about ownership governance in Chapter 5).

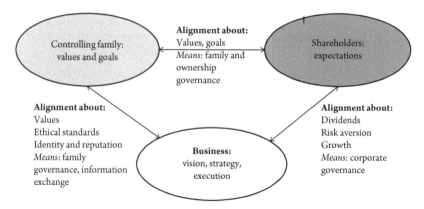

Figure 6.22 Alignment of family, shareholder and business goals

These guidelines pave the way for professional corporate governance. Corporate governance mainly refers to the collaboration between shareholders, the board and the top management to ensure the efficient working of the firm.

From family involvement to operative execution

Based on the guidelines determined in the previous steps, actual family involvement—and in particular next-generation involvement—takes place at the execution and operating levels. On the side of the firm, the focus is on financial planning, marketing and production plans and the execution of strategic initiatives. These functions split the overarching strategic goal of the business into distinct, manageable pieces.

In the end, the goal of such an integrated approach is to achieve an alignment between the values and goals of the controlling family, the expectations of the shareholders and the vision and strategy of the firm (Figure 6.22). Ideally, family and ownership governance may be used to help the family and the shareholders establish mutually agreed-upon values and goals.

In the relationship between shareholders and the firm, we expect to see an alignment with regard to dividends, risk aversion, growth intentions and the overall strategy of the firm. Professional corporate governance, and in particular the collaboration between a competent board and the management team, can be used to achieve this goal.

Although the link between the family and the firm is mediated through family, ownership and corporate governance, it may be useful to strengthen the informal ties between the family and the firm as well. Informal ties are a given in the context of smaller family firms, where family members are also shareholders and work in the firm. However, they become a more prominent issue for larger family firms, where it is no longer a given that the values, ethical principles, identities and goals of the family and the firm are aligned. This alignment is important in maintaining the identification of the family with the firm and ensuring that family and firm share a set of common values.

? **REFLECTION QUESTIONS**

1. What is socioemotional wealth (SEW)?
2. When do family firms prioritize SEW considerations over financial considerations? And when do these preferences shift?
3. Are family firms more or less risk averse than nonfamily firms?
4. What is familiness?
5. Discuss the typical resource advantages and disadvantages of family firms.
6. Discuss examples of how familiness drives or hinders the competitiveness of family firms.
7. What are the unique features of financial capital provision in family firms?
8. How are family firms unique with regard to resource management?
9. Why are family firms so concerned with CSR?
10. What image do family firms have in the marketplace?
11. If you were an owner of a family firm, how would you exploit the firm's image as a family firm in the marketplace?
12. Describe the unique strategies of family firms as brand builders and preservers.
13. How should complying with generally accepted norms of doing business contribute to firm performance? Why should family firms be particularly well positioned to comply with such norms?
14. Why are family firms particularly well positioned to exploit institutional voids (i.e., inefficiencies in labor and capital markets, the rule of law, protection of property rights and the like)?
15. Why is the family business group a prominent organizational form in many emerging markets?
16. What kinds of tensions are particularly prevalent in the management of family firms?
17. Why are family firms particularly good at managing these tensions?
18. What are some common paradoxes in the context of family firms?
19. Why is it problematic to solve paradoxes in a non-integrative manner (e.g., by avoiding or adopting one of the aspects of the paradox)?
20. What is the particular problem with arguments such as 'We are a business-first family firm'?
21. How are family firms able to exploit their tradition to come up with innovations?
22. What are the strengths and weaknesses of family firms with regard to innovation?
23. What are some generic business strategies of family firms, and on what family-firm-specific attributes do these strategies build?
24. Let's assume that you are asked to develop an integrated family, ownership and business strategy for a family firm. How would you approach this task? Along what process would you develop the strategy?

NOTES

1 All these works appeared in *Entrepreneurship Theory and Practice*.
2 We will relax the tradeoff assumption later on, but it is useful at this point in helping to clarify our arguments about the central feature of SEW.
3 Hong Kong, Indonesia, Japan, Korea, Malaysia, Philippines, Singapore, Taiwan, Thailand (Carney and Child 2013). Share of family firms from all publicly listed firms.

BACKGROUND READING

Aguilera, R., and R. Crespi-Cladera (2012). Firm family firms: Current debates of corporate governance in family firms. *Journal of Family Business Strategy*, 3 (2): 63–69.

Amit, R., and B. Villalonga (2013). Financial performance of family firms. In L. Melin, M. Nordqvist, and P. Sharma (Eds.), *The Sage Handbook of Family Business*. London: Sage, 157–179.

Anderson, R., and D. Reeb (2003a). Founding-family ownership, corporate diversification, and firm leverage. *Journal of Law and Economics*, 46: 653–684.

Anderson, R. C., and D. M. Reeb (2003b). Founding-family ownership and firm performance: Evidence from the S&P 500. *Journal of Finance*, 58 (3): 1301–1328.

Anderson, R. C., A. Duru and D. M. Reeb (2012). Investment policy in family controlled firms. *Journal of Banking and Finance*, 36 (6): 1744–1758.

Arregle, J. L., M. A. Hitt, D. G. Sirmon and P. Very (2007). The development of organizational social capital: Attributes of family firms. *Journal of Management Studies*, 44 (1): 73–95.

Banalieva, E., K. Eddleston and T. Zellweger (2015). When do family firms have an advantage in transitioning economies? Toward a dynamic institution-based view. *Strategic Management Journal*, 36 (9): 1358–1377.

Berrone, P., C. C. Cruz and L. R. Gomez-Mejia (2012). Socioemotional wealth in family firms: A review and agenda for future research. *Family Business Review*, 25 (3): 258–279.

Berrone, P., C. Cruz, L. R. Gomez-Mejia and M. Larraza-Kintana (2010). Socioemotional wealth and corporate responses to institutional pressures: Do family-controlled firms pollute less? *Administrative Science Quarterly*, 55 (1): 82–113.

Binz, C., J. Hair, T. Pieper and A. Baldauf (2013). Exploring the effect of distinct family firm reputation on consumers' preferences. *Journal of Family Business Strategy*, 4 (1): 3–11.

Carney, M. (2005). Corporate governance and competitive advantage in family-controlled firms. *Entrepreneurship Theory and Practice*, 29 (3): 249–265.

Carney, M., E. R. Gedajlovic, P. Heugens, M. Van Essen and J. Van Oosterhout (2011). Business group affiliation, performance, context, and strategy: A meta-analysis. *Academy of Management Journal*, 54 (3): 437–460.

Carney, M., M. Van Essen, E. Gedajlovic and P. Heugens (2015). What do we know about private family firms: A meta-analytic review. *Entrepreneurship Theory and Practice*, 39 (3): 513–544.

Carney, R. W., and T. B. Child (2013). Changes to the ownership and control of East Asian corporations between 1996 and 2008: The primacy of politics. *Journal of Financial Economics*, 107 (2): 494–513.

Chrisman, J., and P. Patel (2012). Variations in R&D investments of family and nonfamily firms: Behavioral agency and myopic loss aversion perspectives. *Academy of Management Journal*, 55 (4): 976–997.

Chua, J. H., J. J. Chrisman and P. Sharma (1999). Defining the family business by behavior. *Entrepreneurship Theory and Practice*, 23 (4): 19–39.

Claessens, S., S. Djankov, J. P. H. Fan and L. H. P. Lang (2002). Disentangling the incentive and entrenchment effects of large shareholdings. *Journal of Finance*, LVII (6): 2741–2771.

Claessens, S., S. Djankov and L. H. P. Lang (2000). The separation of ownership and control in East Asian corporations. *Journal of Financial Economics*, 58: 81–112.

Craig, J., C. Dibbrell and P. S. Davis (2008). Leveraging family-based brand identity to enhance firm competitiveness and performance in family businesses. *Journal of Small Business Management*, 46 (3): 351–371.

Deephouse, D. L., and P. Jaskiewicz (2013). Do family firms have better reputations than non-family firms? An integration of socioemotional wealth and social identity theories. *Journal of Management Studies*, 50 (3): 337–360.

Duran, P., N. Kammerlander, M. Van Essen and T. Zellweger (2016). Doing more with less: Innovation input and output in family firms. *Academy of Management Journal*, 59 (4): 1224–1264.

Dyer, W., and D. Whetten (2006). Family firms and social responsibility: Preliminary evidence from the S&P 500. *Entrepreneurship Theory and Practice*, 30 (6): 785–802.

Faccio, M., and L. H. P. Lang (2002). The ultimate ownership of Western European corporations. *Journal of Financial Economics*, 65 (3): 365–395.

Feldman, E. R., R. R. Amit and B. Villalonga (2016). Corporate divestitures and family control. *Strategic Management Journal*, 37 (3): 429–446.

Feldman, M. S., and B. T. Pentland (2003). Reconceptualizing organizational routines as a source of flexibility and change. *Administrative Science Quarterly*, 48 (1): 94–118.

Gedajlovic, E. R., and M. Carney (2010). Markets, hierachies and families: Toward a transaction cost theory of the family firm. *Entrepreneurship Theory and Practice*, 34 (6): 1145–1172.

Gedajlovic, E., M. Carney, J. Chrisman and F. Kellermanns (2011). The adolescence of family firm research: Taking stock and planning for the future. *Journal of Management*, 38 (4): 1010–1037.

Gomez-Mejia, L. R., K. T. Haynes, M. Nunez-Nickel, K. J .L. Jacobson and J. Moyano-Fuentes (2007). Socioemotional wealth and business risks in family-controlled firms: Evidence from Spanish olive oil mills. *Administrative Science Quarterly*, 52 (1): 106–137.

Habbershon, T. G., and M. L. Williams (1999). A resource-based framework for assessing the strategic advantages of family firms. *Family Business Review*, 12 (1): 1–25.

Kellermanns, F., K. Eddleston and T. Zellweger (2012). Extending the socioemotional wealth perspective: A look at the dark side. *Entrepreneurship Theory and Practice*, 36 (6): 1175–1182.

Khanna, T., and K. Palepu (2000). Is group affiliation profitable in emerging markets? An analysis of diversified Indian business groups. *Journal of Finance*, 55: 867–891.

Khanna, T., and Y. Yafeh (2007). Business groups in emerging markets: Paragons or parasites? *Journal of Economic Literature*, 45 (2): 331–372.

Koenig, A., N. Kammerlander and A. Enders (2013). The family innovator's dilemma: How family influence affects the adoption of discontinuous technologies by incumbent firms. *Academy of Management Review*, 38 (3): 418–441.

Luo, X., and C. N. Chung (2005). Keeping it all in the family: The role of particularistic relationships in business group performance during institutional transition. *Administrative Science Quarterly*, 50 (3): 404–439.

March, J. G. (1991). Exploration and exploitation in organizational learning. *Organization Science*, 1 (1): 71–87.

Masulis, R., P. Kien Pham and J. Zein (2011). Family business groups around the world: Financing advantages, control motivations, and organizational choices. *Review of Financial Studies*, 24 (1): 3556–3600.

Miller, D., and I. Le Breton-Miller (2005). *Managing for the Long Run: Lessons in Competitive Advantage from Great Family Businesses*. Boston, MA: Harvard Business School Press.

Miller, D., I. Le Breton-Miller and R. H. Lester (2013). Family firm governance, strategic conformity and performance: Institutional versus strategic perspectives. *Organization Science*, 24 (1) 189–209.

Miller, D., I. Le Breton-Miller, R. H. Lester and A. A. Cannella (2007). Are family firms really superior performers? *Journal of Corporate Finance*, 13: 829–858.

Miller, D., J. Lee, S. Chang and I. Le Breton-Miller (2009). Filling the institutional void: The social behavior and performance of family versus non-family technology firms in emerging markets. *Journal of International Business Studies*, 40 (5): 802–817.

Morck, R. K., D. Wolfenzon and B. Yeung (2005). Corporate governance, economic entrenchment, and growth. *Journal of Economic Literature*, 43 (3): 655–720.

Peng, M. W., and Y. Jiang (2010). Institutions behind family ownership and control in large firms. *Journal of Management Studies*, 47 (2): 253–273.

Schulze, W. S., and T. Zellweger (2016). On the agency costs of owner-management: The problem of holdup. Working paper, University of Utah and University of St. Gallen.

Schulze, W. S., M. H. Lubatkin, R. N. Dino and A. K. Buchholtz (2001). Agency relationships in family firms: Theory and evidence. *Organization Science*, 12 (2): 99–116.

Schuman, S., S. Stutz and J. Ward (2010). *Family Business as Paradox*. New York: Palgrave Macmillan.

Sciascia, S., and P. Mazzola (2008). Family involvement in ownership and management: Exploring nonlinear effects on performance. *Family Business Review*, 21: 331–345.

Scott, R. W. (1995). *Institutions and Organizations*. Thousand Oaks, CA: Sage.

Sirmon, D. G., and M. A. Hitt (2003). Managing resources: Linking unique resources, management, and wealth creation in family firms. *Entrepreneurship Theory and Practice*, 27 (4): 339–358.

Sirmon, D. G., M. A. Hitt, R. D. Ireland and B. A. Gilbert (2011). Resource orchestration to create competitive advantage breadth, depth, and life cycle effects. *Journal of Management*, 37 (5): 1390–1412.

Smith, W. K., and M. W. Lewis (2011). Toward a theory of paradox: A dynamic equilibrium model of organizing. *Academy of Management Review*, 36 (2): 381–403.

Stewart, A., and M. A. Hitt (2010). The yin and yang of kinship and business: Complementary or contradictory forces? (And can we really say?) *Advances in Entrepreneurship, Firm Emergence and Growth*, 12: 243–276.

Sundaramurthy, C., and G. E. Kreiner (2008). Governing by managing identity boundaries: The case of family businesses. *Entrepreneurship Theory and Practice*, 32 (3): 415–436.

Verbeke, A., and L. Kano (2010). Transaction cost economics (TCE) and the family firm. *Entrepreneurship Theory and Practice*, 34 (6): 1173–1182.

Villalonga, B., and R. Amit (2006). How do family ownership, control and management affect firm value? *Journal of Financial Economics*, 80 (2): 385–417.

Whiteside, M. F., and F. H. Brown (1991). Drawbacks of a dual systems approach to family firms: Can we expand our thinking? *Family Business Review*, 4 (4): 383–395.

Zellweger, T. M. (2007). Time horizon, costs of equity capital, and generic investment strategies of firms. *Family Business Review*, 20 (1): 1–15.

Zellweger, T. (2013). Toward a paradox perspective of family firms: The moderating role of collective mindfulness of controlling families. In L. Melin, M. Nordqvist and P. Sharma (Eds.), *The SAGE Handbook of Family Business*. Thousand Oaks, CA: SAGE Publications, 648–655.

Zellweger, T., K. Eddleston and F. W. Kellermanns (2010). Exploring the concept of familiness: Introducing family firm identity. *Journal of Family Business Strategy*, 1 (1): 54–63.

Zellweger, T., F. Kellermanns, J. Chrisman and J. Chua (2012). Family control and family firm valuation by family CEOs: The importance of intentions for transgenerational control. *Organization Science*, 23 (3): 851–868.

Zellweger, T., R. Nason, M. Nordqvist and C. Brush (2013). Why do family firms strive for non-financial goals? An organizational identity perspective. *Entrepreneurship Theory and Practice*, 37 (2): 229–248.

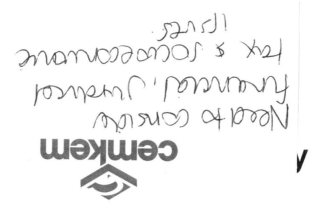
Succession is one of the most dominant topics in family business practice and research. Controlling a company with the intent to transfer it to the next family generation is often seen as one of the defining characteristics of family firms. Some even argue that the transgenerational outlook is what distinguishes family control from other types of corporate control (Chua, Chrisman and Sharma 1999). But beyond these definitional considerations, transferring the control of a business—whether to the next family generation, or to some other type of controlling body—represents a critical managerial challenge. This challenge is significant not only because it represents a once-in-a-lifetime event for many entrepreneurs, but also because it requires the consideration of a wide array of issues, including financial, strategic, juridical, tax and socioemotional issues. In consequence, dealing with succession requires a very broad range of competencies, which entrepreneurs rarely possess all by themselves. Even succession advisors often lack the full expertise required to guide firm owners through the succession process.

Every business succession is unique to a certain extent given the idiosyncrasies of firms, people and families. There is no one-size-fits-all solution. What is more, transferring control in a family firm is not like selling some shares in a public company—that is, it is not a transaction that can be confined to the seller and buyer. In many smaller family firms, succession impacts a wide set of stakeholders, including employees, clients, capital providers and, more broadly, the wider social environment. These stakeholders may have distinct expectations and demands concerning succession. Finally, succession is a transfer of corporate control that in many ways defies a purely financial logic. In one sense, of course, the succession is a financial transaction. But a multi-generational family firm is an asset from which many owners derive meaning that exceeds financial value. Many incumbent owners in family firms enter the succession process with specific goals for their firms and ultimately themselves. This creates a context in which feelings and emotions may bias decision making.

From a very practical standpoint, succession is a highly challenging process in family firms. The present chapter intends to shed some light on the sources of this complexity and to provide practical and integrative guidance on how to manage it.

7.1   Succession options

To fully grasp the complexity of the succession process, we must first consider the array of succession options. Family business scholars and practitioners tend to equate succession with a parallel transfer of ownership and management of a firm from one family generation to the next. In many countries, this is still the preferred option because it is often seen as the safest way to perpetuate the incumbent owners' vision for the firm and to create a long-term family legacy. In Poland, for instance, about 87% of all family firms are passed along this way. In Western Europe and the United States, however, this share is significantly lower and ranges between an estimated 30% and 50%.

Despite its perceived prevalence, the parallel transfer of ownership and management within a family is only one of several succession options. A two-dimensional typology can help distinguish between ownership and management transfers, and whether the transfer of control takes place inside or outside the family. Allowing for mixed combinations of family and external managers and owners, we identify the following succession options (Figure 7.1):

		Leadership		
		Family internal	**Combination**	**Family external**
Ownership	**Family internal**	Family succession	Mixed management	Professional management
	Combination	Partner or private equity	Mixed management and ownership (e.g., publicly listed family firm)	Financial investment
	Family external	Ongoing family involvement after succession		Transfer to employees, MBO, sale to co-owner, sale to financial or strategic buyer, liquidation

Figure 7.1 Succession options

Considering these various succession options in full is an essential step that increases the scope of action for both incumbent and successor. Next to the prototypical intra-family succession, we find various external exit options, such as the transfer of control to the firm's employees, the sale to the existing management (management buyout, or MBO), the sale to a new management (management buy-in, or MBI), or the sale to a financial (such as private equity) or strategic (such as a competitor) buyer. Alternatively, the incumbent owner may decide to sell to a co-owner, whether from inside or outside the family.

Next to these options, various combinations of family and nonfamily involvement are conceivable on both management and ownership levels. For example, ownership can remain in the hands of family while management is shared or completely turned over to nonfamily managers. But incumbent owners may also consider opening up ownership. Financial investors such as other families, institutional investors or private equity can take over fractions of ownership ranging from minority to majority stakes. Alternatively, family firms may consider listing the firm on the stock market, thereby selling out fractions of family ownership, or establishing a trust/foundation that serves as the ultimate owner.

Often, partially selling out or publicly listing the company is a viable succession option when parts of the family (e.g., branches of the family tree) want to relinquish their investment in the firm. These options thus serve both a succession and a governance motive, which is to simplify the shareholding structure.

The availability of these options is contingent on the firm itself, the interests of the involved parties and the institutional environment. For a small company, the intra-family transfer, the transfer to employees or the sale to a co-owner may be the sole options available. As firms grow larger, it may become increasingly difficult to transfer all ownership to an individual family successor. In these cases, ownership may be split up among children or (partially) opened up to external investors. Management may be kept in the family or passed to nonfamily managers, depending on the availability of management expertise. But size is not the only constraint on the availability of exit options. Profitability is important, too. For example, a failing firm will have difficulty finding a successor, whether from inside or outside the family. In this case, liquidation may be the best option.

The availability of exit options also depends on the interests of the involved parties. For instance, an incumbent owner may wish to pass on complete ownership and management involvement and the related responsibilities. Alternatively, the incumbent may want to keep a minority ownership stake. More broadly, the incumbent may have a preferred order of succession options.

Finally, the availability of exit options is contingent on the institutional environment and, in particular, the availability of legal instruments (Carney, Gedajlovic and Strike 2014) and external capital. In institutional environments with weak capital supply, as evidenced by an underdeveloped banking sector and a small equity capital market, transferring the business to nonfamily buyers will be challenging because of limited capital availability. Similarly, in the absence of qualified human capital, that is, well trained and experienced nonfamily managers, a family member will be the most efficient succession option, as he/she will have some knowledge about the firm and a trust-based relationship with the incumbent owner and other involved family members.

7.2 Opportunities and challenges of succession options

The succession options displayed in Figure 7.1 all come with specific advantages/opportunities and disadvantages/challenges. These are compiled in Table 7.1.

For many owners, the liquidation of the company—for instance, by progressively selling assets, not renewing job openings and reducing overall business activity—is still seen as a failure. But from the stakeholders' perspective (in particular, employees and customers), an orderly and timely liquidation may seem more responsible than a forced continuation of the business. This is especially the case for companies in decline. However, a timely exit through liquidation may also be the most reasonable option for the many small firms whose owners have reached retirement age and which lack any employees interested in taking over.

As the succession options listed above illustrate, the switch from an intra-family transfer of management and ownership to nonfamily involvement comes at a price for the family in most instances. While from a financial standpoint it can make sense to open up the firm to nonfamily influence, from a socioemotional viewpoint this choice involves loss. Family owners who derive socioemotional wealth (SEW) from the firm—for example, in the form of the wish to secure transgenerational control in family hands, ties between the firm's and the family's reputations, benevolent ties to

Table 7.1 Opportunities and challenges related to selected succession options

Description	Opportunities	Challenges
Family ownership and management	• No need to search for successor • Continuation of family's entrepreneurial legacy • Preservation of firm's independence and jobs • Willingness to compromise on sale price facilitates financing • Knowledge transfer from incumbent to successor • Low information asymmetries • Seamless and closely followed succession	• Qualification and interest of successor not necessarily given • Need for long-term planning • Conflicts due to unequal treatment of children (role in the firm and financial compensation), especially if the succeeding child is preferred • Conflicts between senior and junior generations
Mixed management, family ownership	• Family remains in control and sets strategic goals • Relief for family regarding operating responsibilities • Access to wider talent pool • Temporary solution when next generation is too young to take over management responsibility	• Selection of managers • Distrust between family and nonfamily managers • Differing degrees of identification and goals within management • For the family, reduced influence but equal risk
Nonfamily management, family ownership	• Preservation of family control • Unbiased focus on managerial expertise, independent of family concerns • Reduced operating pressure for family • Opportunity to resolve (family) ownership issues independent of management issues	• Limited insight and influence of family owners • Potential distrust between owners and managers • Agency problems between owners and managers regarding risk taking, goals and incentives • Threats to family-influenced corporate culture, short-termism • Loss of managerial competencies in family • Limited commitment and identification of nonfamily managers
Family management, mixed ownership	• Pruning the family tree: short-term or long-term solution for partnership with investor to finance exit of parts of family	• Divergent interests between family and nonfamily investors • Differing (higher) return expectations among nonfamily investors in comparison to family investors

Table 7.1 (continued)

Description	Opportunities	Challenges
Family management, mixed ownership	• Capital influx to finance expansion, increased liquidity for firm • Distribution of investment risk • Increased stability of financial structure	• Manipulation of managerial decision making by investors • Exit of nonfamily investors
Mixed management and mixed ownership	• Capital influx to finance expansion • Renewed managerial impetus and expertise	• Loss of influence for family • Potential for conflict in case of diverging management and ownership priorities • Potential for conflict in case of diverging priorities among owners
Nonfamily management and mixed ownership	• Capital influx to finance expansion • Renewed managerial impetus and expertise • Combination of powers to enhance competitive position	• Loss of influence for family • Incentive and control issues with managers • Limited proceeds from sale if only small ownership stake sold • Reduction in dividend and control rights
Transfer to employees, MBO	• Independent survival of the firm, with management that shares the values and vision of the incumbent owner • Stability for stakeholders (e.g., employees and clients) • Management well informed about firm and related challenges: low levels of information asymmetry • Performance of managers-turned-owners improves	• Often only feasible with seller financing (e.g., seller loan) • No maximization of sale price: loyalty discount to managers; financing mainly from firm's cash flows • Conflicts between incumbent and new owners: (1) during negotiation as management is engaged on both the buyer and the seller side; (2) after deal is closed as a consequence of role changes
Sale to financial or strategic buyer	• Larger number of potential buyers • Opportunity to maximize sale price • Freedom to start new period in owner's life • Opportunity to start new venture with proceeds from sale	• Loss of entrepreneurial legacy • Privacy issue in preparing sale • Publicity and eventual threats to family reputation • Hardly any way back to family control

Table 7.1 (continued)

Description	Opportunities	Challenges
Sale to co-owner	• If co-owner available: availability of potential buyer • Often valuation predetermined as part of buy–sell agreement • Simplification of ownership structure, 'pruning the family tree'	• Financing: does co-owner have the funds to pay out the incumbent?
Initial public offering (IPO)	• Capital influx • Professionalization of the firm • Exit opportunity for family, 'pruning the family tree' • Tradability of shares, even for remaining family shareholders	• Administrative costs • Public exposure of firm and family • Analyst pressure for short-term performance • Loss of family business culture
Liquidation	• Orderly wind up of firm, especially if not performing	• Loss of firm, eventually assets and jobs

stakeholders or emotional attachment to the company—may find it hard to accept nonfamily owners or management. A succession option that appears promising from a financial standpoint may thus appear harmful from a socioemotional standpoint. Depending on the level of SEW that the family has tied up in the firm, the family may prefer a succession option that preserves family control despite the eventual financial benefits of nonfamily involvement.

In many cases, and often as a consequence of firm growth, the pattern of succession choices alters over time. While first-generation family firms are often passed down within the family, as a firm increases in size and complexity, management is often shared with and then completely handed over to nonfamily managers. With growing funding needs, ownership is progressively opened up to nonfamily investors, ultimately culminating in the sale of the firm and the complete exit of the family. Over time, financial considerations usually come to the fore, while socioemotional concerns around the core business tend to recede.

7.3 Significance of succession options

The significance of different succession options varies widely across countries and therefore across institutional settings. As mentioned above, in Poland, a country in which a first generation of founders is giving way to a second generation of entrepreneurs after a period of communist rule, 87% of all ownership and management successions take place within the family. These figures drop to significantly lower levels in other European countries; for instance, the rate is 43% in Germany, 40% in both Sweden and Switzerland, and 33% in Denmark (for some background on these figures, see Bennedsen et al. 2007; Wennberg et al. 2012).

Data collected in 26 countries as part of the Global University Entrepreneurial Spirit Students' Survey (GUESSS) project sheds additional light on the relevance of intra-family successions across the globe. This large-scale international dataset suggests a curvilinear relationship between the countries' GDP and the strength of succession intentions among potential successors (see Figure 7.2) (Zellweger, Sieger and Englisch 2012). Interestingly, in relatively

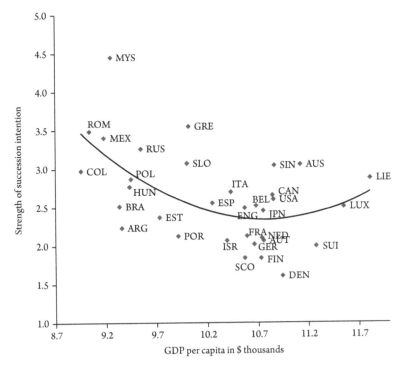

Source: Zellweger, Sieger and Englisch (2012).

Figure 7.2 Strength of succession intention among students with family business backgrounds

poor countries such as Pakistan, China, Romania and Chile, we find relatively high levels of succession intention among students whose parents own a company. Those in very rich countries, such as Singapore and Luxembourg, share this relatively high level of succession intention. However, in countries with medium levels of GDP per capita, succession intentions are rather low among students with family business backgrounds.

In poorer countries, the succession career path is relatively attractive compared to other career paths. In these countries, a potential successor may choose between joining the parents' company, seeking employment in an underdeveloped labor market or founding a firm in the context of a weak banking system, underdeveloped capital markets and weak protection of property rights. In contrast, in more developed and wealthier countries such as the United Kingdom, Germany, France, the Netherlands and the United States, potential successors typically find job alternatives that are often more attractive to taking over the family firm. Thus, in countries with medium levels of GDP per capita, succession intentions are relatively weak. Finally, in the context of very rich countries, potential successors may be inclined to take over the family firm for reasons that are not solely financial, such as legacy creation. Alternatively, in these countries taking over the family firm may seem attractive because it represents an opportunity to pursue an entrepreneurial career without immediate financial pressure. At the same time, because these very rich countries tend to be smaller in size (especially Luxembourg and Liechtenstein), the succession career path may seem relatively attractive due to a smaller labor market.

7.4   Declining relevance of intra-family succession

For an intra-family succession to take place, the first requirement is a successor willing to take over. Despite international variance, an international survey on the topic reveals that, overall, next-generation family members do not show a strong intention to take over the business (Zellweger, Sieger and Englisch 2012). As shown in Figure 7.3, only 22.7% of all students with family business backgrounds in a global sample of students whose parents own a firm have thought about taking over their parent's firm. In addition, 47.9% of students with firms in their families have never considered succession as a career path. When we asked all the students with a family business background about what they intend to do as new graduates in comparison to what they intend to do once they are five years out of school, we find that only 6.9% among the new graduates intend to take over straight after school, whereas this share rises to 12.8% five years after graduation.

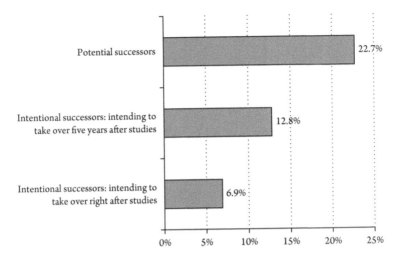

Notes: Potential successors defined as students with a family business background who could see themselves at the helm of their parents' firm or have already started to take over their parents' firm. The sample includes all 5363 respondents across 26 countries, all with family business backgrounds (mean age of respondent = 23.5 years). The mean firm size is 31 employees, and the standard deviation is 96 employees.

Source: Zellweger, Sieger and Englisch (2012).

Figure 7.3 Succession intention immediately after graduation and five years later

The relatively weak intention of potential successors to take over the family business is also interesting to explore from a dynamic point of view. Indeed, we can think of several underlying trends in developed economies that make the family-internal succession career path progressively unattractive for potential family successors.

1. **Decreasing family size**

    The drop in intra-family succession may be linked to underlying demographic trends toward lower fertility rates in developed and most Western economies. The mean fertility rate in Organisation for Economic Co-operation and Development (OECD) countries in 2012 was 1.76 births per woman, while it was 3.04 in 1970. As a direct result, the pool of direct family successors in OECD countries has been falling.

2. **Changing family structures**

    While marriage rates are decreasing in most developed economies, divorce rates have increased significantly over the past century. For instance, in the United States, divorce rates have doubled since the 1950s. In parallel, the number of out-of-wedlock births is increasing. For example, in the European Union in 2010, some 38.3% of children were born outside marriage, while the corresponding figure for 1990 was 17.4%. The result is a sharp increase in nontraditional family structures.

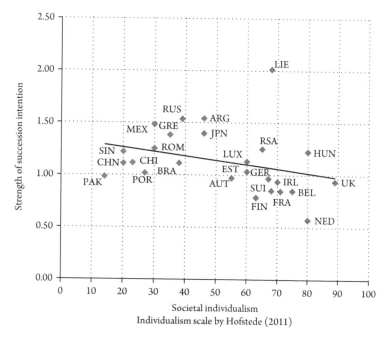

Source: Zellweger, Sieger and Englisch (2012).

Figure 7.4 Societal individualism and strength of succession intention

This does not mean that the family as a social category is necessarily less significant, but it does indicate that social networks may alter and reconfigure throughout a person's life. In the context of business succession, it may be that nontraditional families have less clear 'heirs' to succession. In these families, a firm may be viewed more as a utilitarian asset and less as a legacy asset to be passed down within the family.

3. **Individualism in society**

With progressing economic development, societies tend to become more individualistic. In individualistic societies, the ties between individuals are looser and independence is highly valued. In contrast, in collectivist societies, strong, cohesive groups such as extended families dominate; in these groups, unquestioning loyalty and acceptance of strict power structures are valued. In a recent study on succession intentions, we found that students who grow up in individualistic societies are less likely to choose the succession option (Figure 7.4). Entering the family firm means accepting, at least to some degree, the structures and norms that have been established by the family, a context which runs counter to the ideal of an independent life valued in an individualistic society.

One consequence of individualism is a weaker inclination to take on responsibility for the social group. Taking over the family firm often comes with the responsibility of successfully continuing the business as well as honoring familial achievements. Thus, individualistic potential successors will likely avoid the succession path and instead choose to work outside the family firm or to start their own firm (Zellweger, Sieger and Halter 2011).

4. **Multioptional society**

As contemporary sociology emphasizes, individualistic societies come with an increase in options or choices. This multioptionality manifests itself prominently in career patterns that are less linear and predictable. Driven by a strong desire for flexibility and self-realization in their life course, younger professionals with many options are less likely to aspire to a lifetime job. This sociological trend runs counter to the career of a successor in the family firm, a role in which the successor is often expected to persist until retirement.

5. **Demographic trends**

A further trend reducing the attractiveness of a career as a successor can be found in the aging of the workforce. Workers now remain in the workforce longer, and parents may not be willing to step back from their leadership roles at the time when their children are graduating and taking their first jobs. By the time the incumbent generation vacates their leadership roles, their children will have likely started their own specialized careers, raising the costs of a career switch into the family firm.

In part, the above trends are counteracted by the more egalitarian treatment of male and female offspring in succession. While in earlier generations many family firms followed the unwritten rule of primogeniture, and hence the succession of the eldest son, gender and birth order preferences have fortunately been decreasing in recent years.

It is important to note that the declining relevance of intra-family succession does not necessarily lead to the decline and failure of family firms. Rather, the general decline in intra-family succession goes hand in hand with an increase in mixed and external successions, in particular sales, MBOs and MBIs in many developed economies. The institutional context in these developed economies is characterized by well-functioning capital and labor markets that support the efficient allocation of resources. Interestingly, a large-scale longitudinal study from Sweden shows that firms transferred to external owners outperform those transferred within the family, but that survival is higher among intra-family transfers (Wennberg et al. 2012). These performance differences are attributed to the perseverance of family firms passed on to the next generation and to the entrepreneurial impetus and abilities of nonfamily acquirers. More efficient resource allocation in developed labor and capital markets includes better matches between the abilities of potential successors and jobs or entrepreneurial opportunities outside the family business. At the same time, efficient capital markets make it more probable that family firms that enter the market find a buyer capable of financing the takeover.

7.5 Sources of complexity in family business succession

In contrast to the strictly financial sale or acquisition of shares of a publicly quoted company, succession has a highly social aspect. For instance, buyer and seller, that is, successor and incumbent, are often interdependent and know each other well. The transfer of the firm, especially in intra-family successions, is an exchange that involves give and take on both sides. The result is a significant amount of complexity in the succession process. We explore some causes of this complexity below.

1. **Multiple stakeholders with diverging claims**
   Because most successions concern the transfer of large ownership stakes or even the entire firm, stakeholders will likely be impacted by the succession and will want to voice their claims. The group of affected stakeholders may include the individual owner, the owner's family, the firm and the society in which it is embedded.

   At the individual level, incumbent owners most often seek to preserve the independence of the firm. At the same time, they seek financial compensation for their ownership stake, which may form part of their pension. The family of the incumbent owner most often emphasizes harmony within the family and the fair treatment of the next generation. Individual firm managers will be concerned about their salaries, their future role in the firm's hierarchy and, more broadly, their employment. Employees, customers, suppliers and banks are concerned about employment, continued supply, timely payment and continued debt service respectively. In addition, stakeholders at the social level may have legitimate claims and exercise pressure on how the succession is executed. For instance, the media will be interested in knowing how the firm is passed on, when and to whom, and what the implications are for jobs and local engagement. Similarly, the government will be interested in tax income and externalities of the succession such as eventual unemployment.

   The complexity of succession in family firms stems from the involvement of multiple stakeholders with diverging claims. Notably, these concerns are not financial alone—consider, for instance, the claims at the family level or the goal of many sellers to preserve the independence of the firm. The stakeholders involved cannot always be satisfied with money.

2. **Role complexity**

   Most importantly, the complexity of the succession process arises because the incumbent entrepreneur is a decision maker who occupies several roles simultaneously: owner, manager, family member and citizen. Unlike many advisors, who tend to only consider a specific technical aspect of the succession challenge (e.g., valuation, tax aspects), the incumbent owner is confronted with multiple and often competing claims. For instance, the incumbent may be caught between family and business logic when choosing a successor: as a parent he/she would most likely prefer a child as successor, but as a CEO he/she will likely prefer the most competent person, who is more likely to be found among the large pool of managers outside the family. The owner often has to choose 'which hat to wear' in these situations. In other words, which logic—family or business—should they adhere to in a specific decision context?

3. **Not one, but multiple successions: ownership, board, management and wealth succession**

   Succession not only implies the transfer of a firm as an impersonal, legal entity, but also the transfer of roles—in particular, ownership, management and board roles. While these role transfers can be planned according to a timeline, family firm owners often overlook the effect that transferring roles has on their personal wealth. For most owners, the firm represents the largest fraction of their personal wealth; thus, passing the company to a successor has an immediate impact on their wealth and that of their family. This impact comes in two distinct forms. First, the transfer price affects the amount of wealth that can be extracted (e.g., used for the incumbent's pension) and eventually distributed within the family. Second, there may be fairness concerns within the family about which next-generation members receive which share of total family wealth. In the presence of multiple children, passing the firm on to a single child implies a significant material disadvantage for any other existing children.

4. **Technical complexity**

   Unlike many other business-related decisions, succession touches upon a multitude of topics and technical questions across a broad range of disciplines. Actors involved in the process need to tackle interpersonal and governance questions and deal with the current and future strategic position of the firm. Financial, legal and tax aspects interfere in the process as well. Incumbents and their families are challenged with a multi-disciplinary decision context in which it is very difficult for a single person to contribute all the necessary expertise. In consequence, many incumbent and even next-generation owners have to rely on third-party advice to deal with the full complexity of the situation.

5. **Imperfect capital market**

The transfer of private family firms takes place in a capital market that is far from perfect in terms of liquidity and transparency. Family firm shares are often completely or highly illiquid. Many private firm characteristics are hidden, and the data used to assess the financial health of such firms is often incomplete and flawed. In addition, the matching between buyer and seller takes place in a private context, often through a specialized broker or advisor. In consequence, the valuation of private family firms is based on more or less justifiable proxies and assumptions. What further complicates valuation and ultimately the transfer of the firm is the assessment of an eventual value premium/discount attributed to family involvement.

6. **Information asymmetries**

Significant information asymmetries complicate the transfer of power in family firms. On the one hand, there is significant information asymmetry on the side of the buyer/successor in relation to the quality of the firm (Dehlen et al. 2012). The successor often has limited insight into the firm's financial details. The successor also faces a moral hazard risk imposed by the post-transaction behavior of the incumbent owner. For instance, the incumbent owner may start a competing firm after exiting and try to poach the best managers from the original firm.

On the other hand, because most sellers/incumbent owners of private firms are concerned with the successful and independent continuation of their firms ('their baby') in the future (Graebner and Eisenhardt 2004), they are also confronted with information asymmetries. For instance, incumbent owners face uncertainty about the ability of the new owner-manager to successfully run the firm.

These information asymmetries tend to be smaller in an intra-family transfer of ownership and management. But for the growing number of transfers outside the family, they engender significant complexity; for example, successors must signal their abilities and incumbents must screen successors in some way before closing the transaction. At the same time, contractual elements such as earn-out structures and penalty clauses have to be negotiated to align the incumbent's and successor's post-transaction behavior.

7. **Long and often uncertain timeframe for completion**

Succession is often not a simple transaction but a process that spans multiple years, in many cases with an uncertain outcome and completion date. Searching for, selecting and training a potential successor, preparing the incumbent's retirement, negotiating a contract, and other elements of the succession are all steps that may take years to complete. Momentary set-backs, such as when a successor steps out of the process, may stretch the timeline even farther. Of course, succession may take place over shorter time periods as well; many necessary steps can be executed in parallel, and a trade sale to a financial or industrial investor can be finalized in a relatively short time span (i.e., months). But for intra-family successions, MBOs and MBIs, incumbent owners should anticipate five to ten years for the full completion of a structured succession process. For instance, and as further elaborated upon in section 7.9, in a study about succession in central Europe we found that the average length is 6.5 years for intra-family successions, 3.3 years for transfers to employees and 1.6 years for sales. This makes sense when we consider that most successions are sequential transactions, with management and ownership control being transferred over extended periods of time, often several years. Not surprisingly, the sale is the succession path completed within the shortest timeframe. These rather long timeframes are not primarily induced by contract negotiations. Rather, the search for a successor, the withdrawal of the incumbent and the taking over of responsibility by the successor take multiple years.

7.6 Structuring the succession process: succession framework

The sources of complexity listed above bring us closer to a structured approach to succession management in family firms. The opportunities and challenges tied to various succession options highlight the need to determine the preferred succession option early in the process, as this choice will have consequences for later steps such as financing, taxes and legal processes. Accordingly, any structured approach needs to incorporate a logical sequence starting with broad questions in which values, preferences and boundary conditions for the involved parties are made explicit. These initial reflections then logically lead to more strategic and execution-oriented questions.

In light of these considerations, the succession framework depicted in Figure 7.5 should provide some guidance on what needs to be addressed in the succession process and when. This succession framework builds on some of the exemplary work on succession by De Massis, Chua and Chrisman (2008) concerning the factors preventing intra-family succession, the integrative succession model by Le Breton-Miller, Miller and Steier (2004), the work by Chua, Chrisman and Sharma (2003) on succession and non-succession concerns in family firms and the work by Halter and Schroeder (2010) which includes their own succession framework.

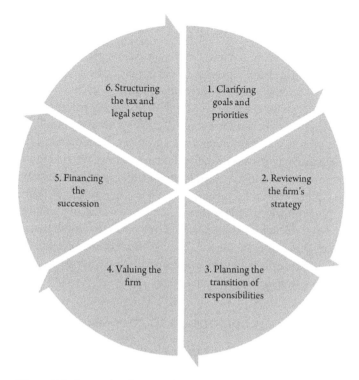

Figure 7.5 Succession framework

In this six-step process, the first two steps are the most time consuming. They are also the most critical ones in terms of keeping related decision processes on track (or delaying them). For example, if the incumbent has to switch the succession option, there will be a substantial delay in the overall succession process. As the above overview indicates, the topics to be addressed change significantly throughout the succession process, from very personal topics at the beginning to very technical ones toward the end.

Too many succession processes start with or are dominated by legal and tax considerations. But as we show below, the tax, legal and financial implications are themselves dependent on the succession option chosen. Thus, it is important to start the succession process by reflecting on and choosing the preferred succession options—only then should the actors involved move on to strategic and governance issues and ultimately transactional questions. In what follows, we discuss these six steps in more detail, moving from normative, to strategic, and finally to operational questions.

7.7   Clarifying goals and priorities

A critical step in an effective succession process is the consideration of various succession options, in particular options other than an intra-family succession. Each succession option comes with particular opportunities and challenges (for details, see Table 7.1). Each option also depends upon the satisfaction of certain preconditions (e.g., an intra-family succession requires the presence of competent and interested children). The motivations and preferences of the incumbent and successor may vary significantly depending on the option chosen, with some options appearing much more attractive to one party than to another. Moreover, the choice of succession option has implications for the length and sequence of the ownership and management transfer, the achievable transfer price of the ownership stake, and the financing of that price. In Table 7.2, these aspects are detailed for intra-family succession, transfer to employees, sale to co-owner or individual outsider, and sale to a strategic or financial buyer.

7.7.1   Which succession option to choose?

One way for incumbents to deal with the complexity of exiting their business and make an informed choice about succession options is to ask themselves two important questions: 'Am I financially ready to let go?' and 'Am I mentally ready to let go?'

The rationale for the first question is that different succession options provide vastly different financial options to the incumbent. For instance, if the firm is gifted to a child or put into a trust without financial recompense of the incumbent, the incumbent receives zero or a very limited financial return. At the other end of the spectrum, the incumbent may receive a significant premium if a strategic buyer sees an opportunity to leverage synergies with the existing operations and makes an offer for the firm.

The rationale for the second question is that entrepreneurs vary in their ability and willingness to mentally distance themselves from their firm. After all, for many entrepreneurs the firm is their baby. Some incumbents are more than happy to let go, for instance because they would like to have more time for themselves after years of dedication to the firm. For other incumbents, however, the firm represents their entire life; what that life might be without the firm is hard to envisage.

From these two perspectives, the attractiveness of various succession options varies dramatically (Figure 7.6). Owners who are neither mentally nor

Table 7.2 Precondition, motivation, timing, price and financing of various succession options

	Family-internal succession	Transfer to employee(s)	Sale to co-owner or individual outsider	Sale to strategic or financial buyer
Description	Transfer to next-generation family member(s)	Transfer to nonfamily employees	Transfer to co-owner or nonfamily manager not previously involved in firm	Transfer to strategic buyer (e.g., competitor) or financial buyer (e.g., private equity)
Precondition	• Competent and interested children • Intact family relationships • Clear responsibilities for senior and junior generations	• Competent and interested manager(s) • Funds available to employees • Willingness of incumbent to support financing	• Match between buyer and seller (availability and fit) • Funding available • Strategic and financial fitness of the firm	• Strategic and financial fitness of the firm • Willingness of incumbent to let go rapidly
Motivation of incumbent	• Ensure independence of firm • Family tradition • Personal legacy	• Ensure independence of firm • Honor management's loyalty • Secure employment	• Ensure independence of firm • Simplify ownership structure	• Seize attractive exit opportunity • Maximize sale price
Motivation of successor	• Tradition • Personal legacy • Entrepreneurial career	• Entrepreneurial career • Self-fulfillment	• Increase control (co-owner) • Start an entrepreneurial career (MBI)	• Seize attractive investment opportunity
Timing	About 5 to 10 years	About 2 to 5 years	About 1 to 2 years	About 1 year
Price	Gift: price = 0* Market value – Family discount	Market value – Loyalty discount	Market value – Sympathy discount	Market value
Financing	Gift, inheritance (in this case no financing at all); otherwise equity, debt, vendor loan	Equity Debt Vendor loan	Equity Debt	Equity/shares of acquiring firm Debt

Note: * In case estate or gift taxes are levied in a state, firms cannot be simply gifted to children, as this would mean an attempt to circumvent tax obligations. Still, even under legislations that levy such taxes, family-internal transfers tend to be generous and thus often do not seek to maximize the transfer price.

Source: Leonetti (2008).

Figure 7.6 Exit quadrant

financially ready to let go may stay and grow the firm to prepare for an exit at a later stage. Other incumbents may be financially ready to let go if they have extracted substantial wealth from the firm over their career or count on doing so upon their departure. However, owners may wish to preserve some ties to the firm and resist options that would cut off their involvement (e.g., a sale to a third party). This type of incumbent should prefer an intra-family transfer or transfer to employees, as these options should allow for some continued involvement in the firm even if they do not maximize the sale price.

The exit preferences should look very different in cases when the incumbent is mentally ready to leave the firm but seeks to maximize the financial proceeds from the sale. In these cases, the incumbent has an incentive to sell to the buyer offering the highest price, whoever that is, and even if this implies a complete and rapid loss of control.

Finally, an incumbent who is both mentally and financially ready to let go has the most succession options to choose from. In this situation, the incumbent may or may not seek to maximize the returns from the exit. Similarly, the incumbent may be willing to give over complete control to the next generation of owner(s) but remain available for support if the successor desires it. These four options are depicted in Figure 7.6.

Whatever their financial or mental readiness, incumbent entrepreneurs usually have in mind some kind of order of preference in relation to exit options. Many

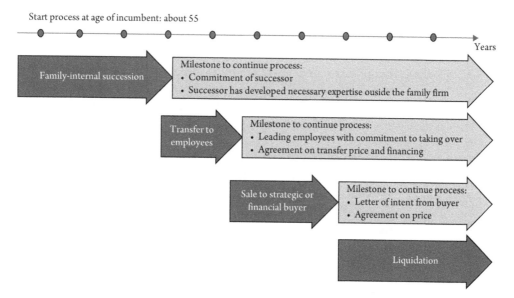

Start process at age of incumbent: about 55

Years

Family-internal succession

Milestone to continue process:
• Commitment of successor
• Successor has developed necessary expertise ouside the family firm

Transfer to employees

Milestone to continue process:
• Leading employees with commitment to taking over
• Agreement on transfer price and financing

Sale to strategic or financial buyer

Milestone to continue process:
• Letter of intent from buyer
• Agreement on price

Liquidation

Figure 7.7 Example of succession scenarios

incumbents would prefer an intra-family transfer if they were completely free to choose. After the intra-family transfer, many smaller firms prefer to pass the firm on to co-owners, co-founders or other family members. The next preferred option in this pecking order is usually the employees. Employees have deep insights into the firm, and thus know what they will be taking over; they may also be the sole possible candidates/buyers given the limited number of parties interested in taking over small family firms. Alternatively, the incumbent may decide to sell the firm to a strategic or financial buyer. Of course, the fact that an incumbent has a preference about succession options does not mean that this preference will be feasible. Nevertheless, it is useful for incumbents to reflect on their preferred order of succession options.

Given the significant uncertainty about the feasibility of preferred succession options, the incumbent must consider various options and exit scenarios and sort them along a timeline. For instance, and as depicted in Figure 7.7, an incumbent entrepreneur may wish to follow through on an intra-family succession in the next two years. In order to achieve this goal, the incumbent and the successor will have to carry out several important action points. For instance, the successor will have to complete his or her studies and work in another firm to gain relevant industry experience before entering the firm. The incumbent may have to professionalize leadership within the firm by installing a second management level, separate operating from non-operating assets, and set up a management accounting system. Note that all of these preparations are reasonable even if the parties conclude that they will continue with another exit option.

If the action points noted above are fulfilled before the two-year mark, the process toward an intra-family succession continues. If they are not achieved, the incumbent entrepreneur will pursue the next preferred succession option—the transfer of the firm to employees.

In the next sections of our succession journey, we will focus more closely on the prototypical cases of a transfer from an individual owner-manager to another individual owner-manager (e.g., intra-family succession), transfer to an employee(s), MBOs, and MBIs, or the sale to co-owners. We choose to focus on these particular succession options as they represent the majority of successions in family firms. They are especially relevant to the context of small to mid-sized family firms, which represent more than 90% of all family firms.

Of course, there are other succession options, including a mix of family and nonfamily involvement, the outright sale of the firm, listing on the stock market and liquidation. The challenges and opportunities tied to these options were addressed in detail in the first section of this chapter (see Figure 7.1 and Table 7.1). Firm sales and acquisitions have also been widely discussed in the corporate finance and mergers and acquisition literatures.

7.7.2 Goals of incumbent and successor

Succession often defies the typical assumptions about a transfer of corporate control. In particular, in the case of an intra-family transfer, the incumbent/seller and successor/buyer know each other well; are often interdependent, with a relationship that extends beyond the succession transaction; and exhibit goals that embrace nonfinancial as well as financial considerations. Recognizing this particular dyad is important, as the considerations of incumbents and successors are often diametrically opposed. For an overview of the considerations of incumbents and successors, see Table 7.3.

While in anonymous markets sellers simply pursue the maximum sale price, many owners of private firms want to be sure that they are placing their firm in the right hands. Incumbents often seek a fit between their own personal values and preferences and the characteristics of the successor. In addition, in many cases only a single party is interested or considered for succession (i.e., a child for intra-family succession, or a manager in the case of a transfer to employees). As a result, incumbent and successor are mutually dependent; both parties need to acknowledge each other's goals and concerns. If

Table 7.3 Typical considerations of incumbent and successor regarding succession

Considerations of incumbent	Considerations of successor
Tends to think and act in a backward-looking manner	Tends to think and act in a forward-looking manner
Has become tired over the years	Is full of energy and ideas
Primarily considers threats to the firm as life achievement; preservation oriented	Considers risks and opportunities for the firm; change oriented
Tends to be older	Tends to be younger
Ample experience running the firm	Limited experience running the firm
Loses control and responsibility	Gains control and assumes responsibility
Social standing eventually decreases after succession	Social standing eventually increases after succession
Strong emotional ties to the firm	Few emotional ties to the firm
Evaluates firm value in terms of past personal achievements and efforts	Evaluates firm value in terms of future financial opportunities and risks

incumbents fail to acknowledge the concerns of the potential successor, they may easily end up without a successor at all, resulting in the increased costs of an alternative search. But successors also need to acknowledge the concerns of the incumbent. If they do not, they may forgo an attractive opportunity to start their entrepreneurial career.

Thus, it is critical to make the goals, considerations and fears of both sides clear and explicit. If such an understanding is lacking, it will be difficult if not impossible to close the deal to the satisfaction of both parties. In the best case, both sides will walk away from the negotiation table frustrated and confused—most often after having spent significant amounts of time and money on operating expertise, such as financial or legal advice. In the worst case, the parties close the deal only to realize that it was a mistake. In this case, they may be bound to each other via, for instance, the incumbent's remaining ownership stake, his/her advisory role or backseat driving, or the incompetence of the successor.

7.7.3 How incumbent and successor determine acceptable transfer prices

An eye-opening way to illustrate how personal goals, preferences and values impact seemingly technical questions is to investigate acceptable sale prices when a firm is transferred from one family generation to the next. As we will see, these prices are subjectively determined by the incumbent and the successor respectively.

The incumbent's view: emotional value

In a study conducted in Germany and Switzerland, we asked incumbent owners about acceptable sale prices for their firms[1] (Zellweger et al. 2012) and found that their assessment of firm value was about 30% higher than an estimated market value. This value premium attributed by the incumbent owner to the firm, labeled emotional value (Zellweger and Astrachan 2008), is driven by a complex set of the owner's value and compensation considerations.

Notably, when incumbent owners sell outside the family, they seek compensation for the subjective benefits of their position, in particular the opportunity to continue a family legacy. In the aforementioned empirical study, we found that the intention to pass the firm on to some future family generation had a massive positive impact on emotional value. That is, owners dramatically overvalued their companies if they had the opportunity to pass the firm on to a next-generation family member. At the same time, incumbents were more inclined to let go and reduce their value expectations to avoid negative effects such as physical and psychological firm-related stress. Both of these effects worked in the expected direction: socioemotional advantages (e.g. having the opportunity to pass the firm on within the family) increased emotional value, while socioemotional disadvantages (e.g. stress) reduced emotional value.

Remarkably, however, incumbent owners also indicated socioemotional disadvantages that resulted in higher, not lower, emotional values. For instance, in the presence of severe conflicts among family owners, incumbents sought compensation for the 'costs' and hence the discomfort and anger tied to the conflict. This part of their emotional accounting was an attempt to seek compensation for sunk costs. Take, for example, the owner of a small firm that was largely unsuccessful in financial terms—the company had lost money over the last five years—who nevertheless had very explicit ideas about the acceptable sale price for his company. In an interview, he argued:

The firm is not worthless, even if we have been losing money in the recent years. You need to consider the fact that my company is the last firm in my region that has survived and remained independent—all my former competitors are either bankrupt or were taken over by large multinationals over the last few years. And you know, I have been working hard, over the weekends, putting in many extra hours and dedicating large parts of my private life to the company. Don't tell me this is worth nothing.

Conversely, some owners may be willing to trade some socioemotional advantages against a value decrease. For instance, marketing studies have shown that in the presence of emotional attachment to a posses-

Table 7.4 Drivers of emotional value for the incumbent owner[2]

	Impact on emotional value	
	Positive	Negative
Socioemotional Advantages	Compensation for lost benefits Example: status, control, family legacy	Benevolence and altruism Example: 'Putting the firm in the right hands'; 'Having the opportunity to pass the firm on inside the family means a lot to me'
Socioemotional Disadvantages	Compensation for sunk costs Example: escalating conflicts	Avoidance Example: responsibility, stress

sion, owners are willing to let go at a lower price if they feel that they are putting the cherished possession in the right hands. Similar findings have been reported for the transfer of ownership in US entrepreneurial firms (Graebner and Eisenhardt 2004). In our study of central European incumbent owners, we found that they were willing to 'sell' at a discount of 20% to 30% in comparison to some nonfamily buyer if the successor was a next-generation family member. Alternatively, owners may be willing to honor the loyalty of long-term employees who are willing to take over in an MBO. In this case, the transfer price most often includes a loyalty discount. These cognitive mechanisms driving emotional value are depicted in Table 7.4.

What is important to note here is that personal goals and preferences—more broadly termed behavioral biases—impact seemingly purely financial considerations. Owners cannot capitalize on high levels of emotional value per se. However, their biased value perceptions do have an impact on their negotiation position and on the likelihood of finding a successor.

The family successor's view: family discount

Asking potential successors about the price they expect to pay when taking over the firm from parents is less straightforward. Some may say: 'Why pay a price at all? There should be no money involved. Children should get the firm as part of their inheritance, and hence without having to pay anything!' Others may argue: 'Although parent–children relationships may be involved, we are talking about a firm, and hence an asset that can have significant value. Ultimately, children should not get favorable treatment. The parents have worked hard and need to get some money out of the succession.' As for the case of emotional value, next-generation family successors do exhibit particular preferences and biases when

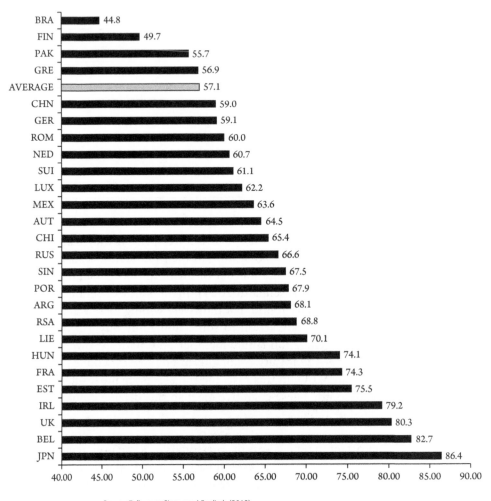

Source: Zellweger, Sieger and Englisch (2012).

Figure 7.8 Expected family discounts of students with family business backgrounds

considering an acceptable transfer price. In a recent study conducted in 20 countries with 4500 potential successors, we found that, on average, potential successors expect to receive a 57% discount in comparison to some nonfamily buyer when taking over the parents' firm (Zellweger, Sieger and Englisch 2012). Figure 7.8 provides an overview of this international comparison of expected family discounts.[3]

These expected discounts are significant. For instance, the mean numbers for Japan, Belgium, the United Kingdom, Ireland and the other countries with high expected family discounts suggest that in these countries next-generation members simply expect to inherit the family firm, without any compensation of the incumbent. A follow-up study in Germany and Switzerland suggests that the expected discounts as reported in Figure 7.8 are not wishful thinking by potential next-generation owners. Indeed, we find that family discounts in actual transfers of small to mid-sized family firms in Germany and Switzerland across family generations amount to roughly 60%. This figure is in line with the above-reported data on expected discounts for these two countries.

These reflections and the empirical evidence on emotional value at the incumbent and family discounts at the successor further suggests that behavioral biases have dramatic effects on intergenerational transfers of family firm control. For sure, tax regulations may limit the degree to which intergenerational transfer prices can deviate from some market value.[4] Still, given that so many private firms are passed on within the family from parents to children, and given that wealth transfers to direct descendants are tax exempt under many legislations around the world, these findings provide a more behaviorally accurate account of many organizational ownership transfers. They suggest that it is critical to unearth the behavioral biases and preferences of the actors involved and take them seriously, as they contradict the rhetoric of price supremacy and the ubiquity of self-interest.

7.7.4 What motivates and discourages family successors from joining?

Many family business succession studies focus on the incumbent owner, for instance by exploring the owner's goals for succession. However, this focus is limited by its one-sidedness. Most successions—in particular, intra-family transfers—are of a dyadic nature, involving two mutually interdependent actors. Thus, it is useful to examine the underlying motivations of successors in more detail and ask what (still) motivates and what deters successors from joining the parent's firm.

Recent studies exploring the antecedents of intra-family succession find a wide set of criteria on personal, company, family and societal levels that impact succession intention among students with family business backgrounds (Zellweger et al. 2012). At the individual level, we find that the more confident potential successors are in their entrepreneurial potential, the *less* likely it is that they will want to become successors. Similarly, the higher the students' internal locus of control—meaning the more they are convinced that their fate is in their own hands, rather than decided by others or by luck—the lower their succession intention. These two findings suggest that individuals with attributes that are normally seen as highly desirable for an entrepreneurial career may be more likely to opt *against* joining the parents' firm. On the other hand, as expected, the stronger the emotional attachment to the firm, and the more positively parents perceive their children's desire to pursue an entrepreneurial career, the stronger the students' succession intention.

The familial context may further discriminate between next-generation family members with strong and weak succession intentions. While an individual's experience of family tradition has a positive effect on succession intention, highly cohesive families tend to deter next-generation family members from joining. This is because such families may pressure offspring to join, causing them to resent their dependency on the firm and the family. Simply put, standing in the shadow of a cohesive family may lead some next generation family members to feel smothered by their involvement in the firm. This insight on the 'family handcuff' is important, because many entrepreneurial families strive to uphold family cohesion, with parents assuming that stronger cohesiveness will motivate children to follow in their footsteps.

Also, there is evidence that the more elder siblings a child has, the lower his or her succession intention. This insight points to the relevance of birth order. Elder and, in particular, first-born children are often more willing to comply with parental demands in comparison to later-born children. Also, when first-borns make their career choices, there may be more vacant employment niches in the family firm than when later-borns are ready to enter. Consequently, later-born heirs often pursue a career outside the family's firm.

At the firm level, we find that the larger the firm, and the more firms a family controls, the more attractive succession is for next-generation family members. Again, this points to potential successors' desire to find a sufficiently large scope of action and discretion—that is, to make their own marks outside the immediate influence of their parents.

At the societal level, we find that the stronger the degree of uncertainty avoidance in a society, the more children are motivated to join the family firm. The level of tolerance for uncertainty and ambiguity in a given society indicates the extent to which culture 'programs' people to feel (un)comfortable in unstructured situations. Joining the family firm is a relatively stable choice compared to other career paths. This makes it an appealing choice in nations where people tend to dislike uncertainty, such as Germany, Japan and France. Also, as shown in Table 7.2, individualistic societies such as the

Table 7.5 Drivers of succession intention among next-generation family members

Positive impact on succession intention (SI) ➕	Negative impact on succession intention (SI) ➖
Individual level	
Attitude toward entrepreneurial career The more positive the attitude toward an entrepreneurial career, the higher the SI	**Entrepreneurial self-efficacy** The higher the entrepreneurial self-efficacy, the lower the SI
Subjective norm (parents' reaction) The more positive the parents' reaction toward children's entrepreneurial aspirations, the higher the SI	**Internal locus of control** The higher the internal locus of control (i.e., the stronger students' conviction that their fate is in their own control), the lower the SI
Affective commitment The more positive the students' emotional relationship with the firm, the higher the SI	
Family level	
Family tradition The more important the family tradition is to students, the higher the SI	**Family cohesion** The stronger the family cohesion, the lower the SI
	Number of older siblings The more older siblings a person has, the lower the SI
Firm level	
Firm size The larger the firm, the higher the SI	
Portfolio of firms The more firms are part of the family portfolio, the higher the SI	
Societal level	
Uncertainty avoidance The higher the uncertainty avoidance in a society, the higher the SI	**Individualism** The stronger the individualism in a society, the lower the SI

Source: Zellweger, Sieger and Englisch (2012).

Netherlands and the United Kingdom tend to deter succession. Table 7.5 summarizes these findings.

The above findings suggest that parents are critical role models for their children. First and foremost, supporting an entrepreneurial career entices offspring to envisage such a career for themselves. But parents also need to provide offspring with sufficient control over their own lives to motivate them to follow in their footsteps. Interestingly, emphasizing family cohesion is an effective way to *discourage* next-generation family members from joining the firm. Another way that parents can impact the attractiveness of joining the firm is through venture size and diversity. Larger firms and portfolios of companies are more attractive for next-generation family members than a single small firm.

7.7.5 Successor willingness and ability

The above discussion of next-generation family members' interest in joining the family firm points to various mechanisms that make joining the firm more or less attractive. In consequence, successors differ significantly in their willingness to join the family firm. But willingness may not be enough to successfully run a firm; ability is at least as important. Thus, when reflecting on the 'right' successor we are well placed to consider two dimensions: the successor's willingness and ability to take over.

7.7.5.1 *Successor willingness: it is the type of commitment that matters*

At first sight, successor willingness seems to be a simple way to assess whether a successor is qualified for a job inside the family firm. For sure, some level of motivation is important for a successful family-internal succession to take place. But even more so than simple willingness, it is the quality of this willingness and the successor's type of commitment that matters for a successful succession. In fact, potential successors may have significantly different motives for wishing to join the firm. Exploring these motives is important, because when there is variation in the motive for joining, we have reasons to assume that there will be variation in the next generation's behavior and effort put into the family business.

In a particularly interesting study on this topic, Sharma and Irving (2005) distinguish four motivational bases for joining the family firm: affective, normative, calculative and imperative commitment. *Affective commitment* is based on a strong belief in and acceptance of the organization's goals, combined with a desire to contribute to them and the confidence in one's ability to do so. In essence, the successor '*wants to*' pursue such a career. Affective commitment should be more pronounced when the next-generation family member's career interests and identity are aligned with the opportunities and the identity of the firm.

Normative commitment is based on a feeling of obligation to pursue a career in the family business. By pursuing a career within the family firm, the successor attempts to foster and maintain good relationships with the senior generation. In short, successors with high levels of normative commitment feel that they *'ought to'* pursue such a career. Strong family norms regarding upholding a family legacy, birth order (first-born succession) or gender (male succession) should drive the feeling of obligation among the affected offspring.

Calculative commitment is based on successors' perceptions of substantial opportunity costs and threatened loss of investments or value if they do not pursue a career in the family business. Successors with high levels of calculative commitment feel that they *'have to'* pursue such a career. Higher opportunity costs, such as a lower salary outside the family firm, should instill calculative commitment.

Imperative commitment is based on a feeling of self-doubt about one's ability to successfully pursue a career outside the family business. Individuals with high levels of imperative commitment perceive that they lack alternatives to a career in the family business. The underlying mindset in this case is a *'need to'* pursue such a career.

Sharma and Irving (2005) suggest that the type of commitment experienced by next-generation family members who wish to join the family firm should have a strong effect on their willingness to exert discretionary behavior, and hence the effort they will put in beyond the call of duty (Figure 7.9). It is assumed that next-generation family members with strong affective commitment will exhibit the strongest discretionary behavior, because their personal interests are intrinsically aligned with those of the firm. A slightly lower level of engagement should be expected for normative and calculative commitment. For these two types of commitment, the potential successor feels that there are good reasons to join, but these reasons are mainly provided by external sources (e.g., social and economic pressures). Finally, successors with imperative commitment, and hence a lack of alternatives, should have the lowest—or even negative—engagement for the effectiveness of the firm.

For these reasons, it is essential to keep an eye on the underlying motives of next-generation family members who express an interest in joining the family firm. Given the impact on future firm prosperity and also on the likely pleasure the potential successor will experience working for the family firm, senior- and junior-generation family members should have an open discussion about the type of commitment at play.

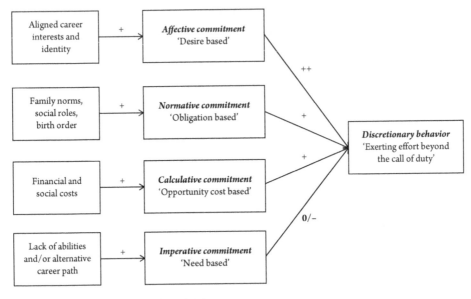

Source: Sharma and Irving (2005).

Figure 7.9 Successor commitment and discretionary behavior

7.7.5.2 Successor ability: it is the job profile that matters

It is similarly intuitive to ask whether a successor has the required abilities to take over the family firm. Required abilities, however, vary widely depending on the job profile. For a CEO position in a larger firm, management expertise and leadership experience may be critical. In contrast, for a subordinate and administrative job in the same firm, leadership skills may be less of a concern. In contrast, as the sole owner-manager of a small company, technical skills may be particularly important. In consequence, when assessing the ability of next-generation members we have to ask whether the successors have the required abilities for the specific job that they are expected to take on.

7.7.5.3 The willingness and ability diagram

Combining these arguments on willingness and ability, we may thus assess the fit of a successor for the job in the family business by asking:

1. **Willingness**: How strongly is the successor committed to the family firm? This is best assessed in terms of the successor's intrinsic desire to pursue a career inside the firm.

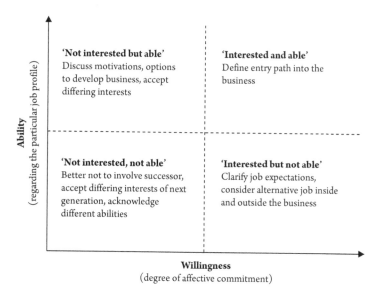

Figure 7.10 Willingness and ability of the successor

2. **Ability**: To what degree does the successor have the required capabilities? This is best assessed in light of the job that they are expected to take over.

We can think of four combinations of willingness and ability, as depicted in Figure 7.10. Of course, the ideal successor is both highly willing and committed to take on a role inside the firm. For such successors, it is important to clarify their entry path into the firm so that their commitment and abilities can be put to the most efficient use. But this ideal successor is often not available inside the family, and a successor may exhibit lower levels of willingness or ability.

Able but not interested successors see a misfit between their private and their professional passions on the one hand and a job inside the family firm on the other. For instance, the successor may have no affective commitment to the firm, its products or the particular industry. In most cases, such individuals may be better off with a career outside the family firm. Still, given their abilities it may be important to provide such potential successors with the opportunity to get engaged with the firm early on, for instance on a part-time basis or for a limited timeframe. Families with such successors should also consider various job alternatives inside the firm and in governance roles, and think through ways to develop the business so as to increase the successor's interest in the firm. Most importantly, however, for junior and senior generations it is important to accept the limited interest on the part of the successor and in this case unconditionally support a career outside the family firm.

Interested but insufficiently qualified successors are not ideal successors either. In such a constellation, we have to ask whether the successor can take on a certain job inside the firm for which his/her abilities are sufficient. It is easy to imagine entrepreneurial parents who think their children do not have the required abilities to run the firm; and the children's abilities may indeed not be satisfactory especially for a top management position inside the firm. But the judgment by parents may easily be biased: parents may underestimate the qualifications of their children, especially when thinking of various jobs inside the firm, or the collaboration of their children with a management team with complementary skills. At the same time, parents may also overestimate the qualifications of their children, simply because they love them. In such cases, it is important to ask first what type of challenges the firm is facing and what skills are required to successfully tackle these challenges. In a next step, it is important to objectively assess the qualifications of children in light of these required skills, for instance with the help of a professional human resource advisor.

Given that entrepreneurial abilities and the passion for a firm's products are only imperfectly inherited from one generation to the next, most incumbent entrepreneurs will have to deal with family internal successors with lower and less than perfect ability and willingness to take over.[5] Hence, the 'interested but not able' and the 'not interested but able' successor is not the exception among potential successors.

Having such successors in prospect we should ask whether an imperfectly motivated or an imperfectly qualified successor is worse for the firm? We may come closer to answering this intricate question by asking ourselves whether it is easier to develop motivation and commitment to a firm, or to develop the necessary skills to run it. From many real-life examples, we can conclude that skills may be learned or added by hiring people with complementary skills in management or on a board. In contrast, motivation and commitment to a firm seems to be much harder to build. Consider the following story about Karl Lagerfeld, the famous French couturier, about why he did not join his father's firm.

CASE STUDY

Ability and commitment at Karl Lagerfeld

This willingness/ability dilemma among successors is famously summarized in an interview with Karl Lagerfeld, a famous German/French couturier. The interviewer asked him: 'Your father had a firm producing condensed milk. Could you imagine yourself taking the firm over from him?' Karl Lagerfeld famously replied: 'Condensed milk was not my passion.'

In this case, it was probably better that the firm was not taken over by the next generation. In any case, the worst scenario we can think of is the one of an incompetent and careless successor, a scenario under which even the most successful firms are doomed to fail.

CASE STUDY

Succession at Gardner Bakers

Paul Gardner has been in business since he was 21, when he started his first bakery shop, Gardner Bakers, in a small Midwestern town. Paul quickly learned that supermarkets were his main competitors and that they could drive him out of business if he failed to position his growing bakery in a unique way. By focusing on freshness, store ambiance and innovation in his bakery products, he managed to build a group of 15 bakeries with a combined sales volume of $40 million. Now, at the age of 58, he realizes that he has to think about stepping back—not immediately, but in a planned and ordered way. Asked about his goals concerning the business, Paul mentions: 'I have reached a lot, and I am very grateful for that. But now it is time to think about passing the reins, not immediately, but progressively. It would be nice if one or even several of my kids took over. But not all three of them have an interest in the business, and probably it is not wise to bring them all into the firm.'

Paul realizes that he needs help navigating the challenging succession process and calls on Sandra Reynolds, a senior advisor with many years of experience advising family firms on succession issues. Together, Paul and Sandra lay out a long-term process for the succession. The intended process starts with a definition of Paul's preferences about the succession options. Paul indicates: 'I do have a clear preference for my kids to take over. But if none of them is interested or able, it would be my wish to pass the firm on to my employees. They are a very important part of our story and success at Gardner Bakers. Their loyalty and support should be acknowledged.' Sandra and Paul come up with a

CASE STUDY *(continued)*

timeline for pursuing these two priorities. Given Paul's preference for intra-family succession, Sandra's advisory plan includes individual discussions with the three children about their respective interest and abilities in taking over the bakery chain. Afterward, she plans to report back to Paul about her assessment of each child as a potential successor.

Together with Paul, she sets up a milestone plan for their pursuit of the intra-family succession. Two of the children work in related industries and express an initial interest in taking over. In a first joint discussion, Paul, Sandra and the two interested heirs agree on the next phase, which Sandra summarizes as follows: 'Given that both of them signaled their eventual interest in taking over, we defined the next steps thus: for two years, they both continue their professional careers outside the family business. At the end of those two years, they enter the firm in roles still to be defined. Over these two years we will assess how they are performing in their jobs and how committed they are toward taking over. Are they doing it for lack of other attractive career prospects, or out of real affection for the business? For this particular firm, we think that one of the children has to become the CEO. The other could eventually take on a different role, but this will be decided at a later stage. If we cannot agree on a natural distribution of responsibilities, we agreed that we would involve a human resource expert who will assess the individual capabilities of the two siblings. The assessment could even suggest that neither of them is capable of running the firm. But what matters now is that we have clear priorities for succession options, and that all parties have an opportunity to openly express their respective goals and interests. The timeline and milestones help in creating some accountability early in the process when much is still open.'

Paul and Sandra have set the first milestone two years from now. They realize that if intra-family succession does not work out, they have to be ready to switch to the next preferred option—passing on the firm to employees. In fact, some months ago Paul was approached by two of his managers who asked about the outlook of the firm, and whether the two of them could play a role as future owner-managers. Both of them were crucial to the firm and Paul feared that he would lose them if he rejected their request. He initially thought about giving them some shares to bind them to the firm. But after laying out these first steps in the succession process with Sandra, he informs his two managers about the timeline, the milestones and his first and second priority with regard to succession options.

 REFLECTION QUESTIONS

The following reflection questions for the incumbent owner and the successor are intended to help clarify goals and priorities for succession.

Reflection questions for the incumbent owner

1. What are my goals related to succession?
2. What are my fears related to succession?
3. What will I do after passing the baton?

4. What succession option(s) do I have? What are the related opportunities and challenges?
5. What are the implications of the succession options in terms of timing, achievable price and financing?
6. What roles do different family members play in the various succession options?
7. What are the family members' opinions and interests with regard to succession?
8. What is my preferred succession option? What is the next option I will try to pursue in case the preferred option cannot be executed?
9. What milestones need to be reached to achieve the preferred succession option? What about the milestones of the second preferred succession option?
10. What factors influence my calculation of an acceptable sale price? Are these considerations impacted by emotional biases?
11. What is my timeframe to complete the succession?
12. How do I define 'successful succession'?
13. Have I talked about these considerations with the successor?
14. Who could support and advise me along the succession process?

Reflection questions for the successor

1. What are my goals for my (professional) life?
2. What are my fears related to the succession?
3. What challenges and opportunities will I face by taking over the company?
4. What are my family members' opinions about succession?
5. How will I ensure a sustainable work–life balance?
6. What is my timeframe to complete the succession?
7. Who could support and advise me along the succession process?
8. How do I define 'successful succession'?
9. Have I talked about these considerations with the incumbent?

Combined perspective of incumbent and successor

1. What are the challenges that we see with regard to succession?
2. What are our shared goals?
3. How do we both define 'successful succession'?
4. Do we want to engage a single advisor to help us through the succession process, or should each party engage their own advisor?
5. For what parts of the process do we need help?

The answers of incumbent and successor could be compiled in separate workshops. Then, a joint discussion could bring their viewpoints together.

Reflection questions for students

1. Why is intra-family succession decreasing in many developed countries?
2. What drives the complexity of the succession process?
3. Will family firms disappear as a consequence of the relatively low interest among next-generation family members in taking over the parents' firm?
4. When advising in the succession context, why is it inappropriate to start with topics such the legal setup or tax considerations?
5. What are the critical abilities an advisor needs to have to professionally advise in the succession context?
6. Describe the differences in viewpoints of incumbent and successor with regard to succession.

7. In addition to the type of successor, how is intra-family succession different from transferring the firm to employees?
8. What questions should the incumbent address when clarifying goals and priorities for succession?
9. What questions should the successor address when clarifying goals and priorities for succession?
10. What makes the succession career path attractive for next-generation family members?
11. Why are next-generation family members from very cohesive families less inclined to join their parent's firm?
12. Why do incumbent and successor have such different perceptions about the fair value of the firm?
13. Describe the types of commitment that successors can have vis-à-vis the family firm, and explain how the type of commitment relates to work effort.
14. Ability and willingness are both critical characteristics for a successor. What are the likely consequences when insufficiently qualified or committed successors enter the firm?

7.8 Reviewing the firm's strategy

In the second step in the succession framework outlined in Figure 7.5, the involved parties have to deal with the current and future strategy of the firm. Reviewing the firm's strategy is important, as this will prepare the firm for succession from a business management point of view. The goal is to make the firm an attractive target for a transfer of control, whether from within or outside the family.

In practice, the firm's strategic position will not necessarily be attractive for a successor. Some parts of the firm may not have much to do with the main operations and may be uninteresting for the successor. These components may be kept in the firm, spun off or closed down before the succession. The exercise of reviewing the firm's strategy thus clarifies three important questions that are relevant both for the incumbent and the successor:

● What are the current strengths and weaknesses of the firm?
● What are the future opportunities and threats for the firm?
● Which parts of the firm are to be passed on?

Like their owner-managers, firms often follow a lifecycle: inception, a growth phase, a phase of saturation and, most often, a partial decline before succession. Throughout this process, organizations often mirror the incumbent's goals, preferences, aspirations and abilities. Firms that enter the succession process therefore do not necessarily fit the goals and aspirations of the successor. From a strategic point of view, firms face several strategic challenges when approaching the succession phase. These challenges are outlined below.

7.8.1 Stagnating performance

As succession and hence retirement approaches, the incumbent has little personal incentive to invest in further growing the firm. While this may be partly mitigated if a child is taking over, from an individual owner's point of view it is rational to ask whether it pays to invest this type of effort if they can only partly benefit from the returns. In addition, the physical and mental abilities of entrepreneurs to innovate and compete in a dynamic marketplace may have decreased over the years. Not surprisingly, as a result of all these factors, we often observe that performance stagnates or decreases when firms enter the succession phase.

7.8.2 Leadership vacuum

In many cases, family firm succession affects not only the CEO, but also the broader top management of the firm. Many owner-managed firms, independent of their size, heavily depend on their (founding) entrepreneurs. The entrepreneur represents a significant resource for the firm, for instance through their technical abilities, customer relationships, leadership or networking skills. This points to a sad irony that many successful entrepreneurs face toward the end of their careers: because they are a significant source of competitive advantage for their firm, they also become a source of liability when they leave. In this context, the incumbent and successor must discuss the circumstances under which the incumbent will continue to contribute to the firm: in which role, for how long and under what conditions.

But the exit of the owner-manager is not the only cause of the leadership vacuums that can arise during or after succession. Many owner-managers fail to establish a second layer of managers able to run the firm in their absence. Often, second-level managers are either nonexistent or not competent enough to step up and take on leadership roles. If there are competent second-level managers, they are often members of the 'old guard' approaching retirement age along with the incumbent. Both cases result in a significant leadership vacuum.

7.8.3 Diversified product/market portfolio

Over the years, many firms engage in a relatively wide set of business activities, resulting in a relatively diversified product and market portfolio. Products or markets that serve narrow, less attractive customer segments may seem obvious targets for trimming. However, incumbents may be hesitant to cut off long-term customer relationships or fire loyal employees associated with these products or markets. In consequence, product and market segments tend to be fairly broad and include some financially unattractive components.

7.8.4 Intertwined operating and non-operating assets

Firms entering the succession phase are often characterized by intertwined operating and non-operating assets. Owner-managers who see their firms as their main source of wealth often fail to differentiate between assets that mainly serve the fulfillment of business operations and assets that are private in nature and not needed for operations. Such non-operating assets include, for example, unnecessary liquid wealth or real estate that is not required for the firm's current operations.

In the context of succession, the existence of non-operating assets may be a significant obstacle. The successor may be unwilling (given the assets' lack of relevance for operations) or unable (given the successor's limited financial capital) to take them over. From a strategic point of view, non-operating assets may have to be spun off from the main business before succession to simplify the transfer, streamline the firm and free resources to satisfy the financial needs of family members not involved in the succession. These family members are important to consider, as they may be legally entitled—or feel emotionally entitled—to receive a share of the family's wealth that is tied up in the firm.

7.8.5 Firm as incumbent's retirement fund

Because owner-managers exercise strong control over their firms, they do not see the need to draw strict boundaries between the wealth they have invested in the firm and the wealth they have vested to private assets. As a result, they often invest large parts of their total wealth in the firm; for family business owners, the average amount of total wealth invested in the firm is roughly 80%. Family business owners also tend to reinvest profits in the firm rather than transferring them to the private sphere, for instance through dividend payments or salary increases to feed their pension plans. This behavior is perceptible in firms' balance sheets when they are heavily equity financed and especially when there are reserves and undistributed profits accumulated over the years. This problem may appear to be limited at first sight, as some laws allow firms to amortize large parts of their assets to lower their tax bill so that only very limited assets and equity levels appear on the balance sheet. And, indeed, this strategy can work well as long as the owner is able to control and run the company.

However, as succession and hence the exit of the owner-manager approaches, the concentration of total wealth in the firm may become an issue. Owner-managers count on capitalizing on the funds that they have (re)invested in the firm over the years. But this assumption can prove problematic, especially for small firms. First, there may be no successor in sight who is willing and able to take over. The problem intensifies if the firm is only marginally profitable. In that case, the valuation based on earnings, which often defines the successor's willingness to pay for the firm, is lower than the net asset value, which the incumbent often perceives as the relevant valuation of the firm (for more details, see the valuation section—section 7.10—of this chapter). In addition, the incumbent often hopes to unearth hidden reserves in the firm's balance sheet in the form of undisclosed reserves. When realized, these reserves are heavily taxed under many tax regimes. In consequence, and in particular in the context of small-firm succession, the concentration of total wealth in the firm may become a liability. Owners who expect to finance their pensions from the proceeds of the sale of the firm and/or from undisclosed reserves are often disappointed.

All of the challenges above need to be addressed in order to prepare the firm for succession. The incumbent bears the most responsibility for considering these challenges and removing obstacles toward succession. But the successors should also consider these challenges in order to prepare for the strategic complications they will encounter during and after the succession process. The overview and reflection questions in Table 7.6 should help both incumbents and successors in this area.

7.9 Planning the transition of responsibilities

After addressing the current and future strategic position of the firm, it is critical to define how governance (management, ownership and board) and functional roles are passed down from incumbent to successor. In many cases, especially when the succession is familial, there is a relatively prolonged time period during which incumbent and successor are both involved in the firm. As many firms will attest, this transition period can involve misunderstandings about roles and responsibilities, confusion about who is in control, and frustration and irritation on the part of the incumbent, successor, employees and further stakeholders. However, this period of collaboration is not all negative. The parallel involvement of the incumbent and successor also represents a unique opportunity to pass on relevant resources, such as knowledge and networks.

Table 7.6 Reflection questions for incumbent and successor on the strategic setup of the firm

Strategic challenge	Commentary	Reflection questions for incumbent	Reflection questions for successor
Stagnating performance	Declining performance as a result of outdated technology and facilities; lack of innovation and decreasing entrepreneurial spirit	• What makes the firm an attractive organization for a takeover? • In what areas should we invest or innovate in before passing the firm on?	• What are the firm's strengths and weaknesses? • What are the strategic opportunities and threats? • In what areas can I increase efficiency? • In what areas will I have to innovate? • What are my objectives for the first year? • What are the obstacles to these changes?
Leadership vacuum	Leadership vacuum as a result of incumbent exiting the firm; absence of second-level managers willing and able to lead the firm in the future	• What are the opportunities and threats for the firm when I leave? • Is the leadership team willing and able to step up and take responsibility to support the succession? • What role am I willing to play after passing the baton?	• Is the current leadership team able to establish the necessary strategic changes? • What managers will form the new leadership team with me? • In what areas is the incumbent a critical resource for the firm? • In what role, for how long and under what conditions should the incumbent stay involved?
Diversified product/market portfolio	Broad range of offerings with partly unsatisfactory performance	• Are there product lines or markets that we should exit? • Have we been hesitant to exit businesses for emotional reasons, such as long-term customer or employee relationships, despite the economic benefits of doing so?	• How does the firm earn money today, and how will it earn money in the future? • Are there parts of the firm that I am not interested in taking over? • Are there activities I want to exit after taking over the firm? • What areas should I invest in after taking over? What are the associated costs?

Table 7.6 (continued)

Strategic challenge	Commentary	Reflection questions for incumbent	Reflection questions for successor
Intertwined operating and non-operating assets	Liquid assets and real estate not necessary for operations appear in the firm's balance sheet	• Do I have assets invested in the firm that are not used for operations? • How can I separate these non-operating assets from the firm? • Would separating these assets simplify succession and/or satisfy the financial needs of family members not involved in succession? • What are the legal and tax implications?	• Are there revenues or costs stemming from non-core/non-operating activities that cloud the actual operating performance of the firm? • Does separating operating and non-operating assets reduce the valuation of the firm and simplify financing the succession? • Are some parts of non-operating assets critical or valuable for the future success of the firm?
Firm as incumbent's retirement fund	Undiversified incumbent wealth; incumbent hopes to finance pension with the proceeds from succession	• How do I finance my pension? • Are there many undisclosed reserves in the firm's balance sheet? • To facilitate succession and satisfy pension needs, should we pay out dividends/salary before succession? • What are the tax implications? • Do I have to untangle private and business finances?	• Are the private and business finances of the incumbent intertwined? • Are there related-party transactions by the incumbent that conceal the actual financial health of the firm? • What do the financials look like when the incumbent's private affairs are separated from firm? • Is the incumbent counting on a maximized sale price?

CASE STUDY

Succession at Software Ltd.

Software Ltd. was founded in the 1990s by Louis Brenner. Louis based his business on the realization that small firms needed a cheap software solution to support customer relationship management. Over the years, Louis's firm managed to become the leader in its niche market. While Louis began by installing all the software locally at the client, with the advent of internet technology he moved his offering to a pure cloud-based solution. Software Ltd. hosted the software and the clients' data on its own servers, which proved to be a highly scalable business model. In the best years, the firm generated operating margins of 40%. But over the last few years, the firm had lost market share, in part because Louis was unable to update the security systems and increase the reliability of his offerings. Also, the software—which at the core was still the original software Louis had programmed in the late 1990s—could not keep up with more graphically pleasing interfaces and sophisticated analytics.

The firm's balance sheet for the previous year is listed in Table 7.7 (figures in $).
Last year, Software Ltd. generated sales of $3.5 million and an EBIT of $500 000. The company currently has ten employees. Asked about the significant amount of real estate and cash on the firm's balance sheet, Louis reflects: 'You're right. We don't need all that real estate for our software business. But over the years, I always decided to reinvest the money from our successes in the firm or in some real estate projects—even if they did not have much to do with our core activity. In terms of risk, it made sense to me to leave all my money inside the firm. There is no better and more secure investment than the one you control yourself.'

Table 7.7 Balance sheet for Software Ltd.

Assets		Liabilities	
Liquid assets	4 500 000	Short-term debt	350 000
Accounts receivable	250 000	Bank debt (mortgage)	1 500 000
IT & office infrastructure	500 000	Distributable reserves	8 900 000
Real estate	6 000 000	Share capital	500 000
Total assets	11 250 000	Total liabilities	11 250 000

Louis Brenner sees three options for his succession. The first is to pass the firm to one of his four children, and one of them is indeed interested. However, the children not interested in the business point out: 'What about us? It can't be that our sister gets the whole firm, including its cash and real estate. It would be completely unfair given that our dad's wealth is completely tied up in the firm.'

CASE STUDY (continued)

Louis's second option is to pass the firm to one of his leading employees, who had signaled interest in the company. This employee, however, sees other challenges: 'This is an interesting company to take over. But there are two important problems I see here. The first relates to our product: it is not up-to-date anymore; it needs a significant overhaul and then a re-launch. The second problem is the structure of the company: effectively, the firm is a real estate company with some smaller software activity tied to it. I am interested in the software part only. I have no interest in or familiarity with the real estate aspect—and anyway, I don't have the capital to take over the real estate part as well.'

Louis has also talked to a strategic buyer, a larger competitor who may be interested in taking over the firm. Looking at the financials of Software Ltd., this competitor replied: 'Congratulations for building up this company, Louis. But it is impossible for us to judge how your business is doing. What does it mean that you are generating an EBIT of $500 000? It is hard to see whether you are earning or losing money in the software business given that operating and non-operating (real estate) activities are interwoven. We are only interested in your software, your clients, and your engineers.'

The feedback on the three succession options is frustrating for Louis. He has built a profitable company, is a rich man (at least on paper), and yet nobody wants to acknowledge his success by taking over the firm. The problems become even more apparent when Louis mandates his accountant to value the company. The accountant replies: 'It is very hard to value this company. Assuming that the assets are valued at fair market value, your company has a net asset value of roughly $9.4 million (= $8.9 million distributable reserves + $500 000 share capital). But looking at the EBIT of the firm, it has an estimated value of roughly $2.5 million only (EBIT of 500 000 * estimated industry multiple of 8 − 1.5 million mortgage). You have a big problem here. It will be hard for you to unlock the value of your real estate when passing the firm to somebody interested in the software activity alone.' Louis realized he had to do some homework along the following lines before he could move toward exiting his business. Specifically, he defined the following steps:

1. Create transparency: set up income statement separately for software and real estate activities.
2. Allocate fixed assets, mainly real estate, to the two activities.
3. Spin off software activity from real estate activity by setting up two distinct legal entities. Minimize the tax consequences of this move.
4. In parallel: initiation of innovation process for product rejuvenation.
5. Once the above steps are executed, which Louis estimates will take two years, he would restart discussions with potential successors.

Table 7.8 Sequence of ownership and management transfer in Swiss successions

Percentage of all observed successions	Ownership and management transferred simultaneously	Management first, then ownership	Ownership first, then management
Intra-family succession	51%	43%	6%
Transfer to employees	47%	41%	12%
Sale	66%	28%	6%

Source: Christen et al. (2013).

In many cases, management and ownership is passed along in sequential steps. For many successions, the management transfer precedes the ownership transfer. Alternatively, management functions and ownership, at least part of it, may be passed on simultaneously. Table 7.8 presents some data for Switzerland that may shed further light on the sequence of ownership and management transfers.

When we make a single assessment of the time elapsed between some initial discussion about succession and the actual handover of both management and ownership control, we find that the average length is 6.5 years for intra-family successions, 3.3 years for transfers to employees and 1.6 years for sales. This makes sense when we consider that most successions are sequential transactions, with management and ownership control being transferred over extended periods of time, often several years. Not surprisingly, the sale is the succession path completed within the shortest timeframe.

7.9.1 The succession road map

The consequences of extended succession timeframes and sequential transfers of control are significant. First, there is the potential for conflict in relation to roles, responsibilities and economic incentives. To avoid these conflicts, it is important to plan succession well ahead of the intended exit of the incumbent. Problems are often aggravated if the first-priority succession path cannot be completed and an alternative path has to be chosen, or if the process has to be restarted from beginning. A setback along the succession path can significantly extend the timeframe until succession is completed, with important personal and financial consequences for the incumbent.

When the incumbent and successor are both involved in the firm for extended periods, there are the uncertainties about roles and responsibilities at the helm of the firm. If it is unclear when the successor will be appointed as CEO, he or she may feel stalled and frustrated and eventually leave the firm. Alternatively, if the successor is appointed to a top management role but the ownership timeline remains unclear, the successor may feel punished for his or her efforts. That is, when increased efforts by the successor result in heightened profitability for the firm, firm value will rise. The successor is effectively 'punished' for improving the firm's performance if he or she has to acquire firm ownership at a valuation that has grown because of that improvement.

Table 7.9 shows an example of a detailed succession roadmap defining the sequential transfer of governance and functional roles. The incumbent and the successor of a mid-sized French manufacturer drafted this roadmap early in the succession process. The roadmap helped address the inevitable governance challenges that came up before the succession was complete.

It specifies who has decision authority and defines the changing roles and responsibilities along the whole succession process. It also specifies when one party should consult the other or bring a question to the attention of the board. This system can help incumbent and successor address investment decisions, divestment decisions, the hiring and firing of top management team members, and other decisions with a significant impact on the strategy of the firm.

As Table 7.9 suggests, succession at the governance level generally moves through three phases. First, there is a 'freeze' phase in which the incumbent largely controls the firm. Second, there is a 'thaw' phase in which incumbent and successor sort out the firm's strategic challenges and progressive changes in the governance structure. In the example of the French manufacturer, this second phase lasts from year T+1 to year T+5. Finally, there is a 'refreeze' phase when the successor takes the helm at the firm.

Not surprisingly, the second step is particularly critical for the succession process, as the governance roles and functional responsibilities are progressively passed from the incumbent to the successor. This phase holds many traps for both parties. For instance, the roles and responsibilities for each party may lack clear definition, and the successor may be tempted to engage in backseat driving, thus undermining the successor's decisions. Of particular concern are the financial implications of the transfer of ownership rights. If ownership is gradually passed from one generation to the next, as in the example above, the valuation of shares can become an issue, in particular if

Table 7.9 Succession roadmap example (mid-sized French manufacturer)

		Year T	Year T+1	Year T+2	Year T+3	Year T+4	Year T+5	Year T+6
Age	Incumbent (Peter)	62	63	64	65	66	67	68
	Successor (Petra)	35	36	37	38	39	40	41
Governance transition								
Ownership (%)	Incumbent (Peter)	100	100	80	80	20	20	0
	Successor (Petra)	0	0	20	20	80	80	100
Board	Incumbent (Peter)	President	President	President	Member	Member	Member	–
	Successor (Petra)	Member	Member	Member	Member	Member	Member	Member
	Nonfamily member		Member	Member	President	President	President	President
CEO/ Management	Incumbent (Peter)	CEO	CEO	CEO	CEO	Advisor	Advisor	Advisor
	Successor (Petra)	Management	Management	Management	Member	CEO	CEO	CEO
Transition of functional responsibilities								
Human resources		Peter	Peter	Both together	Both together	Petra	Petra	Petra
Business strategy		Peter	Peter	Both together	Both together	Petra	Petra	Petra
Marketing		Peter	Peter	Petra	Petra	Petra	Petra	Petra
Research & development		Peter	Peter	Petra	Petra	Petra	Petra	Petra
Transition miscellaneous								
Private expenses	Incumbent (Peter)	Car	Car	Car	Car	Fuel	Fuel	–
	Successor (Petra)	–	Car	Car	Car	Car	Car	Car
Dividend		100k to Peter	50k to Peter	0	0	0	0	0

Monica – 50% – 5 = 30 – 25 = 25
Mike – 10%
Elizabeth – 5% +25
David Jr – 10% +10 =20
Timothy – 5% +15 =20
Louis – 0 + 5%
Managers – 10% +10 /20

the value of the shares alters (e.g., increases) due to the involvement of the successor. This may cause successors to feel that they are being punished for their efforts through higher share acquisition prices.

For all of these reasons, a succession roadmap such as the one outlined above is helpful. It helps reduce the typical uncertainty inside and outside the firm about the progress of the succession. In brief, the succession roadmap defines the succession process in terms of:

- *who* is responsible,
- *what* the incumbent and successor are responsible for, respectively, and
- *when* responsibilities are transferred on the way to the transfer of full control.

The third dimension in the above list, which deals with timing, is particularly critical. Some argue that the shorter the transition process, the more likely it is to be successful. There are good arguments for this assumption: the leadership vacuum should be filled and the interests of the controlling owner and CEO should be realigned as quickly as possible. Furthermore, successors who are put on probation for a prolonged period will inevitably become frustrated with the process. Such a trial period is especially costly for the most competent successors, in light of the opportunity cost to their careers (Dehlen et al. 2012). Thus, it is usually better to entrust the firm to the successor within a reasonable timeframe.

As shown above, however, in practice most successions take several years to complete—and not all of these successions are failures. There may be good reasons not to finalize the transfer of power prematurely. First, incumbents can be a critical resource for the firm, and this resource can be easily lost in a hastened succession (Cabrera-Suarez, De Saa-Perez and Garcia-Almeida 2001). Second, if the incumbent and successor work well together, senior experience with junior innovation may be paired for the 'best of both worlds'. Third, to ensure a smooth continuation of operations and to uphold an established corporate culture, it may be important that the incumbent stays involved, at least to some degree. For instance, the senior owner may serve as the firm's ambassador to important clients and opinion leaders even though he or she has already passed on most operating obligations. Thus, depending on the type of succession, there may be good reasons not to minimize the transition period during which incumbent and successor are both involved in the firm.

Whatever the optimal duration of this transition period, it is crucial to identify the roles and responsibilities of the incumbent and to define entry and exit paths for both parties on a timeline. If these questions are sorted out appropriately, the length of the transition period itself may be less of an issue.

7.9.2 Entry paths for the successor

The succession roadmap above charts the entry and exit paths for future and incumbent owners. When considering the entry path of the next generation, it is important to examine the pros and cons of family members entering at the shop floor versus the top level (see Figure 7.11).

Family members who enter the firm at the level of the shop floor will still be seen as part of the owning family, and will most likely not be treated as regular employees. In this case, the successor is unlikely to receive objective feedback and may be promoted more easily. Worse, he or she is likely to be pulled into political power games by parties who hope that the successor's influence will benefit them.

Alternatively, when family successors enter at the top management level, they may not be respected by long-time nonfamily managers. Nonfamily managers may be hesitant to confer legitimacy on heirs who have limited experience inside (and sometimes outside) the firm. Long-term managers may see the successor as undeserving of a senior management position that they were aspiring to themselves. At worst, the successor may become the incarnation of the 'nonfamily ceiling' (sometimes also called 'blood ceiling'), defined as the career limitation experienced by nonfamily employees when

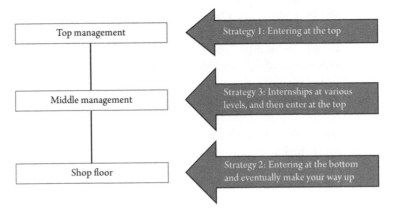

Figure 7.11 Entrance paths for family successors

top positions are reserved for family members. At best, the family successor may be seen as a symbol of the family's continued commitment to the firm, which in turn suggests continuity, good prospects for job security and a stable strategic outlook.

Given the downsides of both these approaches, a kind of intermediary approach works well in practice, especially in mid- to large-sized firms. In the first phase, the successor pursues a career outside the firm with the intention to gain as much management experience as possible, learn what it takes to run a firm and see whether a job at the helm suits them. This outside experience will signal their professional track record when they enter the firm at a later stage. In the second phase, the successor will receive firm- and successor-specific training inside the company in preparation for a leadership role. In this phase, the successor works temporarily in several key departments (e.g., a few months each in the finance, production and sales departments) to familiarize him-/herself with the firm, its operations and key employees. In the third phase, the successor assumes a top position at the family firm. This position will depend on the jobs available and the career planning of other top executives. It will eventually lead to the CEO job if the successor's performance is satisfactory.

7.9.3 Adapting roles for incumbent and successor

The above succession roadmap describes succession as a fairly technical process. What makes the transition challenging, however, is that the change in roles not only implies a change in functions and responsibilities, but also a change in the self-understanding of the people involved, which reaches beyond their immediate governance roles inside the firm. According to Handler (1990), the incumbent moves from the role of leader/chief, to monarch, to overseer/delegator, to consultant (Figure 7.12). In contrast, the successor moves from having no role, to being a helper, manager and, ultimately, the new leader/chief.

As the incumbent has the formal power in the firm at the outset of the succession process, he or she is also the one to initiate this transition process. It is the incumbent who must realize that the firm requires new managerial talent. At first, the successor will be engaged in a helping role. This helping role signals to the incumbent that it is time to delegate some formal power and to progressively move to the role of monarch. The successor's support provides the security the incumbent needs to ask the successor to step up and become a manager, which in turn allows the incumbent to delegate even

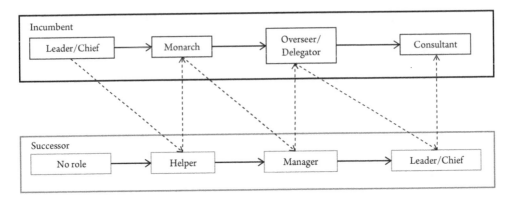

Source: Handler (1990).

Figure 7.12 Role adaptation in the succession process

more tasks and to move to the role of overseer. When the incumbent realizes that the firm is working well even as they become less engaged, the successor can step up to the role of new leader and chief. In turn, the incumbent takes on an even more passive role as a consultant, offering advice only when it is required by the successor.

7.9.4 Grooming the successor

In an increasing number of family firms, and especially in small firms with limited financial success, it cannot be taken for granted the successor will be a child of the incumbent. Even in larger, more prestigious firms, potential successors often have problems identifying with the firm and its products and assimilating into the firm culture once they decide to join. While a governance transition roadmap and an understanding of changing roles may be helpful to some extent, challenges often arise at a more subtle, psychological level, for example when the successor does not get the needed support and grooming to identify with the firm and the new role.

This leads to an important question: is there a way to groom successors so that they evolve from the position of outsider to intrinsically motivated leader? The answer to this question is not an easy one, as it has both a normative and functional dimension. From a normative point of view, one may ask whether parents should try to groom successors. Shouldn't becoming an entrepreneur or successor be a completely independent and self-determined choice? Certainly, being coerced into the role of successor will never be a satisfactory solution for any of the parties involved or for the firm. Coercion is likely to end in drama at all levels.

From a functional point of view, however, if the junior family member shows some initial interest and capability, the question is how he or she may be best assimilated into the firm. In the end, this is the challenge that any employee faces when joining a new employer. Psychologists Edward Deci and Richard Ryan (2000) developed a self-determination theory for such cases that describes the assimilation processes of individuals who approach new tasks, groups and organizations. Their conceptual model suggests that individuals who face new contexts move from being external to the new context, to intro-jection (where they act out of guilt, anxiety, to maintain self-worth, or because others want them to do so), to identification (where action is personally rel-evant), to integration (where actions are aligned with personal values) and, ideally, to intrinsic motivation (where actions are enjoyable, satisfactory and aligned with personal interests). Adapting their model to the succession context would suggest that parents and other external parties have three levers to facilitate the assimilation and grooming process (Figure 7.13):

1. **Support feelings of autonomy**
   Successors are more likely to identify with and eventually develop intrin-sic motivation for the firm if they feel that their decisions, and more broadly their life and fate, are determined by themselves, and not by others, in particular not by parents. Feelings of autonomy are supported by freedom in career choice and the de-emphasis of control mechanisms once the successor joins the family firm.

2. **Support feelings of competence**
   Successors are more likely to identify with and eventually develop intrin-sic motivation for the firm if they are given demanding but solvable challenges. Evaluations should be fair and focused on promotion; they should not be condescending or paternalistic. The successor should get adequate training outside and inside the firm and receive objective and supportive feedback.

3. **Support feelings of relatedness**
   In addition, successors are more likely to identify with and eventually develop intrinsic motivation for the firm if they work in a welcoming, interpersonal environment. Colleagues inside the firm can help junior family members develop a feeling of belonging by being supportive. But prospective heirs must also be supported by their parents. Ideally, parents should show unconditional support and communicate that the successor/child is loved even if the succession does not work out as originally intended.

Internalization and assimilation process

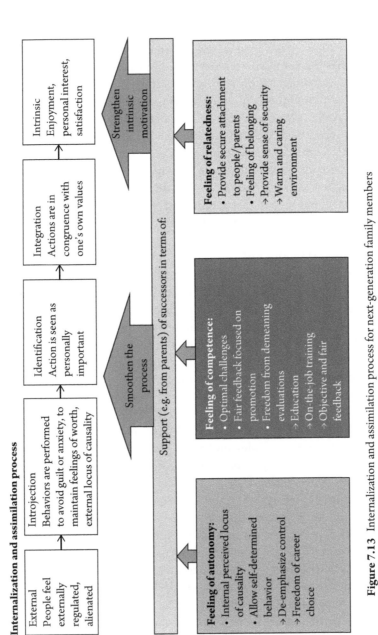

Figure 7.13 Internalization and assimilation process for next-generation family members

CASE STUDY

Grooming the successor at Filter Corp, Italy

When his friends asked Pietro about whether he wanted to join his parents' firm, Filter Corp, after graduation, he used to instantly reply: 'Not before I get some professional experience elsewhere.' But a few weeks before graduation, his father asked Pietro whether he could take over an important job inside the family firm. A couple of years ago, his father had acquired a former distributor of Filter Corp's products in China. This firm was run by a local manager overseeing a team of ten employees. Unfortunately, it had serious financial problems, stemming mainly from unsatisfactory customer service and inefficient logistics with multiple warehouses.

His father asked Pietro whether he would be interested in taking on the challenge and moving to China for some years to fix these problems. At first, Pietro was hesitant; he'd always been determined to make his mark outside the firm first. On the other hand, this was a tempting opportunity: he would be far away from his father's influence and could prove himself on his own terms. The business problem seemed to be a real challenge, but one that was commensurate with his limited experience. Wouldn't this be a great opportunity to do something autonomously and prove his competence at the same time? His father promised to support Pietro and not to interfere with his decisions regarding the Chinese acquisition. But the two of them agreed that Pietro had to consult his father about investment decisions exceeding a certain amount of money. They also found a local business consultant who could help with some of the restructuring of the Chinese operations.

Then, Pietro and his father set up a long-term succession plan. Once the Chinese turnaround was complete—presumably in two to four years—Pietro would return to Europe and head the Italian headquarters, which included about 100 people. After heading the Italian operations for about three years, Pietro would assume responsibility for the whole group.

When Pietro moved to China, he became a member of the board of the holding company, which owned the whole business group. His father also gave him some group shares. Both of them signed a shareholder agreement that regulated the conditions under which shares could be transferred between them.

? **REFLECTION QUESTIONS**

The following list includes some of the most relevant questions for the incumbent and successor regarding the transition of governance roles.

Reflection questions for the incumbent (see also questions in Table 7.6)

1. How long should I stay on as CEO? When will I pass on the CEO role?
2. At what level should the successor enter the firm? What are the pros and cons of the proposed entry path?

3. What are my roles and responsibilities when I am involved in the firm at the same time as the successor?
4. Will I stay involved on the board? If so, in what role, and for how long?
5. How do I communicate with the successor inside and outside the firm?
6. On the timeline, how do we move from me being 100% owner to the successor being 100% owner?
7. What tasks do I want to pass on to the successor first? What next?
8. How do changes in the valuation of the firm during succession impact the successor's acquisition of (remaining) ownership later in the process?
9. Is the current management team supporting the successor? Do we need to find new managerial talent at a second managerial level?
10. Is the successor able to step up to the leadership role?
11. What will I do with my time after my complete exit from the firm?
12. Can I ensure my retirement income without significant proceeds from the sale of the firm?
13. How can we support the successor's integration into the firm?

Reflection questions for the successor (see also questions in Table 7.6)

1. At what level should I enter the firm? What are the pros and cons of the proposed solution?
2. Is the current management team supporting me? Do I need to reconfigure the management team in the future?
3. What are my roles and responsibilities in the firm when the incumbent is still involved?
4. How do I communicate with the incumbent inside and outside the firm?
5. Will I become involved on the board? If so, in what role?
6. Do I want to become the new CEO?
7. Do we need external additions to the board?
8. When and under what conditions do I acquire ownership in the company?
9. How do changes in the valuation of the firm during succession impact my acquisition of (remaining) ownership?

Reflection questions for students

1. Why is reviewing the firm's strategy important for the succession process?
2. What strategic challenges do owner-managed family firms typically face when approaching the succession phase?
3. Given these strategic challenges, what questions do the incumbent and successor need to address?
4. 'Parallel engagement of the incumbent and successor in the firm should be minimized.' Do you agree or disagree? Why?
5. How do the roles of incumbent and successor change throughout the succession process?
6. Consider a firm you know well. What does the roadmap for management, ownership and board succession look like?
7. What are the potential sources of conflict if management and ownership succession are not well defined between successor and incumbent?
8. What can parents do to help integrate their children into the family firm?

7.10 Valuing the firm

Sooner or later, any succession will be confronted with a difficult question: at what price will the firm be passed down to the next owner? The price that is ultimately paid in the transaction, as for any other economic good, will be determined by the offer and the demand. The stronger the demand, for example when there are competing buyers/successors, the higher the price. Often, we observe a discrepancy between the valuation of the firm and the price that is ultimately paid in the transaction. Put differently, what is determined to be a 'fair' price in a valuation serves only as a proxy for what is ultimately paid. Still, to obtain an approximate idea about the price or price range, a company valuation may be helpful.

In the present chapter, we cannot explore the subtleties of every valuation method in detail. Instead, we aim to highlight the most relevant valuation methods and their unique characteristics when it comes to the valuation of private family firms. Valuing a private family firm is a challenging endeavor on many fronts. First, many incumbent owners fail to set up sophisticated accounting and control systems, leading to a lack of solid financial information. Second, once financial information is available, it will be hard to judge its quality given the absence of external scrutiny. What is more, because the firm is privately held and there is no liquid market for the shares, there are severe constraints on ownership transfers. In addition, there may be firm-specific challenges such as a narrow segment of product offerings, growth financing restrictions, or the intertwinement of business and private affairs. Some private expenses may run through company accounts, or the firm may possess assets that are not used for operations. Incumbent owners may have taken advantage of accounting practices that reduce tax burdens, most often by inflating the cost structure, which makes firm value even more difficult to assess. Finally, there may be undisclosed reserves in the firm's books, for instance due to excessive depreciation of assets or inflated accruals.

It is therefore of paramount importance to review the financial data that is used for the valuation of the firm and adjust it as necessary. With regard to the balance sheet, accounts receivable, raw materials and real estate have to be set at their replacement values. This will involve reassessing the risk of default and adapting related accruals. Similarly, the market value of machinery must be estimated. Accruals must be set at a level that reflects the risks they are intended to cover.

In addition, the income statement has to be reviewed and adjusted. In particular, the salaries of the owner and other family members involved in the firm need to be examined. Incumbent owners often apply salary levels to family members that deviate from market levels. Higher-than-market salaries are paid out to transfer liquidity from the business to the owner.

Alternatively, lower-than-market salaries are paid out to support and subsidize the firm. For many small firms, reviewing and adjusting the incumbent owners' salaries to market levels can have a significant impact on firm profits, and ultimately the value of the company. Similarly, related-party transactions—that is, those with other firms controlled by the incumbent, or with acquaintances of the incumbent—must be reviewed for the appropriateness of transfer prices. Eventually, value-increasing expenses can be capitalized in the balance sheet. Depreciation must be reviewed, and changes in accruals must be booked into company accounts. Ultimately, the tax expenses have to be reassessed.

These changes to the balance sheet and income statement are necessary to reevaluate the firm's profitability. From the perspective of the next owner, the firm's relative attractiveness must be assessed in the absence of the previous owners and with market-based cost and income estimates. This is not to say that there is a 'right' or 'wrong' empirical evaluation of the firm. Rather, any valuation is the result of more or less reasonable assumptions about the firm's financial situation. Critically reviewing the valuation, understanding its assumptions and assessing their plausibility are essential tasks for those involved in the succession process. For an overall understanding of a given valuation, the following questions may be helpful:

- Who executed the valuation? Is the evaluator advising the buyer, the seller or both? Depending on the evaluator's position at the negotiation table, he or she may have incentives to either deflate or inflate firm value.
- How biased are the financial data used to calculate firm value? What adjustments have been applied to the balance sheet and income statement?
- Do the assumptions for value adjustments and budget figures make sense?
- Have there been separate value assessments for operating and non-operating assets?
- How plausible are the critical parameters in the applied valuation method?
- Does the applied valuation method make sense in light of the firm's business activity?
- Does the valuation apply a single or multiple valuation methods? As different valuation methods make different assumptions about value drivers, it is important to triangulate the valuation using multiple valuation methods.

Below, we will present three of the most common methods used to estimate the value of closely and privately held companies. The explanations
for each method are limited to the most relevant aspects and emphasize the
method's underlying assumptions, critical parameters, and strengths and
weaknesses.

7.10.1 Net asset value

The net asset value of a company estimates the value of a firm's equity according to the firm's balance sheet after disclosure of all previously undisclosed
reserves. This valuation requires the reassessment of the firm's balance sheet
based on market values. The net asset value is calculated as:

Net asset value = Total value of assets − Total value of liabilities

Net asset value is useful for share valuation in sectors where the company
value is based on held assets rather than the profit stream generated by
the business (e.g., property companies and investment trusts). The net
asset value typically represents the floor value of the firm, as it indicates
the amount of money that is left for distribution to shareholders if the firm
stops its operations and sells all its assets after serving all its debts. This
makes it a particularly useful method in determining the liquidation value of
a firm. Technically, net asset value is fairly easy to determine even though the
market value for illiquid assets may be difficult to assess. The disadvantage
of a valuation based on net asset value is that it neglects the profitability of
the firm, and hence the firm's ability to generate profits with the assets. This
valuation also neglects earnings prospects and thus the future of the firm's
operations.

Still, net asset valuation is a commonly used technique in the valuation of
small to mid-sized family firms, as it helps estimate changes in undisclosed
reserves and verify depreciation procedures; these findings can then be used
in other valuation methods. It is a particularly useful method for valuing
family firms, which tend to be asset heavy. Compared to a market value estimate, net asset value can be an important indicator in determining whether
the firm is a cheap or expensive investment. In well-run and profitable firms,
net asset value should be below the market value of the firm (when market
value is estimated based on some valuation of the firm's profitability). If the
net asset value of a firm is *larger* than a reasonable market value estimate,
family investors in the firm should ask whether their funds are being put to
efficient use and how efficiency could be improved. In extreme cases, from a
short-term financial standpoint, it may make more sense to wind operations

up and sell off the firm's assets individually rather than continue to run it as a going concern.

Summing up, the critical parameters in a net asset valuation are the following:

Critical parameters:
- Reassessment of the value of balance sheet items.
- Treatment of undisclosed reserves, including from a tax standpoint (as they may be taxed in a transfer of assets).

Advantages of the method:
- Indicates a floor value of the firm.
- Provides useful estimations for other valuation methods, for example discounted cash flow.
- Relatively easy to apply; no sophisticated technical skills required.
- Useful for asset-heavy firms, especially in comparison to market value.

Disadvantages of the method:
- Neglects firm profitability.
- Cannot provide insights into operating strengths/weaknesses of the firm.
- Neglects the firm's future prospects.

7.10.2 EBIT or EBITDA multiple valuation

A commonly used method to approximate the value of a closely held firm is to multiply some earnings base, such as profit (after tax), sales volume, or most often EBIT or EBITDA,[6] by a multiple. Of course, the determination of the multiple is a key challenge. Stock market valuations of publicly quoted companies in the same industry and of more or less comparable size can serve as one source of data for deriving the multiple. For instance, EBITDA and EBIT multiples of publicly quoted companies for many industries and geographic regions can be found on the website www.damodaran.com. Given the particular risks of private firms, their multiples tend to be smaller than those of public firms. Multiples for German private firms, for instance, can be found on the website of *Finance Magazin*. For UK private firms, BDO's Private Company Price Index is helpful. Many other sources can be found on the web or via professional service providers.

Two caveats on the use of multiples to value companies are in order. First, no company is perfectly comparable to another company. In consequence, selecting peer companies that are comparable in terms of industry, business model and size to determine multiples can be challenging. Second, the earnings base (e.g., profit after tax, EBIT, EBITDA or even sales) that is multiplied with the multiple determines whether the resulting value estimate represents the enterprise value (EV, sometimes also called entity value) or the market value of equity (= the value of the shares). EV is the sum of the market value of equity plus the book value of debt minus unused cash (see formula below). Applying EBITDA or EBIT multiples results in EV, whereas a multiple for profit after tax directly results in the firm's equity value.

This distinction is based on whether the earnings base (e.g., EBIT, EBITDA, sales, profit) is valuable to equity *and* debt holders, or to equity holders alone. Because EBIT, EBITDA and sales are valuable to equity and debt holders, the resulting value is EV. In contrast, multiplying profit after tax (as represented by the price earnings ratio) directly results in equity value, as profit is only value creating for equity holders; debt holders have already been paid through interest.

The following formulas indicate the relationship between EV, equity value, EBITDA, and the EBITDA multiple (the formula applies equally to EBIT).

$$EV = \text{Market value equity} + \text{Book value of debt} - \text{Unused cash}$$

$$EV = EBITDA * \text{Multiple}_{EBITDA}$$

$$\text{Market value equity} = EBITDA * \text{Multiple}_{EBITDA} - \text{Book value of debt} + \text{Unused cash}$$

Often, the average EBITDA or EBIT over the last three years are used for valuation.

Summing up, the critical parameters in a multiple valuation are the following:

Critical parameters:
- Plausible estimation of the multiple.
- Distinction between enterprise and equity value.

Advantages of the method:
- Technically, relatively easy to apply.
- Availability of multiple estimates from various data sources.
- Based on achieved market prices.

Disadvantages of the method:
- Neglects the firm's future prospects.
- Neglects the firm's assets.
- Difficulty in finding comparable transactions (e.g., size, industry, geography).

CASE STUDY

EBIT multiple valuation

Assume a firm with an average EBIT of 550 over the last three years, with long-term debt of 450, a shareholder loan of 350 and unused cash of 100. Assuming an EBIT multiple of 6.4, the following values result:

Enterprise value: $6.4 * 550 = 3520$
Equity value: $3520 - 450 - 350 + 100 = 2820$

If the firm owns assets that are not used for operations, these would be valued separately and then added on top of the above equity value.

7.10.3 Discounted free cash flow (DCF) valuation

The discounted free cash flow (DCF) valuation method estimates the current value of the future free cash flows (FCFs) of the firm. This valuation method comes with two peculiarities. First, the DCF method does not take into consideration the profit of the firm, but its free cash flows. This is an important distinction from the two methods discussed above, as free cash flows represents the amount of liquidity generated over a year and available for distribution among *all* the securities holders (debt holders and shareholders) of a firm after all other expenses and investments have been paid. As such, the DCF method uses a profit measure that is of central interest to the capital providers of a firm. Second, the DCF method does not measure the past performance of the firm, but its profit outlook. More specifically, through a DCF valuation we try to estimate today's value of future FCFs.

To understand the mechanics of the DCF method, let's first examine the determination of FCF, starting with EBIT (Table 7.10).

An example may shed further light on the calculation of FCF (see Table 7.11). Starting with the last available balance sheets and income statements,

Table 7.10 Determination of free cash flow

Element	Data source
EBIT	Income statement
− Tax rate	Marginal tax rate, given local tax regime
+ Depreciation and amortization	Income statement
− Capital expenditures	Prior and current balance sheet: property, plant and equipment accounts
− Changes in working capital	Prior and current balance sheet: current assets and liability accounts
Free cash flow (FCF)	

estimated balance sheets and income statements are set up for the next five years. The five-year planning period represents a more or less predictable timeframe for which detailed balance sheets and income statements can be prepared to ultimately deduct future FCF.

The resulting future FCFs will be discounted to current values. The discount rate takes into account the risks (which correspond to the costs) that the security holders incur to attain these FCFs. As a discount rate, we estimate the weighted average cost of capital (WACC), which is determined as follows:

$$WACC = D \,/\, (D + E) * C \text{ of } D * (1 - t) + E \,/\, (D + E) * C \text{ of } E$$

With D = market value of debt; E = market value of equity; C of D = cost of debt; C of E = cost of equity; and t = marginal tax rate.[7]

The above WACC formula takes into account the capital structure of the firm by weighing costs of equity and costs of debt against their relative presence in the firm's balance sheet.[8] Costs of equity capital are normally higher than costs of debt capital, as debt is secured by assets such as machinery, real estate or inventory. In contrast, equity is unsecured. Also, debt holders get a predetermined and fixed interest payment, while equity holders do not benefit from predetermined payments, but only from uncertain dividends and value increases in their ownership stake. While in recent years mid-sized private firms in the West have had interest rates between 3% and 7% on operating debt, equity holders often expect returns of 10% to 25% from their investments. The actual interest rates always depend on the specific risk profile of the firm.

Table 7.11 Calculation of operating free cash flow (example)

in $ million	History	Planning				
Balance Sheet	-1	1	2	3	4	5
Assets						
Fixed assets	361.2	364.8	381.7	384.6	384.5	374.4
Liquid assets	466.3	472.0	485.6	516.5	540.6	565.3
Total Balance Sheet	827.5	836.8	867.3	901.1	925.1	939.7
Liabilities						
Equity	184.5	200.7	220.1	245.9	273.4	300.7
Other equity	13.0	13.0	13.0	13.0	13.0	13.0
Accruals	103.1	108.0	113.0	120.6	127.1	133.2
Liabilities	526.9	515.1	521.2	521.6	511.6	492.7
Total Balance Sheet	827.5	836.8	867.3	901.1	925.1	939.7
Income Statement	-1	1	2	3	4	5
Total Sales	1496.8	1516.9	1573.9	1682.0	1762.7	1834.2
(–) Materials	759.8	773.6	802.7	857.8	899.0	935.4
(–) Third-party services	61.0	68.3	67.7	69.0	72.3	75.2
Gross Margin	676.0	675.0	703.5	755.2	791.5	823.6
(–) Personnel	365.2	375.1	386.8	406.9	423.8	439.4
(–) Depreciation	56.6	64.8	68.5	75.7	79.2	81.9
(–) Depreciation on goodwill	10.1	10.1	10.1	10.1	10.1	10.1
(–) Other operating expenses	179.6	184.7	190.4	198.2	209.3	220.2
(+) Other operating income	11.3	12.8	12.0	9.8	7.4	2.4
EBIT	75.8	53.1	59.8	74.0	76.4	74.4
(+) Financial income	0.4	-15.4	-14.7	-13.9	-12.5	-10.6
EBT	76.2	37.8	45.1	60.1	63.9	63.7
(–) Taxes	27.5	14.6	17.4	23.2	24.7	24.6
EAT	48.7	23.2	27.7	36.9	39.2	39.1
(–) Other	0.9	0.0	0.0	0.0	0.0	0.0
Annual Profit	47.8	23.2	27.7	36.9	39.2	39.1
Net Working Capital	-1	1	2	3	4	5
Net Working Capital	318.3	313.3	319.6	341.4	357.8	370.4
Change in Net Working Capital		-5.0	6.4	21.7	16.4	12.5
Capital expenditures (CAPEX)	-1	1	2	3	4	5
Immaterial assets	106.8	96.7	86.6	76.5	66.4	56.3
Fixed assets	241.3	255.0	282.0	295.0	305.0	305.0
Depreciation	56.6	64.8	68.5	75.7	79.2	81.9
Depreciation on goodwill	10.1	10.1	10.1	10.1	10.1	10.1
CAPEX		78.5	95.5	88.7	89.2	81.9

Table 7.11 (continued)

in $ million Balance Sheet	History -1	Planning 1	2	3	4	5
Operating FCF		1	2	3	4	5
EBIT		53.1	59.8	74.0	76.4	74.4
(−) Adapted taxes on EBIT (38.65%)		20.5	23.1	28.6	29.5	28.7
NOPLAT		32.6	36.7	45.4	46.9	45.6
(+) Total depreciation		74.9	78.6	85.8	89.3	92.0
(+) Change in long-term accruals		3.0	3.0	3.0	3.0	3.0
(+) Change in short-term accruals		1.9	2.1	4.5	3.5	3.1
Cash Flow		112.4	120.4	138.8	142.7	143.7
(−) CAPEX		78.5	95.5	88.7	89.2	81.9
(−) Change in net working capital		-5.0	6.4	21.7	16.4	12.5
Operating FCF		38.9	18.5	28.3	37.0	49.3

Notes: CAPEX Year i = Fixed assets Year i − Fixed assets Year (i − 1) + Depreciation Year i; NOPLAT = Net operating profit after tax.

The fact that equity is more expensive and hence more risky than debt is significant for family firms, which tend to rely more heavily on equity for their financing. While a strong equity base reduces bankruptcy risk because of a low debt burden, financial risks are undistributed and carried by the equity holder alone. Consequently, a firm that is solely financed with equity is not necessarily worth more than a firm that is financed with a balanced mix of equity and debt.

Of course, the positive relationship between leverage levels and firm value has its limits, as the costs of equity and debt may vary depending on the leverage level. With extreme leverage levels, the costs of debt may increase dramatically to levels comparable to equity capital, so that highly leveraged firms are ultimately penalized on their weighted average costs of capital. Highly self-financed firms, including many family firms, often face lower firm values because of high WACCs given the high proportion of relatively expensive equity in their balance sheets. But highly leveraged firms can face lower firm values as well, as under high leverage costs of debt start to increase dramatically. This observation points to a curvilinear (inverted U-shaped) relationship between debt/equity levels and firm value.

At very low debt/equity ratios, the financial risks are concentrated with the equity investors alone, which reduces the attractiveness of the investment. With increasing leverage levels, financial risks are split across several entities, and firm value increases in turn. But at very high leverage levels, the firm faces a growing bankruptcy risk given its heavy debt burden and the increasing costs of debt. We find optimal leverage levels to be around 0.7 to 1.5.

Up to now, we have estimated the future FCFs for the next five years and the WACC at which these FCFs are discounted. We can now proceed with discounting these future FCFs using WACC to derive the present value of the future FCFs. The present values of the five future FCFs are calculated as follows:

$$NPV_{1-5} = FCF_1 / (1 + WACC)^1 + FCF_2 / (1 + WACC)^2 + FCF_3 / (1 + WACC)^3 + FCF_4 / (1 + WACC)^4 + FCF_5 / (1 + WACC)^5$$

Because the firm will not end its operations after these five years, we have to estimate the terminal value (TV) of the firm. TV captures that part of the firm's value that accrues after year five. To derive TV, we assume that the FCF in year five (FCF_5) will be sustainable in perpetuity. Of course, this is an extreme assumption; in consequence, the value we set for FCF_5 will have a decisive influence on the resulting firm value. The TV of this perpetual income stream is calculated as follows:

$$TV = FCF_5 / WACC - g$$

With TV = terminal value; g = terminal growth rate.

The terminal growth rate allows us to account for industries that are expected to grow steadily at an estimated rate g over the coming years. The present value of TV is derived as follows:

$$Present\ value\ of\ TV = TV / (1 + WACC)^5$$

Building on the above example, assuming a WACC of 9%, we arrive at a value of 131.4 for the net present values of the next five years of FCF (for details, see Table 7.12). Assuming a terminal growth rate of 0%, we find a TV of 547.8 (= 49.3/0.09), and a present value of TV of 356.0. In a DCF valuation, enterprise value is derived from the sum of the present values of free cash flows (the five years of detailed planning, 131.4) plus the present value of TV (the remaining years, 356.0).

It is important to reiterate that the FCF that we used as our earnings base in a DCF valuation creates value for all security holders (debt and equity

Table 7.12 Discounting future FCFs to determine entity and equity value

	-1	1	2	3	4	5	TV
Operating FCF		38.9	18.5	28.3	37.0	49.3	547.8
Discount rate		1.09	1.19	1.30	1.41	1.54	
Present value of free cash flow		35.65	15.60	21.85	26.24	32.04	
Sum of present values of free cash flows	131.4						
(+) Present value of TV	356.0						
Enterprise value	487.4						
(+) Cash	32.9						
(−) Interest-bearing debt	259.7						
Equity value	260.6						

holders).[9] Thus, the immediate result from discounting our FCF is enterprise value, and not yet equity value. To derive equity value, as was the case for EBIT and EBITDA multiple valuations, interest-bearing debt has to be deducted and unused cash must be added.

To reiterate, DCF valuation is calculated according to the following steps:

1. Estimate the next five years' operating free cash flows.
2. Estimate the weighted average cost of capital.
3. Determine the terminal value.
4. Calculate present values of the next five years' free cash flows (present value part 1).
5. Calculate the present value of the terminal value (present value part 2).
6. Add the two present values to obtain *enterprise value.*
7. Add unused cash and subtract interest-bearing debt to obtain *equity value.*

Summing up, the critical parameters in a DCF valuation are the following:

Critical parameters:
- WACC, with a significant impact on the present value of future FCF and TV.
- FCF_5, as this FCF also enters into the estimation of TV.
- Terminal growth rate g, which enters into the estimation of TV.
- TV, which often represents the largest fraction of enterprise value (in the above example, TV represents 73.1% of enterprise value).

Advantages of the method:
- Focuses on free cash flows, and hence profits distributable to security holders.
- Focuses on future and not past profits.
- Accounts for the occurrence of profits and investments on the timeline.

Disadvantages of the method:
- Technically more challenging than other methods.
- Estimation of WACC, and therein particularly cost of equity capital.
- Sensitive to few but critical parameters (in particular, WACC, g and FCF_s).

7.10.4 Combining different valuations to get a fuller perspective

The above presented valuation methods differ in their assumptions about 'what is valuable' in a firm. They all have particular strengths and weaknesses, and are sensitive to a few but critical parameters. It is therefore advisable to compare several valuations in order to obtain a more complete picture of the firm's value. Note that the choice of valuation methods should depend on the specific firm in question. While net asset valuation is a good choice for an asset-heavy firm, a DCF valuation seems more appropriate for a firm that finds itself in a strong growth phase with significant future investment.

7.10.5 From valuation to price

From the above remarks, it should be clear that valuation cannot be understood as a scientific endeavor. Valuations operate with more or less reasonable assumptions to accommodate the particularities of a case, and different valuation methods result in differing firm values. Valuations can only provide a range within which a transaction price will likely fall. Still, and as mentioned at the outset of this chapter, transaction prices may sometimes differ significantly from the results of a valuation. As for any other economic good, offer and demand are central to the determination of firm value. In the absence of demand, the price will fall even in the presence of seemingly valuable assets. And in the presence of demand, the price will increase even when such assets are lacking. Ultimately, the valuation depends on what a willing buyer is prepared to pay a willing seller.

In family firm successions, and in particular when a firm is passed from one owner-manager to the next, the transaction price often represents a compromise between several factors, of which valuation is only one. More specifically, transaction prices in family firm successions are often contingent on the following four factors:

1. **Valuation**

   Valuations as introduced above set the margins within which an efficient transaction price will likely fall. Depending on the type of firm, different valuation methods are more or less appropriate.

2. **Emotional value**

   We have seen that incumbent owners account for their emotional attachment to the firm, over and above financial considerations, when considering the acceptable sale price. They also tend to overestimate the value of their firms. For example, a sample of German owner-managers estimated the value of their firms at a rate of 30% above market value estimates. For further details, see section 7.7.3. Notwithstanding the efficient market perspective that is applied for valuation, the incumbent may have significant emotional attachment to the firm, and will be hesitant to let go at a market price that does not reflect or compensate for perceived emotional value.

3. **Type of successor**

   Strategic buyers, such as former competitors, may be willing to pay a synergy premium on top of market value. Similarly, a financial buyer with access to significant amounts of capital, such as a private equity fund, may be willing to pay a premium. In these two cases, the incumbent has significant opportunities to maximize the sale price.

   In a contrast to the case of a strategic or financial buyer, in an MBO, the incumbent may be willing to discount the sale price in return for the knowledge that the firm will be under the control of a long-term loyal employee. The discount may be even deeper when the firm is passed down to a family member who perpetuates the family's entrepreneurial legacy. For more details on the expected family discount among next-generation family members, see section 7.7.3.

   These hypotheses are borne out by the evidence. For example, in a study of 455 Swiss and German small to mid-sized private firms that were passed on from one owner-manager to the next, we found transaction prices to be significantly lower than market value. The highest discounts (42%) occurred when the successor was a family member and the lowest when the firm was sold to a business partner through an MBI (22%). It is important to note that tax authorities limit the depth of these discounts to some extent. This is because a highly depressed transfer price limits the tax income from the transaction.

4. **Financing opportunities**

   Even though incumbent and successor may largely agree on a fair transaction price, in many successions of small to mid-sized firms the transaction price ultimately depends on the financing constraints of the successor. The successor may simply not have the equity or the access to debt

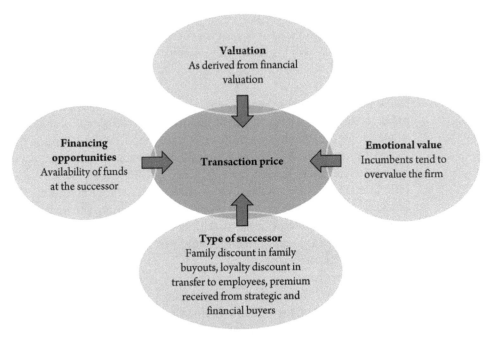

Figure 7.14 Drivers of transaction prices in private family firm successions

financing to fund the transaction. In the absence of alternative buyers, or in cases when the incumbent prefers a successor who lacks financing, the incumbent will have to adjust the transaction price or otherwise help to finance the transaction (e.g., through a seller loan).

Even with a sophisticated valuation, transaction prices in private firm successions, especially when one owner-manager passes the firm to the next, depend on several factors. These factors are summarized in Figure 7.14.

? REFLECTION QUESTIONS

Reflection questions for the incumbent

1. What critical assumptions are linked to each valuation method?
2. What is a reasonable value estimate as assessed by an independent advisor?
3. Do I agree with the price estimate? If not, could emotional biases potentially be affecting my valuation?
4. Depending on the succession option, am I willing to compromise on the sale price?
5. What level of discounts do tax authorities accept compared to a fair market valuation?

Reflection questions for the successor

1. What is the financial outlook of the firm (balance sheet, income statement and cash flow statement) for the next five years?

2. What are the specific risks of the firm which have an impact on future cash flows?
3. What are the appropriate valuation methods? What critical assumptions are linked to each valuation method?
4. What is a reasonable value estimate as assessed by an independent advisor?
5. Are there any assets (e.g., real estate) that have to be valued differently than the operating business?
6. How do the incumbent's private expenses impact the valuation of the firm?
7. Has the incumbent paid him-/herself an above-market-level salary? If so, what would the firm's cash flow look like if a market-level salary were paid?

Reflection questions for students

1. Why does corporate value appear so different for incumbent and successor?
2. How do you assess the net asset value of a firm? What are the advantages/disadvantages of this valuation method?
3. How do you assess the EBIT multiple value of a firm? What are the advantages/disadvantages of this valuation method?
4. How do you assess the DCF value of a firm? What are the advantages/disadvantages of this valuation method?
5. What assumptions in a DCF valuation have an important impact on the resulting firm value?
6. What is the difference between equity value and enterprise value?
7. How do you calculate free cash flow, starting with EBIT?
8. How do you calculate the weighted average cost of capital of a firm?
9. Why is a fully equity-financed firm not necessarily worth more than a partly leveraged firm?

CASE STUDY

Transfer to employees—Valuation and incentive setting

Three years ago, Sandra and one of her colleagues on the management team took over an interior design studio from their former boss. They acquired 60% of the shares at the time and intended to acquire the remaining 40% four years later. The value of this residual ownership stake would be contingent on the firm's financial performance during the first three years of operations after the acquisition of the 60%.

Today, Sandra and her friend are considering acquiring the remaining 40% of shares next year. The former owner wants $450 000 for these shares. The firm holds interest-bearing debt of $100 000 and is free from non-operating assets. In the past three years, the firm reached EBITs of $120 000 (T-3), $120 000 (T-2) and $150 000 (T-1). The current year is likely to end at the same EBIT as last year.

 REFLECTION QUESTIONS

1. Is $450 000 a realistic price for the remaining shares?
2. What do you think of the structure of this succession agreement? What incentives does it set?

7.11 Financing the succession

Once the parties have agreed on a transaction price, it will be essential to establish the financing of the transaction. In what follows, we discuss the most relevant financing options when it comes to the transfer of private firm ownership from one owner-manager to the next. Our focus is on the many small to mid-sized family firms in which succession financing takes place outside of public markets. The most relevant financing options for these firms, as we will discuss, are equity, vendor loan, bank loan and mezzanine capital. We put less emphasis on succession in large family firms, where the incumbent or part of the family can be paid out through an IPO.

To be clear, financing is a challenge mainly for the successor, who has to secure the financial means to pay for the firm he/she wants to take over. It will be less of a concern if the firm is given to or inherited by the successor. But even in these cases, the gift often comes with strings attached, for instance in the form of annual installments to the (ex-)incumbent. These expenses also have to be financed. However, and as will be further explained below, the incumbent also has a role to play in facilitating the transaction and its financing. In small to mid-sized firms, incumbents often have to be actively involved in crafting a deal structure. Otherwise, there may be no deal at all, given the limited liquidity of the firm's shares and the potentially limited interest of buyers. The incumbent may need to demonstrate flexibility in terms of:

1. The purchase price itself (i.e., he/she must be willing to forgo a maximized sale price).
2. The payment structure for the purchase price across time. For instance, does the successor have to pay the complete purchase price at the moment the deal is closed, or can parts of the deal be paid at a later point in time?
3. Co-financing the deal via a vendor loan.
4. The sequential sale of the firm's shares, so that the successor acquires complete ownership in more than one step.
5. The requirements to secure the deal.
6. Various combinations of the above elements.

7.11.1 Financing with equity

It would be hardly conceivable for one owner-manager to take over from another without putting up any equity at all. The successor has to bring a minimum amount of equity to secure the deal and signal to all other capital providers (e.g., banks) that he/she is willing to make a significant personal investment in the target firm. For such owner-manager successors, we differentiate between three sources of equity:

1. **Equity provided by the successor**: The successor invests his/her own money in the target firm. This money may come from personal savings or from the successor's family or friends.
2. **Equity provided by the incumbent**: The incumbent sells less than 100% of the shares in order to facilitate succession. That is, the incumbent may retain some shares so that the successor does not have to finance the whole transfer all at once. As a result, the incumbent retains some control, but also has an ongoing responsibility in the firm. Such a stepwise sale raises a question about the price at which the remaining shares will be acquired by the successor at a later point in time.
3. **Equity provided by a third party**: A third-party investor acquires equity alongside the successor. For instance, a private equity fund acquires an ownership stake in a firm alongside the successor.

In small to mid-sized firm successions, equity providers (such as the successor, eventually in combination with a third-party equity investor) often contribute between 10% and 50% of the purchase price in the form of equity.

7.11.2 Financing with vendor loan

A vendor loan, also called vendor finance, is designed to allow the purchase price to be paid over time. The vendor finances the whole (as is sometimes observed in intra-family transfers of small firms) or part of the purchase price by agreeing to accept payment by installments from the successor. The idea is to structure the loan so that the repayment period is short enough from the vendor's point of view and long enough from the successor's (i.e., the successor can repay the loan from the firm's cash flow).

To further support the successor, the incumbent may agree to subordinate the vendor loan to a bank loan that may be further required to finance the transaction. In case of a default, the bank loan is senior to the vendor loan. In this case, the bank often considers the vendor loan to be equity, and may increase the amount of the senior loan and/or lend it with more favorable conditions. If the vendor loan is subordinate to some other loan, the interest rate on the vendor loan will also rise.

7.11.3 Financing with bank loan

Bank debt is a lower cost-of-capital (lower interest rates) security than subordinated debt and equity. However, it often comes with more onerous conditions. Bank debt requires full amortization, and hence payback typically over a five- to seven-year period. The size of the bank loan is most often determined by the firm's debt capacity, which is defined as follows:

$$\text{Debt capacity} = \text{SUM}_{1 \to t} \left(\text{FCF} / (1 + \text{C of D})^t \right)$$

FCF = free cash flow of the firm, assumed to remain stable across the repayment period; C of D = cost of bank loan; t = repayment period of loan.

Debt capacity thus represents the debt ceiling or, put differently, the amount of debt that a company can repay in a reasonable amount of time (most often five to seven years). This calculation uses current resources (in particular, FCF) and assumes income neither increases nor decreases. The bank will conservatively estimate the firm's FCF over the expected repayment period of the loan and discount future FCF to obtain current value, which in turn informs debt capacity. Debt capacity can be extended if pledgeable assets such as real estate are available to secure the bank loan.

One rule of thumb is that the debt ceiling should be two to three times the EBITDA of the firm to be acquired. The interest rate charged on bank debt (cost of debt) is often a floating rate equal to the London Interbank Offered Rate (LIBOR) plus some premium, depending on the credit characteristics of the borrower. Depending on the credit terms, bank debt may or may not be repaid early without penalty.

Banks often put strict conditions (covenants) on their credit line. In private firm successions, such conditions come in various forms, such as:

- Restrictions on making further acquisitions.
- Restrictions on raising additional debt.
- Restrictions on dividend distributions.
- Maintenance condition: quarterly performance report to the bank.
- Performance condition: minimum EBITDA level (e.g., total debt outstanding = max 2 * EBITDA), maximum leverage.
- Pledging of assets by the borrower, such as shares of a company, life insurance or personal assets.

It goes without saying that these conditions are not in the interest of the successor, who will try to avoid them. In a reasonably valued company, bank loans will make up around 50% of the transaction price.

7.11.4 Financing with subordinated debt and mezzanine capital

Subordinated debt, or mezzanine debt, is a type of debt that has both debt and equity characteristics and sits between senior debt and equity in the firm's balance sheet. Since the risk exposure of mezzanine debt is greater than for senior debt, it carries a higher interest rate and some form of equity 'kicker' to obtain risk-adjusted returns. This equity kicker may come in the form of an adjustable interest rate, which rises when performance improves, or an option to convert the loan into equity at a later point in time. Mezzanine debt combines features of debt financing, such as the regular payment of interest, with features typical of equity financing, such as the opportunity to benefit when the firm performs well.

Given the risk incurred by mezzanine debt lenders, the successor should expect a comprehensive list of conditions to protect the lender. Typical conditions would likely include the ones mentioned for bank loans (see above), but could additionally cover restrictions on joint ventures, changes to employee compensation plans, changes in officers, investments above a certain threshold level and overall changes to important business agreements.

Mezzanine financing can be an attractive option for financing succession in firms with fairly stable cash flows that are able to finance the cash drain incurred by interest payments. It can help bridge the gap between the purchase price on the one hand and equity and bank loans on the other.

Convertible loans are one form of mezzanine capital often observed in succession financing. These loans are issued by the incumbent and provide the incumbent with the right to convert the loan into equity if the successor is unable to satisfy contractual agreements, such as regular payments on a vendor loan. Converting the loan into equity allows the incumbent to regain ownership and hence control over the company. We will look more closely at this tool in the next chapter, which focuses on combinations of various financing options.

Summing up, Table 7.13 shows the key tools used to finance succession from one owner-manager to another in private family firms.

Total debt is typically in the range of 3.0 × to 6.0 × LTM[10] EBITDA, with an interest coverage ratio of at least 2.0 × LTM EBITDA/first-year interest. However, total debt varies by sector, market conditions and other factors.

Table 7.13 Financing options and their key terms in family firm succession[11]

Source of funds	Key terms	Comments
Common equity	• Typically 20–50% of purchasing price • 20–30% internal rate of return (IRR) on an approximately 5-year holding period	
Bank debt	• Typically 30–50% of purchasing price • Based on asset value (e.g., mortgage on real estate) as well as free cash flow (debt capacity) • Often LIBOR-based interest rate (i.e., floating rate) • 5–7-year maturity, with annual amortization and interest payments • 2.0 × to 3.0 × EBITDA (varies with industry, ratings and economic conditions) • Sometimes secured by pledge of stock and assets • Maintenance and incurrence conditions	• Bank debt will also include short-term revolving credit facility to fund working capital needs • Generally, no minimum size requirement
High-yield and subordinated debt (i.e., vendor loan)	• Typically 20–30% of purchasing price, if needed at all • Generally unsecured • Fixed coupon • Often subordinated • Longer maturity than bank debt (7–10 years) • Amortization with various options: none, but bullet payment at maturity; once bank debt is repaid; progressive • Incurrence conditions • IRR: 14–19%	• Most often for mid-sized and larger transactions
Mezzanine debt	• Can be preferred equity (i.e., equity with preferred dividend, liquidation rights, anti-dilution rights) or convertible bond • IRRs in the high teens to low twenties on 3–5-year holding period	• Occasionally used in place of high-yield debt • Generally, a combination of cash payment and PIK*

Note: * Payment in Kind (PIK) = periodic form of payment in which the interest payment is not paid in cash, but rather by increasing the principal amount by the amount of the interest (e.g., a $100 million bond with an 8% PIK interest rate will have a balance of $108 million at the end of the period but will not pay any cash interest).

7.11.5 Combining multiple financing options

In reality, financing a succession in a family firm most often combines a series of financing instruments. The central question in these cases is the following: what financing option(s) will allow us to match the gap between purchase price and the successors' equity, assuming that the firm is not given to the successor outright and that the successor's equity is insufficient to cover the complete purchase price?

In Figure 7.15, we assume that a firm should be passed on at a price of 100. The successor can only provide 20% of the price using his/her own equity. How can the financing gap be bridged?

To bridge the financing gap of 80 and to match the purchase price of 100, the transaction partners have several options. We have touched upon some of these, including bank loans, vendor loans, convertible loans and private equity.

To avoid the involvement of outsiders, especially in small firms and in particular in intra-family successions, successor and incumbent may simply renegotiate the purchase price so that it can be matched by the successor's equity plus a vendor loan (by parents as sellers).

Alternatively, successor and incumbent may determine an earn-out model that assumes the purchase price will vary with the profitability or growth of the firm over some predefined period of time (e.g., two to three years). The two parties may also agree that the ownership transfer will take place in several steps, with the successor acquiring 100% of ownership in a sequential manner.

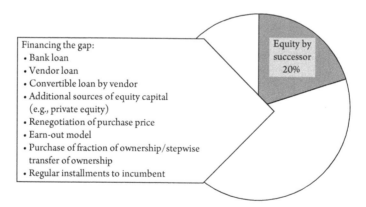

Financing the gap:
- Bank loan
- Vendor loan
- Convertible loan by vendor
- Additional sources of equity capital (e.g., private equity)
- Renegotiation of purchase price
- Earn-out model
- Purchase of fraction of ownership/stepwise transfer of ownership
- Regular installments to incumbent

Equity by successor 20%

Note: Assumed purchase price of 100.

Figure 7.15 Options to bridge the financing gap in family firm successions

A very simple option for small firm successions is to define yearly installments to be paid by the successor to the incumbent. These payments are financed with the cash flows of the firm. In effect, this form of financing is like a vendor loan with no coupon.

As a rule of thumb, we find that the higher the level of trust and mutual benevolence between successor and incumbent, the higher the incumbent's willingness to support the transfer of the firm at conditions favorable to the successor. Examples of such favorable conditions are below-maximum sale prices in intra-family transfers (gifts), the issuance of vendor loans, favorable earn-out clauses and the sequential sale of the firm.

In practice, small to mid-sized firms often opt for fairly simple financing structures. We discuss some of these financing combinations below.

Successor equity and vendor loan

The prototypical case is one where the owner wants to transfer the firm to a family member or to a loyal employee and grants a vendor loan to help finance the succession. Issuing a vendor loan spares the successor from the need to raise a bank loan. This solution is particularly suited for intra-family successions, where the firm and hence the purchase price is limited, the incumbent trusts the successor, the incumbent remains involved in the firm after the transfer, and the incumbent does not have immediate pension needs that would have to be financed by a large bullet payment at the moment the deal is closed.

The incumbent will thus only receive 20% of the purchase price at the moment of contract signature. He will have to wait for the remaining 80% to be paid through annual installments over the duration of the vendor loan.

Successor equity, bank loan and vendor loan

For larger firms, and for those where the incumbent is more interested in cashing out, the successor will have to secure a bank loan to finance the purchase price. As discussed above, banks may be willing to lend up to 50% of a reasonable purchase price. The remainder may then have to be secured via a vendor loan, which may be subordinated to the bank loan (see Figure 7.16). In this case, upon signature of the contract, the incumbent receives 70 (20 equity from successor + 50 bank loan). The remaining 30 is financed through the vendor loan. Typically, the successor will have to repay the bank loan within five to seven years via the firm's free cash flows. The vendor loan is repaid either in parallel to the bank loan or in a deferred manner.

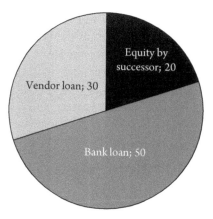

Figure 7.16 Succession financing with successor equity, bank loan and vendor loan

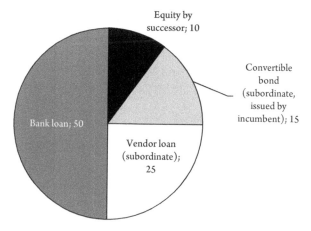

Figure 7.17 Succession financing with equity, bank, vendor and convertible loans

Successor equity, bank loan, vendor loan and convertible loan

The incumbent may wish to structure the transfer so that he/she can regain control if the new owner breaches some predetermined conditions. In the example displayed in Figure 7.17, the convertible loan is the 'emergency brake' that allows the incumbent to regain majority ownership in such a case. Once the breach of some condition causes the convertible loan to be exercised, the incumbent converts the loan into equity and thereby regains majority ownership of $15/(15+10)$ (= 60% ownership for the incumbent, 40% for the successor, after conversion). In addition to the convertible loan, a bank loan of 50 and a vendor loan of 25 are needed to match the purchase price of 100.

The monetary stream is comparable to the previous case: the successor will have to repay the bank loan within the typical maturity range of the bank loan using the free cash flows of the firm. The vendor and convertible loans are repaid in a deferred manner, with the convertible loan coming last.

CASE STUDY

Financing the MBO at Wood Corp

Andy Yu took over Wood Corp from its previous owner about 15 years ago. With about 50 employees in the wood construction business, the company was an important local player with a strong market position. The local demand for wood constructions was fairly strong, giving the firm a good economic outlook for the next few years. It was a good time to pass on the firm.

For Andy, the preferred succession method would be to transfer the firm to his employees. Two of his leading employees knew the firm well and wanted to carry it on. There was no doubt that they had the abilities to take the firm to the next level. In addition, the two had found the capital to finance the purchase of the firm at about $8 million. The combination of finance options they had secured was as follows:

Equity by the two managers:	$1 million
Bank loan:	$4.5 million
Vendor loan by Andy Yu:	$2.5 million

The vendor loan had made a big difference in convincing the bank to support the deal. By providing a vendor loan, and by making it subordinate to the bank loan, Andy signaled to the bank that he was willing to support the deal and believed in the abilities of his successors. Given the subordination of the vendor loan to the bank loan, the bank considered Andy's loan as equity. The bank's risk was thus only 56% of the transaction volume (= 4.5/8). The liquidity flows and the schedule for the amortization and interest payments on the credits were as follows (Table 7.14).

Upon signature of the purchase agreement (T0), the vendor thus receives the equity injections by the two managers and the bank credit, in total $5.5 million. The remaining $2.5 million in the form of the vendor loan is paid back over five years and at a 5% interest rate, once the bank loan is paid back. From year T1 on, however, the vendor receives interest on the vendor loan.

The two managers hope to finance the bank loan via the cash flows of the firm. The bank asks for a five-year repayment period and an interest rate of 7%. Thus, the yearly payments Wood Corp has to make to the bank will be $1.215 million, $1.152 million, $1.089 million, $1.026 million and $963 000 in the years T1 to T5 respectively.

In year T6, the two managers then start to repay the vendor loan. The annual payments

Table 7.14 Liquidity flows and the schedule for the amortization and interest payments

In thousand USD, Year	T0	T1	T2	T3	T4	T5	T6	T7	T8	T9	T10
Payments to seller:											
Equity injection manager 1	500										
Equity injection manager 2	500										
Bank Credit	4500										
Amortization of vendor loan (over 5 years)		–	–	–	–	–	500	500	500	500	500
Outstanding credit amount beginning of period		2500	2500	2500	2500	2500	2500	2000	1500	1000	500
Interest of 5% on outstanding amount		125	125	125	125	125	125	100	75	50	25
Payments to bank:											
Amortization of credit (over 5 years)		900	900	900	900	900					
Outstanding credit amount beginning of period		4500	3600	2700	1800	900					
Interest of 7% on outstanding amount		315	252	189	126	63					
Overview all cash flows											
Source: Equity injections and bank; paid to vendor	5500										
Source: Free Cash Flow of Firm; paid to bank		1215	1152	1089	1026	963					
Source: Free Cash Flow of Firm; paid to vendor		125	125	125	125	125	625	600	575	550	525
Total cash out from firm		1340	1277	1214	1151	1088	625	600	575	550	525

CASE STUDY *(continued)*

(credit amortization and interest rate) will be $625 000, $600 000, $575 000, $550 000 and $525 000 in the years T6 to T10 respectively.

For the two managers, it was critical to assess whether they could finance these annual payments in the years T1 to T10, when the financing of the succession would finally be concluded. The question thus was whether the firm earned at least 1.34 million in free cash flow after tax (the maximum total cash flow needed to serve all the credits across the ten-year repayment period) to support this financing plan.

? REFLECTION QUESTIONS

Reflection questions for the incumbent

1. Am I looking for a fast exit, without any further involvement in the firm?
2. Am I willing to help finance the succession, for example via a vendor loan, stepwise sale, earn-out or convertible bond?
3. If so, how should I secure my ongoing risk exposure?
4. What are the critical deal-breakers?
5. What advisors do I need to understand the financial implications of the succession?

Reflection questions for the successor

1. How much equity do I have available?
2. What financing options do I have?
3. How could I structure/combine various financing options so that they match the purchase price?
4. What are the pros and cons of involving other equity investors?
5. In the presence of multiple equity investors, what are the critical terms of a shareholder agreement?
6. What is the sustainable free cash flow of the firm, that is, the amount that I could use to repay debt?
7. For how long do I have to repay debt before I am debt-free?
8. Are the free cash flows of the firm sustainable, even in an economic downturn, to support all financing obligations?
9. What advisors do I need to understand the financial implications of the succession?

Reflection questions for students

1. Assuming that the successor is unable to fully finance the succession with his/her own equity and a bank loan, how could the financing gap be closed?
2. How can the incumbent facilitate the financing of the transfer?
3. What typical financing options are available in private firm successions?
4. How do banks assess the debt capacity of a firm?
5. Describe the typical conditions that banks impose to secure their credit.

6. Explain the various combinations of financing options in private firm successions, and the characteristics, advantages and challenges of each.

7.12 Defining the legal and tax setup

Legal and tax aspects play a prominent role in family firm successions. In addressing this topic, however, we face the challenge that the legal and tax codes relevant for family business succession vary greatly among countries, sometimes even within a country. Moreover, the legal and tax codes often treat the various succession options differently. Despite these challenges, the topic is so important that leaving legal and tax aspects unaddressed would be a gross omission. One way to simplify things is to link the most important succession options to their typical legal structure (Table 7.15).

In what follows, we will explore four very prominent exit routes, namely transfers to family members, employees, co-owners and financial/strategic buyers, and explore the related legal and tax implications of each option. Given our focus on family business succession, we will give particular attention to the intra-family transfer of shares/wealth and related estate planning vehicles such as gifting, inheritance and trusts.

Because of the considerable international variance in the availability and particularities of various exit methods, a caveat is in order. The following discussion is not a definitive guideline, but rather a high-level overview of the typical legal and tax implications of certain succession options. Ultimately, the legal setup will depend upon local circumstances.

Table 7.15 Succession option and typical legal structure

Succession option: transfer of firm to	Legal structure
Family	Gift, inheritance, trust, sale
Key employee group	Employee stock ownership plan (ESOP), management buyout (MBO), leveraged buyout (LBO)
Co-owners	Buy–sell agreements
Financial or strategic buyer	Negotiated sale, auction, unsolicited offer
Public market	Initial public offering (IPO)
Liquidation	Partial liquidation, fire sale

Source: Adapted from Niemann (2009).

Transfer to family members

An incumbent who wishes to transfer the firm to family members can typically choose one of the following three exit methods: gift, trust (mainly in common law countries, such as the United Kingdom or the United States) or sale to family members.

7.12.1.1 *Giving shares to family members*

Traditionally, family wealth is simply inherited from one generation to the next. In the family business context, this means that shares are passed from one owning generation to the next as a gift, without material compensation. In part, this default case is evidence of parental altruism toward children.

From a legal and tax perspective, however, transferring shares as a gift—and more broadly, the transgenerational handover of assets—can trigger significant taxes. These taxes come in two main forms: estate/inheritance tax and gift tax.

Estate/inheritance tax

Estate/inheritance taxes are levied on the transfer of the estate of a deceased person. They apply to property that is transferred via a will or laws of intestacy. Many countries have exemption amounts that waive taxes if the estate is valued below a certain threshold. Taxes are due only for the amount above that threshold. In the United States, for instance, the federal exemption amount in the year 2009 was $3.5 million, and the federal estate tax top rate was a hefty 45%. Some laws allow further exemptions to this general rule. For instance, US tax law waives all taxes if the entire estate is left to a spouse. In addition, parts of an estate that go to charities may be exempt from estate taxes. Note also that the way the estate is treated under tax laws may depend upon the legal form of the firm—whether the business is a sole ownership, partnership, corporation, limited partnership and so on. For further details on estate (and also gift) tax in selected European countries, refer to the KPMG family business tax monitor (2014). This report features a wide variety of tax regimes across Europe and shows that, in many countries, estate/gift taxes depend on the proximity of the relationship between the deceased/donor and the beneficiary/inheritor. As a rule of thumb, the closer the familial ties, the lower taxes tend to be.

Gift tax

The premise of the gift tax is to levy taxes on portions of an estate that are given while the owner is still alive. It prevents owners from avoiding the estate tax by parceling out its value before death. The gift tax is thus linked to the estate tax, and countries that have abolished estate taxes have typically abolished gift taxes as well. As with the estate tax, there are exemption amounts on gift taxes that allow a certain threshold of tax-free gifts per year and per person. Also, some gifts, for instance to charities, political parties and spouses, may be excluded from taxation.

Note that tax authorities pay careful attention to the valuation of a gift. For instance, according to US tax law, stock in a privately held family business will be valued by fair market valuation. Tax authorities will accept discounts on this baseline valuation for minority interests or lack of marketability only. Any difference beyond these two discounts should incur the gift tax. This is why one may also make a gift if one makes a reduced interest rate loan.[12]

Excursus: Some background information on estate/ inheritance tax

Around the globe, some of the most vocal conflicts over taxation center on estate/inheritance tax, despite the fact that inheritance taxes have rarely ever contributed more than 2% to the budget of any modern state. The profoundly contentious character of this tax is rooted in the way it relates to the normative fabric of societies. In his influential study on inherited wealth, Beckert (2008) suggests four different principles that either legitimize or contest the intergenerational transfer of wealth and the imposition of an inheritance tax.

The *family principle* states that the property of the testator is not really individual property, but property of the family that outlives the testator. It follows, then, that descendants have the right to have property transferred to them. The family principle delegitimizes inheritance taxes. It is very prominent, for instance, in Germany.

The *equality of opportunity principle* states that inequality in society is only justified by differential achievements. This principle calls for the redistribution of inheritances, if need be through taxation. Taxing inheritance leads to more equal material starting positions, which is the precondition for meritocracy. This principle is very prominent, for instance, in the United States.

The *social justice principle* seeks to correct the unequal success of market participants. This principle is particularly prominent in France, with the social norm of 'égalité', an outflow of the French revolution. It attempts to curb the power of the nobility and the landed class, and more broadly the rich. Here, inheritance taxes are justified on the basis that heirs have the financial means to pay.

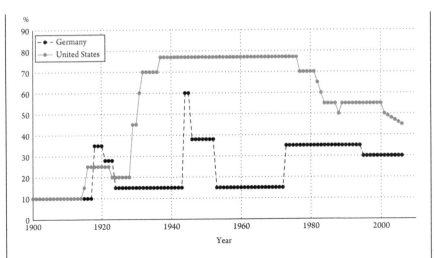

Data source: Piketty (2014); Internal Revenue Services; Beckert (2008); figures for Germany calculated based on inheritance tax for close relatives.

Figure 7.18 Inheritance tax in % in the United States and Germany in the twentieth century

The *community principle*, finally, states that testators are obliged to dedicate their wealth to the promotion of the common good by establishing charitable foundations or trusts. This principle is prominent in the United States, where inheritance taxes serve as a fallback option to create incentives for the establishment of charitable entities (Beckert 2008). To further encourage this type of giving, philanthropic institutions benefit from inheritance tax exemptions.

The use of these principles in the public discourse varies across countries and has a strong impact on tax systems. For example, while the family and the social justice principles are common in Germany, the equality of opportunity and community principles are more strongly anchored in North American society.[13] These differing justifications for or against inheritance taxes help us understand the important international differences in inheritance tax law, as for instance between Germany and the United States (Figure 7.18).

Some further international comparisons of inheritance taxes are available. In a study we conducted with Ernst & Young's (EY's) global family business center of excellence (Figure 7.19) we found the following maximum levels of inheritance taxes upon family business succession.[14]

While taxes are absent or nil in many countries around the globe, some countries stand out with rather high inheritance taxes. However, this tax landscape changes dramatically when we introduce country-by-country tax exemptions and reliefs. In fact, the tax burden virtually disappears or is significantly reduced in many countries besides, for instance, France, Taiwan, Iceland and Argentina.

Advocates of inheritance taxes base their arguments on the principle of the equality of opportunity, the upholding of an entrepreneurial spirit and economic

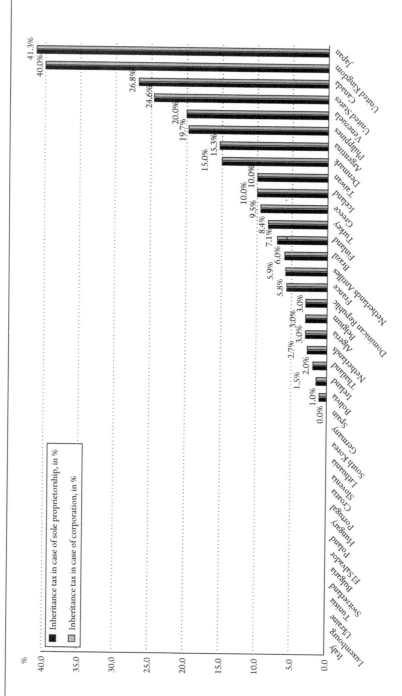

Figure 7.19 Tax due upon inheritance of family firm, without exemptions

ambition, concerns over the undemocratic consequences of the concentration of wealth, and the social desirability of progressive taxation (Piketty 2014).

Opponents of inheritance taxes suggest that they reduce the stock of capital available for investment, which impedes economic incentives for investment and development (Tsoutsoura 2009). Estate/inheritance taxes may also reduce the incentives for saving and increase incentives for consumption, spendthrift behavior and the depletion of property near the end of life.

CASE STUDY

A gift with unexpected consequences

The third-generation family members of the Gallo family were all excited when they heard that they would inherit some shares of the family business. They were grateful to their grandfather for this generous gift. At their age, they had never owned anything more valuable, at least not in financial terms. But it was only at the end of the year that they realized this was a gift with some strings attached. When they compiled their tax files, they also had to list the shares in the family business. Given the heavy estate taxes in their country, the stock gift led to a high tax bill. As the third-generation family members were all still studying and had no regular income, the well-intentioned gift thus had an unexpected downside.

Testamentary freedom

Testamentary freedom is a further legal aspect to consider in the context of transfers of family wealth. Testamentary freedom refers to the extent to which individuals are free to dispose of their wealth upon death—for instance, whether they can allocate all wealth to a single heir. Restrictions on testamentary freedom usually take the form of compulsory shared or equal inheritance among children and spouses, consistent with norms of social justice (Carney, Gedajlovic and Strike 2014). Inheritance law may force the incumbent owner to give a minimal stake in the estate to non-controlling heirs rather than giving it all to one controlling owner/successor. The social tension with regard to testamentary freedom is between the testator's individual rights on the one hand and the claims of spouses and relatives on the deceased's property on the other (Carney, Gedajlovic and Strike 2014). Generally speaking, testamentary freedom is greater in countries with English common law origins than in countries with civil law (most of continental Europe) and Sharia law origins (Table 7.16).

Table 7.16 Testamentary freedom around the world

Australia	1	Taiwan	0.667
Canada	1	Venezuela	0.667
Hong Kong	1	Estonia	0.667
India	1	Latvia	0.667
Israel	1	Monaco	0.667
Mexico	1	France	0.66
New Zealand	1	Luxembourg	0.66
South Africa	1	South Korea	0.643
Thailand	1	Chile	0.625
UK	1	Japan	0.625
USA	1	Malta	0.583
Bulgaria	1	Romania	0.583
Cayman Islands	1	Argentina	0.556
Costa Rica	1	Iceland	0.556
El Salvador	1	Peru	0.556
Guatemala	1	Portugal	0.542
Jamaica	1	Italy	0.5
Kenya	1	Spain	0.5
Sri Lanka	1	Switzerland	0.5
Finland	0.75	Uruguay	0.5
Sweden	0.75	Bolivia	0.5
Hungary	0.75	Cyprus	0.5
Lebanon	0.7	Liechtenstein	0.5
Greece	0.688	Slovak Republic	0.5
Lithuania	0.688	Norway	0.417
Croatia	0.68	Colombia	0.375
Austria	0.667	Belgium	0.333
Brazil	0.667	Philippines	0.333
Denmark	0.667	Bangladesh	0.333
Germany	0.667	Jordan	0.333
Ireland	0.667	Kuwait	0.333
Netherlands	0.667	Saudi Arabia	0.333

Note: Figures indicate the largest share of the estate that a testator can bequeath to a single child in the presence of a surviving spouse and two children in total. Results are largely comparable in the presence of other numbers of children or in the absence of a spouse. For further details, see Ellul, Pagano and Panunzi (2010).

7.12.1.2 Trusts

Trusts (in many common law countries), and to some degree foundations (in many civil law countries), are common tools to legally structure the transfer of family firms, and more broadly speaking family wealth, from one generation to the next. The reasons for and benefits of installing a trust[15] are multiple:

1. Personal and familial legacy-building.
2. Limiting wealth-related conflict inside the family.
3. Protecting wealth from family (e.g., from children who may be incapable of managing the family firm).
4. Protecting family from wealth (e.g., to discourage a spendthrift lifestyle in children).
5. Limiting the tax burden tied to estate/inheritance/gift taxes.
6. Protection of wealth from outside parties (e.g., lawsuits, creditors).

As outlined in our reflections on the governance challenges of trusts in Chapter 5 on governance, however, trusts have several important disadvantages as well:

1. **Disloyalty of the trustee**: The trustee is appointed as the custodian of all the wealth that is placed in the trust. Trustees, however, are hard to monitor because trusts have no owners and because monitoring of the trustees by legal authorities tends to be limited. To some degree, trustees are managers without owners. Children, who are most often the beneficiaries of the trust, have very limited control over the trust and the dealings of the trustee (Sitkoff 2004). Trustees could be tempted to progressively abuse their power over the trust corpus and start to behave as the 'owners' of the wealth, in particular once the settlor is incapacitated or dead (see Chapter 5 on governance for details of these double-agency costs).
2. **Risk aversion**: Trusts are meant to secure the status quo, and thus do not allow for the risk taking that is required to manage an entrepreneurial venture. In fact, trustees are tasked with diversifying risks, which stands in conflict to the concentrated investment required by a family firm. Trusts limit the beneficiary's willingness and ability to take risks, and tend to encourage a conservative use of wealth (Zellweger and Kammerlander 2015). As a result of the conservative allocation of capital, wealth in trusts gradually depletes over time and is unable to keep up with the financial aspirations or growth of the family.
3. **Rigid instructions by settlor**: The trustees are accountable for the execution of the ex ante instructions of the settlor who established the trust. While these ex ante instructions are often well intended, such as, for instance, securing jobs in a certain industry, the instructions may become outdated. The trustees, however, are largely bound by the trust deed and the instructions stated therein, whether or not they are functional under the current circumstances.
4. **Incapacitation of descendants**: Trusts deprive descendants of the decision about what happens to family wealth. To some degree, then, trusts are a sign of the settlor's doubt about the abilities of the next generation.

Paradoxically, setting up a trust can fuel family conflicts rather than solve them.

Trusts can be double-edged swords: they solve some problems, but they create new ones. Families who struggle with the challenges that trusts are meant to solve often underestimate the disadvantages of trusts. As Hartley and Griffith (2009) write: 'Families struggling with these issues often choose trusts as an easy way to continue a pattern of behavior rather than doing the hard work of moving toward a more functional pattern.'

In the pursuit of transgenerational wealth creation, trusts play a controversial role. The limited evidence that we have from families who have been wealth creators for generations shows that they use trusts sparingly. Instead, the family itself remains at the wheel, and each generation (re)defines family, corporate, ownership and wealth governance for its specific needs. This approach may be more time consuming, but it allows the family to avoid the pitfalls tied to trusts.

Types of trusts

There is significant variance in the availability of trusts as legal instruments for the transfer of wealth within families. For instance, in some European countries, such as Switzerland, family trusts that serve to preserve wealth within a family are forbidden out of fear of an excessive concentration of wealth in the hands of an aristocratic elite and the return of feudal social structures. In contrast, in Austria, 30% of the 100 largest family firms are held via foundations (the trust-like equivalent in civil law countries). In the United Kingdom, and in particular in the United States, family trusts are some of the most prominent vehicles for structuring the transfer of wealth within families. Below, we will look at three types of trusts that are regularly used in the United States for estate planning, that is to say to transfer family wealth from one generation to the next.

Grantor retained annuity trust

Grantor retained annuity trusts (GRATs) allow exiting owners to remove a block of shares from their estates by transferring them to a trust. Exiting owners receive an income stream from the GRAT for a set number of years. After that period has passed, the remaining assets in the trust transfer to the beneficiaries of the trust, usually the children of the exiting owner. GRATs allow assets to be removed from the estate and placed in the hands of intended beneficiaries in a very tax-efficient manner (Leonetti 2008).

Charitable remainder trust

Upon exiting the business, some incumbent owners seek to support a particular charity with their wealth. In this case, the incumbent owner transfers some shares of his/her stock to a charitable remainder trust (CRT). Although tax incentives are not the main consideration here, a CRT results in a significant tax benefit for the value of the shares that are placed in it. The incumbent owner can receive an income stream from the CRT for 20 years. In addition, he or she may even sell the stock that is placed in the CRT at a later point in time. In fact, the incumbent will save on capital gains tax when these shares are sold.

Intentionally defective grantor trust

Intentionally defective grantor trusts (IDGTs) allow a grantor to place shares in a trust with a purposeful flaw that ensures that the grantor continues to pay income taxes for the wealth in the trust. Because the grantor pays the income taxes incurred by the IDGT, the assets held in the IDGT can grow unreduced by income taxes. This, in turn, increases the value of the assets available for the trust's beneficiaries (e.g., children and grandchildren). For estate tax purposes, however, the value of the grantor's estate is reduced by the amount of the asset transfer. The individual will 'sell' assets to the trust in exchange for a note of some length, such as 10 or 15 years. In a typical sale to an IDGT, the grantor sells an asset with potential for appreciation at its fair market value to the trust in exchange for a note at a very low interest rate. As with any estate freeze technique, assets that are either depressed in value and/or are expected to appreciate substantially should be selected. The goal is to remove future asset appreciation above the mandated interest rate from the grantor's estate. The IDGT can be a very effective estate planning tool that lowers the taxable estate while allowing the grantor to give assets to beneficiaries at a locked-in value (Niemann 2009).

US trust law, and even more so international trust law, allows for additional types of trusts that family business owners can use for estate planning (for more details, see the wide literature on this topic). Regardless of the specific vehicle, trusts used for estate planning should be structured with the assistance of a certified financial planner or an estate attorney.

7.12.1.3 Selling shares to family members

In some cases, the lifecycle of the business or the family requires a sale. For example, an exiting owner may depend on the income of a sale for retirement. Alternatively, parents sometimes use this approach to guarantee equal treatment of children when not all of them have an interest in continuing the business. The attempt to compensate non-successors has its motivation in parents' wish to ensure that each child gets the same proportion of the parents' wealth. Since the parents' wealth is usually concentrated in one asset, the firm, when a family has multiple children, passing the firm to a single child as a gift would prevent parents from treating all their children equally.

In addition, from a more psychological perspective, selling may allow the incumbent a graceful exit. For the successor, purchasing the business outright clarifies 'who is in charge' (Hartley and Griffith 2009). The intra-family sale most often takes the form of a sale of equity interests, and thereby the transfer of all business risks, in contrast to the asset sale structure most commonly used in sales to outsiders. In an intra-family sale, a portion of the purchase price may be allocated to an ongoing consulting or employment arrangement for the previous owner. Next to the taxes mentioned above, the sale of the firm within the family may make the sellers (parents) responsible for income tax. Depending on the legal form of the firm, capital gains taxes may also apply.

In the United States, there is a legal vehicle—the self-canceling installment note (SCIN)—through which the senior generation can save taxes when selling the family within the family. The SCIN is a debt obligation which, in the event of the death of the seller/creditor, will be extinguished with the remaining note balance automatically canceled. While the noteholder (typically the parents) is alive, the SCIN is treated the same way as any other installment note and parents receive income from the sale of the business via the SCIN. This vehicle has various tax benefits: it freezes the estate tax value of the property being sold. It also removes a portion of that value from the seller's estate in the event whereby a seller dies before the note is paid in full. In other words, if the seller dies while an installment note is outstanding, future appreciation on property will escape being taxed. The seller possesses only the right to receive payments for the rest of his or her life. Since ownership ends at death, nothing remains to include in the estate. This adds a substantial benefit in the use of an intra-family installment sale (for more details refer to the related estate planning literature).

> ## Excursus: Share deal versus asset deal
>
> In a share deal, the buyer purchases the shares of the company from the previous owner. With the purchase, the buyer becomes the owner of the legal entity, and thus purchases not only the firm's assets, but also all existing and potential liabilities, obligations and debts.
>
> In an asset deal, the buyer is solely interested in certain assets the previous owner held. In this case, the buyer and seller could agree that the buyer will take over these assets and eventually some precisely defined liabilities, contracts, employees, etc. The buyer does not purchase the entire legal entity and thereby limits the risks of the acquisition.

Setting the price for intra-family sales

Under a pure market regime, assets are transferred from one owner to the next at their market value. The market value reflects today's value of future FCF (see the section on valuation—section 7.10—in this chapter for more details). But within the family, the laws of the market are partly suspended and often superseded by familial norms of exchange. Family sociologists suggest that there are four central family norms that impact the characteristics of intergenerational transfers (Bengtson 1993; Zellweger et al. forthcoming):

1. **Parental altruism** induces parents to care for their children. This suggests that parents should be generous to their children.
2. **Generativity** elicits parents' desires for legacy creation. According to this norm, parents should have a strong desire for their children to take over, as this keeps firm control in the family. This suggests that parents should be generous to their children.
3. **Filial reciprocity** is the familial expectation that the child reciprocates parental support. From this point of view, children must reciprocate favors they have received from parents in the past. Thus, children cannot expect to get the firm for free without reciprocating the gift in some manner.
4. **Filial duty** constitutes the child's responsibility to support aging parents. Under the norm of filial duty, parents who are in financial need upon retirement have a legitimate claim for material support from their children.

These social norms are partly reflected in familial conversations about the price that is 'sustainable for the successor and the firm' or about 'what the owners need for retirement'. Given the prominent norms of parental altruism and generativity, even if a third-party valuation is available, parents tend to prefer that their children enjoy the lower end of that range. For further details, see our reflections on family discounts in section 7.7.3.

To reiterate: under some legal regimes, intra-family price determination cannot be decoupled from economic realities, even when the family wishes to do so. This is because the firm transfer may be subject to estate or gift taxes. According to US law, for instance, the tax authorities may levy estate or gift taxes if assets are transferred to the next owner without adequate compensation. As mentioned above, US tax authorities will undertake their own assessment of the 'fair' value of the firm and will accept value discounts only for minority stakes and for the non-marketability of shares. Further discounts would be subject to taxes.

7.12.2 Transfer to co-owners

One way for business owners to exit the firm is to pass it on to other current owners. These co-owners can stem from the same family or from outside. Whether or not they are family, co-owners are often the first party the incumbent will approach, because they often have a right of first refusal as determined in a shareholder agreement. Selling to co-owners effectively simplifies the shareholding structure of a company. In the simplest case, one of two co-owners offers his/her stake to the other owner.

The consolidation of shareholdings (i.e., the sale of shares among co-owners) is particularly important to consider in the family business context. As a business passes to succeeding generations, the number of family shareholders naturally expands. The fragmentation of ownership that ensues leads to three central problems:

1. **Incentive**: When the share of ownership is small, the incentive for a particular shareholder to increase the value of his/her ownership stake is limited. Think of a family CEO who only owns 5% of the firm compared to a family CEO who owns 80%. In the latter case, the CEO has a much higher incentive (and ability in the form of power) to ensure the prosperity of the firm.
2. **Governance**: A large number of family shareholders makes governance—for example, coordination and decision making among shareholders—more difficult. A large number of family shareholders may require the family to install a family council and other expensive governance mechanisms.

3. **Identification**: It is challenging to keep a large number of family share-holders identified with and committed to the firm. However, these qualities are important if the family is to act as a controlling group of shareholders with a joint vision.

The transfer of shares to family co-owners and hence the consolidation of family shareholdings can be an efficient way to address the problems listed above. This process of consolidation is sometimes called 'pruning the family tree'.

Buy–sell agreements

One way for families to avoid the fragmentation of ownership is to predefine an orderly exchange of stock in the corporation for cash. To prevent the stock from ending up in unwelcome hands, a buy–sell agreement often includes provisions that the stock will be first tendered to family members from the nuclear family, then to the extended family, or alternatively to the company. Also, buy–sell agreements can be thought of as pressure-relief valves.

As outlined by Poza and Daugherty (2014), the obvious advantage of a buy–sell agreement is that it allows some family members to remain shareholders while providing liquidity to family members with other interests. The ability to sell, whether exercised or not, often makes the difference between owners who are committed to and identified with the firm and owners who feel enslaved and controlled by it (and by other family shareholders). Even a minority shareholder who feels locked in can create turmoil within the shareholder group, for instance by trying to create alliances with more important blockholders to provoke quarrels inside the family.

A buy–sell agreement may have provisions for triggering events, such as if one of the owners is disabled, dies, retires, divorces, files for private bankruptcy, loses a professional license needed to operate the firm or receives an offer by a third party to buy the business. As with shareholder agreements (see Chapter 5 on governance), buy–sell agreements should specify a method for determining the sale price, such as an industry-specific sales multiple, or simply state that the business will be valued by a third party. After a triggering event, it may be risky for the remaining shareholder(s) to finance the purchase of the remaining stock. Next to obvious choices such as equity and bank credit, one way to arrange the purchase is to establish a first-to-die life insurance policy in which the survivor receives a death benefit if the business partner dies.[16] Other forms of buy–sell agreements include entity-purchase buy–sell agreements, in which the company rather than the owners purchase the life insurance.

Before we move on, two important caveats are in order. First, whatever the exact legal form, the agreement must specify whether it applies to current owners alone or to future ones as well (e.g., a junior family member who joins the firm after the agreement is in place). Second, it is important to specify the time period in which payment must occur in the event of a triggering event.

Dual-class shares

One way for families to avoid the fragmentation of ownership and related problems is to create two classes of stock: voting and nonvoting. Such dual-class share structures are prevalent around the world, although they are prohibited by some national regulations. For example, UK law follows the principle that each share should be equipped with one vote.

The particular advantage of dual-class shares is that parents can pass nonvoting shares during their life to children removing the bulk of ownership during their life while holding voting shares until their death. This also allows the incumbent to continue making important strategic decisions for the business while slowly bringing the next generation on board. Also, dual-class shares allow parents to divide the estate equally among heirs in terms of value (justice principle of equality), but differently in terms of control (justice principle of equity). This characteristic helps owners deal with active and inactive next-generation inheritors (Poza and Daugherty 2014).

7.12.3 Transfer to employees

Incumbents who choose to exit the firm by transferring shares to nonfamily employees can do so either through an employee stock ownership plan (ESOP) or through an MBO.

7.12.3.1 *Employee stock ownership plans (ESOPs)*

An ESOP is a mechanism that places all or part of the ownership of a company into the hands of employees. Usually, the ESOP takes the form of a trust arrangement through which the firm purchases shares for employees' retirement accounts. A sale of stock to an ESOP can have significant tax advantages for the seller. It can also help a family liquidate its ownership interests while rewarding long-time employees who have contributed to the growth of the family's wealth.

One of the central benefits of installing an ESOP is that it allows the incumbent to literally create a buyer for the company's stock. Thus, it helps the incumbent plan for retirement while remaining in control of the firm and without involving an outsider. To finance the purchase of the incumbent's stock, the ESOP may have to borrow money. The ESOP can also be established as a savings vehicle, where each year employee contributions are made to the ESOP trust and the savings are later used to purchase the company's shares. ESOPs have many undisputed advantages, and they are particularly popular in the United States. However, setting one up requires technical expertise in estate planning. More information about ESOPs is available on the website of the ESOP association and in Leonetti (2008, pp. 120–134).

7.12.3.2 *Management buyouts (MBOs)*

The central motive behind the MBO is to pass the firm on to the firm's management team. In contrast to an ESOP, in an MBO the managers buy the shares from the incumbent and thus become direct owners unmediated by a trust. An MBO can be a very rewarding succession option for incumbents who are financially ready to let go and are not interested in maximizing the financial proceeds from their exit. The benefits tied to an MBO include the following (Leonetti 2008):

- Continuity of business operations: the managers who are currently running the company will be taking over.
- Flexibility: the deal structure can be tailored to the unique situation of the firm.
- No outside party required.
- Loyalty to a group of individuals who have helped the incumbent grow the business.

However, there are also some serious downsides tied to an MBO:

- Employees may not have the funds to buy the business.
- Employees may be unable to think and act like entrepreneurs.
- Employees may suddenly become negotiation parties, with partly opposed interests.
- The business may serve as collateral to finance the MBO.

When considering an MBO as an exit option, incumbents must take into consideration the fact that the buyers will most likely not have the funds necessary for the purchase. A significant percentage of the sale price will most likely be structured as future—that is, deferred—payment, such as through a vendor loan (see section 7.11.2 for more details). Thus, even though the incumbent will be liberated from the day-to-day operations of the business, he or she will depend on its performance under new management. The MBO's success will thus largely depend on the ability of the new owner(s) to run the firm.

The financing of most MBOs in the small family business context takes place with a limited amount of equity contributed by the manager(s) taking over, some bank credit and a vendor loan, that is, deferred payment to the vendor that is usually subordinate to the bank loan. For an example of MBO financing, see section 7.11.5 and the short case study on Wood Corp therein. From a legal standpoint, it is critical to remember that the business serves as collateral for the bank loan. Banks will seek to secure the credit they provide. To this end, they will either estimate the firm's fixed assets and accounts receivable or its sustainable future cash flows.

CASE STUDY

MBO at Parentico

Parentico is a small group of private kindergartens and elementary schools. Its founder, Anthony Maas, seeks to pass on the firm to his two key managers, Claire and Deborah, via an MBO. Claire and Deborah have a proven track record and are interested in taking over the firm. Parentico is valued at $7 million.

The two entrepreneurs-to-be can only contribute $500 000 in total to the purchase. However, a banker has reviewed Parentico's balance sheet in assessing the possibility of a loan for the MBO. The banker estimates the firm's fixed assets and accounts receivable at about $5 million, and offers a loan of $4 million at 6% to be repaid within a seven-year period. Anthony thus faces a gap of $2.5 million ($7 million – $4 million – $500 000). He offers a vendor loan to the two new owners for the missing $2.5 million, which is subordinate to the bank credit, to be repaid over seven years at a 7% annual interest rate. Anthony's accountant then analyzes whether the firm's cash flows are sufficiently strong to repay the bank credit and the vendor loan.

Anthony's vendor loan also includes a pledge of the company stock against the loan. If the loan is not paid back, Anthony can take back a percentage of the stock and retain the rights to reclaim control of the business.

7.12.4 Private equity, recapitalizations and leveraged buyouts

Another way to plan for succession and exit a firm is to bring in private equity. Private equity companies are financial investors that typically have a five- to seven-year investment horizon after which they will seek to exit from their investment at the highest price possible. The benefits tied to involving a private equity company are:

- For the incumbent, the opportunity to cash out, stay involved with the firm and share the risks of the future strategy with a partner.
- Significant amounts of capital to fund a growth strategy that incumbents could not pursue themselves.
- Increased focus on results.
- Private equity's experience with growth financing and execution of growth strategies.
- Important financial incentives for the management of the target company.

Despite these undisputed benefits, for business owners who are about to exit their firms, private equity investors may not be the right choice. When private equity gets involved, the incumbent who used to be an independent entrepreneur becomes largely dependent on the new, high-performing partners, who will install rigid monitoring systems and will significantly leverage the company to achieve their expected rate of returns of 20% to 40%. Given the relatively high fixed costs of private equity transactions, the lower end for involving such an investor is an EBITDA of at least $1 million at the target company (Leonetti 2008).

7.12.4.1 Private equity recapitalizations

One way to involve private equity is to recapitalize the target company. In a recapitalization, the private equity company replaces the owner's equity with its own mixture of debt and equity. The owner's stock is turned into cash for personal diversification. Such recapitalizations do not have to mean a complete sale of the company. Rather, the private equity company typically takes over a majority of the firm, and the incumbent owner stays on with a minority stake. The incumbent and the private equity firm then proceed to grow the firm together.

7.12.4.2 Leveraged buyouts (LBOs)

A LBO is a transfer of ownership that usually involves a significant amount of external funding—in particular, debt—as well as outside equity investors, such as private equity. From a legal point of view, a leveraged buyout often involves the creation of a new company to acquire all the shares of the target company. For the sake of parsimony, let us call this new company NewCo. NewCo is only created for the sake of the LBO transaction and

CASE STUDY

Private equity recapitalization at Homebrewers

The owner of Homebrewers wishes to monetize a large part of the illiquid wealth in his brewing business. He finds a private equity company willing to purchase 80% of the firm, leaving him with the remaining 20%. As the owner knows the business well and has a proven track record, the private equity company also wants him to stay on as CEO, promising him a large bonus for reaching growth and profitability targets. In this way, the private equity company and the owner of Homebrewers have aligned interests.

This solution is perfect for the owner, as he was neither financially nor mentally ready to let go. Now, with the involvement of private equity, he has found a way to harvest some of the financial value he has created and at the same time stay involved in the firm. He remains CEO and now has access to further growth financing.

aside from its stake in the target company does not execute any operating activity. Typically, NewCo will have no assets other than the shares of the target company it has acquired, the money invested by the financial buyer and, to a lesser extent, the management team.

In consequence, the investors (e.g., private equity investors and management) do not become direct owners of the target company. Rather, they are owners of NewCo, which holds the shares of the target company. The acquirer and the target company do not merge into one legal entity in this scenario. Figure 7.20 depicts the complete structure of an LBO.

In most LBOs, incumbents will try to avoid granting a vendor loan. However, we include this form of financing in Figure 7.20 for the sake of completeness. As outlined in the short case study of Homebrewers above, in a private equity recapitalization the incumbent may stay on as a minority owner. Alternatively, former top managers may become the minority owners in the firm. Such structures look complex, but they have two important advantages:

- **Risk mitigation**: The financial risks to the investors are limited because they are not the owners of the target company—rather, NewCo is. Because NewCo takes on the bank loans to pay for this purchase, the financial assets of the investors beyond their investment in NewCo are protected from the deal. This is particularly important for managers, who tend to have limited private assets available for investment.

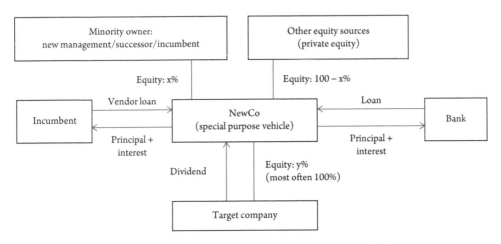

Figure 7.20 Legal setup of LBO with special purpose vehicle

- **Tax advantages**: The investors circumvent double taxation by structuring NewCo as a pass-through entity such as a partnership or holding company (depending on legislation). As dividend income is not taxed in the holding company, the full dividends distributed by the target company can be used to repay the bank loans. In the absence of such a pass-through entity, the dividends would be taxed as income.

To clarify the relationship between the minority owners and the private equity company, the parties may also enter into a shareholder agreement.

Any bank making a loan to NewCo to finance the succession will want to install effective security measures over NewCo's assets and, to the extent possible, those of the target company. Typically, the bank will be looking for the following security measures:

- A share pledge agreement concerning the shares held by the investors (minority owners and private equity company) in NewCo.
- A guarantee from the target company and its subsidiaries with respect to the obligations of NewCo.
- A share pledge agreement concerning the shares held by NewCo in the target company.
- Security over the assets of the target company and its subsidiaries with respect to the guarantee obligations.
- If needed, a vendor loan to be subordinated to the bank loan.[17]

7.12.5 Complete sale to financial or strategic buyer

Finally, the incumbent may decide to let go of the firm completely without any further involvement. This solution is a preferred option for incumbents who are happy to let go of the firm quickly and completely and to maximize the proceeds from the sale. From a financial standpoint, a complete sale may be especially attractive if a strategic buyer, such as a competitor, sees important synergies between his/her own company and the target firm. This exit option requires a strategic fit with the acquirer, for instance in terms of product offerings or geographic scope. Alternatively, a financial buyer such as a private equity company or pension fund may wish to take over the firm through either an asset or share deal. An asset deal can help limit the risks to the acquirer when the target is a privately held firm.

 REFLECTION QUESTIONS

Reflection questions for the incumbent

1. If the firm is transferred to family members:
   a. What are the applicable estate taxes and gift taxes?
   b. How much testamentary freedom do I have?
   c. How are the family members who are excluded from the firm treated?
2. If the firm is sold to family members: what is an appropriate price?
3. When setting up a trust:
   a. Which trust structure suits my goals?
   b. What are the pros and cons of setting up a trust?
4. If the firm is sold to a co-owner: what type of buy–sell agreement do we have in place? How do we finance the buyout of the other owner(s)?
5. If the firm is transferred to employees: should an employee stock ownership plan (ESOP) be set up? What are the pros and cons of a an MBO?
6. Does my firm qualify for private equity investment? If yes, should I go for a private equity recapitalization, or do I want to exit completely?
7. How will I manage the proceeds from the sale?
8. What financial, legal and tax advice do I need to set up the succession?

Reflection questions for successor

1. What is the legal setup of the takeover?
2. What are the opportunities and risks for me?
3. What are the legal and tax implications for me?

Reflection questions for students

1. Describe the differences between estate and gift tax.
2. What are the arguments in favor of and against estate tax?
3. What are the pros and cons of trusts?
4. What is the difference between an employee stock ownership plan (ESOP) and an MBO?

5. Why is the fragmentation of shareholdings problematic for family firms? What can the owner/managers do about it?
6. What are the pros and cons of a private equity recapitalization?
7. Describe the use of a pass-through entity in a leveraged buyout (LBO).

7.13 CASE STUDY

Bernet's choice—Valuation, emotional value, family discount and fair distribution of assets within the family

Twenty-five years ago, Peter and Susan Bernet took over a family firm that had been founded by Peter's grandfather as a forge and continued on by his father. Peter and Susan own 100% of the firm and have developed Bernet AG into a successful plastics company. Within the last four years, sales reached an average of $30 million. During the same period, EBIT amounted to an average of $2.5 million and earnings after tax to approximately $1.9 million. The company holds $3 million in debt in the form of bank loans due to an investment in machinery. Furthermore, property that is not used for company purposes appears in the firm's balance sheet with a value of $3.5 million, with a $1.5 million mortgage. The firm's balance sheet also shows non-operating liquidity of $1 million.

Some time ago, an investor tried to acquire Bernet AG for $16 million. In some ways, the offer was alluring. At 60, Peter was conscious of the fact that he had to think about pulling back from the business. When he had started out in his parents' firm, it hadn't been with any special passion; rather, it seemed like the most rational choice at the time. In fact, his parents exerted significant pressure on him to join the company. Peter used to say: 'I would have preferred to become an architect. I stayed with the firm primarily because of my family, first for my parents and later for my children.'

In terms of succession planning, Peter strongly prefers that the firm be passed on within the family. If he has to sell it to an external buyer, he will hold out for a price he considers fair. He says: 'Bernet AG has been in the family for three generations and carries the family name. I won't sell it at the first best price.' He adds: 'I want the time and effort I've put into the firm to be recognized. The firm doesn't generate a lot of profit, but it has been enough to get along to date. This is an achievement in such a battered industry.' During challenging phases, however, Peter also mentions: 'I wonder, why I am doing this to myself? It's time to pass on the responsibility.' From his personal perspective, an acceptable sale price to a buyer outside the family would be closer to $21 million than the $16 million offered by the investor. If one of his children took over, he would be willing to forgo a significant amount of money—'but of course not all', he explains.

Peter and Susan Bernet have three children: Marc, Paul and Pearl. Marc has already started a career within the family firm and holds the position of Vice-President of Marketing and Sales. Paul on the other hand pursues his own business activities and has founded an IT

CASE STUDY (continued)

startup. He sees his future outside the family firm. Pearl does not work in the family firm and has no entrepreneurial plans. She has been working as a ballet dancer and now wants to start a career in sports management.

Marc has already been thinking about stepping into his parents' shoes and about what he would consider a fair price for the firm. He is aware of the fact that his parents invested a huge amount of their wealth in the company, and he wants to compensate them for that. But on the other hand, he doesn't want to overextend himself. He thinks that the price should be assessed in a way that allows him to lead the company in the future without mountains of debt. When reflecting on his personal view of an appropriate sale price, he mentions:

> I am very interested in the firm, but this is no dream job. My passion for plastics and our products is limited. I think I can expect some support from my parents when it comes to the transfer of the firm, and that includes a favorable price. But I'm aware of the fact that I have to contribute financially as well and ensure that the firm remains successful.
>
> To be honest, I'm not completely sure that I should take on this responsibility. If I do, I know that I can't expect my parents to pass on the company for free. They have to finance a big part of their retirement through the sale. Overall, I think that a maximum price of $10 million is adequate—if it's possible to finance.

Since Marc is interested in taking over the company, Peter and Susan Bernet decline the investor's offer. They then initiate a family discussion about the fair distribution of their wealth.

The Bernet family wealth is composed of the following assets: the company, and Peter and Susan's beautiful $4 million villa. Peter and Susan also possess liquid assets amounting to $2 million.

? **REFLECTION QUESTIONS**

1. What is the equity value of Bernet AG?
2. What are Peter Bernet's considerations concerning a fair sale price?
3. What does Marc Bernet consider to be a fair price?
4. According to which sale price should the company be passed on within the family?
5. For the legal context in which you are embedded, how would you legally structure the succession?
6. How could the succession be financed if Marc takes over?
7. What is the value of the Bernet parents' total wealth?
8. What form of wealth distribution would you recommend for the Bernet family?

NOTES

1 We asked 431 entrepreneurs the following question: 'What is the minimum acceptable sales price at which you are willing to sell 100% of your company's equity to a nonfamily member?' This question made it clear that we were looking for (1) the value of the firm's equity (2) when selling the entire firm (3) to parties outside the family. Subjective value assessment = Market value + Emotional value.

2 Emotional value is defined as the difference between the minimum acceptable sale price as perceived by the incumbent owner and the financial value of the firm. Put differently: Minimum acceptable sale price = Emotional value + Financial value.

3 Family discount was measured as follows: We asked respondents (all with family business backgrounds) the following question: 'Assuming that a nonfamily buyer would have to pay 100 for complete ownership in your parents' firm, how much do you expect to pay?' Answers were then deducted from 100 to derive the family discount.

4 In the United States, for instance, tax authorities would only accept a discount on firm value if it can be justified by the fact that a minority stake is passed on, or if the shares are illiquid. But even under such regulations there is some leeway in terms of calculating firm value, and families will tend to opt for the lower end in the value estimate when passing the firm to a child.

5 The expected drop in entrepreneurial abilities and interests to average population levels should be particularly drastic for highly successful and passionate entrepreneurs. It follows that stellar entrepreneurs face a particularly high likelihood that their children will have lower entrepreneurial skills and passion than they have themselves.

6 EBIT = Earnings before interest and taxes; EBITDA = Earnings before interest, taxes, depreciation and amortization.

7 The marginal tax rate accounts for the fact that interest payments on debt are tax deductible. This makes debt a more attractive financing option in comparison to equity.

8 Often the target and not the actual capital structure of the firm is used in this calculation.

9 Note: we did not deduct interest rate on debt when we calculated FCF. See Table 7.10 for details about the calculation of FCF.

10 LTM: Last twelve months.

11 Part of the information in this table has been retrieved from macabacus.com. Please note: the indicated IRRs may be lower for larger or less risky firms.

12 In some countries, a *generation-skipping tax* is levied when people wish to transfer their estate directly to their grandchildren. This may be the case in wealthy families, in which children already have substantial wealth. Such a transfer could potentially save taxes, as the estate would be taxed only once and not twice (i.e., from parents to children and from children to grandchildren). Generation-skipping taxes close this tax loophole.

13 In his work on inherited wealth, Beckert (2008) writes that in the United States, 'opponents of inheritance taxation argue primarily with an interpretation of property law that includes the unrestricted right to dispose of property after the owner's death. This reasoning is linked with the concern that this kind of taxation could have negative effects on the entrepreneurial spirit. Inheritance taxes, so the argument goes, discourage economic ambition and endanger small companies in particular, whose existence is supposedly the very backbone of the economic foundation of democratic freedoms. The United States has a long tradition of criticism of the transfer of wealth between generations, one that is grounded primarily in the equality of opportunity principle and the community principle. Inheritances seem "un-American," because they violate the principle of equal opportunity and in a sense perpetuate feudal privileges.'

14 We asked EY's tax advisors from around the globe to estimate the tax upon inheritance of a small family firm. The case study we presented to the tax experts read as follows: 'Bob Smith (58) is 100% owner of the business and is resident of the capital city of your country. Bob's business is a corporation. The taxable value of the business is $10 million. Bob has two children: Mike (28) and Molly (25). Unexpectedly, Bob passes away and his will passes the shares to his children, who do not want to continue the business and decide to sell off the business right after succession. What is the inheritance tax due in US dollars in this case?' We put the answers in proportion to the taxable firm value of $10 million, which provided us with the figures displayed in Figure 7.18.

Please note that the scenario describes the selloff of the firm after inheritance. Some countries such as Ireland, the Netherlands or Spain levy lower taxes in cases where the firm is continued and not sold by the inheritors. Still, the overall international pattern remains comparable also under this alternate scenario.

15 For simplicity's sake, we focus on trusts alone.

16 Of course, this gets more complicated in the presence of more than two owners. For instance, if there are five owners, there are 20 individual life insurance policies, which raises administrative costs. In US estate planning, trusteed cross-purchase agreements allow firms to circumvent this problem (i.e., a trust owns all the individual insurance policies and the company pays the insurance premium).

17 The primary aim of the bank is to put in place a security structure that will give it direct access to the cash flows of the target company. Simply entering into a share pledge agreement regarding the shares held by NewCo in the target firm does not achieve this aim. If that was the only security held by the bank and NewCo was to default, the bank would not have access to the target firm's cash flows; it would only have the right to sell the shares in the target firm. Any creditors of the target firm would have first call on the target firm's cash-generating assets. For further details on the legal structure of MBOs and LBOs, see for example DeMott (1988).

 BACKGROUND READING

Bennedsen, M., K. M. Nielsen, F. Perez-Gonzalez and D. Wolfenzon (2007). Inside the family firm: The role of families in succession decisions and performance. *Quarterly Journal of Economics*, 122 (2): 647–691.

Cabrera-Suarez, K., P. De Saa-Perez and D. Garcia-Almeida (2001). The succession process from a resource- and knowledge-based view of the family firm. *Family Business Review*, 14 (1): 37–48.

Carney, M., E. Gedajlovic and V. Strike (2014). Dead money: Inheritance law and the longevity of family firms. *Entrepreneurship Theory and Practice*, 38 (6): 1261–1283.

Christen, A., F. Halter, N. Kammerlander, D. Künzi, D. Merki and T. Zellweger (2013). Success factors for Swiss SMEs: Company succession in practice. Credit Suisse and University of St. Gallen, Zurich.

Chua, J. H., J. J. Chrisman and P. Sharma (1999). Defining the family business by behavior. *Entrepreneurship Theory and Practice*, 23 (4): 19–39.

Chua, J. H., J. J. Chrisman and P. Sharma (2003). Succession and nonsuccession concerns of family firms and agency relationship with nonfamily managers. *Family Business Review*, 16 (2): 89–107.

De Massis, A., J. H. Chua and J. J. Chrisman (2008). Factors preventing intra-family succession. *Family Business Review*, 21 (2): 183–199.

Dehlen, T., T. Zellweger, N. Kammerlander and F. Halter (2012). The role of information asymmetry in the choice of entrepreneurial exit routes. *Journal of Business Venturing*, 29 (2): 193–209.

DeMott, D. (1988). Directors' duties in management buyouts and leveraged recapitalizations. *Ohio State Law Journal*, 49: 517–557.

Ellul, A., M. Pagano and F. Panunzi (2010). Inheritance law and investment in family firms. *American Economic Review*, 100: 2414–2450.

Graebner, M. E., and K. M. Eisenhardt (2004). The seller's side of the story: Acquisition as courtship and governance as syndicate in entrepreneurial firms. *Administrative Science Quarterly*, 49 (3): 366–403.

Handler, W. C. (1990). Succession in family firms: A mutual role adjustment between entrepreneur and next generation family members. *Entrepreneurship Theory and Practice*, 15 (1): 37–51.

Hartley, B. B., and G. Griffith (2009). *Family Wealth Transition Planning: Advising Families with Small Businesses*. New York: Bloomberg Press.

Kotlar, J., and A. De Massis (2013). Goal setting in family firms: Goal diversity, social interactions, and collective commitment to family-centered goals. *Entrepreneurship Theory and Practice*, 37 (6): 1263–1288.

KPMG (2014). KPMG European family business tax monitor: Comparing the impact of tax regimes on family businesses. KPMG.

Le Breton-Miller, I., D. Miller and L. P. Steier (2004). Toward an integrative model of effective FOB succession. *Entrepreneurship Theory and Practice*, 28 (4): 305–328.

Minichilli, A., M. Nordqvist, G. Corbetta and M. D. Amore (2014). CEO succession mechanisms, organizational context, and performance: A socio-emotional wealth perspective on family-controlled firms. *Journal of Management Studies*, 51 (7): 1153–1179.

Poza, E. J., and M. S. Daugherty (2014). *Family Business*. Mason, OH: Southwest Cengage Learning.

Sharma, P., and P. G. Irving (2005). Four bases of family business successor commitment: Antecedents and consequences. *Entrepreneurship Theory and Practice*, 29 (1): 13–33.

Tsoutsoura, M. (2009). *The Effect of Succession Taxes on Family Firm Investment: Evidence from a Natural Experiment*. New York: Columbia University.

Wennberg, K., J. Wiklund, K. Hellerstedt and M. Nordqvist (2012). Implications of intra family and external ownership transfer of family firms: Short-term and long-term performance differences. *Strategic Entrepreneurship Journal*, 5 (4): 352–372.

Zellweger, T., and J. Astrachan (2008). On the emotional value of owning a firm. *Family Business Review*, 21 (4): 347–363.

Zellweger, T. M., F. W. Kellermanns, J. J. Chrisman and J. H. Chua (2012). Family control and family firm valuations by family CEOs: The importance of intentions for transgenerational control. *Organization Science*, 23 (3): 851–868.

Zellweger, T., M. Richards, P. Sieger and P. Patel (forthcoming). How much am I expected to pay for my parents' firm? An institutional logics perspective on family discounts. *Entrepreneurship Theory and Practice*.

Zellweger, T., P. Sieger and P. Englisch (2012). Coming home or breaking free? Career choice intentions of the next generation in family businesses. Ernst & Young.

Zellweger, T., P. Sieger and F. Halter (2011). Should I stay or should I go? Career choice intentions of students with family business background. *Journal of Business Venturing*, 26 (5): 521–536.

8

Change and transgenerational value creation

Thus far, our discussions of strategy and succession in family firms have been driven by certain perspectives on family firms. For instance, our strategy discussion has revolved around managing family influence with the aim of fostering the family firm's competitive advantage. In that regard, we implicitly assumed that the firm possesses a viable business model and operates in a relatively stable environment. Obviously, this is not necessarily the case. Change and adaptation are essential prerequisites for prospering and surviving in today's dynamic marketplace. As with any other type of firm, the ability to handle change is critical for family firms. However, in light of their focus on tradition and their longer-term business outlook, family firms find dealing with change to be a particularly challenging and pressing task.

Also, in our detailed discussions of how to pass a firm from one generation to the next, we have assumed, at least to some degree, that the transfer of the firm within the family is the not only the best option for both the firm and the family, but also the option that is most preferred. However, the natural rise and decline of markets, products and technologies give rise to the question of how to approach succession when the family-internal transfer of the firm is no longer advisable. This occurs not only when an internal successor is missing, but also when alternative routes to family-internal succession may be more advisable. For instance, given certain familial, business and environmental circumstances, a family-external transfer, such as a (partial) sale, a stock market listing, or the exit and closure of the business, may be the best choice for the firm and the family and, hence, a way for the family to harvest or protect wealth.

As a consequence of the dynamic context in which they operate, family firms and their owners must embrace change. This is important for the future of the firm and for the continued success of the family as a collective of people controlling a business activity. Therefore, the following pages on change and transgenerational value creation deal with two key issues: (1) how family firms deal with change and (2) how families create value across generations from their control over the firm.

8.1 Change and adaptation in family firms

by Nadine Kammerlander[1]

Many family firms can look back upon decades, sometimes even a century, of business success in which they have grown to a respectable size, established renowned brands and impressive networks of customers and suppliers, and earned substantial profit. Therefore, it is not surprising that owners and managers of family firms often emphasize the importance of stability and sticking to the firm's traditional roots—recipes that have guaranteed outperformance in the past. However, in today's volatile and uncertain world, an excessive focus on tradition can be a serious threat to family firms, as it can impede the implementation of required changes within the organizations.

In the twenty-first century, firms in high-tech industries with fast 'clock speeds' (Fine 1998) are not the only firms that need to prepare for change. Firms in more traditional industries that have historically been relatively rather stable must also address this need. For instance, in the hotel industry, established players feel an increasing threat from new competitors such as Airbnb, a peer-to-peer provider of hotel services. Alternatively, consider the agricultural sector in which revenues depend on international trade agreements and can thus be substantially affected by political change. These examples illustrate that various stakeholders introduce change for a variety of reasons.

In principle, any of the five forces described by Porter (1979)—new entrants, bargaining power of suppliers, bargaining power of clients, substitute products or services, or rivalry among existing competitors—can change over time, resulting in a need for organizational change. For instance, change can be triggered by the entrance of new, large (potentially international) competitors with significant purchasing power. New products or technologies can serve as substitutes for existing offerings or production technologies. Customer needs and preferences may change over time, such that previously profitable markets dry up. Changes in the political system, the introduction of new laws and industry regulations, or raw-material shortages can challenge established, successful family firms. Only family firms that master adapting to changing environments can survive in the long term.

While organizational change is a challenge for any type of firm (see Miller and Friesen 1980 for an overview), several change-related hurdles are more pronounced in family firms. Consider, for example, the emotional barriers that lead family firms to prefer the status quo. However, family firms also possess some advantages when it comes to dealing with change. For instance, the family firm's focus on socioemotional wealth (SEW, see Chapter 6 on strategy) induces it to pursue specific goals. Moreover, this focus endows the firm with several abilities and constraints that either foster or impede organizational change.

8.1.1 The sensemaking of family firms in changing environments

In the following, the advantages and disadvantages of family firms are outlined along the sensemaking process (Figure 8.1). The discussion extends recent findings presented by Koenig, Kammerlander and Enders (2013) to include a broader range of changes. In the sensemaking process (Thomas, Clark and Gioia 1993), key decision makers, such as the family firm's CEO, need to (1) recognize the need to change, (2) interpret it as a relevant trend that requires a reaction and (3) make a decision about how to adapt. Ultimately, (4) the organization needs to implement the proposed changes.

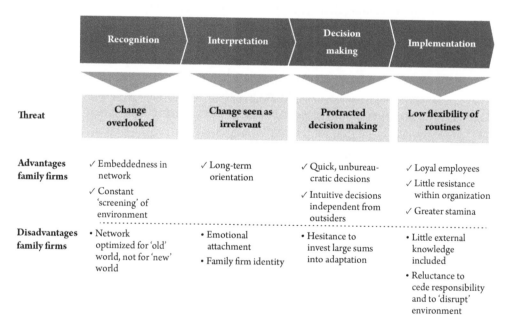

Figure 8.1 Sensemaking and adaptation to change in family firms

8.1.2 Recognition—the ambiguous role of the family firm's network

In order to recognize relevant upcoming changes in a timely manner, decision makers need to 'screen' or 'scan' their firms' environments on a regular basis. Such screening provides important information on upcoming trends and their characteristics. Family firms have both advantages and disadvantages in this regard.

Family firms are often deeply embedded in a strong network of suppliers, customers and other family firms in the region. Often, such ties to external actors are established and strengthened over the course of several years. In many cases, the family firm owner-manager serves as the firm's representative and takes, for instance, important positions in industry associations. Such engagement ensures that family firms become aware of upcoming changes, such as potential industry regulations.

At the same time, however, the family firm's network can become a significant liability that hinders the early recognition of changes. In this regard, the firm's information-exchange partners are as important as its actual embeddedness in a network because many industry changes are not triggered by established players, but by new entrants. Consider, for example, innovations in online retailing that are introduced by startup companies. If such 'industry externals' are not part of the family firm's network, the firm and its decision makers are likely to overlook the new trend. In fact, embeddedness in a network of established firms can strengthen a firm's myopia if it lulls decision makers into a false sense of security. Therefore, family firm owners and managers are advised to critically review their networks and scrutinize whether they are equipped to detect a broad range of potential changes.

8.1.3 Interpretation—long-term orientation versus socioemotional wealth

One of the biggest challenges for decision makers in family firms facing environmental changes is interpreting the resulting turmoil. Decision makers need to recognize that a new trend is important, that it will affect the family firm in the near or medium term, and that the firm needs to adapt. Many cognitive and emotional barriers lead decision makers to either slander the upcoming trend (e.g., 'Digital cameras will never offer the same quality as analog cameras') or assess the changes as occurring only in the distant future (e.g., 'We can wait to consider how climate change will affect our ski resort').

How do family firms generally interpret the relevance of change? Some family firms, particularly those with a long-term focus and an emphasis on continuity and sustainability, can overcome such misinterpretations and biases, and quickly assess emerging trends as relevant issues (Kammerlander and Ganter 2015). Decision makers in such long-term-oriented family firms are particularly attentive to what might affect or threaten the family firm in the long run because they want to hand over the business to their children, and they want that business to be in good shape. Given this lengthy horizon, which often spans beyond the current generation of family leaders, change is likely to be of relevance for the current leaders, even if that change only materializes well into the future.

However, adverse attitudes toward required changes tend to be particularly common in family firms. Many family firm owners and managers feel emotionally attached to their firms' products and established ways of running the business. Therefore, considering potential changes to what the founders established and developed is not an easy task. In addition, adaptations to the changing environment may contradict the family firm's organizational identity. Moreover, changes in certain aspects, such as product features, often entail a string of consequences for the organization. Such changes can result in 'disruptions' in the firm's internal and external networks, or they might require the family to cede responsibility to family and firm outsiders who are better trained in what the 'new world' requires. This requires recognition that the current staff members do not possess the newly required skills and that loyal suppliers may need to be replaced with new suppliers who better fit the new conditions.

Given these consequences, which contradict the family firm's desire to maintain SEW, family firms can easily fall into the trap of misinterpreting important trends. Even if they recognize a new trend in the industry, family firms might find (erroneous) reasons to avoid adapting to that trend. To overcome this barrier, decision makers in family firms need to critically assess how their attachments to the firm and their own views about the firm might bias their decision making.

8.1.4 Decision making—the key advantage of family firms

After interpreting an ongoing change as relevant, decision makers need to agree on how the firm should adapt to the change. In this regard, the ability to make quick decisions is one of the most important advantages of family firms. In nonfamily firms, decisions typically need to be based on extensive calculations and business plans. In other words, they are often based on information that might not be readily available while the environment is still changing. Moreover, as decisions in those firms need to pass through various hierarchical levels, ultimate agreement is likely to be delayed by political, power-based fights among managers.

The structure of family firms typically allows for fast, undisturbed and non-bureaucratic decision making. Family firms that are open to change and able to screen the environment can build on their intuitive decision-making capabilities to react to emerging but still uncertain trends. This is particularly true for private or majority-owned family firms that can make decisions independent of the views of external investors and security analysts, who might be overly cautious given the lack of deterministic and reliable data about the economic impact of the adjustments.

Notably, the socioemotional aspect of family firms also carries one important pitfall—adaptation to change often requires substantial investments upfront. For instance, new employees may need to be hired, new machinery might be required or marketing activities may be needed. As family firm owners wish to avoid involving external investors, the amount of money available for the firm's adaptation is likely to be limited. This limited investment capability might hamper the family firm's adaptation depending on the type of change. Hence, decision makers in family firms need to carefully check whether the amount of planned investments is sufficient to guarantee successful adaptation.

8.1.5 Implementation—the double-edged sword of experience and loyalty

One major but sometimes overlooked challenge in the adaptation process is the implementation of changes within the organization. The organizational members need to understand and accept the required changes, and adapt their working behavior and routines accordingly. In this regard, family influence acts as a double-edged sword.

In some situations, family firms can benefit from their networks, their extensive experience in the market and their loyal and often highly motivated employees. Such resources can, for instance, help firms quickly implement changes required by new laws and regulations, or improve products to meet new standards. Consequently, family firms are particularly well equipped to deal with incremental change.

However, this capability can become a liability when the change is radical, or when it substantially alters the skills and competencies required as well as the criteria customers use to evaluate the products and services. In such cases, long-tenured employees and managers might stick to their old routines and be unable to search for or identify flexible and often highly successful solutions. This, together with family firm's reluctance to bring in external actors, implies that the family firm's implementation might be relatively rigid and inflexible. For instance, many US newspapers struggled when trying to adapt to the emergence of online news. Instead of providing short news pieces soon after an event and offering readers an opportunity to comment on events and interact, these news outlets uploaded their (long) printed texts with a delay of one to two days—an approach that was not appreciated by customers.

Given such observed patterns, family firms need to ask themselves 'How radical is the change?' before engaging in adaptation. Depending on the answer to this question, they can either build on their natural advantages or find ways to overcome their disadvantages.

Independent of the extent to which a certain change is radical and the resulting (dis)advantages, family firms can benefit from their high levels of 'stamina' or perseverance when implementing changes. Abandonment of adaptation in the early stages is not only inefficient, but can also threaten the firm's long-term success. In nonfamily firms, attempts to adopt internal routines are often disrupted by the introduction of new managers, political infighting or budgetary changes. Family firms are less likely to suffer from such disruptions because they have a high level of control concentrated at the top of the company and they are often independent of external investors. Therefore, adaptation in family firms can occur in a more seamless manner over an extended period of time.

8.1.6　Summary: family firms and change

In general, family firms have both advantages and disadvantages when making sense of change. In the recognition stage, family firms need to deal with an ambiguous network. In the interpretation stage, they must find ways of exploiting the long-term view to embrace change while compromising on their SEW. In the decision-making stage, family firms tend to have major advantages, as they can exploit their fast decision-making processes. However, even in this stage, the family's involvement has a downside—the family owners are likely to be hesitant to commit significant resources. Finally, in the implementation stage, family firms benefit from the presence of loyal employees and their greater stamina in terms of persisting with a chosen strategy. However, these firms often have limited access to qualified personnel who can implement that strategy.

Given the above, dealing with change is particularly challenging in family firms, which need to deal with a number of questions.

 REFLECTION QUESTIONS

For family firms on dealing with change

About recognizing change

1. How closed is our network?
2. Do we openly discuss trends with partners outside our established network?
3. Do we take new entrants and technologies seriously?

About interpreting change

1. Do we understand our long-term focus as a means to embrace change or negate change?
2. How does a particular change affect our SEW? More specifically, how does it affect our family firm's identity, our relationships with stakeholders (e.g., employees, suppliers or family members) and our family's control over the firm?
3. How do the threats to our SEW affect our interpretation of change? Are we led to negate the need for change or to try to postpone it?

About decision making in the face of change

1. How fast are we in our decision making in the face of change?
2. Do our bureaucracy and hierarchy slow decision making?
3. What are the maximum investments that we are willing to make as a family to adapt to the changing environment?
4. Where can we obtain the capital and knowledge required to invest in the future?

About implementing change

1. How helpful are our networks and our employees when it comes to implementing incremental change?
2. How helpful are our networks and are our employees when it comes to implementing radical change?
3. What are the radical innovations in our industry? How are we going to implement the required changes?
4. How persistent are we in implementing change?

Excursus: Family firms and disruptive technologies

One particularly threatening type of change is the emergence of disruptive technologies (Christensen 1997; also known as 'radical' or 'discontinuous' technologies). Such technologies are often introduced by new entrants in an industry, and
they tend to change the entire market structure in such a way that former market
leaders ultimately lose their dominant positions. Prominent examples of such disruptive technologies include no-frills airlines, generic drugs and digital cameras.

Several cognitive-emotional and economic-rational barriers impede the adoption of disruptive technologies in established firms (see Hill and Rothaermel 2003
for an overview). Decision makers often overlook or misinterpret such discontinuous changes because products based on disruptive technologies often initially
perform poorly in terms of established performance criteria (compare lines A and
B in Figure 8.2). However, as many examples of disruptive technologies show,
both 'new' and 'old' technologies can improve their performance over time
through incremental innovations. Therefore, while the disruptive technology may
still be regarded as 'inferior' to the established technology in terms of established
performance criteria, a point may be reached at which the new technology may
be viewed as sufficient for meeting customers' requirements (cross-section of
lines B and C in Figure 8.2). As a consequence, customers will start to shift from
the old technology to the new technology and leave established firms that are
still focused on the outdated technology and are still operating in a shrinking
market niche.

While a loss of customers and market share can occur for any established firm,
family business are particularly prone to this trap. Several aspects of the sensemaking process contribute to this 'family innovator's dilemma'. While decision

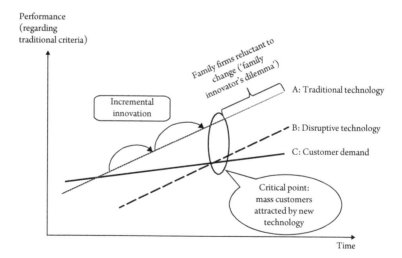

Figure 8.2 Disruptive technological innovations

makers in family firms can easily decide to engage in adoption, their reluctance to disturb established networks inside and outside the firm, and their unwillingness to cede control, restrain them from adopting a disruptive technology. Therefore, decision makers in family firms who sense an emerging disruptive change need to decide whether to retreat into a potentially small, upmarket niche (with potential downsizing risks for the firm) or to adopt the new technology.

CASE STUDY

Hugendubel booksellers

One particularly impactful disruptive change was the shift from bricks-and-mortar bookstores to the electronic trading of books. In Germany, this change began to affect the bookseller industry when the US company Amazon entered the local market in 1998.

In line with the idiosyncratic characteristics of disruptive technological changes, the service provided by the online traders was initially assessed as inferior to that offered by bricks-and-mortar stores, as the online service did not include personalized advice for customers. Moreover, customers could not just 'flip through' a book's pages in order to assess whether it was worth buying.

However, the online service did offer several benefits, which customers quickly learned to appreciate. For example, customers were able to purchase books from home at any time, and they could choose from a large variety of books. More importantly, Amazon (and other online booksellers) improved over time in terms of the traditional performance criteria for retail book sales—customer ratings and extensive reader reviews were introduced to serve as substitutes for a sales person's advice. In addition, as the technology advanced, 'previews' allowed the customers to flip through at least some pages in books of interest. Consequently, the share of book purchases made online increased significantly. Just 15 years after Amazon's market entrance, the company's book-related revenues in Germany amounted to almost $2 billion and the company held a market share of more than 15% (www.buchverein.ch; www.boersenverein.de).

One firm that was particularly challenged by this development was the German book retailer Hugendubel, a family firm that currently has around 1700 employees. Hugendubel was founded in 1893 when Heinrich Karl Gustav Hugendubel acquired a bookstore in the center of Munich, and its ownership and management were transferred from generation to generation. In 1964, Heinrich Hugendubel was appointed manager and started to expand the business by founding branches in Munich and other German cities. Hugendubel's large 'worlds of book experience' shops with self-service and reading corners were said to revolutionize the book-retailing sector.

In the 1980s, the company expanded into publishing and acquired several other retailers. By the turn of the century, Hugendubel had become one of the largest German book

CASE STUDY *(continued)*

retailers. Its success was grounded in a mix of quality products and products offered at low prices. The family manager, Nina Hugendubel, commented in a 2004 interview: 'We will continue to work this way because it is the right mixture.' In interviews given at the beginning of the twenty-first century, Nina Hugendubel emphasized that physical book retailers would remain the 'heart of the business'. Her brother, Maximilian Hugendubel, admitted that the sector was less profitable than others, but he stressed the joy he experienced when observing customers in the stores. He also mentioned that, in his opinion, cinemas and cafeterias, rather than Amazon, were the firm's main competitors—an assessment that, in hindsight, is debatable.

The company's success came to an end shortly after Amazon successfully entered the German market, when its revenues began to shrink. In a first attempt to oppose the growing competition in the changing environment, Hugendubel merged with another established player, Weltbild, in 2006. As the owner-managers of Hugendubel explained, this merger 'aimed at preserving the unique variety as well as jobs in the German book retailing sector'. However, this marriage of two established book retailers lasted for only a few years, as Weltbild filed for bankruptcy in 2014.

Hugendubel appears to have fallen into the 'upmarket trap' (see excursus on 'Family firms and disruptive technologies' as well as Figure 8.2) by the end of the first decade of the twenty-first century. In 2009, Hugendubel launched a large downsizing project. Moreover, the company has closed several of its 50 bookstores, including the original company building in Munich.

However, the family firm's owner-managers, Maximilian and Nina Hugendubel, never gave up. As they explained in several interviews with the press, they adopted a trial-and-error approach in order to improve their understanding of which concepts might work in the future. When they realized that there would be no other sustainable option than adopting online book retailing, they built an online and mobile sales platform for the company. The Internet platform is designed to offer not only the services provided by Amazon, but also a broad range of other services. To be successful with this new channel, the owner-managers invested substantial resources in convincing their own employees that Hugendubel's web platform should not be viewed as a competitor to the core business. As of the autumn of 2014, Hugendubel appears to have found a way to escape the family firm innovator's dilemma.

? REFLECTION QUESTIONS

1. Can Amazon's entrance into the German market be assessed as the emergence of a disruptive technology for German book retailers? If so, why?
2. What (family-specific) elements can you identify that impeded Hugendubel's adaptation to the changing environment?
3. What advantages specific to the family firm could Hugendubel leverage when aiming to ultimately adopt the new technology?

8.2 Longevity of family firms

In his study of family firm succession, Ward (1987) analyzed success rates in intra-family business succession and, hence, the longevity of family firms. He found that 30% of firms survive through the second generation, while 13% survive the third generation and only 3% survive beyond that point. This pessimistic view is captured by the saying 'from shirtsleeves to shirtsleeves in three generations', a saying used in many cultures to describe the decline of family firms in just three generations (Zellweger, Nason and Nordqvist 2012). In general, firms, regardless of type, rarely survive more than one hundred years. An examination of the world's oldest firms (Table 8.1) reveals long-living firms are indeed a rare phenomenon.

Despite the impressive longevity achieved by the firms listed in Table 8.1, only Marinelli is still under the control of the founding family, which raises an important question for family firms: what does it take to achieve family firm longevity, defined as the continuation of a family firm across multiple generations? In an intriguing study of German family-controlled wineries that have been under the control of the same family across 11 generations on average, researchers Peter Jaskiewicz, Jim Combs and Sabine Rau (2015) find that there are three strategic drivers of family firm longevity:

Table 8.1 The oldest companies in the world

Founding year	Name of company	Country of origin	Industry	Still under founding family control	Firm size
705	Nishiyama Onsen Keiunkan	Japan	Hotel	No	Small
717	Koman	Japan	Hotel	No	Small
718	Hoshi Ryokan	Japan	Hotel	No	Small
760	TECH Kaihatsu	Japan	Machinery	No	Small
771	Genda Shigyo	Japan	Paper bags	No	Small
803	Stiftskeller St. Peter	Austria	Restaurant	No	Small
862	Staffelter Hof	Germany	Wine	No	Small
885	Tanaka-Iga	Japan	Religious goods	No	Small
900	Sean's Bar	Ireland	Pub	No	Small
953	The Bingley Arms	UK	Pub	No	Small
970	Nakamura Shaji	Japan	Construction	No	Small
1000	Château de Goulaine	France	Wine	No	Small
1000	Marinelli	Italy	Foundry	Yes	Mid-sized
1000	Ichimonjiya Wasuke	Japan	Confectionery	No	Small

Source: Adapted from Wikipedia.

1. **Strategic education**

   In all the long-living family firms successors pursued studies that were valuable to the family firm. In the winery context, many next-generation family members either graduated from a technical school or from university/college and thus attained a relatively high level of general education. Alternatively, the successors had work experience in the domestic or the international wine industry before joining the family firm.

2. **Entrepreneurial bridging**

   Upon entrance into the family firm, the incumbent mentors the successor, whereby the incumbent keeps the overall responsibility for the firm for some time. During this time, the successor gets resources and the power from the incumbent to start his/her own projects in the firm. Most importantly, the incumbent accepts the changes implemented by the successor. In the case of the wineries this parallel involvement of the senior and junior generation lasted several years (up to three years), during which the junior family members sometimes worked at the firm on a part-time basis. This idea of entrepreneurial bridging reminds us of our discussion of 'How to groom the successor' in Chapter 7 on succession, and the need for parents to create feelings of autonomy, competence and relatedness among the next-generation family members.

3. **Strategic transition**

   The long-lived family firms also had a particular stance toward the treatment of the successor. In particular, the older generation supported the younger generation by integrating potential in-laws into the family (to preserve the successor as resource). For instance, the successor's partner regularly participated in family events. Most importantly, the senior generation also protected the successor from the burden of having to buy out siblings (to preserve capital within the firm).

On sibling buyouts the families who had been in business for a very long time were of the opinion that it is critical that the succession does not create firm or successor indebtedness that cripples future entrepreneurship. The authors go on to write:

> Although several parents expressed concern about the disproportional treatment among children, they did so believing that even those children and grandchildren who received less were better off because they benefit greatly from the social and, if necessary, financial support from being part of an on-going, entrepreneurial, and successful family firm. These parents view the firm's success as essential for carrying on the family's entrepreneurial legacy and as a central source of long-term support for all family members. If they harm the family firm in the name of equal treatment, the long run result might be more harm to more family members. The

firm and its cash flow would disappear as it is divided into ever-smaller portions across generations. Instead family members, along with inheriting a disproportionate share of the wealth, also inherit a social obligation to protect their siblings and their families. (Jaskiewicz, Combs and Rau 2015, p. 44)

Vis-à-vis the other siblings this uneven treatment of the siblings was justified on the grounds that the successor was not really an owner but a caretaker of the firm. In this way, the transfer of full ownership to a single child was legitimized as a 'gift with strings attached', namely, that the successor was not supposed to sell the firm and to harvest the disproportionate value that was given to him or her, and that family firm continuity came with some implicit obligations. One of the successors in the winery study justified his preferred treatment by arguing:

> I inherited the entire winery from my father and thus my siblings had to give up their legitimate portion of the inheritance. Although they did not receive a material value in exchange, they received something else, but it did not equal the true value of their shares. If one proceeded according to the legal code, they could have asked for more. That means that I have a responsibility to maintain an open house for my siblings. It is and remains their childhood home. I am also responsible for maintaining, further developing, and passing on the firm—but I cannot sell it. (Jaskiewicz, Combs and Rau 2015, p. 44)

Strategic transition, so the authors of the study conclude, that does not involve buyouts is critical in order for the successor to pursue entrepreneurial opportunities without worrying about debt or family infighting.

This finding is intriguing for multiple reasons: first, in Germany inheritance law limits the uneven transfer of an estate to offspring. The families controlling these long-lived family firms thus had to craft their own family-internal estate planning regulations, which are in conflict with the official legal code. Apparently, the disfavored siblings were willing to accept such unfavorable treatment to support the family's entrepreneurial tradition. In this case, the siblings typically had to sign a contract of inheritance, whereby we can assume that this was more likely to be feasible in cohesive families.

Such idiosyncratic regulations seem to be needed to keep ownership concentrated, especially in countries with a restrictive and less permissive law of intestacy, such as many civil law countries. In contrast, such family-internal regulations should not be required in countries with a more permissive law of intestacy, with higher levels of testamentary freedom, such as in the United States, United Kingdom and Australia, but also Hong Kong, Israel and

Mexico (for more details on testamentary freedom refer to Chapter 7 on succession). In these civil law countries, keeping ownership concentrated and in consequence preserving an entrepreneurial spirit should thus be easier.

This study on the longevity of family firms in the hands of the same family proposes further factors that imprint an entrepreneurial legacy on the next generation. For instance, it seemed to help for the longevity of the family firms in cases where the families could be proud of the previous generations' entrepreneurial behaviors and achievements and knew how the family and the firm survived past perilous times and calamities. Also, mutual support in the family and hence cohesive families facilitate discussions about who is taking over and under what conditions. This is evidenced by the involvement of family members in each other's lives and frequent interactions among family members. Furthermore, childhood involvement of next-generation family members in the family firm proved to be useful for the long-lasting success of the family firms. For instance, the successors worked or helped out in the firm during holidays (Jaskiewicz, Combs and Rau 2015).

Taking a step back from this discussion it is important to keep in mind that this study was conducted in a rather stable industry, wine-making, which has undergone relatively little change across time, and is very much locally rooted. This context may be particularly well suited for family firms that are passed on from one generation to the next. With this observation in mind, the next section departs from the discussion of the longevity of a family firm and discusses long-term, or more precisely transgenerational, value creation of entrepreneurial families.

8.3 Transgenerational value creation in family firms

Our above discussions and the worldwide data hence suggest that true longevity of family firms is a rare phenomenon. However, there is more to be learnt from these examples: in fact, the long-term survival of a firm is no guarantee for equally impressive value and wealth creation. Most of the firms listed in Table 8.1 are small companies that employ a very limited number of people. For example, the mean number of employees of the wineries analyzed in the study by Jaskiewicz, Combs and Rau (2015) is about eight. In many instances, longevity and firm survival thus mean persistence with a traditional business in which growth opportunities are often limited or even forgone.

8.3.1 Value creation versus longevity

The depressed view of family firms' apparent inability to prosper and create value across generations thus deserves a second look. Most centrally, we must recognize that the 30% survival rate alluded to above is not a reason for despair. Aronoff (2001) shows that the survival rates of (publicly listed) nonfamily firms are no higher. Furthermore, entrepreneurship studies report that only around 50% of all newly founded firms survive beyond the first five years.

Notably, given natural changes in technologies, customer demands and the broader social environment in which a firm is embedded, holding on to a firm at any price may not be the best way forward. In fact, continually attempting to turn around a failing firm may be a sign of irresponsible behavior, not only for the owners themselves, but also for other stakeholders. In this regard, we highlight the relentless process of creative destruction described by Schumpeter (1934) through which new organizations emerge. New entrants into an industry first weaken and then destroy the incumbent firms. As such, giving up, exiting and selling out may be the opposites of failure, but they represent key strategies for embracing the future of a firm that will inevitably fail. Therefore, they serve as important methods of protecting wealth.

Notably, some of the most successful entrepreneurs and (family) business owners chose to exit their original firms at some point in time. This deliberate exit choice cannot be put on an equal footing with a case in which owners come to realize that they are on a sinking ship from which they have to disembark. Rather, such exits can come in the form of an attractive opportunity to step aside, sell and harvest the value that has been created over time. For instance, a (partial) sale of the firm or a stock market listing implies that the family loses full control over ownership and management. Nevertheless, the family may be able to maintain some influence on the firm, perhaps via a minority stake or seats on the board. In any case, such exits cannot be equated with failure. They create significant value for the former owners and generate new growth opportunities for the firm under the control of new owners, who may be better equipped to bring the firm to the next level.

In brief, exiting and thereby limiting the longevity of a venture in the hands of the family may be the opposite of failure but is a relevant strategy for either (1) avoiding an unprofitable future for the firm and the owner, or (2) seizing an attractive opportunity to create value for all of the firm's stakeholders. Conversely, seeking longevity for a firm can mean forgoing value creation and, in extreme cases, can result in value destruction on a massive scale.

8.3.2   Some evidence on transgenerational value creation

A first descriptive study of the transgenerational value creation phenomenon offered impressive evidence to support the above arguments, especially with regard to the need for change and rejuvenation in a family's business activities (as evidenced, for instance, by a change in industry focus across time), the parallel control of multiple companies, and the role of exit and entry for transgenerational value creation (see Zellweger, Nason and Nordqvist 2012 for additional details).

In that study, which we conducted mainly in the United States, we interrogated a number of wealthy families that had been in business for 60 years on average and had created businesses with a current combined sales volume of $174 million on average. We thus considered these families to be good exemplars of transgenerational entrepreneurship. When taking a closer look at how this wealth was created, some interesting patterns emerged.

First of all, this current sales volume was not tied to a single firm, but on average split between three firms under the control of the same family. On average, each family controlled not just one but 3.4 firms, and total sales volume of a family's businesses was split 74%/18%/8% (on average) among the three largest companies in the family's portfolio. Also, we found that each family has divested 1.5 firms since the inception of the family's entrepreneurial activities. In addition, these families have controlled 6.1 companies across their lifespans, which implies that there have been an average of 2.7 (= 6.1 − 3.4) 'failures' per family if we consider closure or divestment as a failure.

We cannot be absolutely sure that such evidence really discriminates between families who have been successful in creating massive value across generations and families who have failed in this dimension—there may indeed be a survivor bias in the analysis. However, numerous observations, including the case studies discussed later, seem to support the conclusion that transgenerational value creation requires continuous change, alterations and, in particular, exit from business activity.

8.3.3   Transgenerational value creation defined

Thus far, we have learned that transgenerational value creation is not necessarily concerned with avoiding the 'shirtsleeves to shirtsleeves' paradigm, as represented by the downward arrow in Figure 8.3. Moreover, this perspective does not ask how to perpetuate an existing business and,

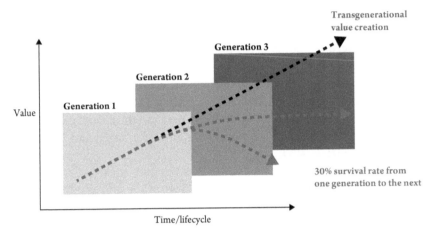

Source: Adapted from Tim Habbershon's early work on transgenerational entrepreneurship.

Figure 8.3 From longevity of firm to transgenerational value creation

consequently, forgo growth opportunities, as represented by the horizontal arrow in Figure 8.3. Rather, it focuses on how a family can generate value across generations by controlling businesses, as represented by the upwards arrow in Figure 8.3.

As an extension to the concept of transgenerational entrepreneurship (see Nordqvist and Zellweger 2010 for more details), we can define 'transgenerational value creation' as follows:

> Transgenerational value creation captures the processes, structures and resources through which a family creates economic and social value across generations.

8.3.4 Transgenerational value creation: a model

In light of the above discussion, we can take a closer look at the components of transgenerational value creation and explore what it takes to create value across generations. This perspective departs in multiple ways from the traditional longevity perspective and related concerns about the stability of the firm, family-internal succession and value preservation (Zellweger, Nason and Nordqvist 2012). The central building blocks of transgenerational value creation are depicted in Figure 8.4.

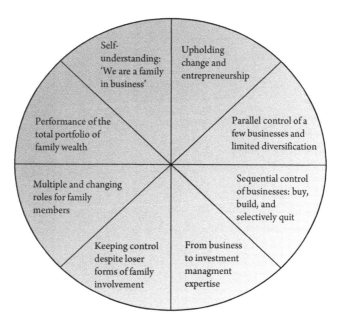

Figure 8.4 Elements of transgenerational value creation

8.3.4.1 *Upholding change and entrepreneurship*

The traditional longevity perspective emphasizes the persistence of the firm, ideally within the original business activity. Firms seeking longevity expend a significant amount of energy on continuously improving existing technologies and production processes in an exploitative manner. In contrast, the transgenerational value creation perspective focuses on change and entrepreneurship. This perspective thus values exploration in which the resulting change and new ventures take place within the existing firm or in a new firm. For families in the pursuit of transgenerational value creation it is thus important to keep in mind that each generation thus is the first generation—each generation has to reengage in entrepreneurship, and thus innovate and take risks.

From studies about corporate entrepreneurship, such as Lumpkin and Dess (1996), we know that the critical features of an entrepreneurial company include decision-making autonomy (at the top and at lower hierarchical levels), innovation, proactiveness and risk taking. Scholars and practitioners alike assume a positive link between entrepreneurship and performance. On the basis of the centrality of change and entrepreneurship for transgenerational value creation, we have developed a tool for analyzing a company's level of entrepreneurship (Table 8.2).

Table 8.2 Entrepreneurship self-assessment

Entrepreneurship dimension	low	medium	high	Commentary
Autonomy Freedom of individuals inside a firm to be creative, to push for ideas and to change ways of doing things				Satisfaction with current level: Obstacles against further increase:
Innovativeness Tendency to engage in and support new ideas, experimentation and creative processes that may result in new products, services or technological processes				Satisfaction with current level: Obstacles against further increase:
Proactiveness Taking strategic initiatives by anticipating and pursuing new opportunities; acting in anticipation of future problems				Satisfaction with current level: Obstacles against further increase:
Risk tasking The degree to which managers are willing to make resource commitments that have a reasonable chance of failing				Satisfaction with current level: Obstacles against further increase:

? REFLECTION QUESTIONS

Barriers to entrepreneurship

1. To what degree does the desire to retain transgenerational control in family hands hamper entrepreneurship? In what ways does it do so?
2. To what degree do reputational concerns related to the family and firm hamper entrepreneurship? In what ways do they do so?
3. To what degree does the wish to uphold personal ties in the family and firm hamper entrepreneurship? In what ways does it do so?

Excursus: Fortune and misfortune of Dynasties

In his 2008 book entitled *Dynasties: Fortune and Misfortune in the World's Great Family Businesses*, David Landes, a professor of business history at Harvard University, discusses the rise and fall of dynasties in business. His historic account shows that it is not so much lack of managerial skill, but rather disinterest in the business among next-generation family members who pursue careers and lavish lifestyles outside the family business that leads to the demise of many dynasties in business. David Landes argues that 'there lay the path of social promotion and commercial demotion in a society that confused rank with merit and sacrificed achievement to eminence'. Indeed, many later generation family firms, ironically the particularly successful ones, progressively tended to see the industrial world and the world of business as 'a crude, second-class activity, beneath the dignity of the aristocracy' into which the successful families progressively moved given their capital and power.

Exploring the fate of dynasties such as the Barings, Rothschilds, Morgans, Fords and Agnellis he finds that each dynasty

> exerted remarkable financial and social power for some generations, and then ultimately suffocated on its own success, as the few offspring who might have proved worthy successors were drawn off to more appealing pursuits made possible by their wealth and station. This is a model that is repeated time and time again throughout the history of family dynasties, and it is one we will encounter in other parts of this study. The issue of continuity is a constant problem for family firms. Failure will, of course, kill the business. But so will success, with all the diversions and temptations of fortune.

Landes finds that the disinterest in the business, the pursuit of more 'noble' activities among later generation family members, is not only the result of personal vanity, but also of the societal attitudes toward money and industry. The trend to flee industrial activity and to spend money and time on political careers, cultural endeavors and the ascent into nobility (in particular, in England, France and Germany) reflects the attempt to shed the image of being a snob, a parvenu, and to definitely enter the local establishment and elite.

8.3.4.2 *Parallel control of several businesses and limited diversification*

Transgenerational value creation captures the family's complete portfolio of business activities and, more broadly, all of the family's assets. It does not limit the focus to a single company (the 'family firm'). Families that create value across generations often control multiple firms *in parallel*. Therefore, they control a portfolio of businesses and, often, other assets, such as real estate and liquid wealth. This important point implies that we cannot necessarily equate the decline of a single company with the decline of the family's overall economic fate. Assets can be transferred and redeployed across the portfolio to fuel growth and mitigate portfolio risk. Even though there may be a focal firm inside the portfolio—often the largest, most visible firm and the one that is central to the family's history—it may not be the most profitable or the most dynamic company in the family's portfolio. Future growth and value can originate from more ancillary investments in the family's portfolio.

Section 8.3.2 documented the importance of parallel control of businesses for transgenerational value creation among companies in the United States. However, this is by no means a phenomenon solely seen in the United States. For instance, in Southeast Asia, families controlling a publicly listed company often do not own just that one firm—on average, they control 1.58 publicly listed companies (Carney and Child 2013). Similar evidence is also available for Europe. For example, the Wallenberg family controls more than 20 firms in Sweden.

Families that engage in transgenerational value creation have to decide whether to concentrate or diversify their wealth. In other words, they must consider whether they should put their assets into a single business or multiple businesses. A priori, predicting whether the concentration or diversification of business activities will lead to higher financial returns and create more value is difficult. Diversification reduces fluctuations in the value of the portfolio and putting wealth into multiple baskets limits the damage if businesses fail. However, diversification can also be detrimental for performance, as a diversified portfolio is harder to control and, therefore, makes governance more expensive. Moreover, diversification limits opportunities for synergies and learning across the unrelated activities, which hampers growth. In addition, diversification is unattractive from a socioemotional standpoint, as it requires opening control up to nonfamily experts and eventually nonfamily owners, leads away from the original business focus and dilutes a family firm's otherwise consistent image and reputation.

In practice, families pursuing transgenerational value creation resolve the dilemma of whether to diversify or focus by opting for a relatively concentrated wealth position (Gomez-Mejia, Makri and Kintana 2010). Even though families may hold multiple ventures, the largest portion of their wealth is typically tied to a single investment. For instance, among the US families mentioned above, an average of 70% of total sales in each family's portfolio was tied to a single firm.[2] A similar trend is evident among wealthy German families in business (Zellweger and Kammerlander 2014). Even though wealthy German families may control a large number of companies (75 companies on average, most of which are holding companies, investment vehicles, family offices and similar organizations), two-thirds of total controlled assets and 45% of total sales volume are tied up in a single investment, on average.

When pursuing a limited level of diversification, families sometimes seek to diversify the firm itself. In this case, the main firm engages in unrelated businesses and operates as a type of diversified conglomerate. As an example, consider Henkel, a German publicly listed family firm. At one point, Henkel's family shareholders decided to be active in three businesses held under the same roof: laundry and homecare, beauty care, and adhesive technologies. These businesses offer only limited synergies, but they have different risk profiles and follow different industry cycles, which reduces the overall portfolio risk for the family.

Alternatively, a family may decide to invest in multiple independent businesses in unrelated industries. In such situations, the diversification occurs at the level of family wealth and, hence, outside the main business, which allows each business to focus on its strengths. Such families may set up investment offices or holding companies to undertake direct investments in other, often unrelated fields. For instance, the Wallenberg family in Sweden controls more than 20 investments in a wide range of industries through Investor, a publicly listed holding company, which is controlled by the Wallenberg foundation (for additional information on how the Wallenbergs pursue transgenerational value creation, refer to the case study found in this chapter). The Kristiansen family in Denmark follows a similar approach. It established a holding company that controls Lego and several other investments.

Given the above, we find that many families that have been able to create value across generations typically hold more than a single business. At the same time, they do not generally hold a widely diversified portfolio of assets.[3] Rather, these families control a limited number of businesses in parallel. In other words, these families put most of their eggs in very few baskets and then watch those baskets very carefully.

8.3.4.3 *Sequential control of businesses: buy, build and selectively quit*

Ward's (1987) important analysis of the longevity of family firms finds that only 13% of the firms studied remained intact and under family control through the third generation. This statistic is the basis for the argument that only 30% of family firms remain family firms from one generation to a next. However, this study overlooked the fact that a total of 20% (rather than 13%) of the firms survived, but some were no longer held by the original family owners after three generations. Some (5%) were sold to outsiders, while others (2%) went public. From a transgenerational value creation perspective, these 7% cannot be viewed as failures for two reasons. First, the family may retain control of a firm that goes public through voting rights or other control mechanisms. In fact, 35% of publicly traded Fortune 500 companies remain family controlled (Anderson and Reeb 2003b). Second, and more importantly, a strategic move to exit a business may greatly increase family wealth and resources, which can then be redeployed in a new venture.

Of course, transgenerational value creation may be achieved by starting new ventures inside the focal family firm itself. However, an exit and corresponding redeployment of assets in a new business may be an attractive strategy when the company is declining or an attractive exit opportunity presents itself. The exit and the entry into a new business can take place sequentially, with assets being gradually transferred from one business to the next business. Alternatively, these steps can be achieved through a complete sale followed by the acquisition of another firm. In sum, families that generate value across generations *sequentially* engage in business investments, such that they enter and exit business activities with the intent to generate value across time and generations.

Therefore, families pursuing transgenerational value creation need to pay attention to the resource flows between the family and the firm. For instance, a firm may benefit from the financial resources provided by the family or the social capital that is available to the company through the family's network. Conversely, the family may benefit from the company's financial success, or it may be able to extend its network thanks to contacts established by the firm. In other words, some of the resources available to the firm are provided by the family and vice versa (Nordqvist and Zellweger 2010). In this trans-level perspective, family and firm serve as both suppliers and recipients of resources.

This mutual resource exchange is particularly important from a transgenerational perspective because the types of resources, as well as the amount and direction of resource flows between family and firm, change over time. In the founding stage, many firms benefit from family involvement to a certain degree, and resources flow from family to firm. Family members are often the only investors to finance and provide cheap labor for a newly established firm. However, as the firm succeeds over time, the family starts to benefit from the resources generated by the firm in the form of dividends, social capital and reputation. Consequently, the resource flow shifts direction over a company's lifecycle and the types of resources exchanged can change.

For the family, the crucial question for transgenerational value creation is whether resources mainly flow from the business to the family or from the family to the business. In other words, does the firm exist for the family or does the family live for the firm? This question is best answered from a dynamic point of view. When the business is young or in a turnaround phase and therefore has some growth potential, the family ideally helps the firm by injecting the required resources. In contrast, a business that is operating in a saturated or declining market mainly serves as a resource provider for the family. In that situation, the family harvests the resources in order to redeploy them in another venture.

Most importantly, transgenerational value creation implies that families are willing to *reinvest* the resources they have generated into another business activity. Too many families are satisfied with seeing wealth creation as a one-way street, such that the business is viewed as existing for the family and not vice versa. Truly great families in business are willing to launch new entrepreneurial activities either inside the main business or outside—they maintain their entrepreneurial spirit and their willingness to take risks over generations.

As alluded to above, this implies that families in business are willing to keep the funds that are generated in the business together in, for instance, a family holding company. While the controlled companies may pay healthy dividends, the family does not pay out all of the dividend income to the individual shareholders. Instead, at least some of the funds are kept together with the aim of reallocating them to a new promising business.

CASE STUDY

Transgenerational value creation at Gallus Group

Gallus and Heidelberg work closer together

Gallus and Heidelberg work closer together: focus on the accelerated development of a digital label printing press in cooperation with Heidelberger Druckmaschinen AG, Ferdinand Ruesch brings in his 70% Gallus shares and will become thereby an anchor shareholder of Heidelberger Druckmaschinen AG.

Ferd. Ruesch AG, a Swiss company controlled by Ferdinand Ruesch, will contribute its 70% stake in Gallus Holding AG as contribution in kind into Heidelberger Druckmaschinen AG—against the issue of new Heidelberg shares. After the transaction Heidelberger Druckmaschinen AG will hold directly and indirectly 100% of the Gallus Holding AG shares. Ferdinand Ruesch will thereby hold approx. 9% of the shares of Heidelberger

CASE STUDY *(continued)*

Druckmaschinen AG and become an anchor shareholder. Already since 1999 Heidelberger Druckmaschinen AG held 30% of Gallus Holding AG and both companies cooperated closely in technology and sales.

The planned complete takeover of Gallus Holding AG accelerates the development and use of Heidelberg's digital products in the growing labels sector. In September of this year, Heidelberg and Gallus will be unveiling at the Gallus Innovation Days a new digital printing system for the label market that incorporates Fujifilm technology. Gallus will continue to operate under its brand name and under its current management. Gallus will continue to focus on development, production and sales/service of narrow reel-fed printing presses targeted for the label printer as well as on wide reel-fed printing presses and die-cutting machines for folding carton converters.

Background information about Gallus Group

The Gallus Group is the world market leader in the development, production and sale of narrow-web, reel-fed presses designed for label manufacturers. Its folding carton business offers a range of presses and die-cutters for the cost-effective in-line production of folding cartons and cardboard products. The machine portfolio is augmented by a broad range of screen printing plates (Gallus Screeny), globally decentralized service operations, and a broad offering of printing accessories and replacement parts. The comprehensive portfolio also includes consulting services provided by label experts in all relevant printing and process engineering tasks. Gallus employs around 560 people, of whom 260 are based in Switzerland.

 REFLECTION QUESTIONS

1. How do you assess the sale of Gallus Holding AG from: (a) a succession perspective and (b) a transgenerational value creation perspective?
2. Would you consider the sale of Gallus Holding AG to Heidelberg to be a failure? Why or why not?
3. How can Ferdinand Ruesch ensure transgenerational value creation given the new stake in Heidelberg?

Source: Press release from the Gallus Group, June 10, 2014.

The above investment behavior may be best described as a process of 'buying, building and selectively quitting' businesses. In the founding phase, we find the well-known image of a founding entrepreneur who establishes an owner-managed company. This constellation sometimes continues beyond the founding generation. However, in most cases, families move through a three-step investment cycle:

1. **Buy**: The family purchases a stake in an established company with growth potential. Note that the core investments of these families are not in startup companies.
2. **Build**: The stake in that company is developed through, for instance, acquisitions of complementary businesses, spin-offs and mergers over several years and sometimes over generations.
3. **Selectively quit**: The family partially or completely exits the investment by actively creating exit opportunities through, for example, the entry of other investors or an initial public offering (IPO).

The individual investments held by the family run through these three steps, regardless of whether those investments are held inside the main business or in an investment company. Step 2, the building phase during which the respective businesses are patiently developed and nurtured, can take many years and even multiple generations. For instance, the family may increase its stake in a business that is flourishing, acquire complementary activities, spin-off incompatible activities or merge the business with another firm in order to increase market share. All of these measures aim to create value in the long run.

The third step in the 'buy, build and selectively quit' investment cycle, in which families actively create exit opportunities, is of particular importance and somewhat unexpected for family firms. Instead of eternally holding on to their businesses, families actively seek ways to bring in outside investors who are willing to progressively support the firm's growth. For instance, a partial sale of a company, or a stock market listing and gradual reduction of the family's share in the firm, enables the family to harness the value it has created.

In the philosophy of reinvestment and continued entrepreneurship described in the sections on the components of transgenerational value creation, the investment cycle of 'buying, building and selectively exiting' does not end with step 3. Instead, the families redeploy the funds generated in steps 2 and 3 so as to restart the value creation engine through a new business opportunity. This three-stage investment process is depicted in Figure 8.5.

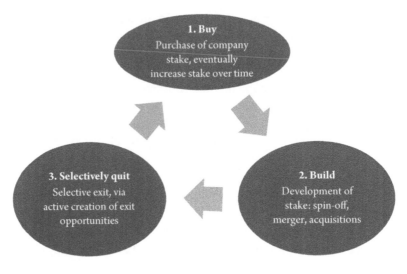

Source: Zellweger and Kammerlander (2014).

Figure 8.5 Buy, build and selectively quit

CASE STUDY

The Quandts of Germany—Transgenerational value creation since 1883

The Quandt family is one of the most illustrious families in business in central Europe. Based in Germany, the family is known for its controlling stake in BMW. However, a close look at the emergence of this family's fortune, which was estimated at roughly €20 billion in 2013, reveals massive adaptations and sequential control of various businesses across the family's history, which spans more than a century.

The family's involvement in business started when Emil Quandt purchased a textile firm in 1883. The business activities grew with the acquisitions of chemical and industrial companies, selective mergers, the acquisition and resale of a stake in Mercedes, the acquisition of a stake in BMW, and developments and exits from several other business activities. The sequential control of businesses and the 'buy, build and selectively quit' investment process are illustrated through the family's business-involvement timeline, which starts with the initial investments in 1883 and goes through to 2013 (Figure 8.6).

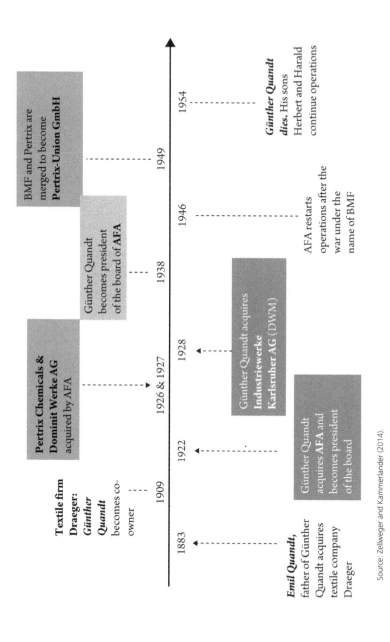

Source: Zellweger and Kammerlander (2014).

Figure 8.6 Quandt family's business-involvement timeline

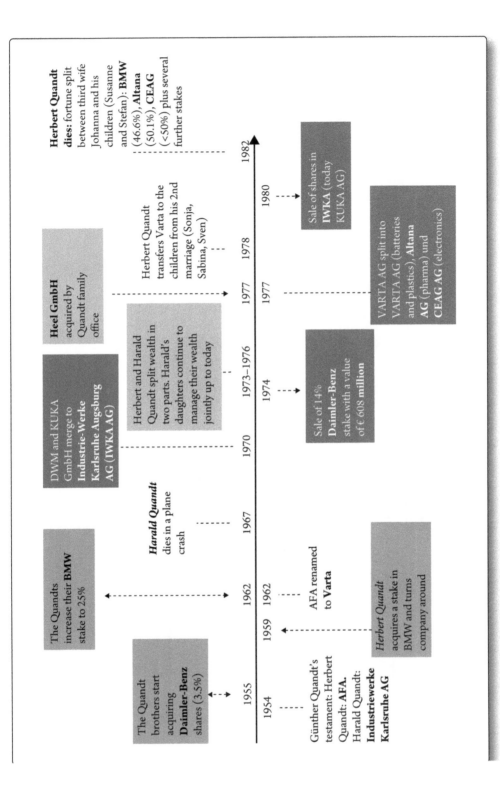

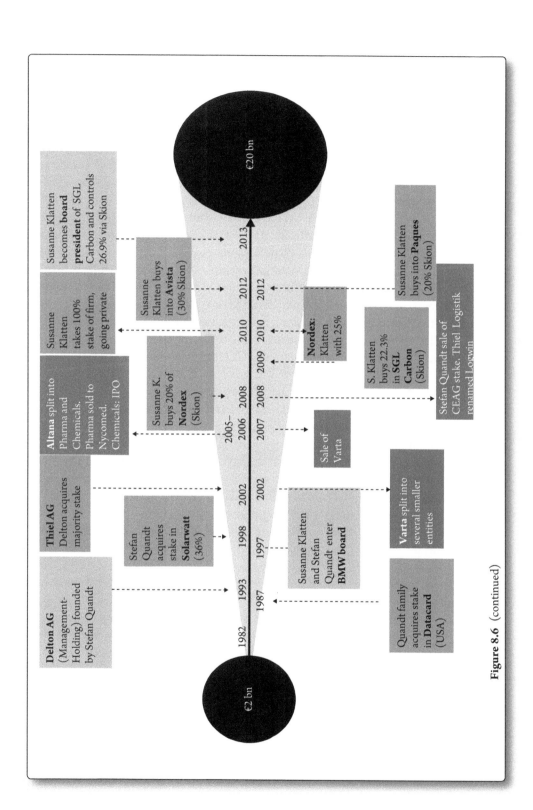

Figure 8.6 (continued)

8.3.4.4 *From business management to investment management expertise*

From the longitudinal point of view that underlies the transgenerational perspective, we have to ask whether the resources and capabilities needed to ensure an established firm's existence are equally valuable for managing a changing and somewhat diverse portfolio of business activities. For the creation and persistence of a firm, industry-specific knowledge is key, as it encompasses knowledge about production and processes, and more general knowledge about what it takes to successfully run that type of company in the focal industry. However, given ongoing and sometimes disruptive changes in technology, client demands and institutions, this knowledge may become obsolete, such that it even restricts value creation. The unlearning of skills is important for sustained success because experienced individuals rely on heuristics and mental shortcuts, which leave them more likely to fall prey to mental ruts (Shepherd, Zacharakis and Baron 2003). These dangers become particularly pressing in dynamic contexts. In addition, a need to unlearn old skills and learn new ones arises for firms with a long-term focus because, over time, the probability of encountering a change that requires adaptation rises.

Context- and industry-specific knowledge is likely to be particularly problematic for the successful administration of a dynamic portfolio of businesses. The management of such assets requires 'meta-industry expertise'. Meta-industry expertise includes generic knowledge about business management, such as knowledge of strategic planning, portfolio management, investment and risk analysis, mergers and acquisitions, accounting, and motivating management. More broadly speaking, it also requires knowledge about corporate-level strategy making and governance. Therefore, while firm- and industry-specific resources become obsolete and often even restraining over time, other resources, such as meta-industry expertise, gain relevance.

In an analysis of business families from Ireland, Chile, Guatemala and France that have been able to create significant value across multiple generations, Sieger et al. (2011) find that meta-industry networks, and the reputation of the family and the firm become increasingly relevant over time. For instance, with the continuing success of their operations, families become reputable and well-connected beyond their industries' boundaries, which results in a steady flow of business opportunities.[4] The shifting relevance of resources across time and generations is depicted in Figure 8.7.

This shift from running a particular business to overseeing a portfolio of investments is far from easy. In many family firms, the buildup of invest-

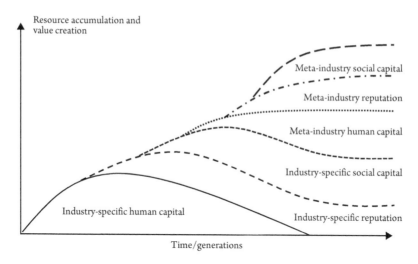

Source: Adapted from Sieger et al. (2011).

Figure 8.7 Changing relevance of resources for transgenerational value creation

ment management activities happens gradually over a number of years, in line with the continued success of the main business. This gives families the time needed to develop the necessary structures and competencies.

The switch from entrepreneurship to investment management is much harder to handle when roles change quickly, such as when a family sells all of its business activities in a single transaction. In such cases, the former entrepreneur or entrepreneurial family trades its business activities for a pile of cash. Typically, the entrepreneurs and families going through such a liquidity event underestimate the challenges tied to their new investor role. As described in Table 8.3, the challenges pertain to a wide range of domains, such as the social roles of those involved, the liquidity and diversification of wealth, the required expertise, the regulatory context, career opportunities for the next generation and governance.

8.3.4.5 *Maintaining control despite looser forms of family involvement*

The ownership of multiple businesses represents a significant challenge with regard to monitoring and maintaining control. The operations of a large, somewhat diversified group of companies are difficult for a single family to handle on its own, as the activities may be too complex and too vast. Therefore, nonfamily expertise is a critical ingredient for transgenerational value creation. Families pursuing transgenerational value creation understand

Table 8.3 Differences between business management and investment management

	Business management (Before liquidity accumulation and event)	Investment management (After liquidity accumulation and event)
Social role	Entrepreneur	Investor
Liquidity of wealth	Mostly illiquid	Mostly liquid
Asset class	Mainly equity, own firm	Diversification across assets
Diversification	Low	High
Risk–return profile	High	Low to moderate
Risk aversion	Limited: 'Much to gain' attitude	High: 'Much to lose' attitude
Identification with asset	Very high in most cases	Lower and decreasing over time
Emotional value	High	Lower
Required expertise	Business management	Asset management
Compensation	Salary, dividend, private benefits of control	Total return
Regulatory context	Private and corporate law	Bank law, financial market regulations, tax law
Career opportunities for next generation	Available	Very limited
Governance	Corporate governance	Wealth and family governance

that they have to open up and accept looser forms of family control in, for example, their management teams, boards and ownership.

However, ownership of a business with the intent to create value brings with it the responsibility of oversight and control of activities for the benefit of the family. In the absence of control and accountability, entrepreneurial efforts lack focus and fail to have their full effect. Financial investments may fuel stagnation and inertia instead of innovation and growth. Given their economic and socioemotional incentives, families have good reason to ensure the efficient and far-sighted management of their business(es). This equips the family with the motivation to control and monitor the owned assets.

Unfortunately, too many families believe that the delegation of board and management functions to hired experts is enough. This view tends to be naïve in many instances. When solely deferring to hired experts, families delegate control and, consequently, risk losing control. Outsiders tend to have less to lose should the operations fail and, therefore, have less incentive to ensure the efficient deployment of company resources. However, in light of the larger talent pool outside the family, nonfamily members should be able to contribute critical knowledge that is otherwise lacking. Hence, while outsiders may not be the best watchdogs, they may be indispensable as managers and advisors.

Efficient corporate governance for transgenerational value creation thus combines family involvement in monitoring and control with nonfamily involvement in management and advisory roles. While family involvement in governance remains necessary at all times, nonfamily experts should enter and exit board and management roles depending on the required expertise. Therefore, corporate governance for transgenerational value creation means delegation of control without a loss of control.

8.3.4.6 *Multiple and changing roles for family members*

The preferred succession path within the traditional longevity view of family firms is that next-generation family members take over the top management functions, especially the CEO position, from the preceding generation. In contrast, from the transgenerational value creation perspective, a successful family-internal succession involves assigning more than the top management positions to next-generation family members. Active owner, board member, family officer, and manager are all possible roles for next-generation family members. As such, transgenerational value creation creates various succession options for members of the next generation.

Given our considerations on family firm governance (see Chapter 5 on governance for more details), family members may be considered for various jobs. Family members have various roles to play depending on what is expected in terms of family, corporate, ownership and wealth governance. With regard to the firm's operations, such roles could be regular employee, top management team member or CEO. At the board level, family members can be involved as board members or as president of the board. At the ownership level, family members can be passive owners or serve as the representative of the family's shareholder pool. At the family level, some family members may serve on the family council, while others might coordinate the family's social or philanthropic activities. At the family wealth level, family members may take on some role related to the administration of family wealth.

Moreover, family members' jobs might not be fixed. Family members may be elected for a certain period of time, after which they rotate into a new role.

8.3.4.7 Focus on the overall performance of family wealth

The transgenerational value creation perspective is distinct from the traditional family business perspective because it shifts the level of analysis from the firm to the family as the driver of value creation. Therefore, the family's ability to initiate, administer and harvest value is central, rather than the firm's performance or longevity. Whereas we have traditionally viewed the firm as the engine behind growth (i.e., the performance of the family firm), the ultimate measure of success from a transgenerational value creation perspective is the degree to which a family is able to generate value.

Accordingly, it is insufficient to use firm-level outcomes, such as survival, independence, size or performance, to measure the success of a family's value creation abilities. Families focus on the overall performance of family wealth, as depicted, for instance, in Table 8.4. The reporting tool used in Table 8.4 summarizes the performance of one family's total portfolio of assets, which consists of three business operations, three office buildings and liquid wealth.

8.3.4.8 Renewed identification: we are a 'family in business'

The shift in focus from the firm to the family as the central actor in value creation requires the family to develop a new self-understanding. Families that wish to create value in a dynamic business environment over the long run must progressively adapt their self-understanding. In moving toward a role that resembles the one of an investor who enters and exits businesses, families will struggle, as they tend to see themselves as nurturers of a family firm with a traditional core activity that goes back to the founders. Eventually, the family will find it challenging to identify 'the family business'. The family will need to perceive itself as a group of individuals active in the administration of businesses, a view that will allow it to move progressively from a 'family business' to a 'business family' self-understanding. In the traditional longevity perspective, the family defines itself using statements like 'We control a family business' or 'We own company XYZ'. In contrast, in the transgenerational value creation perspective, the family defines itself using statements along the lines of 'We are a business family', meaning that the family is active in the administration and development of businesses.

Identification with the family's business activities will become a growing concern across generations and as the focus of the business changes. It will gradually become harder to identify with the family's business. This is even more relevant when the current business activities are unrelated to the original activity and when the portfolio of activities is diversified.

Table 8.4 Overview of total family wealth—an example

Business operations

	Business 1	Business 2	Business 3	Total
Sales	10 500	20 000	25 000	55 500
EBITDA	2 000	1 300	8 000	11 300
EBIT	1 500	500	5 000	7 000
Profit	1 200	400	4 000	5 600
Cash	500	2 000	2 000	4 500
Net working capital	200	1 200	1 500	2 900
Order entry	5 000	8 000	15 000	28 000
Inventory	1 000	2 000	780	3 780
ROE	8%	4%	15%	
ROS	3%	2%	6%	
Leverage	1	1.5	1.2	

Planning and reporting for business operations
Monthly reporting of profit and loss statement
Monthly reporting of cash flow statement
Monthly short commentary of individual companies on: sales, marketing, competition, finance
   & controlling, human resource, production

Real estate

	Location 1	Location 2	Location 3	Total
Income from rent	350	800	1 200	2 350
Maintenance	100	200	100	400
Interest expenses	100	240	450	790
Profit	150	360	650	1 160
Mortgage remaining	2 000	4 000	10 000	16 000
Interest rate on mortgage	5%	6%	4.50%	
Estimated fair value	5 000	10 000	15 000	30 000
Return	3.0%	3.6%	4.3%	

Planning and reporting for real estate
Monthly reporting of profit and loss statement

Liquid wealth

Cash	5 000
Shares publicly listed companies	2 500
Investment funds	4 000
Bonds	6 000
Venture capital funds	2 000
Total	19 500

Planning and reporting for liquid wealth
Monthly reporting of balances

Therefore, any attempt to create value across generations will have to address the threats of fragmentation, defamiliarization, and dilution of ownership and wealth. This is particularly true for families that shift their focal area from serving as 'entrepreneurs' to 'investors', as such shifts tend to lower the level of identification. For such families, therefore, it is paramount to continually renew identification and ensure family cohesion.

CASE STUDY

Transgenerational value creation in the Quandt family, main shareholders of BMW

Germany's Quandt family has been in business since 1883. The first firm the family owned was in the textile industry, but the family moved into the chemical, electrical and automotive industries over the years. Interestingly, during the second half of the twentieth century, the family was an important shareholder in Daimler-Benz, one of BMW's main competitors. In 2013, the family's wealth was primarily invested in BMW, the famous German automaker, in which it had a total stake of about 46.6%.

The current generation includes a group of around 20 family shareholders with assets in various industries. The family tree is grouped into four main branches and each branch controls significant wealth. The branch of Johanna Quandt, a third-generation family member, has probably been the most successful in terms of creating value across time. In 2013, this branch's wealth amounted to about €30 billion, which was mainly in the hands of three family members: Johanna Quandt and her two children, Stefan Quandt and Susanne Klatten.

The portfolio held by this branch of the family includes much more than BMW. Stefan Quandt, either directly or through his investment business Delton, controls several other companies. These companies are active in such areas as pharmaceuticals (Heel), logistics (Logwin) and digital security (Gemalto, Datacard). Stefan Quandt holds some of these investments together with his sister Susanne (e.g., Gemalto, Datacard). In turn, Susanne Klatten holds stakes in wind energy (Nordex), carbon fiber production (SGL Carbon) and specialty chemicals (Altana) either directly or through her investment business, Skion. The details of these main investments are displayed in the following figure (Figure 8.8).

Even though the family has stakes in multiple businesses (and the family has other investments that are relatively minor in value), its wealth is rather undiversified. An estimated 83% of the Johanna Quandt family branch's total wealth is tied to the BMW stake.

Given this wealth exposure, the fact that the family wishes to exercise rigorous influence over BMW through active involvement in its corporate governance is not surprising. Upon their mother's retirement from BMW's board, Stefan Quandt and Susanne Klatten both joined the board. Stefan serves as vice-president of the board and is a member of all of the board's subcommittees, including the presidential committee (preparing board meetings),

CASE STUDY *(continued)*

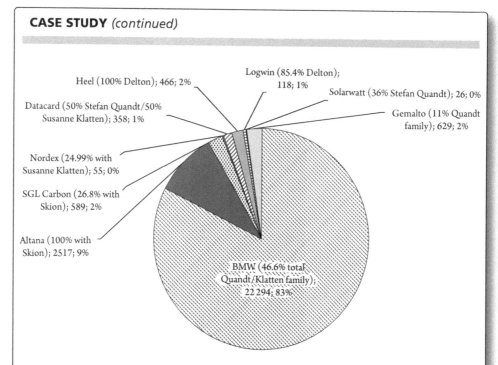

Notes: Name of business, ownership share held by the Johanna Quandt family branch, equity value in millions, fraction of total wealth of Johanna Quandt family branch (as of 2013).

Figure 8.8 Investments of the Johanna Quandt family branch

personnel committee (preparing appointments and revocation of appointments of members of the management board, compensation, and review of the management board's compensation system), audit committee (supervision of the financial reporting process, effectiveness of the internal control system, risk management system, internal audit arrangements and compliance) and the nomination committee (identification of suitable candidates for the board). Susanne also sits on the nomination committee.

In the other investments, at least one of the two siblings is involved on the board. However, the family is not involved in the operational management of the portfolio companies.

? REFLECTION QUESTIONS

1. How would you assess the diversification of the family's wealth?
2. How would you assess the Quandt family's ability to control its wealth?
3. Which features of transgenerational value creation do you recognize in this case?

Source: Adapted from Zellweger and Kammerlander (2014); thank you also to Maximilian Groh for helping with the data collection and analysis.

8.3.5 Transgenerational value creation from a dynamic point of view

In the previous section, we outlined the central building blocks of transgenerational value creation but paid relatively little attention to the process along which families should operate. More specifically, we have yet to investigate the steps families take to achieve transgenerational value creation.

Therefore, in the following, we develop a process model of transgenerational value creation (Figure 8.9). This process model consists of two reinforcing and intertwined management spheres: business management and investment management. It describes the phases that families typically pass through while managing corporate assets (businesses) on the one hand and managing non-corporate assets on the other.

The business management sphere
Sequential steps pursued by the family on the side of controlled businesses:

1. The establishment of a new company by a founder entrepreneur represents the first step toward value creation.

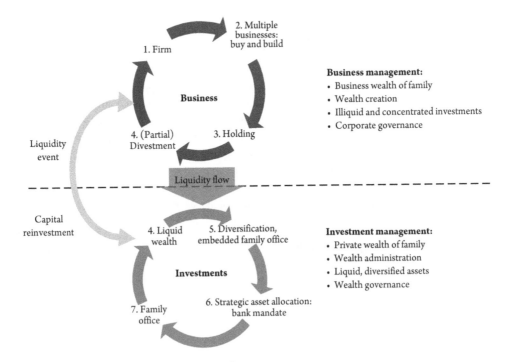

Figure 8.9 Business and investment management

2. Initial success with the original business sparks growth beyond the core activity, often via diversification through the establishment or acquisition of additional businesses over time.

3. Over the years, these businesses reach a respectable size through organic growth, acquisitions, mergers and strategic rearrangements. The resulting complexity requires the establishment of a distinct organization, such as a holding company, to handle the integration of all of the business activities. This organization centralizes a limited number of corporate functions, including strategic planning, finance and accounting.

4. Over time, some of the businesses become less attractive. Growth may stall and some businesses may experience losses as product and industry cycles expire. Consequently, some of the businesses are closed, opened up to outside investors, listed on the stock market or divested. The family thus creates exit opportunities that enable it to harvest the value it has created over the years. It then continues with a revitalized set of activities.

The upper part of Figure 8.9 illustrates these four wealth creation steps within the business management sphere. Not all firms make it through this cycle of value creation—some cease to exist along the way. There are also variations in the speed with which firms advance through the cycle, such that some complete the cycle within a few years, while others take several generations.

The investment management sphere

Firms that manage to successfully move through the business cycle progressively generate wealth for their family owners through salaries, dividends, private benefits of control and, in particular, the proceeds from liquidity-related events (e.g., partial divestments or stock market listings). This progressive accumulation of wealth over time renders management of the family's private wealth increasingly important (see the lower part of Figure 8.9). Such investment management activities typically develop as follows:

1. At the outset, the wealth generated in the business sphere is typically held inside the firm. By the end of the owner-manager stage, the business assets are basically equal to the entrepreneur's private assets.

2. While the liquid wealth is kept inside the firm, its management is typically handled by dedicated employee(s), usually from the finance department. We refer to this as an embedded family office (see Chapter 5 on wealth governance for additional details). The

3. As the volume and complexity of nonbusiness-related assets grows, the desire to separate family wealth from business operations in order to satisfy the financial needs of the family and to finance succession increases. The administration of the family's wealth is then outsourced to asset managers, who are mandated to handle strategic asset allocation.
4. As accumulation of wealth continues, the family insources wealth administration and sets up a single family office. The office is a separate organization under the direct control of the family that serves as the family's own wealth administration vehicle.

Business management *and* investment management are important for transgenerational value creation, but for different reasons. Business management is essential because wealth creation primarily takes place in the world of business and entrepreneurship. Entrepreneurial endeavors promise significant economic and social rents that are hard to achieve and sustain via a diversified portfolio of liquid assets. Many families incorrectly assume that the passive administration and diversified investment of liquid wealth, including real estate, will be sufficient to create value over time. In addition, for many families in business, the flow of resources is a one-way street from the business sphere to the investment sphere, or from the firm to the family. As they build on past achievements, many families become complacent over time, consume the reserves accumulated in the business sphere or live on the dividends from the business in the absence of a material need to pursue a professional career. Families that view their firm(s) as a pension fund designed to enable an extravagant lifestyle tend to lose their interest, their economic aspirations, their willingness to take risks, and their desire to rejuvenate and reinvest in the entrepreneurial activities that are so essential for transgenerational value creation. In the end, such families cease their business activities (upper cycle) in the false hope that they will generate sufficient returns through their liquid investments (lower cycle). This is a sure way to significantly diminish a large fortune.

A combination of effective business asset management with the investment sphere is an essential prerequisite for transgenerational value creation. In fact, investment management fulfills several important tasks for transgenerational value creation. First, it serves as a security buffer, which enables the firm and the family to ride out economic downturns. Second, the family's private wealth represents the reservoir of patient capital that is needed to support the long-term innovative strategies that make family firms successful. Third, the pooling of family interests and assets, instead of their distribution among individual family members, promotes the continued economic power of the family. Continual asset pooling enables the family to seize new business opportunities either through (re)investments inside the main firm or engagement in new activities outside the firm. Finally, pooled family assets provide the family with economies of scale in the administration of their wealth by, for instance, lowering asset management fees or justifying the hiring of expert advisors who would be too costly for a family member to engage alone.

Given the above, transgenerational value creation can be seen as a dynamic process in which families need to dynamically manage two interlinked managerial processes: business management and investment management. Let us take a closer look at the evolution of business and investment management.

8.3.5.1 Evolution of business management

The evolution of business management starts with the founding stage, and then moves through the buying and building stage to the selective exit and reentry stage. For each of these stages, we can map the typical diversification level, corporate governance structures, succession and required expertise (Figure 8.10).

Diversification: In the early stages, diversification is limited, but it tends to widen as the business grows. When exit opportunities are seized, diversification is cut back to focus on the most promising businesses.

Governance: Corporate governance starts with founder- or entrepreneur-centric ownership, and management and board configuration. In fact, the entrepreneur may simultaneously be the owner, CEO and a board member. Over time, expert nonfamily managers are hired, and ownership is diluted through extension to the growing family and, sometimes, to nonfamily investors. The governance structures must change accordingly (for additional details, please refer to Chapter 5 on governance).

Succession: In the early stages of business management, succession is challenging, as management succession and ownership succession coincide. The challenge stems from the unwillingness of incumbent entrepreneurs to let go and from the difficulty of finding a capable and willing successor inside the family. In later stages, when management is passed to nonfamily managers whose tenures are not bound to the lifecycle of family members, family-internal succession primarily concerns the ownership sphere. Ownership succession then either takes place via the splitting of assets among family members or through the transfer of shares within the family.

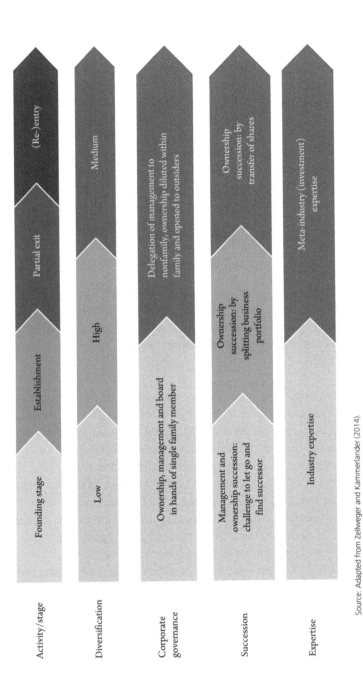

Activity/stage	Founding stage	Establishment	Partial exit	(Re-)entry
Diversification	Low	High		Medium
Corporate governance	Ownership, management and board in hands of single family member		Delegation of management to nonfamily, ownership diluted within family and opened to outsiders	
Succession	Management and ownership succession: challenge to let go and find successor	Ownership succession: by splitting business portfolio	Ownership succession: by transfer of shares	
Expertise	Industry expertise		Meta-industry (investment) expertise	

Source: Adapted from Zellweger and Kammerlander (2014).

Figure 8.10 Evolution of business management for transgenerational value creation

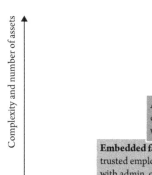

Figure 8.11 Evolution of investment management for transgenerational value creation

Expertise: As business activities evolve, the required expertise shifts from industry- and firm-specific expertise to investment management expertise (Figure 8.10).

8.3.5.2 *Evolution of investment management*

We can also take a closer look at the evolution of investment management. For families, the challenge in this regard is less about the allocation of (mostly liquid) assets—many banks and asset managers have specialized in this type of advisory activity—and more about finding the right wealth administration structure, which we labeled 'wealth governance' in Chapter 5 on governance (Figure 8.11).

Many entrepreneurs are so involved in business management that they fail to set up appropriate investment management structures. Some families have no principles or structures for the administration of wealth in place (labeled the 'uncoordinated family' in Chapter 5 on wealth governance). In such situations, the means that are generated through the business are mostly held inside the business in the form of cash and slack resources.

As family wealth accumulates over time, many business owners seek advice on private financial issues or other private family matters from business employees. The advantage for the family is that the respective costs are passed on to the firm and, thereby, split among all owners and stakeholders. In addition, some employees in the operating business, typically the chief financial officer (CFO), treasurer or accountant, have all the necessary information as well as the family's trust that they can take care of the family's financial affairs. Such structures have been labeled 'the embedded family office' (see Chapter 5 on governance for details).

As a consequence of further growth in the family's wealth, the family opts to outsource the administration of family wealth to banks, asset managers and multi-family offices. The purpose of doing so is to professionalize the administration of their wealth and to limit the risks associated with having all private wealth invested in the business.

With additional accumulation of wealth, the family may come to a point where a (partial) insourcing of services into a single office is sensible. Given the amount of assets at stake, the family concludes that it can afford to set up an investment office that renders all of the services the family requires at costs comparable to an outsourced solution but in a more tailor-made, flexible and private manner.

In the final stage, the family works with an integrated structure in which all business and family assets are under one roof. Figure 8.11 illustrates these stages in the investment management process.[5]

8.3.6 Integrated business and investment management for large fortunes

Large fortunes that accrue as a consequence of transgenerational value creation are often composed of two components: business assets and investment assets. The management of these two types of assets is typically handled by two separate organizational and legal entities, such as a holding company that administers business assets and a family office that administers family assets.

The roles of the holding company are to structure and develop the business investments, to provide business-related corporate finance and treasury services, and to implement new entrepreneurial ventures. The holding company is typically controlled by a top management team with a CEO who is appointed and controlled by a board of directors, to which family members are appointed via the family council (Figure 8.12).

In contrast, the role of the family office is to administer and allocate the mostly liquid family wealth, including real estate and minor investments. This function includes defining the strategic asset allocation, selecting asset managers, structuring investments, consolidating assets, accounting and reporting. In close cooperation with family members, the family office sometimes also offers such 'concierge' services for family members as cash management, tax filing and relocation. Family offices sometimes also provide educational programs on the governance system, family matters and professional ownership for next-generation family members. Moreover, large family offices may have an investment advisory board that serves as a sounding board for important investment decisions.

This integrated administration system is held together by governance structures. *Family governance* provides the overarching values and goals of the family, and sets the boundaries for family member involvement in business management, ownership and wealth management. *Ownership governance* defines the entry and exit of shareholders, the transfer of shares and the execution of voting rights through a legally binding shareholder agreement. *Corporate governance* primarily regulates the interaction and decision-making power of the board and management. In relation to family wealth, *wealth governance* defines the decision-making power and processes with regard to investment decisions, defines the setup of an eventual investment advisory committee, sets broad guidelines for asset allocation and the compensation of family officers, and bills family office services to the family.[6] An integrated business and wealth governance structure is described in the following case study.

CASE STUDY

The Brenninkmeijer family

The Brenninkmeijer family is one of the oldest European families in business. It has been able to generate significant wealth since it took its first entrepreneurial steps in 1841. It is well known in Europe and Latin America for its ownership of C&A, a private, 100% family-owned fashion retailer. In 2013, C&A's sales reached about €5.2 billion.

C&A is held by the family's investment company, Cofra Holding. On its website, Cofra states: 'COFRA is a global family-owned and -led business, creating sustainable economic value for its owners and exciting career opportunities for its employees through a dynamic portfolio of investments in retail, real estate, financial services and corporate investments, with the unique ability to attract, retain, develop and promote exceptional talent both from within and outside the family.' Cofra was founded in 2001 to oversee the family's various investments. Today, it controls three main business activities—retail (C&A), real estate

CASE STUDY *(continued)*

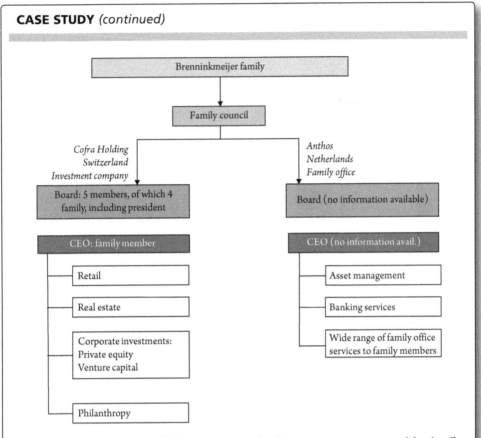

Figure 8.12 The Brenninkmeijer family's investment company and family office

(Redevco) and corporate investments (Bregal Investments and Entrepreneurs Fund)—just as philanthropic activities.

Given the size and the business opportunities tied to the real estate and retail activities, the family must have decided to keep its real estate under the purview of Cofra rather than under the control of the family office, Anthos. In the corporate investment arm, Cofra manages significant private equity investments (Bregal investments) and a venture capital fund (Entrepreneurs Fund).

Anthos, the family office, is located in the Netherlands, where some of the family members live and where the company has its roots. The office manages the family's liquid wealth and provides a wide range of services to family members.

Family members are welcome to work for the company. However, only those demonstrating business success are entitled to become shareholders. Family members who wish to become shareholders must acquire shares of Cofra and obtain a loan from Anthos to finance the purchase.

? **REFLECTION QUESTIONS**

Reflection questions for practitioners

Building on the framework depicted in and given the dynamics at play, transgenerational value creation is more likely to be achieved when:

1. The family renews its entrepreneurial spirit in later generations

Reflection questions for the family:
- Are we innovative enough?
- Do we take enough entrepreneurial risks?
- Do we delegate decisions making to lower hierarchical levels and businesses?
- Are we proactive and tackle opportunities before others do so?
- What are the impediments to being more entrepreneurial and what can we do about them?
- How do we ensure that next-generation family members stay interested in the business?

2. The family pursues concentrated corporate investments

Reflection questions for the family:
- Do we invest most of our assets in a limited number of businesses, thereby avoiding excessive diversification?
- What are the opportunities and the risks related to holding a very limited number of investments?
- How risky are our combined activities?

3. The family jointly invests, harvests and reinvests its resources in business(es)

Reflection questions for the family on business management:
- Do we invest sufficient resources in our firm(s) so that we can enter promising new businesses?
- Are we willing to exit a business that is declining or when there are more attractive alternative business opportunities?
- Do we reinvest the harvested resources in promising future businesses?
- Are we willing to keep our business assets together so as to invest as a family group?

Reflection questions for the family on investment management:
- Have we set up a wealth governance structure that keeps liquid family wealth together with the aims of protecting wealth, supporting the firm and eventually investing in new businesses?
- Do we possess the necessary expertise inside the family and from nonfamily experts for business and investment management?

4. The family possesses and develops business and investment expertise

Reflection questions for the family:
- Do we have the expertise needed to run a company outside our original industry?
- Who inside or outside the family has the business intelligence needed to run a portfolio of businesses?

5. The family keeps control despite delegation of authority

Reflection questions for the family:
- Do we ensure professional governance over the businesses through tight monitoring by the family and the involvement of nonfamily experts?

- Are the corporate and ownership governance regulations up to date so that we have good control over the assets we control?
- What reporting, incentive, control and sanctioning systems do we need to run our investments?

6. The family defines roles for family members

Reflection questions for the family:
- What roles do we expect family members to take in the management and supervision of the firm(s), ownership, family committees and wealth administration?
- What are the requirements for family members to enter these roles?
- For how long can family members execute a certain role?

7. The family monitors the performance of total family wealth

Reflection questions for the family:
- How good is our ability to monitor the performance of total family wealth?
- How do the returns from our various businesses compare to alternative investments with comparable risk profiles?

8. The family acts as an identified group of owners

Reflection questions for the family:
- Are we a cohesive family?
- How do we ensure that our family identifies with our business activities?
- Which family governance structures and activities should we set up to support cohesion and identification?

Reflection questions for students

1. Please describe the advantages and disadvantages of family firms with regard to the management of change?
2. Family firms and disruptive change: what is meant by the term 'family innovator's dilemma'?
3. What are the three strategic drivers of family firm longevity?
4. Why is a focus on longevity of the family firm limiting for families pursuing transgenerational value creation?
5. Why is the performance of a single firm not the most critical measure of success in the context of transgenerational value creation?
6. What are the building blocks of transgenerational value creation? Please include an example for each element.
7. What are the critical attributes of resources and resource management in the longevity perspective? What are they in the transgenerational value creation perspective?
8. Why is it challenging for entrepreneurs to switch from the role of business manager to the role of investment manager?
9. Which arguments speak against diversification of family wealth if a family seeks to achieve transgenerational value creation?
10. Transgenerational value creation emphasizes business and investment management. What are the respective roles that these two management spheres play in transgenerational value creation?
11. What are the risks if a family only focuses on business management and neglects investment management?

12. What are the risks if a family only focuses on investment management and neglects business management?
13. How does business management evolve throughout the process of transgenerational value creation?
14. How does investment management evolve throughout the process of transgenerational value creation?

8.3.7 CASE STUDIES

Transgenerational value creation at Ahlstrom (Finland)

by Philipp Sieger[7]

In 1851, Antti Ahlstrom started his entrepreneurial career by establishing a grain mill, a rag paper mill and a ceramics workshop in Finland. He also acquired a share in a sawmill. In the 1860s, his focus shifted to the shipping business, which generated significant profits that enabled Ahlstrom to expand his business. He built a new sawmill and ironworks, and purchased three additional ironworks. In the 1880s and 1890s, he acquired 18 more sawmills and became one of the major Finnish industrialists of the time.

After Ahlstrom's death in 1896, his wife Eva took over the company. She was followed by Walter Ahlstrom, Antti's eldest son, who also proved to be a true entrepreneur. Under his leadership, the company started paper production in 1921, and it diversified into machinery and glassworks. By the time of Walter Ahlstrom's death in 1931, Ahlstrom Oy was Finland's largest industrial conglomerate with more than 5000 employees.

After World War II, the expansion continued with the company launching activities in engineering and chemical technologies. Moreover, Ahlstrom Oy became a Finnish pioneer in internationalization when it acquired a majority stake in a large Italian paper mill in 1963. In the 1980s, Ahlstrom left the newspaper and magazine paper market—its paper-producing units were sold in 1987 in order to allow the company to fully concentrate on specialty papers and engineering. In the 1990s, the company diversified into nonwoven products, and it acquired other firms in France, Germany, the United Kingdom and other countries.

In 2001, the company was split into three parts. The manufacturing businesses formed the new Ahlstrom Corporation, which was listed on the Helsinki Stock Exchange in March 2006. In 2013, it employed around 3500 people in 24 countries, and generated revenue of €1 billion. The second part, Ahlstrom Capital Oy, was created as a private investment company. It invests internationally in such areas as the industrial sector, real estate and cleantech. The third part, A. Ahlstrom Osakeyhtiö, was established to handle the family's real estate and forests. All three companies are owned by Antti Ahlstrom Perilliset Oy, a private holding company that is owned by members of the Ahlstrom family. It administrates assets with a combined revenue of $4 billion.

The following figure (Figure 8.13) and table (Table 8.5) display the current governance structure (as of 2013) and the most critical events in Ahlstrom's history.

CASE STUDY *(continued)*

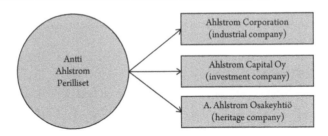

Figure 8.13 Current governance structure

Table 8.5 Critical events in Ahlstrom's history

Year	Event
1851	Antti Ahlstrom is established with several mills and a ceramics workshop
1860s	Focus on shipping business
1880s–1890s	Strong expansion, industrialist career
1896	Death of Antti Ahlstrom
1921	Start of paper production, diversification
1931	Ahlstrom becomes Finland's largest industrial conglomerate
1963	First internationalization activities
1980s	Exit of paper market/paper production
2001	Company split into three parts
2006	IPO of Ahlstrom Corporation

According to company documents, one of the aims of the governance structure is to separate ownership and family issues from business issues. On the holding-company level (Antti Ahlstrom Perilliset, which is held as a private firm), the vision, mission and owner strategy are developed. These three elements then affect the three operating companies. From a screening of the Ahlstrom Corporation's annual reports, we can conclude that the financial performance of the business is strong.

Today, the family includes around 340 members who belong to the fourth, fifth, sixth and even seventh generations. The family group includes children and in-laws, and approximately 230 of its members are shareholders. At the board level, the fifth generation has taken over, with 14 family members serving on the holding company's board. In total, three family members are employed in the family's companies.

The family defines its role as 'superstakeholder' as follows: 'In a listed, or a privately

CASE STUDY *(continued)*

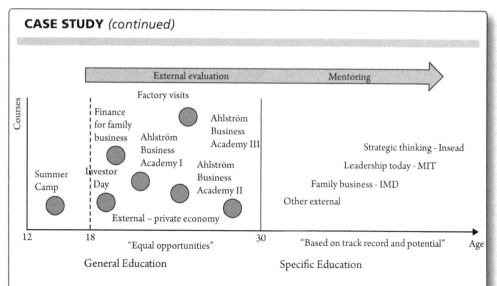

Source: Taken from Thomas Ahlstrom's presentation from the FBC Family Business Conference, Helsinki, 2014.

Figure 8.14 Onboarding and involvement of the next generation at Ahlstrom

held company, there is always a possibility to exit [. . .] whereas the fundamental idea about family ownership—in its purest form—is to keep the company, own it as a going concern, and pass it on to the next generation'. The family also explains its approach toward governance: 'If you can't (or are not supposed to) vote with your feet—you probably want to exercise influence over the company, and ideally, in a much more rigorous way than the average shareholder in the average company.'[8]

The family has adopted a systematic approach to onboarding and involving the next generation (see Figure 8.14).

From your reading of this brief description:

1. Which elements of the transgenerational value creation framework do you recognize in the case?
2. What roles do entrepreneurship and resources play for transgenerational value creation in this case?
3. Why is the family and not the firm particularly useful as a level of analysis in this case?
4. Do you believe the current governance structure is appropriate for ensuring the family's future success? Why or why not?
5. What is your evaluation of the family's approach to the engagement/inclusion of the next generation?

CASE STUDY

The Wallenberg family and Investor AB (Sweden)

The Wallenberg family is one of Sweden's most eminent business families. Its wealth originates from its holdings in Stockholms Enskilda Bank (SEB), which was founded in 1856. Over the years, the bank acquired ownership stakes in a wide range of companies. To control these investments, Investor was founded as an industrial holding company in 1916. It was originally established as a subsidiary of SEB. In the 1970s, Investor was spun off from SEB and has since served as the Wallenberg's main investment vehicle. Today, Investor is a publicly listed investment company in which the Wallenberg family has a dominant stake, either directly or through the Wallenberg foundations.

The Wallenberg foundations, which are controlled by the Wallenberg family, are the largest owners of Investor. The three largest Wallenberg foundations own a combined 23.3% of the capital and hold 50% of the votes in Investor. Investor itself is governed by Jacob Wallenberg, who is chairman of the board, while a nonfamily member serves as CEO.

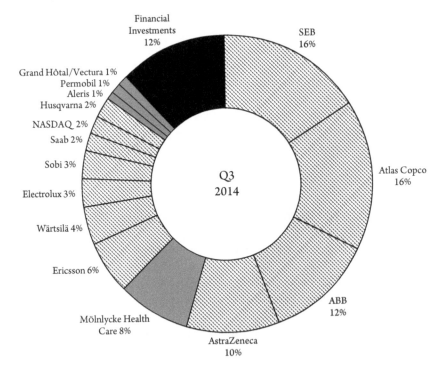

Source: www.investorab.com

Figure 8.15 Split of assets as of Q3 2014

CASE STUDY *(continued)*

At the end of 2013, Investor's total net asset value amounted to roughly $33 billion. These assets were split as shown in Figure 8.15 (as of Q3 2014).

In order to analyze transgenerational value creation in the Wallenberg family, take a look at Investor AB's website (www.investorab.com). What elements of the transgenerational value creation framework do you recognize from the information on the website and your other research on Investor and the Wallenbergs?

CASE STUDY

Cargill (USA)

Cargill is said to be the largest privately held company in the world. Its sales reached $135 billion in 2013, while earnings totaled about $2 billion. It employs approximately 145 000 people in 67 countries. The company provides food, agriculture, financial and industrial products and services. Cargill was founded in 1865 with the opening of a grain storage facility in Iowa. However, it has adapted its activities over the years. Take a look at Cargill's corporate website (www.cargill.com) and do some additional search on the web for information on the firm and its family. Then reflect on the following questions:

1. What elements of the transgenerational value creation framework do you recognize in this case?
2. In what way do the cultural and institutional contexts of the United States support or hinder the pursuit of transgenerational value creation?

CASE STUDY

Your own family firm

If your family controls a business activity, consider the following questions:

1. What do you think needs to be done to prepare the firm for transgenerational value creation?
2. What are the obstacles?

CASE STUDY

Transgenerational value creation in a family firm near you

Think about a long-term value-creating family from your region or your cultural context, and consider the following questions:

1. What elements of the transgenerational value creation framework do you recognize in this case?
2. In what way do the cultural and institutional contexts hinder or support transgenerational value creation?

NOTES

1   Thank you to Dr. Nadine Kammerlander for contributing this intriguing section on 'Change and Adaptation'. Nadine Kammerlander is a Professor of Business Administration at WHU Otto Beisheim School of Management, Germany, and has a special focus on strategic management, innovation and family business.
2   We therefore assumed that sales volumes served as a reasonable proxy for value.
3   This observation of the low level of diversification is important and intriguing, as it partly challenges portfolio theory, which suggests that investors should hold highly diversified portfolios.
4   This shift toward general-management acumen is also perceptible in the education of next-generation members who obtain university degrees, often in business administration or engineering, which equip them with more generic management know-how and less industry-/firm-specific knowledge.
5   Please refer to Chapter 5 on governance and, therein, the section on wealth governance for a detailed discussion of the advantages and disadvantages of the uncoordinated family, embedded family office and single-family office. That section also contains a discussion of family trusts and foundations.
6   For additional information on these governance aspects, please refer to Chapter 5 on governance.
7   Thank you to Dr. Philipp Sieger for this rich case study. Philipp Sieger is a Professor of Business Administration at the University of Bern, Switzerland, and has a special focus on entrepreneurship and family business.
8   See Thomas Ahlstrom's presentation from the FBC Family Business Conference, Helsinki, 2014.

 BACKGROUND READING

Aronoff, C. (2001). Understanding family-business survival statistics. *Supply House Times*, July.

Carney, R. W., and T. B. Child (2013). Changes to the ownership and control of East Asian corporations between 1996 and 2008: The primacy of politics. *Journal of Financial Economics*, 107: 494–513.

Christensen, C. M. (1997). *The Innovator's Dilemma*. Cambridge, MA: Harvard University Press.

Hill, C. W. L., and F. T. Rothaermel (2003). The performance of incumbent firms in the face of radical technological innovation. *Academy of Management Review*, 28: 257–274.

Jaskiewicz, P., J. G. Combs and S. B. Rau (2015). Entrepreneurial legacy: Toward a theory of how some family firms nurture transgenerational entrepreneurship. *Journal of Business Venturing*, 30 (1): 29–49.

Kammerlander, N., and M. Ganter (2015). An attention-based view of family firm adaptation to discontinuous technological change: Exploring the role of family CEOs' non-economic goals. *Journal of Product Innovation Management*, 32 (3): 361–383.

Koenig, A., N. Kammerlander and A. Enders (2013). The family innovator's dilemma: How family influence affects the adoption of discontinuous technologies by incumbent firms. *Academy of Management Review*, 38 (3): 418–441.

Landes, D. (2008). *Dynasties: Fortune and Misfortune in the World's Great Family Businesses.* London: Penguin.

Lumpkin, G. T., and G. G. Dess (1996). Clarifying the entrepreneurial orientation construct and linking it to performance. *Academy of Management Review*, 21 (1): 135–172.

Nordqvist, M., and T. Zellweger (2010). *Transgenerational Entrepreneurship: Exploring Growth and Performance in Family Firms across Generations.* Cheltenham, UK and Northampton, MA, USA: Edward Elgar Publishing.

Shepherd, D. A., A. Zacharakis and R. A. Baron (2003). VCs' decision processes: Evidence suggesting more experience may not always be better. *Journal of Business Venturing*, 18 (3): 381–401.

Sieger, P., T. Zellweger, R. Nason and E. Clinton (2011). Portfolio entrepreneurship in family firms: A resource-based perspective. *Strategic Entrepreneurship Journal*, 5 (4): 327–351.

Ward, J. (1987). *Keeping the Family Business Healthy.* San Francisco, CA: Jossey-Bass.

Zellweger, T., and N. Kammerlander (2014). Family business groups in Deutschland. Working paper, University of St. Gallen.

Zellweger, T., R. Nason and M. Nordqvist (2012). From longevity of firms to transgenerational entrepreneurship of families. *Family Business Review*, 25 (2): 136–155.

9

Financial management in the family business

What is different about the financial management of family firms? After all, family firms are firms—owners and managers are concerned about their returns, the related risk and, ultimately, the value of their investments. Even though family firms are unable to suspend the fundamental laws of finance, such as the positive relationship between risk and return, it is still interesting to revisit the fundamental assumptions of corporate finance, which have shaped much of our understanding of financial management in companies. In this chapter, we will show that some of these assumptions are not helpful for explaining the typical family firm. In fact, some of these assumptions are even misleading in relation to family firms.

We raise one caveat upfront: the following pages emphasize, first and foremost, financial considerations and economic rationality. This focus represents a deliberate choice aimed at providing actors in the family business realm with economically rational tools and arguments that can help reduce the complexity of decision making. Nevertheless, we acknowledge that nonfinancial, or socioemotional, concerns can influence, bias and sometimes outright cloud decision making in this type of firm. Chapter 6 on strategy has shown how socioemotional biases, such as concerns regarding identity and reputation, may lead to better financial performance through, for instance, brand building and relational ties with clients. Behavioral biases clearly matter in family firms and are not necessarily detrimental to the firm's financial performance. However, for family business practitioners and scholars alike, it is important to understand what economically rational choices are in order to make informed decisions about whether they want to comply with the principles of economic rationality or deviate from those principles. Practitioners also need to understand the consequences of such nonfinancial preferences. In this regard, this chapter investigates some of the most important tools and concepts related to the financial management of family firms.

9.1 Why finance is different for family firms

As alluded to in the introduction above, an examination of the assumptions behind modern corporate finance theory is useful for understanding the particularities of financial management in family firms. These assumptions, such as those ingrained in the capital asset pricing model (CAPM), influence many of the tools that we use to make financial decisions today. The CAPM is a financial model that helps decision makers assess the value of an investment.[1] The most critical assumptions of the CAPM and their appropriateness for family firms are displayed in Table 9.1.

The CAPM makes additional assumptions: taxes and commissions are absent, investors cannot influence prices, investors can borrow and lend at the risk-free rate, and investors can short any asset and hold any fraction of an asset. One can challenge these assumptions as well, but as they are equally appropriate for both nonfamily and family firms, they are not of interest here. In contrast, the assumptions outlined in Table 9.1 are particularly critical and deserving of a brief discussion.

Table 9.1 The CAPM's assumptions and their appropriateness for family firms

Assumption	Appropriateness for family firms
There are many investors. These investors invest in many assets in order to diversify their risks, and each investor only holds a small fraction of each asset.	Family firms have a low number of investors (usually the family members, especially in private family firms). The family has an undiversified wealth position and holds a large fraction of the asset (i.e., the firm).
All investors look ahead over the same one-period planning horizon.	Family firm owners invest for the longer run, usually with the intent of passing the firm on to another family generation.
All investors maximize economic utility.	Family firm owners are concerned about socioemotional utility as well as economic utility.
All investors have the same information about investment opportunities.	The controlling shareholder (i.e., the family) is often involved in management and has an information advantage over outside investors.
Assets can be sold at the market price at any time, and investors have equal access to all assets.	The market for ownership stakes in family firms is illiquid. Investments in private family firms are closed to nonfamily investors and 'not for sale'.

9.1.1 Concentrated and active majority owners

The assumption that owners have diversified their wealth across a multitude of assets and that they are passive minority owners stands in flagrant contradiction to the family firm reality. The shareholders of a closely held company, a characterization applicable to the great majority of family firms, have a concentrated wealth position. This also holds true for publicly listed firms in which a family holds a controlling stake. As such, family business owners are not diversified. Rather, given the controlling stake they have in their firms, they are often undiversified majority owners (see descriptive data on this point later in this chapter). Moreover, one element of the 'diversified minority owner' assumption is that owners are generally passive and do not contribute managerial services. However, this is not an accurate depiction of the family firm reality, as most family firms are managed by the controlling families themselves.

The consequences of these assumptions are significant. Given the undiversified wealth, family owners and, by extension, their firms should be relatively risk averse. In addition, given that these owners often act as the firm's managers, they are not passive *risk takers* but rather active *risk shapers*. Families have a strong financial incentive to tightly control and limit the risks their firms take. The active involvement of the family in operations also means that the value of the investment is contingent on the family itself. As Ahlers, Hack and Kellermanns (2014) describe, taking the family out of a family firm may lead to a loss of family-related strengths, such as human capital, social capital and patient financial capital. At the same time, replacing the family with another type of owner (such as a private equity firm) creates options to improve the financial condition of the firm, as wealth preservation concerns can be overcome. In sum, the value of the family firm should be contingent on the family itself and, hence, on who owns the firm.

9.1.2 Owners with a long-term view

The CAPM assumes that investors do not care about the time horizon of their investments. Again, this assumption stands in striking contrast to many family business practitioners who emphasize that they are not overly concerned about quarterly earnings, as they plan and manage their companies for the long run (Miller and Le Breton-Miller 2005).

To understand why the time horizon matters, consider two extreme types of investors. The first is a computer that automatically buys and sells shares depending on market sentiment within the timeframe of a few minutes. The second is a family with the goal of passing the firm on to a future generation. The first investor will generally be unconcerned with innovation and operating improvements in the firm because the benefits of those activities will only materialize long after the investor has sold the asset. If this investor has an opportunity or the motivation to make him-/herself heard as a shareholder, he/she may even counter such long-term projects (Belloc 2013). In contrast, the latter investor will not be concerned about the short-term fluctuations in the stock price, as he/she plans to hold on to the asset for several years.

The inappropriate assumption about the irrelevance of the time horizon has drastic consequences for investing and, more broadly, for corporate strategy. Many people seem to forget that an extended time horizon provides firms with a unique competitive advantage—the opportunity to invest in projects that are more risky (but, ultimately, more profitable) than the projects of interest to the short-term competitor. If we assume that firms have sufficient capital to weather difficult periods, those that have a long-term perspective can engage, for instance, in projects for which the payback will materialize at an uncertain time in the future (such as innovation projects) or at a distant time in the future (such as the development of a forestry or winery business, as well as international expansion).[2] Similarly, an extended time horizon may provide the firm with significant options, such as the option to expand the scale or scope of a project, the option to abandon a project, or the option to wait for the right timing to seize an investment opportunity (consider, for instance, a family engaged in real estate that has no need to buy or sell a property, but can wait until the price is particularly attractive).

9.1.3 Owners who value economic *and* socioemotional utility

The assumption that investors maximize economic utility is a parsimonious simplification useful for explaining and ultimately predicting individual and organizational decision making. However, even though many investors exhibit behavioral biases in their decision making, family business owners are particularly inclined to emphasize nonfinancial considerations. For instance, Koropp and colleagues (2014) found that family norms and attitudes toward external debt and external equity affect the financing behavior of family firms. Factors singled out in various studies included entrepreneurs' prior experiences in capital structure, wish to retain control, risk propensity, personal net worth of the owner, and social norms (for an overview of arguments refer to Romano, Tanewski and Smyrnios 2001 and Matthews et al. 1994). Put differently, normative beliefs about the usefulness of the various financing instruments had an immediate impact on the adoption of a certain financing mix.

As discussed in Chapter 6 on strategy, decision making in family firms can be quite accurately depicted as weighing the expected gains and losses of an investment in financial and socioemotional terms. The parallel concerns regarding financial and socioemotional wealth (SEW) imply that decisions are hard to make, as it is impossible to come up with a deterministic ordering of preferences in a single currency, such as money. For instance, what is the monetary value of not firing long-term employees and instead honoring them for their loyalty to the firm? In addition, the two utility dimensions—money and SEW—trade off against each other in many circumstances. For instance, hiring a child with mediocre talent may increase SEW but detract from financial wealth. In reality, decision makers have to deal with two non-fungible utility dimensions, where a change in one dimension often leads to an opposite change in the other dimension.

This complexity has important consequences for how family firms make decisions. Caught in a dilemma over which utility dimension to prioritize, decision makers must carefully consider the firm's vulnerability. Under conditions of strong financial performance and/or abundant slack resources, family firms should feel securely ensconced in their current investment preferences and see no need to engage in financial improvements. The continued pursuit of SEW is secure and any change would be unnecessary. In this case, family firms are risk averse. However, under conditions of weak financial performance and/or the absence of slack resources, which represents a situation characterized by high vulnerability, family firms should turn to strategies aimed at improving the financial conditions. This is because not only money but also lifeblood would be lost if the firm were to fail. In this case, family firms are willing to take large risks. In summary, given that family firms consider noneconomic utility as well as economic utility, their risk aversion is not constant (Gomez-Mejia, Patel and Zellweger 2015).

9.1.4 Owners with privileged access to information

The CAPM's equal information assumption postulates that all investors have equal and, therefore, simultaneous access to information. This is a useful assumption for minority investors of large firms, who receive information about the firm through various channels, such as the media, analyst reports and the company's press releases. However, in the case of closely held firms, such as family firms, this assumption is too narrow. Through their involvement on the board and in management, controlling families have privileged information access. In fact, family owners may be the originators of information themselves.

This fact is important because information is thus unevenly distributed among investors. The group of insider owners has privileged access to information, while the group of outsider owners are caught outside the information loop, at least to some extent. Often, the distinction between insiders and outsiders is linked to management involvement. Owners who are active in the firm's operations have privileged access to information, which sometimes gives rise to mistrust among outsiders about the dealings of those insiders (even within a family if some members feel they are left out of the information loop), and an opportunity for insiders to exploit their information access. For instance, insiders may preselect firm-specific information in a way that puts their actions in a favorable light and promotes their own agendas in relation to, for instance, risk taking, investments or dividends.

9.1.5 Illiquid market for shares

The assumption that markets are liquid implies that investors can buy and sell any asset at any time. This implies, for instance, that entry into an asset is possible at any time. However, this is not necessarily the case for family firms. Many of these firms are 'not for sale' and no investor other than a family member is allowed to hold shares. Hence, there is no market for such shares or only a very illiquid one.

The consequences of such market illiquidity are numerous. For instance, investors have to plan an exit ahead of time and actively seek buyers for their stakes. In addition, the illiquidity of the market for such shares implies that exit is only feasible at a significant discount. Investors are thus locked in to some extent. This creates incentives on several levels. First, it motivates owners to ensure the profitability of the firm. Second, these firms will experience a push for dividends, as dividends are a less costly way for family owners to benefit from firm performance than selling their shares. Moreover, as a market that would reveal the price for these shares is largely missing, there is often uncertainty about the appropriate price for the firm.

In summary, family firms violate some of the most fundamental assumptions about how assets are priced and financial decisions are evaluated. This point is important to keep in mind when we turn to the tools and concepts that help family firms make sound financial decisions.

9.2 Family equity as a distinct asset class

The above discussion of the features of family equity capital prompts us to suggest that family equity is a distinct type of asset. Positioning the attributes

Table 9.2 Family equity as a distinct asset class

	Public equity	Private equity	Family equity
Description/type of investor	Fund manager or small private investor	Professional investor	Family
Ownership stake	Low minority	Mostly majority	Mostly 100%, declining over time
Number of company stakes held in parallel	Many	Up to 15	1 to 3, of which one tends to be the largest by far
Wealth diversification	High	Medium	Low
Risk aversion	Very low	Low	High
Financing	High leverage	Medium leverage	Equity, low leverage
Control over investments	Very low	Medium	High
Managerial involvement	Nonexistent	Medium	Medium to high
Time horizon	A few days up to a few months	About 5 years	Up to multiple generations
Strategic rationale	Opportunistic trading	Buy, build, rapidly quit	Buy, build, selectively quit

of family equity against the typical attributes of private equity and public equity helps to clarify this point (Table 9.2). Family equity is distinct from these other forms of capital at the level of ownership concentration, the number of company stakes, the owners' wealth diversification, the owners' risk aversion, financing preferences, the control the owners have over investments, the managerial involvement of the owners, the time horizon and the strategic rationale.

The investment approach of business families is thus distinct from equity held for opportunistic trading purposes, which looks for short-term returns without active involvement in the firm. Family equity is also distinct from private equity, which has to achieve a satisfactory return within about five years to compensate the fund investors within the promised timeframe. Private equity investors often seek to generate a return, in part by leveraging the company and then obliging the firm to pay back the heavy debt burden within a relatively short period of time. In contrast, family equity seeks to create value via the strategic repositioning of the firm and primarily via operational improvements. Such benefits are tricky and time consuming to realize, but they generate more sustainable returns. Family investors are more hesitant to seek financially engineered returns that limit the availability of capital for alternative and more value-creating uses, such as innovation.

The above comparison is not meant as a statement about the best asset class. Rather, it serves to show that family investors pursue an investment strategy that is distinct from those pursued by other types of investors. From the concentration of wealth in a single legacy asset or only a few assets flows a particularly cautious investment approach that seeks to build firms that are sustainable in the long run.

CASE STUDY

Family Equity in Haniel

Haniel is a private strategic investment management company that is 100% controlled by the Haniel family. It currently invests in five types of activities (as of June 2015).

- **Bekaert Textiles** (100% owned by Haniel) Bekaert Texties is the world's leading specialist for the development and manufacturing of woven and knitted mattress textiles.
- **CWS-boco** (100% owned by Haniel) CWS-boco ranks among the leading service providers for washroom hygiene products, dust control mats, workwear and textile services.
- **ELG** (100% owned by Haniel) ELG is one of the world's leading specialists in trading and recycling raw materials, in particular for the stainless steel industry.
- **Takkt** (50.25% owned by Haniel) Takkt is the market-leading business to business (B2B) direct marketing specialist for business equipment in Europe and North America.
- **Metro Group** (25% owned by Haniel) Metro Group is among the premier international merchandisers.

On its website Haniel positions itself as follows:

Family equity—the best of both worlds

Haniel has changed radically since it was founded back in 1756: the trader of colonial goods in Duisburg has become a German family equity company that combines the best of the two worlds of private equity and family companies. Haniel has a strategic and highly professional approach, is adaptable and has a clear claim to leadership. At the same time, it is the values of a tradition going back almost 260 years, as well as high stability and a sense of responsibility for people, the environment and returns, that are essential to the company. This combination is what makes Haniel unique—and therefore enkelfähig [literally translated: 'competent for grandchildren'.]

A family owned investment company

Haniel manages a diversified portfolio, pursuing a sustainable long-term investment strategy as a value developer. With the expertise of the employees at the holding company, Haniel offers its shareholdings crucial added value in development and professionalization, a clear value orientation as a framework for activities, and a high level of reliability in terms of the holding period for its shareholdings.

CASE STUDY *(continued)*

Haniel has set itself the goal of expanding the portfolio to comprise up to 10 shareholdings. Investments come into question only if they are a good fit for the company and the values it puts into practice. This ensures a close-meshed investment filter that examines the potential business models with regard to criteria including how much of a contribution they make to the diversification of Haniel's portfolio, how sustainable they are, and whether they can generate an appropriate value contribution for further growth.

Owing to the long-term development prospects, Haniel—in contrast to private equity companies, which generally operate with a focus on short-term optimization of returns—can offer different versions and special forms for the integration of new shareholdings. These may take the form of a step-by-step transition in ownership structures, special forms of involvement in committees such as an Advisory Board, or acquisition with an additional investor—there are many different options. However, they always come on the condition of becoming the majority owner.

The fundamental objective for current and future shareholdings is always to develop the company into a market leader in its segment. But Haniel also sees the divestment of parts of the portfolio as a component of successful and active management. If Haniel is no longer the best owner for an investment after a long time spent following a development course together, Haniel seeks a suitable new owner in order to create new scope for further growth—for both parties.

The new Haniel worlds

When it comes to possible future investments, Haniel also has clear expectations combined with a high degree of openness—in Haniel's good old tradition. For example, all economic sectors are essentially of interest, although the level of capital intensity sets limits. As a family equity company, Haniel wishes to focus its investments on regions whose legal and governance standards are reliable and comprehensible to us and which represent a familiar language area (Europe, North America). Different types of sustainable business model in both the business-to-business and the business-to-consumer segment are of equal interest to us. The respective companies should be medium-sized businesses that have already successfully emerged from the start-up phase of their lifecycle.

Investment strategy

There is a clear division of responsibilities: the divisions focus on their operational business while the holding company is in charge of strategic management. In the process, Haniel applies the fundamental principle of active portfolio management with a long-term focus.

 REFLECTION QUESTIONS

- Which aspects of family equity, as outlined in Table 9.2, do you recognize in the Haniel case?

9.3 Performance of family firms: a short review of the evidence

The performance of family firms has nearly become a field of academic research in its own right. In an interesting meta-analysis of public family firms in the United States, van Essen et al. (2015) found 'modest but statistically significant' positive performance effects for family involvement. In contrast, a meta-analysis of studies of private firms by Carney et al. (2015) found no significant performance effects of family involvement.

Probably one of the most robust reviews on the topic combines the findings of 380 studies. The review, published by Wagner et al. (2015), suggests that family involvement has a positive, albeit small, effect on firm performance. The authors suggest that whether one finds a positive or a negative performance effect for family firms depends on whether the firm is publicly listed (publicly listed family firms seem to outperform publicly listed nonfamily firms) and on the performance measure applied. For instance, when measured in terms of return on assets (ROA), the performance of family firms tends to be more positive, while their performance tends to be weaker when measured in terms of return on equity (ROE). This is because ROA is less contingent than ROE on the capital structure of the firm.

An additional robust feature of performance studies on family firms is that when the family is entrenched in ownership through control-enhancing mechanisms, such as dual-class shares or pyramid structures, performance tends to suffer. Similarly, family firms in which the founders are in control tend to outperform family firms controlled by later generations (for overviews of performance studies, refer to Amit and Villalonga 2013; Anderson and Reeb 2003b).

This overview of performance studies is far from complete, and the above references point to a wide variety of additional literature on this important topic. Regardless of one's view on the performance consequences of family involvement, it is much more insightful to move beyond the comparison of family versus nonfamily firms to ask what drives or hinders family firm performance. Chapter 6 on strategy holds some insights that are useful for answering this fundamental question.

9.4 Risk taking in family firms

Are family firms more or less risk averse than their nonfamily counterparts? This question is best addressed by first identifying the type of risk in question.

9.4.1 High wealth concentration

Bitler, Moskowitz and Vissing-Jorgensen (2005) find a mean ownership stake among US entrepreneurs of roughly 85% and that, on average, 40% of an entrepreneur's total wealth is tied up in firm equity. In family firms, which tend to be more established and larger than firms in the founding stage, we can assume that the wealth concentration is even greater. We can therefore conclude that family business owners' wealth is highly concentrated and, consequently, highly exposed to the risks the firm is running.

9.4.2 Low leverage

A firm's leverage captures the relationship between total debt and total equity. High leverage (i.e., debt/equity higher than 2 ×, although this level varies across industries) can lead to the company defaulting on its debt. However, do family firms have higher or lower leverage levels than their nonfamily counterparts?

There are two competing views on this question. The first emphasizes the fact that family owners often have an undiversified wealth position, as outlined above. Consequently, family owners have an important incentive to avoid taking on excessive leverage in order to limit the risk to their wealth, as the firm can go bankrupt if it defaults on its debt. The second view suggests that family business owners have an incentive to take on debt. This is because family firms view external equity—an alternative to debt for financing growth—as unattractive because it dilutes family control. As such, debt becomes relatively more attractive.

The empirical evidence shows that, on average, the leverage levels of US family firms are lower than those of nonfamily firms (e.g., Anderson, Duru and Reeb 2012). In contrast, Croci, Doukas and Gonenc (2011) find that the leverage levels of a large number of European family firms are higher than those of European nonfamily firms. Despite these divergent findings, there is additional evidence for the United States that family firms are more likely than nonfamily firms to have zero leverage (Strebulaev and Yang 2013). A prominent argument among researchers and practitioners alike is that family owners derive utility from passing on the family legacy and, thus, from the long-term survival of the firm, which increases the perceived risk of default-risky debt (e.g., Bertrand and Schoar 2006). Even though the evidence is ambiguous, it seems safe to assume that family firms tend to be rather reluctant to increase their level of debt.

CASE STUDY

Schaeffler acquires Continental

Schaeffler Group is a German family controlled company that manufactures rolling elements, such as bearings, for automotive, aerospace and industrial uses. In 2008, with sales of €8.9 billion, Schaeffler decided to acquire 75.1% of the tire producer Continental for €12 billion. In 2008, Continental had sales of €28 billion, which made it about three times larger than Schaeffler.

As a 100% privately owned family firm, Schaeffler had no access to the equity capital market and, therefore, had to heavily leverage its balance sheet in order to finance the acquisition. While the company's net financial debt was just €316 million in 2007, the figure grew to a whopping €6.1 billion by 2009. The acquisition was clearly a risky move, and the economic downturn of 2008 and 2009 added to the risk. Schaeffler was close to defaulting on its debt.

To overcome its financial problems, Schaeffler decided to reduce its stake in Continental to 60.3% in 2011. The company held a stake of only 46% by 2015. The remaining 54% was publicly listed. Nevertheless, the debt burden was still too heavy. On October 5, 2015, Schaeffler decided to list 25% of its own shares on the German stock exchange to further reduce its debt burden and increase its flexibility to seize further growth opportunities.

? REFLECTION QUESTIONS

- Assume you are one of the family owners of Schaeffler. Would you have agreed to the acquisition in 2008?

9.4.3 Low investment risk

Investment risk captures the degree to which firms make risky strategic choices. As outlined above and in our exploration of the consequences of making decisions based on socioemotional considerations (see Chapter 6 on strategy), we find that family firms tend to be more risk averse than non-family firms (for a discussion of risk taking in family firms, see Naldi et al. 2007). The argument is clear: because family firm owners are highly exposed to the risks their firms are running in terms of both undiversified wealth and SEW, the firms they control tend to be more cautious in their strategic decisions.

In summary, we can conclude that family firms generally tend to prefer low leverage levels and less risky strategic investments because of their concentrated investments in the firm and the resulting undiversified wealth.

9.5 Debt financing

For many established firms, debt is an important part of the financing mix. This is not surprising because debt financing bears some important advantages. Notably, however, it also has some disadvantages.

9.5.1 Advantages of debt financing

- **Control**: When increasing debt, a firm's owners maintain control over the firm. Banks that provide the financing will not require a seat on the board or a say in the general assembly.
- **Cost**: As a financing instrument, debt is cheaper than external equity financing. This is because debt is senior to external equity, meaning that it is paid back before equity in the case of bankruptcy.
- **Tax shield**: As the interest payments on debt are typically tax deductible, debt financing can lower the firm's tax burden.
- **Profit discipline**: Regular interest payments and the repayment of the debt serve as disciplining mechanisms. These payment requirements induce managers to ensure that the firm is performing.
- **Leverage effect**: As long as the cost of debt is lower than the return on total capital, it makes sense to increase a firm's leverage because the firm's ROE will rise. We return to the leverage effect in section 9.7.1.

9.5.2 Disadvantages of debt financing

At the same time, debt financing comes with certain disadvantages:

- **Bankruptcy risk**: In contrast to equity, debt has to be repaid by following a strict payment schedule. This is not much of an issue if the firm performs well and has the necessary funds, but if a firm is unable to adhere to the agreed payments, it can go bankrupt.
- **Lack of flexibility**: Given the strict payment policy (interest and repayment of nominal amount), debt is most helpful for financing projects for which the payback is certain and can be aligned with the terms of the debt financing. Debt's strict payment terms do not fit well with entrepreneurial projects or innovation, which are more uncertain but nevertheless critical for the prosperity of the firm.

It is important to note that debt financing has both advantages and disadvantages. Despite the general hesitation of family firms to increase their level of debt, it can be the right source of financing for larger projects for which the firm does not have the necessary funds and for which the financial implications are relatively predictable.

9.5.3   Cost of debt capital

There are several reasons to believe that family firms have advantages in terms of access to debt, such as their strong links to the community in which they are embedded, and in terms of the cost of debt. In a study of US publicly listed family firms, Anderson, Mansi and Reeb (2003) find that, on average, the cost of debt financing for family firms is about 32 basis points lower than for nonfamily firms. These authors write that 'the combination of undiversified family holdings, the desire to pass the firm onto subsequent generations, and concerns over family and firm reputation suggest that family shareholders are more likely than other shareholders to value firm survival over strict adherence to wealth maximization' (Anderson, Mansi and Reeb 2003, p. 264). For these reasons, family owners who raise debt have little incentive to deviate from the debt financing they get from banks and invest in high-risk/high-return projects (asset substitution) and, thus, default on their debt.

Banks may, however, be more critical with the supply of debt to privately held family firms and seek more collateral when lending to this type of firm. Given the limited transparency of private family firms in combination with the unfettered discretion of their owners (for instance, to appoint a limitedly qualified successor), banks should fear that the owners can divert the funds to other than the promised efficient uses, which may threaten the repayment of the loan. In the absence of the close scrutiny by the capital market, banks should be particularly concerned about the professional conduct of an owner-manager. Indeed, in a study of loan terms of Belgian private family firms, Steijvers and Voordeckers (2009) found that banks demanded systematically more personal collateral from the owner in private family versus private nonfamily firms, while the interest rate and business collateral was not significantly different between the two groups of firms.

9.6   Equity financing

Given their hesitation to increase debt, family firms have to rely more on equity in their financing. To qualify this preference for equity, we first explore the advantages and disadvantages of equity financing.

9.6.1 Advantages of equity financing

- **No fixed payments**: Firms that rely on equity do not have to service bank loans, which allows them to use the funds for their investment projects. The likelihood of going bankrupt from not being able to service financing is nonexistent.
- **Interest alignment toward value creation**: As equity providers are interested in increasing the value of their equity stakes, they have an incentive to make the firm successful. This is in contrast to debt claimants, whose primary interest is the servicing of the debt. In contrast to debt claimants, equity investors benefit from an increase in firm value.
- **Flexibility**: Equity financing increases the strategic flexibility of the firm. A strong equity base makes it easier to weather difficult periods; to invest in high-risk/high-return projects, such as innovation; and to increase debt if needed in the future.
- **Control, in the case of internal equity providers**: If equity is provided by insiders, such as family members who may also work within the firm, it allows the family to maintain tight control over the firm.

9.6.2 Disadvantages of equity financing

We can subsume the principal disadvantages of equity financing under the following points:

- **Cost**: In contrast to what many family business owners believe, especially those who have inherited a stake in a family firm and thus did not have to spend money on the asset, equity capital is expensive. As equity capital carries the full risk of the investments and is junior to all other forms of capital, equity investors seek a risk equivalent and a relatively high return.
- **No tax shield**: Given that equity does not bear interest payments that are tax deductible, equity does not carry a tax shield.
- **Profit discipline**: Firms that are heavily financed by equity do not experience pressure to pay interest and repay debt. They may therefore become complacent and hesitant to push for strategic change that would increase the firm's profitability.
- **Loss of control, in the case of external equity**: Equity investors who come from outside the firm will want to have a level of control over the firm that is proportionate to their investments. These external investors will expect regular information on results, forecasts and strategic projects, which allows them to monitor activities inside the firm and to probe the firm's management. Therefore, in contrast to a case in which

equity is provided by insiders, equity provided by outsiders entails some loss of control.

9.6.3 Cost of equity capital

Many family firms are hesitant to raise debt capital from nonfamily members, such as banks, because of the risk of bankruptcy. At the same time, family firms are cautious about raising equity capital from nonfamily members, such as private equity providers or the stock market, primarily because such equity entails a loss of control for the family over the firm. In many family firms, the family thus represents the primary market from which the firm raises capital. What is then an adequate return on the capital that the family invests in the firm?

The cost of equity capital reflects the return an equity investor desires in order to offset the risks the investor runs from investing in the firm. According to the CAPM, the cost of equity is:

$$i + \beta \, (\mu m - i)$$

where i is the risk-free interest rate; β indicates whether the investment is more or less volatile than the market; and μm is the market rate of return.[3] According to the CAPM, the relationship between the risk and return of an investment can be depicted as shown in Figure 9.1, where it is denoted by the capital market line (CML).[4]

As the main equity provider in the firm, family business owners may be willing to deviate from the above efficiency considerations. Some family owners, in particular those who have vested much SEW into their ownership stake, may be willing to compromise on the financial returns they expect from the firm and be satisfied with less than a risk-equivalent rate of return. In such cases, family business owners trade financial returns for socioemotional returns. Such tradeoffs may occur, for instance, when the firm holds on to an underperforming activity or underperforming employees. Thus, the family may have its own views on the adequate rate of return for the equity it has invested (see Figure 9.1, family market line, FML).

We can assume that this inclination to deviate from the CML and accept returns on capital that are lower than risk-equivalent returns is particularly prominent in cases where the firm is privately held (i.e., public scrutiny of firm performance by analysts is nonexistent), the family controls 100% of the equity (i.e., there are no other shareholders who can push for more efficiency) and

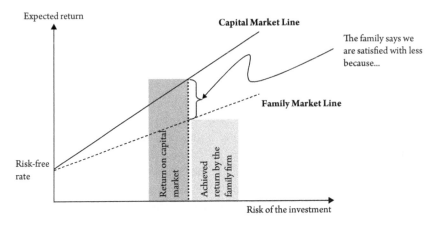

Figure 9.1 Family market line, FML

the ownership stake in the firm has been inherited from previous generations (i.e., the owners did not have to pay for the investment).

Some family business owners may argue that investments at lower than efficient returns on capital can still be rational and efficient when the firm wishes to:

- Benefit from higher returns in the longer run. In such cases, the owners accept some years with unsatisfactory returns in the hope of high returns in the future.
- Take on more investments projects, or detect and then exploit a priori undervalued projects.
- Diversify capital across a number of projects.
- Create value for stakeholders who are important for the functioning of the firm, such as employees.

However, systematically underinvesting and accepting a return on invested capital that is lower than the efficient rate becomes problematic for a firm, at least in the long run. This is because:

- Competitors who invest in more efficient ways will outcompete the firm. For instance, competitors will generate more funds to invest and, thereby, grow their businesses.
- Family owners will eventually realize that their money is tied to an unsatisfactory, if not failing, investment. Family owners may then decide to sell or liquidate their investments. This can be particularly disruptive for family firms if family owners active in operations are willing to accept

lower-than-efficient returns, while 'passive owners' who are not involved in operations seek a maximum financial return on their investments.

9.7   Leverage

One of the holy grails within the theory of corporate finance is the question of how a firm should finance itself in terms of the right mix of debt and equity. In the following, we explore this question by first looking at the leverage effect in detail. We also discuss the typical strategic challenges faced by two types of firms—one that is highly leveraged and another that has very low leverage. Finally, we offer several pieces of advice regarding the appropriate leverage of family firms.

9.7.1   Leverage effect

Leverage is typically defined as a firm's debt in proportion to its equity. A firm might find itself tempted to increase leverage for a fairly simple reason: if the firm's profit remains constant, then increasing debt and, thereby, reducing the proportionate share of equity means that profit accrues on a reduced equity base. In turn, the ROE rises, which is beneficial for shareholders. This effect has been labeled the 'leverage effect'. It suggests that as long as the interest rate on debt is lower than the return on total capital, an increase in leverage increases the ROE. This is subsumed in the following formula:

$$ROE = ROI + debt/equity * (ROI - cost of debt)$$

As shown in the formula, as long as ROI (return on investment), which is synonymous with return on total capital in this context, is higher than the cost of debt, the term within the brackets will be positive. In this case, a firm can increase its leverage and ROE will increase. Put differently, as long as the return on total capital is higher than the interest rate on debt, the higher the amount of debt the firm should rationally accept.

However, accepting high leverage levels can be a dangerous strategy. Interest rates on debt generally rise as leverage increases. More importantly, given the uncertainties associated with running a firm, return on total capital can fluctuate from year to year and can, in actuality, drop below the interest rate on debt. This is an uncomfortable situation for all types of firms, but it is particularly uncomfortable for family firms, which are very concerned about the continuity of the firm. Bankruptcy as a consequence of an inability to service or repay debt is the worst-case scenario for family firms, as family owners lose not only money but also SEW. For this reason, family firms must have a good understanding about the upsides (especially in terms of increased ROE) and downsides (especially in terms of bankruptcy risks) of increased leverage.

9.7.2 Leverage, risk and firm value

The above discussion suggests that increasing a firm's leverage is a double-edged sword. At low levels of leverage, the firm forgoes important opportunities for growth and higher returns for shareholders. Also from an owner's risk perspective, it is unreasonable to finance a firm solely with equity. If a firm is solely financed using equity (a zero-leverage firm), the equity holders carry all of the financial risks. If a zero-leverage firm goes bankrupt, it is the equity investors' money that is lost. To the contrary, if a bank also lends money to the firm, the losses are spread between the bank and the equity investors. Consequently, zero-leverage firms are not necessarily more valuable than firms that exhibit some leverage. In many studies, the optimal capital structure and, hence, the capital structure that results in the highest firm value has been found to be in the range of 25% to 50% of equity from total assets.

9.7.3 Practical advice on the appropriate leverage level of family firms

The above considerations regarding the leverage effect may appear to be fairly theoretical. In fact, they may seem to ignore legitimate questions among family business practitioners about the adequate leverage level. Given the central concern of family business owners in securing the continuity of the firm, we may ask how likely it would be that a firm would be unable to service its debts and, therefore, go bankrupt.

Banks are fairly good at answering this question, as they share a central concern with the family business owners—they do not want the firm to go bankrupt, as that would most likely mean that the firm would default on its debt. To assess the likelihood of a firm defaulting on its debt, banks develop credit ratings that typically range from AAA (very secure investments with a high certainty of payback) to C or D (very high-risk investments with highly uncertain payback). Banks then assign default rates to these rating categories, where a default rate is defined as the probability that a firm will default on its debt from, for instance, one year to the next (a one-year default rate). Credit ratings are also mapped in relation to the firm's interest coverage, which defines how many times a firm can service its annual debt obligations using its cash flow, as proxied by EBITDA.[5] Interest coverage is therefore defined as follows:

$$\text{Interest coverage} = \text{EBITDA/interest on debt paid per year}$$

Table 9.3 Credit rating, default rate, interest coverage and spread on risk-free rate

Rating	Default rate	Interest coverage from . . . . to		Spread on risk-free rate
Aaa/AAA	0.000	12.5		0.75%
Aa2/AA	0.015	9.5	12.49	1.00%
A1/A+	0.048	7.5	9.49	1.10%
A2/A	0.062	6	7.49	1.25%
A3/A−	0.078	4.5	5.99	1.75%
Baa2/BBB	0.281	4	4.49	2.25%
Ba1/BB+	0.683	3.5	3.99	3.25%
Ba2/BB	0.891	3	3.49	4.25%
B1/B+	2.444	2.5	2.99	5.50%
B2/B	7.279	2	2.49	6.50%
B3/B−	9.972	1.5	1.99	7.50%
Caa/CCC	22.671	1.25	1.49	9.00%
Ca2/CC		0.8	1.249	12.00%
C2/C		0.5	0.79	16.00%
D2/D			0.49	20.00%

Source of interest coverage and spread data, spring 2016: http://pages.stern.nyu.edu/~adamodar/New_Home_Page/datafile/ratings.htm. The link between interest coverage and ratings was developed by looking at all rated companies in the United States.

Source of default rate data: Standard and Poors (2014). Default, Transition, Recovery: Annual Global Corporate Default Study and Rating Transitions. New York; global one-year default rates.

Table 9.3 links rating categories to default rates and interest coverage. The table also displays the interest rate spread that accompanies each rating, whereby the interest rate spread is the difference between the interest to be paid on a certain debt instrument such as a loan and some benchmark debt (such as the risk-free interest rate). The addition of the interest rate spread to the risk-free rate yields the typical pre-tax cost of borrowing for a firm.

Given family firms' concerns regarding firm survival in light of the concentrated wealth position of the owners, they should aim for an A rating. An A rating indicates that firms are unlikely to default and that they have sufficient capital to survive a few difficult years. An A rating implies an expected default rate of 6.2% and interest coverage of about 6 × (Table 9.3).

CASE STUDY

Financial guidance for strategic management

The CEO of a publicly listed family firm wishes to know how far he can go in expanding the firm. The controlling family is concerned that the CEO might take excessive risks. To limit the manager's risk propensity, the family decides to ask the CEO and the CFO of the firm to manage the company so that it always receives an A rating from rating agencies. This kind of financial guidance is useful for the firm's management team, as it sets clear guidelines regarding the firm's strategic options, especially with regard to the amount of debt it can take on in order to finance growth.

In the course of the firm's evolution, management considers multiple acquisitions. The CFO calculates how much debt the firm could accept in order to finance an acquisition while keeping an A rating. The firm reaches an EBITDA of $12 million, and the CFO knows that if the firm's debt were to increase, the firm would have to pay an interest rate on that debt of 5%. Given an expected A rating and, hence, interest coverage of 6x, the firm can service debt at an amount of $2 million per year ($12/6 = 2$). Given the interest rate of 5%, it can thus increase its debt by a total of $40 million ($2/0.05 = 40$).

9.7.4 Leverage and strategic challenges

A firm's financing mix—its mix of debt and equity—alters the strategic challenges it typically experiences. To illustrate this point, let us look at two types of firms. Firm 1, which we name Petra Ltd., has a relatively solid equity base. Roughly 50% to 60% of its balance sheet is financed by equity. From a liquidity standpoint, the firm also looks rather solid. The value of its short-term assets is roughly double the amount of its short-term debt, which means that it has positive net working capital (net working capital = short-term assets – short-term debt). Firm 2, which we call Mara Ltd., is active in the same industry as Petra Ltd. It has an equity ratio of only about 10%. The remaining 90% of its balance sheet is short-term and long-term debt. Mara's net working capital is slightly negative, as its short-term debt is greater than the value of its short-term assets.

Now, let us assume that both firms generate the same profit. Consequently, both firms reach the same ROI (ROI = profit/total capital). However, the firms differ significantly in terms of ROE (ROE = profit/equity), as Mara's ROE is far larger than Petra's ROE (for an illustration, see Figure 9.2).

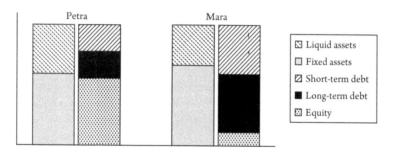

Figure 9.2 Strategic challenges depending on the financing mix

Assume that you are the owner of Petra. What are your main concerns? You would probably be quite happy with the liquidity of your firm and its solid equity base. However, you would most likely be unsatisfied with its profitability, at least as measured in terms of ROE. This is because you realize that a competing firm, Mara, is able to achieve a much higher ROE with much less equity. Your analysis would probably go in two directions. You would first assess how the efficiency of the firm can be improved, perhaps by cutting costs or increasing production output. You would also have to search in a second direction focused on how efficiently the firm's capital is deployed. You would investigate whether all of the capital that is invested in the firm is well allocated and actually needed for the operation of the firm. You would also ask whether some of the equity should be distributed to shareholders, so that they can allocate the capital to more profitable uses. Alternatively, you might push for investment projects, such as innovation or internationalization, so that the funds available to the firm are used more efficiently.

Let us now turn to the second company, Mara. As its owner, your concerns are quite different. The profitability of the firm is impressive, as the ROE is high. However, Mara faces a severe liquidity shortage given the negative net working capital. This can cause the firm to go bankrupt in the near future. Therefore, you have to act quickly and move in a number of directions. You need to collect your accounts receivable as quickly as possible, pay your accounts payable as late as possible and try to sell some of the fixed assets in order to generate cash. Eventually, you may even turn to your short-term creditors and swap the short-term credits into long-term credits. You might also consider asking the long-term debt claimants to convert their debt into equity. Of course, you could also inject more equity. However, given the firm's strong profitability, its operational performance seems to be in good shape.

These two examples demonstrate that management faces different strategic challenges depending on the financing mix. Would you prefer to be the owner of Petra or Mara? Probably, you would sleep soundly as Petra's owner given the solid financial circumstances. However, it would most likely be more time consuming to increase Petra's efficiency and bring it up to speed. In contrast, as Mara's owner, you would not have much time to reflect on what has to be done. Nevertheless, after you put the necessary measures into place in order to improve the liquidity of the firm, you would find yourself in calmer waters with a very profitable firm.

How are these examples linked to family firms? Many family firms prefer equity and a solid, conservative financing policy. They therefore tend to resemble Petra rather than Mara. For too many family business owners, low vulnerability in the form of high levels of liquidity and equity serves as a security margin and a cushion that spares the firm the need for change, innovation and efficiency improvements. However, such improvements could be desirable in light of the often unsatisfactory performance (Gomez-Mejia, Patel and Zellweger 2015).

9.8   Value management

Undisputedly, profit is an essential figure for the management of a company. However, does the fact that a firm makes a profit tell us much about the company? The profit line simply indicates whether the firm's expenses are greater or less than its revenue. Clearly, it does not serve as a very good measure of profitability, as the same profit could be achieved with various amounts of capital.

One way to overcome this limitation is to measure profit in relation to invested capital. For instance, ROE indicates the percentage of profit that is generated on every monetary unit of equity. We can then compare the ROE of the firm to other investment opportunities and, thereby, assess whether we could generate a higher return at equal risk through an alternative investment. Nevertheless, profitability ratios, such as ROE, ROI and ROS (return on sales), are also limited in their usefulness because they do not tell us how much value the firm has created from one period to the next. For instance, an increase in ROE from 5% to 10% does not indicate how much value the firm has generated. We are only able to conclude that the firm has doubled its profitability—what does that mean in monetary terms?

The concept of economic value added (EVA) tries to address the shortcomings of profit and profitability ratios. Instead of measuring profit, EVA measures in a first step a firm's net operating profit after tax (NOPAT).[6] It thus captures the firm's operating income and deducts estimated tax, but not the interest rate on debt. As such, it captures a measure of profit that is valuable to debt and equity claimants. It then compares NOPAT with the cost of capital. The cost of capital is defined as:

$$\text{Cost of debt * interest-bearing debt + cost of equity * equity}$$

where equity and interest-bearing debt represent the firm's capital employed. Capital employed can be calculated as:

$$\text{Equity + interest-bearing debt}$$

or as:

$$\text{total assets – short-term liabilities}$$

Table 9.4 provides an example of the calculation of EVA.[7]

Table 9.4 Economic value added (EVA)—an example

	Year 1	Year 2	Year 3
Sales	2600	3000	3500
Cost of goods sold	1400	1600	1800
Sales and general administration expenses	400	600	750
Depreciation	150	200	250
Other operating expenses	100	150	150
Operating income	550	450	550
Interest expenses	200	200	200
Income before tax	350	250	350
Income tax (25%)	87.5	62.5	87.5
Net profit after tax	262.5	187.5	262.5
Operating income	550	450	550
Income tax (25%)	137.5	112.5	137.5
NOPAT	412.5	337.5	412.5
Equity (cost of equity: 12%)	3000	2700	2400
Interest-bearing debt (cost of debt: 6%)	1000	900	600
Capital employed	4000	3600	3000
Cost of capital = Cost of equity * equity + cost of debt * interest-bearing debt	420	378	324
EVA = NOPAT – cost of capital	–7.5	–40.5	88.5

As shown in Table 9.4, net profit after tax is positive in all three years. However, if we take the amount and type of capital that are used to generate this profit into consideration, we realize that this company is actually destroying value (at least in years 1 and 2). This is because the cost of capital is greater than the NOPAT for these years. As a result, EVA is negative in years 1 and 2. Only in year 3 is the firm able to meet and, in this case, exceed its cost of capital.

The core takeaway from the distinction between profit and EVA is that even though a firm may make a profit, it can still destroy value. Only if a firm earns more than its cost of capital can it create economic value.

Despite the undisputed merits of EVA as a tool for financial analysis, it suffers from a limitation. Assume that, as an owner of a family firm, you decide to link management compensation to EVA, such that you pay out a proportion of EVA to managers every year. As the cost of capital is typically lower for debt than for equity, managers have an incentive to increase the firm's leverage. The replacement of equity with debt drives down the cost of capital and increases EVA. It could, therefore, be tempting for managers to steer toward higher leverage in order to pocket the bonus tied to the related increase in EVA. If EVA is used as a tool for financial decisions, it could make sense to provide management with guidance regarding the maximum leverage. Given their security concerns, family firms would be well served to focus on operating improvements instead of increasing leverage.

9.9 Key financial indicators

Financial ratios are essential tools for the financial management of family firms, as they give concise indications of how well a firm is doing. Financial ratios can be divided into five major categories: operational efficiency, profitability, liquidity, security and value creation. However, before we discuss some of the central financial ratios within each of these categories, some general considerations about the use of financial ratios are in order. For financial ratios to be useful and meaningful, they must be:

- Calculated using reliable, accurate financial information,
- Calculated consistently from period to period,
- Used in comparison to internal benchmarks and goals,
- Used in comparison to other companies in the same industry,
- Viewed at both a single point in time and as indication of trends over time,
- Carefully interpreted in the given context, as there are many important factors and indicators involved in assessing performance, and
- Viewed as a reflection of the past.

Private firms often struggle to find the right peer group against which to benchmark their own financial ratios. The only reliable data available typically stems from publicly listed firms. However, benchmarking against publicly listed firms can be challenging given the different accounting standards adopted by private and public firms. Therefore, private family firms have to carefully triangulate their own financial position with various sources of data and take the results with a grain of salt.

Table 9.5 highlights some of the most relevant financial ratios for assessing the financial status of a firm. Depending on the particular business in which the firm is active, additional financial ratios may be required. For instance, in real estate, a vacancy rate would probably be required, while inventory turnover should probably be observed in manufacturing companies. Nevertheless, the financial ratios presented in Table 9.5 should enable owners of a family firm who are not very involved in the firm's daily operational activity to monitor its financial viability.

Table 9.6 compares some key financial indicators of US publicly listed family firms with those of their nonfamily counterparts. The table shows that, on average, family firms are more asset light, smaller, less leveraged and more profitable (in terms of cash flow) than nonfamily firms. Moreover, they pay higher dividends, are less transparent, invest less in research and development (R&D) and have higher capital expenditures.

9.10 Dilemmas in the financial management of family firms

In the ideal case, a firm has limited leverage, is highly profitable and is highly liquid. In practice, however, there are important tradeoffs among these three goals and firms are often unable to achieve these goals in parallel. For instance, the firm's growth and profitability can be enhanced by increasing leverage, but increasing leverage runs counter to the interests of shareholders who are concerned about the firm's survival. Financial management typically deals with goal conflicts among three key dimensions: the firm's growth and profitability; the liquidity needs of the owners; and the security of the firm (Figure 9.3).

These goal conflicts are rather tricky to resolve because they do not avail themselves to a linear solution. Decisions in one of the three dimensions often have repercussions for the other dimensions. Therefore, we need an integrated understanding of financial management in family firms that seeks to solve the dilemmas that arise from the parallel pursuit of growth, liquidity

Table 9.5 Key indicators for assessing the financial viability of firms

Type	Financial ratio	Description	Definition
Efficiency	Sales	Total financial proceeds from products/services sold	
	Gross margin	Amount of money earned to cover the indirect costs	(Sales – direct costs)/sales
	EBIT margin	Amount of money earned to cover interest on debt and taxes	EBIT/sales
	Operating expense ratio	Operating costs as a percentage of sales	Operating expense/sales
	Sales of new products	Extent to which sales are driven by new products	Sales from new products/sales
Profitability	EBITDA	Earnings before interest, taxes, depreciation/amortization; serves as a proxy for the firm's cash flow	
	EBIT	Earnings before interest and tax	
	Return on assets (ROA)	Measures ability to turn assets into profit; often synonymous with ROI	Profit/total assets
	Return on equity (ROE)	Rate of return on investments by shareholders	Profit/equity
	Return on sales (ROS)	Amount of money made per every monetary unit of sales	Profit/sales
Liquidity	Accounts receivable turnover	Number of times receivables turn over during the year	Sales/average accounts receivable
	Days in accounts receivable	Number of days until payment; serves as a proxy for customer payment habits; can be compared to own payment habits	Average accounts receivable/sales * 365
	Quick ratio	Cash, bank deposits, bankable securities, accounts receivable; as a percentage of short-term debt	(Cash + bank deposits + bankable securities + accounts receivable)/short-term debt
	Current ratio	Current assets = short-term assets, such as cash, bank deposits, bankable securities,	Current assets/short-term debt

Table 9.5 (continued)

Type	Financial ratio	Description	Definition
		accounts receivable, inventory; as a percentage of short-term debt	
	Net working capital	Ability to pay short-term debt using short-term assets	Current assets – short-term debt
Security	Leverage	Indebtedness of firm	Total debt/equity
	Equity ratio	Equity from total assets	Equity/total assets
	Interest coverage	Number of times EBITDA could pay interest on debt	EBITDA/interest on debt
Value creation	ROCE	Return on capital employed; capital employed = equity + interest-bearing debt	EBIT/capital employed
	EVA	Economic value added; indicates whether firm profit is above or below the cost of capital	Net operating profit after tax – cost of capital

and security needs. As owners and managers may not always have the same preferences (consider, e.g., the reinvestment of profits vs. the payout of dividends), these two parties must jointly address the three dilemmas and seek constructive solutions through open communications.

9.10.1 The growth versus liquidity dilemma: the role of dividends

The growth rate of firms is determined by its growth capacity, which is defined as:

$$\text{Growth capacity} = \text{ROE} * (1 - \text{payout ratio})$$

This relationship posits that the firm will only be able to grow at the rate that remains after all expenses and all dividends to shareholders have been paid. In particular, the higher the dividends, the more the firm's growth is restrained. For instance, in a family firm, the firm's growth will be lower if the family has a lavish lifestyle and, thus, a greater need for dividends. In this regard, there is a direct link between the family's lifestyle choices and the growth of the firm. Let us look at some figures: if the family wishes the firm to grow at a rate of 10% and the firm achieves an ROE of 15%, then the firm can pay out 33% of its profit. To achieve 12% growth, it must limit the dividend payout to 20%.

Table 9.6 Financial indicators of publicly listed family and nonfamily firms in the United States

Financial ratio	Definition	Family firms	Nonfamily firms	Significant difference ** at 5% *** at 1%	Interpretation
Total assets ($ millions)	Book value of total assets	2956	6434	**	Family firms are more asset light
Total sales ($ millions)	Annual total of net sales	2968	5538	***	Family firms are smaller
Firm age	Number of years since foundation	42.22	49.77	***	Family firms are younger
Debt ratio	Long-term debt/total assets	15.22	18.33	***	Family firms are less leveraged
Cash flow	(Net income + annual depreciation)/total assets	8.52	6.82	***	Family firms have higher cash flows
Dividend payout ratio	Annual cash dividends/total assets	1.26	1.03	**	Family firms have higher dividend payouts
Asset tangibility	Liquidity proxy: (0.715 * accounts receivable + 0.547 * inventory + 0.535 * PP&E + net cash)/total assets	49.85	48.63		
Return volatility (firm risk)	Standard deviation of monthly stock returns for previous 36 months	12.43	12.25		
Tobin's Q	(Market value of common stock + book value of preferred stock + book value of long-term debt)/book value of total assets	1.86	1.83		
Transparency index	Relative transparency of firm using three proxies: trading volume, bid–ask spread and analyst following	14.10	17.12	***	Family firms are less transparent
Total investment/total assets (%)	(R&D expenditures + capital expenditures)/total assets	9.01	9.62		
R&D expenses/total investment (%)	R&D expenditures/(R&D expenditures + capital expenditures)	26.46	35.73	***	Family firms have lower R&D expenditures
Capital expenditure/total investment (%)	Capital expenditure/(R&D expenditure + capital expenditure)	73.54	64.27	***	Family firms have higher capital expenditures

Note: PP&E = Property, plant and equipment.

Source: Anderson, Duru and Reeb (2012); data for 2003 to 2007; for data on European family firms refer to Croci, Doukas and Gonenc (2011).

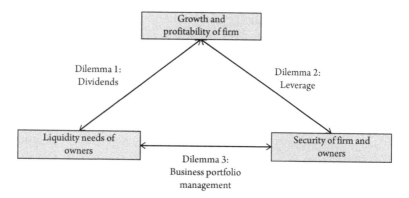

Figure 9.3 Three dilemmas in the financial management of family firms

The few available empirical studies show that, with data on public US family firms, family firms have higher payout ratios than nonfamily firms (see Table 9.6); similar findings for Europe are available in Pindado, Requejo and de la Torre (2012). Most of the available studies focus on publicly listed family firms, while very little data is available on the payout ratios of private family firms (for an exception refer to Michiels et al. 2015).

The central argument in favor of dividend payout is that dividends are a way for the controlling family owners to signal to minority owners that the family adheres to good corporate governance standards and that it does not expropriate minority owners by filling the family's pockets with money that belongs to all shareholders. This argument not only applies to public firms, but also to private family firms. It seems that dividend policy often starts to become an issue when active and passive family owners coexist in a private family firm. Active family members typically have the incentive to invest and let the firm grow while passive family owners prefer a dividend.[8] Another reason next to the signaling effect that speaks in favor of dividend payout is that because the shares are typically not for sale and the family does not directly benefit from increases in the share price, dividends are one of the few ways besides salaries paid to employed family members to provide financial benefits to family shareholders.

Given the tradeoff between the dividend payout and the firm's growth capacity, it is paramount that owners and managers establish a dividend policy that is aligned with the target growth rate. An analysis of data covering large publicly listed firms (S&P 500) shows that, on average, family firms pay out roughly 30% of their net income.

Discussions of dividends should not only deal with the *level* of dividends, but also their *stability* from one year to the next. There is some evidence that family firms prefer to smooth dividends, and that they therefore move slowly from current dividend levels to some desired or optimal dividend level (Pindado, Requejo and de la Torre 2012). When profits rise, the firm increases dividends in a less than proportionate way. When profits fall, the firm decreases dividends in a less than proportionate way. Dividend smoothing may be a cautious way of adapting the payout policy to the firm's changing profitability.

Private family firms may sometimes decide to continually pay out a certain level of dividends, irrespective of the firm's profitability. The idea behind such a dividend policy is to guarantee the shareholders a steady stream of income and, thereby, to keep shareholders happy. If these payouts are low enough, this dividend policy will not endanger the firm. If the firm's reserves are large enough, the family may be able to maintain such a dividend policy over a number of years even if the firm is losing money. Over time, however, family shareholders will view the dividend income as a given and adapt their lifestyles to that expected income. They will therefore eventually become risk averse and oppose (necessary) strategic change that would require them to relinquish dividends for some time. Therefore, stable dividends that are paid out irrespective of firm performance may not only endanger the survival of the firm over time, but also entice family shareholders to adopt a lavish lifestyle or to view the firm more as a pension fund than as a risky equity investment.

Excursus: Can firm growth keep up with family growth? The family CAGR

Biological systems, such as families, are known to grow at exponential rates. We assume that the average lifespan of each individual is 80 years, that parents have children at the age of 25, and that children inherit shares in their parents' firms at the age of 20. The shares are equally distributed among offspring upon the death of a family member. In-laws do not receive any shares.

The following table (Table 9.7) estimates the number of family shareholders, their individual ownership stakes and the required compound annual growth rate (CAGR) of the firm that ensures that the firm's profit can keep up with the family's growth over a period of 100 years.

As is evident in the table, the compound annual growth rate of the firm varies depending on the average number of children per offspring. The family CAGR indicates how quickly a firm's profit has to grow from one year to the next to ensure that the value of the individual ownership stake remains stable despite the dilution of ownership with the arrival of new family shareholders.

The family CAGR is not the actual growth rate of the firm because it is before inflation and industry growth. Instead, the family CAGR indicates how much

Table 9.7 Firm profit and family growth

Average number of children per family member	Number of shareholders after 100 years	Ownership stake of individual shareholder after 100 years	Required compound annual growth rate over 100 years—Family CAGR
2	6	16.66%	1.10%
3	12	8.33%	1.81%
4	20	5.00%	2.33%

faster a firm needs to grow than its competitors if it wants to ensure that the firm's profit can keep up with the growth of the family tree.

Obviously, this goal is hard to achieve. Therefore, family shareholders need to accept the fact that if they are welcoming to new generations of family shareholders, their ownership stake will be diluted not only in terms of ownership percentage but, most likely, also in terms of value.

From this perspective, it makes sense for family business owners to emphasize the growth of the firm. At the same time, family owners have to consider raising external capital to grow the firm more quickly so that the value of the firm is able to keep up with the growth of the family tree. Alternatively, families may decide to 'prune the family tree' and buy out some family shareholders who are less committed to the firm. The ultimate insight is, however, that the growth of the firm is normally insufficient to keep up with the growth of the family tree.

9.10.2 The profitability versus security dilemma: the role of leverage

The second dilemma explores the tension between the firm's profitability and its security. A firm creates value whenever it generates a return on capital above the weighted average cost of capital (WACC), as outlined in our discussion of EVA.

There are two ways to achieve this goal. The first is to enhance the firm's profit through operational improvements, innovation, internationalization and other strategic actions. The second is to reduce the firm's cost of capital by, for example, leveraging the company. This is because the cost of debt is typically lower than the cost of equity. Therefore, by replacing equity with debt, the WACC will fall. As outlined in section 9.7.1 on the leverage effect, a firm can increase its ROE by increasing leverage as long as the ROI is higher than the cost of debt.

Consequently, family firms are caught in a dilemma. On the one hand, the family is concerned about the security of its ownership stake, which would suffer with increasing leverage. On the other hand, the family may be tempted to increase leverage in order to increase ROE. As outlined in section 9.7.3 on the appropriate amount of leverage, family firms should solve this dilemma by limiting the amount of leverage, even though more leverage would theoretically increase ROE. It makes sense for family firms to target an A rating and, thus, an interest coverage of about 6 × (for additional details refer to section 9.7.3).

9.10.3 The liquidity versus security dilemma: the role of portfolio management

Industries and businesses typically evolve along a lifecycle that is characterized by specific phases, including inception, growth, maturity and decline. This means that, at some point, business owners have to deal with a context that challenges the firm's prosperity. Thus, it is essential for the far-sighted management of a company to consider the finite nature of the current business activities. If business owners wish to counter this seemingly inescapable decline, they have to determine where their business(es) are in the lifecycle, and they must pump the capital generated by maturing and declining businesses into new activities that hold promise.

The pursuit of such a portfolio approach is easier said than done. Founders tend to be skilled marketers or engineers, but they often lack the finan-

---

Excursus: Deriving strategic actions by comparing profitability and the cost of capital

One straightforward way to assess whether a firm's profitability meets the firm's cost of capital is to measure return on capital employed (ROCE, often termed ROIC) and compare it to the firm's weighted cost of capital (WACC). ROCE is defined as follows:

$$ROCE = EBIT/(equity + debt)$$

ROCE is useful for comparing the relative profitability of a company after taking the amount of capital used into account. It also serves as a useful benchmark against which alternative investment opportunities can be evaluated. Depending on whether a firm's ROCE fails to meet, meets or exceeds its WACC, different strategic measures must be considered (see also Axelrod and McCollom-Hampton, FFI Conference 2013):

1. **ROCE > WACC**: Stay on course, do not become complacent, grow.
2. **Cost of debt < ROCE < WACC**: Ask hard questions, watch the trends, examine overhead costs, review/adapt incentives.
3. **ROCE < cost of debt**: Identify root causes, reduce leverage and investments, shrink to the profitable core, examine competences of finance team, consider exiting.
4. **ROCE** < 0: Urgently implement corrective action, turn around/wind down if more than one year or if credible action plan is lacking, examine competences of leadership team.

cial and strategic skills needed to manage a portfolio of businesses. More importantly, the owners may simply not see the need to move toward a portfolio strategy, or they may be too complacent or risk averse to reinvest in new businesses. From the perspective of the sound, long-term development of family wealth, however, the owners need to face the fact that the businesses they are operating will decline sooner or later if they do not invest in new activities.

As such, families in business face another dilemma in the financial management of the firm. One option is to extract as much capital as possible from the firm and transfer those funds to the private sphere to increase the liquid wealth of family members and diversify wealth away from the family firm. The other option is to reinvest the funds and build a portfolio of businesses, perhaps within the same firm, with great future potential.

This portfolio management approach ideally follows what has been called the 'successful sequence'. Firms are typically founded as 'question marks', and hence as firms with low market share but operating in high-growth markets. Such businesses must be turned into 'stars', which are defined as businesses in growth markets and with large but neutral cash flows. In other words, they generate significant cash flows but also require substantial investments in order to flourish. When the business matures, stars hopefully become 'cash cows', which generate large, positive cash flows. At this stage, it is paramount for the owners to maintain a sense of urgency and risk propensity, and to reinvest the accumulating capital into new question marks in order to prepare for the next cycle of growth.

Unfortunately, many family firms fail to maintain a competitive position by adequately reinvesting. This can be deadly. Consider, for instance, a case in which a star company never manages to establish a business model that generates substantial cash and makes it a cash cow. Instead, it turns into a question mark and, finally, a dog. Cash cows can become dogs if a firm holds on to a shrinking business.

9.11 Principles for the sustainable financial management of family firms

In summary of the above discussion of key financial aspects, we present the following general principles for the sustainable financial management of a family firm.

1. **Keep an eye on the key financials**
   Measure and track the key financial ratios related to operational efficiency, profitability, security, liquidity and value.
2. **Use leverage carefully**
   Given the undiversified wealth of the owners, be careful with using debt. Define a target rating and derive the maximum debt level.
3. **Focus on value, not just profit**
   Keep in mind that a firm that generates a profit does not necessarily create value. Compare the firm's net operating profit after tax to its cost of capital.
4. **Grow the firm**
   Growth is important, especially given the expansion of the family tree and the resulting dilution of wealth.
5. **Establish a dividend policy that is in line with the growth aspirations for the business**
   Remember that dividends reduce the firm's growth potential. Set a growth target for the firm and then calculate the resulting sustainable payout ratio.
6. **Use portfolio-management thinking**
   Businesses mature and decline over time. Analyze (potential) sources of current and future cash flows.

9.12 The role of the CFO in family firms

At the founding stage, most family firms will not have a dedicated CFO. A CFO may simply not be required, as the financial function is restricted to record keeping, bill payment and payroll. In addition, founders often want to keep their financial affairs private. As the firm grows and matures, more sophisticated financial management techniques are needed, such as cost accounting, reporting systems, budgeting, allocation of excess liquidity and identification of appropriate sources of growth capital. Moreover, firms must deal with banks and equity investors, and negotiate business transactions (Fischetti 2000).

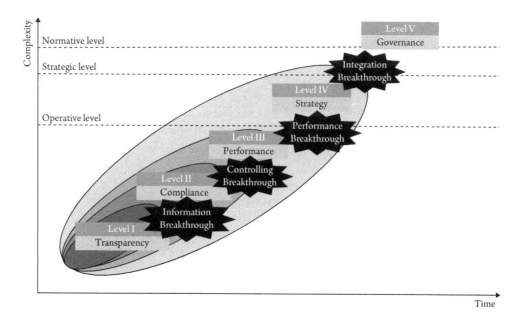

Figure 9.4 The evolutionary role of the CFO

The financial function thus evolves in line with the evolution of the firm. Ohle (2012) suggests that the role of the CFO in family firms evolves as complexity increases, especially in terms of the size of the family business (Figure 9.4). At low levels of complexity, the CFO's primary role is to create transparency so that the firm can execute its basic financial functions, such as cash collection, bill payment and basic bookkeeping. Transparency is crucial, as a lack thereof hinders the development of the finance function toward best-in-class support of the overall development of the family firm. Only if these basic tasks are addressed can the CFO's role move toward improving the effectiveness and efficiency of the business through, for example, cost accounting, budgeting, and implementation of compliance and internal audit capabilities.

In moving beyond such operating tasks, the CFO will eventually become able to take part in strategic issues. In this respect, the CFOs role is to provide in-depth information about the various functions of the firm and its organizational entities. This information is important for the strategic management of the firm in such aspects as sales, marketing and production, and for the financial function itself. At this stage, the CFO will most likely also be coordinating a multi-business or multi-product firm, and will therefore need to keep track of the growth and profitability of the various businesses.

Ultimately, the CFO will have to integrate the normative claims that different stakeholders have vis-à-vis the firm, especially those of the family, and ensure that the various goals and demands are aligned. At this stage, the CFO's role shifts again and may even include the management of the private assets of the family, as well as advising on the overall structure of the firm. Thus, CFOs in successful family firms are often involved in operational, strategic and normative questions. Such CFOs thus become trusted advisors to the family in business matters as well as private issues (Figure 9.4).

In the family business, the CFO must also develop a skill set that goes beyond financial acumen. He or she must navigate the dilemmas outlined above (see section 9.10), especially when the controlling family's interests are not perfectly aligned with those of other stakeholders. The dividend policy is one such focal point, as the CFO needs to keep an eye on the growth aspirations of the business and on the dividend requirements of the family members. Similarly, risk taking can be an important discussion point for the CFO, as family owners may be cautious when faced with risky strategic decisions. The firm may, for example, need to invest in new, somewhat uncertain activities if it wishes to prosper in the long run. In this situation, the CFO's role is to communicate with shareholders, and to demonstrate that the business risks are not excessive and are within the limits set by the shareholders. The extraction of private benefits of control by the family, such as when the firm pays part of the family's private expenses, represents a particularly fertile ground for conflict between the CFO and the controlling family. Within the confines of law, the owner is free to decide on how to run the firm. How should a nonfamily CFO react when a family owner, who may even be the CFO's boss, uses the firm's capital to finance private projects that have nothing to do with the firm? A similar issue can arise if the owner asks the CFO to manage private family wealth, a task for which the CFO is typically neither originally hired to handle nor trained to address.

Interaction with the family's shareholders is of crucial importance for the CFO. Shareholders of family firms are often limited in their willingness and ability to trade their shares. It follows that family shareholders often feel locked into their investments. Even when the firm grows and pays decent dividends, some shareholders, especially those who are not involved in the daily operations, may be dissatisfied with the firm's development and may not trust the firm's management. This is simply because they do not receive sufficient information about what is going on inside the firm and, consequently, feel excluded from decisions and downgraded to passive bystanders. To avoid the disruptive effects of dissatisfied family shareholders, the CFO, eventually together with the CEO, should regularly inform all shareholders of the firm's strategic initiatives and treat all shareholders equally in this regard.

In addition, CFOs in family firms will encounter the importance of SEW and the fact that families in business often focus on nonfinancial utility in the firm. In particular, CFOs will come face to face with the wish to keep control in the hands of the family across generations and the focus on reputational benefits arising from being associated with the firm. Often, the pursuit of SEW runs counter to the financial interests of the firm. Consider, for example, the preservation of a legacy activity that is losing money. What should the CFO's stance be in such a situation?

In light of the above dilemmas, the CFO should serve as an impartial advisor to all of the firm's stakeholders. The CFO should not be aligned with any family faction or with a particular shareholder group. The CFO's role is to serve as the trusted custodian of the firm's finances, and as someone who brings rationality and clarity into discussions that can easily be clouded and biased by emotions. The CFO has to creatively devise solutions that all parties can accept, and he or she must be a gifted communicator able to address all relevant stakeholders. As the advocate for the financial health of the firm, the CFO is primarily concerned with the financial consequences of strategic decisions. The impartiality of the CFO becomes all the more important when the firm has multiple shareholders, especially when some shareholders do not work inside the firm or when the family firm is publicly listed.

The CFO must also have the stamina to oppose suggestions made by the owners that are not aligned with the corporate governance or the agreed strategy of the firm, such as when owner suggestions will unilaterally benefit only one group of (family) shareholders. Ideally, such issues should be officially discussed and resolved by the management board, the board of directors or even the general assembly. Family owners are normally the most powerful stakeholders within the firm. As such, they are capable of overruling or bypassing the governance bodies, and pushing the CFO toward unilaterally steering decisions in their favor. Whether the CFO gives in to the demands of the owners then becomes a matter of the CFO's personality and his/her work ethic.

CASE STUDY

An interview with a long-standing CFO in a large family firm

In an interview, the long-standing nonfamily CFO of a Singaporean family firm was asked about dealing with the family owners. He replied:

> In contrast to the case of a publicly listed company, the owners in my firm are very present and powerful. It is not that I have to spend a great deal of time on investor relationships like my colleagues in publicly listed family firms—for instance, they spend days and weeks on road shows to meet their pension-fund investors. The presence and power of my owners brings other challenges. Here is a dilemma that I feel quite prominently in my case: on the one hand, I need to subscribe to the values of the company, which I happily do. I also want to be loved by the owner. If he thinks I am disloyal to the firm and dislikes me, he will fire me. He has the power to do so—there is no doubt about it. At the same time, however, I need to make myself heard, to have the owner's ear . . . I try to be the trusted advisor who walks the fine line between dependence and independence. I have earned the trust of the owners over the many years I have been working here.
>
> My role here is to prepare the decisions, to show the owners the various options they have, to keep a discussion going and to make the owners think through the various options so that they can make informed decisions. In so doing, I try to be as rational as possible and I do not take sides.
>
> Sometimes if the owners do not want to listen to an important piece of advice I have for them, it gets tricky. In the past, I have asked the owner of another family firm to speak to my owners. I have also asked the chairman of a large auditing company to talk to the owners about the issue so that they hear the concerns from other people they trust or respect. In this way, there is some level of diplomacy in my job.'
>
> Asked about whether he likes this situation, the CFO replied: 'It is not a question of whether I like it. It is the price we pay for being a private family firm. The owners are very present and powerful, and they will not fully delegate their ownership rights to a board. Therefore, we need to ensure that everyone is informed and aligned. There may be some potential problems in such a constellation, such as when the owners are very irrational or incompetent. In our case, the biggest risk may thus be the owners. However, in the end, this is still a more efficient collaboration between owners and managers than in the case of a widely held firm. Let's face it—in such firms, the owners simply have to hope that the managers will act in their best interests. They have very limited control over the managers. In such firms, the biggest risk is not the owners but the managers.

9.13 Management compensation in family firms

Management compensation is of utmost importance for the strategic management of a firm for at least two reasons. First, personnel costs are often the greatest expense item in firms. Second, and of central concern here, compensation systems serve to pay and incentivize a firm's managers and employees.

Over the last years multiple studies have explored the employment practices of family firms. Some suggest that family firms are areas full of stewardship behavior, whereby family owners are able to create a very caring and supportive atmosphere ('we treat our employees as if they were family'). This is because family owners identify strongly with their firm, are motivated to ensure its long-run survival, and tend to be deeply embedded in their social context. These attributes nurture a stewardship culture that motivates family members to care for the concerns of their employees, and stimulate high levels of commitment, trust and loyalty among employees (Corbetta and Salvato 2004). In sum, family firms should be great places to work.

But there is also a more pessimistic view about family firms' employment practices. Drawing from arguments primarily rooted in economics, other observers suggest that the unrestrained power that family owners have over their firms makes anyone who contracts with a family firm, especially the nonfamily managers, vulnerable to the unilateral exercise of that power. Because ultimately no one can control the owner besides the owner him-/herself, and because (employment) contracts do not specify all eventualities, nonfamily managers are exposed to the particularistic and changing preferences of owners, honest disagreements about the best strategy for the firm, even unprofessional conduct by the owner, or outright owner opportunism. In the case of owner opportunism the owner would, for instance, not hold promises he/she has made to the manager and exploit the manager who has made firm-specific investments, such as, for instance, buying a house close to the firm. Typically, the owner may make promotion promises to the non-family manager but then appoint a family member to the promised position. Such threats of owner holdup, whether as a consequence of disagreements between owner and manager or opportunism by the owner, should make it difficult for family firms to hire, retain and motivate highly skilled managers (Chrisman, Memili and Misra 2014; Schulze and Zellweger 2016).

Whether the bright or the dark side prevails in the average family firm is still a matter of debate. It is clear, however, that it is the owners themselves who must sometimes curb their power so as to bring out the best in their employees and make them commit to the firm, which ultimately is in the owners own best interest.

9.13.1 Some findings and reflections on compensation practices in family firms

Studies comparing pay levels in family versus nonfamily firms have consistently found lower pay levels in exchange for higher job security in family firms. This pattern of employment practices is rather robust, both at the level of managers and regular employees (Sraer and Thesmar 2007; Bassanini et al. 2013).

Exploring the relationship between compensation of family managers and the risk of the firm, Gomez-Mejia, Larraza-Kintana and Makri (2003) find that family managers earn less than nonfamily managers but that their compensation is at least partially insulated against risks.[9] Such risk averse compensation contracts are not surprising if we keep in mind that such owner-managers have a largely undiversified wealth and income position.

Defining the compensation package of family members is a tricky issue, especially if some family member has to decide about the pay level of some other family member. Too often family members are excessively insulated against any risks, earn a fixed salary and are thus not particularly motivated to take risks to grow the firm. In the extreme case family members earn a high salary independent of their performance.[10] Alternatively, to keep family peace and treat family members equally, family members in the business earn the same salary despite differing responsibilities and abilities. In other words, family members' compensation is not determined by merit, but by family status.

For families in business it is important to keep in mind that such compensation practices frustrate family and nonfamily managers who feel underrewarded given their contributions to the firm. It is a sign of professional family ownership if family members are paid on a level commensurate with their performance and responsibilities and in line with what is paid to nonfamily employees.

9.13.2 Base salary

An essential part of any compensation package is the base salary, which is a fixed amount of money that the employer pays to the employee regardless of the performance of the firm or the employee. Even though employees can often earn more than the base salary through various incentive schemes, the base salary serves as an important reference point in compensation negotiations, and in the social comparison of the employee with his or her peers. Because family owners want to avoid excessive risk taking and keep control in family hands, nonfamily managers in family firms sometimes earn a relatively high base salary but do not get any performance-related bonus or even common stock.

9.13.3 Bonus plan and supplemental benefits

The idea of bonus plans is to reward managers and employees for their performance, for instance in proportion to EBIT or some other profit measure. Alternatively, the firm may decide to set goals for growth, value creation or profitability, and state that if the firm reaches these goals over, for instance, three consecutive years, a substantial bonus will be paid to management. Attractive compensation plans sometimes also include some supplemental benefits, such as non-qualified retirement plans ('non-qualified' for tax purposes), medical savings accounts and other firm-specific benefits. To limit managerial risk taking, bonuses are oftentimes capped.

9.13.4 Common stock

For large firms, especially those that are publicly listed, making employees co-owners of the firm is an obvious way to align the incentives of managers with those of owners. However, many family firms are reluctant to hand stock over to managers or employees for multiple reasons. First and foremost, employee stock ownership is often not desirable for family owners because opening up ownership dilutes family control over the firm. Second, employee stock ownership may not be possible because the firm is not a stock company but has some other legal form, such as a partnership or a limited liability company. Third, stock ownership plans can be costly, as value has to be shared with third parties and the stock plan has to be administered by the firm, which creates administrative costs. Fourth, in the case of private family firms, the determination of firm value can pose a problem and lead to disagreements. Finally, stock ownership plans may create frustration among managers and employees who are not eligible for the plan.

Does it pay for a firm to give stock to employees? After centuries of practice and decades of research on whether firms that have a stock ownership plan perform better than those without, the results are rather disenchanting. If there is any effect at all, it is minor (for an overview of the related research, see Dalton et al. 2007). In sum, despite the intuitive appeal of stock owner-ship plans aimed at aligning the financial incentives of owners and manag-ers, they come with important disadvantages, especially in family firms, and often do not lead to the desired effects.

9.13.5 Phantom stock and stock appreciation rights (SARs)

For many family firms, employee ownership plans are not the best fit, espe-cially because they entail a loss of control for the family. For such firms, phantom stock or stock appreciation rights (SARs) may be attractive alter-natives (for a discussion of the practicalities, refer to the US-based National Center for Employee Ownership, for instance). Phantom stock is a cash bonus plan that can be introduced when the owners want to share the eco-nomic value of equity but not equity itself. The most obvious benefit is that phantom stock plans enable owners to create an incentive for managers without giving control away. As explained by Fischetti (2000), a phantom stock plan is a contract between a company and its managers in which the company promises to pay the employee a sum of money that is reflective of the rise in the firm's stock value over a specified period of time. Such plans thus often also include dividend payments.

Assume, for example, that a firm's value is $5 million, which is divided into 10 000 units of phantom stock. The value of one phantom stock is thus $500. Paul, the firm's nonfamily CEO, gets 100 phantom stocks, so that the total value of his phantom stocks is $50 000. Under Paul's leadership, the firm's value triples over the next three years, as does the value of the phantom stocks. Paul's phantom stocks are now worth $150 000. As Paul's contract states that he has a three-year vesting period, he can only start to sell his phantom stocks in year four. Also, he cannot sell all of his stocks at once, but only 33% of the phantom stocks per year. If he leaves the firm before the end of the vesting period of three years, he has to hand all of the phantom stocks back to the firm without any compensation.

Just like phantom stock, SARs are a type of cash bonus plan. In contrast to phantom stock, which emulate common stock, SARs emulate stock options. However, in contrast to stock options, the recipient does not have to pay an option premium when the SAR is awarded. As in the case of options, the employees have the flexibility to decide when to exercise a SAR after it vests. While phantom stocks often pay dividends, SARs do not. SARs give the participant the right to receive a cash or equivalent stock amount equal to the appreciation on a specified number of shares of company stock over a speci-fied period of time. The advantages of phantom stocks and SAR are evident:

- They create an incentive for managers to increase firm value.
- They do so without diluting the control in the hands of family.
- They are relatively flexible.

However, these programs also have important disadvantages. Some of the disadvantages are comparable to those evident for common stock ownership plans, such as disagreements about the appropriate firm value, the cost of the plan's administration and managers' eligibility to take part in the plan. But here are further disadvantages:

- These plans foster a focus on the short term despite the vesting period. Managers may oppose value-creating investments that will only pay off after they have left the company.
- If a phantom stock or SAR is only a promise of a future cash payment, employees might believe that the benefit is as 'phantom' as the stock, especially in the context of powerful family owners who can hardly be held accountable if they change their minds, for instance about the incentive plan itself.
- The company needs to create cash reserves and contribute to those reserves at a rate commensurate with the increase in firm value, which limits the firm's growth potential.
- While the reserves for the phantom stock are typically tax deductible for the firm, the employee who receives the benefits must often pay income tax.

In practice, it is also important to consider the potentially destructive effects of incentive plans. Consider, for example, a difficult year for the firm in which firm value decreases but the manager does an excellent job of solving the problems. In this case, there is a mismatch between individual performance and the bonus, which results in frustration at the manager level. This, in conjunction with the limited evidence of the overall benefits of sophisticated incentive plans, leads us to conclude that such plans often do not live up to their promises. It is therefore not surprising that many family firms have simple management compensation plans with decent fixed salaries that are sometimes complemented with bonuses that vary with the performance of the firm. In such situations, the bonus is often capped.

9.13.6 Psychological ownership

In light of the limitations of stock ownership, phantom stock and SARs, firms seek alternative ways to encourage their employees and managers to behave like owners. Psychological ownership taps into this idea by asking what makes employees feel and act like owners even though they do not hold stock or any other rights in the firm.

There is mounting evidence that people will only change their behaviors and start acting like owners if they feel that the company is theirs. Only if they are psychological owners will they, for instance, act more entrepreneurially and go the 'extra mile' for the firm. This has important implications for the structure of compensation systems. The fact that someone holds shares in a firm does not necessarily mean that he or she will feel and act as expected of an owner. For instance, an owner may have so little impact on firm value that he or she simply has no incentive to exert more effort. Alternatively, someone may inherit shares in a firm but have no feeling of ownership. For such an owner, the shares may come with undesired obligations and responsibilities, which might lead the owner to sell the shares as quickly as possible. However, there is another way of thinking about the incentive effects of ownership. As legal ownership has no behavioral impact without feelings of ownership ('I feel this is my company'), we may be able to directly foster feelings of ownership without having to hand out shares and without the hassles that come with doing so.

Recent research shows that people who feel they are owners, even though they have no legal ownership, actually behave like owners (Sieger, Zellweger and Aquino 2013). Thereby, feelings of ownership grow in line with employee tenure in a company and in line with hierarchical position. Moreover, men typically score higher than women on psychological ownership for a firm (Van Dyne and Pierce 2004). Research finds three actionable levers that can increase psychological ownership (Pierce, Kostova and Dirks 2001): (1) the presence of a just compensation system that pays people based on their performance, (2) a culture of proactive, open communication and information access, and (3) delegation of control. Prior to installing sophisticated incentive systems, such as stock ownership, phantom stock or SARs, family firms should thus consider whether they have done enough to ensure that managers and employees can feel like psychological owners.

9.14 The responsible shareholder in the family firm

From a legal perspective, the sole responsibility of shareholders is to pay for the shares. In exchange for this transfer, the shareholder receives the right to participate in the general assembly and to vote on the issues discussed therein, for example appointments to the board of directors. As the typical minority shareholder only owns a very small stake in the firm, he or she typically does not have the power or the incentive to take an active role in the firm's activities. For management, this situation is quite comfortable and provides it with important leeway to run the firm at its own discretion. None of the shareholders are able and motivated to actively challenge management's decisions or to hold it accountable beyond the legally binding obligations.

The situation looks quite different in family firms, where owners control a majority stake and, thus, have both the power and the incentive (given their undiversified wealth) to hold management accountable for its decisions. If we assume that family firm owners should monitor the firm's management, challenge management's decisions, and critically discuss and even provide guidance regarding the direction of the firm, then they need to have the abilities to do so. Some family business owners may be happy with delegating these tasks to the board of directors. However, at least some of the family owners should be able to engage in direct dialogue with management. They should not only monitor the firm's strategy and managerial behavior ex post, but also engage in strategy formulation before any malfeasance can occur. What, then, are the required competences for family shareholders?[11] Here is a list of some of the most important attributes of responsible family shareholders:

1. Clarify values for the family and firm.
2. Translate values into strategic goals.
3. Hold management accountable to the goals.
4. Establish family, ownership and corporate governance rules—and stick to them.
5. Understand the key financials and value drivers of the firm.
6. Be mindful.

9.14.1 Clarify values for the family and firm

A family firm's values are often reflective of the founder's personal values and idiosyncratic vision about what he or she wants to achieve with the firm. In the case of L.L. Bean, the US outdoor apparel firm, the founder's values are ingrained in the value statement, which remains valid for the company today: 'We do not want you to have anything from L.L. Bean that is not completely satisfactory.' Another good example is IKEA, which honors the following values: 'Humbleness and willpower, leadership by example, daring to be different, togetherness and enthusiasm, cost-consciousness, constant desire for renewal, accept and delegate responsibility.' Over the years, IKEA has stood by a set of values that affect the way people work inside the company, as well as the firm's hiring policy. These values are as important in a design studio in Sweden as they are in a retail store in the United States or at a production site in China.

Value statements serve as a credible reflection of the company's values. In the case of L.L. Bean, those values are customer service and quality. For IKEA, they are a willingness to be different, determined, enthusiastic and daring. Value statements provide guidance for management on strategic questions, offer a sense of purpose and serve as a motivation for stakeholders, especially clients and employees, to identify and engage with the firm. Values help increase the efficiency of a firm because they foster a mutual understanding of how things are done and how people work inside the firm.

In many family firms, the link to the founder's values remains because the founder is still active in the firm or descendants of the founder run the firm in a way that reflects the founder's inspirational business philosophy. Many family firms therefore have the opportunity to draw from a particularly personal, tangible and credible set of values, which they can use to differentiate themselves in the marketplace.

Values have to be renewed from time to time. Consider, for example, the value statement of Tamedia, a Swiss family controlled media company. As part of its current value and mission statement, the company writes: 'Through independent reporting and critical investigations, our media make an important contribution to the formation of opinions.' A previous version of the mission statement also included the term 'newspaper' and mentioned the metropolitan region in which the firm is based. However, these aspects of the original value statement became obsolete with the shift from newspapers to online media and with the internationalization of the firm. However, the core value statement on independent reporting and critical investigations has not lost its topicality. Clearly, value statements need to be reviewed periodically to assess whether their meaning remains relevant and functional in the current context, and whether family members can identify with them.

9.14.2 Translate values into strategic goals

Values have to be made tangible to have an impact. Value statements risk becoming toothless rhetoric if they are not translated into specific goals that are reflective of those values. Responsible owners must therefore establish goals based on the firm's values and hold people, especially the firm's board members and management, accountable for them. For instance, a family firm that values entrepreneurship can translate that value into an emphasis on innovation and proactiveness. In turn, the strategic goals of innovation and proactiveness should be measured, for instance, in terms of the number of new products the company launches over a certain period of time. Similarly, if a family emphasizes independence as part of its value statement, that value can be translated into limits on leverage. Relatedly, the family might also have to define whether it views the sale of part of the firm to external investors as an option.

The above example of the media company is useful for illustrating the importance of translating values into strategic goals. As mentioned, the company's value statement emphasizes critical investigations and the formation of an independent opinion in the public sphere. What does this mean with regard to the political orientation of the various news outlets and magazines the company owns? Moreover, what happens when a news outlet discusses a certain topic in a way that contradicts the family's own political convictions? It is exactly for these types of situations that values need to be operationalized and translated into goals and behavioral principles for both the owners and the managers.

In addition to family- and firm-specific goals, family firms—just like nonfamily firms—should spell out financial goals for the firm. In smaller companies, this can take the form of a budget with which all shareholders agree. In larger companies, where the owners are less involved in management, stated goals should typically cover growth aspirations, dividend payouts and leverage. They might also include noneconomic goals, such as location and ethical behavior.

9.14.3 Hold management accountable to the goals

Based on the guidance provided by the owners, the board of directors must translate the owners' values into strategic goals. However, only if the board holds management accountable to those goals can the family owners be sure that the firm is being run in a way that takes the issues that matter to the shareholders into account (Poza 2013).

To define goals and hold management accountable to them, owners and board members must have a good understanding of the business, the industry and the trends affecting the firm. This requires owners who are able to critically assess the firm's strategy. Otherwise, goals may be unrealistic or not sufficiently ambitious. Even though owners, especially owners of large, professionally run family firms, often have limited experience in strategy *implementation*, they need to be involved in the *formulation* of strategy and in its *monitoring*.

The formulation of a firm's strategy should ideally be neither a purely top-down process (i.e., the board dictating the strategy to the management) nor a purely bottom-up process (i.e., management dictating the strategy to the board). Based on the value statements defined by the owners, the board should develop a set of tangible goals. These goals should then be critically discussed, refined and substantiated in conjunction with management. Management then has to come up with a strategic plan for achieving the defined goals. That strategic plan should be discussed and refined with the board. Through this type of iterative process, family firms can ensure the alignment of family values, goals and business strategies.

Owners wishing to maintain control should monitor the execution of the strategy and hold management accountable to the goals. In other words, owners should not be passive recipients of results—they should carefully monitor the course of the firm, keeping their 'nose in the business, but their hands out of the business'. While owners and the board should not interfere in management's day-to-day work, they should maintain a regular dialogue with key decision makers inside the firm.

9.14.4 Establish family, ownership and corporate governance rules—and stick to them

In Chapter 5 on governance, we learned about the importance of family, ownership, corporate governance and even wealth governance. In the absence of proper governance, family firms risk becoming inefficient and are ultimately doomed to fail. Responsible owners will therefore carefully consider which types of governance regulations are needed and stick to those regulations after they are defined.

A central goal linked to the governance of family firms is defining the roles family members should play in the firm today and in the future. This is not only important in terms of avoiding confusion within the family, but also for nonfamily managers and employees, who will appreciate the clarity and predictability of the family's stance toward the firm. In the end, such governance regulations determine the nonfamily managers' and employees' own job security and career prospects inside the family firm.

Many family members who are deeply involved in the operations of the firm naturally know about the firm's governance, and the roles played by owners, board members and managers. However, for family shareholders who are not involved in operations, knowing the principles of good governance and the specific regulations for the firm is crucial. Such shareholders must familiarize themselves with the governance regulations and take part in meetings during which these regulations are discussed or changed.

9.14.5 Understand the key financials and value drivers of the firm

Owning a company without proper knowledge of its financial health is like flying a plane without looking at the instruments. The decisive measures for assessing the financial health of the company are outlined in the above sections, especially section 9.9 on measures of efficiency, profitability, liquidity, security and value. However, do not be fooled—financial ratios are only as informative as the quality of the data used for their calculation. They have to be calculated consistently from period to period, used in comparison to firm-internal and firm-external benchmarks and goals, and viewed at both a single point in time and as an indication of trends over time. As owners with a long-term view, family business owners should pay particular attention to long-term trends in financial ratios and search for information about the outlook for the firm, keeping in mind that today's financial ratios are only a reflection of the past.

9.14.6 Be mindful

A key takeaway from the definition and strategy chapters (Chapters 2 and 6, respectively) was that family influence is a double-edged sword.[12] In the best case, it is a guarantor of efficiency, innovation and firm growth. In the worst case, it can be a source of inefficiency, inertia and stagnation. How can we ensure that the best case side prevails? Governance structures are an integral part of the solution, but they are not foolproof. They are only as good as the people who establish them, interpret them, (dis)respect them and eventually adapt them. The most successful family business owners not only establish appropriate governance structures, but also exhibit certain attitudes and behaviors toward their firms, which we might call 'mindfulness'.

As outlined in Brown and Ryan (2003), mindfulness is defined as the state of being particularly attentive to and aware of what is taking place in the present. A core characteristic of mindfulness is *open* or *receptive* awareness and attention, which may be reflected in a more regular or sustained consciousness of ongoing events and experiences (Brown and Ryan 2003). For example, in speaking with a relative or, for the sake of argument, with a manager of a family firm, one can be highly attentive to the ongoing communication and sensitively aware of the subtle emotional tones underlying the interaction. This is the kind of attitude and behavior responsible family business owners exhibit relative to their firms. Let us look at this facet of responsible family business ownership in more detail. Collective mindful families in business typically exhibit the following characteristics:

1. Be aware of the bivalence of family involvement.
2. Seek synergies between family and business.
3. Be hesitant to simplify things.
4. Consider the affordable loss and ensure the firm's resilience.
5. Adopt a long-term view.
6. Develop a sense of responsibility for the firm.

1. Be aware of the bivalence of family involvement

Family influence is not, per se, good or bad for a firm. Family influence is bivalent in that a single attribute, such as a long-term perspective, can have both positive and negative impacts on the firm (see our discussion of bivalent attributes of family firms in Chapter 4 on strengths and weaknesses of family firms). In the positive case, a long-term view implies an opportunity to innovate, while it is a recipe for complacency and inertia in the negative case. Mindful families in business understand that there is a fine line between business and family, and that there is always a threat that things could derail or a negative momentum could emerge.

Mindful families are therefore highly aware of the fragility of the situation in which they operate. As they understand that family influence is Janus faced, they are often worried that the family and the firm could be on the wrong track, even if all looks fine. This leads them to regularly challenge the current course of action, even if doing so seems unnecessary. This represents a responsible and mindful way to test the stability of the system against alternative interpretations. For families in business, concerns about the bivalent attributes sometimes result in repetitive, frustrating discussions. Such discussions start to make sense when seen in light of a mindful concern about the bivalent attributes of family influence.

2. Seek synergies between family and business

Mindfulness reasoning assumes that tensions persist within complex and dynamic systems. It shifts attention from identifying the conditions under which organizations are driven by certain factors (e.g., stability vs. change orientation; family vs. business interests) toward an examination of how firms simultaneously engage in these competing factors in order to reap synergies, flexibility, unity and creativity advantages. If all simultaneous contradictions are removed in management and if managers consistently pursue logical consistency, then excellence may be inhibited by the elimination of creative tensions.

This tension is best illustrated by considering the fundamental tensions between family and business. Some people argue that family firms should adopt a business-first philosophy, which would always give precedence to business over family matters. The opposite view can also be found in practice. However, both of these extreme positions forgo impor-

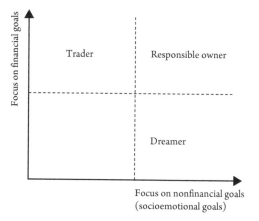

Source: Kammerlander et al. (2015).

Figure 9.5 Dreamer, trader and responsible owner

tant synergies between the family and the business. Responsible owners are permanently concerned about how to exploit the synergies between family and business. Family owners who adopt a business-first perspective and only focus on the short-term financial performance may become 'traders' who earn a decent living over a short period of time but forgo important opportunities that might arise from thinking beyond the daily trading gains. In the opposite case, family businesses adopt a family-first perspective, and are thus primarily concerned with the maintenance of family harmony, family reputation and family-internal leadership succession. These families close their eyes to the economic realities and related opportunities (Figure 9.5). Responsible owners thus seek synergies between family and business.

3. **Be hesitant to simplify things**

   Mindful families in business are reluctant to simplify interpretations. They appreciate multiple interpretations and perspectives, and are open to ambiguity stemming from the interaction between the family and the business (Farjoun 2010). As a consequence of this reluctance to simplify, mindful families are highly aware of the force of habit, history and tradition.

   Less mindful families easily confuse the stability of their emotionally rigid, rule-based assumptions with stability in the world, which provides them with a false reading of their surroundings. Less mindful families trust that management checklists will address their challenges (the 'checklist fallacy'). In contrast, mindful family business owners do not trust quick fixes. Rather, they adopt an inclusive approach, welcome opposing opinions and try to accommodate multiple views by seeking creative, new solutions. They are suspicious of their own and others' biased perspectives on circumstances.

4. **Consider the affordable loss and ensure the firm's resilience**

   Mindful families in business are preoccupied with the affordable loss, just as they are concerned with success. Responsible family business owners will not risk their total wealth (i.e., the family firm) in the pursuit of extreme but highly uncertain profits. Rather, responsible owners are concerned with profit only to the degree that the complete failure of a project is within the means of the family and the firm. As a consequence of their risk exposure, responsible family business owners also exhibit a high concern for reliability and continuation of the firm. In addition, they show a high commitment to resilience and, hence, an ability to rebound from setbacks.

5. **Adopt a long-term view**

   It seems almost naïve to believe that a controlling family would consistently put its own interests behind those of the firm. However, the future prosperity of the firm are integral parts of the family's utility function. Consequently, mindful families are less likely to seek immediate financial returns, and are more willing to accept a future and, hence, more uncertain payback. They are also less likely to fall prey to fallacies, such as the inappropriately high discounting of future returns.

6. **Develop a sense of responsibility for the firm**

   An integral part of a liberal understanding of economic activity is that owners' rights are protected. As long as the owners behave in accordance with the law, no one can stop them from unilaterally weakening the firm through either well-intended but mistaken strategic decisions or deliberate extraction of private benefits of control. The first type of inefficiency may be solved by, for example, installing a professional board and management team. The second inefficiency is often more difficult to address because the extraction of private benefits of control is sometimes rooted in a sense of entitlement among owners. Such irresponsible behaviors are also perceptible if the owners do not follow their own professional careers, but pursue a lavish lifestyle while living on the various financial benefits they receive from the firm. Mindful family business owners who are not involved in the operations of the firm ensure that they make a living and generate income from sources other than the firm. In addition, mindful families are more likely to view their status as owners of a family firm as a privilege, to develop a sense of responsibility for the firm and to care about the firm's long-term success.

Excursus: The mindless family business owner—A caricature

Mindless family business owners:

- Believe that family has to be separated from the business.
- Seek simple solutions, shortcuts and quick fixes.
- Strictly follow rules, regardless of the situation.
- Are convinced of the value of their own opinions.
- Aim for the maximum return, even if doing so involves high risks.
- Are willing to risk the continuation and reliability of the firm's operations.
- Emphasize short-term benefits.
- Feel entitled to benefits from the firm.
- Believe in checklists (like this one).

CASE STUDY

Developing responsible future family owners

The owners of a UK family firm decided to work toward developing the competences of the next generation of family owners. The related education concept held the following information.

Ideal competences of family owners

Ideally, an owner of our family firm:

- Knows the products and services our firm offers.
- Understands the trends in our industry in order to make the right strategic decisions.
- Is able to challenge management and ask critical questions.
- Provides guidance to management in terms of the values and goals of the owners.
- Knows the governance regulations in the firm, takes them seriously and serves as a role model.
- Knows and is able to interpret the key financial ratios of the business.
- Understands and is able to critically reflect on the firm's compensation system.
- Is willing to constructively and openly address conflicts within the family and the business.

Principles for the education of the next generation of family owners

We assume that not all family members who will hold shares in our firm in the future will be equally interested in our firm. The present concept on the education of next-generation family business owners therefore represents a nonbinding offer to our shareholders.

CASE STUDY *(continued)*

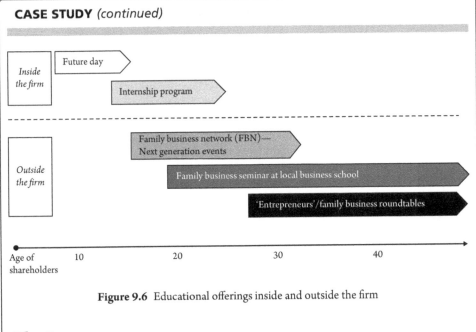

Figure 9.6 Educational offerings inside and outside the firm

Education program

We intend to prepare the next generation of family members for their roles as owners in a stepwise manner. With regard to the managerial involvement of family members, we refer to the governance regulations. In the following, we describe various educational offerings inside and outside the firm in terms of the audience attending the event/program, the content, the required prior knowledge, the ideal age and additional information sources (Figure 9.6).

9.15 CASE STUDY

Tom's world

After a number of years in banking and with an international auditing company, Tom was ready for a change. He received an offer to become the CFO of a family-controlled company. In addition to the decent salary, Tom was attracted by the opportunity to work directly for and with the owners of the company. His task, according to the family CEO, would be to 'professionalize' the firm.

Soon after joining the company, Tom realized that the firm had a very unique structure and he started to understand what it meant to be the CFO of a family firm. He realized that family topics interfered with his activities in various ways. For instance, Tom needed to establish a more in-depth and transparent reporting system. Without solid figures, it was difficult to compare the different activities and to increase the level of accountability among the different business units. This system showed that some of the firm's activities had been in the red for years. When Tom presented these figures to the management board and suggested that these operations come to an end as quickly as possible, the family CEO did not oppose Tom's suggestion. However, the CEO was unwilling to actually make this decision or to communicate it to the relevant departments. The decision was postponed—part of the CEO's hesitation had to do with his own involvement with a certain part of those businesses. Tom realized that there was not much he could do, and he decided to accept the underperforming activity because the losses were minor when seen in relation to the overall size of the firm.

The firm was owned by 15 family shareholders stemming from three family branches. The first family branch owned 55% of the firm, while the second held 35% and the third held 10%. Each branch had one representative on the board of directors. The family CEO was representative of the first branch. As a producer of dental implants, the firm was quite profitable and paid out roughly 40% of its net profit to the shareholders. The dividends had risen steadily over the years. However, when Tom met the shareholders on various occasions, he realized there were two rival groups: the shareholders representing branch 1 and the remaining shareholders who together controlled 45% of the firm. Despite the increasing dividends, the second group appeared to be dissatisfied, and members of that group were latently (and sometimes overtly) suspicious of the majority owners and the CEO.

Moreover, Tom was surprised to realize that, as CFO, he was partly responsible for the management of the family's private wealth in addition to running the firm's finance department. Apparently, the family shareholders had concluded that the CFO should handle some of their private financial matters. His department therefore had to manage the private wealth of some of the shareholders and file tax returns for others. Not all shareholders took advantage of this opportunity. For those who did, it was unclear whether the firm should charge them for the services. Tom felt uncomfortable with the situation—he was not an asset manager. What if his team backed the wrong horse when allocating private family assets? The problem threatened to get out of control when those shareholders who had not previously used these services decided to hand over their financial affairs to Tom's department, as the services seemed to be of good quality and were free for the shareholders. This trend was worrying for Tom, as the services consumed nearly an entire full-time position on his team.

Tom's collaboration with the family CEO worked well and the two seemed to like each other. However, one day, the CEO mentioned a private investment project to Tom. Apparently, the CEO's wife wanted to invest in a hotel project that had nothing to do with the firm's operations. To finance the project, the CEO asked Tom to prepare a loan contract in which the firm would lend $400 000 to the CEO. The CEO mentioned that he had approval from the board of directors and that he would repay the loan within two years. However, Tom was hesitant. The amount was manageable for the firm, but it was clear to

CASE STUDY *(continued)*

Tom that this was beyond any good governance standard. How should he approach the topic? The CEO was his boss and one of the firm's majority owners.

These questions were disturbing for Tom, as there was simply no textbook answer about how to solve them. He had never considered the possibility that such issues would become relevant for him as a CFO one day. Probably the trickiest challenge Tom faced was when he was invited to a board of director's meeting to present an acquisition project. The company was exploring an opportunity to buy a firm in an industry that was relatively unrelated to the current activities. The business outlook for the acquisition target looked fine, but the board members ended in a heated debate about whether to acquire the company. The representative of family branch 1 complained: 'This new business is not sufficiently close to what we are currently doing. There are hardly any synergies. Moreover, we are known as a producer of dental implants and have been in this industry for more than 50 years. Why should we dilute our image?' The representative of family branch 2 saw more advantages than disadvantages: 'We are so concentrated in a single industry. This is a great opportunity for us to diversify our business and thus limit the risks to our wealth.' The representative of the third family branch was more hesitant: 'Our part of the family does not see much value in diversification. We can diversify on our own. For many of us, our investment in the firm today primarily has financial meaning.' Toward the end of the discussion, Tom was asked for his opinions and feedback on the different points of view.

? **REFLECTION QUESTIONS**

1. What should Tom do about the underperforming activity in which the CEO was involved?
2. What could be the underlying reasons for the dissatisfaction of shareholder groups 2 and 3? What could Tom, as CFO, do about it?
3. With regard to the rendering of private financial services to the family, what are the risks for Tom and the firm?
4. Should Tom oppose the loan to the CEO? If so, how should he proceed?
5. With regard to the acquisition, what are the underlying motives for the arguments brought up by family branches 1, 2 and 3? How should Tom position himself?

? **REFLECTION QUESTIONS**

1. Discuss the assumptions of the capital asset pricing model (CAPM) and the degree to which they apply to family firms.
2. What is family equity? How is it distinct from private and public equity?
3. What does the empirical evidence say about the financial performance of family and non-family firms?
4. Are family firms more risk averse than nonfamily firms?
5. What are the advantages and disadvantages of debt financing?
6. Why do family firms typically have a lower cost of debt financing?

7. Explain the differences between the capital market line (CML) and the family market line (FML).

8. What are the risks associated with applying a lower than risk equivalent cost of equity capital?

9. Under which conditions does it pay for the owners to increase the firm's leverage?

10. How do the leverage levels of family firms compare to those of nonfamily firms?

11. What could the arguments for family firms to increase leverage be?

12. Explain the links among credit ratings, interest coverage and the amount of debt a firm should raise. Assume that the firm is required to achieve an A rating, has an EBITDA of $20 million and the risk-free rate is 4%.

13. Consider a family firm with which you are familiar. What are the informative financial ratios that can be used to measure its operational efficiency, profitability, liquidity, security and value creation?

14. Under which conditions can a firm destroy value while still generating a profit?

15. Explain the link between a firm's dividend policy and its growth?

16. How much dividend should a family firm pay out?

17. How should a family resolve the dilemma related to the leveraging of the firm? On the one hand, increased leverage normally increases return on equity (ROE). On the other hand, higher leverage increases the firm's default risk.

18. Why is portfolio management important for family firms?

19. What are the six principles of sustainable financial management in family firms?

20. On employment practices in family firms: discuss the competing views about whether family firms are great places to work.

21. What are the pros and cons of stock ownership plans in family firms?

22. Describe the functioning of phantom stock for a firm.

23. What are the pros and cons of phantom stock and stock appreciation rights (SARs)?

24. What is psychological ownership? What are the three levers for increasing it?

25. How is the role of a CFO in a family firm distinct from the role of a CFO in a nonfamily firm?

26. What are the attributes of responsible owners in family firms?

27. What does mindfulness mean in the context of family firm ownership?

NOTES

1   For an application of the CAPM, please refer to the Chapter 7 on succession, especially section 7.10.3 on discounted free cash flow valuation.

2   For a more detailed discussion of the strategic opportunities tied to an extended investment horizon, see Zellweger (2007).

3   For private, mid-sized firms in Europe and the United States with an established business model, the cost of equity ranges from 10% to 20% depending on the firm's risk profile.

4   Actually, the CML represents the risk–return relationship from the point of view of a diversified investor. Therefore, the opportunity cost of capital is much higher for an undiversified investor, such as the typical owner of a family firm, even the family owner of a listed family firm.

5   EBITDA = earnings before interest, tax, depreciation and amortization. EBITDA often serves as a proxy for cash flow.

6   For the sake of simplicity, we do not consider additional adjustments, such as value-increasing expenses.

7   For background information on cost of equity and debt capital, refer to Chapter 7 on succession and that chapter's section on valuations (section 7.10).

8   The challenge is to keep the family owners together with a shared vision (investing vs. paying out dividend). Family governance practices can help in maintaining such a shared vision on what to do with the cash. For example, it may be more optimal for all shareholders to invest (and grow) and keep the cash in the firm (for further information refer to Michiels et al. 2015).

9   More specifically, Gomez-Mejia, Larraza-Kintana and Makri (2003) find that family managers' compensation was more closely tied to systematic risks, and hence risks that are induced by industry and market forces. The same study also found that compensation of family managers was not tied to the risks that are specific to the firm (= unsystematic risks). This incentive pattern is distinct from the one typically found in nonfamily firms where unsystematic rather than systematic risk is related to executive pay. Family managers are thus protected against risks they cannot influence or diversify away and are not motivated to engage in firm-specific risks.

10 We have discussed the negative behavioral consequences such as free riding by the family manager in Chapter 5 on governance under the category of altruism-induced governance problems.

11 For an interesting discussion as well as two intriguing interviews on the topic of responsible ownership, see Koeberle-Schmid, Kenyon-Rouvinez and Poza (2014).

12 See also Zellweger (2013).

 BACKGROUND READING

Ahlers, O., A. Hack and F. W. Kellermanns (2014). 'Stepping into the buyers' shoes': Looking at the value of family firms through the eyes of private equity investors. *Journal of Family Business Strategy*, 5 (4): 384–396.

Amit, R., and B. Villalonga (2013). Financial performance of family firms. In L. Melin, M. Nordqvist and P. Sharma (Eds.), *The SAGE Handbook of Family Business*. London: SAGE Publications, 157–178.

Anderson, R. C., and D. M. Reeb (2003b). Founding-family ownership and firm performance: Evidence from the S&P 500. *Journal of Finance*, 58 (3): 1301–1328.

Anderson, R. C., A. Duru and D. M. Reeb (2012). Investment policy in family controlled firms. *Journal of Banking and Finance*, 36 (6): 1744–1758.

Anderson, R. C., S. A. Mansi and D. M. Reeb (2003). Founding family ownership and the agency cost of debt. *Journal of Financial Economics*, 68 (2): 263–285.

Bassanini A., T. Breda, E. Caroli and A. Rebérioux (2013). Working in family firms: Paid less but more secure? Evidence from French matched employer–employee data. *Industrial and Labor Relations Review*, 66 (2): 433–466.

Belloc, F. (2013). Law, finance, and innovation. *Cambridge Journal of Economics*, 37 (4): 863–888.

Bertrand, M., and A. Schoar (2006). The role of family in family firms. *Journal of Economic Perspectives*, 20 (2): 73–96.

Bitler, M. P., T. J. Moskowitz and A. Vissing-Jorgensen (2005). Testing agency theory with entrepreneur effort and wealth. *Journal of Finance*, 60 (2): 539–576.

Carney, M., M. van Essen, E. R. Gedajlovic and P. P. Heugens (2015). What do we know about private family firms? A meta-analytical review. *Entrepreneurship Theory and Practice*, 39 (3): 513–544.

Chrisman, J. J., E. Memili and K. Misra (2014). Nonfamily managers, family firms, and the winner's curse: The influence of noneconomic goals and bounded rationality. *Entrepreneurship Theory and Practice*, 38 (5): 1103–1127.

Croci, E., J. A. Doukas and H. Gonenc (2011). Family control and financing decisions. *European Financial Management*, 17 (5): 860–897.

Dalton, D. R., M. A. Hitt, S. T. Certo and C. M. Dalton (2007). The fundamental agency problem and its mitigation: Independence, equity, and the market for corporate control. *Academy of Management Annals*, 1: 1–64.

Fischetti, M. (2000). *Financial Management for Your Family Company*. Philadelphia, PA: Family Business Publishing.

Gomez-Mejia, L., M. Larraza-Kintana and M. Makri (2003). The determinants of executive compensation in family-controlled public corporations. *Academy of Management Journal*, 46 (2): 226–237.

Koropp, C., F. W. Kellermanns, D. Grichnik and L. Stanley (2014). Financial decision making in family firms: An adaptation of the theory of planned behavior. *Family Business Review*, 27 (4): 307–327.

Michiels, A., W. Voordeckers, N. Lybaert and T. Steijvers (2015). Dividends and family governance practices in private family firms. *Small Business Economics*, 44 (2): 299–314.

Miller, D., I. Le Breton-Miller, R. H. Lester and A. A. Cannella Jr. (2007). Are family firms really superior performers? *Journal of Corporate Finance*, 13: 829–858.

Naldi, L., M. Nordqvist, K. Sjöberg and J. Wiklund (2007). Entrepreneurial orientation, risk taking, and performance in family firms. *Family Business Review*, 20 (1): 33–47.

Pindado, J., I. Requejo and C. de la Torre (2012). Do family firms use dividend policy as a governance mechanism? Evidence from the Euro zone. *Corporate Governance: An International Review*, 20 (5): 413–431.

Romano, C. A., G. A. Tanewski and K. X. Smyrnios (2001). Capital structure decision making: A model for family business. *Journal of Business Venturing*, 16 (3): 285–310.

Schulze, W., and T. Zellweger (2016). On the agency costs of owner-management: The problem of holdup. Working paper, University of Utah and University of St. Gallen.

Sieger, P., T. Zellweger and K. Aquino (2013). Turning agents into psychological principals: Aligning interests of non-owners through psychological ownership. *Journal of Management Studies*, 50 (3): 361–388.

Sraer, D., and D. Thesmar (2007). Performance and behavior of family firms: Evidence from the French stock market. *Journal of the European Economic Association*, 5 (4): 709–751.

Steijvers T., and W. Voordeckers (2009). Private family ownership and the agency costs of debt. *Family Business Review*, 22 (4): 333–346.

Strebulaev, I. A., and B. Yang (2013). The mystery of zero-leverage firms. *Journal of Financial Economics*, 109 (1): 1–23.

Van Essen, M., M. Carney, E. R. Gedajlovic and P. P. Heugens (2015). How does family control influence firm strategy and performance? A meta-analysis of US publicly listed firms. *Corporate Governance: An International Review*, 23 (1): 3–24.

Villalonga, B., and R. Amit (2006). How do family ownership, control and management affect firm value? *Journal of Financial Economics*, 80 (2): 385–417.

Wagner, D., J. H. Block, D. Miller, C. Schwens and G. Xi (2015). A meta-analysis of the financial performance of family firms: Another attempt. *Journal of Family Business Strategy*, 6 (1): 3–13.

Zellweger, T. (2007). Time horizon, costs of equity capital, and generic investment strategies of firms. *Family Business Review*, 20 (1): 1–15.

10

Relationships and conflict in the family business

The previous chapters have taken an in-depth look into business-related aspects of family firms. Although those discussions always defined the family-specific elements of the administration of firms, a closer look at the family itself is warranted. Thereby, our voyage into the anthropology of kinship and family relationships risks becoming a superficial endeavor if we do not acknowledge the heterogeneity of family structures. In other words, we need to clarify what we mean when we talk about 'family', especially because variations in the structural features of families (e.g., conjugal family, in-laws, extended family) give rise to variations in relationship dynamics across family types. These relationship dynamics, in turn, are important for the efficient functioning of family firms. For instance, healthy family relationships, such as those in families where members support each other and openly discuss various views on business-related topics, will probably exhibit more comprehensive strategic decision making. In contrast, conflictual family relationships that spill over to the business can undermine the effectiveness of even the most successful family firms. Family feuds are believed to be one of the greatest threats to family firms (Gordon and Nicholson 2010). Given this background, our chapter starts with a discussion of the social structure of the family in an attempt to clarify family heterogeneity.

10.1 The social structure of the family

The study of the family is a vast field of research. Researchers from sociology, anthropology, psychology, medicine, biology, management and economics have looked into the topic and made significant contributions to our understanding of this very basal social system. Therefore, we offer a highly selective compilation of insights into elements of the family that appear central in the context of families that are in business.

Anthropology offers a wide range of definitions of family and kinship, and these terms are often used interchangeably. A loose usage of the term 'family' distinguishes between the family of procreation and the family of orientation. The *family of procreation* is formed through partnership or marriage and by having or adopting children. Members of the family of procreation are linked by *affinity*. In contrast, the *family of orientation* is that family into which one is born and in which early socialization takes place. Members of the family of orientation are linked by *consanguinity*. Kinship and, thereby, family are thus defined as 'the network of genealogical relationships and social ties modeled on the relations of genealogical parenthood' (Holy 1996, p. 40).

In terms of attempts to sort out the structural distinctiveness of families, the foundational work by Parsons (1943) is key. As an anthropologist, Parsons worked to untangle the structural particularities of families. Even though his thinking dates back to the middle of the twentieth century, it offers a compelling logic that helps us better understand how families work. To be clear, Parsons and, therefore, the following considerations focus on very broad types of family structures, within which the typical Western middle-class family falls. However, the structural approach advocated by Parsons has retained its appeal as a tool useful for understanding the basic functioning of modern family structures, including family structures from other cultural contexts.

Central to Parson's work is the observation that the 'ego' (i.e., a person) is born into a family of orientation. After the person enters a partnership or marriage, he or she also enters a family of procreation. As such, the person is the only common member of the two families[1] (Figure 10.1). *Families of orientation* consist of the focal individual, as well as his or her father, mother, grandfather, grandmother, uncles and aunts (Figure 10.1). Therefore, the family of orientation is that part of the family that exists regardless of whether the person is in a partnership, has siblings or has children. From the perspective of the individual, it represents a rather stable part of the kinship system. It is that part of the family in which one grows up and shares many experiences and acquaintances. It is also that part of the family that the individual is usually unable to leave. Parsons (1943) points to the lack of terminological distinction between the paternal and the maternal families of orientation—grandparents, uncles and aunts are alike regardless of whether they are on the maternal or paternal side. The only exception to this rule lies in the patrilineal inheritance of the family name, which is typical in many Western societies and which gives rise to a unilateral name line (Figure 10.1).

Families of procreation, in turn, consist of the individual, as well as his or her partner, sons, daughters, daughters-in-law, sons-in-law, grandsons and grand-daughters. Parsons (1943) also points to the importance of what he calls the

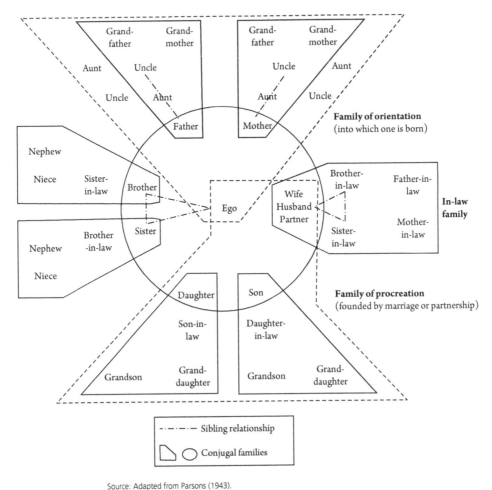

Source: Adapted from Parsons (1943).

Figure 10.1 The social structure of the family

inner circle, which is composed of the father, mother, brothers, sisters, spouse or partner, sons and daughters. Notably, each member of an individual's inner circle in the kinship system connects with the *conjugal family* (comprising the individual's father, mother and children) and with a separate conjugal family (Parsons 1943).

In the social structure of the family, the *in-law family* plays a particular role. It is the only part of kinship to which the person is linked not by consanguinity but by affinity. As such, the in-law family is a fragile part of the kinship system in the sense that its presence is contingent upon the existence of the relationship between the individual and his or her partner. It is through the arrival of partners and, often, through the act of marriage that new conjugal families come into being. The family system becomes an open system through the addition of the in-law family.

Parsons (1943) explains that the extent of this interwoven kinship system largely depends on the cultural context and, therein, the tendency to emphasize the role of clans in society. As mentioned above, in the Western social structure of the family, there is no distinction between grandparents, uncles and aunts who stem from the maternal or paternal side. Westerners tend to only distinguish between the degrees of relationship (e.g., first, second, third cousins; great-great grandfather). We can therefore assume that people from Western cultures will primarily think of the inner circle or, even more restrictively, the conjugal family when asked to describe their family. In contrast, the term 'relatives' does not refer to any particular family unit, but instead to anyone who is part of the wider kinship system (Parsons 1943).

The conjugal family has a somewhat isolated status in the kinship system, as it is normally the household unit. Therefore, the conjugal family not only occupies a socially central position within the kinship system, but also an economically central position. As the household is the unit of residence, resources (e.g., income, wealth, labor) are redistributed and sometimes even pooled within it. In the Western context, the typical conjugal family lives in a home segregated from the homes of both pairs of parents and is economically independent of both.

As mentioned, this structural analysis of the family is reflective of the rather traditional Western middle class, which suggests that kinship structures are highly interdependent with other structural aspects of the same society. However, the above approach to understanding families is useful, as it points to multiple structural features that families from other cultural contexts should share in some form.

For instance, this analysis highlights the importance of *inclusiveness* and, consequently, how far we dig into the 'onion layers' of the kinship system when we talk of family. The level of inclusiveness is important with regard to families in business, as it has an impact on who is entitled to occupy a role or have a say within the business. This is particularly true of next-generation members who may not yet be shareholders. Distant family members, who are traditionally referred to as 'relatives', may admittedly be part of the kinship system, but they would probably be left out of a genogram and should therefore not have a role in the business.

Even though family members may all be part of the same kinship system and even the same inner circle, *identification* may vary depending on the norms along which family names are passed on to other family members. In Western societies, the name line traditionally follows the patrilineal lineage, which long ago was also associated with preferential treatment of male descendants via the transfer of property and wealth. However, in the case of partnership dissolution (e.g., through divorce), mother-centered family structures in which children stay with their mothers often emerge. We can expect that in such situations different types of identification patterns emerge.

The structural analysis of family also points to conflicts of *loyalty* within families. A person belongs to multiple families, most importantly the family of orientation and the family of procreation, as well as the inner circle and the conjugal family. At times, these different systems will have different opinions on various matters related to the firm, such as strategic priorities, risk taking, dividends, managerial involvement of family members, or even the continuation of the firm. The individual may therefore be caught in loyalty conflicts about which point of view to follow, which part of the family to favor and, ultimately, where one belongs within the kinship system. The loyalty conflicts and potential repercussions increase if the individual holds the opinion of more distant relatives and, thus, is in opposition to the opinions of closer family members.

We are also reminded of the *openness* of the kinship system. The arrival of new partners typically means the creation of new conjugal families. The entry of a new partner normally means that the person removes himself from his or her family of orientation to some extent. The first kinship loyalty is then to the partner or spouse and to the couple's children. However, this unilateral shift in loyalty raises a question about the impartiality of the status of the two families of orientation (i.e., the own family of orientation and the in-law family). But also the departure of partners alters the structure of the family, which is a feature of family life that has become more prominent in the last decades (we will return this point in section 10.2). The openness of the kinship system through the arrival and departure of members and partners implies that the familial network and relationships alter over time. This openness of the system becomes particularly visible when a person divorces or changes partner(s), whereby stepfamily members come into being and the distances within the kinship system change. This, in turn, should have repercussions on mutual proximity, identification and loyalty.

When looking at families through the structural lens, we also recognize problems associated with accessing, mobilizing, pooling and transferring *resources* within the family. Altruism is an exchange norm that calls for generous transfers from parents to children. This might have financial implications in terms of ownership transfer from one generation to the next. Children are sometimes expected to reciprocate favors from their parents by supporting parents, especially as they age (Kohli and Künemund 2003).[2] A particularly problematic aspect of resource allocation within families relates to the transfer of wealth upon death and, hence, the departure of family members. Inheritance laws and related laws therefore touch upon a fundamental understanding within society about what constitutes family and the importance of its various members—in this case, via the redistribution of wealth upon death within the family. In some societies, the testator has full testamentary freedom and, hence, unfettered discretion to dispose of his or her wealth. In such contexts, individuals can allocate their wealth in a completely uneven way to their descendants and other relatives, or to actors outside the kinship system (for a more detailed discussion of inheritance law and taxes, refer to Chapter 7 on succession).

Taken together, the structural features of family have an immediate impact on fundamental aspects of how we exist in the family realm. These structural features give rise to tensions in various forms, such as how close or distant we are to relatives, who we identify with, those to whom we are loyal, the extent to which we are open to the arrival and departure of family members, and how we allocate resources within the family. In the following, we explore these structural and relational aspects in more detail for the cases of spousal teams, sibling teams and extended families in business. As discussed in the governance chapter, these family types figure prominently in the context of family firms.

10.1.1 The spousal team in business

The most common type of family firm involves spouses who are in business together. For instance, Ruef (2010) finds that more than 50% of all entrepreneurial teams in the United States are composed of spousal couples. In this regard, it is essential to recognize that relationships between spouses are social and voluntary, in contrast to family relationships based on biological linkages.[3] Spousal relationships have both advantages and disadvantages in business (Dahl, van Praag and Thompson 2014; Sharifian, Jennings and Jennings 2012).

The bright side of being in business with a spouse

Individuals engage in spousal relationships because of personal affinity and, often, romantic love. Therefore, spousal relationships often embody loyalty, solidarity and care. In addition, spousal couples typically have frequent and close interactions, which increase the level of trust and mutual support, deepen fine-grained information exchange and facilitate joint problem solving. All of these elements have been found to support firm growth (Bird and Zellweger 2016). In addition, spousal entrepreneurs are inclined to work toward economic gains from their firm. This is because the firm typically represents the most vital and undiversified source of income for both spouses, and it finances a shared household and, perhaps, even child rearing (Ruef 2010). The shared economic aspirations and the resource-redistribution commitments among spouses also tend to harmonize interests within the spousal team, thereby limiting possible opportunistic behavior and free riding. Spousal relationships also entail certain behavioral norms, such as benevolence and solidarity. Therefore, spouses enjoy some important advantages that support the likelihood of their success as an entrepreneurial team.

The downside of being in business with a spouse

There are also important downsides to being in business with a spouse. In particular, spousal entrepreneurs experience work–family conflict, a form of conflict in which the role pressures from the work and family domains are mutually incompatible in some respect (Greenhaus and Beutell 1985). Participation in one role (work or family) is made more difficult by virtue of participation in the other role. Work–family conflicts surface at the intersection of the family and business systems. They arise when the business supersedes the family's needs for an extended period of time or when business managers face high demands in both systems simultaneously (Carr and Hmieleski 2015).

As spouses who own family businesses share both their professional and their private lives, tensions and conflict experienced in one setting (family or work) are almost certain to bleed into the other setting. For the business-owning couple and for immediate family members (e.g., children), this means 'that tension cannot be abandoned for the sanctity of home life, nor can one leave a difficult family conflict for the steady drone of the workplace; rather these conflicts are woven throughout both of these contexts, making success and high functioning in either more challenging' (Danes and Morgan 2004, p. 243). Such work–family conflict and feelings of being unable to, for example, perform satisfactorily as both owner-manager and parent are likely to be prominent among business-owning couples. This is especially true when the family and business systems share the same location (e.g., farms, hotels), as the boundaries between the family and the work spheres are blurred in such cases. Feelings of guilt and of being undervalued may therefore be prominent among business-owning couples.

In addition, couples can experience severe relationship conflicts. Moreover, solidarity, support, goal congruence and, ultimately, trust often suffer over time, not least because of growing frustrations and disillusion-ment about the incompatibility of personal, spousal, family, household and business demands, but also once the shared goal of child rearing has been reached and the children are out of the house. Divorce is only a visible reflection of such tensions. One particular area of conflict relates to feelings of injustice, which might arise when a family member works for the firm and receives an unsatisfactory level of compensation or, in extreme cases, no compensation at all. Such an individual may feel that he or she does not 'count' at all.

10.1.2 The sibling team in business

As siblings are related by blood, the affiliation between them is endur-ing and persists irrespective of family members' life choices. For example, while it is possible to divorce a spouse, siblings do not have a similar option. Sibling relationships exist because of biology and not necessarily because of affinity. Individuals generally do not view their siblings as core family because the sibling relationship is not the structural basis for the formation of families or for their continuation (Bird and Zellweger 2016). Despite their blood ties, siblings often do not see each other as central to their own families.

The bright side of being in business with siblings

Sibling partnerships are common among family firms and in the best case entail relational qualities, such as companionship, admiration and trust. These qualities are, however, fragile, as we will explore below. Sibling teams in business have been found to perform best in mature firms that have often developed a division of labor and introduced formal control systems that measure performance and create accountability in order to keep sibling tensions and rivalry within an acceptable scope, reduce the likelihood that family conflicts will spill over to the firm, and limit opportunistic behavior. Similarly, established firms often have planning and budgeting systems, which generally help align otherwise incongruent goals and strategic preferences. In sum, while young firms are particu-larly vulnerable when siblings are at the helm, such relationships are less of a problem in older firms. Indeed, in a study of private family firms in Sweden we found that the relational challenges of sibling partnerships are particularly destructive when firms are young, as young firms cannot afford the distractions caused by conflicts, a lack of shared vision, or goal incongruence if they want to survive and prosper (Bird and Zellweger 2016).

The downside of being in business with siblings

Sibling relationships often entail quarreling and antagonism, and tend to be rather fragile. Sibling conflicts often stem from involuntary membership and social comparisons, such as the need to differentiate themselves from family expectations and the need to be an independent, autonomous person. Sibling conflicts may also arise as a consequence of rivalries for parental love, attention and resources (for a more in-depth discussion, see Bird and Zellweger 2016).

Siblings are also less likely to cohabit than spouses—they often have their own spouses with whom they share a household and have their own conjugal family. In turn, siblings are unlikely to redistribute resources among themselves. Instead, they may experience conflicts in terms of whether they should be loyal to their siblings or to their own spouses—a conflict between the family of orientation and the conjugal family. Among themselves, siblings will typically experience somewhat limited solidarity and cohesion, which makes it more difficult to develop a joint vision for the firm, at least when compared to spouses. While spouses are typically interdependent, siblings are rather independent and tend to follow their individual goals. Consequently, joint problem solving is often rather challenging among siblings.

Sibling feuds can also easily escalate (Gordon and Nicholson 2010), while the unconditional existence of blood ties makes it impossible to fully withdraw from a conflict. Siblings in business together often have a history of some form of antagonism as well as destructive family baggage, which can undermine trust and solidarity. Conflicts are sometimes even seen as inevitable and natural in sibling relationships. In sum, sibling entrepreneurs are prone to embeddedness mechanisms that typically have a negative impact on the effectiveness of the firm.

The epic sibling feud between Mukesh and Anil Ambani

Dhirubhai Ambani was the founder of Reliance Industries, one of the largest Indian industrial conglomerates. When he died in 2002 without leaving a will, his oldest son, Mukesh Ambani, became chairman and managing director of Reliance Industries Ltd., while his younger son, Anil Ambani, was made vice-chairman. Mukesh reportedly tried to oust Anil from the Board. In November 2004, the private rift between the brothers became public when Mukesh Ambani admitted that the brothers could not agree on how the firm should be run. In June 2005, their mother, Kokilaben, intervened and split Reliance Group into two. Mukesh was put in charge of Reliance Industries and IPCL, while Anil became head of Reliance Infocomm, Reliance Energy and Reliance Capital.

In November 2006, Anil and Mukesh came to blows over a gas-supply agreement signed between Mukesh's Reliance Industries Ltd. and Anil's Reliance Natural Resources Ltd. at the time of the demerger. Mukesh's exploration company was reportedly expected to sell gas to Anil's power company at a reduced rate, which would supposedly lead to high profits in Anil's part of the firm. When the government would not approve the deal and instead set higher prices, Anil suspected covert dealings between the government and his brother Mukesh.

In June 2008, another of Anil's companies lost a deal, perhaps because of Mukesh's involvement. Anil's company, Reliance Communications, called off merger talks with South Africa's MTN to form a large, international, mobile tele-communications company. Reliance said the failed talks were the result of legal and regulatory issues, but Mukesh's claim on the shares of the telecom firm was also blamed for the failed deal. Moreover, in September 2008, Anil filed a $2 billion defamation suit over statements Mukesh made to *The New York Times*.

In another episode of this heated conflict, in the summer of 2009, Anil blamed his brother's company for power cuts sweeping across India. In a letter to the Indian prime minister, Anil said: 'Major power cuts, especially in north India, have become commonplace, causing grave hardship to hundreds of millions of consumers—sadly, all a result of RIL's corporate greed.' Anil's Reliance Natural Resources Ltd. even placed daily advertisements in *The Times of India*, India's largest newspaper, and 32 other papers alleging that the Indian government had sided with Mukesh's Reliance Industries to raise the price of gas. During this time, even the Indian finance minister begged the brothers to stop feuding for the sake of India's capital markets.

The brothers went to the Indian Supreme Court over the gas dispute. The Supreme Court ruled in Mukesh's favor and declared that Reliance Industries could sell gas to Anil Ambani's Reliance Natural Resources Ltd. at government-set prices that were higher than those agreed on in the 2005 family agreement. Anil said that he would not request a review of the verdict. The companies were given six weeks to renegotiate their agreement.

Throughout this period, the two brothers lived near each other in an upscale neighborhood in southern Mumbai. Nevertheless, they rarely spoke to each other except at family meetings and conferences. However, in 2010, their mother, Kokilaben, was able to broker a peace agreement between them. Officials of Reliance Industries Ltd. and Anil Dhirubhai Ambani Group both received notes stating that the Ambani brothers would draft a non-compete agreement to replace an earlier one that obviously did not work. Consequently, Anil Ambani agreed to withdraw his defamation suit.

 REFLECTION QUESTIONS

1. What are the origins of the sibling dispute?
2. What kinds of behaviors do you recognize in this conflict, especially among the brothers?
3. What is the mother's role in this conflict?
4. What dynamics lead to the escalation and, later, to the de-escalation of the conflict?

10.1.3 The extended family in business

By 'extended families in business', we typically refer to later-generation family firms, with multiple family owners. In such cases, some of the owners are often also involved in the firm's management. The extended family business is typically organized in a way that reflects the branches of the founder's family tree. For instance, the owning family of Henkel, a publicly listed, diversified German family firm, has three branches that reflect the three children of the company's founder, Fritz Henkel. Three members of the owning family are still active on the board of directors, as each branch of the family tree can send one delegate to the board. For family member(s) in charge of overseeing and running the firm, such as the three Henkel family members, this constellation most likely creates loyalty conflicts around whose viewpoints (i.e., which parts of the family tree) to prioritize. Each family member on the board represents an individual family branch with particular preferences related to, for example, the staffing of the board, members of management, and the firm's strategic orientation. At the same time, as the family branch representatives sit on the board of the firm, they should have the overall success of the firm in mind. This means that the opinions expressed by a different family branch representative or a third party may appear more appropriate than the preferences of their own family branch.

Levels of affection and emotionality in general should be lower in the extended family than in the other two family constellations. In the context of an extended family, members are generally more distant, and may not even know each other. Progressively, relational ties transform into contractual ties, whereby legal documents, such as shareholder agreements, company bylaws and family constitutions, regulate interactions among family members. As a result, families become more like organizations. As in the case of sibling partnerships, members of the extended family do not cohabitate and are unlikely to redistribute resources across the extended family. However, the owners will be progressively aligned in their economic and shareholder-value-enhancing aspirations. Therefore, they should view the firm as a utilitarian asset rather than as an asset to which they attach strong emotions.

In this constellation, relationship dynamics should make themselves felt along the branches of the family tree and along name lines. They are also likely to affect whether someone is part of the inner or outer circle from the individual's point of view. Relative to the sibling team, power struggles and interlocking conflicts that undermine the effective working of the firm should be less likely in the constellation of the extended family. This is because establishment of a controlling ownership stake, which is required to steer the firm in a desired direction, requires coalitions among multiple family members, each of whom holds only a small stake in the firm given the progressive dilution of ownership stakes across generations. In this case, conflicts can more easily be resolved than in the case of the sibling team. Such a resolution may involve, for instance, buyouts of family members' stakes.

10.1.4 Family embeddedness

In summary, spouses, siblings and extended families in business exhibit unique structural and relational features, which we subsume under the term 'family embeddedness' (refer to Table 10.1 for an overview). We define family embeddedness as follows:

> Family embeddedness is defined as the firm's exposure to familial relationships that either support or constrain the firm's economic development.

As should be clear from the above discussion of three prototypical family types in business (i.e., spousal team, sibling team and extended family), family firms vary significantly in the extent of their family embeddedness depending on the structural and relational features among the family members. Families in business typically vary along the following dimensions of family embeddedness (Table 10.1):

- Type of family or families involved,
- Dependence among family members,
- Distance among family members,
- Loyalty concerns within the family,
- Socioeconomic aspirations,
- Relational attributes, and
- Types of conflict.

Type of family or families involved
A firm's embeddedness within the family varies dramatically depending on the type of family involved. For instance, the size and, thereby, the complexity of the kinship system grows as we move from the spousal team to siblings to the extended family constellation. The kinship system in a spousal team consists of the conjugal family. This is a fairly simple setup, at least from a structural point of view, as it solely consists of the spouses and, eventually, their children. The sibling constellation includes not only the conjugal families of the individual siblings, but also their shared family of orientation, typically parents and other siblings. In the

Table 10.1 Family embeddedness of spousal team, sibling team and extended family

	Typical attributes of spousal team	Typical attributes of sibling team	Typical attributes of extended family
Involved family or families	Conjugal family	Family of orientation (including sibling) Conjugal family	Family of orientation (extended) Conjugal family
Dependence among family members	High	Medium	Low
Distance among family members	Low	Low–medium	Medium–high
Loyalty concerns	Low	Medium	Medium–high
Socioeconomic aspirations	Shared socioeconomic aspirations to sustain household and eventually rear children Resource redistribution Undiversified income and wealth Cohabitation	Limited sharing of socioeconomic aspirations Limited resource redistribution Partly diversified income and wealth No cohabitation	Alignment with regard to economic goals No resource redistribution Diversified income and often diversified wealth No cohabitation
Relational attributes	Affinity, respect, support, loyalty, warmth and love	Warmth but also conflict and rivalry	Heterogeneous levels of affection Arm's-length relationships
Conflict patterns	Limited jostling for power in firm because of interdependence	Jostling for power in firm Opportunism and free riding Path-dependent conflict reinforced by inability to withdraw	Limited jostling for power in firm Coalitions needed for influence Individual ownership stakes smaller, which makes withdrawal easier

case of the extended family, the kinship system with ties to the business is even further expanded, as not only the person's own conjugal family, but also an extended family of orientation involving multiple branches of the family tree tend to be involved, often as passive shareholders.

Dependence among family members

The three constellations also vary in terms of dependence among the involved family members. Spouses in business together are often highly interdependent because they usually share the same household. They also have an undiversified income stream and, often, an undiversified wealth position. In contrast, siblings tend to be more independent when in business together, as they typically do not cohabitate and they often have their own families of procreation. In the case of the extended family, family members tend to be even more independent. As members of the extended family often only hold a minority stake in the firm, they typically have a more diversified wealth position, as well as independent income streams from jobs outside the business.

Distance among family members

Whereas spouses engage in their relationships voluntarily and typically as a consequence of feelings of proximity and connection, sibling relationship are not necessarily characterized by high levels of proximity. This is particularly true among adult siblings. Members of extended families may not even know each other personally, not necessarily owing to a lack of personal affection, but simply because of geographical location and related lifestyle choices.

Loyalty concerns within the family

Loyalty concerns within the family are of crucial importance for our understanding of family relationships, as are tension and conflict. In the case of a spousal team in which a single family is involved in the business, the spouses are spared the dilemma of whether they should be loyal to a certain part of the kinship loyalty system. Such concerns should be more prevalent in sibling and extended family constellations. In the former case, siblings in business may be torn between the demands of their sibling partnership, which is grounded in the family of orientation, and their respective conjugal families. In the case of the extended family, loyalty conflicts should be even more numerous and nuanced, as the family of orientation is composed of multiple branches that are more or less distant from the individual's own branch, plus also the conjugal family. The issue then becomes one of loyalty to a certain part of the family, which is likely to be a particularly intricate problem in the case of sibling and extended family constellations.

Socioeconomic aspirations

Spouses typically share strong socioeconomic aspirations to sustain a common household and, often, to rear children, which represents a clear motivation to ensure the successful operation of the firm. This should be especially true for spouses controlling a young firm, as young firms benefit significantly from informal ties, relational support among the founders and an ability to withstand setbacks. In contrast, siblings—who are less interdependent, unlikely to cohabitate, and tend to have income streams from outside the business (such as from a spouse)—do not necessarily have aligned socioeconomic aspirations. One sibling may want to sell the firm to harvest firm value, while the other may wish to continue running the firm. In the extended family case, we can assume that family members—who tend to be more distant—will also view the firm as a progressively utilitarian asset, such that individual family members should be aligned with regard to the financial benefits they expect from the firm (e.g., dividends, stock-price appreciation).

Relational attributes

Spousal relationships are typically characterized by such attributes as affinity, respect, support, loyalty, warmth and love. In contrast, sibling relationships often entail warmth as well as rivalry, pointing to the tensions built into many sibling relationships. In the case of the extended family, we would expect heterogeneous levels of affection depending on the part of the kinship system in focus. For instance, the level of warmth should be much higher in relation to parents than in relation to distant relatives. With progressive growth of the family tree, personal relations should generally become arm's-length, contractual relations, whereby family members are bound to each other merely by contract and not by affection.

Undoubtedly, these descriptions ignore much of the variance within the three constellations, as well as cultural discrepancies and changes in these relational attributes over time. However, they may be useful for illustrating the basic relational attributes and dynamics against which we can compare individual situations.

Conflict patterns

Conflict patterns are a direct consequence of differences in terms of the type(s) of family involved, dependence, distance, loyalty concerns, socioeconomic aspirations and relational attributes. In the prototypical case, spouses should experience limited feuds with regard to the firm because of a fairly simple family constellation, mutual interdependence, high proximity, low loyalty concerns, and shared aspirations. In contrast, sibling partnerships should typically be characterized by jostling for power inside firm, and path-dependent conflict reinforced by an inability to withdraw from the relationship. For the case of the extended family, jostling for power with regard to the firm should be limited. However, in contrast to the spousal case, conflicts should be less prominent because it is more difficult to build powerful coalitions out of a dispersed group of minority family shareholders. In the extended family constellation, family members may also have more options to sell their shares, which makes withdrawal from the conflict easier.

The above considerations are summarized in Table 10.1.

This discussion of family embeddedness foreshadows appropriate conflict-management approaches. As spouses tend to be highly dependent on each other, a breach of trust appears particularly harmful and questions the foundational core of the couples' strength, especially as entrepreneurs. Relational support, intimate information exchange and joint planning toward a shared socioeconomic goal all come into question. A breach of trust can therefore easily turn the centripetal forces within a spousal couple into centrifugal forces.

The tensions embedded in sibling relationships, which stem from their dependence in business and their independence in private matters, have to be stabilized through in-depth discussions and the definition of joint goals. As one sibling may be tempted to free ride on the efforts of the other sibling, systems of accountability (e.g., budgeting, reporting and performance-based pay) should be implemented. In addition, each sibling should have his/her own sphere of responsibility.

In the case of the extended family, conflict management means making provisions to avoid the breakup of the family. Conflict prevention in this context means giving family members good reasons to stay together. One way to facilitate this goal is to establish ongoing communication within the extended family, and to set up systems of governance that work against the dissolution of the family or infighting among its members. This may entail defining shared values and goals, introducing shareholder agreements regulating the entry and exit of shareholders, and developing provisions regarding the involvement of family members in the management of the firm (see the Chapter 5 on governance for more details).

10.2 Trends in the social structure of the family

In large parts of the Western world during the mid-twentieth century, 'family' typically meant a nuclear, two-generational group with parents and children sharing the same household (Aldrich and Cliff 2003). This form of family came under pressure in the second half of the century. Today, families take more diverse forms and the traditional family has lost much ground to other forms of partnerships and households.

These trends have an immediate impact on what constitutes family and how family members relate to each other, which in turn affects the governance of the firms they control from a structural and relational point of view. In the following, we look into the most important societal trends surrounding families and households, and try to disentangle their consequences for family firms. In so doing, we build on the important work by Aldrich and Cliff (2003), who explore the pervasive effects of family trends on entrepreneurship. We limit our discussion to five major trends evident among families in much of the Western world: (1) fewer children and smaller households, (2) the retreat of marriage and advance of divorce, (3) childbirth without marriage, (4) more diverse household forms and (5) women entering the labor force.

Fewer children, smaller families and smaller households

An important trend in the evolution of families is the decline in fertility rates across large parts of the world. In Organisation for Economic Co-operation and Development (OECD) countries, the average number of children born per woman over a lifetime was 3.23 in 1960, but this number had dropped to 1.68 by 2013 (OECD Family Database).[4] There are large variations in international fertility rates. At the lower end within the OECD, we find Korea and Portugal, with 1.2 children per woman in 2013. India and Israel, with 2.3 and 3.0 children per woman, respectively, occupy the upper end of that list.

Lower fertility rates are important for our understanding of interpersonal relationships within business-controlling families and of the firms themselves, as they imply that the average size of conjugal families is in retreat. A decrease in this family size has multiple structural consequences for family firms. From a succession point of view, the pool of potential family internal successors shrinks, making it less likely that a willing and able successor can be found in the close family. When ownership is passed on to the next generation, ownership fragmentation should be less of a problem. Relatedly, family-external transfers of ownership and management should become more prominent.

Retreat of marriage and advance of divorce

As noted by Lundberg and Pollak (2007), frameworks that consider sex and childbearing only within the context of a committed partnership have become increasingly disconnected from reality since the 1960s. In 1960, an average of 7.8 marriages or legal civil unions took place per 1000 inhabitants in the OECD annually. By 2012, this number had dropped to 4.6. In parallel with the decline of marriage, the divorce rate grew from 0.8 to 2.0 per 1000 inhabitants per year over the same time period[5] (OECD Family Database). There is also international variation in divorce rates. By 2012, divorce rates were at 0.1 in Chile and 0.6 in Ireland. At the upper end of the scale, we find the United States, Lithuania and Latvia with divorce rates of 2.8, 3.5 and 3.6, respectively.

In light of these trends, the family as described by Parsons (1943) appears to be becoming a more open system. The arrival of new partners means that families are less likely to resemble close-knit clans in which externals only become members after they have committed to a socially and legally regulated arrangement, such as marriage. In modern families, memberships in a family of procreation and in a conjugal family are structurally less stable because individuals can change partners over the course of their lives, which means that new members can enter and previous members can (partially) leave the family. This openness of the family also means that families become more extended, and what used to be called stepfamily members are becoming more prevalent. For instance, Aldrich and Cliff (2003, p. 583) report that as of the beginning of the millennium, 50% of all children in the United States 'will spend at least some time in a single-parent family, and about one-third of U.S. children will live in a remarried or cohabiting stepfamily household before they reach adulthood'. The trend toward non-marital spousal relationships is also reflected in recent adaptations to matrimonial and family law in many Western countries, which grant more flexibility in the formation (e.g., marriage among same-sex couples) and dissolution (e.g., a shift toward no-fault divorces, legal enforcement of prenuptial agreements) of a marriage.

For family firms, these trends are important. For instance, the emergence of partners who stem from outside the traditional family network means that the network that is potentially accessible for the business (e.g., in terms of access to business opportunities and managerial talent) is growing. As such, firms should have access to an expanded pool of current and former 'family' members, which may facilitate the resource-mobilization process (Aldrich and Cliff 2003). At the same time, the fragility of current familial structures should make family members more reluctant to pool and transfer resources within the family. In addition, people often lose touch with nonresident family members after a divorce, which means that 'former' family members are likely to be less accessible across time.

Childbirth without marriage

The increase in childbirth outside of marriage represents another long-term trend with important consequence for family firms. Across the OECD countries in 1960, the mother's marital status at the time she gave birth was not 'married' in only 5.8% of all births. By 2012, this figure had risen to 37.9%. Again, the international variance is striking. In 2012, the share of out-of-marriage births amounted to 69.6% in Chile, while the corresponding figures for Korea and Japan were only 2.1% and 2.2%, respectively (OECD Family Database).

This increase in non-marital childbearing in conjunction with growing divorce rates has altered the living arrangements of children. Children may experience multiple transitions in terms of where and with whom they live, as most unmarried parents eventually marry and divorced parents sometimes remarry. With multiple partnerships among parents, families become more open and complex.

From a family business standpoint, the increase in childbirth outside of marriage is likely to raise questions around the transfer of resources from parents to children, especially with regard to the transfer of business ownership from parents to children upon death. Given that parents may have children from different partners, determining who the natural family-internal successors of the family firm are may be more difficult. We therefore expect litigation over family business inheritance among children from multiple partnerships to rise in the future.

More diverse household forms

A direct outcome of the aforementioned trends is the emergence of smaller households and new household forms, especially a growing proportion of single-person and cohabiting couple households. In the United States, for instance, the average household size fell from 3.4 in 1960 to 2.6 people in 2005 (Lundberg and Pollak 2007).

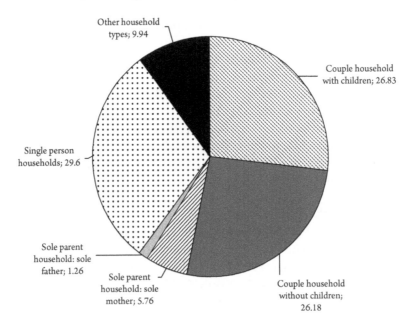

Data source: OECD Family Database; distribution (%) of households by household type.

Figure 10.2 Types of households across OECD countries, 2011.

With regard to the prevalence of various household forms, OECD data for 2011 are shown in Figure 10.2. Moreover, in 2011, 74.4% of children aged 11–15 in OECD countries lived with both parents, 14.9% lived with a single parent and 8.8% lived with a stepfamily (the remaining 1.9% lived in other household forms).

There are three important trends behind these figures: (1) the trend toward cohabitation of unmarried couples (in the United States, 11% of these couples are same-sex couples), (2) the trend toward single-person households, and (3) the trend toward single-parent households. For the United States, Aldrich and Cliff (2003, p. 583) report that 'the stereotypical "married couple with children" household dropped from approximately 44% of all households in 1960 to only 24% in 1999'.

The overall effect of the smaller and changing compositions of households for family firms is challenging to predict. From a family business perspective, these changes should have ambivalent effects on the ability to mobilize family resources. On the one hand, access to family human capital and family financial capital should be more restricted because of decreasing household size, changing household composition and weaker ties among members. On the other hand, the family network should be more open given the changes in household and family composition, which should help individuals access non-redundant, novel information, and uncover opportunities to grow the firm.

However, the consequences of these household trends are not purely structural. As people within a household not only get to know each other intimately, and develop warmth and trust, but also experience conflict, changes in household composition are likely to have an impact on relational quality. These trends in relationship quality are just as important as the structural trends, as tensions at the family level can easily spill over to the business. Moreover, as children in many Western countries typically stay with the mother and her household if their parents separate, we should see growing matrilineal alignment of loyalty and support.

Women entering the labor force
Another important trend is the growth in the women's employment rate. In 1960, 39.5% of women in the United States were employed, while this rate was 63.4% in 2014 (OECD Labour Market Statistics).[6] Over time, the gender wage gap has narrowed in virtually all OECD countries, but women still earn, on average, 16% less than men per hour worked (Lundberg and Pollak 2007). These authors suggest that about half of this gap can be explained by individual characteristics, job experience and occupational choices. The source of the unexplained residual—labor market discrimination or the continuing gender disparity in family and

household responsibilities—remains the subject of considerable controversy. Women are spending less time on housework than they used to in the 1960s, but they still assume the primary responsibility for this task.

The fact that women play a more active role in the labor market has an impact on family businesses as well. In some societies, the natural form of succession is still for a son to take over the business. With the arrival of women in the workforce, the option of female successors taking over should hopefully become a more widespread option.

All in all, what do these five trends mean for family firms? The Western family has been radically altered by these changes. Family structure has become more heterogeneous and less stable (Lundberg and Pollak 2007), and these trends have most likely weakened the inclination among family members to commit and pool resources. Given the long-term trends since the 1960s, we can assume that the economic role of the family continues to decrease as the market and the state supplement or replace an increasing number of family functions, such as food preparation, old-age support, child rearing, education and security provision.

Interestingly, while these changes have diminished the role of marriage as a tool for forming family alliances, they have increased the importance of love and companionship as a basis for spousal teams. In addition, as the instrumental value of children falls—for instance, children are no longer viewed as a source of cheap labor—parents have fewer children and invest more in each child. This is a reflection of what has been termed the 'quantity–quality' tradeoff (Becker and Lewis 1974). The bright side of these trends may be a turn toward higher relational quality within families.

10.3 International variance in family values

The world is an intriguing amalgam of value systems, which vary widely across cultures (refer also to the foundational work by Geert Hofstede). These value systems are important, as they have an impact on the interpersonal relationships in a society. They also affect the social standing of the individual vis-à-vis the collective and, of particular importance in the family business context, the dominance of family values.

Collectivism versus individualism
An important cultural value that affects the social acceptance of family firms in general and family-internal business succession in particular is the degree of collectivism in society. A collectivist culture, such as those prominent in Brazil, the Philippines, Pakistan and Greece, is one in which there is a pref-

erence for tightly knit social networks in which individuals can expect their relatives, clan or other in-groups to look after them in exchange for unquestioning loyalty. In contrast, individualistic cultures, such as the culture in the United States, emphasize the rights of the individual, the right to free speech and the achievement of personal freedom and personal goals regardless of the demands of the collective. Collectivist cultures should favor the emergence and persistence of family firms, especially the intention among next-generation family members to take over a parental firm.

High and low power distance

Power distance is the extent to which the lower-ranking individuals of a society accept that power is distributed unequally. People in societies with high power distance are more likely to conform to a hierarchy and require no further justification of that hierarchy. In societies with low power distance, individuals tend to try to distribute power equally. In such societies, inequalities of power among people require additional justification.

Pakistan is a society with a high power distance. Afghan and Wiqar (2007, p. 8) describe Pakistani family values and suggest that power distance supports

> a structure of hierarchy with the father being the head of the family and the eldest son having more say in decision making than the younger ones. Children are expected to respect and obey their parents and refrain from questioning their authority. The elders of the families (*buzurg*), such as paternal or maternal grandparents or great grandparents, are also considered wise and experienced and are to be treated with respect and reverence. Sibling rivalry is discouraged and siblings are instructed to respect each other from an early age.

In societies with a high power distance, next-generation family members typically have to honor the achievements of the parents by, for example, taking over the family business.

Family values

The international variance in value systems is particularly striking when looking at societal values that directly deal with family. Based on World Values Survey data, Figure 10.3 compares two types of family values across a selection of countries: the general importance of family in a person's life, and a person's desire to make his or her parents proud.

Figure 10.3 strikingly demonstrates the importance of family as a social category around the world. Interestingly, there is notable variance with regard to children's desires to make their parents proud. As such, family

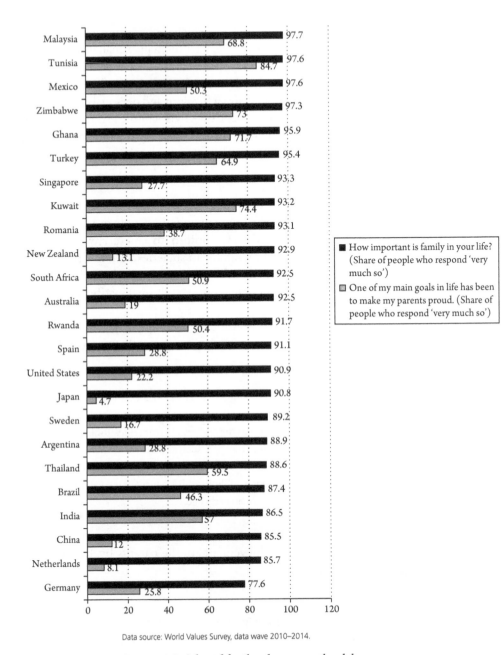

Data source: World Values Survey, data wave 2010–2014.

Figure 10.3 Selected family values across the globe

seems to be important to a lot of people, but this does not mean that there is equal agreement about what the importance of family means. For instance, Kuwaitis not only seem to value family in everyday life, but children also put a great amount of emphasis on trying to make their parents proud. In contrast, New Zealanders value family nearly as much as Kuwaitis. However, next-generation New Zealanders do not seem to pay much attention to parental expectations. Given the prevalence of individualistic values in this Anglo-Saxon country, breaking free from parents seems to be as important as valuing family.

One way to dig deeper into the international variance in family values is to look at gender stereotypes. Relative to other biases, gender stereotypes are insightful, as they point to deeply rooted preferences about who the 'best' successor in the family firm would be. The World Values Survey asks people about their level of agreement with the following statement: 'On the whole, men make better business executives than women do.' The share of respondents who agreed completely with this statement is indicated in Figure 10.4.

Based on the these results one cannot help but wonder how much was lost to the economic development of the countries that top this list by this traditional division of entrepreneurship by gender.

The above discussion does not attempt to provide a complete overview of family values. Rather, this discussion reminds us that family firms operate within societies with widely varying value systems, which have an important impact on how family firms operate and are passed on from one generation to the next.[7]

10.4 Understanding interpersonal dynamics in the family firm: a systemic view

To understand interpersonal dynamics—especially conflict patterns and their possible resolution—in family firms, it is fruitful to return to the three-circle model of family firms (see Chapter 2). That model suggests that we view a family firm as a system of multiple subsystems, most prominently the family, the firm and ownership. The subsystems of family, firm and ownership are inextricably linked in family businesses—each one is indispensable for the existence of the overall family business system (in systems theory, this is typically called 'structurally coupled systems').

This parallel presence of the three systems gives rise to various problems because the three systems function according to different logics. These logics materialize as conflicting conditions of membership (entry and exit of people into the system), communication styles and channels, justice principles, decision principles and behavioral principles. They are also evident in differences in the importance of individual personality, compensation currencies and time horizons, as depicted in Table 10.2.

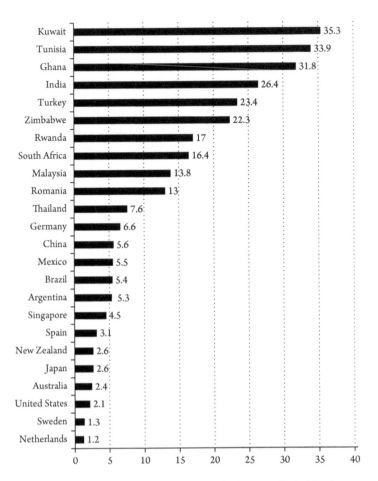

Note: Share of respondents who replied 'completely agree' with the following statement: 'On the whole, men make better business executives than women do.'

Data source: World Values Survey, data wave 2010–2014.

Figure 10.4 Gender stereotypes about men's and women's business acumen

For instance, equality is established in the family realm by asking for a favor, saying thanks, caring and forgiving. In the ownership context, in contrast, it typically involves a transfer of money. In their communications, families tend to be inclusive and to talk about everything simply to confirm the bonds among family members and to assure each other that the world is in order (von Schlippe and Frank 2013). It follows that in the family context, the individual personality—with all of its facets—counts.

The business system, in contrast, is more selective. Communication is meant to bring the strategy that is expected to generate the highest economic value

Table 10.2 Logics of family, business and ownership systems

	Family	Business	Ownership
Conditions of membership	Birth, partnership, marriage, adoption divorce, death	Application, hire, promotion, fire	Inheritance, acquisition, sale
Communication style	*Bonding* communication: informal, about everything, inclusive	*Decision* communication: hierarchical, selective depending on functional responsibility and ability to make strategic decisions	*Legal* communication: formal, selective depending on ownership concentration
Communication channel	Oral	Strategic plans	Contracts supported by law
Justice principle	Equality, need	Equity (= performance based)	Equality, legality
Decision principle	Seniority	Economic value	Majority
Behavioral principle	Solidarity	Competition	Authority
Importance of individual personality	All facets of personality acknowledged	Personality acknowledged to the extent that it is performance related	Personality acknowledged to the extent there is an ownership stake
Compensation currency	Love, affection, recognition	Performance	Ownership/voting stake, shareholder value, dividend, money
Time horizon	Long term (generation)	Short term (months)	Medium term (years)

Source: Adapted from Groth and von Schlippe (2012).

to light. Moreover, communication is formalized and spelled out in the form of strategic plans. The individual personality matters only to the extent that it contributes meaningfully to the detection and pursuit of the economically promising strategic plan. As such, the business system is more selective than the family system with regard to communication topics, valued contributions, just as the promotion of issues and people.

The ownership system, in turn, is less concerned with decision making. Instead, it focuses on the setup and enforcement of legally binding agreements about who has status and power within the firm. This results in more formalized ways of communicating, such as contracts. These contracts often cover individual rights and obligations, as well as the legal consequences for not adhering to the agreed principles.

Most importantly, the appropriate justice principle varies across the three systems. In the family system, the principle of equality prevails, as typically observed in solidarity-oriented, caring groups. In contrast, the equity principle, which we can also refer to as the performance principle, applies to the business system. Those who contribute more should also have more say. In turn, in the ownership system, legality and the equal treatment of shareholders within their respective asset class prevail.

Therefore, what is accepted as legitimate behavior varies substantially across the three systems. While solidarity is the guiding behavioral principle in the family system, competition for the best performance counts in the business system. The situation is further complicated by the presence of the third system, the ownership system, in which the power ingrained in various levels of ownership status rules. As a result, competing justice principles, behavioral principles and expectations exist in parallel in the family business system, which explains part of the complexity of interactions and relationships in the family business context.

10.4.1 Systems in conflict and ambiguous context markers

Central to a systemic understanding of family firms is recognition of the fact that the structurally coupled systems of family, business and ownership provide multiple reasons for misunderstandings and, ultimately, conflicts among the people who interact in the integrated family business system. As the three systems (family, business and ownership) are present in parallel, people struggle to recognize which behavior is appropriate in certain situations.

This problem is intensified in the family business context because the family business system does not automatically provide information on which system the actor finds him-/herself in. Such an ambiguous situation is challenging for individuals because the social context is much less ambiguous in everyday life. We go to work, where we know that the logic of business prevails. When we come home (a location typically geographically distant from the workplace; it may even be clearly marked with our name on the door; we may change our clothing when coming home), we know that different behavioral norms apply (context markers; Bateson 1972). As individuals who live in societies with a high level of labor division, we normally have no problems understanding which world we are in: job, private life, hobby etc. Therefore, we usually easily understand the 'rules of the game' that apply in a particular situation.

The family firm context does not unambiguously mark the system in which we find ourselves and, thus, we struggle to understand which behavior is appropriate. This provides fertile ground for misunderstandings, perceptions of injustice and, ultimately, conflict. In fact, in many business-controlling families, business-related matters are discussed at the family's kitchen table. Simon (2002, p. 30) provides another example: 'If you meet your boss and father in the firm, you cannot tell whether he is a loving father right now or a strict boss. If in one role he had red spots on his face, and in the other green, everything would be much easier.' The context is ambiguous because the roles that people play (e.g., family member, manager, owner) in a specific situation are not detectable or are blurred. A drastic example from a Mexican family business serves to illustrate this dilemma. In a board meeting of the focal family firm, both a mother and her son are present. The mother is the president of the board, while the son is the CEO. As the meeting starts, the mother asks her son: 'Have you brushed your teeth?' This statement may have a legitimate basis in the context of the family, but it appears inappropriate in the context of the business.

A fundamental misunderstanding

In the quiet days after Christmas a couple approached their son and his fiancée and made an offer: 'We would like you to take over our hotel in the future that we have built up and run for about 30 years.' The young people, hearing this for the first time, were delighted. Four weeks later, they came back to the parents with an elaborate business plan. They had outlined strategic options, milestones for the further development of the business, and suggestions for the gradual handover of control. The parents were deeply hurt: 'How dare you approach us like this?' This, in turn, was confusing for the members of the younger generation as they were not aware of having made a mistake. Both parties accused each other of being 'false' or even 'not normal.' The mutual feelings of being hurt and misunderstood grew to a point where they required external support. After a while, it was obvious that the two parties had communicated from within different contexts: The parents had made their offer within the 'family' field of meaning (expecting gratitude and willingness in response to their offer), the youngsters had done so from the field of 'business' (seeing the opportunity and expecting a business relationship). Both were 'right' but within different systems of logic.

Source: Example taken from von Schlippe and Frank (2013, p. 392).

Thus, the meaning that arises from a statement or an action and its appropriateness depends on the context in which it is understood. Von Schlippe and Frank (2013) suggest that

> confusion and susceptibility to conflict can arise when one and the same act is received under different (or blurred) context markers, apparently depending on whether the communication takes place within the logic of the family, the business, or the ownership. Communication might be evaluated as normal according to the one logic but possibly as mad in the other.

Thus, the overlap of the family, business and ownership systems means that a communication can be interpreted differently depending on the system in which it is understood.

10.4.2 Who is speaking? The challenge of skewed communications

The possibilities for confusion, misunderstandings and, ultimately, severe conflict are numerous given the parallel presence of three systems with widely differing working principles. One person may speak as a family member but another may receive the message as a business manager or owner. For instance, a father who sees himself in the role of a caring parent may wish to give his son some advice about how to run the firm. However, the son may interpret the statement as a disrespectful subversion of his capabilities as an entrepreneur. Similarly, the son, acting in the role of future owner-manager, may tell his father that he feels that the father is not capable of understanding the technical details of a recent investment. The father may understand the son's statement as a sign of disrespect. Thus, a person may wear three hats, one for each system, and the hat that they are wearing when speaking is not always clear. Consequently, skewed communications arise—the sender and receiver of a message misunderstand each other as they are not operating in the same system. In Figure 10.5, skewed communications occur when people do not horizontally communicate within the same system. Rather, they communicate diagonally across systems and are unaware of the related confusion.

Misunderstandings can be avoided if the parties clarify the context in which they are talking to each other. This is important from a practical point of view, as the parties can improve their mutual understanding when they realize that their opponent is not 'bad' or 'mad', but is simply acting from a different systemic point of view (von Schlippe and Frank 2013).

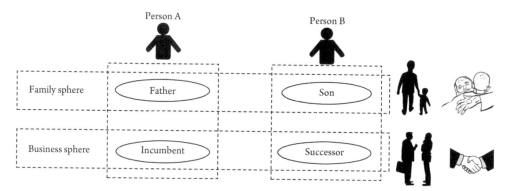

Figure 10.5 Horizontal and skewed communications

In sum, systems theory provides a useful way to unravel the underlying reasons for interpersonal dynamics and fundamental misunderstandings in the family business context. At the same time, it guides us toward a way to overcome the related problems. The following learning points summarize our arguments:

1. The meaning of a certain statement or action changes depending on the systemic context in which it is interpreted.
2. In family firms, three systemic contexts exist in parallel: the family context, the business context and the ownership context. Each context is characterized by different and sometimes opposing conditions of membership, communication styles, communication channels, justice principles, decision principles, behavioral principles, currencies and time horizons.
3. Typically, context markers (e.g., being at home or being at work) provide signals to the actors about the systemic context, and guide them to the appropriate interpretations and actions.
4. In family firms, context markers are sometimes absent or blurred, as people are simultaneously family members, managers and owners. In addition, families and businesses are often not clearly separated in space and time.
5. Perceptions of justice and functional family relationships are more likely when a discussion or the outcome of a decision are consistent with the implicit norms that are expected to prevail in a certain context.

> ## Workshop: Making people aware of the systemic reasons for their misunderstandings[8]
>
> A useful way to clarify 'who is speaking' and to make families in business aware of related misunderstandings is to hold a workshop in which each family member has multiple chairs on which to sit. Each family member is given three chairs representing the roles of family member, manager and owner. When sitting on a certain chair, family members are obliged to take on that role and to discuss application of the corresponding logic (e.g., language, arguments, justice principles; refer to Table 10.2) of that particular chair.
>
> For instance, if all workshop participants sit on the family chairs and are therefore obliged to apply the family logic to their arguments, a constructive dialogue emerges in which people speak the same 'language'. Of course, the chairs can be switched so that all workshop participants can be asked to sit on the business or ownership chairs, and then have dialogues as managers or owners, respectively.
>
> This setup can be altered further by placing one family member on, for instance, the manager chair and another family member on the family chair. Thereafter, attempts to have a dialogue should make family members aware of the reasons for misunderstandings in such situations.

10.5 Justice perceptions

Disagreements within families are a universal phenomenon and a normal part of family life, although the level of conflict generated by such disagreements and how disagreements are resolved may vary considerably across families or even within the same family at different points in time. A particularly important source of conflict in families is differing justice perceptions. In particular, perceived injustice (Fondacaro, Jackson and Luescher 2002)[9] fuels hostility and anger. Over time, such anger and hostility can contribute to a toxic family atmosphere characterized by high levels of conflict and low cohesion. In turn, high family conflict and low family cohesion tend to result in problematic behaviors both within and outside the family context.

For families in business, the concern for justice and the focus on avoiding injustice are particularly important. As we discuss below, what is perceived as fair within the business is not necessarily viewed as fair in the family. Moreover, during periods of transition and change, such as when the business is handed down from parents to children, people in close relationships become more concerned about issues of justice (Fondacaro, Jackson and Luescher 2002). As such, justice perceptions are an important trigger for relational dynamics in business-controlling families, especially at the time of succession. To understand the dynamics of family conflicts resulting from perceived injustice, we first need to acknowledge the distinctions among three types of justice:[10] distributive justice, procedural justice and interactional justice.

10.5.1 Distributive justice

Distributive justice refers to the fact that whether a decision is perceived as fair depends on the outcome of that decision. In this distributive point of view, people draw from one of three distributive allocation rules to determine whether a solution is fair: equity, equality and need.

Equity: the justice principle of the business
The allocation rule of *equity* suggests that whether a solution is seen as fair does not primarily depend on the absolute outcome. Rather, what matters is the ratio between one's input and the related output. Thus, people who view an outcome as fair from an equity point of view would argue that the outcome reflects the effort they have put into their work and is thus reflective of their performance.

Although this understanding of fairness is in line with the seemingly objective efficiency concerns that prevail in the business world, it is often problematic in practice. The conclusion that the rewards received are proportional to the investments undertaken can only be drawn if one has a reference value. This reference value is given by the rewards and investments of others. In addition, what are viewed as valuable inputs and valuable outputs can differ significantly among individuals. For example, a daughter who has loyally complied with her parents' wishes by following a certain educational program that prepares her for a job inside the firm could view her education as a valuable contribution that justifies her appointment as a successor (the output). However, from another person's point of view, the fact that someone has completed an educational program may not qualify as valuable input, perhaps because that person lacks practical experience. Therefore, many contributions may subjectively qualify as inputs, such as skill, effort, education, experience, age, gender, ethnic background and (in the family business context) birth order. Output can also have various subjective dimensions. With regard to the business context, we can think of growth, profit, dividends, corporate culture, customer satisfaction and job creation. In sum, the idea of equity and, hence, the perception of fair compensation for one's input is an often-contested topic in practice.

Despite these drawbacks, the justice rule of equity is particularly prominent in the business sphere. The idea of an output commensurate with a certain input is in line with the idea of efficiency and the effective allocation of resources. The idea of equity is reflected in many compensation systems, which often reward the outcome of an individual's inputs.

Equality and need: the justice principles of the family

Distributive fairness according to an *equality* principle is based on dividing outcomes evenly among people, regardless of input or need. This principle is often well intended, especially among caring parents who would like to avoid any discrimination among children. The problem is that the equality principle does not take different preferences and needs into account.

The distributive principle of *need* tries to address this problem, with those in greatest need getting more. For instance, one child might require more attention and support than another owing to developmental problems. In this case, the attention and support provided by the parents to that child would be considered legitimate within the family, even when such support comes at the expense of 'less' needy children. Need-based allocation of resources often constitutes a compromise aimed at accommodating individual differences with the ultimate goal of reaching equal distributions. Research in inheritances, for instance, shows that the equality principle most often serves as the default justice principle (Drake and Lawrence 2000). Therefore, the norm of equality is the default justice principle in the family context.

CASE STUDY

Who should get the family firm? Distributive justice principles in play

Three children—Anne, Bob and Carla—all claim a right to their parents' business and would like to become the next owner-manager, but on different grounds. Anna has completed an MBA and, through jobs outside the family firm, has proven her capacity to successfully lead a complex organization. Bob is in need of the position, as he does not have a job that would give him the same social standing and income. Carla has worked in the firm for the last few years and has contributed to its current success. Who should be the successor?

The answer varies based on the favored justice principle. If we apply the principle of equity, two solutions are conceivable: (1) Anna gets the firm, as she gains the greatest benefit from managing it (a utilitarian argument), or (2) Carla gets the firm, as she contributed most (the Aristotelian solution). If we apply the principle of need, the recipient would be Bob, as this would reduce inequality among the siblings. From the perspective of equality, justice can only be achieved if all three siblings are equally involved in the firm.

CASE STUDY *(continued)*

Therefore, the pluralism of justice principles leads to completely different outcomes, all of which are defendable on moral grounds.

We learn the following from this example:

1. Justice perceptions compete for influence. Selection of one justice principle can always be attacked on moral grounds by referring to another justice principle. This is particularly true in family firms given the parallel presence of multiple justice principles.
2. Even though people in the family business context are typically quick to suggest that the equity principle should be applied, this principle often does not help as much as expected. If we only look for the most favorable input/output relationship, both Anna and Carla could claim the position.
3. Given the fundamental misunderstanding about which solution is a fair solution, picking one option without going through a fair decision process will most likely lead to a severe family feud.

10.5.2 Procedural justice

In the case of distributive justice, people are only concerned with the outcome of the decision process. However, people often care at least as much about *how* they are treated during a process that results in a certain outcome. People are more likely to view a solution as fair if they have the opportunity to express their views and feelings during the process that leads to the outcome, when the process is applied consistently and is free from bias, and when the process is based on accurate information. For a solution to be considered procedurally just, five criteria must be met by the procedure that leads to the focal outcome:[11]

1. Applied consistently across people and over time,
2. Free from bias—no vested interests in a particular solution,
3. Ensures accurate information is collected and used in decision making,
4. Conforms to personal or prevailing standards of ethics or morality, and
5. Takes the opinions of the various groups affected by the decision into account.

Therefore, fair process means that people feel that their opinions are respected throughout a decision-making process—from problem formulation to the final decision. With regard to succession, families in business could, for instance, define the meaning of each criteria in a particular decision-making process. A particular threat to perceptions of fair process is the exclusion of important stakeholders from the decision. Therefore, an important element for ensuring fair process is defining who will be involved in which parts of the decision process. Moreover, if some parties are excluded, transparent explanations must be given (Van der Heyden, Blondel and Carlock 2005).

10.5.3 Interactional justice

Interactional justice reflects the idea that sensitivity, truthfulness and justification can make people feel better about an unfavorable outcome. People who are familiar with each other, such as family members, expect to be treated in a polite manner, and with dignity and respect, and they expect the person who enacts a certain decision (e.g., other family members or advisors) to refrain from improper and scathing comments. In addition, a situation in which people are not truthful, or decisions are not explained in a thorough and timely manner, is dangerous in any decision context, especially among people who are familiar with each other.

CASE STUDY

Procedural and interactional fairness in three family-internal successions in Switzerland

While studying fairness in three family-internal successions in Switzerland, Nicole Faessler (2014) found that procedural and interactional fairness were absolutely key for avoiding family conflict. A next-generation family member stated that 'in some situations, emotions ran high [. . .] and we had to sit together at one point to thoroughly discuss all of the issues until everything was worked out.'

A family member who did not take on a role inside the family business after succession emphasized the role of communication: 'Communication is always crucial. You have to be on speaking terms, and you have to talk things out at a single table instead of everyone walking off and doing his own thing.' For one family, interaction during the transition process had many facets: 'Sometimes, it was seething and sometimes it really was ablaze [. . .] Then you simply needed the situation to cool off [. . .], sometimes by putting your foot down and sometimes by examining the whole issue with everyone around one table and talking about it. Every now and then, you have to keep it under wraps and not speak about it anymore.'

Another family member mentioned that he appreciated being kept informed about the various financial discussions even though he was not personally involved. He felt that he always knew what was going on and that he understood what the other family members

---

CASE STUDY *(continued)*

were talking about. As he was able to approach his father with any information request, he 'knew what he wanted to know.'

The families also emphasized that they appreciated some formality in the process, such as formal rules for meeting minutes and procedures for signing an agreement.

Interestingly, some families found it useful to be able to build on family traditions, which served as guiding principles for solving conflicts. For instance, one family had a tradition in which only those family members working inside the firm could get shares. This principle spared the members from numerous discussions.

10.5.4 The importance of procedural and interactional justice in the family

To illustrate the relative importance of procedural and interactional justice as opposed to distributive justice, consider the example of a family that needs to plan the transfer of the family business from one generation to the next. As the firm is managed by its owners, the family deals with succession questions at the management and ownership levels and, ultimately, at the level of family wealth. For the senior generation, it is of paramount importance to find a solution that is fair for all involved parties, especially all children. Many parents require a solution that upholds family cohesion and avoids family conflict.

In many such cases, it is impossible to devise a solution that treats all children equally (i.e., all children get the same share of the parents' wealth). The firm often represents the largest part of family wealth and it is often unsuitable to split firm ownership among multiple parties (i.e., children), especially for smaller firms. Fragmented ownership complicates the firm's management (e.g., owing to different goals among the owners) and waters down the incentives of the owner-manager in charge, as he or she has to share the value created with all other owners. In addition, depending on the firm's legal format (e.g., a sole proprietorship), it may be legally impossible to split ownership.

From a distributive point of view, therefore, succession solutions often lead to an uneven distribution of wealth that tends to favor the child that continues the family firm. Often, such unequal solutions are defended on the grounds of the equity principle and, hence, on the grounds that the child taking over has contributed more than his or her siblings by working inside the firm, has the appropriate education and experience, or takes greater risks by continuing the firm. From a distributive point of view, successions often take the form of compromises in which equity, equality and need considerations are blended.

Nevertheless, even though successions may be skewed in the sense that they infringe on the distributive norm of equality that typically prevails in the family context, they may be acceptable to the disfavored parties in cases where the solution was reached in a procedurally just way. Indeed, numerous studies in the general population and within families have shown that procedural and interactional justice are more important for perceptions of fairness than distributive fairness (e.g., Fondacaro, Jackson and Luescher 2002). Apparently, people are particularly attuned to considerations of procedural and interactional justice when they deal with in-group members, such as close family members. How family members are treated in the course of resolving intra-family disputes, especially disputes between parents and children, is often more important than dispute outcomes.

This finding is crucially important for families in business. Instead of only focusing on distributive questions, such as who will get ownership and managerial responsibility inside the firm, it is critical to define a decision process that satisfies the criteria for distributive fairness. Moreover, treating people with disrespect, systematically keeping them from giving their opinions and excluding them from information flows are sure ways to create feelings of injustice, which in turn lead to anger and conflict.

An unequal outcome that is reached using either fair procedures or fair interactions has no effect on a person's reaction. Only a reliance on unfair procedures in combination with unfair interactions results in negative reactions and dissatisfaction with the results. This leads us to Figure 10.6, which summarizes the extent to which solutions are likely to be accepted by the parties involved in a decision-making process.

Figure 10.6 holds some crucial information. A solution that is unfair from a distributive point of view may still be acceptable if the decision process and the interactions among the involved parties is fair. Therefore, in trying to manage a conflict, the focus should be on ensuring a fair process and respectful interactions among people, especially if the distributive effects lead to unequal treatment of the parties.

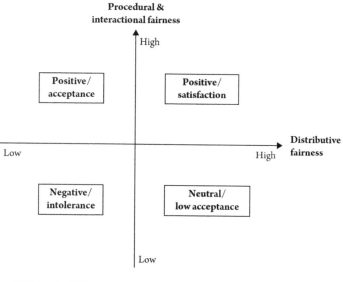

Source: Faessler (2014).

Figure 10.6 Fairness and behavioral reactions

CASE STUDY

The fair distribution of family wealth

This is the story of a family-owned private firm run by a father who has two sons. With regard to the fair distribution of the family firm, Son A argues: 'I have worked in the firm, I have made it big, and I deserve to get the firm.' Son B contends: 'I am not interested in the firm. However, I want to be treated fairly. I therefore expect to get something that is of equal value to what my brother is getting.' Hence, while Son A argues in line with the equity principle and, hence, in line with the justice principle that prevails in the business context, Son B emphasizes the principle of equality, which is salient in the family context. Therefore, both offer arguments that can be considered legitimate in the family business context.

Note how different the discussion would be if Son A and Son B were unrelated and no parents were involved. The parents would be the sellers of a firm, while Son A and Son B would be potential buyers. In this case, neither Son A's arguments on his contributions nor Son B's claims for equal treatment would have much legitimacy. The discussion would simply revolve around who makes the highest bid for the firm.

Also note that the situation would be much simpler if the family's wealth was not tied up in a firm, but was simply an amount of money. However, as the firm represents the largest part of family wealth in this case and as the firm is private, splitting family wealth in an equal way is difficult.

CASE STUDY *(continued)*

In this case, the family tried to find a compromise. As Son A is interested in continuing the firm, the family decides to allocate a majority stake in the firm to Son A, while Son B is given a minority stake. An alternative that the family also considered but then rejected was to give both sons an equal ownership stake, but equip son A's stake with superior voting rights.

To compensate for the uneven distribution of family wealth, Son B receives a loan from the firm, which the firm will repay in the coming years. Son B also receives some other family wealth, including money and real estate, in order to move as close as possible to an equal distribution of family wealth. Upon further scrutiny, however, it is clear that Son A receives something more valuable than Son B.

In light of the challenges of finding a fair solution upon the transfer of the family firm, many families adopt the solution of last resort: the sale of the firm. A pile of money is easier to distribute than a family firm. Even though this may be catastrophic for the family's business tradition, it may be one way to keep the family together.

 REFLECTION QUESTIONS

1. As a family business consultant, you are called to moderate the discussion within the family about the fair distribution of the family firm between the brothers. How would you go about it?
2. What options would you present to the family, and what are their specific advantages and disadvantages?

10.5.5 Injustice perceptions and their consequences

Perceptions of injustice or unfairness are one of the most effective destroyers of families in business. This is because unfairness leads to hostility, anger, distrust and sometimes deviant behavior, which over time can contribute to a toxic family atmosphere characterized by high conflict and low cohesion. Notably, however, solutions that are unfair from a distributive point of view may still be accepted if there is procedural and interactional fairness in decision making.

Perceptions of unfairness can have a lasting impact and are by no means fleeting emotions. Adolescents can often easily point to circumstances in which they felt unfairly treated. Memories of these episodes of injustice are accessible to people long after they occur, and they may even be passed on within the family from one generation to the next. Conversely, resolving family problems in a manner that is viewed as fair may contribute to a family environment characterized by low conflict, high cohesion, cooperation, trust, reciprocative behavior and psychological well-being (Jackson and Luescher 2002).

Injustice perceptions lead to emotional reactions in the person who feels under-rewarded and in the person who feels over-rewarded. Under-rewarded people tend to experience anger, while over-rewarded people tend to experience guilt. Such emotionality motivates people to try to reduce perceived injustices (Adams 1965). Consequently, over-rewarded people who feel guilty experience pressure to increase their own inputs (e.g., by working harder), to reduce their own outcomes (e.g., limit their salaries), to accept the fact that the under-rewarded people will reduce their inputs (e.g., free ride on the guilt of the over-rewarded and work less), or to increase the outputs of the under-rewarded (e.g., by paying higher salaries).

In contrast, under-rewarded people who feel angry may seek a mirroring strategy to address the perceived injustice. They may, for instance, reduce their own efforts. Consider, for example, two brothers taking over a family firm from their parents. One of the brothers feels unjustly treated, as he was only given a secondary job in the firm while his brother was appointed CEO. The former may limit the effort that he puts into his work, and he may feel entitled to more favorable treatment. He may also remind the brother who was appointed CEO that he was over-rewarded and, therefore, has to prove that he is worthy of that favorable treatment and has to work harder. Alternatively, the under-rewarded brother may ask his over-rewarded brother to limit his payouts.[12]

In sum, justice matters in family firms, especially in the context of succession. The results of perceived injustice materialize in negative emotions, decreased family functioning, and dysfunctional behaviors among both under-rewarded and over-rewarded people, which severely limit the efficient working of the firm.

The Fredo Effect

Fredo is the middle son of the Corleone family in the 1972 American crime movie *The Godfather*. He is deeply insecure and not very bright, and is considered the weakest of the three sons in his family. As he is viewed as the black sheep in the family and as a failure, Fredo is denied a leadership role in the business and is sent away from the family's main business operations to take care of some side activity. Deeply hurt from being passed over in the family firm's succession, Fredo breaks organizational norms, pursues a lavish lifestyle, and even betrays his brother.

> In an intriguing set of papers on what they call the 'Fredo effect', Kim Eddleston, Franz Kellermanns and Ronald Kidwell develop the idea that many families in business have to deal with a Fredo. They show that the presence of a Fredo in the family firm tends to not only lead to a destructive family climate, but also to a destructive effect on the family firm. Why are Fredos so hard to stop?
>
> The authors suggest that parents are often very generous to such children and put more faith in them than is justified. One possible reason for the family's forbearance with a Fredo is that the other family members, especially parents, feel guilt toward that child. They therefore offer the child undeserved rewards and spoil them. These authors write: 'The rub is that continuing to reward Fredos while ignoring their damaging behavior leads to more problems: the child's sense of entitlement increases, higher levels of conflict in the family firm result, and more problems with productivity and teamwork emerge because of the family Fredo.' (Kidwell et al. 2013, p. 6). The Fredo effect can thus be viewed as an outcome of a justice-restoration mechanism following from the guilt toward the under-rewarded child.

10.6 Why family firms are fertile contexts for conflict

Disagreement and conflict are a universal experience in families. Small and large, poor and rich families all experience the strain of conflict, where we define 'conflict' as perceived incompatibilities or discrepant views among the parties (Jehn and Bendersky 2003). The popular press is replete with stories about business-owning family members who engage in more or less overt and escalated feuds. We might, therefore, wonder why family firms serve as fertile grounds for conflict. We laid some foundations for answering this question when we discussed family firms from a systemic perspective and when we explored the issue of justice in family firms. In this section, we offer a more complete overview of why family firms are fertile fields for conflict.

1. **Intertwinement of multiple systems with conflicting logics**
   As outlined in the previous sections, family, business and ownership systems each come with their own inherent logic. The challenge lies in the fact that these logics make conflicting predictions about appropriate behavior. For more details, refer to section 10.4.
2. **Absent or blurred context markers**
   As the same people occupy multiple roles (e.g., two brothers who are also co-CEOs), it is challenging for people to identify the logic within which a certain conversation or action should be interpreted (e.g., in the family or business logic). Behavior that appears appropriate in one logic may appear inappropriate in another logic.

3. **Spillover effects of interpersonal dynamics**

   The vanishing boundaries between business and private or family life facilitate the spillover of behaviors from one system to another. In the positive case, functional behavior spills over from the family to the business and vice versa. For instance, a proactive problem-solving approach to conflict management in the family provides a basis for a positive problem-solving orientation in the firm (Sorenson 1999). Unfortunately, dysfunctional behavior may also bleed into other systems.

4. **Unforeseen types of conflict**

   Family firms are prone to psychodynamic effects that arise in any family, such as from sibling rivalry, children's desires to differentiate themselves from their parents, marital discord and identity conflict. Nonfamily businesses do not suffer from these effects. These types of conflicts significantly disturb the business system, as they cannot be controlled through the standard managerial practices typically learned in business school.

5. **People with high levels of informal power**

   Even family members without high formal positions can wield informal power in the business because of their family connections. Power exerted by family members can overshadow the authority vested in roles and positions within the organization (Sorenson 1999). For instance, founders who have left the firm—grandparents, mothers or fathers with no formal decision-making authority—can exert influence on high-level business decisions.

6. **Insider information**

   Family members tend to have access to business-related insider information. This information offers its holder some level of influence in the organization, which can be used to steer decisions in opportunistic directions.

7. **Sustained conflict over time and across domains**

   Relationship conflict may be particularly harmful to family firms because conflicts among family members tend to be sustained over time by the repetitive and inevitable interactions occurring both at work and away from the business (Eddleston and Kellermanns 2007). Sometimes, family conflicts are even passed on across generations through stories and storytelling and are, therefore, inherited.

8. **High exit costs**

   Except in the case of spousal couples, it is virtually impossible to leave one's family. This is particularly true for families that are in business together. In economic terms, exiting the family business may be costly because of an illiquid market for the firm's shares and, hence, a depressed value of the ownership stake upon exit. Moreover, selling out and leaving the family business may mean also cutting family bonds.

Consequently, family firms are not only fertile fields of conflict. They also provide the background against which conflicts can carry very destructive potential.

10.7 Types of conflict

As people have individual views about the world, discrepant views, incompatibilities and conflict are inevitable parts of social life. For our understanding of conflict's destructive as well as constructive effects, we distinguish between two types of conflict: relationship conflict and task conflict.

10.7.1 Relationship conflict

Relationship conflicts exist when there are interpersonal incompatibilities among individuals. This type of conflict often reflects personality differences as well as differences of opinion and preferences regarding non-task issues (e.g., religion, politics, fashion) (Jehn and Bendersky 2003). Examples that illustrate this type of conflict between two individuals include constant bickering, snide comments, mocking or a failure to talk with each other because of dislikes.

Relationship conflict is a dysfunctional form of conflict that includes affective components, such as annoyance, frustration, personal animosity, incompatibility and irritation with others. It is emotionally charged, and often includes interpersonal clashes characterized by anger, resentment and worry (Eddleston and Kellermanns 2007). In such situations, time is often spent on interpersonal aspects rather than on technical and decision-making tasks. Moreover, relationship conflict often clashes with work efforts, as it redirects efforts related to work toward the reduction of threats, politics, coalition and cohesion. In turn, relationship conflict hampers people's abilities to focus, to act creatively, and to process information. Therefore, personal performance and the performance of the group suffer.

Relationship conflict is always dysfunctional for firms and hampers their performance. However, such conflicts are particularly destructive in the family firm context, as relationship conflicts among family members tend to be sustained over time and to take place among the top decision makers in the firm (see section 10.6).

10.7.2 Task conflict

Task conflict (also called 'cognitive conflict') involves disagreements among group members about the tasks being performed, including differences in viewpoints, ideas and opinions. Employees often describe these conflicts as 'work conflicts', 'work disagreements' and 'task problems' (Jehn and Bendersky 2003).[13] In other words, task conflicts represent diverging views about appropriate behaviors and strategies with regard to the firm, including disagreements about the proper speed of performing a task, the importance and meaning of financial data, the meaning of governance regulations, and the content and importance of strategic plans and goals.

The most important distinction between relationship conflict and task conflict is that task conflicts can be beneficial for firm performance if they increase the number of opinions, prevent premature consensus, increase member

---

Excursus: Typical patterns and dynamics of escalated relationship conflict in family firms[14]

Triangulation: In this conflict pattern, a third party becomes involved in a conflict that initially occurred between two parties. For instance, instead of directly speaking to the opposing person, one of the original parties may choose to go through a third party and start a conflict with that third party. The conflict with the third party has an integrating effect with the internal parties, who can then coalesce against the third party. Triangulation also occurs when each one of two conflicting parties (e.g., two siblings) seeks to bring a third party (e.g., a mother) onto their side in an attempt to build a coalition against the other party. Often, advisors are brought into the third-party role.

Projection: Projection occurs when people place their own wishes, such as wishes about career choices, capabilities, behaviors and attitudes, on other people. The most common case is when parents project their own wishes on their children. Typically, individuals react either by adapting and compromising on the development of their own identities, or by extreme differentiation from these expectations and the people who express them.

Identification and differentiation: Identification may result in extreme imitation, such as when a son wants to be like his father. Such attempts are typically doomed to failure given the natural differences between people. In the case of differentiation, the opposite behavior occurs—people try to be different at any price.

Splitting and connecting: By splitting, people try to create ruptures within a group, such as a family, and develop a 'us against them' atmosphere. Extreme splitting has the power to simultaneously split and connect. On the one hand, people are split along the lines of the conflicting parties. On the other hand, a tight coalition is formed that is motivated to fight. It is the connecting aspect of splitting that motivates groups to escalate conflicts.

Denial: When people are in denial, they tend to be unwilling to face the facts. Better denying the facts than being overwhelmed by the emotions from acknowledging them. Denial is a short-sighted, fragile way of trying to uphold a certain worldview or group constellation.

> **Demonization**: An important component of escalating relationship conflict is to demonize the opponent in an attempt to rationalize the opponent's behavior. When demonizing, people often resort to depicting the opponent as stupid, bad or sick.
>
> This list is by no means complete. For instance, various levels of aggression could be added (from sarcasm to physical aggressiveness). This list is meant to illustrate typical conflict patterns and their origins.

involvement or improve decision quality (Kellermanns and Eddleston 2004). In general, cognitive conflict improves the decision-making process by increasing discussions of which tasks should be performed, and which work and strategies should be pursued (Jehn and Bendersky 2003). In a set of influential studies, Kellermans and Eddleston (2004 and 2007) suggest that task conflict facilitates the critical evaluation of issues, and ensures that superior alternatives are not overlooked and creative solutions are considered. This is extremely important for family firms, which tend to let their core competencies develop into core rigidities. If key issues are viewed differently but those differences are discussed openly and without emotion, groupthink can be avoided and consensus can be reached. In addition, task conflict may help maintain the identity and boundaries of groups, act as a safety valve, increase in-group cohesion, establish and maintain the balance of power, and create allies and coalitions. By initiating an engaging dialogue on the work to be done, task conflict can also foster learning.

Despite the many positive aspects of task conflict, it can still be emotional, and give rise to anxiety, tension, antagonism and discomfort among the parties. This is because a person's normal reaction to disagreement or the questioning of one's viewpoints is dissatisfaction, regardless of the advantages of the confrontation (Jehn and Bendersky 2003). It is therefore important to avoid downplaying the negative effects of task conflict.

The overall effect of task conflict on the performance of groups and the organizations they work for seems to be a matter of degree (Kellermanns and Eddleston 2004). In fact, only moderate levels of task conflict are beneficial for the performance of top management teams. Firms with high levels of task conflict tend to have problems completing tasks and reaching goals, while firms with low levels of task conflict often become stagnant and are unable to develop new strategies. Moderate levels of task conflict in family firms may be particularly important, as family and business interests often collide and need to be considered simultaneously.

Table 10.3 Relationship conflict and task conflict

Relationship conflict	Task conflict
'We cannot stand each other'	'We disagree about the best way forward'
Negative emotions	Negative and positive emotions, no emotions
Withdrawal, clash, escalation, aggression, destruction	Argument with opposing party
Undermines cooperation, benevolence and solidarity	Comprehensive discussion of possible actions
Only negative consequences known at group and organizational levels	Improved decisions, creativity and performance at group and organizational levels

The message for family firms is that it is important to distinguish between types of conflict (see Table 10.3). While relationship conflict can unfold in particularly destructive ways in family firms and has no apparent positive effect, task conflict is an important and valuable part of family firm conduct. As long as people are able to keep conflicts impersonal and task-centered, and as long as they can avoid escalating task conflicts to extreme levels, they should be able to harness advantages from a constructive conflict culture.

10.7.3 Connection between task and relationship conflict

Despite the clear-cut distinction between relationship conflict and task conflict, we find important links between the two conflict types. For instance, what may start as a constructive task conflict may turn into personal animosity and, finally, a heated relationship conflict. Alternatively, relationship conflicts may intensify task conflict. For instance, a relationship conflict between siblings that dates back many years may erupt from time to time and interfere with task-related problem solving in the firm. Relationship conflict may thus impede the positive effects of moderate levels of task conflict on firm performance. Relationship conflict can, for example, prevent family members from implementing others' ideas for performing tasks or handling business processes.

Notably, the simplest models of conflict resolution assume that people are really fighting about the issue at hand (Kaye 1991). This may be true of disputes between strangers who happen to transgress upon one another's rights or threaten one another's interests, but it is rarely the case between spouses, or among relatives or long-time business partners. In fact, a task conflict can be a relationship conflict in disguise and vice versa.

Moreover, relationship conflict and task conflict may be more or less legitimate forms of conflict depending on whether they play out in the family or business spheres. For instance, a task conflict involving arguments about performance would appear legitimate in the business sphere. However, in the family sphere, with its emphasis on inclusive and benevolent relationships, the same arguments may seem misplaced. Conversely, a relationship conflict may reflect a legitimate misunderstanding in the family sphere, but it may be seen as a dysfunctional way to solve disagreements in the business sphere. Thus, relationship-or task-related arguments may appear more legitimate for resolving disagreements depending on the context in which they unfold.

10.8 Conflict dynamics

Conflicts are about something and occur with someone. In other words, they have a topic and happen within relationships, which gives rise to the distinction between task and relationship conflict. However, the conflict topic is not always clear. It is generally useful if people can delineate the topic and disagree about a very specific issue or task. After the topic is delineated, debates are less likely to escalate because the level of identification with the topic is most often limited and factual discussions become possible. However, in addition to the issue and relationships, conflicts have a third critical dimension—time.

10.8.1 The role of time in conflicts

As noted by Simon (2012), conflicts always take place in the present, but they normally deal with the past or the future. When we ask 'Who is responsible for this situation?', we typically reconstruct today's reality by referring to past events. If the cause lies prior to the consequence in time, then conflicts may arise about the temporal ordering of events. People fight about the temporal order of events because their understanding of the past allows them to legitimize their present behavior. In their ordering and retention of past events, people tend to be selective, not always because of ill will but because of selective memory. The past matters for conflicts that take place in the present, as the person who is believed to be the wrongdoer in the past has to pay the price today. Alternatively, the person who has not been indulgent in the past is entitled to restorative transfers today.

As people tend to remember the past very selectively and as the subjectively memorized past is important for people's perceptions about fair behavior today, discussions about the past are often not useful for resolving conflicts or deriving solid plans for the future. If discussions about the past take place, they should occur without time pressure, as they could be abused and may lead to biased decisions related to the future.

10.8.2 Conflict and the lifecycle of the firm

Conflict issues and conflictual relationships change across a firm's lifecycle. In the founding phase, task conflict revolves around such issues as the feasibility of the venture, the raising of capital and the willingness of family members to invest capital. In this new-venture stage, relationship conflict may arise in the founding team. If family members are involved, conflict may emerge around mutual expectations. In particular, family members who invest in the new firm may be willing to do so on favorable terms. However, such family capital often has strings attached—the continuous involvement of family members, the need to inform them about the firm's progress, and the expectation that the new firm will also be 'their' venture.

In the growth phase, task conflicts typically deal with the mobilization of resources, such as who to hire, which technology to adopt, which machinery to buy and where to establish the firm. In the growth phase, demands from work may interfere with demands from the family and vice versa, leading to feelings of stress and guilt because neither the demands of the business nor the demands of the family are satisfied.

After a firm is established, its professionalization, the delegation of authority and efficiency concerns move into focus and may give rise to task conflicts. With regard to relationship conflicts, the cooperation within the growing top management team may not be as harmonious as expected. In addition, family members could clash with each other in the private sphere on lifestyle choices and the use of accumulated private wealth. The owner-managers may also ask themselves about what the future may bring to them personally. Some may even experience a midlife crisis, which might lead them to fundamentally question their relationships.

In the maturity stage, rejuvenation and continued innovation typically become conflict-laden issues. Most importantly from a family business perspective, succession takes center stage, giving rise to questions about who should take over the business, when, in what role(s), and under what conditions. In terms of relationship conflict, the involvement of the next generation poses a particular challenge, especially with regard to the constructive collaboration of senior and junior generations.

Thus, each stage in the firm's lifecycle has its own topics and relational dynamics that have the potential to lead to conflict. For a practitioner, this overview may be used to put his or her own experience into perspective. An entrepreneurial career is a life choice with many opportunities for conflict. In other words, conflict is a natural part of an entrepreneurial career. As discussed above, as conflict may have positive aspects, the question is not how to avoid it at any price, but how to accept it, keep it within an acceptable scope and make the best out of it.

10.8.3 Conflict escalation

Conflicts can take on a life of their own. A minor misunderstanding can escalate in certain circumstances. Multiple conceptual models explain how conflicts escalate and typically refer to a sequence of events along the following lines: starting from a normal, nonconflictual situation, a person feels impaired by the behavior of another person. The former signals that he/she is unwilling to leave that behavior unacknowledged and asks for a reparation. If he/she receives a satisfactory response, the two will return to the normal state. If he/she does not receive a satisfactory response, he/she will make some sort of threat. If he/she does not receive a satisfactory response at that point, both parties will escalate the conflict. Thus, before conflicts escalate, we observe multiple opportunities for reconciliation that could return the parties to the original nonconflictual state.

Glasl (1982) describes nine steps of conflict escalation from the hardening of the situation at the outset to a status in which both parties seek mutual destruction (Figure 10.7).

In the early stages, the parties are able and willing to end the process in a way that will enable them both to exit the conflict with their heads held high. The focus in these stages with modest conflict intensity is on issues and tasks, and a win–win outcome is possible. In later stages, the conflict becomes more heated and confrontational, and the parties come to understand that only one of them can exit the dispute as a winner. Relational issues interfere with task-related issues, which undermines the potential benefits of task-related discussions.

The lose–lose situation is particularly worthy of exploration in the family business context given the multiple reasons for why conflicts escalate and are hard to resolve in this organizational context (refer to section 10.6). In

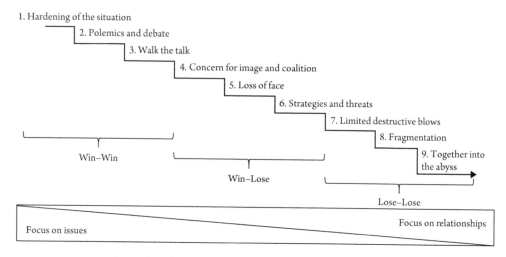

Source: Adapted from Glasl (1982).

Figure 10.7 Conflict-escalation model

the presence of profound antagonism, parties will be willing to accept their own losses only if the other party is destroyed. In such a situation, the parties might even be willing to accept their own financial ruin if doing so may help ruin the other party as well. The conflicting parties may conclude that if they go into the abyss together, 'nothing is left, and we will finally achieve justice'. Each party's own perceptions and opinions are biased to such a degree that the parties are no longer concerned with their own gains. Instead, they are only focused on the losses of the other party. Such a conflict is primarily driven by relational considerations—it is only driven by tasks to the extent that they support the destruction of the other party. As the threat of conflict escalation is immanent if families in business come to blows, any conflict-moderation strategy must foresee opportunities for the conflicting parties to go their separate ways by, for example, predefining ways to exit management and ownership positions.

10.9 Conflict-management styles

Language use and our cultural backgrounds typically lead us to believe that conflicts should be 'resolved'. However, 'conflict resolution' may be an unfortunate choice of words for dealing with conflict because the term suggests that conflicts should be eliminated. This goal may be appropriate when conflict is destructive, such as in the presence of relationship conflict. Nevertheless, there are many instances in which conflict should be encouraged and utilized

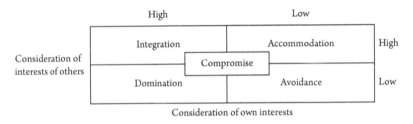

Source: Rahim (1983).

Figure 10.8 Conflict-management styles

to improve decisions (Cosier and Harvey 1998). Therefore, it is more useful to talk about the 'management' of conflict—the pursuit of strategies to organize conflict in the most constructive way.

Regardless of whether we are dealing with task or relationship conflict, it is useful to distinguish between the degree to which one considers one's own interests and the degree to which one considers the interests of others (Rahim 1983). These two dimensions are critical for the choice of an appropriate conflict-management style, and their combination results in five prototypical conflict-management styles: integration, accommodation, domination, avoidance and compromise (Figure 10.8), which vary in their ability to address family and business-related conflict.

10.9.1 Domination

The domination conflict-management style is assertive and uncooperative. It involves a unilateral concern for one's own interests and, hence, the pursuit of a win–lose outcome. In trying to address the conflict, domination is unlikely to address the many issues associated with the business and family because the desired outcome is a 'winner-takes-all' solution, which would leave behind both winners and losers. Moreover, as domination blocks others from achieving their goals, this conflict-management style generates negative emotions, such as anger, stress and distrust. Therefore, this approach is unlikely to build relationships, accommodate varied interests or lead to positive family outcomes such as cohesion and harmony.

Nevertheless, domination may be an appropriate conflict-management style in extreme conflict situations in which the family and/or the business are suffering. This is the case when the family is unable to make a necessary but controversial decision and when the family is willing to accept the tensions that may result from authoritative conflict resolution and, perhaps, even the separation of the parties. This patriarchic approach to conflict management should be more acceptable in cultural contexts with high power distance, such as those in which junior family members are required to unconditionally respect the power of senior family members. The enforcement of a decision may then be an acceptable way to regain the capacity to act.

When people opt for domination as their approach to managing family business conflict, the owner with the most votes typically retains ultimate control rights and, hence, authority. Therefore, under a dominating conflict-management style, the owner with the highest stakes will typically be the party imposing his or her preferences upon the others.

10.9.2 Accommodation

As the extreme opposite of competition, accommodation represents an attempt to manage conflicts in unassertive, cooperative ways. Accommodation is based on concern for others rather than oneself, and may even include a willingness to neglect personal desires. When accommodating, people are willing to make concessions so as to orientate themselves toward the interests of others. In his study of conflict in family firms, Sorenson (1999) suggests that accommodation typically involves a conciliatory tone, a willingness to get along, supportiveness and acknowledgment of others' concern. If all parties are accommodating, good relationships and cohesiveness should result. This, in turn, should generally support the resolution of conflict.

However, too much accommodation may prevent some parties from asserting themselves, even on important issues. For example, a highly accommodative owner might sacrifice business success to satisfy family members or employees. Therefore, even though accommodation may be a signal of deep compassion for the (justified) concerns of others, it is frequently an expedient outcome that does not result in the best solution for both parties. In other words, accommodation often prevents fruitful discussion and the search for creative alternatives that can accommodate the interests of all parties.

10.9.3 Avoidance

Avoidance refers to a lack of interest in one's own position or those of others, and refers to a failure to address a conflict. Individuals may deny that conflicts exist or simply avoid discussing them. If avoidance is used, the issues that sparked the conflict may go unaddressed. There are multiple motivations for engaging in avoidance, such as an ideal that the family must always be in harmony, a fear that the family is not strong enough to deal with the conflict and will fall apart, or a hope that everything will turn out fine over time.

When individuals need time to 'cool down' or when an issue is not important, avoidance can be an effective strategy. However, avoidance postpones conflicts and, consequently, frustrations increase. Although avoidance limits direct face-to-face confrontations, it can escalate frustrations, which can spill over in other ways. For example, family members might avoid discussing conflicts at work but vent their feelings with spouses, thereby adding to overall negative feelings within the family (Sorenson 1999). When avoided, conflicts reemerge at some other point, often when the family constellation changes, such as when a senior family member who kept all parties together dies.

Given the above discussion, avoidance is clearly not a relationship-building strategy. Too much avoidance leaves important business and family issues unresolved, which can heighten tensions and limit productive action. Kaye and McCarthy (1996) find that a strategy of conflict avoidance is associated with relatively low family satisfaction, high sibling rivalry and low levels of mutual trust. Therefore, avoidance does not contribute to positive family or business outcomes.

10.9.4 Compromise

Forging a compromise requires intermediate levels of assertiveness and cooperativeness. This means considering one's own interest as well as those of others to a medium degree, so that no one can be viewed as a winner or loser. Each party gives in to the other in order to find an acceptable solution. Compromises reflect a 'fixed-pie' approach, and because each party gives something up, no one feels fully satisfied. The solutions that are adopted are the result of a search for the least common factor. Compromises have the flavor of 'giving in to keep the peace' and may be a way to reduce relationship conflict, as both parties have the impression that their concerns have at least been considered. In sum, compromises may contribute to achieving desired business and family outcomes, but not to the same extent as integration in which a new, creative solution can be found that more fully satisfies the parties (Rahim 1983).

10.9.5 Integration

Integration means that the conflicting parties try to integrate their mutual interests in order to achieve a solution in which everyone wins. As such, it is an approach that attempts to fully satisfy the concerns of all involved parties. Like accommodation, integration indicates a willingness to adapt. However, it does not involve yielding to others' concerns. Instead, it is an active search for 'win–win' solutions—the parties jointly search for a fully satisfactory solution that goes beyond a compromise. Integration requires time and effort on the part of participants, as well as good interpersonal skills, including open communication, trust and mutual support. Integration is more likely to occur under conditions of mutual trust, open communication, and creativity (to identify win–win outcomes), and in cultures that value teamwork over individualism.

Undoubtedly, integration contributes to desirable family outcomes, including positive relationships and cohesion. As it requires mutual sharing and openness, it is more likely than accommodation to promote organizational learning and adaptation, which should also enhance the firm's effectiveness (Sorenson 1999). The advantage of integration is that a 'win–win' solution may be reached by asserting one's own position while attempting to meet another's needs. Thus, it should positively contribute to family and business outcomes.

10.9.6 Which conflict-management style is best in the family business context?

While the first four conflict-management styles outlined above have negative effects, collaboration offers the highest likelihood of lasting, positive effects for both the family and the business. Multiple studies of conflict in family firms find that the firms with higher growth and better performance are more likely to use integration as their conflict-management style, suggesting that integration is the most productive conflict-management style for family businesses.

Interestingly, Sorenson (1999) finds that accommodation and compromise are highly correlated with positive family outcomes (Kellermanns and Eddleston 2007). At the same time, many firms that adopt one of these approaches suffer from performance shortfalls. Businesses with negative business/positive family outcomes seem to place a premium on resolving conflict and maintaining family relationships. They therefore appear to accept poorer performance in exchange for family functioning. The worst outcomes for business and family are found for the avoidance strategy, which again serves to highlight the importance of open and sincere communication.[15]

Sometimes, families in business view the use of a mediator as taboo for privacy reasons, or because engaging a mediator signals an inability to solve a problem on one's own and, hence, is viewed as an admission of weakness. However, as integration requires a high level of competency among all parties in relation to communicating and dealing with the conflict, and carries a risk that the conflict could escalate, a professional mediator may help keep the discussion constructive in the pursuit of win–win solutions.

10.10 Communication strategies

Particularly critical for our understanding of conflict in family firms is the observation that not all conflict is destructive. In fact, moderate levels of task conflict may help family firms to develop creative solutions for advancing the business. In practice, however, task conflict is unlikely to keep us awake at night, while relationship conflict might. Successfully dealing with relationship conflict may not be directly related to improved firm success. However, better relationships make it more likely that families will engage in constructive, inclusive dialogues about the business. Therefore, harmonious interpersonal relationships have an indirect, positive effect on the firm.

In the following, we discuss ways of managing relationship conflict. Our discussion of conflict-management styles and the promise of integrative approaches to conflict reminds us of the importance of open and sincere communication. As communication is key to the successful management of relationship conflict, we focus on ways to ensure constructive dialogues in the presence of relationship conflict.

10.10.1 Moving across time using conflict rooms

In our discussion of conflict dynamics, we learned that even though conflict takes place in the present, it often deals with the past, especially the ordering of past events and past individual behavior. From this (selective) interpretation of the past, people deduct and legitimize their current behavior and expectations. One way of taking into account the effect of time in the face of conflict is to segregate discussions based on whether they deal with the past, the present or the future. We can then ask:

- **When referring to the present**: What is happening? What is the issue at the core of the conflict?
- **When referring to the past**: What happened? What past events continue to have an effect on us?

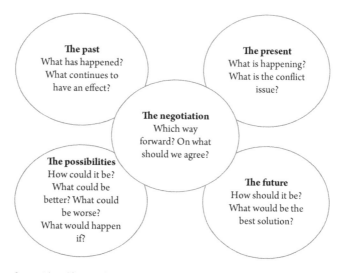

Source: Adapted from Noecker et al. (2012).

Figure 10.9 Temporal rooms for conflict communication

- **When referring to the future**: How could the future be? What would be the best outcome?

In a workshop setting, different rooms can be used to represent the present, past and future. People who would like to address a focal conflict in a certain room would then ask: where are we now? Where should we start our discussion?

In an article about fruitful communication in the face of conflict, Noecker et al. (2012) propose locating conflict communication in five different rooms. In addition to the past, present and future, the authors also include rooms for discussions of possibilities and for negotiation (Figure 10.9).

As outlined in section 10.8.1 on the role of time in conflicts, discussions about the past are rarely fruitful. The interpretation of the past tends to be subjective and selective. Ideally, conflict discussions should focus on the possibilities and the future. On the basis of those considerations, participants can then come up with acceptable ways to move forward. In the room of possibilities, participants could discuss:

- What could be done to improve the situation?
- What could make things worse?

- Assume that the conflict has ended: what has changed in comparison to the current situation?
- What are the consequences if the conflict is not resolved?
- What are the opponent's minimum goals? What would have to be achieved so that the opponent can still feel some sense of victory?
- How would another person approach this issue?
- What options do we have?

In the room of the future, participants can also discuss the following questions:

- What are my dreams with regard to the situation?
- What is the best outcome?
- What is the worst outcome?
- Which behaviors should we avoid in the future?

In the negotiation room, participants can try to consolidate their discussions and develop answers to the following questions:

- What options do we have?
- Which way forward now?
- What are the next steps?

10.10.2 Principles of constructive and destructive communication

In communication handbooks, you will find a list of the behaviors appropriate for ensuring constructive dialogues. Typically, you will find some of the following suggested behaviors, especially when in conflict with family members (refer also to Rosenberg 2012):[16]

- **Everyone gets about the same time to speak**: Within any group, especially in families with patriarchal power structures, not everyone is used to speaking up, or expressing opinions and feelings. As such, some individuals are systematically bypassed in discussions. Therefore, an important rule is that everyone gets about the same amount of time to speak.
- **Listen**: Listening signals that one respects and takes what other people do and say into account. Speech is silver, while silence is golden. The positive signal of listening can be strengthened by reframing what the other party has said using one's own words and by asking whether the other party's statements have been understood correctly.
- **Saying nothing equals agreement**: When emotions run high, and two

individuals or groups come to blows, a third person who takes a side in the conflict can escalate it. In this case, the symmetry of the conflict is disturbed and the unsupported party often feels deeply hurt. The challenge is that people should be able to freely express even a controversial opinion in a way that does not hurt the opposing party or hurts that party as little as possible. One way to solve this dilemma is to agree that if someone expresses an opinion, anyone who agrees with it can remain silent and does not have to overtly state his/her agreement. In this case, silence means agreement.

- **Right to take a break**: When emotions run high and people are overwhelmed by emotion, everyone has the right to ask for a break in the discussion. Breaks are useful because they allow people to collect themselves and to regain control of their emotions so as to have a constructive dialogue. During the break calm down and halt the negative cycle of your thoughts by replacing distress-maintaining thoughts with positive ones such as, 'He's frustrated at the moment, but is not always like this', or 'He's not really mad at me. He just had a bad day' (Gottman 1994).

- **Speak nondefensively**: Listen and speak in a way that does not engender defensiveness but, instead, fosters healthy discussion. Remind yourself of the other person's positive qualities to help keep negative thoughts at bay. Empathize and try to realize that your partner's anger might be an effort to get your attention. Adopt a receptive body posture and an open facial expression. Limit yourself to a specific complaint rather than a multitude of criticisms, such as by trying to remove the blame from the opponent's comments; saying how you feel; not criticizing the opponent's personality; not insulting, mocking or using sarcasm; being direct; not mind-reading (Gottman 1994).

- **Validate**: Validate the other person's emotions by looking at the situation from his or her viewpoint. Often, simply empathizing is enough. You don't have to solve the problem. Validation halts criticism, contempt and defensiveness. You validate also by taking responsibility for your words and actions, and by apologizing when you are at fault (Gottman 1994).

- **Overlearn**: What Gottman (1994) calls overlearning means trying to learn the techniques of fighting fair, practicing them until they become second nature. Your objective is to be able to use these techniques during the heat of a battle instead of resorting to your old, ineffective ways. Try to (re)discover your delight in each other.

Just as there are principles of *constructive* communication, there are also principles for *destructive* communication. In his work on long-lasting family relationships, psychologist John Gottman (1994) highlights four principles of communication that are highly destructive. Gottman calls these principles the 'four horsemen of the apocalypse':

- **Criticism**: Criticisms attack someone's personality or character—rather than a specific behavior—usually with some element of blame. Criticisms may take the form of unrestrained accusations or a list of negative comments. They are often expressed using global statements, such as 'you never' or 'you always'.
- **Defensiveness**: Defensiveness is a self-protective response to an opponent's actions that appears in the guise of denying one's own responsibility, making excuses, making (and responding to) negative assumptions about what the other party is feeling or engaging in counter-attacks.
- **Contempt**: Contempt aims to cause a partner psychological pain through expressions of disgust. It may be conveyed verbally (e.g., via insults, name calling, moaning or mockery) or nonverbally (e.g., by rolling one's eyes). Behind these behaviors is a lack of respect for the partner. Sarcasm and cynicism often lead to a reduction of conflict volume and intensity, which makes this behavior dangerous for the relationship because one may easily fail to recognize the deeply rooted antagonism.
- **Stonewalling**: Stonewalling involves creating psychological or physical distance from a partner by being unresponsive to efforts to communicate, responding in grunts or withdrawing from interaction. Physically, people may turn away from each other, become silent, and harden so that the other party feels like he or she is talking to a wall.

10.10.3   Why governance is not always the best solution

The typical managerial response to conflict is to call for regulation, typically in the form of some sort of governance mechanisms for family, ownership, corporate and wealth issues (for more details, refer to Chapter 5 on governance). However, when people have come to blows and conflicts are present, it may be quite difficult to develop a decent governance structure among the conflicting parties. Even well-intended proposals will be rejected and marked as insidious attempts to sideline or outsmart the opposing party.

In fact, family business advisors often report that the first impulse of families is to 'escape into organization' by attempting to address emotional issues through structural fixes. Families may want to reconfigure boards or restructure shareholder agreements. These are 'power solutions to love problems'. In contrast to collaborative conflict-management processes, such rights-based conflict management (Jehn and Bendersky 2003) has the effect of suppressing both the positive effects of task conflict and the negative effects of relationship conflict. It relies on some independent, legitimate standard (such as governance regulations, laws, contracts or social norms) to determine if one side's rights have been violated in an effort to end the conflict. Unlike collaborative conflict-management processes, which require the disputing parties to generate solutions, the goal of rights-based conflict management is to basically squelch or end all conflict.

In practice, such solutions may indeed end the task-related aspects of family business conflicts. However, in families that continue to interact (or hope to interact) after the intervention, the relational dynamics tend to undo the structural fixes. This is typically the case among family members who live near to each other, or between parents and children who interact on a private basis, and for governance regulations that are not legally binding but nevertheless of critical importance for the firm, such as family charters and family employment policies.

10.11 How to behave in the face of conflict

Our discussion of conflict in the family business context is far from complete, and it is certainly possible to expand the list of conflict-management styles and communication strategies. However, let us highlight two key observations. First, tensions are an inevitable part of family life. Second, given the effect of positive emotions on openness and creativity, they may distract people from fulfilling a task. The question, therefore, is not one of who is best at avoiding the tensions and negative emotions, but who is best at managing them. The goal is to learn how to address conflict and use it as an opportunity to grow. Remember that two (or more) heads are better than one only if they can disagree (Kaye and McCarthy 1996). Therefore, we provide a few practical tips for how to behave in the face of conflict:[17]

1. **Slow down.** If you are pulled into a conflict and you feel that you have to act rapidly, refrain from doing anything. This creates an opportunity to de-escalate the conflict and gives you time to think carefully about the appropriate reaction.
2. **Gentle in manner, firm in action.** Show that you do not take offenses personally and do not denigrate your opponent. This is one way to untangle the issue from the relationships in a conflict.
3. **Try to ensure a gain for your opponent in an aspect that matters to that opponent.** You thereby give your opponent rational and emotional reasons to end the conflict.

4. **Think about the worst-case scenario before you act**. If the consequences of further escalating the conflict are not predictable, try to exit the conflict.

5. **Take the risk of attributing positive motives to your opponent and be prepared to be disappointed**. You may still be surprised.

6. **A third (external) party is most useful when the escalation of the conflict is costly for the parties**, or when a stalemate is in sight and none of the parties expect to achieve ultimate victory.

7. **If you are the third party in a conflict and you are equipped with authority over the other parties, set clear limits to the conflict**. For example, you can suggest that if no solution has been found by a specific day, you make the decision yourself.

8. **If you are the third party in a conflict and you are not equipped with authority over the other parties (e.g., you are brought in as an advisor), stay neutral and hand responsibility for resolving the conflict over to the opponents**. Hold regular discussions with the opponents about whether they feel they are making progress and what needs to be improved.

9. **You may have a solution in mind**. Present your ideas by asking whether the solution they entail is conceivable. Do so by referring to other cases you have seen, but do not fall in love with your own ideas.

10. **Look for the acceptable solution**. Conflict resolution may not end in perfect solutions. However, the solutions have to be pragmatic. Try to seek an acceptable solution, even though it might not be perfect.

11. **Watch out when things start moving**. When things start moving and improving, the situation can become tricky. A single inconsiderate word or a misunderstood gesture may lead to a reemergence of the original conflict.

10.12 CASE STUDY

Conflict in the Solomon family

When the Solomon family called Mary Spencer, a certified family therapist, she knew it would be a tricky job. She had been advising the Solomon family for some time, and many of those discussions had centered around the involvement of the third family generation in the business. However, this call was about the second generation, which was the main owner of the family firm and which had apparently come to blows.

The Solomon family controlled a significant industrial company with about $500 million in sales, located in the Midwest of the United States. The family patriarch, Rudi Solomon, started this entrepreneurial saga. He was 75 years old at the time Mary received the call, and his three children (i.e., the second generation) were already in their late forties. Apparently,

CASE STUDY *(continued)*

Charles and Mike, two brothers in the second generation, had come to blows over a family dinner during the holiday season. Charles, the older of the two who served on the board of the firm, had accused Mike of forgetting to inform his siblings and their father about an investment decision he made with the family's liquid wealth. It is not that much had gone wrong with the investment, but apparently Mike had forgotten to inform the other family members about the investment and this issue had come up repeatedly between the two brothers.

The family had put all of its corporate investments, including the ownership in the main firm and its further investments in smaller companies, into a private holding company. This private holding company was run by a family officer, and was owned by the father and the three children in equal proportions. It also had a board of directors consisting of all four Solomons (the father and his three children) and a distant relative who worked as a business consultant. The latter served as the president of the board of directors. The board of this family holding company met every few months, whereby each of the two sons also served on boards of the various firms in which the private holding company had stakes. Charles served on the board of the main company. Susan, the third child, was a board member for the private holding company but did not have any other role in any further company. She stated:

> I was never actually asked whether I wanted to become more active in the firms. I might have more to do in the family's foundation and doing some charity work. Other than that, I have my private life and my private activities. However, you know, this is also a bit of a gender issue. As a daughter, I was never considered in terms of taking responsibility for our firms.

Over the years, Mike had become progressively frustrated with his brother's work attitude. Charles was supposed to be active on the boards of various investments, especially the main firm, which represented about 70% of the family's wealth. Apparently, however, Charles was often not well prepared for the board meetings, had missed some meetings, and could be very aggressive toward the firm's top management. At one point, a board member of one of the non-core firms had called the father, Rudi Solomon, to complain about Charles' behavior in the board meetings. Mike was deeply troubled by his brother:

> Whenever we have a board meeting in the private holding company, Charles seems to be ill-prepared. More importantly, he freaks out whenever my sister and I tell him that we are not happy with his work ethic. He prefers golfing and is unable to fulfill his various roles. He is my brother, but we have reached a point where I can no longer stand him. Keep in mind that these conflicts have been going on for years! Enough is enough. Our feud showed me that we cannot continue like this. I want to be independent of my brother. My suggestion is that we pay him out. He might get some of the firms and maybe some money, but that is it. I simply do not want to continue working with him.

CASE STUDY *(continued)*

The father was also deeply worried about the recent escalation, although he had seen the tensions coming for years. Apparently, he had never put his foot down or made any tough decisions such as telling his oldest son to leave the board of the main firm. However, in private discussions, Rudi Solomon had told Mary Spencer that this step should have been taken years prior to the escalation of the conflict, but that the family had unfortunately never been able to tackle the delicate issue. Rudi seemed to be concerned about what would happen to his eldest son if he lost his only 'real' job as a board member of the main firm, a position that came with prestige both within the firm and in local society.

Mary called the family's advisor, who served as the board president for the family's private holding company, Henry Rogolski. Henry stated:

> We all feel that Charles is no longer up to the task of being a valuable board member in the various firms. I tried to give him my assessment of the situation a few years ago, and we nearly reached a decision for him to move out of the board of the main firm. However, Charles went to see his father after our conversation and apparently found a way to convince his father that such a move would be unfair. There is also a father–son problem here.

Mary met the three second-generation family members for a preparatory meeting and finally had the chance to talk directly with Charles. He acknowledged the tensions, but indicated:

> I do not see an immediate need to change anything now. If Mike wants to be more independent from the rest of the family, he can take some money out of the private holding company and do whatever he wants with it. That would be completely fine with me. I would be happy to pass on the baton in the board of the main firm in five years or so. However, overall, I do not see a real problem here.

In this preparatory meeting, Mike once again aired his frustrations:

> I am unable to work with my brother anymore. I want to be more independent. It is tough, but this whole thing gives me sleepless nights. It is getting deeply psychological—I am suffering from this issue.

When Susan heard that her brother Mike wanted to split the private holding company into pieces, she said:

> I partly understand Mike's point of view. If he wants to move on, I would rather move on with him than stay with Charles with my share of the wealth and all of the investments. However, I

CASE STUDY *(continued)*

must say that I am also disappointed by the fact that Mike wants to break up what has been built here.

Your assignment: Put yourself in the shoes of the family therapist Mary Spencer and reflect on the following questions:

1. What are the issues in this case?
2. What type of conflict do you recognize in this case?
3. What roles do the various individuals play? What are their individual goals?
4. How should Mary approach the tensions in the Solomon family?

? REFLECTION QUESTIONS

1. What are the typical relational strengths and weaknesses of teams of spouses, siblings and extended families who are in business together?
2. Why are spouses better equipped to start a company than siblings?
3. What does the term 'family embeddedness' in relation to a firm mean?
4. How do societal trends in the structure of the Western family influence the governance of family firms?
5. Given the cultural context in which one is embedded, how do power distance, individualism/collectivism, family values and gender stereotypes shape preferences for certain types of succession solutions and the governance of family firms?
6. Consider family firms from a systemic perspective. What can be learned about the functioning of the family, business and ownership systems?
7. In what way do context markers play different roles in family firms and nonfamily firms?
8. What are the differences between the justice principles of equity, equality and need?
9. Why does the equity principle often lead to disputes about fair treatment?
10. Why are procedural justice and interactive justice of utmost importance in the family firm context?
11. Why are family firms fertile grounds for conflict?
12. What is the difference between task and relationship conflict?
13. How are task and relationship conflict interrelated?
14. How are the past, present and future interrelated in conflict situations? Why are discussions about the past often not helpful for addressing conflict?
15. What steps are often seen in conflict escalation?
16. With regard to conflict-management styles, what are the advantages and disadvantages of domination, accommodation, avoidance and compromise?
17. Why is integration often the most promising conflict-management style?
18. In what way can the idea of 'conflict rooms' help in addressing conflict?
19. What are the principles of constructive communication?
20. What are the principles of destructive communication?
21. Why are governance mechanisms often not useful for addressing an existing relationship conflict?

NOTES

1 Although siblings may intermarry, that case has limited structural significance and little empirical significance.
2 For an intriguing discussion of familial exchange norms, refer to Kohli and Künemund (2003).
3 The trend toward acceptance of nontraditional spousal relationships is reflected in recent changes in matrimonial and family law in many Western countries, which grant more flexibility in the formation (e.g., marriage between same-sex individuals) and dissolution (e.g., no-fault divorces, legal enforcement of prenuptial agreements) of a marriage. The resulting heterogeneity decreases the structural stability of families as well as the inclination of spouses to commit or pool resources. However, matrimonial law still governs the division of property and imposes child support on cohabitating couples who split up regardless of the type of spousal relationship. For additional reflections, see Lundberg and Pollak (2007).
4 The average number of children born per woman over a lifetime given current age-specific fertility rates and assuming no female mortality during the reproductive years.
5 Crude divorce rate (CDR), defined as the number of legal civil unions or marriages that are dissolved each year per 1000 people.
6 For other countries, no such long-term data is available.
7 For an intriguing discussion of the impact of family values on the economic growth of a nation, refer to Bertrand and Schoar (2006).
8 I am indebted to Professor Arist von Schlippe of the University of Witten, Germany, for making me aware of this highly effective workshop design.
9 In line with the related research, we use the terms 'justice' and 'fairness' synonymously.
10 For an in-depth discussion of the dimensions of justice, refer to Colquitt (2001).
11 For more information, refer to Colquitt et al. (2001).
12 I would like to thank Sonja Kissling for making me aware of the importance of justice-restoration mechanisms and their governance consequences in family firms.
13 A third type of conflict is process conflict, which is about the means used to accomplish tasks, but not about the content or substance of the task itself (Jehn and Bendersky 2003). Process conflicts are less critical for our discussion of conflict in family firms.
14 I would like to thank Santiago Perry for making me aware of some of these patterns.
15 For more information, refer to Frank et al. (2010).
16 For further insights into productive family communication refer also to Gottman (1994). Although Gottman's considerations about family communication is originally set in the context of marriages, it is also applicable to other relationships and communication settings. I am also indebted to Joe Astrachan for pointing me to some of these principles.
17 I am thankful for various interactions with academics, family business owners and advisors, in particular Rudi Wimmer and Arist von Schlippe from the University of Witten-Herdecke, Germany. For further information please also refer to Simon (2012).

BACKGROUND READING

Afghan, N., and T. Wiqar (2007). *Succession in Family Businesses of Pakistan: Kinship Culture and Islamic Inheritance Law*. Centre for Management and Economic Research, Lahore University of Management Sciences.

Aldrich, H. E., and J. E. Cliff (2003). The pervasive effects of family on entrepreneurship: Toward a family embeddedness perspective. *Journal of Business Venturing*, 18 (5): 573–596.

Bird, M., and T. Zellweger (2016). Social embeddedness and family firm growth: comparing spousal and sibling entrepreneurs. Working paper, University of St. Gallen.

Carr, J. C., and K. M. Hmieleski (2015). Differences in the outcomes of work and family conflict between family- and nonfamily businesses: An examination of business founders. *Entrepreneurship Theory and Practice*, 39 (6): 1413–1432.

Cosier, R. A., and M. Harvey (1998). The hidden strengths in family business: Functional conflict. *Family Business Review*, 11 (1): 75–79.

Dahl, M. S., M. van Praag and P. Thompson (2014). Entrepreneurial couples. Discussion paper, Tinbergen Institute.

Eddleston, K. A., and F. W. Kellermanns (2007). Destructive and productive family relationships: A stewardship theory perspective. *Journal of Business Venturing*, 22 (4): 545–565.

Fondacaro, M. R., S. L. Jackson and J. Luescher (2002). Toward the assessment of procedural and distributive justice in resolving family disputes. *Social Justice Research*, 15 (4): 341–371.

Gordon, G., and N. Nicholson (2010). *Family Wars: Stories and Insights from Famous Family Business Feuds*. London: Kogan Page Publishers.

Gottman, J. M. (1994). *Why Marriages Succeed or Fail*. New York: Fireside.

Grossmann, S., and A. von Schlippe (2015). Family businesses: Fertile environments for conflict. *Journal of Family Business Management*, 5 (2): 294–314.

Harvey, M., and R. E. Evans (1994). Family business and multiple levels of conflict. *Family Business Review*, 7 (4): 331–348.

Jehn, K. A., and C. Bendersky (2003). Intragroup conflict in organizations: A contingency perspective on the conflict-outcome relationship. *Research in Organizational Behavior*, 25: 187–242.

Jehn, K. A., and E. A. Mannix (2001). The dynamic nature of conflict: A longitudinal study of intragroup conflict and group performance. *Academy of Management Journal*, 44 (2): 238–251.

Kaye, K. (1991). Penetrating the cycle of sustained conflict. *Family Business Review*, 4 (1): 21–44.

Kellermanns, F. W., and K. A. Eddleston (2004). Feuding families: When conflict does a family firm good. *Entrepreneurship Theory and Practice*, 28 (3): 209–228.

Kellermanns, F. W., and K. A. Eddleston (2007). A family perspective on when conflict benefits family firm performance. *Journal of Business Research*, 60 (10): 1048–1057.

Kets de Vries, M. F. R. (1993). The dynamics of family controlled firms: The good and the bad news. *Organizational Dynamics*, 21 (3): 59–71.

Kidwell, R. E., K. A. Eddleston, J .J. Cater and F. W. Kellermanns (2013). How one bad family member can undermine a family firm: Preventing the Fredo effect. *Business Horizons*, 56 (1): 5–12.

Levinson, H. (1971). Conflicts that plague family businesses. *Harvard Business Review*, 49: 90–98.

Lundberg, S., and R. A. Pollak (2007). The American family and family economics. National Bureau of Economic Research, Work paper No. 12908.

Olson, P. D., V. S. Zuiker, S. M. Danes, K. Stafford, R. K. Heck and K. A. Duncan (2003). The impact of the family and the business on family business sustainability. *Journal of Business Venturing*, 18 (5): 639–666.

Ruef, M. (2010). *The Entrepreneurial Group. Social Identities, Relations, and Collective Action*. Princeton, NJ and Oxford: Princeton University Press.

Sharifian, M., P. D. Jennings and J. E. Jennings (2012). Should women go into business with their family partner. In K. D. Hughes and J. E. Jennings (Eds.), *Global Women's Entrepreneurship Research: Diverse Settings, Questions and Approaches*. Cheltenham, UK and Northampton, MA, USA: Edward Elgar Publishing, 114–134.

Sorenson, R. L. (1999). Conflict management strategies used in successful family businesses. *Family Business Review*, 12 (4): 133–146.

Van der Heyden, L., C. Blondel and R. S. Carlock (2005). Fair process: Striving for justice in family business. *Family Business Review*, 18 (1): 1–21.

Von Schlippe, A., and H. Frank (2013). The theory of social systems as a framework for understanding family businesses. *Family Relations*, 62 (3): 384–398.

References

Adams, J. S. (1965). Inequity in social exchange. *Advances in Experimental Social Psychology*, 2: 267–299.

Afghan, N., and T. Wiqar (2007). *Succession in Family Businesses of Pakistan: Kinship Culture and Islamic Inheritance Law*. Centre for Management and Economic Research, Lahore University of Management Sciences.

Aguilera, R., and R. Crespi-Cladera (2012). Firm family firms: Current debates of corporate governance in family firms. *Journal of Family Business Strategy*, 3 (2): 63–69.

Ahlers, O., A. Hack and F. W. Kellermanns (2014). 'Stepping into the buyers' shoes': Looking at the value of family firms through the eyes of private equity investors. *Journal of Family Business Strategy*, 5 (4): 384–396.

Albert, S., and D. A. Whetten (1985). Organizational identity. *Research in Organizational Behavior*, 7: 263–295.

Aldrich, H. E., and J. E. Cliff (2003). The pervasive effects of family on entrepreneurship: Toward a family embeddedness perspective. *Journal of Business Venturing*, 18 (5): 573–596.

Amit, R., and B. Villalonga (2013). Financial performance of family firms. In L. Melin, M. Nordqvist and P. Sharma (Eds.), *The SAGE Handbook of Family Business*. London: SAGE Publications, 157–178.

Amit, R., Y. Ding, B. Villalonga and H. Zhang (2015). The role of institutional development in the prevalence and performance of entrepreneur and family-controlled firms. *Journal of Corporate Finance*, 31: 284–305.

Amit, R., H. Liechtenstein, M. J. Prats, T. Millay and L. P. Pendleton (2008). *Single Family Offices: Private Wealth Management in the Family Context*. Research report. Philadelphia, PA: Wharton School.

Anderson, R., and D. Reeb (2003a). Founding-family ownership, corporate diversification, and firm leverage. *Journal of Law and Economics*, 46: 653–684.

Anderson, R. C., and D. M. Reeb (2003b). Founding-family ownership and firm performance: Evidence from the S&P 500. *Journal of Finance*, 58 (3): 1301–1328.

Anderson, R. C., A. Duru and D. M. Reeb (2012). Investment policy in family controlled firms. *Journal of Banking and Finance*, 36 (6): 1744–1758.

Anderson, R. C., S. A. Mansi and D. M. Reeb (2003). Founding family ownership and the agency cost of debt. *Journal of Financial Economics*, 68 (2): 263–285.

Aronoff, C. (2001). Understanding family-business survival statistics. *Supply House Times*, July.

Aronoff, C. E., S. L. McClure and J. L. Ward (1993). *Family Business Compensation*. New York: Family Business Consulting Group.

Arregle, J. L., M. A. Hitt, D. G. Sirmon and P. Very (2007). The development of organizational social capital: Attributes of family firms. *Journal of Management Studies*, 44 (1): 73–95.

Ashforth, B. E., and F. A. Mael (1996). Organizational identity and strategy as a context for the individual. *Advances in Strategic Management*, 13: 19–64.

Astrachan, J. H., and M. C. Shanker (1996). Myths and realities: Family businesses' contribution to the US economy—A framework for assessing family business statistics. *Family Business Review*, 9 (2): 107–123.

Astrachan, J. H., and M. C. Shanker (2003). Family businesses' contribution to the US economy: A closer look. *Family Business Review*, 16 (3): 211–219.

Astrachan, J. H., S. B. Klein and K. X. Smyrnios (2002). The F-PEC scale of family influence: A proposal for solving the family business definition problem. *Family Business Review*, 15 (1): 45–58.

Au, K., and C. Y. J. Cheng (2011). Creating 'the new' through portfolio entrepreneurship. In P. Sieger, R. Nason, P. Sharma and T. Zellweger (Eds.), *The Global STEP Booklet, Volume I: Evidence-based, Practical Insights for Enterprising Families.* Babson College, 17–21.

Axelrod, A., and M. McCollom-Hampton (2013). Five principles of sustainable financial management of family-owned enterprises. Presentation given at Annual Conference of the Family Firm Institute, San Diego.

Balunywa, W., P. Rosa and D. Nandagire-Ntamu (2013). 50 years of entrepreneurship in Uganda, ten years of the Ugandan global entrepreneurship monitor. Working paper, University of Edinburgh.

Banalieva, E., K. Eddleston and T. Zellweger (2015). When do family firms have an advantage in transitioning economies? Toward a dynamic institution-based view. *Strategic Management Journal*, 36 (9): 1358–1377.

Barney, J. (1991). Firm resources and sustained competitive advantage. *Journal of Management*, 17 (1): 99–120.

Bassanini A., T. Breda, E. Caroli and A. Rebérioux (2013). Working in family firms: Paid less but more secure? Evidence from French matched employer–employee data. *Industrial and Labor Relations Review*, 66 (2): 433–466.

Bateson, G. (1972). *Steps to an Ecology of Mind: Collected Essays in Anthropology, Psychiatry, Evolution, and Epistemology.* Chicago, IL: University of Chicago Press.

Becker, G. S., and H. G. Lewis (1974). Interaction between quantity and quality of children. In T. W. Schultz (Ed.), *Economics of the Family: Marriage, Children, and Human Capital.* Chicago, IL: University of Chicago Press, 81–90.

Beckert, J. (2008). *Inherited Wealth.* Princeton, NJ: Princeton University Press.

Belloc, F. (2013). Law, finance, and innovation. *Cambridge Journal of Economics*, 37 (4): 863–888.

Bengtson, V. L. (1993). Is the 'contract across generations' changing? Effects of population aging on obligations and expectations across age groups. In V. L. Bengtson and W. A. Achenbaum (Eds.), *The Changing Contract across Generations.* New York: Aldine de Gruyer, 3–23.

Bennedsen, M., K. M. Nielsen, F. Perez-Gonzalez and D. Wolfenzon (2007). Inside the family firm: The role of families in succession decisions and performance. *Quarterly Journal of Economics*, 122 (2): 647–691.

Berle, A., and G. Means (1932). *The Modern Corporation and Private Property.* New York: Macmillan.

Berrone, P., C. Cruz, L. R. Gomez-Mejia and M. Larraza-Kintana (2010). Socioemotional wealth and corporate responses to institutional pressures: Do family-controlled firms pollute less? *Administrative Science Quarterly*, 55 (1): 82–113.

Berrone, P., C. C. Cruz and L. R. Gomez-Mejia (2012). Socioemotional wealth in family firms: A review and agenda for future research. *Family Business Review*, 25 (3): 258–279.

Bertrand, M. and A. Schoar (2006). The role of family in family firms. *Journal of Economic Perspectives*, 20 (2): 73–96.

Bertrand, M., S. Johnson, K. Samphantharak and A. Schoar (2003). Mixing family with business: A study of Thai business groups and the families behind them. *Journal of Financial Economics*, 88 (3): 466–498.

Binz, C., and J. C. Schmid (2012). From family firm identity to the family firm brand. In *12th Annual IFERA World Family Business Research Conference*, Bordeaux, France.

Binz, C., J. Hair, T. Pieper and A. Baldauf (2013). Exploring the effect of distinct family firm reputation on consumers' preferences. *Journal of Family Business Strategy*, 4 (1): 3–11.

Bird, M., and T. Zellweger (2016). Social embeddedness and family firm growth: comparing spousal and sibling entrepreneurs. Working paper, University of St. Gallen.

Bitler, M. P., T. J. Moskowitz and A. Vissing-Jorgensen (2005). Testing agency theory with entrepreneur effort and wealth. *Journal of Finance*, 60 (2): 539–576.

Boston Consulting Group (2013). *Global Wealth: Maintaining Momentum in a Complex World*. Boston, MA: Boston Consulting Group.

Bourdieu, P. (1996). On the family as a realized category. *Theory, Culture and Society*, 13 (3): 19–26.

Brown, K. W., and R. M. Ryan (2003). The benefits of being present: Mindfulness and its role in psychological well-being. *Journal of Personality and Social Psychology*, 84 (4): 822–848.

Cabrera-Suarez, K., P. De Saa-Perez and D. Garcia-Almeida (2001). The succession process from a resource- and knowledge-based view of the family firm. *Family Business Review*, 14 (1): 37–48.

Cameron, K. S. (1986). Effectiveness as paradox: Consensus and conflict in conceptions of organizational effectiveness. *Management Science*, 32 (5): 539–553.

Carlock, R. S., and J. L. Ward (2010). *When Family Businesses Are Best: The Parallel Planning Process for Family Harmony and Business Success*. Basingstoke, UK: Palgrave Macmillan.

Carney, M. (2005). Corporate governance and competitive advantage in family-controlled firms. *Entrepreneurship Theory and Practice*, 29 (3): 249–265.

Carney, M., E. R. Gedajlovic, P. Heugens, M. Van Essen and J. Van Oosterhout (2011). Business group affiliation, performance, context, and strategy: A meta-analysis. *Academy of Management Journal*, 54 (3): 437–460.

Carney, M., E. Gedajlovic and V. Strike (2014). Dead money: Inheritance law and the longevity of family firms. *Entrepreneurship Theory and Practice*, 38 (6): 1261–1283.

Carney, M., M. Van Essen, E. Gedajlovic and P. Heugens (2015). What do we know about private family firms: A meta-analytic review. *Entrepreneurship Theory and Practice*, 39 (3): 513–544.

Carney, R. W., and T. B. Child (2013). Changes to the ownership and control of East Asian corporations between 1996 and 2008: The primacy of politics. *Journal of Financial Economics*, 107 (2): 494–513.

Carr, J. C., and K. M. Hmieleski (2015). Differences in the outcomes of work and family conflict between family- and nonfamily businesses: An examination of business founders. *Entrepreneurship Theory and Practice*, 39 (6): 1413–1432.

Chemla, G., M. A. Habib and A. Ljungqvist (2007). An analysis of shareholder agreements. *Journal of the European Economic Association*, 5 (1): 93–121.

Chrisman, J., and P. Patel (2012). Variations in R&D investments of family and nonfamily firms: Behavioral agency and myopic loss aversion perspectives. *Academy of Management Journal*, 55 (4): 976–997.

Chrisman, J. J., E. Memili and K. Misra (2014). Nonfamily managers, family firms, and the winner's curse: The influence of noneconomic goals and bounded rationality. *Entrepreneurship Theory and Practice*, 38 (5): 1103–1127.

Christen, A., F. Halter, N. Kammerlander, D. Künzi, D. Merki and T. Zellweger (2013). Success factors for Swiss SMEs: Company succession in practice. Credit Suisse and University of St. Gallen, Zurich.

Christensen, C. M. (1997). *The Innovator's Dilemma*. Cambridge, MA: Harvard University Press.

Chua, J. H., J. J. Chrisman and A. De Massis (2015). A closer look at socioemotional wealth: Its flows, stocks, and prospects for moving forward. *Entrepreneurship Theory and Practice*, 39 (2): 173–182.

Chua, J. H., J. J. Chrisman and P. Sharma (1999). Defining the family business by behavior. *Entrepreneurship Theory and Practice*, 23 (4): 19–39.

Chua, J. H., J. J. Chrisman and P. Sharma (2003). Succession and nonsuccession concerns of family firms and agency relationship with nonfamily managers. *Family Business Review*, 16 (2): 89–107.

Claessens, S., S. Djankov, J. P. H. Fan and L. H. P. Lang (2002). Disentangling the incentive and entrenchment effects of large shareholdings. *Journal of Finance*, LVII (6): 2741–2771.

Claessens, S., S. Djankov and L. H. P. Lang (2000). The separation of ownership and control in East Asian corporations. *Journal of Financial Economics*, 58: 81–112.

Colli, A. (2003). *The History of Family Business, 1850–2000*. Cambridge: Cambridge University Press.

Colquitt, J. A. (2001). On the dimensionality of organizational justice: A construct validation of a measure. *Journal of Applied Psychology*, 86 (3): 386–400.

Colquitt, J. A., D. E. Conlon, M. J. Wesson, C. O. Porter and K. Y. Ng (2001). Justice at the millennium: A meta-analytic review of 25 years of organizational justice research. *Journal of Applied Psychology*, 86 (3): 425–445.

Corbetta, G., and C. Salvato (2004). Self-serving or self-actualizing? Models of man and agency costs in different types of family firms: A commentary on 'Comparing the Agency Costs of Family and Non-family Firms: Conceptual Issues and Exploratory Evidence'. *Entrepreneurship Theory and Practice*, 28 (4): 355–362.

Cosier, R. A., and M. Harvey (1998). The hidden strengths in family business: Functional conflict. *Family Business Review*, 11 (1): 75–79.

Craig, J., C. Dibbrell and P. S. Davis (2008). Leveraging family-based brand identity to enhance firm competitiveness and performance in family businesses. *Journal of Small Business Management*, 46 (3): 351–371.

Croci, E., J. A. Doukas and H. Gonenc (2011). Family control and financing decisions. *European Financial Management*, 17 (5): 860–897.

Cyert, R. M., and J. G. March (1963). *A Behavioral Theory of the Firm*. Englewood Cliffs, NJ: Prentice-Hall.

Dahl, M. S., M. van Praag and P. Thompson (2014). Entrepreneurial couples. Discussion paper, Tinbergen Institute.

Dalton, D. R., M. A. Hitt, S. T. Certo and C. M. Dalton (2007). The fundamental agency problem and its mitigation: Independence, equity, and the market for corporate control. *Academy of Management Annals*, 1: 1–64.

Danes, S. M., and E. A. Morgan (2004). Family business-owning couples: An EFT view into their unique conflict culture. *Contemporary Family Therapy*, 26 (3): 241–260.

De Massis, A., J. H. Chua and J. J. Chrisman (2008). Factors preventing intra-family succession. *Family Business Review*, 21 (2): 183–199.

Deci, E. L., and R. M. Ryan (2000). The 'what' and 'why' of goal pursuits: Human needs and the self-determination of behavior. *Psychological Inquiry*, 11 (4): 227–268.

Deephouse, D. L., and P. Jaskiewicz (2013). Do family firms have better reputations than non-family firms? An integration of socioemotional wealth and social identity theories. *Journal of Management Studies*, 50 (3): 337–360.

Dehlen, T., T. Zellweger, N. Kammerlander and F. Halter (2012). The role of information asymmetry in the choice of entrepreneurial exit routes. *Journal of Business Venturing*, 29 (2): 193–209.

DeMott, D. (1988). Directors' duties in management buyouts and leveraged recapitalizations. *Ohio State Law Journal*, 49: 517–557.

DiMaggio, P., and W. W. Powell (1983). The iron cage revisited: Collective rationality and institutional isomorphism in organizational fields. *American Sociological Review*, 48 (2): 147–160.

Drake, D. G., and J. A. Lawrence (2000). Equality and distributions of inheritance in families. *Social Justice Research*, 13 (3): 271–290.

Duran, P., N. Kammerlander, M. Van Essen and T. Zellweger (2016). Doing more with less: Innovation input and output in family firms. *Academy of Management Journal*, 59 (4): 1224–1264.

Dyer, W., and D. Whetten (2006). Family firms and social responsibility: Preliminary evidence from the S&P 500. *Entrepreneurship Theory and Practice*, 30 (6): 785–802.

Eddleston, K. A., and F. W. Kellermanns (2007). Destructive and productive family relationships: A stewardship theory perspective. *Journal of Business Venturing*, 22 (4): 545–565.

Ellul, A., M. Pagano and F. Panunzi (2010). Inheritance law and investment in family firms. *American Economic Review*, 100: 2414–2450.

Faccio, M., and L. Lang (2002). The ultimate ownership of Western European corporations. *Journal of Financial Economics*, 65 (3): 365–395.

Faessler, N. (2014). Fairness in transgenerational family business transitions. Unpublished master's thesis, University of St. Gallen.

Fama, E. F., and M. C. Jensen (1983). Separation of ownership and control. *Journal of Law and Economics*, 26 (2): 301–325.

Farjoun, M. (2010). Beyond dualism: Stability and change as a duality. *Academy of Management Review*, 35 (2): 202–225.

Feldman, E. R., R. R. Amit and B. Villalonga (2016). Corporate divestitures and family control. *Strategic Management Journal*, 37 (3): 429–446.

Feldman, M. S., and B. T. Pentland (2003). Reconceptualizing organizational routines as a source of flexibility and change. *Administrative Science Quarterly*, 48 (1): 94–118.

Fine, C. H. (1998). *Clockspeed: Winning Industry Control in the Age of Temporary Advantage*. New York: Perseus Books.

Fischetti, M. (2000). *Financial Management for Your Family Company*. Philadelphia, PA: Family Business Publishing.

Flanagan, J., S. Hamilton, D. Lincoln, A. Nichols, L. Ottum and J. Weber (2011). *Taking Care of Business: Case Examples of Separating Personal Wealth Management from the Family Business*. London: Family Office Exchange (FOX).

Flören, R. (1998). The significance of family business in the Netherlands. *Family Business Review*, 11 (2): 121–134

Flören, R. (2002). Family business in the Netherlands. *Crown Princes in the Clay: An Empirical Study on the Tackling of Succession Challenges in Dutch Family Farms*. Breukelen, the Netherlands: Nyenrode University, Chapter 1.

Flören, R., L. Uhlaner and M. Berent-Braun (2010). *Family Business in the Netherlands: Characteristics and Success Factors*. A Report for the Ministry of Economic Affairs. Breukelen, the Netherlands: Centre for Entrepreneurship, Universtity of Nyenrode.

Fondacaro, M. R., S. L. Jackson and J. Luescher (2002). Toward the assessment of procedural and distributive justice in resolving family disputes. *Social Justice Research*, 15 (4): 341–371.

Frank, H., C. Korunka, M. Lueger, L. Nose and D. Suchy (2010). *Erfolgsfaktoren österreichischer Familienunternehmen. Das Zusammenspiel von Familie und Unternehmen in Entscheidungs-und Konsens-bzw. Konfliktprozessen* [Success Factors of Austrian Family Firms. The Interplay of Family and Business in Decision-Making and Conflict Processes]. Forschungsinstitut für Familienunternehmen an der WU Wien.

Franks, J., C. Mayer, P. Volpin and H. F. Wagner (2012). The life cycle of family ownership: International evidence. *Review of Financial Studies*, 25 (6): 1675–1712.

Frey, U., F. Halter, T. Zellweger and S. Klein (2004). *Family Business in Switzerland: Significance and Structure*. IFERA, Copenhagen.

Gedajlovic, E. R., and M. Carney (2010). Markets, hierachies and families: Toward a transaction cost theory of the family firm. *Entrepreneurship Theory and Practice*, 34 (6): 1145–1172.

Gedajlovic, E., M. Carney, J. Chrisman and F. Kellermanns (2011). The adolescence of family firm research: Taking stock and planning for the future. *Journal of Management*, 38 (4): 1010–1037.

Glasl, F. (1982). The process of conflict escalation and roles of third parties. In G. B. J. Bomers and R. B. Peterson (Eds.), *Conflict Management and Industrial Relations*. Dordrecht: Springer, 119–140.

Gomez-Mejia, L. R., C. Cruz, P. Berrone and J. De Castro (2011). The bind that ties: Socioemotional wealth preservation in family firms. *Academy of Management Annals*, 5 (1): 653–707.

Gomez-Mejia, L. R., K. T. Haynes, M. Nunez-Nickel, K. J .L. Jacobson and J. Moyano-Fuentes (2007). Socioemotional wealth and business risks in family-controlled firms: Evidence from Spanish olive oil mills. *Administrative Science Quarterly*, 52 (1): 106–137.

Gomez-Mejia, L., M. Larraza-Kintana and M. Makri (2003). The determinants of executive compensation in family-controlled public corporations. *Academy of Management Journal*, 46 (2): 226–237.

Gomez-Mejia, L. R., M. Makri and M. L. Kintana (2010). Diversification decisions in family-controlled firms. *Journal of Management Studies*, 47 (2): 223–252.

Gomez-Mejia, L. R., P. C. Patel and T. M. Zellweger (2015). In the horns of the dilemma socioemotional wealth, financial wealth, and acquisitions in family firms. *Journal of Management*, forthcoming.

Gordon, G., and N. Nicholson (2010). *Family Wars: Stories and Insights from Famous Family Business Feuds*. London: Kogan Page Publishers.

Gottman, J. M. (1994). *Why Marriages Succeed or Fail*. New York: Fireside.

Graebner, M. E., and K. M. Eisenhardt (2004). The seller's side of the story: Acquisition as courtship and governance as syndicate in entrepreneurial firms. *Administrative Science Quarterly*, 49 (3): 366–403.

Greenhaus, J. H., and N. J. Beutell (1985). Sources of conflict between work and family roles. *Academy of Management Review*, 10 (1): 76–88.

Groth, T., and A. von Schlippe (2012). Die Form der Unternehmerfamilie—Paradoxiebewältigung zwischen Entscheidung und Bindung [The form of the business family—managing the paradox between decision-making and relationships]. *Familiendynamik im Focus*, 37: 2–14.

Habbershon, T. G., and M. L. Williams (1999). A resource-based framework for assessing the strategic advantages of family firms. *Family Business Review*, 12 (1): 1–25.

Halter, F., and R. Schroeder (2010). *Unternehmensnachfolge in Theorie und Praxis: das St. Galler Nachfolge Modell* [Firm Succession in Theory and Practice: The St. Galler Succession Model]. Bern: Haupt.

Handler, W. C. (1990). Succession in family firms: A mutual role adjustment between entrepreneur and next generation family members. *Entrepreneurship Theory and Practice*, 15 (1): 37–51.

Hartley, B. B., and G. Griffith (2009). *Family Wealth Transition Planning: Advising Families with Small Businesses*. New York: Bloomberg Press.

Hill, C. W. L., and F. T. Rothaermel (2003). The performance of incumbent firms in the face of radical technological innovation. *Academy of Management Review*, 28: 257–274.

Hitt, M. A., R. D. Ireland, S. M. Camp and D. L. Sexton (2001). Strategic entrepreneurship: Entrepreneurial strategies for wealth creation. *Strategic Management Journal*, 22 (6–7): 479–491.

Hofstede, G. (2011). Dimensionalizing cultures: The Hofstede model in context. *Online Readings in Psychology and Culture*, 2(1).

Holy, L. (1996). *Anthropological Perspectives on Kinship*. London: Pluto.

Hoy, F., and T. G. Verser (1994). Emerging business, emerging field: Entrepreneurship and the family firm. *Entrepreneurship Theory and Practice*, 19 (1): 9–23.

Hughes, J. E. (2004). *Family Wealth—Keeping It in the Family*. New York: Bloomberg Press.

Institute for Family Business (2011). *The UK Family Business Sector*. Oxford Economics.

Jaskiewicz, P., J. G. Combs and S. B. Rau (2015). Entrepreneurial legacy: Toward a theory of how some family firms nurture transgenerational entrepreneurship. *Journal of Business Venturing*, 30 (1): 29–49.

Jehn, K. A., and C. Bendersky (2003). Intragroup conflict in organizations: A contingency perspective on the conflict-outcome relationship. *Research in Organizational Behavior*, 25: 187–242.

Kammerlander, N., and M. Ganter (2015). An attention-based view of family firm adaptation to discontinuous technological change: Exploring the role of family CEOs' non-economic goals. *Journal of Product Innovation Management*, 32 (3): 361–383.

Kammerlander, N., P. Sieger, W. Voordeckers and T. Zellweger (2015). Value creation in family firms: A model of fit. *Journal of Family Business Strategy*, 6 (2): 63–72.

Kaye, K. (1991). Penetrating the cycle of sustained conflict. *Family Business Review*, 4 (1): 21–44.

Kaye, K., and C. McCarthy (1996). Healthy disagreements. *Family Business*, Autumn: 71–72.

Kellermanns, F. W., and K. A. Eddleston (2004). Feuding families: When conflict does a family firm good. *Entrepreneurship Theory and Practice*, 28 (3): 209–228.

Kellermanns, F. W., and K. A. Eddleston (2007). A family perspective on when conflict benefits family firm performance. *Journal of Business Research*, 60 (10): 1048–1057.

Kellermanns, F., K. Eddleston and T. Zellweger (2012). Extending the socioemotional wealth perspective: A look at the dark side. *Entrepreneurship Theory and Practice*, 36 (6): 1175–1182.

Khanna, T., and K. Palepu (2000). Is group affiliation profitable in emerging markets? An analysis of diversified Indian business groups. *Journal of Finance*, 55: 867–891.

Khanna, T., and J. W. Rivkin (2001). Estimating the performance effects of business groups in emerging markets. *Strategic Management Journal*, 22 (1): 45–74.

Khanna, T., and Y. Yafeh (2007). Business groups in emerging markets: Paragons or parasites? *Journal of Economic Literature*, 45 (2): 331–372.

Kidwell, R. E., K. A. Eddleston, J. J. Cater and F. W. Kellermanns (2013). How one bad family member can undermine a family firm: Preventing the Fredo effect. *Business Horizons*, 56 (1): 5–12.

Klein, S. (2000). Family businesses in Germany: Significance and structure. *Family Business Review*, 13: 157–181.

Koeberle-Schmid, A., D. Kenyon-Rouvinez and E. J. Poza (2014). *Governance in Family Enterprises*. New York: Palgrave Macmillan.

Koenig, A., N. Kammerlander and A. Enders (2013). The family innovator's dilemma: How family influence affects the adoption of discontinuous technologies by incumbent firms. *Academy of Management Review*, 38 (3): 418–441.

Kohli, M., and H. Künemund (2003). Intergenerational transfers in the family: What motivates giving. In V. L. Bengtson and A. Lowestein (Eds.), *Global Aging and Challenges to Families*. Piscataway, NJ: Aldine Transaction, 123–142.

Kormann, H. (2008). *Beiräte in der Verantwortung: Aufsicht und Rat in Familienunternehmen*. [The Responsibility of Advisory Committees: Oversight and Advice in Family Businesses]. Heidelberg: Springer-Verlag.

Koropp, C., F. W. Kellermanns, D. Grichnik and L. Stanley (2014). Financial decision making in family firms: An adaptation of the theory of planned behavior. *Family Business Review*, 27 (4): 307–327.

KPMG (2013a). *Family Business Survey 2013: Performers, Resilient, Adaptable, Sustainable*. Melbourne: Family Business Australia

KPMG (2013b). *CII's Family Business Network* (India chapter). New Delhi: Confederation of Indian Industry.

KPMG (2014). KPMG European family business tax monitor: Comparing the impact of tax regimes on family businesses. KPMG.

La Porta, R., F. Lopez-De-Silanes and A. Shleifer (1999). Corporate ownership around the world. *Journal of Finance*, 54: 471–517.

Landes, D. (2008). *Dynasties: Fortune and Misfortune in the World's Great Family Businesses*. London: Penguin.

Le Breton-Miller, I., D. Miller and L. P. Steier (2004). Toward an integrative model of effective FOB succession. *Entrepreneurship Theory and Practice*, 28 (4): 305–328.

Lee, J. (2006). Impact of family relationships on attitudes for the second generation in family businesses. *Family Business Review*, 19 (3): 175–191.

Leonetti, J. M. (2008). *Exiting Your Business, Protecting Your Wealth*. Hoboken, NJ: Wiley.

Lumpkin, G. T., and G. G. Dess (1996). Clarifying the entrepreneurial orientation construct and linking it to performance. *Academy of Management Review*, 21 (1): 135–172.

Lumpkin, G. T., W. Martin and M. Vaughn (2008). Family orientation: Individual-level influences on family firm outcomes. *Family Business Review*, 21 (2): 127–138.

Lundberg, S., and R. A. Pollak (2007). The American family and family economics. National Bureau of Economic Research, Work paper No. 12908.

Luo, X., and C. N. Chung (2005). Keeping it all in the family: The role of particularistic relationships in business group performance during institutional transition. *Administrative Science Quarterly*, 50 (3): 404–439.

Mandl, I. (2008). *Overview of Family Business Relevant Issues: Final Report*. Conducted on behalf of the European Commission, Enterprise and Industry Directorate-General: KMU Forschung Austria.

March, J. G. (1991). Exploration and exploitation in organizational learning. *Organization Science*, 1 (1): 71–87.

Masulis, R., P. Kien Pham and J. Zein (2011). Family business groups around the world: Financing advantages, control motivations, and organizational choices. *Review of Financial Studies*, 24 (1): 3556–3600.

Matthews, C. H., D. P. Vasudevan, S. L. Barton and R. Apana (1994). Capital structure decision making in privately held firms: Beyond the finance paradigm. *Family Business Review*, 7 (4): 349–367.

Meyer, J. W., and B. Rowan (1977). Institutionalized organizations: Formal structure as myth and ceremony. *American Journal of Sociology*, 83 (2): 340–363.

Michiels, A., W. Voordeckers, N. Lybaert and T. Steijvers (2015). Dividends and family governance practices in private family firms. *Small Business Economics*, 44 (2): 299–314.

Miller, D., and P. H. Friesen (1980). Momentum and revolution in organizational adaptation. *Academy of Management Journal*, 23 (4): 591–614.

Miller, D., and I. Le Breton-Miller (2005). *Managing for the Long Run: Lessons in Competitive Advantage from Great Family Businesses*. Boston, MA: Harvard Business School Press.

Miller, D., and I. Le Breton-Miller (2014). Deconstructing socioemotional wealth. *Entrepreneurship Theory and Practice*, 38 (4): 713–720.

Miller, D., I. Le Breton-Miller and R. H. Lester (2013). Family firm governance, strategic conformity and performance: Institutional versus strategic perspectives. *Organization Science*, 24 (1) 189–209.

Miller, D., I. Le Breton-Miller, R. H. Lester and A. A. Cannella (2007). Are family firms really superior performers? *Journal of Corporate Finance*, 13: 829–858.

Miller, D., J. Lee, S. Chang and I. Le Breton-Miller (2009). Filling the institutional void: The social behavior and performance of family versus non-family technology firms in emerging markets. *Journal of International Business Studies*, 40 (5): 802–817.

Montemerlo, D., and J. Ward (2010). *The Family Constitution: Agreements to Secure and Perpetuate Your Family and Your Business*. New York: Palgrave Macmillan.

Morck, R., and B. Yeung (2003). Agency problems in large family business groups. *Entrepreneurship Theory and Practice*, 27 (4): 367–382.

Morck, R. K., D. Wolfenzon and B. Yeung (2005). Corporate governance, economic entrenchment, and growth. *Journal of Economic Literature*, 43 (3): 655–720.

Naldi, L., M. Nordqvist, K. Sjöberg and J. Wiklund (2007). Entrepreneurial orientation, risk taking, and performance in family firms. *Family Business Review*, 20 (1): 33–47.

Niemann, N. (2009). *The Next Move for Business Owners*. Omaha, NE: Briefback Business Institute.

Noecker, K., H. Molter, A. von Schlippe and T. Rüsen (2012). Wie kann ein Gespräch zu einem Spaziergang werden? [How a talk can become a walk]. *Familiendynamik*, (1): 50–52.

Nordqvist, M., and T. Zellweger (2010). *Transgenerational Entrepreneurship: Exploring Growth and Performance in Family Firms across Generations*. Cheltenham, UK and Northampton, MA, USA: Edward Elgar Publishing.

North, D. C. (1990). *Institutions, Institutional Change and Economic Performance*. Cambridge: Cambridge University Press.

Ocasio, W. (1997). Towards an attention-based view of the firm. *Strategic Management Journal*, 18 (S1): 187–206.

Ohle, M.-P. (2012). The role of the CFO in large family firms. Unpublished doctoral dissertation, University of St. Gallen.

Parsons, T. (1943). The kinship system of the contemporary United States. *American Anthropologist*, 45 (1): 22–38.

Peng, M. W., and Y. Jiang (2010). Institutions behind family ownership and control in large firms. *Journal of Management Studies*, 47 (2): 253–273.

Pierce, J. L., T. Kostova and K. T. Dirks (2001). Toward a theory of psychological ownership in organizations. *Academy of Management Review*, 26 (2): 298–310.

Piketty, T. (2014). *Capital in the 21st Century*. Cambridge: Harvard University Press.

Pindado, J., I. Requejo and C. de la Torre (2012). Do family firms use dividend policy as a governance mechanism? Evidence from the Euro zone. *Corporate Governance: An International Review*, 20 (5): 413–431.

Porter, M. E. (1979). The structure within industries and companies' performance. *Review of Economics and Statistics*, 61 (2): 214–227.

Poza, E. J. (2013). *Family Business*. Mason, OH: Cengage Learning.

Poza, E. J., and M. S. Daugherty (2014). *Family Business*. Mason, OH: Southwest Cengage Learning.

Rahim, M. A. (1983). A measure of styles of handling interpersonal conflict. *Academy of Management Journal*, 26 (2): 368–376.

Ramachandran, K., and N. Bhatnagar (2012). Challenges faced by family businesses in India. Indian School of Business, Hyderabad.

Ravasi, D., and M. Schultz (2006). Responding to organizational identity threats: Exploring the role of organizational culture. *Academy of Management Journal*, 49 (3): 433–458.

Raven, P., and D. H. B. Welsh (2006). Family business in the Middle East: An exploratory study of retail management in Kuwait and Lebanon. *Family Business Review*, 19 (1): 29–48.

Richards, M. M., T. M. Zellweger and J. P. Gond (2016). Maintaining moral legitimacy through words and worlds: An explanation of firms' investment in sustainability certification. *Journal of Management Studies*, forthcoming.

Romano, C. A., G. A. Tanewski and K. X. Smyrnios (2001). Capital structure decision making: A model for family business. *Journal of Business Venturing*, 16 (3): 285–310.

Rosa, P. (2014). The emergence of African family businesses and their contribution to economy and society: An overview. Working paper, University of Edinburgh.

Rosenberg, M. B. (2012). *Gewaltfreie Kommunikation: Eine Sprache des Lebens* [Nonviolent communication: A language of life]. Paderborn: Junfermann Verlag.

Rosplock, K. (2013). *The Complete Family Office Handbook: A Guide for Affluent Families and the Advisors Who Serve Them*. New York: Bloomberg Financial.

Ruef, M. (2010). *The Entrepreneurial Group. Social Identities, Relations, and Collective Action*. Princeton, NJ and Oxford: Princeton University Press.

Schulze, W. S., and K. W. Kellermanns (2015). Reifying socioemotional wealth. *Entrepreneurship Theory and Practice*, 39 (3): 447–459.

Schulze, W., and T. Zellweger (2016). On the agency costs of owner-management: The problem of holdup. Working paper, University of Utah and University of St. Gallen.

Schulze, W., M. Lubatkin, R. Dino and A. Buchholtz (2001). Agency relationships in family firms: Theory and evidence. *Organization Science*, 12 (2): 99–116.

Schuman, S., S. Stutz and J. Ward (2010). *Family Business as Paradox*. New York: Palgrave Macmillan.

Schumpeter, J. A. (1934). *The Theory of Economic Development: An Inquiry into Profits, Capital, Credit, Interest, and the Business Cycle*. New Brunswick, NJ: Transaction Publishers.

Scott, R. W. (1995). *Institutions and Organizations*. Thousand Oaks, CA: Sage.

Sharifian, M., P. D. Jennings and J. E. Jennings (2012). Should women go into business with their family partner. In K. D. Hughes and J. E. Jennings (Eds.), *Global Women's Entrepreneurship Research: Diverse Settings, Questions and Approaches*. Cheltenham, UK and Northampton, MA, USA: Edward Elgar Publishing, 114–134.

Sharma, P., and P. G. Irving (2005). Four bases of family business successor commitment: Antecedents and consequences. *Entrepreneurship Theory and Practice*, 29 (1): 13–33.

Shepherd, D. A., A. Zacharakis and R. A. Baron (2003). VCs' decision processes: Evidence suggesting more experience may not always be better. *Journal of Business Venturing*, 18 (3): 381–401.

Sieger, P., T. Zellweger and K. Aquino (2013). Turning agents into psychological principals: Aligning interests of non-owners through psychological ownership. *Journal of Management Studies*, 50 (3): 361–388.

Sieger, P., T. Zellweger, R. Nason and E. Clinton (2011). Portfolio entrepreneurship in family firms: A resource-based perspective. *Strategic Entrepreneurship Journal*, 5 (4): 327–351.

Simon, F. B. (2002). *Die Familie des Familienunternehmens: Ein System zwischen Gefühl und Geschäft*. Heidelberg: Carl-Auer.

Simon, F. B. (2012). *Einführung in die Systemtheorie des Konflikts*. [Introduction to the Systems Theory of Conflict]. Heidelberg: Carl-Auer.

Simon, F. B., R. Wimmer, T. Groth and J. Baumhauer (2005). *Mehr-Generationen-Familienunternehmen: Erfolgsgeheimnisse von Oetker, Merck, Haniel ua* [Multi-generation Family Firms: Secrets of Success from Oetker, Merck, Haniel and Others]. Heidelberg: Carl-Auer.

Sirmon, D. G., and M. A. Hitt (2003). Managing resources: Linking unique resources, management, and wealth creation in family firms. *Entrepreneurship Theory and Practice*, 27 (4): 339–358.

Sirmon, D. G., M. A. Hitt, R. D. Ireland and B. A. Gilbert (2011). Resource orchestration to create competitive advantage breadth, depth, and life cycle effects. *Journal of Management*, 37 (5): 1390–1412.

Sitkoff, R. H. (2004). An agency costs theory of trust law. *Cornell Law Review*, 69: 621–684.

Smith, W. K., and M. W. Lewis (2011). Toward a theory of paradox: A dynamic equilibrium model of organizing. *Academy of Management Review*, 36 (2): 381–403.

Sorenson, R. L. (1999). Conflict management strategies used in successful family businesses. *Family Business Review*, 12 (4): 133–146.

Sraer, D., and D. Thesmar (2007). Performance and behavior of family firms: Evidence from the French stock market. *Journal of the European Economic Association*, 5 (4): 709–751.

Steijvers, T., and W. Voordeckers (2009). Private family ownership and the agency costs of debt. *Family Business Review*, 22 (4): 333–346.

Stewart, A., and M. A. Hitt (2010). The yin and yang of kinship and business: Complementary or contradictory forces? (And can we really say?) *Advances in Entrepreneurship, Firm Emergence and Growth*, 12: 243–276.

Strebulaev, I. A., and B. Yang (2013). The mystery of zero-leverage firms. *Journal of Financial Economics*, 109 (1): 1–23.

Strike, V. M. (2013). The most trusted advisor and the subtle advice process in family firms. *Family Business Review*, 26 (3): 293–313.

Sundaramurthy, C., and G. E. Kreiner (2008). Governing by managing identity boundaries: The case of family businesses. *Entrepreneurship Theory and Practice*, 32 (3): 415–436.

Sundaramurthy, C., and M. Lewis (2003). Control and collaboration: Paradoxes of governance. *Academy of Management Review*, 28 (3): 397–415.

Tagiuri, R., and J. Davis (1996). Bivalent attributes of the family firm. *Family Business Review*, 9 (2): 199–208.

Thomas, J. B., S. M. Clark and D. A. Gioia (1993). Strategic sensemaking and organizational performance: Linkages among scanning, interpretation, action, and outcomes. *Academy of Management Journal*, 36 (2): 239–270.

Thornton, P. H., W. Ocasio and M. Lounsbury (2012). *The Institutional Logics Perspective: A New Approach to Culture, Structure, and Process*. Oxford: Oxford University Press.

Tsoutsoura, M. (2009). *The Effect of Succession Taxes on Family Firm Investment: Evidence from a Natural Experiment*. New York: Columbia University.

Van der Heyden, L., C. Blondel and R. S. Carlock (2005). Fair process: Striving for justice in family business. *Family Business Review*, 18 (1): 1–21.

Van Dyne, L., and J. L. Pierce (2004). Psychological ownership and feelings of possession: Three field studies predicting employee attitudes and organizational citizenship behavior. *Journal of Organizational Behavior*, 25 (4): 439–459.

Van Essen, M., M. Carney, E. R. Gedajlovic and P. P. Heugens (2015). How does family control influence firm strategy and performance? A meta-analysis of US publicly listed firms. *Corporate Governance: An International Review*, 23 (1): 3–24.

Verbeke, A., and L. Kano (2010). Transaction cost economics (TCE) and the family firm. *Entrepreneurship Theory and Practice*, 34 (6): 1173–1182.

Villalonga, B., and R. Amit (2006). How do family ownership, control and management affect firm value? *Journal of Financial Economics*, 80 (2): 385–417.

Villalonga, B., and R. Amit (2010). Family control of firms and industries. *Financial Management*, 39 (3): 863–904.

Von Schlippe, A., and H. Frank (2013). The theory of social systems as a framework for understanding family businesses. *Family Relations*, 62 (3): 384–398.

Wagner, D., J. H. Block, D. Miller, C. Schwens and G. Xi (2015). A meta-analysis of the financial performance of family firms: Another attempt. *Journal of Family Business Strategy*, 6 (1): 3–13.

Ward, J. (1987). *Keeping the Family Business Healthy*. San Francisco, CA: Jossey-Bass.

Ward, J., and C. Aronoff (2010). *Family Business Governance: Maximizing Family and Business Potential*. New York: Palgrave Macmillan.

Wennberg, K., J. Wiklund, K. Hellerstedt and M. Nordqvist (2012). Implications of intra family and external ownership transfer of family firms: Short-term and long-term performance differences. *Strategic Entrepreneurship Journal*, 5 (4): 352–372.

Westhead, P., and M. Cowling (1998). Family firm research: The need for a methodological rethink. *Entrepreneurship Theory and Practice*, 23 (1): 31–56.

Whiteside, M. F., and F. H. Brown (1991). Drawbacks of a dual systems approach to family firms: Can we expand our thinking? *Family Business Review*, 4 (4): 383–395.

Willers, M. (2011). The significance of family firms across industries. Unpublished master's thesis, University of St. Gallen.

Williamson, O. E. (1985). *The Economic Institutions of Capitalism*. New York: The Free Press.

Yates, R. E. (1998). *The Kikkoman Chronicles: A Global Company with a Japanese Soul*. New York: McGraw-Hill.

Zellweger, T. M. (2007). Time horizon, costs of equity capital, and generic investment strategies of firms. *Family Business Review*, 20 (1): 1–15.

Zellweger, T. (2013). Toward a paradox perspective of family firms: The moderating role of collective mindfulness of controlling families. In L. Melin, M. Nordqvist and P. Sharma (Eds.), *The SAGE Handbook of Family Business*. Thousand Oaks, CA: SAGE Publications, 648–655.

Zellweger, T. M., and J. H. Astrachan (2008). On the emotional value of owning a firm. *Family Business Review*, 21 (4): 347–363.

Zellweger, T., and U. Fueglistaller (2007). Die volkswirtschaftliche Bedeutung der Familienunternehmen in der Schweiz [The economic significance of family firms in Switzerland]. *Schweizer Arbeitgeber*, (15): 30–33.

Zellweger, T., and N. Kammerlander (2014). Family business groups in Deutschland. Working paper, University of St. Gallen.

Zellweger, T., and N. Kammerlander (2015). Family, wealth, and governance: An agency account. *Entrepreneurship Theory and Practice*, 39 (6): 1281–1303.

Zellweger, T., K. Eddleston and F. W. Kellermanns (2010). Exploring the concept of familiness: Introducing family firm identity. *Journal of Family Business Strategy*, 1 (1): 54–63.

Zellweger, T., F. Kellermanns, J. Chrisman and J. Chua (2012). Family control and family firm valuation by family CEOs: The importance of intentions for transgenerational control. *Organization Science*, 23 (3): 851–868.

Zellweger, T., R. Nason and M. Nordqvist (2012). From longevity of firms to transgenerational entrepreneurship of families. *Family Business Review*, 25 (2): 136–155.

Zellweger, T., R. Nason, M. Nordqvist and C. Brush (2013). Why do family firms strive for non-financial goals? An organizational identity perspective. *Entrepreneurship Theory and Practice*, 37 (2): 229–248.

Zellweger, T., M. Richards, P. Sieger and P. Patel (forthcoming). How much am I expected to pay for my parents' firm? An institutional logics perspective on family discounts. *Entrepreneurship Theory and Practice*.

Zellweger, T., P. Sieger and P. Englisch (2012). Coming home or breaking free? Career choice intentions of the next generation in family businesses. Ernst & Young.

Zellweger, T., P. Sieger and F. Halter (2011). Should I stay or should I go? Career choice intentions of students with family business background. *Journal of Business Venturing*, 26 (5): 521–536.

Index